Collections for young Scholars®

FRAMEWORK FOR EFFECTIVE TEACHING®

Teacher's Guide, Grade 5 Book 1

Collections for young Scholars®

FRAMEWORK FOR EFFECTIVE TEACHING®

Teacher's Guide, Grade 5 Book 1

PROGRAM AUTHORS
Carl Bereiter
Valerie Anderson
Ann Brown
Marlene Scardamalia
Joe Campione

CONSULTING AUTHORS
Michael Pressley
Iva Carruthers
Bill Pinkney

Open Court Publishing Company

CHAIRMAN
M. Blouke Carus

PRESIDENT
André W. Carus

EDUCATION DIRECTOR
Carl Bereiter

CONCEPT
Barbara Conteh

SENIOR EXECUTIVE EDITOR
Sheelagh McGurn

EXECUTIVE EDITOR
Shirley Graudin

SENIOR PROJECT EDITORS
Wiley Blevins
Linda Cave
Theresa Kryst Fertig
Nancy H. Johnson

PROJECT EDITORS
Joseph Barron
Nita Garvin
Jennifer Johnson
Janette McKenna
Karen Sapp
Ana Tiesman

ASSESSMENT PLANNING
Karen Herzoff

ASSESSMENT DEVELOPMENT
Bernard Fletcher

SUPERVISOR, EDITORIAL SERVICES
Janice Bryant

SENIOR COPYEDITOR
Lucille Alaka

ART DIRECTOR
John Grandits

DESIGN
Diane Hutchinson

VICE-PRESIDENT, PRODUCTION
AND MANUFACTURING
Chris Vancalbergh

COVER ARTISTS
Mary Beth Schwark
and Bob Kuester

Contents

● Award-winning author and/or illustrator
▲ Full-length trade books
■ Dramatized on audiocassette

● Award-winning author and/or illustrator
▲ Full-length trade books
■ Dramatized on audiocassette

● Award-winning author and/or illustrator

▲ Full-length trade books

■ Dramatized on audiocassette

● Award-winning author and/or illustrator
▲ Full-length trade books
■ Dramatized on audiocassette

● Award-winning author and/or illustrator
▲ Full-length trade books
■ Dramatized on audiocassette

optional - difficult

● Award-winning author and/or illustrator
▲ Full-length trade books
■ Dramatized on audiocassette

Using Open Court's *Collections for Young Scholars*®

A Program for the 21st Century

Open Court's *Collections for Young Scholars*® represents a profound depar-
ture from mainstream reading programs. Its completely new approach to the
teaching of reading demands more of students. Yet if a reading program is to
prepare students to lead productive lives in twenty-first century society, it
must be demanding. Basic literacy skills are not enough. Traditional
approaches are not adequate.

Students who experience *Collections for Young Scholars*

- learn how to read and respond to a variety of text
- acquire strategies for accessing information and for exploring concepts
  from many areas of knowledge—including some that do not even
  exist today
- learn how to communicate effectively in both oral and written language
- learn how to work both independently and collaboratively
- give sustained effort to thinking and problem solving

THE PRINCIPLES

Collections for Young Scholars is built upon principles that reflect the consensus of leading literacy researchers and practitioners on what is essential
for reading success.

No Assumptions

In *Collections for Young Scholars,* initial reading instruction relies on the
explicit teaching of sounds, on the blending of sounds into words, and on the
leverage of using this knowledge for reading and writing.

For phonics instruction to work, it has to be systematic. It cannot start
somewhere in the middle. It cannot assume that students will "pick it up
somehow." *Collections for Young Scholars* does not assume that students
already know the letters or can distinguish individual sounds. It systematically teaches letter knowledge and phonemic awareness before and during
the introduction of sound/spelling associations. The introduction of sounds
and spellings is also systematic. And, because young students find it difficult
to analyze the phonemic structure of words, the program offers direct
instruction in blending. The teaching of writing begins with interactive
dictation. All of these techniques are used together in predictable and
recurring activities that teach students how to think about the sound/spelling
associations and about their connections with word meanings.

Authentic Literacy Experiences

Young students need to be reminded every day that literacy is a powerful tool. They need to see that attaining literacy is the goal of their hard work in learning the written code. Students participate daily in reading authentic, high-quality literature in Big Books or student anthologies. Beginning in kindergarten, students experience a range of text genres, including nonfiction. There are also many opportunities for writing, allowing students to understand the uses of writing even as they are learning to write. These experiences help to reinforce students' print awareness and their understanding of the structure and conventions of written language.

Throughout the program, students are encouraged to construct meaning by interacting with and responding to outstanding literature. They read widely, write frequently, and listen and speak effectively. The focus is always on building knowledge rather than on routinized performance.

Integrated Instruction

The use of learning frameworks, or predictable teaching techniques, ensures substantive integration of instruction. Lessons in which learning is presented as isolated, unrelated bits and pieces are replaced with learning units tied to important concepts that call on students to make connections across all areas of the curriculum and to acquire knowledge that can be used beyond a single lesson. Activities within a unit are integrated through reading, writing, discussion, and exploration activities that become increasingly complex and demanding.

Intentional Learning

Learning to read empowers students. Learning to learn enables them to use that power intelligently and to take charge of their own lives and their own learning process as soon as possible. In *Collections for Young Scholars,* learning is the goal of instruction, rather than an incidental outcome. Students explore critical areas for depth and understanding rather than march through large amounts of material for superficial learning. The intent of instruction is to engage the students in the kinds of activities that will prepare them for the reading, thinking, and problem-solving typical of real-world situations.

Support and Challenge for *All* Students

Collections for Young Scholars is designed so that every student is able to participate fully in class. No student gets bogged down in repetitive practice. Grouping is flexible and based on interest, not ability. The top priority of the program is to give all students important insights into the vast amount of knowledge available so that they can set learning goals for themselves.

Diverse and individual needs are met by varying the time and intensity of instruction, not by using watered down content or by having students read simplified and pointless texts or complete boring skill sheets. In addition, the students have access to a variety of activities that provide for differing language proficiencies and abilities. Multicultural activities are a natural part of the curriculum, not an add-on. Students for whom English is the primary language work with and learn from their classmates who are learning English as a second language. Conversely, English Language Learners have opportunities to practice their new language in an environment in which their ideas and contributions are sought and valued by their classmates and teacher.

Plentiful and Relevant Practice Opportunities

It is important to give students time during the day in which to practice what they are learning. Time for practice, called Workshop, is an integral part of *Collections for Young Scholars.* In Workshop, students work independently, collaboratively, or with the teacher to practice and review material taught in their lessons. Practice materials are also important, and the program contains a number of such materials that can be used by individual students or small groups as needed.

The goals are to use all class time as efficiently and productively as possible. No time is wasted on mindless repetition and seat work.

Teacher Leadership, Collaborative Learning

In *Collections for Young Scholars* classrooms, the learning environment is established by the teacher. The powerful learning frameworks in the program help you to focus the students' attention on real learning and away from busywork. The program encourages you to model how to pursue both personal and collaborative learning and how to communicate that learning to others. Equally important, the program provides students with ample opportunities to learn from and work with classmates in collaborative learning groups. These groups allow students to work on topics of mutual interest, to share ideas, and to help each other gain understanding of complex concepts. Learning groups composed of both English-speaking students and English Language Learners encourage the students to learn more about each other's languages and backgrounds and make it possible for those learning English to ask questions they might be reluctant to raise in a whole-class setting. Carefully structured activities involve special-needs students in learning groups in ways that make their ideas and efforts crucial to the group's success.

Home/School Connections

Families are kept informed of their children's classroom activities and are consulted on matters of importance to their children. Homework assignments are extended in ways that invite family members to become closely involved in their children's learning. In turn, families are expected to participate actively in helping their children attain full literacy.

High Expectations, Positive Assessment

Students perform to the level of expectations set by their surroundings. It is unfair to them not to expect their best. Open Court has a long tradition of respecting the intelligence of students and of their teachers. *Collections for Young Scholars* continues that tradition by providing high-quality literature and meaning-based, relevant activities that honor the abilities of the program's users.

Although expectations are high, assessment is positive. It focuses on what the students do right, not on what they do wrong. Above all, it helps them to move continuously up the learning ladder.

THE LEARNING FRAMEWORKS

In *Collections for Young Scholars,* principles are translated into instruction by means of powerful learning frameworks, or teaching techniques that recur frequently. The use of learning frameworks frees students to focus on the content of a lesson without the distraction of learning a new format for its presentation. The framework used to introduce key skills and concepts is also used to present increasingly complex or expanded versions of the skills and concepts as the students progress through the curriculum. For you, this means that the time spent setting up a lesson is minimized.

In each teacher's guide, the learning frameworks are noted by an asterisk (✶). The learning frameworks for the program, kindergarten through grade 6, are shown in the following chart, with the grade 3-6 frameworks highlighted. The grade 3-6 learning frameworks are discussed in detail on pages 34F–39F.

The Learning Frameworks

	Kindergarten	Grade 1
Reading Skills and Fluency	* Phonemic Awareness	
	* How the Alphabet Works: Part 1	
	* How the Alphabet Works: Part 2	
	* Introducing the Sounds and Using the Alphabet Cards	
	*	Introducing the Sounds
	*	Blending
	* Using the First-Step Stories	
	*	Reading Phonics Minibooks
Writing Skills and Fluency	*	Dictation and Spelling
	* Writing	
	*	Sentence Lifting
Knowledge Building	*	
	*	
	*	
	*	
	*	Research
Authentic Literacy Experiences	*	Reading the Student Anthol...
	*	
	* Exploring Through Discussion	
	*	
	* Reading Aloud	
	*	Reading Big Books
	* Using the Big Book and Print Awareness	
Monitoring, Assessment, and Individualization	* Assessment and Monitoring	
	* Workshop	
	* English Language Learners	

	Grade 2	Grades 3–6

Using the Sound/Spelling Cards

and Step-by-Step Practice Stories

Writing Process

Writing Seminar

Exploring Through Reflective Activities

Exploring Through Research

Cognitive and Responsive Reading

Reading Roundtable

Formative Assessment (Separate Teacher's Guide)

Senior Author Team

If schools are going to change in any direction that's relevant to the future, it has to be in helping students work toward deeper knowledge in whatever they are studying. That's why I'm excited about the research component of this reading series. It's unique in that it does move the students toward deeper and deeper knowledge in some area that they're working on.
—Carl Bereiter

Carl Bereiter is Professor at the Centre for Applied Cognitive Science at the Ontario Institute for Studies in Education in Toronto and a member of the National Academy of Education. He has co-authored many curriculum projects, including Open Court's reading and mathematics programs. He is coauthor with Marlene Scardamalia of *The Psychology of Written Composition* (1987) and *Surpassing Ourselves: The Nature and Implications of Expertise* (1993); and he has published extensively on the nature of teaching and learning. Computer-supported intentional learning environments and collaborative knowledge building have been the subjects of his most recent classroom investigations and publications.

Valerie Anderson is Research Associate at the Centre for Applied Cognitive Science at the Ontario Institute for Studies in Education and has had extensive experience both in designing curriculum and in training teachers. Her most recent work with children has centered on helping them learn to use thinking strategies to become independent readers.

Throughout this program, not only does the teacher provide and model strategies . . . , he or she encourages children to bring out their own strategies and to apply them to reading. This is unusual in strategy instruction.
—Valerie Anderson

Students in the research class-room, because they are doing their own research, are free to become expert in something that interests them. Our deliberate intent is that everyone is responsible for some part of the curriculum.
—Ann Brown

Ann Brown is Professor of Math, Science, and Technology in the Graduate School of Education at the University of California at Berkeley. She was previously associated with the Center for the Study of Reading at the University of Illinois. Dr. Brown, 1993–94 President of the American Educational Research Association (AERA), is an internationally recognized expert in cognitive science. She has published extensively on such topics as memory strategies, reading comprehension, analogical thinking, self-regulated reading, metacognition, and reciprocal teaching. Ann Brown and her colleague Joe Campione are focusing their current research on students as researchers and teachers, a significant aspect of their study of distributed expertise in the classroom.

Joe Campione is Professor in the School of Education at the University of California at Berkeley. He is also Director of the Berkeley component of the Joint Doctoral Program in Special Education between UC Berkeley and San Francisco State University. Campione has long been known for his work in cognitive development, transfer of learning, individual differences, and assessment. He is working with Ann Brown to discover ways to restructure elementary-school learning environments to take advantage of distributed expertise in the classroom and to use interactive learning to promote scientific literacy within communities of learners.

People aren't happy with the way schools have been run in very traditional ways. We really see a lot of agreement that people want students working on longer-term projects, thinking in depth about things, working collaboratively, and taking responsibility for their own learning. I think that's true of parents, it's true of teachers, and it's true of administrators.
—Joe Campione

The notion of bringing the students up to fine literature, to history, to sociology, to astronomy instead of bringing the content down to them is critical both to the program and to the spirit students can develop. It's a real "I can do it" spirit, and indeed they can. And we believe they will with this program.
—Marlene Scardamalia

Marlene Scardamalia is Professor and Head of the Centre for Applied Cognitive Science at the Ontario Institute for Studies in Education in Toronto. She is currently a Fellow in the Center for Advanced Study in the Behavioral Sciences at Stanford. Her extensive list of publications includes books, journal articles, and papers focusing on cognitive, developmental, and instructional psychology. She is presently engaged in studies of text-based questioning by children; computer technology for collaborative processes; and collaborative, knowledge-building environments for tomorrow's schools.

Consulting Authors

Intentional learning, what's that? Well, it's sort of going around the world as kind of an active, problem-solving thinker. We have become incredibly aware that the best readers, when they're reading, are very active. They're very planful. They're very reactive. They're filtering what they read through prior knowledge. They're thinking about what they're going to do with what they read. The same goes for when they're composing or writing. —Michael Pressley

Michael Pressley is Professor of Educational Psychology and Statistics at the State University of New York at Albany, as well as Principal Investigator for the National Reading Research Center, centralized at the Universities of Maryland and Georgia. He does both basic laboratory research on cognition and learning and applied work in educational settings. Memory development and reading comprehension strategies have received much of his attention.

Iva E. Carruthers is Professor and former Chairperson of the Sociology Department of Northeastern Illinois University. She is also President of Nexus Unlimited, Inc., a human resources development and computer services consulting firm, and of Ed Tech, a computer software development company. In addition to developing educational software aids for teaching history and interdisciplinary subjects, she has produced fourteen study guides on African-American and African history.

Bill Pinkney is the first African American to sail solo around the world, traveling around the five great capes in his sailboat named *Commitment*. Only forty-one individuals have accomplished this feat. More than 30,000 students across the United States were able to share in his legendary voyage, thanks to advanced satellite and computer technologies. Not only did he give these students lessons in math, science, geography, and social studies, but Captain Pinkney also modeled for them the courage, perseverance, skill, and commitment required to realize one's dreams.

Instructional Consultants

Charles Abate, Ed.D.
Elementary Principal
Orchard Elementary School
Ridgewood, New Jersey

Doris B. Ash, M.S.
Assistant Director
Fostering a Community of Learners Research Project
University of California, Berkeley

Mary Lamon, Ph.D.
Project Director
Middle School Curriculum Development Project
St. Louis Science Center
St. Louis, Missouri

Martha E. Rutherford, M.A.
Assistant Director
Fostering a Community of Learners Research Project
University of California, Berkeley

Teacher Reviewers

Barbara Appleberry, *Grade 1*
Mollison Elementary School
Chicago, Illinois

Marie Beacham, *Grade 1*
Ephraim Elementary School
Ephraim, Utah

Joyce Bell, *Grade 1*
Brown School
Newburyport, Massachusetts

Kim Carey, *Grade 6*
Crestmont Elementary School
Northport, Alabama

Peggy Clelland, *Grade 1*
Washington Terrace Elementary
    School
Ogden, Utah

Emmy Daniel, *Grade 1*
South Shores School
Decatur, Illinois

Tony Dillon, *Grade 1*
John Foster Dulles School
Chicago, Illinois

Dorothy Dorsey, *Grade 4*
Glenmount Elementary School
Baltimore, Maryland

Kay Ericksen, *Grade 5*
Ephraim Elementary School
Ephraim, Utah

Debra Evans, *Grade 3*
Goldblatt Elementary School
Chicago, Illinois

Margaret Ewing, *Grade 3*
Abraham Lincoln Elementary School
Palm Desert, California

Sr. Susan Faist, *Grade 2*
Christ the King School
Toledo, Ohio

Mary Fatsi, *Grade 1*
Brooklyn Elementary School
Brooklyn, Connecticut

Susan Fowler, *Grade 2*
Yaquina View Elementary
Newport, Oregon

Bonnie French, *Grade 6*
Carl Sundahl Elementary School
Folsom, California

Lena Gates, *Grade 1*
Crispus Attucks School, P. S. 21
Brooklyn, New York

Lila Gilchrist, *Grade 3*
The Orchard School
Ridgewood, New Jersey

Leticia Gonzalez, *Grade 4*
Saenz Elementary School
Alice, Texas

Lora Gordy, *Grade 5*
Buckingham Elementary School
Berlin, Maryland

Janice Green, *Grade 1*
Francis T. Bresnahan School
Newburyport, Massachusetts

Joyce Haffey, *Grade 4*
St. Therese School
Kansas City, Missouri

Jackie Herath, *Grade 3*
Sunderland Elementary School
Sunderland, Maryland

Karen Horace, *Grade 6*
Goldblatt Elementary School
Chicago, Illinois

Patricia Horst, *Grade 5*
Harding Elementary School
Clinton, Ohio

Hurtice Howard, *Grade 1*
Julia L. Armstrong Elementary
    School
Greenville, Mississippi

Nancy Hughes, *Grade 2*
Eleanor Roosevelt School
Vancouver, Washington

Celeste James, *Grade 1*
John Foster Dulles School
Chicago, Illinois

Christine Johnson, *Grade 1*
Kelley School
Newburyport, Massachusetts

Patricia Johnson, *Grade 3*
Crispus Attucks School, P. S. 21
Brooklyn, New York

Laurie Jones, *Grade 4*
Grantswood Community School
Birmingham, Alabama

Lisa Kane, *Grade 5*
Disney Magnet Elementary School
Chicago, Illinois

Charlotte Lewis, *Grade 1*
L. B. Weemes Elementary School
Los Angeles, California

Rhet Lickliter, *Grade 6*
Park Tudor School
Indianapolis, Indiana

Sandra Loose, *Grade 1*
Indian Lane Elementary School
Media, Pennsylvania

Frank Lopez, *Grade 5*
Parker Elementary School
Panama City, Florida

Kathryn Lopez, *Grade 1*
Millville Elementary School
Panama City, Florida

Mary Ann Luebbert, *Grade 6*
Russell Elementary School
Hazelwood, Missouri

Ruth MacGregor, *Grade 3*
Mildred M. Fox School
South Paris, Maine

Lynne Malone, *Grade 3*
Carver Elementary School
Dawson, Georgia

Pam Martin, *Grade 1*
L. B. Weemes Elementary School
Los Angeles, California

Melony Maughan, *Grade 1*
Grantswood Community School
Birmingham, Alabama

Ursula McClendon, *Grade 3*
George West Primary School
George West, Texas

Phyllis Miles, *Grade 4*
Our Lady of Mount Carmel
Carmel, Indiana

Sue Miller, *Grade 1*
The Valwood School
Valdosta, Georgia

Nancy Mitchell, *Grade 2*
Pleasant Ridge School
Grass Valley, California

Trudy Mockert, *Grade 1*
Nicolaus Copernicus School, P. S. 25
Jersey City, New Jersey

Anna Molina, *Grade 1*
Ezra Nolan School, P. S. 40
Jersey City, New Jersey

Roberta Montoya, *Grade 3*
Alamosa Elementary School
Albuquerque, New Mexico

Carol Neyman, *Grade 5*
Cotton Boll Elementary School
Peoria, Arizona

Margaret Nichols, *Grade 1*
Brown School
Newburyport, Massachusetts

Cindy Noland, *Grade 2*
Jefferson Elementary School
Parkersburg, West Virginia

Bettye Nunnery, *Grade 2*
Otken Primary School
McComb, Mississippi

Jane Offineer, *Grade 5*
Belden Elementary School
Canton, Ohio

Sara Oliveira, *Grade 5*
Portsmouth Elementary School
Portsmouth, Rhode Island

Kathleen Pabst, *Grade 3*
Charles Drew Elementary School
San Francisco, California

Judith Palermo, *Grade 1*
St. Helen's School
Chicago, Illinois

Terri Patterson, *Grade 4*
Paradise Elementary School
Las Vegas, Nevada

Becky Philips, *Grade 2*
Sunderland Elementary School
Sunderland, Maryland

Donna Powell, *Grade 2*
Melville School
Portsmouth, Rhode Island

Barbara Purcell, *Grade 3*
Education Service Center
Corpus Christi, Texas

Caron Reasor, *Grade 6*
La Quinta Middle School
La Quinta, California

Sharon Robinson, *Grade 2*
Flournoy Elementary School
Los Angeles, California

Judith Roy, *Grade 1*
Grantswood Community School
Birmingham, Alabama

Maxine Rushing, *Grade 4*
Plymouth Day School
Detroit, Michigan

Kathy Rodger-Sachs, *Grade 4*
The Orchard School
Ridgewood, New Jersey

Agnes Schutz, *Grade 1*
Alamosa Elementary School
Albuquerque, New Mexico

Donna Sedlacek, *Grade 3*
Bear Creek Elementary School
Lakewood, Colorado

Ruth Seiger, *Grade 1*
Francis T. Bresnahan School
Newburyport, Massachusetts

Cheryl Sheehan, *Grade 1*
Nicolaus Copernicus School, P. S. 25
Jersey City, New Jersey

Margaret Simmons, *Grade 6*
Corpus Christi Elementary School
San Francisco, California

Renee Singer, *Grade 1*
Grantswood Community School
Birmingham, Alabama

Jacqueline Smith, *Grade 1*
John Foster Dulles School
Chicago, Illinois

Patricia Terrell, *Grade 4*
Gatewood Elementary School
Oklahoma City, Oklahoma

Barbara Uhrin, *Grade 2*
Amos Hutchinson Elementary School
Greensburg, Pennsylvania

Celia Waddell, *Grade 5*
Grantswood Elementary School
Birmingham, Alabama

Laurie Walters, *Grade 1*
L. B. Weemes Elementary School
Los Angeles, California

Robin Wexler, *Grade 5*
Roosevelt Elementary School
River Edge, New Jersey

The Grade 5 Program of
Collections for Young Scholars®

If schools are going to change in any direction that's relevant to the future, it has to be in helping students work toward deeper knowledge.

—Carl Bereiter

Students who will graduate into the world of the twenty-first century will need much more than basic reading and writing skills. To participate productively in that world, graduates must know how to go about gaining information, to evaluate it critically, and to adapt it for differing purposes. They must be equipped to deal with a variety of fields, including some that do not even exist today, and to understand and participate in scientific reasoning and problem solving.

THE MATERIALS

The teacher and student materials of the *Collections for Young Scholars*® grade 5 program all focus on developing self-directed, highly motivated students who take primary responsibility for their own learning.

Framework for Effective Teaching®, Grade 5, Books 1 and 2
The teacher's guide for the grade 5 program is contained in two volumes:
* *Framework for Effective Teaching,* Grade 5, Book 1, which accompanies the student anthology *Collections for Young Scholars,* Volume 5, Book 1
* *Framework for Effective Teaching,* Grade 5, Book 2, which accompanies the student anthology *Collections for Young Scholars,* Volume 5, Book 2.

The teacher's guide presents instruction in meaning-based learning units, each of which revolves around compelling explorable concepts from across the curriculum. Each unit leads students to pursue personal and collaborative inquiry, to identify and access the information they need, and to communicate their findings to their classmates.

Each unit is organized so that a reading selection adds more information or a different perspective to the students' knowledge of a concept. Throughout all units, the focus is on intentional learning—that is, learning is the goal rather than an incidental outcome of a lesson.

Lessons within a unit are integrated through reading, writing, discussion, research, and exploration activities that evolve sequentially, becoming increasingly complex and demanding. Individual, collaborative learning group, and whole-class activities encourage the students to bring their own experiences to the learning situation and, through exploration, to gain deeper understandings. The students' responsibility is to learn more, and to help their classmates discover more, about the unit concepts.

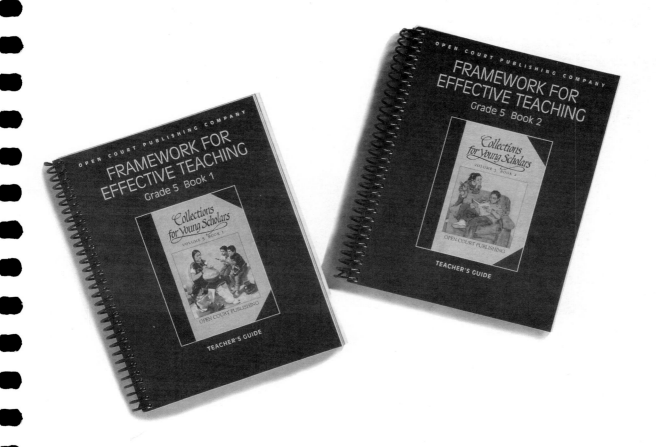

Collections for Young Scholars, **Volume 5, Books 1 and 2**

The student anthologies are filled with beautifully illustrated selections by award-winning authors and artists. Realistic fiction, historical fiction, poetry, nonfiction selections, and full-length trade books captivate students and encourage them to think, wonder, raise questions, learn—and read more. Literature from around the world offers the students differing perspectives on many topics. Fine Art selections included with each unit show students how the topics they are reading about can be represented visually.

Each anthology is organized into learning units that focus on important concepts. By exploring concepts of universal interest and from science and social studies, students build valuable background knowledge through their reading.

The three units in Volume 5, Book 1 are Learning, Astronomy, and Family Heritage. The three units in Volume 5, Book 2 are The Civil War, The American West, and Journeys and Quests.

Teacher Toolbox

The lessons in the teacher's guide are supported by resources contained in the Teacher Toolbox. These resources are as follow:

- **Learning Framework Cards**—convenient reference tools that contain descriptions and discussions of the key learning frameworks that recur throughout the grade 5 program (see pages 34F–39F). The cards also contain suggestions for applying the learning framework to other areas of the curriculum and for working with English Language Learners.

- **Teacher Tool Cards**—cards that provide basic lessons on Writer's Craft/Reading; Grammar, Mechanics, and Usage; Spelling and Vocabulary; Study and Research; and Classroom Supports that can be used to meet individual needs at any time, not just during reading. Tool Cards contain tips for dealing with common problems related to the subject of a lesson and suggestions for working with English Language Learners.

- **Home/School Connection** materials—convenient masters, including letters written in both English and Spanish that explain to families what their children are learning in class; activity sheets that the students and their families can complete together; and bibliographies that list children's literature for families to share at home.

- **Reproducible Masters**—convenient masters that allow you and the students to make choices, based on individual needs. The masters provide pages the students can use to customize their Writer's Notebook, including a table of contents and divider pages, informational pages to be inserted in the Writer's Notebook for future reference, extensive bibliographies for use in exploring unit concepts, and extension pages for use in conjunction with lessons on the Teacher Tool Cards.
- **Assessment** materials—a number of components, including a guide to assessment techniques (Formative Assessment) and materials used in the program and masters of observation logs, performance assessment rubrics, cumulative class folders, and individual student profiles.
- **Instructional Posters**—large wall posters that illustrate reading strategies, the phases of the writing process, the phases of the research cycle, projects and activities that can help in exploring and sharing ideas in units, and discussion starters.

Explorer's Notebook, Volume 5

The intent of *Collections for Young Scholars* is to help students become independent, intentional learners. Each student, individually and as part of a community of scholars, works to build a useful body of knowledge as she or he proceeds through the program.

The Explorer's Notebook helps students build this body of knowledge. Students use the notebook to record information about a particular unit. The completed pages provide students with a cumulative record of their learning and give them a place in which they can respond to a reading selection, record questions they may have about their reading or learning, make connections between and across selections, and plan and organize research.

Reading/Writing Connection, Volume 5

An important goal of *Collections for Young Scholars* is to help students grasp and implement the connections between what they read and what they write. The Reading/Writing Connection workbook encourages students to approach reading with a writer's eye by giving them a place to note, examine, and comment on the techniques used by authors to communicate ideas clearly. Each lesson in the workbook invites students to transfer into their own writing the insights they gain from their reading.

Student Toolbox

Designed for use in a classroom learning center, this resource aids student independence and motivation. The toolbox contains:

- **Student Tool Cards**—cards, written in appropriate language, that provide independent instruction and information about literary techniques, grammar conventions, spelling, vocabulary, research skills, and effective classroom participation.
- **Cross-curricular Activity Cards**—cards that present engaging activities that help students make connections between the reading selections, the concepts they are exploring in a unit, and other curriculum areas.
- **Tradebook Connection Cards**—cards that provide activities to accompany popular trade books and serve as the basis of Reading Roundtable discussions throughout the program.
- **Listening Collections Audiocassette**—tape that contains dramatic readings to enhance students' enjoyment of selections from the anthologies.

Writer's Notebook

To help solidify the reading/writing connection, every student is encouraged to keep a Writer's Notebook—a three-ring binder or folder. This notebook is a personalized writing tool in which students record reactions to their reading, compile writing reference materials based on classroom lessons, compile their own personal word lists from their readings in and out of class, and record ideas for writing.

The Reproducible Masters, Part 1 booklet (in the Teacher Toolbox) contains a table of contents sheet and divider sheets that students can use to organize their notebooks into the following sections:

- Writing Ideas
- Personal Dictionary
- Author's Style
- Story Elements
- Genres
- Checking My Work
- My Response Journal

Optional Materials
Writer's Handbook

The Writer's Handbook is an optional, easily accessible writing reference tool for students to keep and use independently. It provides students with good writing examples for them to examine as they review their own writing. The Writer's Handbook contains three sections:

- Write It Well offers pointers for developing a clear and appealing style
- Write It Right explains correct usage
- Writer's Quick Reference provides proofreading checklists, common abbreviations, commonly confused words, commonly misspelled words, spelling generalities, and synonyms

Researcher™

Researcher is an interactive software program designed to help students organize, direct, and collaborate on the research they do in the classroom. It offers a structure for collaborative research and helps students keep track of key information during every phase of their research. The program also can provide you with a forum for monitoring the level of involvement of individual students in a research group, reviewing the students' progress, and making sure that the students understand and take part in the research process. The program operates on 5 MB RAM, color Macintosh System 7.0 or later.

Book Exchange™

Book Exchange is an interactive software program designed to provide a way for students to share their responses to books and to discover new interpretations of the literature they are reading. The program operates on 5 MB RAM, color Macintosh System 7.0 or later.

Concept Board and Question Board

One of the primary goals of *Collections for Young Scholars* is to help you and your students form a community of scholars. To do this, sharing information is essential. The Concept Board and the Question Board can facilitate classroom communication and allow the students to publicize their learning.

The Concept Board is a bulletin board or chart where the students can share their growing knowledge about a unit concept by posting newspaper clippings, magazine articles, information taken from on-line computer services, and other items that might be of interest to or help for their classmates. As the class progresses through a unit, the Concept Board serves as the place where common interests become evident. As these interests emerge, the students can use them as the basis for forming collaborative groups to explore ideas in greater depth.

The Question Board, a bulletin board or chart, gives students an outlet for questions that arise as they read on their own. The questions can be written directly on a sheet of paper attached to the board, or they can be written on separate slips of paper and pinned to it. Self-sticking note pads can also be used. The Question Board lets the students know that questions are not problems, but a tool for learning. Questions thus become a springboard to further exploration. Collaborative groups can be formed around common questions.

The boards should change constantly, reflecting the developing and changing interests of the class.

Assessment Materials

The *Collections for Young Scholars* grade 5 program provides a multidimensional, continuous assessment system designed to measure change in students' performance and to check their progress in each area of the literacy curriculum. Ongoing assessment is accomplished through teacher observation, portfolios, and student self-evaluation. End-of-unit assessments provide cumulative evaluations of the students' progress as well. A special assessment manual, *Formative Assessment: A Teacher's Guide,* found in the Teacher Toolbox, provides an overview of the types of assessment used in the program and explains how to use each. Also in the Teacher Toolbox, there are convenient observation logs for recording observations of individual students' progress. Comprehension Assessment sheets provide a place to record individual students' reading performance as they read aloud in Workshop or during other available time. Essay and Writing Assessment sheets provide performance assessment rubrics to help organize evaluations of different aspects of students' writing. Research Assessment sheets provide a means to assess students' performance in the research process.

In addition to being assessed by monitoring, performance assessments, and written tests, each child also develops a portfolio of samples of his or her work.

Getting Started

Instruction in *Collections for Young Scholars* is organized by way of key techniques, or learning frameworks that recur frequently. In the grade 5 program, the key learning frameworks are:

1. Cognitive and Responsive Reading
   1A. Setting Reading goals and Expectations
   1B. Responding to Text
   1C. Checking Understanding
   1D. Clarifying Unfamiliar Words and Passages
2. Exploring Through Discussion
3. Exploring Through Reflective Activities
4. Exploring Through Research
   4A. Problem Phase 1 and 2
   4B. Conjecture Phase
   4C. Needs and Plans Phase 1 and 2
5. Independent Workshop
6. Reading Roundtable
7. Writing Process
   7A. Prewriting
   7B. Drafting
   7C. Revising
   7D. Proofreading
   7E. Publishing
8. Writing Seminar
9. English Language Learners

Organizing instruction by learning frameworks means that by varying the time and intensity of instruction, individual and special needs can be addressed without ability grouping. All students receive the same high-quality learning experiences. However, because students learning English occasionally require extra help, the teacher's guide provides **Teaching Tips** for **English Language Learners** whenever the tips are appropriate for a specific lesson.

Throughout *Framework for Effective Teaching*®, Grade 5, Books 1 and 2, the learning frameworks are noted with an asterisk (✱). In addition, Learning Framework Cards found in the Teacher Toolbox contain detailed discussions of each learning framework.

The learning frameworks incorporate and develop all key areas of instruction in grade 5. Although the learning frameworks are each clearly identifiable, as the chart on pages 16F–17F indicates, they often overlap to reinforce learning of key skills and concepts:

Writing Skills and Fluency/Knowledge Building

Writing is a way of learning. When students engage in the process of writing, they gain important insights that promote deeper thinking and reasoning. This is especially true when writing has a clear purpose and is shared with others who respond to it constructively and thoughtfully.

The learning frameworks for writing and knowledge building are Writing Process and Writing Seminar.

✳ Writing Process

Writing Process introduces students to the problem-solving and reasoning activities that writers engage in as they form their ideas and communicate them through print. Students acquire knowledge of writing conventions by reading and examining good writing. Purposeful writing involving **Prewriting, Drafting, Revising, Proofreading,** and **Publishing** connects students to the long tradition of people who capture the wisdom, beauty, humor, and knowledge of many cultures and societies in written language.

Each lesson in a unit contains writing activities that are related to the unit's explorable concept and the specific reading selection used in the lesson. Writer's craft skills are taught in each writing lesson to reinforce a technique or convention important to writing. Optional minilessons relate to the reading selection and explorable concept and expand the use of writing strategies.

Teaching writing as a process allows English Language Learners to break down writing into easily manageable stages. The frequent occasions for individual work with the teacher and for group work offer support and encouragement.

✳ Writing Seminar

Writing Seminar is an activity students can choose during Independent Workshop. It gives students an audience for their writing and a way to share the stages of the writing process with others. Students meet in small groups to read and discuss each other's work. One student reads a piece of writing-in-progress and the other students respond to the writing by asking questions and offering suggestions. The student whose work is being reviewed writes down the comments and suggestions and decides how to use them to make the writing better. Writing Seminar is used during all phases of the writing process. Students use it to generate ideas for writing, proofread revised drafts, and share completed works.

English Language Learners benefit from the frequent peer and teacher tutoring and conferencing made possible by Writing Seminar.

Knowledge Building

The goal of knowledge building is to help students become active participants in a community of scholars by increasing their ability to think about, appreciate, and contribute to the vast richness of human knowledge.

The key learning frameworks for knowledge building are Exploring Through Research and Exploring Through Reflective Activities.

✳ Exploring Through Research

As they progress through units that focus on Exploring Through Research, the students carry out the phases of the research cycle—the **Problem** Phases, in which they determine a problem and generate questions; the **Conjecture** phase, in which they pose explanations and theories about the problem; and the **Needs and Plans** Phases, in which they determine what they have to know and what sources of information might be helpful. At the end of the process, the students plan a project to present what they have learned.

The Research Cycle Poster reminds the students of the phases, and the Explorer's Notebook systematically guides them through the research process. Independent Workshop time is used to conduct ongoing research and to work with the interactive computer software program called *Researcher*™. The program is built around the phases of the research cycle and helps students define a problem, assign individual research tasks, and share their discoveries. It can be used by students independently or in collaborative groups.

Introducing students to the research process gives them access to the tools they need for discovering and learning on their own and as a member of a collaborative group. Research activities provide a systematic structure for inquiry that is driven by the students' wonderings and conjectures.

Research activities are especially important to English Language Learners because they allow the students to display their already-learned competencies and to show their classmates that they, too, have complex and sophisticated ideas.

✳ Exploring Through Reflective Activities

Units that involve Exploring Through Reflective Activities are organized so that each selection in a unit adds more information or a different perspective to the students' growing body of knowledge about a particular concept or topic. Exploring Through Reflective Activities allows students to expand their perspectives by relating what they read to their own experiences. As they explore increasingly complex and challenging unit concepts, students participate in writing, discussing, interviewing, debating, and other individual and collaborative activities that extend their experiences and offer opportunities for reflection.

Exploring Through Reflective Activities gives English Language Learners opportunities to build on their existing knowledge and to use English to expand their understanding of a concept or topic.

Authentic Literacy Experiences/Knowledge Building

As they become more fluent readers and writers, students find out that reading and writing give them power: the power to take control of their learning. From the selections used in the student anthologies, students both gain information that will serve as the underpinning for their later learning and receive an introduction to the world of scholarship and its traditions and joys. Three learning frameworks extend and interweave the instruction found in each of these areas: Cognitive and Responsive Reading, Exploring Through Discussion, and Reading Roundtable.

✳ Cognitive and Responsive Reading

For students to become full members of a community of scholars, they must become *strategic* readers. They must learn how to think about what they read and to use specific reading strategies and behaviors across reading situations. In grade 5, four basic reading behaviors are taught, through teacher modeling, to help students become thoughtful, responsive readers who use key strategies to enhance their understanding and to solve problems that arise during reading: **Setting Reading Goals and Expectations, Responding to Text, Checking Understanding,** and **Clarifying Unfamiliar Words and Passages.** Across the grades, the students have opportunities to apply their strategies to increasingly complex selections and topics.

This learning framework is specifically tied to Volume 5, Books 1 and 2 of *Collections for Young Scholars.* It gives the students opportunities to use their evolving reading strategies with a variety of text types. Biographies and autobiographies; history, geography, and science selections; photo essays; and discussions of art and music introduce the students to the variety of human knowledge and experience. Stories, poems, and nonfiction selections about both familiar and unfamiliar characters, cultures, and events stretch their minds and encourage them to think and reflect about how they interpret the world.

Exploring how written language works in the context of authentic and motivating literature is crucial for English Language Learners. Practice in using the behaviors and strategies they see modeled by expert readers of English is also extremely valuable.

✳ Exploring Through Discussion

Discussing with students what they are learning and how they are learning it allows them to express their doubts and concerns as well as their excitement about ideas and language. Whole-class discussions of a reading selection encourage students to express their opinions and ideas clearly and to listen attentively and to respond appropriately to the opinions expressed by others. These discussions are opportunities for the students to think, predict, and draw connections between the selection they are reading and other selections or with their own experiences.

Exploring Through Discussion is a principal means of helping students tie together all of the things they are learning about language and literacy and to examine the edges of their knowledge and understanding.

Discussion activities are also opportunities to elaborate on content-specific vocabulary, to emphasize the proper vocabulary, and to provide the students with more information about a selection, all of which are important to English Language Learners and special-needs students.

✳ Reading Roundtable

A community of readers can be created in a classroom only if there are regular occasions for students to discuss what they read. Reading Roundtable, an activity students can choose during Independent Workshop, provides them opportunities to discuss what they are reading on their own, sharing opinions and recommending books. Reading Roundtable introduces students to the ways adults think about and analyze texts. If several students have read the same book, they can discuss it. If only one student has read the book, he or she can review it for others.

The interactive computer software program called *Book Exchange*™ provides a way for the students to share their responses to books and to compare their interpretations with those of others.

Reading Roundtable allows English Language Learners to expand the perspectives of their classmates by choosing to share a book written in their primary language, especially if the book relates to the unit concept.

Monitoring, Assessment, and Individualization

Collections for Young Scholars provides for multidimensional, continuous monitoring and assessment to ensure that all students are progressing toward clearly established goals and benchmarks. Individualization of assessment and instruction are accomplished through Independent Workshop. Workshop is especially beneficial for English Language Learners.

The learning frameworks for monitoring, assessment, and individualization are Independent Workshop and English Language Learners.

✳ Independent Workshop

Workshop gives students the experience of managing their own learning process. In Workshop, the students work independently or collaboratively to practice and review material taught in the lessons or to complete projects of their own choosing. As the students gradually take more and more responsibility during Workshop, they learn to set learning goals, to make decisions about the use of time and materials, and to collaborate with their classmates. Of equal importance, Workshop gives you a designated time to work with individuals or with groups to reinforce learning, to provide extra help to those who need it, and to assess and monitor the progress of individuals or of the whole class.

Workshop can be a supportive but open forum in which all students express themselves freely and experiment with different approaches to learning. It is also a good way for students to help each other over hard spots. Placing English Language Learners in pairs and in small groups takes away an emphasis on individual performance, something that can interfere with learning a second language in the initial stages.

✱ English Language Learners

In *Collections for Young Scholars,* English Language Learners receive the same high-quality instruction as do all other students. Instruction respects and builds on English Language Learners' existing knowledge and competencies. A wide range of oral language activities gives them opportunities to hear and to use English for valid communicative purposes—to learn new things from and with their classmates. Frequent reading and writing experiences help the students acquire English vocabulary, learn English spellings, and become familiar with the mechanics of writing and the writing process.

Preparing to Use the Grade 5 Program of *Collections for Young Scholars*®

Before you begin to use the grade 5 program, you should do the following:

BECOME AQUAINTED WITH THE INSTRUCTIONAL GOALS

Clarity and concrete support for helping students become intentional, self-directed learners were the primary goals in the writing of the lessons contained in *Framework for Effective Teaching.* All lessons were thoroughly reviewed by panels of teachers, who are actively involved in the classroom. The Scope and Sequence Chart, found in each book of the teacher's guide, can provide a quick overview of content of the lessons.

CHECK YOUR MATERIALS

You will need the following materials for each student:
- *Collections for Young Scholars,* Volume 5, Book 1
- *Collections for Young Scholars,* Volume 5, Book 2
- Explorer's Notebook, Volume 5
- Reading/Writing Connection, Volume 5
- Writer's Notebook (Each student should keep his or her own Writer's Notebook in a binder or folder, supplied either by the student or by the school. See the directions for assembling the Writer's Notebook in the Organize Student Materials section.)

In addition to the teacher's guides, you should also have the following teacher resources:
- Teacher Toolbox
- Student Toolbox (one per classroom)

You will find it helpful to have the following optional component:
- Writer's Handbook (one per student)

ORGANIZE YOUR MATERIALS AND SET UP YOUR CLASSROOM

- The **Teacher Toolbox** serves as easily accessible storage for your instructional materials. Unpack the materials and use the dividers to organize the box.

- Set aside two areas for a **Concept Board** and a **Question Board,** where the students can share their growing knowledge about unit concepts. If you do not have bulletin board space, two large charts—clearly designated **Concept Board** and **Question Board**—can be placed where they are accessible to students. You will also want to keep a supply of self-sticking note pads for use with these boards.
- Display the **Instructional Posters** in order to make public the strategies and processes that students need to become effective readers, writers, and learners.
- Select an area of the classroom for **Independent Workshop** and a place for keeping Workshop materials. Choose an area with enough space to expand as the year progresses. **Learning Framework Card 5** contains more information about Independent Workshop.

ORGANIZE STUDENT MATERIALS

The students will each need a three-ring binder and a set of dividers for their **Writer's Notebooks.** If the students or the school cannot provide the binders, the students can use folders with brass clasps. Reproducible Masters, Part 1 (in the Teacher Toolbox) contains the following materials for students. For each student:

- Use Reproducible Master 5 to make individual tables of contents.
- Use Reproducible Masters 6-12 to make section dividers.
- Make a supply of copies of Reproducible Master 14, Vocabulary Exploration, for the students to use as they add words to the Personal Dictionary section.

Place the **Student Toolbox** in an area where the students can have access to it during Independent Workshop and at other times when they choose their own activities.

- Unpack the various cards in the Student Toolbox and use the dividers to organize the box.
- Work with your school or local librarian to obtain copies of the trade books mentioned on the Tradebook Connection Cards and to make these books available to your students.

Annotated Lesson

Presented here is an annotated lesson, designed to help you use this guide as efficiently and effectively as possible. This version of lesson 4, *Stevie,* in grade 3, unit 1, takes you point-by-point through a typical lesson, showing you where to locate all the information you'll need for planning and conducting lessons and assessing the progress of your students. The annotations also explain how to find and interpret important author, illustrator, and selection information that you may want to share with your students and their families.

1 Each **selection** in the unit is listed along with its **genre**, **author**, and **illustrator**.

2 Each selection has been chosen to add another perspective or to contribute new information that can be explored about the concepts.

3 A bullet (●) indicates an **award-winning** author and/or illustrator.

4 A triangle (▲) indicates the reproduction of a **full-length trade book**.

5 Each unit contains one selection that is designated especially for **independent reading**. During this lesson, the students demonstrate their ability to use strategies independently and to conduct discussions and skills lessons.

6 A square (■) indicates that a selection is dramatized on the **Listening Collections Audiocassette.**

7 Every unit contains reproductions of **fine-art** pieces that add a further dimension to the unit concepts.

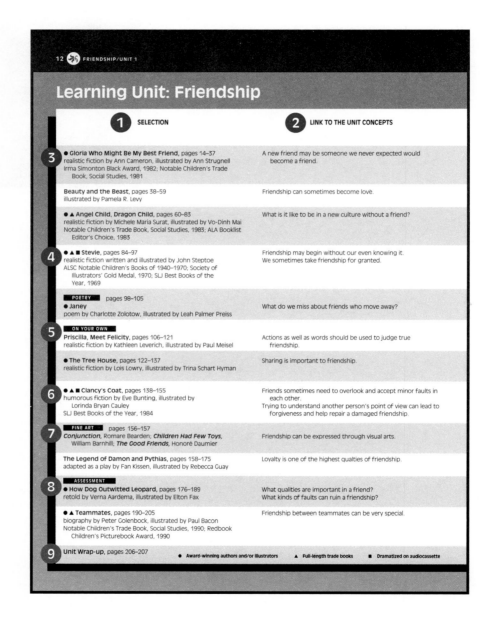

12 FRIENDSHIP/UNIT 1

Learning Unit: Friendship

1 SELECTION	**2** LINK TO THE UNIT CONCEPTS
3 ● **Gloria Who Might Be My Best Friend,** pages 14–37 realistic fiction by Ann Cameron, illustrated by Ann Strugnell Irma Simonton Black Award, 1982; Notable Children's Trade Book, Social Studies, 1981	A new friend may be someone we never expected would become a friend.
Beauty and the Beast, pages 38–59 illustrated by Pamela R. Levy	Friendship can sometimes become love.
● ▲ **Angel Child, Dragon Child,** pages 60–83 realistic fiction by Michele Maria Surat, illustrated by Vo-Dinh Mai Notable Children's Trade Book, Social Studies, 1983; ALA Booklist Editor's Choice, 1983	What is it like to be in a new culture without a friend?
4 ● ▲ ■ **Stevie,** pages 84–97 realistic fiction written and illustrated by John Steptoe ALSC Notable Children's Books of 1940–1970; Society of Illustrators' Gold Medal, 1970; SLJ Best Books of the Year, 1969	Friendship may begin without our even knowing it. We sometimes take friendship for granted.
POETRY pages 98–105 ● **Janey** poem by Charlotte Zolotow, illustrated by Leah Palmer Preiss	What do we miss about friends who move away?
5 **ON YOUR OWN** **Priscilla, Meet Felicity,** pages 106–121 realistic fiction by Kathleen Leverich, illustrated by Paul Meisel	Actions as well as words should be used to judge true friendship.
● **The Tree House,** pages 122–137 realistic fiction by Lois Lowry, illustrated by Trina Schart Hyman	Sharing is important to friendship.
6 ● ▲ ■ **Clancy's Coat,** pages 138–155 humorous fiction by Eve Bunting, illustrated by Lorinda Bryan Cauley SLJ Best Books of the Year, 1984	Friends sometimes need to overlook and accept minor faults in each other. Trying to understand another person's point of view can lead to forgiveness and help repair a damaged friendship.
7 **FINE ART** pages 156–157 *Conjunction,* Romare Bearden; *Children Had Few Toys,* William Barnhill; *The Good Friends,* Honoré Daumier	Friendship can be expressed through visual arts.
The Legend of Damon and Pythias, pages 158–175 adapted as a play by Fan Kissen, illustrated by Rebecca Guay	Loyalty is one of the highest qualties of friendship.
8 **ASSESSMENT** ● **How Dog Outwitted Leopard,** pages 176–189 retold by Verna Aardema, illustrated by Elton Fax	What qualities are important in a friend? What kinds of faults can ruin a friendship?
● ▲ **Teammates,** pages 190–205 biography by Peter Golenbock, illustrated by Paul Bacon Notable Children's Trade Book, Social Studies, 1990; Redbook Children's Picturebook Award, 1990	Friendship between teammates can be very special.
9 Unit Wrap-up, pages 206–207	● Award-winning authors and/or illustrators ▲ Full-length trade books ■ Dramatized on audiocassette

8 One selection in each unit is designed to be used for **assessment** of the students' growing knowledge of the concepts. The focus of these assessments is on connecting new knowledge to existing knowledge.

9 The **Wrap-up** at the end of each unit provides closure of the unit exploration.

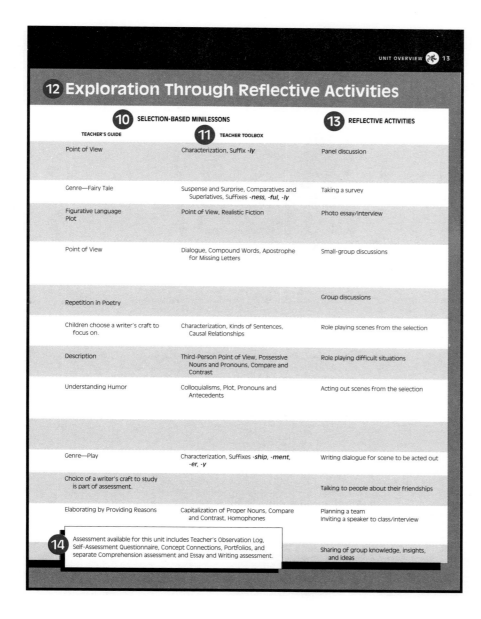

12 Exploration Through Reflective Activities

| 10 SELECTION-BASED MINILESSONS | | 13 REFLECTIVE ACTIVITIES |
TEACHER'S GUIDE	11 TEACHER TOOLBOX	
Point of View	Characterization, Suffix -ly	Panel discussion
Genre—Fairy Tale	Suspense and Surprise, Comparatives and Superlatives, Suffixes -ness, -ful, -ly	Taking a survey
Figurative Language Plot	Point of View, Realistic Fiction	Photo essay/interview
Point of View	Dialogue, Compound Words, Apostrophe for Missing Letters	Small-group discussions
Repetition in Poetry		Group discussions
Children choose a writer's craft to focus on.	Characterization, Kinds of Sentences, Causal Relationships	Role playing scenes from the selection
Description	Third-Person Point of View, Possessive Nouns and Pronouns, Compare and Contrast	Role playing difficult situations
Understanding Humor	Colloquialisms, Plot, Pronouns and Antecedents	Acting out scenes from the selection
Genre—Play	Characterization, Suffixes -ship, -ment, -er, -y	Writing dialogue for scene to be acted out
Choice of a writer's craft to study is part of assessment.		Talking to people about their friendships
Elaborating by Providing Reasons	Capitalization of Proper Nouns, Compare and Contrast, Homophones	Planning a team Inviting a speaker to class/interview
		Sharing of group knowledge, insights, and ideas

14 Assessment available for this unit includes Teacher's Observation Log, Self-Assessment Questionnaire, Concept Connections, Portfolios, and separate Comprehension assessment and Essay and Writing assessment.

10 Selection-Based Instruction is included within the Reading with a Writer's Eye portion of every lesson. You may use this instruction, or select from the Options for Instruction.

11 The contents of the Teacher Toolbox provide support for opportunity-driven instruction. Choose those lessons you believe are the most valuable. The **Options for Instruction** are based on selection text; however, you may choose any minilessons you wish based on your students' needs and/or district requirements. These lessons appear on **Teacher Tool Cards** in the **Teacher Toolbox** for your use whenever the need arises.

12 Each grade contains two ways of exploring the unit concepts: through **research** and through **reflective activities.** The kind of exploration expected from the students differs for each type of unit.

13 In the units involving topics of universal interest, exploration takes place through participation in **reflective activities.**

14 A number of **assessment options** for each unit are available in the Assessment Module of the Teacher Toolbox. The options are designed to actively involve both students and teachers in creating an atmosphere conducive to authentic assessment of the students' growing ability.

1 Link to the Unit Concepts explains the connections between this selection and the concepts discussed in the unit introduction. Each selection has been carefully chosen to add to the students' increasing understanding and knowledge of the unit topic and unit concepts.

Stevie

1 READING THE SELECTION

INFORMATION FOR THE TEACHER

About the Selection

As an only child, Robert is not used to sharing his toys or having to consider the needs and feelings of another child. By the time the young visitor Stevie leaves the household, Robert has learned something about himself and about being a friend. The characters speak an African-American dialect that lends the story its charm; and the illustrations, drawn with chalk in Steptoe's unique style, make this story a delight to read.

1 Link to the Unit Concepts

Stevie, pages 40–45, may lead the children to think about friendships they take for granted and whether it is possible for a friendship to begin without someone knowing it. After reading *Stevie,* children should better understand the friend they have in a younger brother, sister, cousin, neighbor, or schoolmate, even though they may believe they would be far better off without such a friend. At the end of this story, Robert discovers that Stevie wasn't so bad after all. In fact, after Stevie has gone, Robert "kinda" misses him.

About the Author/Illustrator

John Steptoe wrote and illustrated *Stevie* in 1969 at the age of 19. He used the language that many black children speak. He felt there was a need for books that black children could relate to. This dialogue may be difficult for some children to read, but all children will understand the story and the problem it touches on. The book brought Steptoe instant recognition, and he was awarded a gold medal by the Society of Illustrators. *Stevie* was named a best book of the year by both *School Library Journal* and *Publisher's Weekly.* The profile on page 45 of the student anthology tells more about Steptoe and his reasons for writing *Stevie.*

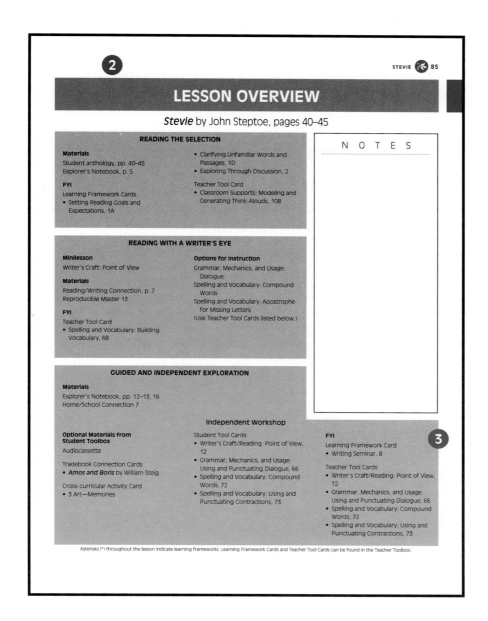

②

LESSON OVERVIEW

Stevie by John Steptoe, pages 40–45

READING THE SELECTION

Materials
Student anthology, pp. 40–45
Explorer's Notebook, p. 5

FYI
Learning Framework Cards
• Setting Reading Goals and Expectations, 1A

• Clarifying Unfamiliar Words and Passages, 1D
• Exploring Through Discussion, 2

Teacher Tool Card
• Classroom Supports: Modeling and Generating Think-Alouds, 108

N O T E S

READING WITH A WRITER'S EYE

Minilesson
Writer's Craft: Point of View

Materials
Reading/Writing Connection, p. 7
Reproducible Master 13

FYI
Teacher Tool Card
• Spelling and Vocabulary: Building Vocabulary, 68

Options for Instruction
Grammar, Mechanics, and Usage: Dialogue
Spelling and Vocabulary: Compound Words
Spelling and Vocabulary: Apostrophe for Missing Letters
(Use Teacher Tool Cards listed below.)

GUIDED AND INDEPENDENT EXPLORATION

Materials
Explorer's Notebook, pp. 12–13, 16
Home/School Connection 7

Optional Materials from Student Toolbox
Audiocassette

Tradebook Connection Cards
• *Amos and Boris* by William Steig

Cross-curricular Activity Card
• 3 Art—Memories

Independent Workshop

Student Tool Cards
• Writer's Craft/Reading: Point of View, 12
• Grammar, Mechanics, and Usage: Using and Punctuating Dialogue, 66
• Spelling and Vocabulary: Compound Words, 72
• Spelling and Vocabulary: Using and Punctuating Contractions, 73

FYI
Learning Framework Card
• Writing Seminar, 8

Teacher Tool Cards
• Writer's Craft/Reading: Point of View, 12
• Grammar, Mechanics, and Usage: Using and Punctuating Dialogue, 66
• Spelling and Vocabulary: Compound Words, 72
• Spelling and Vocabulary: Using and Punctuating Contractions, 73

③

Asterisks (*) throughout the lesson indicate learning frameworks. Learning Framework Cards and Teacher Tool Cards can be found in the Teacher Toolbox.

---

② Each **Lesson Overview** provides a quick look at what you can expect while working with the unit. The Lesson Overview is organized to reflect the three standard parts of each lesson.

• **Reading the Selection** indicates student anthology pages and Explorer's Notebook pages used in the lesson.

• **Reading with a Writer's Eye** indicates minilessons included in the lesson and the materials needed for working on those minilessons. **Options for Instruction** are also offered to help you tailor your curriculum planning to your individual classes.

• **Guided and Independent Exploration** contains information about minilessons presented in this section of the lesson, along with materials references and Student Toolbox materials appropriate to the lesson.

③ **FYI** (For Your Information) indicates relevant Teacher Tool Cards and Learning Framework Cards that might be helpful in teaching the lesson.

1 Information that is pertinent to the understanding of a selection or that would enhance the students' enjoyment of the selection is provided before the students begin reading.

2 **Learning Frameworks** such as Cognitive and Responsive Reading are indicated with an asterisk (✱). Additional information for each learning framework can be found on the Learning Framework Cards stored in the Teacher Toolbox.

3 The **students** are encouraged to **make choices** about how to read the selections. The recommendations found here can help you help the students make that decision.

4 Helping students become mature strategic readers is one goal of this program. The different reading strategies are introduced and discussed in **About the Reading Strategies.**

---

1 **INFORMATION FOR THE STUDENT**

Tell the children that John Steptoe wrote this story and drew the pictures for it. Explain that John Steptoe's writing reflects the speech of city children he grew up with. He wanted to write a book that they could read easily.

2 ✱ **COGNITIVE AND RESPONSIVE READING**

Activating Prior Knowledge

If the children have ever had to "put up with" a younger brother or sister, you might ask them to talk about their experiences.

Setting Reading Goals and Expectations

Explain to the children that before they read they will set reading goals and expectations. To do this, they will browse the first page of the selection. Use the clues/problems/wondering procedure. On the chalkboard under the headings clues, problems, and wonderings, write in brief note form the observations the children generate during browsing. These will be returned to after reading. For a review of **browsing,** see **Learning Framework Card 1A.**

3 **Recommendations for Reading the Selection**

Because the informal language and dialect might be difficult for some children to read at first, oral reading of *Stevie* is suggested. You might begin reading aloud until the children become accustomed to the style. Then have them continue when they feel comfortable doing so. Since this story is full of emotion, encourage expressive reading throughout.

If the children elect to read orally, you should refer to the think-aloud prompts that are provided beneath the page miniatures. Instead of or in addition to using these prompts, encourage the children to provide their own think-alouds while reading.

This would be a good selection for **responding to text by expressing feelings** while reading aloud. Model this response and invite the children to do the same.

If the children elect to read silently, have them discuss problems, reactions, and strategies after reading. Let the children know, however, that they can raise their hands any time during reading to ask questions or to identify problems for discussion with the group.

4 **About the Reading Strategies**

Since the dialect and informal language in this story may be confusing for some children as they read, the **clarifying strategies** may be helpful.

The children should realize that when we read, there are often things we don't immediately understand. Sometimes it's a single word. Sometimes it's a sentence or an idea. Sometimes it's the reason a character does something or why an event happens.

The children should recognize that **clarifying** is something they do often. For example, if a friend were telling them about something that happened and used a name they didn't know, say Josephine, they would probably stop the friend and ask, "Who's Josephine?" This kind of conversation is an example of clarifying.

Introducing Clarifying Strategies

Clarifying requires that readers actively participate in reading a selection by identifying words and ideas that are difficult for them. Be sure the children understand that all readers, even good readers, get confused and occasionally need something clarified.

When good readers don't understand what they are reading, they often stop and ask themselves a question about it and look for the answer. Asking questions is one way to start clarifying something that confuses us. In addition, rereading the other words in the sentence or paragraph will often **clarify** the meaning of a word or a confusing idea. Sometimes if we go back and look, we find that the cause for an action or event has already been stated. Other times we have to keep the question in mind and look for the answer as we read on. If we can't figure it out on our own, we can always ask a friend for help.

Clarifying is an important key to independent comprehension. It is very important to help every child understand and apply these strategies. To review **clarifying**, see **Learning Framework Card 1D.**

Before the children begin reading, be sure to direct their attention to the **reading strategy poster Clarifying Unfamiliar Words and Passages,** which should be displayed in a prominent place along with the other reading strategy posters. Read the poster together and discuss the questions. Remind the children to refer to and use this poster whenever they need to clarify.

Reading Strategy Posters

⑤ Think-Aloud Prompts for Use in Oral Reading

Notice the suggested think-aloud prompts under the page miniatures. Keep in mind that these are merely suggestions for helping the children use the strategies. Remind the children that reading should make sense. Reiterate that using the strategy posters will help them when they have a problem as they read. Explain that you will occasionally model the strategies you use when a problem arises, but that you also want them to take responsibility for using strategies and sharing with others how they solved their reading problems.

Encourage the children to ask for clarification or to use any of the strategies that they've learned so far whenever they feel it is appropriate. Remind them also to stop at any time during reading to share their reactions to the story. Try especially to get the children's opinions about the characters. For a review of **modeling and generating think-alouds,** see **Teacher Tool Card 108.**

TEACHING TIP You should "think-aloud" often as you read, making connections, wondering, and so on. **⑥**

⑤ Think-Aloud Prompts are included with the selection page miniatures. These prompts are placed where the students may need to use the reading strategies. The prompts are only suggestions for handling these text situations. The response of your class should always determine when and why the strategies are used.

⑥ Teaching Tips give you reminders and special teaching hints as you progress through each lesson.

1 **Think-Aloud Prompts** are included to help you encourage the students to think strategically as they read. As you and the students model this thinking, students learn to use this process independently.

2 For your convenience, prompt references are clearly marked on miniature pages of the student text.

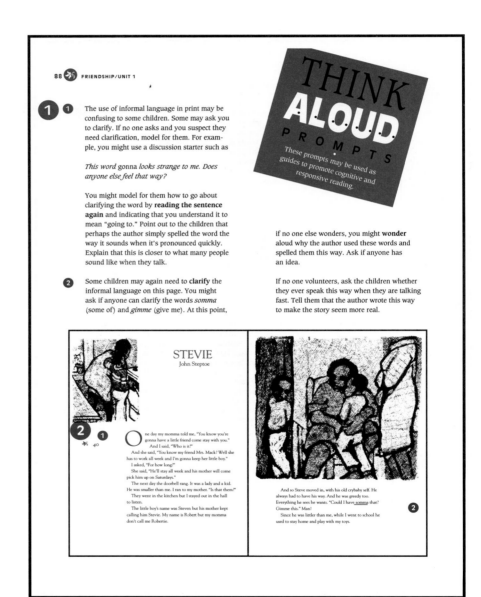

3 If the children seem to be confused, ask a volunteer to **clarify** the word *gotta* (got to).

1 Making thinking public can help the students understand how to use the strategies as they read. After reading the selections, the students are encouraged to **discuss** and share their **strategy use**. They are also encouraged to develop their own strategies and to share them with their classmates.

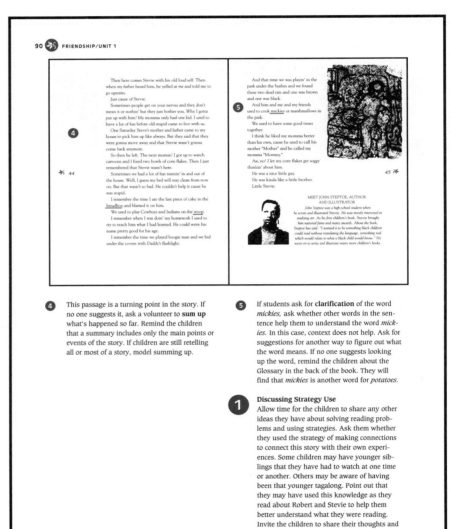

4 This passage is a turning point in the story. If no one suggests it, ask a volunteer to **sum up** what's happened so far. Remind the children that a summary includes only the main points or events of the story. If children are still retelling all or most of a story, model summing up.

5 If students ask for **clarification** of the word *mickies*, ask whether other words in the sentence help them to understand the word *mickies*. In this case, context does not help. Ask for suggestions for another way to figure out what the word means. If no one suggests looking up the word, remind the children about the Glossary in the back of the book. They will find that *mickies* is another word for *potatoes*.

1 **Discussing Strategy Use**
Allow time for the children to share any other ideas they have about solving reading problems and using strategies. Ask them whether they used the strategy of making connections to connect this story with their own experiences. Some children may have younger siblings that they have had to watch at one time or another. Others may be aware of having been that younger tagalong. Point out that they may have used this knowledge as they read about Robert and Stevie to help them better understand what they were reading. Invite the children to share their thoughts and opinions about the characters.

② Students **explore** selections **through** a framework of **discussion** that includes a general response to the text; a return to the clues, problems, and wonderings recorded as part of browsing before reading; and making connections between the selection and the unit concepts.

③ As a group, the **students reflect** on the selection and return to the clues, problems, and wonderings recorded before reading. They raise any additional questions and discuss wonderings that they want to pursue.

④ **Discussion ideas** are presented to help you assess the students' general understanding of the selection.

⑤ Students are encouraged to always record their impressions of the selection in their **Response Journals.**

⑥ When students have discussed the selection and their reaction to it, they form **small groups** and **discuss connections** between the selection and the unit concepts.

⑦ Small groups share their **discussion of the connections** with one another. Similarities and differences of opinion are discussed, and the **links** between the selection and unit concepts take shape.

⑧ For your convenience, possible links to the explorable concepts are noted.

⑨ The students record their ideas and questions on the **Concept Board** and the **Question Board.**

⑩ The students point out and discuss how each selection fits into the unit as a whole and what each selection adds to the understanding of unit concepts.

⑪ For your convenience, possible connections to other selections in the unit are noted. Students also are encouraged to make connections across units.

---

② *

STEVIE 91

EXPLORING THROUGH DISCUSSION

By now you should be familiar with the learning framework for Exploring Through Discussion. Continue the discussion sequence followed in the previous lessons. If you need to review the discussion sequence, see **Learning Framework Card 2, Exploring Through Discussion.**

③ Reflecting on the Selection
Whole-Group Discussion

The **whole group discusses** the selection and any thoughts, reactions, or questions that it raises. During this time, children also **return to the clues, problems, and wonderings** they noted on the chalkboard during browsing.

④ Assessment

To assess the children's understanding of the text, engage in discussion to determine whether the children have grasped the idea of the old saying "You don't know what you have 'til it's gone." The class might discuss its meaning in relation to this story.

⑤ Response Journal

Children may wish to record their personal responses to the selection.

⑥ Exploring Concepts Within the Selection
Small-Group Discussion

Small groups discuss the relation of the selection to friendship. Circulate and observe the small-group discussions. Remind the children to refer to the Concept Board and the Question Board to help keep their discussions focused.

⑦ Sharing Ideas About Explorable Concepts

Have the groups report and discuss their ideas with the rest of the class. It is crucial that the children's ideas determine this discussion.
• The children may point out how Robert and Stevie were alike and how they were different. They may discuss Robert's feelings about Stevie and come to some conclusions about the two boys, particularly regarding their age difference and how this factor affected their relationship.

⑧
• Perhaps the children will discuss the likelihood of becoming friends with someone they don't think they like.
• The children may recognize that Robert was not willing to make friends with Stevie. If he had been, perhaps he and Stevie would have had more fun together before Stevie left.

⑨
As these ideas and others are stated, have the children add them to the Question Board or Concept Board.

⑩ Exploring Concepts Across Selections

Ask the children how this story reminds them of other stories they have read. They may make connections with the other selections in the unit.
• The children may point out that, as in the other stories in this unit,

⑪
time spent together was important. The time Robert and Stevie spent together helped them to become better acquainted, although in this case, Robert didn't realize it until later.

---

1 As a conclusion to each discussion, the students **evaluate the discussion** and comment on its value to their exploration of the unit concepts.

2 As they proceed through the lessons, the students are constantly updating the **Concept Board** and the **Question Board**.

3 Miniature pages of the student ancillaries provide you with the convenience of seeing what the students will be working on in conjunction with the various parts of the lesson.

The **Explorer's Notebook** helps the students to progress through their exploration and research.

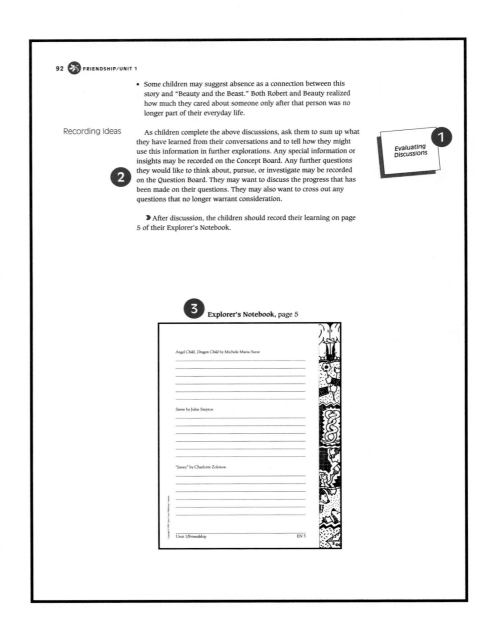

• Some children may suggest absence as a connection between this story and "Beauty and the Beast." Both Robert and Beauty realized how much they cared about someone only after that person was no longer part of their everyday life.

Recording Ideas

As children complete the above discussions, ask them to sum up what they have learned from their conversations and to tell how they might use this information in further explorations. Any special information or insights may be recorded on the Concept Board. Any further questions they would like to think about, pursue, or investigate may be recorded on the Question Board. They may want to discuss the progress that has been made on their questions. They may also want to cross out any questions that no longer warrant consideration.

➤ After discussion, the children should record their learning on page 5 of their Explorer's Notebook.

Evaluating Discussions

3 Explorer's Notebook, page 5

Angel Child, Dragon Child by Michele Maria Surat

Stevie by John Steptoe

"Janey" by Charlotte Zolotow

Unit I/Friendship   EN 5

4 Students are encouraged to always look for examples of writing techniques in their reading and to use these techniques in their own writing.

5 All **Writer's Craft** and writing minilessons depend entirely on selection content, thus providing your students with a wealth of examples to reinforce the lesson content.

Each Lesson Overview lists Teacher Tool Cards, stored in the Teacher Toolbox, that contain alternate lessons. The needs of your class should determine the lessons you choose to teach.

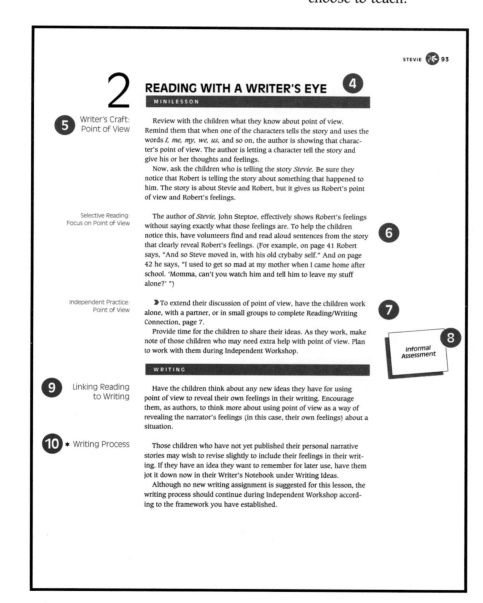

2 READING WITH A WRITER'S EYE **4**

MINILESSON

5 Writer's Craft: Point of View

Review with the children what they know about point of view. Remind them that when one of the characters tells the story and uses the words *I, me, my, we, us,* and so on, the author is showing that character's point of view. The author is letting a character tell the story and give his or her thoughts and feelings.

Now, ask the children who is telling the story *Stevie.* Be sure they notice that Robert is telling the story about something that happened to him. The story is about Stevie and Robert, but it gives us Robert's point of view and Robert's feelings.

Selective Reading: Focus on Point of View

The author of *Stevie,* John Steptoe, effectively shows Robert's feelings without saying exactly what those feelings are. To help the children notice this, have volunteers find and read aloud sentences from the story that clearly reveal Robert's feelings. (For example, on page 41 Robert says, "And so Steve moved in, with his old crybaby self." And on page 42 he says, "I used to get so mad at my mother when I came home after school. 'Momma, can't you watch him and tell him to leave my stuff alone?' ") **6**

Independent Practice: Point of View

➤To extend their discussion of point of view, have the children work alone, with a partner, or in small groups to complete Reading/Writing Connection, page 7. **7**

Provide time for the children to share their ideas. As they work, make note of those children who may need extra help with point of view. Plan to work with them during Independent Workshop.

Informal Assessment **8**

WRITING

9 Linking Reading to Writing

Have the children think about any new ideas they have for using point of view to reveal their own feelings in their writing. Encourage them, as authors, to think more about using point of view as a way of revealing the narrator's feelings (in this case, their own feelings) about a situation.

10 * Writing Process

Those children who have not yet published their personal narrative stories may wish to revise slightly to include their feelings in their writing. If they have an idea they want to remember for later use, have them jot it down now in their Writer's Notebook under Writing Ideas.

Although no new writing assignment is suggested for this lesson, the writing process should continue during Independent Workshop according to the framework you have established.

6 As a group, the **students** find and **discuss** the selection author's use of **writing techniques and conventions.** Not until these techniques and conventions are thoroughly discussed are students asked to work independently.

7 Students use their **Reading/Writing Connection** books to continue their study of the author's use of writing techniques. In continuing their study and discussions, the students may choose to work alone or in small groups.

8 For your convenience, especially good opportunities for **informal assessment** are noted.

9 Students are always asked to link to their writing what they learned from the minilessons. By applying what they have learned to their own writing, the students are given the opportunity to immediately reinforce this new learning.

10 The students are introduced to and encouraged to use the **phases of the writing process** as they produce their own pieces of writing.

1 **The Reading/Writing Connection** gives students the opportunity to identify, analyze, and discuss examples of writing techniques found not only in the student anthology but also in their other reading.

2 The students are asked to view new vocabulary in two distinct ways. First, since unit concepts are critical to all of the work done in *Collections for Young Scholars*, words that are important to understanding these concepts are pointed out and discussed. Then the students are asked to identify and discuss words from the selection that they think will be useful in their writing.

Students are always encouraged to use **Vocabulary Exploration** forms to record and study words they choose and to place these forms in the Personal Dictionary section of their Writer's Notebook.

3 Convenient **Vocabulary Tips** help guide you in working with the students in developing vocabulary.

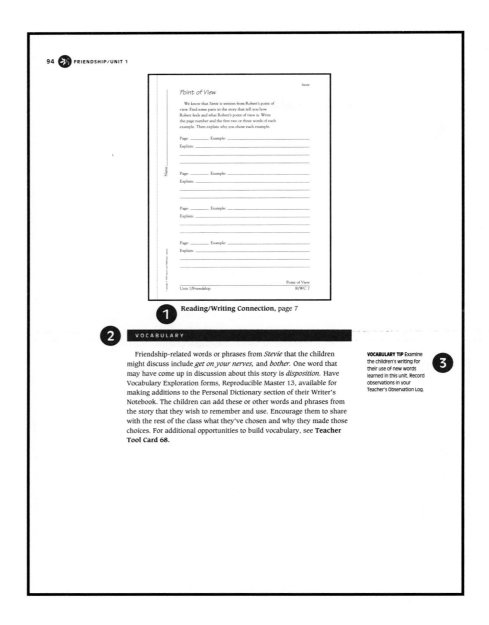

94 🏃 FRIENDSHIP/UNIT 1

Point of View

We know that *Stevie* is written from Robert's point of view. Find some parts in the story that tell you how Robert feels and what Robert's point of view is. Write the page number and the first two or three words of each example. Then explain why you chose each example.

Page: _____ Example: _____
Explain: _____

Page: _____ Example: _____
Explain: _____

Page: _____ Example: _____
Explain: _____

Page: _____ Example: _____
Explain: _____

Unit 1/Friendship   Point of View
                                    R/WC 7

1 **Reading/Writing Connection,** page 7

2 VOCABULARY

Friendship-related words or phrases from *Stevie* that the children might discuss include *get on your nerves,* and *bother.* One word that may have come up in discussion about this story is *disposition.* Have Vocabulary Exploration forms, Reproducible Master 13, available for making additions to the Personal Dictionary section of their Writer's Notebook. The children can add these or other words and phrases from the story that they wish to remember and use. Encourage them to share with the rest of the class what they've chosen and why they made those choices. For additional opportunities to build vocabulary, see **Teacher Tool Card 68.**

VOCABULARY TIP Examine the children's writing for their use of new words learned in this unit. Record observations in your Teacher's Observation Log. **3**

3

GUIDED AND INDEPENDENT EXPLORATION ❹

EXPLORING CONCEPTS BEYOND THE TEXT ❺

STEVIE 95

❻ Guided Exploration

Children will select activities in which they explore concepts related to friendship. Refer them to the exploration activities poster and give them time to discuss what they wish to explore and how they wish to go about it. If the children need further help, here are some suggestions:

❯ Have the children form small groups and discuss their groups of friends and problems they have had with friends. Have them use page 16 in their Explorer's Notebook to extend this discussion. Have the groups share their ideas and conclusions. If students want to write about this, suggest that they write a newspaper advice column.

❯ Distribute Home/School Connection 7. Encourage the children to discuss with adults at home ways to care for younger children.

* Exploring Through Reflective Activities

Continuing Exploration

Have the children review the questions on the **Question Board**. Remove any that they no longer find interesting or appropriate. ❼

Have the children return to Explorer's Notebook, pages 12–13, to continue planning their exploration on friendship. Remind them to add their thoughts about possible ideas to explore.

Explorer's Notebook, page 16

❽ Home/School Connection 7

Exploring Friendship

---

❹ **Exploration** forms the heart of the program. Each lesson guides you and the students in exploring unit concepts and learning how to be a community of scholars.

❺ The students have explored and discussed unit concepts as they apply to the lesson text; the students have also connected the new text to selections they have read previously. Now they take their **exploration beyond the student text** and out into the larger world. Learning doesn't just take place in the classroom.

❻ Suggestions and guidance are supplied to help you and the students at each step of their explorations. Students know what your expectations of them are and why their explorations are important.

❼ **The Concept Board** and the **Question Board** are the focal points and the source of much of the unit exploration. They are a dynamic representation of ongoing exploration. They are also the point of organization for many of the small exploration groups. Through this ongoing public display of questions and information, students with similar research interests are able to identify each other.

❽ Through the **Home/School Connection,** adults at home are not only kept informed of what their children are studying, they are also shown how to take active roles in the unit explorations.

57F

1 **Independent Workshop** gives the students the time they need to pursue their explorations. Students may work individually, in pairs, or in small groups to read, discuss, research, write about, and present ideas pertaining to their exploration and research.

2 The students are always encouraged to take responsibility for their own learning. Part of this growing responsibility is learning to budget and organize their time and energy. **Students** are encouraged to **make choices** about their use of Independent Workshop time. Although most of the time will be spent exploring unit concepts, other options are available as time permits.

3 Adult readers enjoy sharing with friends what they are reading. They discuss their reading, give opinions on it, and recommend books to each other. The students are encouraged at all times to cultivate the habits and behaviors of mature readers. **Reading Roundtable** offers students this opportunity. Tradebook Connection Cards, available in the Student Toolbox, can be used to give students ideas about activities and discussions related to popular trade books and familiar classics.

4 The students may decide to use some of this time to work on writing projects they started earlier in this lesson or in previous ones. During a **Writing Seminar,** students may choose to conference with their peers to gain feedback about their writing. This is also a good time for you to conference with the students about their writing. Guidance is also offered here on using the writing process.

Student Tool Cards contain lessons that the students can use independently to help them in their writing, revising, and proofreading.

5 Both you and the students will be choosing representative work to place in their **portfolios.** Independent Workshop provides the time necessary to carefully consider additions to the portfolio.

6 **Cross-curricular Activity Cards** highlight for the students cross-curricular applications of what they are learning in *Collections for Young Scholars.* Students are given the opportunity to participate in activities related to the selections and the explorable concepts that have broad applications in science, mathematics, social studies, art, drama, and music.

7 Independent Workshop affords you an additional **opportunity to observe the students as they interact in their research groups, discuss literature, and work on their writing.** The Teacher Tool Cards give you the freedom to address the children's individual needs during this time. Tool Cards that work particularly well with the lesson text are listed here. These cards, however, are just suggestions; you and your students will be the best judges of what they need to focus on.

The students should be encouraged to use the Student Tool Card lessons stored in the Student Toolbox to help them in their study.

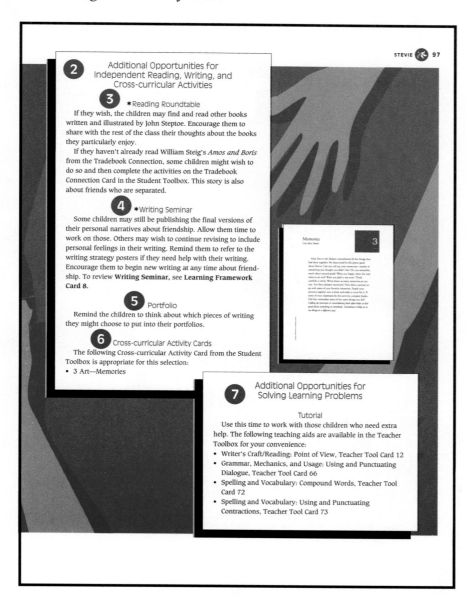

2 Additional Opportunities for Independent Reading, Writing, and Cross-curricular Activities

3 *Reading Roundtable
If they wish, the children may find and read other books written and illustrated by John Steptoe. Encourage them to share with the rest of the class their thoughts about the books they particularly enjoy.
If they haven't already read William Steig's *Amos and Boris* from the Tradebook Connection, some children might wish to do so and then complete the activities on the Tradebook Connection Card in the Student Toolbox. This story is also about friends who are separated.

4 *Writing Seminar
Some children may still be publishing the final versions of their personal narratives about friendship. Allow them time to work on those. Others may wish to continue revising to include personal feelings in their writing. Remind them to refer to the writing strategy posters if they need help with their writing. Encourage them to begin new writing at any time about friendship. To review **Writing Seminar,** see **Learning Framework Card 8.**

5 Portfolio
Remind the children to think about which pieces of writing they might choose to put into their portfolios.

6 Cross-curricular Activity Cards
The following Cross-curricular Activity Card from the Student Toolbox is appropriate for this selection:
• 3 Art—Memories

7 Additional Opportunities for Solving Learning Problems

Tutorial
Use this time to work with those children who need extra help. The following teaching aids are available in the Teacher Toolbox for your convenience:
• Writer's Craft/Reading: Point of View, Teacher Tool Card 12
• Grammar, Mechanics, and Usage: Using and Punctuating Dialogue, Teacher Tool Card 66
• Spelling and Vocabulary: Compound Words, Teacher Tool Card 72
• Spelling and Vocabulary: Using and Punctuating Contractions, Teacher Tool Card 73

STEVIE 97

Volume 5

Framework for Effective Teaching® Grade 5 Book 1

Introducing *Collections for Young Scholars*®

Preview by the Students

Activating Prior
Knowledge

Ask the students whether they are familiar with any kinds of book collections. They may mention some popular series like Little House, Encyclopedia Brown, or a set of encyclopedias. If they are unsure about the meaning of *collection,* explain that a collection is a group of books created to be read, studied, or kept together and that each book is called a volume. Have students who are familiar with collections explain why the different volumes go together.

Setting Reading Goals
and Expectations

Ask the students to tell how they choose a book at the library. Emphasize the aspects of **browsing** mentioned by the students— reading the title, looking at the illustrations, flipping through a few pages to find out what the book is about. Then point out that before they start reading, **good readers** spend some time **setting reading goals** and **deciding what they expect from a text**. A good reader often begins setting reading goals and expectations by looking at and thinking about the **title** of the book or story. Have a volunteer read aloud the title of this book, *Collections for Young Scholars*.

Invite the students to give their definitions or impressions of the word *scholar.* Be sure to allow sufficient time for the students to discuss any ideas they have about scholars. At the conclusion of this discussion, you may want to ask the students whether they consider themselves scholars and why.

Read the following definition to the class:

> Scholars are people who study subjects that are important to them. They interpret, analyze, communicate, reason, and solve problems because these are ways to gain knowledge and understanding.

Have volunteers **paraphrase** this **definition**. Then ask how the definition affects their past ideas about scholars. Tell the students that whether or not they have previously considered themselves scholars, they will be expected to grow as scholars as the year progresses.

Cover Illustration

The cover illustration of *Collections for Young Scholars,* volume 5, book 1, shows three Native-American children in contemporary clothing interviewing a Native-American woman dressed in traditional clothing. Invite volunteers to share their impressions of the **illustration**. Tell the students that the cover illustration was done by **Mary Beth Schwark and Bob Kuester.** Share with the students the following information about Schwark, Kuester, and the illustration:

> "We were trying to capture the dignity of Native Americans and the rich heritage that they pass on to their own children as well as to all races here in America," says co-illustrator Schwark. "The woman in the illustration is explaining to the children the method for making pottery, as she learned from her mother, and as her mother learned from her mother."
>
> Kuester is a native of Iowa. He studied at the Art Center School in Los Angeles and has worked as an artist and illustrator for the past twenty years.
>
> Schwark is a native of Michigan. She studied at Macomb Community College in Warren, Michigan, and served an apprenticeship at the McNamara Art Studio in Detroit. She specializes in children's illustrations and has worked in the field for sixteen years.
>
> Kuester and Schwark live in New Mexico with their thirteen-year-old daughter.

Browsing *Collections for Young Scholars*®

The **purpose** of this initial browsing is to **help** the **students think** about what they will be reading and to **build** a sense of **anticipation** for the reading they will be doing.

Have the students spend a few minutes browsing *Collections for Young Scholars,* volume 5, book 1. Tell the students that when they browse, they should **quickly go through** the book to

- Get an idea of what the book is about
- Think about what they may learn from it
- See what looks interesting
- Notice things that may raise questions or cause problems

When the students have had ample time to browse the entire book, invite volunteers to point out things that they noticed. The students may have noticed particular illustrations, familiar story titles, or familiar unit topics. They may also point out titles that they have never encountered before or topics that they are not accustomed to seeing in a book such as this. As many **students** as possible should be given the opportunity to **comment on what they found** in their browsing.

You may want to **record comments** that have to do with the students' expectations. It will be interesting for the students to go back later to see whether their expectations were fulfilled.

Parts of the Book

Ask the students to look briefly at the **title page** and to tell what information they find there. Do the same for the **copyright page**. Review the meaning of the information given on the copyright page, including the copyright date.

When they have finished looking at these first few pages, have the students look at the table of contents. Ask them to share what they already know about a **table of contents** and its use. They should mention that a table of contents lists the **title of each selection**, the **author of each selection** (and the source of each selection if it is an excerpt), and the **page** on which **each selection begins.** This particular table of contents also lists for each selection the **genre,** the **illustrator,** and some of the **awards** it has won; and for some selections, special **author/illustrator information.** This table of contents also lists the pages on which the **unit opener, bibliography,** and **fine art** can be found. Give the students time to browse the table of contents and pick out titles or information that particularly interests them. Encourage them to share their impressions of the table of contents and the information contained in it.

When they have completed their discussions of the front of the book, ask the students to turn to the **Glossary**, page 356, and spend a few minutes browsing through it. Then ask them to share what they know about glossaries in general and what they noticed about this glossary in particular. If necessary, explain that the words in the glossary are words the students may need help with as they read the selections throughout the year.

Finally, encourage the students to think about the **whole book** and to tell what some of the subjects were and what they noticed that looked particularly interesting. As they respond, **write the titles of specific selections that they mention**. In each case, ask what it was about the selection that caught their attention. It will be interesting for the students to return to this list after they have read the selections.

Other Program Materials

In addition to the anthologies, each student will need one **Explorer's Notebook** and one **Reading/Writing Connection**. This may be a good time to **distribute** these books and have the students spend some time **browsing** them. Encourage the students to share what they notice.

Introduce the **Student Toolbox** to the students, and tell them where it will be permanently located. You may at this time want to tell the students about the **materials** that they will find in the Student Toolbox:

- **Student Tool Cards,** containing lessons in grammar, mechanics, and usage; reading and writing; spelling and vocabulary; study and research; and information about classroom participation that the students can access at any time
- **Cross-curricular Activity Cards,** containing activities that apply information from the selections across the curriculum
- **Tradebook Connection Cards,** containing activities to accompany trade books that can be found in the library
- **Listening Collections Audiocassette,** containing selected readings from anthology selections

To avoid confusion and ensure that everyone has an opportunity to look through the box, you may want to suggest that the students not all try to go through the box at the same time. If possible, allow **small groups** of four or five students each to go through the **Student Toolbox.**

Allow time for **discussion** and **questions** concerning the **contents** of the **Student Toolbox,** and assure the students that they will become very familiar with all of these materials as the year progresses.

At this point, you and your students may want to spend additional time to look over and to discuss *Collections for Young Scholars,* volume 5, book 1; or you may go directly to unit 1, Learning, and begin your explorations.

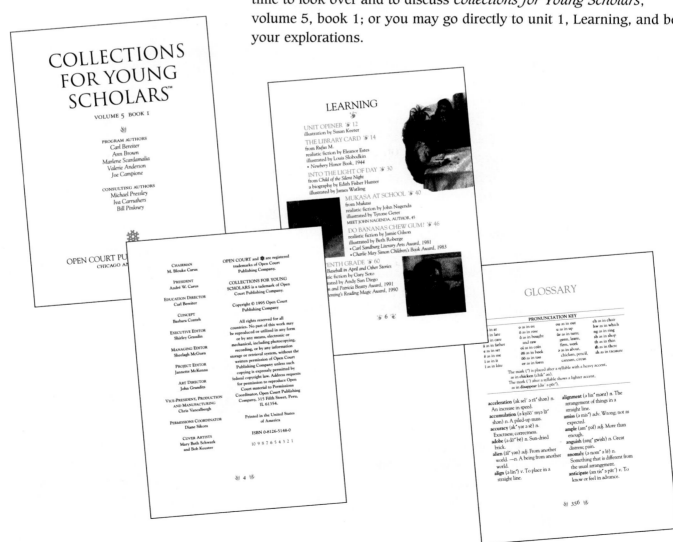

Learning

UNIT INTRODUCTION

BACKGROUND INFORMATION FOR THE TEACHER

Explorable
Concepts

Learning is what children are in school for, yet learning itself is hardly ever a subject for thought or reflection or inquiry for students—in school or out. This unit brings together a number of selections in which learning, mostly by young people, is a central theme. Some of the protagonists take to learning easily; others do not. In each case, a way of learning is as much a part of the person as a face or a voice. Reading these stories should make students reflect on their attitudes toward the ways they learn and on the place learning has in their lives.

Many children believe that learning is "just for kids." They believe that kids are ignorant, and when they get out of school they will no longer be ignorant and will have no need to keep learning. An important goal of this unit is to disabuse your students of that deeply rooted idea. Students might explore the varieties of learning that adults engage in: the training programs undertaken by large firms such as Motorola, the enormous effort and time that goes into getting a professional degree, the hard training and long practice required to become a professional athlete or musician. Compared to these forms of almost full-time learning, most grade school children do very little work.

The scope for inquiry is enormous: what sets human beings apart from all other animals is their prodigious capacity to learn. Scientists and psychologists have marveled at this quality and have studied it carefully, with limited results until the last half-century or so. More recently, they

have tried to model human learning with computers; whether they have achieved any degree of success is an open question. These are fields in which students may legitimately speculate, using their introspection about their own learning processes as evidence.

Learning raises a wide variety of questions. To stimulate your own thinking, you might ask yourself questions like the following, but many others are equally worthy of consideration.

- What would you most like to learn? Why?
- What advice about how to learn successfully would you give a child who was just starting school?
- Could a computer ever tell you what you need to learn (assuming computers get much better than they are now)?
- What is a good way to learn a foreign language?
- If a friend your age didn't know how to read and said there was no point in learning, how would you convince her to change her mind?

Resources   Among the following resources are **professional reference books, read-alouds, and audiovisual materials.** The reference books are intended to help you to organize information to share with students in whatever way you choose. The read-alouds are works that students may enjoy hearing read orally or books that may be too challenging for many students of this age to read independently but that fit the unit subject well and are quality literature. Among the audiovisual materials are some that your students may not be able to obtain and others that will be available to both you and the students. For a complete list of audiovisual sources, see page 567. The community/school resources include people that may be helpful in your exploration.

In addition to the resources listed here, **bibliographies for the students** appear in the student anthology, on **Reproducible Masters 15–19,** and on **Home/School Connection 3–4.** Encourage students to use these bibliographies as they explore learning.

You should also choose and read books from the students' bibliographies. Reading books about learning written for children will help you see and understand the students' point of view.

Professional Reference Books

Anderson, R. C., and others. *Becoming a Nation of Readers: The Report of the Commission on Reading.* Center for the Study of Reading, 1985. This report summarizes research and offers proposals for improving reading instruction.

Bauer, Marion Dane. *What's Your Story?: A Young Person's Guide to Writing Fiction.* Clarion, 1992. The Newbery Honor–winning author discusses the components of fiction and such topics as choosing ideas, revising, and sharing one's work, as she shows how a story works and how to write one.

Bereiter, Carl, and Scardamalia, Marlene. *Surpassing Ourselves: The Nature and Implications of Expertise.* Open Court Publishing Company, 1993. This book can help you create a classroom atmosphere that encourages students to become experts on subjects that interest them.

Zarnowski, Myra. *Learning About Biographies: A Reading-and-Writing Approach for Children.* National Council of Teachers of English, 1990. This teacher's guide will help you to help your students research and write biographies.

Read-Alouds

Dahl, Roald. "Lucky Break: How I Became a Writer," from *The Wonderful Story of Henry Sugar and Six More.* Puffin, 1988. This popular writer describes his school years and the events that led to his becoming a writer, and discusses the importance of writing down story ideas in a notebook.

Hopkins, Lee Bennett, editor. *Good Books, Good Times!* HarperCollins, 1990. Students will enjoy these poems about books and reading.

Juster, Norton. *The Phantom Toll Booth.* Knopf Books for Young Readers, 1988. Milo's trip through the magic tollbooth to the Kingdom of Wisdom changes him from a boy who is always bored to one who is interested in numbers, words, books, and learning.

Once upon a Time: Celebrating the Magic of Children's Books in Honor of the Twentieth Anniversary of Reading Is Fundamental. Putnam, 1986. More than twenty-six authors and illustrators talk about their experiences with books and reading.

Audiovisual Materials

Rufus M., Try Again. Martha Moran, 1977, Phoenix/BFA. This short film is a dramatization of the first selection in the unit. 13 minutes; film.

Booker. Coronet, MTI, 1980. The story of Booker T. Washington is told in this award-winning film. 40 minutes; videocassette.

Community/School

- School principal and other school personnel
- School and local librarians
- Persons in the community who can talk about their experiences in school or in learning a particular subject, such as music, art, science, or a foreign language

Concept Board

Provide space somewhere in the classroom for the Concept Board, which could be a bulletin board or a large sheet of chart paper attached to the wall. **The Concept Board will be a place where the students can post any information they gather and wish to share with their classmates** during their reading of each unit. This information might include written notes or stories, drawings, magazine or newspaper pictures and articles, or anything else that will illustrate the students' growth in knowledge about the subject of each unit. The first Concept Board will have the title Learning. (If you prefer, you may wait to introduce and begin the Concept Board until the students have begun reading and/or exploring and have information to post on it.)

Introducing the Concept Board

Question Board

Designate another area for the Question Board, preferably close to the Concept Board. Explain to the students that on the Question Board they will post any questions they have that are related to learning as they proceed through the unit. Students will take time periodically to review the questions on the board and to organize them, add to them, or remove them if they no longer warrant attention.

Both boards will allow the students to display and share their ideas and questions and to see who has common interests.

For a review of information about the **Concept Board** and the **Question Board,** see **Teacher Tool Card 121.**

Introducing the Question Board

UNIT PREVIEW BY THE STUDENTS

Activating Prior Knowledge

Have the students share what they know about the ways people learn and their ideas about learning in general. Encourage them to express their thoughts about what role learning plays in their own lives. It is important that students feel free to voice their opinions and discuss them. Misconceptions can be addressed as the class proceeds through the unit. On the Concept Board, have the students post learning-related ideas that they feel strongly about.

Setting Reading Goals and Expectations

Share with students the reasons and the procedures for browsing. Emphasize that browsing is not a word-for-word reading but rather a process of looking over a piece before reading it in order to notice things that may be familiar, interesting, unusual, or potentially troublesome.

Procedures for Browsing the Unit

- **Turn to the unit-opener pages. Look first at the unit title and think about what the title means and what kinds of selections may be in the unit.**
- **Look at the illustration on the opener pages.** The illustration may answer questions about the title or prompt more questions.
- **Turn to the selections in the unit. Read the titles and quickly browse the selections, looking briefly at the illustrations and the print.** Encourage students to look not only at content but also at genre: Is the selection a story? A poem? An article? Encourage the students to make any observations that strike them.

For a review of information about **browsing,** see **Learning Framework Card 1A, Setting Reading Goals and Expectations.**

When they have had sufficient time to browse the unit, encourage the students to share their observations. Return to the unit opener on pages 12–13 and discuss what they see in the illustration.

Explain to the students that throughout this unit they will be participating in activities that will extend their experiences and deepen and expand their knowledge of learning. These **exploratory activities** may include writing, drama, art, interviews, debates, and panel discussions. The students will be allowed ample opportunity to reflect on and discuss the activities they complete. **Some selections** in this unit **may** raise questions or **present problems that the students would like to research.** Encourage students who wish to pursue research projects.

For information about the **Research Cycle,** see **Learning Framework Card 4.**

Encourage the students to discuss any questions that they may have about learning. Record on the Question Board questions that they would like to pursue as they read the unit.

Knowledge About Learning

This is what I know about learning before reading the unit.

_____
_____
_____
_____
_____
_____
_____
_____
_____
_____

These are some things about learning that I would like to talk about and understand better.

_____
_____
_____
_____
_____
_____
_____
_____
_____

Reminder: I should read this page again when I get to the end of the unit to see how much my ideas about learning have changed.

Unit 1/Learning   EN 3

Copyright © 1995 Open Court Publishing Company

Explorer's Notebook, page 3

➤ After they have discussed their ideas about learning, have the students do the following:

- Complete page 3 in their Explorer's Notebook.
- Share some ideas related to learning that they would like to talk more about.

Learning Unit: Learning

SELECTION	LINK TO THE UNIT CONCEPTS

● **The Library Card**, pages 14–45
realistic fiction from *Rufus M.* by Eleanor Estes, illustrated by
    Louis Slobodkin
Newbery Honor Book, 1944
	A successful learner must be willing to work hard to
	    meet her or his goals.

Into the Light of Day, pages 46–67
biography from *Child of the Silent Night* by Edith Fisher Hunter,
    illustrated by James Watling
	Different people learn in different ways. Learning can
	    have profound changes on a person's life.

ON YOUR OWN **Mukasa at School**, pages 68–83 realistic fiction from *Mukasa*, by John Nagenda, illustrated by Tyrone Geter	One's first experiences with reading and writing can be very exciting.

● **Do Bananas Chew Gum?**, pages 84–103
realistic fiction from the book by Jamie Gilson, illustrated by Beth Roberge
Carl Sandburg Literary Arts Award, 1981; Charlie May Simon Children's
    Book Award, 1983
	Each person is ultimately responsible for his or her
	    own learning.

● **Seventh Grade**, pages 104–119
short story from *Baseball in April and Other Stories* by Gary Soto,
    illustrated by Andy San Diego
John and Patricia Beatty Award, 1991; Parenting's Reading Magic Award,
    1990
	People have different reasons for wanting to learn.

The Struggle for an Education, pages 120–137
autobiography from *Up from Slavery: An Autobiography* by
    Booker T. Washington, illustrated by Marcy Ramsey
	People often have to overcome many obstacles to
	    obtain education.

FINE ART   pages 138–141
Reading Le Figaro, Mary Cassatt; *Tree of Knowledge*, Terry Chacon and
    Josefina Quezeda; *The Music Lesson*, Johannes Vermeer; **St. Gregory**
    and the Scribes; *The Library*, Jacob Lawrence
	Learning can be expressed through the visual arts.

ASSESSMENT ● **A Real Job**, pages 142–153 autobiography from *Little by Little: A Writer's Education* by Jean Little, illustrated by Ellen Beier ALA Notable Book, 1988	Teachers often learn from those they teach.

● **Storks**, pages 154–181
historical fiction from *The Wheel on the School* by Meindert DeJong,
    illustrated by Maurice Sendak
Newbery Medal, 1955
	Wondering about a subject is the first step to learning
	    about it.

POETRY pages 182–189 **Sam at the Library** poem by Carol Combs Hole, illustrated by Nelle Davis ● **To Young Readers** poem by Gwendolyn Brooks, illustrated by Nelle Davis	Different people have different tastes in books. Good books can add much to their readers' lives.
Unit Wrap-up, pages 190–191	

● Award-winning authors and/or illustrators

Exploration Through Reflective Activities

SELECTION-BASED MINILESSONS		REFLECTIVE ACTIVITIES
TEACHER'S GUIDE	TEACHER TOOL BOX	
Problems and Solutions	Genre—Realistic Fiction; Characterization; Using and Punctuating Contractions	Sharing library experiences Visiting the school library
Indicators of Time and Order Writing Paragraphs	Genre—Biography; Elaboration Through Providing Descriptions; Past-Tense Verbs	Learning about how nonfiction books are organized in a library
Students choose a writer's craft to focus on	Characterization; Compound Words	Conducting library research Interviewing
First-Person Narrative Informal Language	Figurative Language; Elaboration Through Providing Descriptions; Complete and Incomplete Sentences	Conducting library research Group discussion
Setting	Characterization; Dialogue; Adverbs	Visiting a seventh-grade classroom
Providing Specific Facts Genre—Autobiography	Formal Versus Informal Language; Compound Sentences; Clauses and Phrases	Debating an issue Group discussion
		Responding to fine art
Choice of a writer's craft to study is part of assessment	Clauses and Phrases	Group discussion
Characterization Problems and Solutions	Point of View; Setting	Making a picture or photo essay Group discussion
Sound and Meaning in Poetry		Inviting a librarian to talk to the class
		Sharing of group knowledge, insights, and ideas

Assessment available for this unit includes Teacher's Observation Log, Self-Assessment Questionnaire, Concept Connections, Portfolios, and separate Comprehension assessment and Essay and Writing assessment.

The Library Card

1 READING THE SELECTION

INFORMATION FOR THE TEACHER

About the Selection

When young Rufus comes home one summer morning and finds his sisters and brother absorbed in library books, he demands to be taken to the library so that he, too, can get a book. Reminded that he can't yet read, Rufus only becomes more determined to get a book and sets out for the library by himself. Little does he realize the obstacles that he will have to overcome to get a library card. Humorous descriptions and strong characterization lead the reader through this warm, engaging story of a little boy's first experience with formal learning.

Link to the Unit Concepts

"The Library Card," pages 14–29, tells of a young boy's arduous quest for the book he wants and of the learning that occurs along the way. In his determination to achieve his goal and in his willingness to work hard to learn what he needs to know, Rufus models two important qualities of a successful learner.

About the Author

This selection is the first chapter from *Rufus M.,* a book written by Eleanor Estes. Born in New Haven, Connecticut, in 1906, Estes spent many years working in libraries before ever writing about one. Following high school graduation, she was employed for seven years in the children's department of the New Haven Public Library before earning a scholarship to the Pratt Institute Library School. Estes then worked at the New York Public Library until 1941, the year her first book, *The Moffats,* was published. The Moffat family is also featured in *Rufus M.* as well as in *The Middle Moffat* and *The Moffat Museum.* Other popular works by Estes include *The Hundred Dresses* and *Ginger Pye,* which won the Newbery Medal in 1952. Estes died in 1988.

About the Illustrator

Louis Slobodkin began studying to be a sculptor at age fifteen. Much of his three-dimensional work can be found in public buildings in Washington, D.C., and other cities. Slobodkin's friendship with Estes,

LESSON OVERVIEW

"The Library Card" by Eleanor Estes, pages 14–29

READING THE SELECTION

Materials
Student anthology, pp. 14–29
Explorer's Notebook, p. 4
Assessment Master 1

FYI
Learning Framework Cards
- Setting Reading Goals and Expectations, 1A

- Responding to Text, 1B
- Checking Understanding, 1C
- Exploring Through Discussion, 2

Teacher Tool Card
- Classroom Supports: Modeling and Generating Think-Alouds, 116

READING WITH A WRITER'S EYE

Minilesson
Writer's Craft: Problems and Solutions

Materials
Reading/Writing Connection 3
Reproducible Masters 5–14

FYI
Learning Framework Cards
- Writing Process, 7
- Prewriting, 7A
- Drafting, 7B

Teacher Tool Cards
- Spelling and Vocabulary: Building Vocabulary, 75
- Classroom Supports: Writer's Notebook, 120

Options for Instruction
Writer's Craft: Genre—Realistic Fiction
Writer's Craft: Characterization
Spelling and Vocabulary: Contractions
(Use Teacher Tool Cards listed below.)

GUIDED AND INDEPENDENT EXPLORATION

Materials
Explorer's Notebook, pp. 8–9
Home/School Connection 3–4
Reproducible Masters 15–19

FYI
Learning Framework Cards

- Exploring Through Reflective Activities, 3
- Independent Workshop, 5
- Reading Roundtable, 6
- Writing Seminar, 8

Teacher Tool Card
- Classroom Supports: Question Board and Concept Board, 121

Independent Workshop

Optional Materials from Student Toolbox

Tradebook Connection Cards
- *Dear Mr. Henshaw* by Beverly Cleary

Cross-curricular Activity Cards
- 1 Art—Picture Books
- 1 Drama—Dramatizing "The Library Card"
- 1 Science—A Pile of Coal

Student Tool Cards
- Writer's Craft/Reading: Plot, 15
- Writer's Craft/Reading: Reading and Writing Realistic Fiction, 3
- Writer's Craft/Reading: Characterization, 13
- Spelling and Vocabulary: Using and Punctuating Contractions, 80

FYI
Teacher Tool Cards
- Writer's Craft/Reading: Plot, 15
- Writer's Craft/Reading: Genre—Realistic Fiction, 3
- Writer's Craft/Reading: Characterization, 13
- Spelling and Vocabulary: Using and Punctuating Contractions, 80

N O T E S

Asterisks (*) throughout the lesson indicate learning frameworks. Learning Framework Cards and Teacher Tool Cards can be found in the Teacher Toolbox.

who knew him as a sculptor, led to his illustrating her first three books about the Moffats.

Slobodkin describes how he made the Moffats and their surroundings real for himself:

> I consulted with Eleanor and actually drew floor plans and elevations of the yellow house and of all the other houses around and the brick lot, the street, and the surrounding territories that had something to do with the action of the story. It was so clear in my mind that sometime later, after the book had been printed, when a train I was traveling on one summer afternoon stopped on a trestle outside of New Haven, I looked down at a small town which was strangely familiar. It was the actual town of Cranbury out of that book!

Slobodkin went on to illustrate other children's books, including some that he wrote himself. In 1943 he won the Caldecott Medal for his drawings for James Thurber's *Many Moons.* Slobodkin died in 1975.

INFORMATION FOR THE STUDENT

- Tell the students that the story that they are about to read is an excerpt from the book *Rufus M.*
- Before beginning the selection, share any information about the author and illustrator that you think will be of interest to the class. Students may be surprised to learn the great lengths Slobodkin went to in order to make the Moffats and their surroundings more realistic and his illustrations more effective.
- After reading the selection, you may want to mention the other books written by Estes that feature the Moffat family.

In this story, four- or five-year-old Rufus is free to make his way to and from the library without supervision. Students may be surprised at this seemingly risky behavior until they realize that "The Library Card" was set in an earlier time. You might want to mention that the setting of this selection is a small New England town in the early twentieth century.

COGNITIVE AND RESPONSIVE READING

Activating Prior Knowledge   Ask the students to share what they know about library cards and about the process of obtaining a library card from a public library.

Setting Reading Goals and Expectations   Explain to the students that before they read they will **set reading goals and expectations.** Explain that doing this will give them a sense of the story and will help them better understand what they read. To do this, they will **browse the first page** of the selection, **using the clues/problems/wondering procedure.** On the chalkboard under the headings clues, problems, and wonderings, write in brief note form the observations the students generate during browsing. For example, stu-

Introducing the Browsing Procedure

dents might list the genre of the selection under *clues*; they might list unfamiliar words under *problems*; and they might note any questions that arise during browsing under *wonderings.* Students will return to these observations after reading.

Have the students quickly look over the first paragraph or two. They should be able to determine quickly whether the selection is fiction or nonfiction. Fiction pieces should not be browsed in their entirety, since the browsing may ruin the surprise of the story.

For a review of **browsing,** see **Learning Framework Card 1A, Setting Reading Goals and Expectations.**

Recommendations for Reading the Selection

For several reasons, it is recommended that the students read "The Library Card" aloud. This is the first selection in the book, and both you and the students need to hear how they read. It is also a story with many descriptive passages and therefore one that is nice to hear read aloud. Because the selection is rather long, you might consider taking part in the reading.

Note: After this first lesson, give the students the opportunity to decide how they want to read each selection.

Refer to the think-aloud prompts that are provided beneath the page miniatures. Instead of or in addition to using these prompts, encourage the students to provide their own think-alouds. This would also be a good selection for **responding** to text **by making connections and identifying with characters** while reading aloud. Model this response, and then invite the students to respond.

About the Reading Strategies

In this program you will teach reading strategies that will help the students better understand and enjoy what they read. As they read and think about texts, students will become increasingly familiar with reading strategies and how to use them. Like all good readers, they will eventually use these tools automatically.

In subsequent lessons of the teacher's guide, you will find review information about reading strategies in this section. Often, because of the unique demands of a given selection, one or two strategies will be discussed that may be particularly helpful to the students as they try to make sense of the text. Remind the students to refer to the reading strategy posters for help when they encounter reading problems.

All of the reading strategies are introduced in the first unit. If students are familiar with these strategies from previous years, you need only review each strategy briefly to refresh their memories.

Because "The Library Card" is eventful and will have the students guessing at how it will turn out, the strategies of **summing up** and **predicting** may help them follow the story events. Keeping track of what has already occurred and predicting what will happen next will help readers focus their attention on the story and increase their enjoyment.

To keep track of what they are reading, good readers **sum up.** Before reading the selection, ask the students what they know about this strategy. Students should recognize the behavior as something that they do quite often in everyday life. For example, if a friend asks what happened in class while she was sick at home for a day, they would quickly tell the most important events of the day. That's summing up. If they cannot sum up while reading a text, students will know that something is confusing, and they can then try to identify the problem and work to clear it up. Point out that some places in a selection are better than others for summing up. It makes sense, for example, to stop and sum up after something important has happened and before something new starts.

For a review of the strategy of **summing up,** see **Learning Framework Card 1C, Checking Understanding.**

Introducing Summing Up

Direct the students' attention to the **reading strategy poster Checking Understanding**—which should be displayed in a prominent place along with the other reading strategy posters—and read the part about **summing up.** Discuss the strategy, and have a volunteer read the accompanying questions. Explain to the students that they can ask themselves these questions in order to use this strategy effectively.

Reading Strategy Posters

When they read fiction, good readers often use the strategy of **predicting.** Ask the students to tell what they know about predicting. They can use this strategy to help them think ahead and to prepare for new information as they read. Predictions should be based on what they already know and on what the story tells them. Sometimes a story contains clues that help them make predictions about what a character will do or what will happen next. The students should watch for these clues as they read.

Introducing Predicting

Point out the **reading strategy poster Responding to Text,** and read the part about **predicting.** Discuss the strategy, and have a volunteer read aloud the accompanying questions. Encourage the students to ask themselves these questions while reading in order to use this strategy effectively.

To review **predicting,** see **Learning Framework Card 1B, Responding to Text.**

Think-Aloud Prompts for Use in Oral Reading

Notice the suggested think-aloud prompts with the page miniatures. These are merely suggestions for ways to deal with this text. Remind the students that reading should make sense. If it doesn't, they should refer to the **reading strategy posters** for help. Explain that you will occasionally model aloud the strategies that you use when reading becomes difficult or when you want to get more meaning out of a text. They, too, should feel free to share whatever strategies they use to solve a reading problem or to respond to the text. Remind the students to stop and ask for clarification if anything in the story puzzles them. They should also feel free to stop and share their personal reactions to the story. For a review of **modeling** and **generating think-alouds,** see **Teacher Tool Card 116.**

THINK
ALOUD
P R O M P T S

These prompts may be used as guides to promote cognitive and responsive reading.

7.

THE LIBRARY CARD

from RUFUS M. by Eleanor Estes
illustrated by Louis Slobodkin

Rufus M. That's the way Rufus wrote his name on his heavy arithmetic paper and on his blue-lined spelling paper. Rufus M. went on one side of the paper. His age, seven, went on the other. Rufus had not learned to write his name in school, though that is one place for learning to write. He had not learned to write his name at home either, though that is another place for learning to write.

The place where he had learned to write his name was the library, long ago before he ever went to school at all. This is the way it happened.

One day when Rufus had been riding his scooter up and down the street, being the motorman, the conductor, the passengers, the steam, and the whistle of a locomotive, he came home and found Joey, Jane, and Sylvie, all reading in the front yard. Joey and Jane were sitting on the steps of the porch and Sylvie was sprawled in the hammock, a book in one hand, a chocolate-covered peppermint in the other.

Rufus stood with one bare foot on his scooter and one on the grass and watched them. Sylvie read the fastest. This was natural since she was the oldest. But Joey turned the pages almost as fast and Jane went lickety-cut on the good parts.

They were all reading books and he couldn't even read yet. These books they were reading were library books. The library must be open today. It wasn't open every day, just a few days a week.

"I want to go to the library," said Rufus. "And get a book," he added.

"We all just came home from there," said Jane, while Joey and Sylvie merely went on reading as though Rufus had said nothing. "Besides," she added, "why do you want a book anyway? You can't even read yet."

This was true and it made Rufus mad. He liked to do everything that they did. He even liked to sew if they were sewing. He never thought whether sewing was for girls only or not. When he saw Jane sewing, he asked Mama to let him sew too. So Mama tied a thread to the head of a pin and Rufus poked that in and out of a piece of goods. That's the way he sewed. It looked like what Jane was doing and Rufus was convinced that he was sewing too, though he could not see much sense in it.

14

15

Now here were the other Moffats, all with books from the library. And there were three more books stacked up on the porch that looked like big people's books without pictures. They were for Mama no doubt. This meant that he was the only one here who did not have a book.

"I want a book from the library," said Rufus. A flick of the page as Sylvie turned it over was all the answer he got. It seemed to Rufus as though even Catherine-the-cat gave him a scornful glance because he could not read yet and did not have a book.

1 Rufus turned his scooter around and went out of the yard. Just wait! Read? Why, soon he'd read as fast if not faster than they did. Reading looked easy. It was just flipping pages. Who couldn't do that?

Rufus thought that it was not hard to get a book out of the library. All you did was go in, look for a book that you liked, give it to the lady to punch, and come home with it. He knew where the library was for he had often gone there with Jane and some of the others. While Jane went off to the shelves to find a book, he and Joey played the game of Find the Duke in the Palmer Cox Brownie books. This was a game that the two boys had made up. They would turn the pages of one of the Brownie books, any of them, and try to be the first to spot the duke, the brownie in the tall hat. The library lady thought that **2** this was a noisy game, and said she wished they would not play it there. Rufus hoped to bring a Brownie book home now.

"Toot-toot!" he sang to clear the way. Straight down Elm Street was the way to the library; the same way that led to Sunday School, and Rufus knew it well. He liked sidewalks that were white the best for he could go the fastest on these.

16

"Toot-toot!" Rufus hurried down the street. When he arrived at the library, he hid his scooter in the pine trees that grew under the windows beside the steps. Christmas trees, Rufus called them. The ground was covered with brown pine needles and they were soft to walk upon. Rufus always went into the library the same way. He climbed the stairs, encircled the light on the <u>granite</u> arm of the steps, and marched into the library.

Rufus stepped carefully on the strips of rubber matting that led to the desk. This matting looked like dirty licorice. But it wasn't licorice. He knew because once when Sylvie had brought him here when he was scarcely more than three he had tasted a torn corner of it. It was not good to eat.

The library lady was sitting at the desk playing with some cards. Rufus stepped off the matting. The cool, shiny floor felt good to his bare feet. He went over to the shelves and luckily did find one of the big Palmer Cox Brownie books there. It would be fun to play the game of Find the Duke at home. Until now he had played it only in the library. Maybe Jane or Joe would play it with him right now. He laughed out loud at the thought.

"Sh-sh-sh, quiet," said the lady at the desk.

Rufus clapped his chubby fist over his mouth. Goodness! He had forgotten where he was. Do not laugh or talk out loud in the library. He knew these rules. Well, he didn't want to

17

1 A conflict has been set up in the story: Rufus wants a book, whether or not he can read it, because he likes to do whatever his sisters and brother do. Because of the clues in the title and the beginning paragraphs and because of what they have read about Rufus, some students may **predict** that Rufus will try to get a book on his own.

Be sure that the students stop at appropriate points in the story to note whether their predictions were accurate. If they do not follow up on their own, model this behavior for them.

2 **Note:** Author Palmer Cox (1840–1924) first published his Brownie stories in *St. Nicholas* magazine. Children of the time enjoyed the illustrations of such Brownie characters as the Duke, the Chinaman, the Scotsman, the Dutchman, and the Policeman.

stay here any longer today anyway. He wanted to read at home with the others. He took the book to the lady to punch.

She didn't punch it though. She took it and she put it on the table behind her and then she started to play cards again.

"That's my book," said Rufus.

"Do you have a card?" the lady asked.

Rufus felt in his pockets. Sometimes he carried around an old playing card or two. Today he didn't have one.

"No," he said.

"You'll have to have a card to get a book."

"I'll go and get one," said Rufus.

The lady put down her cards. "I mean a library card," she explained kindly. "It looks to me as though you are too little to have a library card. Do you have one?"

"No," said Rufus. "I'd like to though."

"I'm afraid you're too little," said the lady. "You have to write your name to get one. Can you do that?"

Rufus nodded his head confidently. Writing. Lines up and down. He'd seen that done. And the letters that Mama had tied in bundles in the closet under the stairs were covered with writing. Of course he could write.

"Well, let's see your hands," said the lady.

Rufus obligingly showed this lady his hands, but she did not like the look of them. She cringed and clasped her head as though the sight hurt her.

"Oh!" she gasped. "You'll just have to go home and wash them before we can even think about joining the library and borrowing books."

This was a complication upon which Rufus had not reckoned. However, all it meant was a slight delay. He'd wash his

❧ 18 ❧

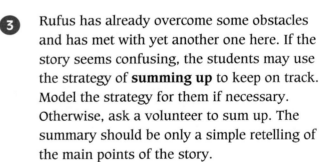

hands and then he'd get the book. He turned and went out of the library, found his scooter safe among the Christmas trees, and pushed it home. He surprised Mama by asking to have his hands washed. When this was done, he mounted his scooter again and returned all the long way to the library. It was not just a little trip to the library. It was a long one. A long one and a hot one on a day like this. But he didn't notice that. All he was bent on was getting his book and taking it home and reading with the others on the front porch. They were all still there, brushing flies away and reading.

Again Rufus hid his scooter in the pine trees, encircled the light, and went in.

"Hello," he said.

"Well," said the lady. "How are they now?"

Rufus had forgotten he had had to wash his hands. He thought she was referring to the other Moffats. "Fine," he said.

"Let me see them," she said, and she held up her hands.

Oh! His hands! Well, they were all right, thought Rufus, for Mama had just washed them. He showed them to the lady. There was a silence while she studied them. Then she shook her head. She still did not like them.

"Ts, ts, ts!" she said. "They'll have to be cleaner than that."

❧ 19 ❧

 Rufus has already overcome some obstacles and has met with yet another one here. If the story seems confusing, the students may use the strategy of **summing up** to keep on track. Model the strategy for them if necessary. Otherwise, ask a volunteer to sum up. The summary should be only a simple retelling of the main points of the story.

Before turning the page, the students may also find it natural to **predict** whether Rufus will give up on his goal or continue to do whatever it takes to get his book. On the basis of what they already know about the library lady, some students may predict that she will sympathize with Rufus and help him with his problem. Others may predict that she will be strict and force him to return home once again.

Rufus looked at his hands. Supposing he went all the way home and washed them again, she still might not like them. However, if that is what she wanted, he would have to do that before he could get the Brownie book . . . and he started for the door.

"Well now, let's see what we can do," said the lady. "I know what," she said. "It's against the rules but perhaps we can wash them in here." And she led Rufus into a little room that smelled of paste where lots of new books and old books were stacked up. In one corner was a little round sink and Rufus washed his hands again. Then they returned to the desk. The lady got a chair and put a newspaper on it. She made Rufus stand on this because he was not big enough to write at the desk otherwise.

Then the lady put a piece of paper covered with a lot of printing in front of Rufus, dipped a pen in the ink well and gave it to him.

"All right," she said. "Here's your application. Write your name here."

All the writing Rufus had ever done before had been on big pieces of brown wrapping paper with lots of room on them. Rufus had often covered those great sheets of paper with his own kind of writing at home. Lines up and down.

But on this paper there wasn't much space. It was already covered with writing. However, there was a tiny little empty space and that was where Rufus must write his name, the lady said. So, little space or not, Rufus confidently grasped the pen with his left hand and dug it into the paper. He was not accustomed to pens, having always worked with pencils until now, and he made a great many holes and blots and scratches.

🦢 20 🦢

"Gracious," said the lady. "Don't bear down so hard! And why don't you hold it in your right hand?" she asked, moving the pen back into his right hand.

Rufus started again scraping his lines up and down and all over the page, this time using his right hand. Wherever there was an empty space he wrote. He even wrote over some of the print for good measure. Then he waited for the lady, who had gone off to get a book for some man, to come back and look.

"Oh," she said as she settled herself in her swivel chair, "is that the way you write? Well . . . it's nice, but what does it say?"

"Says Rufus Moffat. My name."

Apparently these lines up and down did not spell Rufus Moffat to this lady. She shook her head.

"It's nice," she repeated. "Very nice. But nobody but you knows what it says. You have to learn to write your name better than that before you can join the library."

Rufus was silent. He had come to the library all by himself, gone back home to wash his hands, and come back because he wanted to take books home and read them the way the

🦢 21 🦢

others did. He had worked hard. He did not like to think he might have to go home without a book.

The library lady looked at him a moment and then she said quickly before he could get himself all the way off the big chair, "Maybe you can *print* your name."

Rufus looked at her hopefully. He thought he could write better than he could print, for his writing certainly looked to him exactly like all grown people's writing. Still he'd try to print if that was what she wanted.

The lady printed some letters on the top of a piece of paper. "There," she said. "That's your name. Copy it ten times and then we'll try it on another application."

Rufus worked hard. He worked so hard the knuckles showed white on his brown fist. He worked for a long, long time, now with his right hand and now with his left. Sometimes a boy or a girl came in, looked over his shoulder and watched, but he paid no attention. From time to time the lady studied his work and she said, "That's fine. That's fine." At last she said, "Well, maybe now we can try." And she gave him another application.

All Rufus could get, with his large generous letters, in that tiny little space where he was supposed to print his name, was R-U-F. The other letters he scattered here and there on the card. The lady did not like this either. She gave him still another blank. Rufus tried to print smaller and this time he got RUFUS in the space, and also he crowded an M at the end. Since he was doing so well now the lady herself printed the *offat* part of Moffat on the next line.

"This will have to do," she said. "Now take this home and ask your mother to sign it on the other side. Bring it back on

🐚 22 🐚

Thursday and you'll get your card."

Rufus's face was shiny and streaked with dirt where he had rubbed it. He never knew there was all this work to getting a book. The other Moffats just came in and got books. Well, maybe they had had to do this once too.

Rufus held his hard-earned application in one hand and steered his scooter with the other. When he reached home Joey, Jane and Sylvie were not around any longer. Mama signed his card for him, saying, "My! So you've learned how to write!"

"Print," corrected Rufus.

Mama kissed Rufus and he went back out. The lady had said to come back on Thursday, but he wanted a book today. When the other Moffats came home, he'd be sitting on the top step of the porch, reading. That would surprise them. He smiled to himself as he made his way to the library for the third time.

Once his application blew away. Fortunately, it landed in a thistle bush and did not get very torn. The rest of the way Rufus clutched it carefully. He climbed the granite steps to the library again only to find that the big round dark brown doors were closed. Rufus tried to open them but he couldn't. He knocked at the door, even kicked it with his foot, but there was no answer. He pounded on the door but nobody came.

A big boy strode past with his newspapers. "Hey, kid," he said to Rufus. "Library's closed!" And off he went, whistling.

Rufus looked after him. The fellow said the library was closed. How could it have closed so fast? He had been here such a little while ago. The lady must still be here. He did want his Brownie book. If only he could see in, he might see

🐚 23 🐚

4 Clues in the story may lead some students to **predict** at this point. If they do not predict on their own, you might model noticing these clues and predicting what Rufus will do. For example,

Rufus seems so anxious to get his book that I bet he won't wait until Thursday to return with his application. He doesn't seem to mind riding his scooter back and forth to the library as long as it will lead to his getting the book. What do you think?

5 Follow up on students' predictions if they do not do so.

Rufus has encountered another obstacle, and from what they know of his determination, some students may **predict** here what will happen next.

the lady and get his book. The windows were high up but they had very wide sills. Rufus was a wonderful climber. He could <u>shinny</u> up trees and poles faster than anybody on the block. Faster than Joey. Now, helping himself up by means of one of the pine trees that grew close to the building, and by sticking his toes in the ivy and rough places in the bricks, he scrambled up the wall. He hoisted himself up on one of the sills and sat there. He peered in. It was dark inside, for the shades had been drawn almost all the way down.

"Library lady!" he called, and he knocked on the windowpane. There was no answer. He put his hands on each side of his face to shield his eyes, and he looked in for a long, long time. He could not believe that she had left. Rufus was resolved to get a book. He had lost track of the number of times he had been back and forth from home to the library, and the library home. Maybe the lady was in the cellar. He climbed down, stubbing his big toe on the bricks as he did so. He stooped down beside one of the low dirt-spattered cellar windows. He couldn't see in. He lay flat on the ground, wiped one spot clean on the window, picked up a few pieces of coal from the sill and put them in his pocket for Mama.

"Hey, lady," he called.

He gave the cellar window a little push. It wasn't locked so he opened it a little and looked in. All he could see was a high pile of coal reaching up to this window. Of course he didn't put any of that coal in his pocket for that would be stealing.

"Hey, lady!" he yelled again. His voice echoed in the cellar but the library lady did not answer. He called out, "Hey, lady," every few seconds, but all that answered him was an echo. He

24

pushed the window open a little wider. All of a sudden it swung wide open and Rufus slid in, right on top of the coal pile, and crash, clatter, bang! He slid to the bottom, making a great racket.

A little light shone through the dusty windows, but on the whole it was very dark and spooky down here and Rufus really wished that he was back on the outside looking in. However, since he was in the library, why not go upstairs quick, get the Brownie book, and go home? The window had banged shut, but he thought he could climb up the coal pile, pull the window up, and get out. He certainly hoped he could anyway. Supposing he couldn't and he had to stay in this cellar! Well, that he would not think about. He looked around in the dusky light and saw a staircase across the cellar. Luckily his application was still good. It was torn and dirty but it still had his name on it, RUFUS M, and that was the important part. He'd leave this on the desk in exchange for the Brownie book.

Rufus cautiously made his way over to the steps but he stopped halfway across the cellar. Somebody had opened the door at the top of the stairs. He couldn't see who it was, but he did see the light reflected and that's how he knew that somebody had opened the door. It must be the lady. He was just going to say, "Hey, lady," when he thought, "Gee, maybe it isn't the lady. Maybe it's a spooky thing."

25

Then the light went away, the door was closed, and Rufus was left in the dark again. He didn't like it down here. He started to go back to the coal pile to get out of this place. Then he felt of his application. What a lot of work he had done to get a book and now that he was this near to getting one, should he give up? No. Anyway, if it was the lady up there, he knew her and she knew him and neither one of them was scared of the other. And Mama always said there's no such thing as a spooky thing.

So Rufus bravely made his way again to the stairs. He tiptoed up them. The door at the head was not closed tightly. He pushed it open and found himself right in the library. But goodness! There in the little sink room right opposite him was the library lady!

Rufus stared at her in silence. The library lady was eating. Rufus had never seen her do anything before but play cards, punch books, and carry great piles of them around. Now she was eating. Mama said not to stare at anybody while they were eating. Still Rufus didn't know the library lady ate, so it was hard for him not to look at her.

❧ 26 ☙

She had a little gas stove in there. She could cook there. She was reading a book at the same time that she was eating. Sylvie could do that too. This lady did not see him.

"Hey, lady," said Rufus.

The librarian jumped up out of her seat. "Was that you in the cellar? I thought I heard somebody. Goodness, young man! I thought you had gone home long ago."

Rufus didn't say anything. He just stood there. He had gone home and he had come back lots of times. He had the whole thing in his mind; the coming and going, and going and coming, and sliding down the coal pile, but he did not know where to begin, how to tell it.

"Didn't you know the library is closed now?" she demanded, coming across the floor with firm steps.

Rufus remained silent. No, he hadn't known it. The fellow had told him but he hadn't believed him. Now he could see for himself that the library was closed so the library lady could eat. If the lady would let him take his book, he'd go home and stay there. He'd play the game of Find the Duke with Jane. He hopefully held out his card with his name on it.

6

"Here this is," he said.

But the lady acted as though she didn't even see it. She led Rufus over to the door.

"All right now," she said. "Out with you!" But just as she opened the door the sound of water boiling over on the stove struck her ears, and back she raced to her little room.

"Gracious!" she exclaimed. "What a day!"

Before the door could close on him, Rufus followed her in and sat down on the edge of a chair. The lady thought he

❧ 27 ☙

6 Much has happened in the story. **Summing up** is one strategy that will help the students keep the chain of events clear in their minds. They may also want to make another **prediction** at this point. The library lady will either accept Rufus's application or make him leave the library. Clues in the story could support either prediction. On the one hand, the library lady is rather strict; on the other hand, she has already bent the rules once and was very patient with Rufus when he was learning to write his name. If students suggest only one outcome mention the clue that supports the alternative prediction.

had gone and started to sip her tea. Rufus watched her quietly, waiting for her to finish.

After a while the lady brushed the crumbs off her lap. And then she washed her hands and the dishes in the little sink where Rufus had washed his hands. In a library a lady could eat and could wash. Maybe she slept here too. Maybe she lived here.

"Do you live here?" Rufus asked her.

"Mercy on us!" exclaimed the lady. "Where'd you come from? Didn't I send you home? No, I don't live here and neither do you. Come now, out with you, young man. I mean it." The lady called all boys "young man" and all girls "Susie." She came out of the little room and she opened the big brown door again. "There," she said. "Come back on Thursday."

Rufus's eyes filled up with tears.

"Here's this," he said again, holding up his application in a last desperate attempt. But the lady shook her head. Rufus went slowly down the steps, felt around in the bushes for his scooter, and with drooping spirits he mounted it. Then for the second time that day, the library lady changed her mind.

"Oh, well," she said, "come back here, young man. I'm not supposed to do business when the library's closed, but I see we'll have to make an exception."

So Rufus rubbed his sooty hands over his face, hid his scooter in the bushes again, climbed the granite steps and, without circling the light, he went back in and gave the lady his application.

The lady took it gingerly. "My, it's dirty," she said. "You really ought to sign another one."

🍂 28 🍂

"And go home with it?" asked Rufus. He really didn't believe this was possible. He wiped his hot face on his sleeve and looked up at the lady in exhaustion. What he was thinking was: All right. If he had to sign another one, all right. But would she just please stay open until he got back?

However, this was not necessary. The lady said, "Well now, I'll try to clean this old one up. But remember, young man, always have everything clean—your hands, your book, everything, when you come to the library."

Rufus nodded solemnly. "My feet too," he assured her.

Then the lady made Rufus wash his hands again. They really were very bad this time, for he had been in a coal pile, and now at last she gave Rufus the book he wanted—one of the Palmer Cox Brownie books. This one was "The Brownies in the Philippines."

And Rufus went home.

When he reached home, he showed Mama his book. She smiled at him, and gave his cheek a pat. She thought it was fine that he had gone to the library and joined all by himself and taken out a book. And she thought it was fine when Rufus sat down at the kitchen table, was busy and quiet for a long, long time, and then showed her what he had done.

He had printed RUFUS M. That was what he had done. And that's the way he learned to sign his name.

🍂 29 🍂

Discussing Strategy Use

If they do not do so on their own, have the students comment on whether their final predictions were accurate. Also encourage them to discuss whether using the strategies of **summing up** and **predicting** during reading helped them focus their attention on and increased their enjoyment of the story.

*

EXPLORING THROUGH DISCUSSION

For a detailed explanation of **Exploring Through Discussion,** see **Learning Framework Card** 2. Be sure to read the card before beginning the discussion process with your class.

Reflecting on the Selection
Whole-Group Discussion

The **whole group discusses** the selection and any **personal thoughts reactions, problems,** or **questions that it raises.** During this time, students may also be invited to **return** to the **clues, problems, and wonderings** that they noted on the chalkboard during browsing to determine whether the clues were borne out by the selection, whether and how their problems were solved, and whether their wonderings were answered or deserve further discussion and exploration. Avoid treating their ideas like a list to be discussed and eliminated in a linear fashion. Instead, let the **students decide which items deserve further discussion.** To stimulate discussion, the **students** can **ask** one another the kinds of **questions that good readers ask themselves** about a text: **What did I find interesting? What is important here? What was difficult to understand? Why would someone want to read this?** Your own participation in the discussion might take the form of expressing and modeling your reactions to characters or to other aspects of the story. It is important for the students to see you as a contributing member of the group.

Introduce the **handing-off** procedure. (See **Learning Framework Card 2, Exploring Through Discussion.**) To emphasize that you are part of the group, actively **participate in the handing-off process:** Raise your hand to be called on by the last speaker when you have a contribution to make. Point out unusual and interesting insights verbalized by the students so that these insights may be recognized and discussed.

As the year progresses, the **students will take more and more responsibility for the discussions** of the selections. The handing-off process is a good way to get them to take on this responsibility.

Assessment

In a successful discussion, it should not be necessary for you to ask questions to assess the students' understanding of the text. If necessary, however, engage in a discussion to **determine whether the students have grasped**

- what Rufus learns about libraries, writing, and printing
- whether Rufus is a good learner and why

Exploring Concepts Within the Selection
Small-Group Discussion

Have the **students form small collaborative groups** and spend a few minutes **discussing whether this story gave them any new ideas about learning.** Remind them to include in their discussions ideas about learning that have come from their own experiences as well as from experiences they have heard or read about in other books. Have them refer to the **Concept Board and the Question Board.** If they discussed

> Introducing Exploring Through Discussion

> **TEACHING TIP** Encourage students to identify with the selection by asking whether it reminds them of anything in their own lives—people, places, events, relationships, emotions, etc.

> Introducing Handing Off

their ideas about learning before they began the unit and posted these on either board, be sure that they review those ideas now and consider how they have been affected by this story.

▶ **Note:** This may be a good opportunity to observe students working in groups and mark observations on Assessment Master 1, Teacher's Observation Log, which you will find in the booklet Masters for Continuous Assessment. See *Formative Assessment: A Teacher's Guide* for a review of information regarding the purpose and use of the Teacher's Observation Log.

Teacher's Observation Log

Sharing Ideas About Explorable Concepts

Then have the **groups report their ideas and discuss** them with the rest of the class. It is crucial that the students' ideas determine this discussion.

- Students may generalize that people often have a particular goal in mind when they set out to learn something. Rufus's initial goal is to get a library book. He learns to print his name in order to fulfill the library lady's requirements for giving him the book.
- In the process of getting his book, Rufus learns about libraries, writing, and printing. Students may discuss the idea that in trying to achieve their goals, people sometimes learn things they did not expect to learn.

Assessment Master 1

TEACHER'S OBSERVATION LOG

Student _____

Date _____ Unit _____ Activity _____

General Comprehension
Concepts discussed _____

Behavior Within a Group
Articulates, expresses ideas _____

Joins discussions _____

Collaboration (such as works with other students, works alone) _____

Role in Group
Role (such as leader, summarizer, questioner, recorder, critic, observer, non-participant)
_____

Flexibility (changes roles when necessary) _____

Use of Reading Strategies
Uses strategies when needed (either those taught or student's own)/Describe strategies used
_____

Changes strategies when appropriate _____

Changes Since Last Observation
_____
_____

If more space is needed, write on the back or use another sheet.

Teacher's Observation Log   Assessment Master 1

Copyright © 1995 Open Court Publishing Company

As these ideas and others are stated, have the students **add them to the Question Board** or **Concept Board.**

Recording Ideas

As they complete the above discussions, ask the students to **sum up what they have learned from their conversations and to tell how they might use this information in further explorations.** Any special information or insights may be recorded on the **Concept Board.** Any further questions that they would like to think about, pursue, or investigate may be recorded on the **Question Board.** Students may want to discuss the progress that has been made on their questions. They may also want to cross out any questions that no longer warrant consideration.

▶ After discussion, the students should individually record what they have learned on page 4 of their Explorer's Notebook.

Evaluating Discussions

Explorer's Notebook, page 4

Recording Concept Information

As I read each selection, this is what I added to my understanding of learning.

"The Library Card" by Eleanor Estes

_____
_____
_____
_____
_____
_____
_____
_____
_____
_____

"Into the Light of Day" by Edith Fisher Hunter

_____
_____
_____
_____
_____
_____
_____
_____
_____
_____
_____

4 EN   Learning/Unit 1

Be sure to give the students plenty of time to express ideas. Don't be too quick to resort to question asking to end a period of silence. Watch for students' reactions to these periods of silence, and encourage them to spend this time reflecting and thinking.

Notes:

2 READING WITH A WRITER'S EYE

MINILESSON

Writer's Craft: Problems and Solutions

1.

Ask students what they know about plot. Explain that in planning a story one of the most important things a writer must do is to think about the action of the story. Many stories are built around **a problem that the main character must solve.** The events in the story are the steps that the character takes in order to solve the problem.

To start them thinking about the structure of "The Library Card," have the students recall Rufus's ultimate goal: he wants a book from the library. Point out that on his way to achieving his goal, Rufus faces a series of problems, each of which has a solution, and that finding out how he solves each problem helps keep readers interested in Estes's story. Ask what obstacles Rufus faces on his way to getting a book from the library. If necessary, invite a volunteer to read aloud the second paragraph on page 16, which explains his first obstacle (that his siblings will not take him to the library), and the way he solved this problem (by deciding to go to the library by himself).

Selective Reading: Focus on Problems and Solutions

2.

Have the students find other examples of Rufus's problems and solutions in the story. You may wish to help students keep track of the story events by writing them on the chalkboard as the students identify them.

Selection-Based Practice

Problem	Solution
Others won't take Rufus to the library.	He goes by himself.
The librarian refuses to let Rufus fill out an application for a library card because his hands are too dirty.	Rufus goes home and washes his hands.
Rufus learns to print his name but needs his mother's signature.	Rufus goes home again.
The library is locked.	Rufus goes through the basement window.

You may want to illustrate the series of problems and solutions in Estes's story by creating a diagram. To do this, on the lower left corner of the chalkboard or of an overhead transparency, draw a figure to represent Rufus. On the upper right corner, indicate his goal by drawing a book. Show the plot as a series of steps climbing from left to right, with each step labeled with a problem Rufus faced, followed by the solution he devised. The story diagram might resemble the one below.

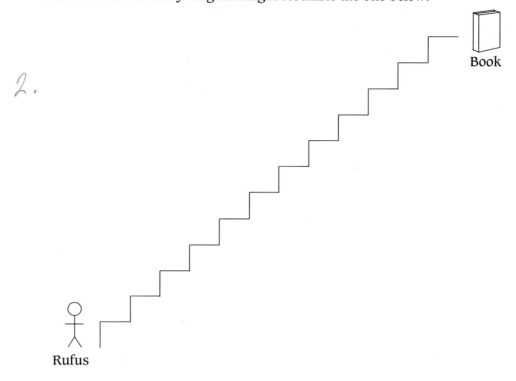

2.

Book

Rufus

Independent Practice: Problems and Solutions

➤ Allow the students to work independently or in small groups, using Reading/Writing Connection, page 3, to extend their study of how writers use problems and solutions in constructing plots. Provide time for the students to share their work. Make note of students who might need more help during Independent Workshop. Tell the students to ask for help whenever they think they need it.

WRITING

Linking Reading to Writing

Tell the students that you will soon ask them to write stories themselves. When they plan and write their stories, it might help them to keep in mind the elements of plot structure that they have been talking about. Suggest that they think about the way Rufus's story is written and about techniques used in the story that they might want to use in their own stories. They might want to briefly note some ideas for a personal narrative. These notes can later be added to their **Writer's Notebook**.

Note: The Writer's Notebook is a three-ring binder that the students supply. They will use and refer to it often. For a review of information regarding its introduction and organization, see **Teacher Tool Card 120.**

➤ Introduce the Writer's Notebook. Explain to the students that they will use these notebooks to jot down ideas they want to remember to use in their writing, to record examples of especially good writing, and to keep track of writing rules and guidelines. Distribute copies of Reproducible Masters 5–12, which contain a the table of contents and the section dividers for the Writer's Notebook. Each section divider represents one entry on the table of contents. Discuss the types of information they may wish to include in each section. If they have other ideas that might help them in their writing, they should feel free to add them to their Writer's Notebook at any time during the year.

Organizing the Writer's Notebook

Reading/Writing Connection, page 3

"The Library Card"

Problems and Solutions

Find examples from "The Library Card" or from any other stories you have read in which the author constructs the plot of the story around a problem and its solution.

Story: _____ Author: _____
What is the character's problem? _____
_____
How does the character solve the problem? _____
_____
_____

Story: _____ Author: _____
What is the character's problem? _____
_____
How does the character solve the problem? _____
_____
_____

Story: _____ Author: _____
What is the character's problem? _____
_____
How does the character solve the problem? _____
_____
_____

Name

Copyright © 1995 Open Court Publishing Company

Story Elements

Unit 1/Learning   R/WC 3

Reproducible Master 5

Writer's Notebook

Contents

Writing Ideas

Personal Dictionary

Author's Style

Story Elements

Genres

Checking My Work

My Response Journal

Name

Copyright © 1995 Open Court Publishing Company

Writer's Notebook   RM 5

Preparing Materials

Tell the students that before they begin writing they must prepare some materials that they will use when they write. Use the following steps to introduce these materials and some of the procedures the class will follow during writing time.

- Have each student prepare two folders for his or her writing, one labeled Writing Folder and the other labeled Portfolio.
- Tell the students that as they work on different writing projects they will keep their works in progress in their writing folders.
- Then explain that as the year progresses, they will take samples of their favorite or best work—both writing projects and research projects—and place them in their portfolios. Tell the students that most artists and professional writers keep portfolios of their best work to show other people or for their own pleasure. Each piece in their portfolio should be accompanied by a brief note explaining why it is in the portfolio.

Folders and Portfolios

Explaining Procedures

You may want to designate a place in the classroom for the storage of the writing folders so that they will be accessible to you and your class at all times.

Once the students have prepared their folders, explain that

- They will write every day on topics related to exploration of learning, the story they are reading, or personal issues.
- To produce writing projects, they may work in groups or they may work individually.
- They will have opportunities to share their work with classmates.
- They will be able to incorporate into their personal writing what they learn during Reading with a Writer's Eye.
- They will have their Writer's Notebooks available at all times and will use them frequently for jotting down ideas, keeping track of rules to remember, and recording examples of good writing. To review the explanation of the Writer's Notebook, see **Teacher Tool Card 120.**

For a review of the information about classroom management and procedures to be followed during **writing,** see **Learning Framework Cards 7 and 8, Writing Process** and **Writing Seminar.**

Classroom Procedures

Presenting an Overview

Overview of the Writing Process

Take some time to review briefly the writing process. Write these phases of the process on the chalkboard:

- Prewriting
- Drafting
- Revising
- Proofreading
- Publishing

Ask volunteers to tell what they understand each phase of this process to involve. Record their ideas on the chalkboard. During discussion, make sure that some of the following points are brought out.

Information About the Phases of the Writing Process

- **Prewriting**—Writers think about, talk about, and develop ideas that they want to write about. They search their store of past experiences, explore their ideas about things outside themselves, participate in brainstorming sessions in order to learn about others' ideas, all in an effort to think about what they are going to write. They should also be encouraged to make their own brief notes on ideas they want to include in their paper and to write a planning statement that briefly describes who their audience will be and what they hope to accomplish in this writing. During this phase, writers jot down ideas in their Writer's Notebook for future use or read over previously recorded ideas when they need a spark.
- **Drafting**—Writers get their ideas down on paper, writing quickly to produce a rough draft and not worrying about handwriting, spelling, or other conventions. As they write, they may use abbreviations, cross out words, or leave blanks.
- **Revising**—Writers go back and make their work better. The students will use writing conferences to get suggestions from their peers or from the teacher for improving their writing. The focus at this step is on ideas and content, not just on mechanical or technical aspects. This is the point at which writers move sentences around, delete, or elaborate. They get additional input and revise again, remembering that writing is a recursive process.
- **Proofreading**—Writers check for and correct errors in capitalization, punctuation, grammar, and spelling. They can use dictionaries or other reference materials. They can also confer with their peers or with the teacher about any questions they have.
- **Publishing**—Finally, writers prepare their writing for sharing with others. They make clean, correct copies of their work, illustrate it if they wish, bind it in some fashion, and read it aloud or place it in the classroom library for others to read.

Make sure that students understand that writers will not go through all the phases of the process for every piece of writing. They may abandon some pieces of writing after the first draft. They may revise other pieces but not publish them.

Brainstorming and Discussing Ideas

Prewriting

Tell the students that they will begin the process of writing a personal narrative (a story about something that really happened to the writer) about learning by prewriting. Remind them that this is the phase of the process during which they will come up with an idea that they want to write about. This means thinking, brainstorming, talking, and jotting down ideas as they come to mind.

➤ At this time, distribute Reproducible Master 13 and have the students insert this page in the Writing Ideas section of their Writer's Notebook. Explain that they will jot on this page specific writing ideas they have throughout the year. Point out the place on

Reproducible Master 13

Writing Ideas

Ideas for _____

	Idea	Check if used
1.		
2.		
3.		
4.		
5.		
6.		
7.		
8.		
9.		
10.		

Name _____

Copyright © 1995 Open Court Publishing Company

Writer's Notebook: Writing Ideas   RM 13

the page to check off each idea if and when they use it. If they wish, they may make some kind of notation to remind themselves in which piece of writing they used an idea. Tell the students they may ask for additional pages whenever necessary and fill one out for any writing ideas they may have. For example, they may want a page with "Ideas for poems," "Ideas for science fiction," or any other writing ideas they may come up with and want to remember.

Model a prewriting activity for the students by thinking aloud about possible ideas to write about.

- Remember out loud personal experiences involving learning that you could write about.
- On the chalkboard or a chart, write down several possible ideas as they come to mind. Remind the students that they will write their prewriting notes in their Writer's Notebook.
- Talk out loud about each idea, telling why it's important to you and listing as you talk key words and phrases that will help you remember later what you want to say. Remind the students that this list does not need to make sense to anyone but the writer.
- Remind the students about the importance of remembering what their purpose for writing is and who their audience will be. This will help them to decide which of their ideas will appeal most to that audience. Emphasize the need to conference and get opinions about their ideas from others.

Modeling Prewriting

Now have the students use this process to come up with personal experiences that they would like to write about. Each experience should be a real event, something that happened to the student. It could be a time when, like Rufus Moffat, the writer learned something in order to get something she or he wanted. It could be a time when, like the librarian in the story, the writer taught someone how to do something. Have students work alone or in small groups. Circulate as they work and comment briefly to let them know whether they're on the right track. Remind them to talk to others about their ideas, just as you talked to the class.

Refer the students to the **strategy poster Planning and Setting Writing Goals,** which should be displayed in a prominent place in the classroom along with the other writing strategy posters. Read the poster with the students. Remind them that as they plan this or any other writing project, they can use the strategies on this poster. It will help them to ask appropriate questions and to solve any problems they may have with the prewriting step of the writing process.

To review information about **prewriting**, see **Learning Framework card 7A.**

Writing Strategy Posters

Drafting

Beginning to Write

If they have had sufficient time to complete their prewriting activities and have decided on an idea for their personal narrative about learning, have the students begin the next phase of the writing process—drafting.

Emphasize these aspects of drafting:

- Students will get their ideas down on paper as fast as they can and will not concern themselves with handwriting or spelling. They may cross out words, leave blanks, and use invented spellings or abbreviations. They will go back and add, remove, correct, or rearrange ideas later.
- Anyone who has trouble thinking of the exact word or phrase needed in a particular sentence should leave space and go on to the next sentence.
- Each student will work individually and silently during the drafting phase of the process.

Model this part of the writing process by writing a draft of your own narrative on the chalkboard, a large chart, or a blank transparency. Think aloud as you try to put your ideas into words. Work as fast as you can. Stress that you are not concerned with handwriting or spelling and that you do not want to be interrupted as you work. Leave a blank in a sentence if you have difficulty thinking of a word. Use abbreviations and invented spellings. Cross out words or sentences. As an afterthought, stick in a new sentence between two sentences that you have already written. If necessary, pretend to have some problems as you write so that it is necessary for you to use these measures. (**Note:** you might want to save the chart or transparency to use in the next lesson on revising.)

Point out the **writing strategy posters Planning and Setting Writing Goals** and **Considering Readers** and discuss them with students. Explain that these are strategies they will want to think about as they begin writing. Remind them to refer to these posters and use the strategies throughout the writing process.

When you think that they are ready, have the students begin writing their own rough drafts. You may want to hand out used computer paper or other used paper to emphasize the fact that students are writing a draft and not a finished paper. Circulate to make sure that every student is writing.

To review information about **drafting**, see **Learning Framework Card 7B.**

Modeling Drafting

Writing Strategy Posters

VOCABULARY

Encourage the students to discuss words or phrases from the selection that they might want to use in their speaking and writing. Words related to learning that you might discuss include the following:

application, librarian, complication, granite, cringed, sprawled, shinny, encircled, reckoned, hoisted, peered, gingerly, obligingly, confidently, dusky, lickety-cut

➤ Have Vocabulary Exploration forms, Reproducible Master 14, available so that students can add their favorite words or phrases from the story to the Personal Dictionary section of their Writer's Notebook. Some students may wish to share their additions and to tell why they chose the words they did. For additional opportunities to build **vocabulary,** see **Teacher Tool Card 75.**

Reproducible Master 14

Vocabulary Exploration

Word: _____

Why you chose this word: _____
_____

Definition as used in the selection: _____
_____

Other meanings: _____
_____

Any antonyms you can think of: _____
_____

Any synonyms you can think of: _____
_____

Where else have you found this word? _____
_____

How might you use this word in your writing? _____
_____

Your sentence using the word: _____
_____

Remember to use this word in speaking as well as in writing.

Name

RM 14   Writer's Notebook: Personal Dictionary

Copyright © 1995 Open Court Publishing Company

3 GUIDED AND INDEPENDENT EXPLORATION

Guided
Exploration

EXPLORING CONCEPTS BEYOND THE TEXT

Students will engage in **activities of their own choosing** that allow them to explore learning more thoroughly and to use the questions they have raised to do so. These explorations may relate to the current selection or to a number of selections, but they must revolve around learning.

The following is a **menu of possible activities** from which the students may choose:

- **A literature search** to pursue a question or a problem. Discussions or writing may follow.
- **An original play or puppet show** based on learning-related situations.
- **A role-playing game** to work out a problem about learning.
- **A panel discussion** with audience participation on a question or a problem. (This discussion would have a leader and could be videotaped.)
- **A debate on an issue** related to learning. (Debaters would form teams. They would be required to follow some basic rules of debate, providing reasoned support for their sides of the issue.)
- **An advice column** dealing with learning-related problems.
- **A personal experience** story related to learning.
- **The questioning of a visiting expert** about learning.
- **An interview** with someone on a subject related to learning.
- **A survey** on an issue or question related to learning.
- **A picture or photo essay** about learning.

For a review of information about **Exploring Through Reflective Activities,** see **Learning Framework Card 3.**

Display the poster listing the **exploration activities** above so that in future lessons the students may readily select from them.

Students may **work alone, in pairs,** or **in small groups** on these activities, with an option to write about them or to present them to the group upon completion. If the students need help in deciding on an activity, here are some suggestions to get them started:

Remind the students that in this story we find out about some of Rufus's early experiences at the library, where he learns to write his name. The students may wish to share some of their own early learning experiences at a library.

Have students discuss what they have learned about their school library. Record this information on the chalkboard. During discussion, make sure that some of the following questions are asked:

- Where are fiction books shelved in the library?
- Where are nonfiction books shelved? How are they organized?
- Where are reference books found in the library?
- Where is the card catalog? How is it used?
- What periodicals does the library receive? Where are they found?

> * Exploring
> Through
> Reflective
> Activities

Mapping the Library

Draw a map of your school library or resource center. Show as many of these sections as you can: fiction, nonfiction, reference, periodicals, card catalog, circulation desk. Then answer the questions on page 9.

8 EN   Learning/Unit 1

Explorer's Notebook, page 8

Answer these questions about your school library.

How are fiction books arranged on the shelves? _____

_____

How are nonfiction books arranged on the shelves? _____

_____

What information is found on a card in the card catalog? _____

_____

What is a call number? _____

_____

What reference books does the library have? _____

_____

What periodicals does the library have? _____

_____

What do I want to find out about the library? _____

_____

_____

Unit 1/Learning   EN 9

Explorer's Notebook, page 9

"The Library Card"

A message from _____

Each unit of stories in our reading anthology centers on an important subject and its explorable concepts. These explorable concepts will be read about, thought about, discussed, researched, and written about. The students will be provided with many opportunities to compare and contrast ideas and to respond in different ways to what they read and find out.

We will try to keep you informed about what your child is learning throughout each unit and will, from time to time, send home activities related to the unit that you can work on and share with your child. This year your child will learn about learning, astronomy, family heritage, the Civil War, the American West, and journeys and quests.

The first unit of the year deals with concepts related to learning. The students will be reading about real people and fictional people whose lives were changed by learning. The first story in this unit is titled "The Library Card" and tells of a small boy who struggles to take out a book from his neighborhood library.

This would be a good time for you to make sure that your child is using your public library. If your child does not have a public library card, please help him or her to get one. Once your child has a library card, encourage her or him to use it. Using the library will help your child become a better learner in science, social studies, and other subjects, as well as a better reader.

Listed here are some books about learning that you might like to locate with your child and further examine. Most should be available in the public library. Add to this list other books that you and your child find together.

Books: From Writer to Reader by Howard Greenfield. Here's an up-to-date book that gives a thorough explanation of how a book is published.

Family Math by Jean Kerr Stenmark and others. You'll have fun with the games and activities in this book.

Great Ideas of Science by Isaac Asimov. These stories show how great thinkers of the past solved problems.

continued

Unit 1/Learning   H/SC 3

Home/School Connection 3

"The Library Card"

continued

Handtalk by Remy Charlip and Mary Beth Ancona. This book is an introduction to finger spelling and sign language.

Mrs. Frisby and the Rats of NIMH by Robert C. O'Brien. A group of laboratory rats learns how to read and escape to form their own community.

A Very Young Musician by Jill Krementz. This book and others in the series use photographs to tell the stories of young people who work hard to learn the skills necessary for their chosen careers.

The Wheel on the School by Meindert DeJong. A class of children in Holland, and eventually the community in which they live, work to realize a dream—storks on the roof of the village school.

The Whole Kids' Future Catalog by Paula Taylor. This book of projects, puzzles, and information is concerned with the future.

A Young Painter: The Life and Paintings of Wang Yani—China's Extraordinary Young Artist by Zheng Zhensun and Alice Low. This book tells the story of how a young girl was encouraged to develop her talent for painting.

You might also enjoy watching with your child the following videos related to learning.

The Miracle Worker. United Artists, 1962. This black-and-white film stars Anne Bancroft as Annie Sullivan and Patty Duke as Helen Keller. Both actresses won Oscars for their performances.

The Phantom Toll Booth. MGM/UA Home Video, 1982. In this animated version of Norton Juster's classic children's novel, Milo travels to the Kingdom of Wisdom where he is changed from a boy who was always bored to one who is interested in numbers, words, books, and learning. 89 minutes; videocassette.

Unit 1/Learning   H/SC 4

Home/School Connection 4

❯ Have the students note any questions that they cannot answer. Arrange to have the class visit the school library in order to find out the answers to these questions and to begin checking out books. When the class returns, have the students use Explorer's Notebook, pages 8–9, to record information about and to make a map of the library, showing the location of the card catalog; the librarian's desk; the fiction, nonfiction, and reference sections; and other important parts of the library.

❯ Distribute Home/School Connection 3–4, which explains the unit focus, includes a brief bibliography, and encourages the students' families to cooperate with them in obtaining cards from their neighborhood libraries.

Generating Questions to Explore

Have the students continue their discussion of learning, raising any new questions that they wish to explore. Tell them that as they read further, they may come up with a variety of ideas for ways to explore, such as interviewing someone on a subject related to learning, talking to people about a subject they would like to learn more about, or discussing the problems and difficulties involved in learning about particular subjects.

Tell the students that this is a good time to post on the Question Board any new questions they may have about learning. Be sure they include their name or initials so that they can find out who has similar interests in order to exchange ideas. Remind them of your earlier discussion about the Question Board and ask them to tell what they remember about that discussion. Point out that they may post a question on the board at any time during the course of their exploration—after they have read a selection in the anthology or after they have done some reading on their own. They should feel free to write an answer or a note on someone else's question or to consult the board for ideas for their own exploration. Remember that you are a part of the group and therefore should feel free to post your own questions from time to time as well. At this point, be sure to explain to the students that throughout the unit they may want to discuss their explorations with one another or to write about them.

To review information about the **Question Board,** see **Teacher Tool Card 121.**

❯ Distribute copies of the unit bibliography, Reproducible Masters 15–19, so that the students will have the bibliographies available as they explore. Remind them also to use the bibliography on pages 118–119 of their student anthology. Some of the books in the bibliographies concern types of learning other than those explored in the unit selections, which are primarily concerned with reading and writing and going to school. Some students may be interested in finding out more about learning mathematics, science, history, a physical skill, or a craft. Some may be interested in learning about schools in other times or places. Spend some time expanding on students' possible questions by discussing items in the bibliographies.

Using the Question Board

BIBLIOGRAPHY

Apple Is My Sign by Mary Riskind. Apple Harry, a ten-year-old deaf boy, goes to a special school in Philadelphia to learn how to speak.

Boy: Tales of Childhood by Roald Dahl. The author of *Charlie and the Chocolate Factory* and other popular books tells the sometimes sad and often hilarious story of his school years.

A Girl from Yamhill: A Memoir by Beverly Cleary. The author of *Dear Mr. Henshaw* and other books tells about her school years in Oregon.

Libby on Wednesday by Zilpha Keatley Snyder. An eleven-year-old girl learns how to work with others in a writer's workshop.

🐚 118 🐚

The Man Who Loved Books by Jean Fritz. Can you imagine how valuable books were when each book had to be printed by hand? This story of Saint Columba, who lived in Ireland about 1,500 years ago, will tell you.

Sideways Arithmetic from Wayside School by Louis Sachar. You'll have fun solving these wacky mathematical puzzles.

Top Secret by John Reynolds Gardiner. What if humans could use photosynthesis to make their own food, just as plants do? You'll laugh at this description of Allen Brewster's science project.

The Winning of Miss Lynn Ryan by Ilene Cooper. How can Carrie make a good impression on her attractive young teacher? In doing research for science and social studies projects, Carrie decides that it is more important to please herself than to please her teacher.

🐚 119 🐚

Bibliography

Books related to learning are listed below. Add other books and magazine articles you find.

Notes

Anastasia Finds the Answers by Lois Lowry. Anastasia Krupnik is determined to learn how to climb a rope and impress her glamorous gym teacher.

Baseball Fever by Joanna Hurwitz. Ezra Feldman makes a deal with his father that he will learn to play chess if his father will learn about baseball.

"The Book That Saved the Earth" by Claire Boiko, from *Space and Science Fiction Plays for Young People*, edited by Sylvia E. Kamerman. You might enjoy performing this play about aliens who do not understand books or reading.

Booker T. Washington: Educator of Hand, Head, and Heart by Shirley Graham. This story of Washington's life is based on his autobiography.

Brain Power: Understanding Human Intelligence by Gail Kay Haines. You'll enjoy these case histories and explanations of how the mind works.

Child of the Silent Night by Edith Fisher Hunter. This biography of Laura Bridgman, who was both blind and deaf, concentrates on the process by which she learned to use language.

Cobblestone magazine, November 1981. The articles in this issue are about early schools in the United States.

Reproducible Master 15

Bibliography *continued*

Notes

Do Bananas Chew Gum? by Jamie Gilson. Sam Mott develops an interest in archaeology and is motivated to improve his reading skills in order to learn about it.

Faces magazine, September 1991. This issue includes articles on education in India, France, and the Arab World; LaGuardia High School of the Arts in New York City; and apprenticeships in Africa and in America. Also provided is a bibliography of other sources of information on learning.

From the Mixed-up Files of Mrs. Basil E. Frankweiler by E. L. Konigsburg. Two children on their own in New York are determined to find out whether a statue in the Metropolitan Museum is by Michaelangelo.

Gee Wiz! How to Mix Art and Science or the Art of Thinking Scientifically by Linda Allison and David Katz. This book explains the scientific method through a set of experiments.

Going to School in 1876 by John Loeper. Photographs and other materials from this time help to tell about schools in the United States in the 1800s. See also *Going to School in 1776* by this author.

Hannah by Gloria Whelan. A nine-year-old blind girl living in the old West learns Braille.

The Helen Keller Story by Catherine O. Peare. This book is based on Helen Keller's autobiography.

Reproducible Master 16

Bibliography *continued*

Notes

Henry Reed's Think Tank by Keith Robertson. Henry Reed and his friend Midge set up a problem-solving service. You'll also enjoy *Henry Reed, Inc.* and *Henry Reed's Journal.*

How a Book is Made by Aliki. Amusing drawings show the stages of writing and publishing a book.

How Do You Know It's True? Sifting Sense from Nonsense by David and Marymae E. Klein. This book helps you to think about what truth is, how to establish it, and who to believe.

How to Think Like a Scientist: Answering Questions by the Scientific Method by Stephen P. Kramer. This book will help you develop a problem-solving strategy.

Little by Little: A Writer's Education by Jean Little. This autobiography covers the author's school years.

The Little Red Schoolhouse: A Sketchbook of Early American Education by Eric Sloane. Detailed drawings provide much information on early schools.

Looking Inside the Brain by Ron Schultz. Photographs, cartoons, and diagrams help to explain how the brain works.

Lyddie by Katherine Paterson. Reading helps a young girl to survive miserable conditions while working in a textile mill.

Name _____

Unit 1/Learning

RM 17

Reproducible Master 17

Bibliography *continued*

Notes

Malcolm X by Arnold Adoff. You may enjoy the story of the African-American leader whose life was changed when he became interested in reading.

Maniac McGee by Jerry Spinnelli. Maniac loves to run and loves to read.

The Moon and I by Betsy Byers. The popular author tells about her childhood and about how she writes a book.

Mukasa by John Nagenda. A boy in Africa finds a way to go to school and learns much during his first year there.

My Side of the Mountain by Jean Craighead George. Sam Grimby is so occupied with learning how to live off the land that he does not much mind living alone for more than a year.

On Their Toes: A Russian Ballet School by Ann Morris. You'll see many contrasts between your school and the one in this book.

The One-Room School at Squabble Hollow by Rosmarie Hausherr. This photo-essay tells about a modern one-room school in Vermont.

The Secret Life of School Supplies by Vicki Cobb. This book shows the kind of information you can find when you ask questions about such ordinary things as paper, ink, pencils, erasers, and glue.

Name _____

RM 18

Unit 1/Learning

Reproducible Master 18

Bibliography *continued*

Notes

Stars Come Out Within by Jean Little. This second volume of the author's autobiography tells the story of her career as a writer and of her struggle to accept her blindness.

Who Stole the Wizard of Oz? by Avi. Clues in children's books help two young detectives track down a thief.

Writing: A Fact and Fun Book by Amanda Lewis. Libraries, literacy, a history of writing, books, printing, and how a fax machine works—all are included in this interesting and amusing book.

Your Two Brains by Patricia Stafford. This book explains the separate function of each half of the brain.

Add books and magazines you find.

• _____
  _____
  _____

• _____
  _____
  _____

• _____
  _____

• _____
  _____
  _____

• _____
  _____

• _____
  _____

Name _____

Unit 1/Learning

RM 19

Reproducible Master 19

* INDEPENDENT WORKSHOP
Building a Community of Scholars

Student-Directed Reading, Writing, and Discussion

Explain to the class that Independent Workshop is a block of time during which they will work alone or cooperatively with their classmates on a variety of activities and in a self-directed manner. The first part of each workshop will be devoted to any collaborative work they wish to do. In small groups they will discuss their explorations. The remainder of Independent Workshop time can be spent on options of their choice, including writing, conferencing, cross-curricular activities, independent reading, and reading roundtable. It is during this block of time that you can work with students who need extra help or tutoring. Remind the students that Independent Workshop is a time for them to work together, to help each other learn more about the concepts, and to build a community of scholars. **Learning Framework Card 5** contains a complete discussion of establishing and conducting **Independent Workshop** and suggestions for helping English Language Learners during Workshop.

WORKSHOP TIPS

Remember that the students should be sharing information freely. They should be encouraged to use the Concept Board and Question Board often. They should write in their Explorer's Notebook any questions, notes, or information from either board that they think will be useful. The students need to get ideas from one another. It is important that they share ideas and information from their Explorer's Notebook with their classmates. After small-group work, some students may wish to locate several of the books listed in their bibliographies or other books about learning. These additional resources may help them think further about learning and ways to explore it.

Remind the students that they may choose at this time to return to their Explorer's Notebook to complete any unfinished pages or to discuss ideas with classmates.

Additional Opportunities for Independent Reading, Writing, and Cross-curricular Activities

If you haven't already done so, take some time at this point to familiarize the students with the Student Toolbox and its contents: the Tradebook Connection Cards, the Cross-curricular Activity Cards, and the Student Tool Cards. Remind the students that during this portion of Independent Workshop, they will be free to work with items from the Student Toolbox.

✳ Reading Roundtable

Encourage the students to read other books by Eleanor Estes. Many of her books feature various members of the Moffat family, including Rufus.

The Tradebook Connection selection *Dear Mr. Henshaw* by Beverly Cleary is particularly appropriate for this unit. It concerns a boy who is influenced to become a better writer through correspondence with his favorite author. Tradebook Connection Cards can be found in the Student Toolbox.

Whenever possible, model good reading habits for the students by doing your own free reading at this time. Share with the students any books you read and especially enjoy.

For information about **Reading Roundtable**, see **Learning Framework Card 6.**

✳ Writing Seminar

The students may continue drafting their personal narratives about learning something or teaching somebody something. For information about **Writing Seminar,** see **Learning Framework Card 8.**

Cross-curricular Activity Cards

The following Cross-curricular Activity Cards in the Student Toolbox are appropriate for this selection:

- 1 Art—Picture Books
- 1 Drama—Dramatizing "The Library Card"
- 1 Science—A Pile of Coal

Additional Opportunities for Solving Learning Problems

Tutorial

Use this time to assist individuals or small groups of students who need help in any area. This is also a good time for peer tutoring. Appropriately match any of your students who would benefit from receiving or providing peer tutoring. The best matches are strong students with average students and average students with weaker students. Have students refer to the proper Student Tool Cards to guide their work together. In addition, encourage them to discuss with you any subject or area in which they need extra help. The following teaching aids are available in the Teacher Toolbox for your convenience:

- Writer's Craft/Reading: Plot, Teacher Tool Card 15
- Writer's Craft/Reading: Genre—Realistic Fiction, Teacher Tool Card 3
- Writer's Craft/Reading: Characterization, Teacher Tool Card 13
- Spelling and Vocabulary: Using and Punctuating Contractions, Teacher Tool Card 80

Into the Light of Day

1 READING THE SELECTION

About the
Selection

Born in 1829 in Hanover, New Hampshire, Laura Bridgman lost both her sight and her hearing at the age of two. Six years later, under the determined tutelage of Dr. Stephen Gridley Howe, this bright and brave little girl would become the first deaf and blind child to learn a formal language. In this inspiring selection, author Edith Fisher Hunter guides the reader through the sometimes playful, often tedious process by which Dr. Howe led young Bridgman from her dark and silent world "into the light of day."

Link to the
Unit Concepts

"Into the Light of Day," pages 30–39, is as much about Dr. Samuel Gridley Howe and his determination to teach Laura Bridgman as it is about the young girl herself. The story dramatically demonstrates that different people learn in different ways. It also emphasizes the profound changes learning can have on a person's life.

About the
Author

"Into the Light of Day" is an excerpt from Edith Fisher Hunter's book *Child of the Silent Night.* Hunter first heard about Laura Bridgman from her mother, who had attended Framington College in Massachusetts, the school at which one of Bridgman's teachers had been educated. The author told her own children Laura Bridgman's story, but when they went to the library to learn more about the blind and deaf child, they could find no books about her. Hunter then decided to write one herself and began a long process of research into old letters, journals, and periodicals. *Child of the Silent Night* is the result of that research.

INFORMATION FOR THE STUDENT

- Tell the students that "Into the Light of Day" is an excerpt from *Child of the Silent Night,* a biography written by Edith Fisher Hunter. Some students may be interested in what inspired Hunter to write this book.

LESSON OVERVIEW

"Into the Light of Day" by Edith Fisher Hunter, pages 30–39

READING THE SELECTION

Materials
Student anthology, pp. 30–39
Explorer's Notebook, p. 4
Assessment Master 1

FYI
Learning Framework Cards
• Setting Reading Goals and
  Expectations, 1A

• Responding to Text, 1B
• Clarifying Unfamiliar Words and
  Passages, 1D
• Exploring Through Discussion, 2

Teacher Tool Cards
• Classroom Supports: Modeling and
  Generating Think-Alouds, 116
• Classroom Supports: Writer's
  Notebook, 120

READING WITH A WRITER'S EYE

Minilesson
Writer's Craft: Indicators of Time and
  Order
Writer's Craft: Writing Paragraphs

Materials
Reading/Writing Connection, pp. 4–6
Reproducible Master 14

FYI
Learning Framework Cards
• Writing Process, 7

• Revising, 7C
• Writing Seminar, 8

Options for Instruction
Writer's Craft: Genre—Biography
Writer's Craft: Elaboration Through
  Providing Description
Grammar, Mechanics, and Usage: Past-
  Tense Verbs
(Use Teacher Tool Cards listed below.)

GUIDED AND INDEPENDENT EXPLORATION

Materials
Explorer's Notebook, pp. 10–11
Assessment Master 1

**Optional Materials from
Student Toolbox**
Tradebook Connection Cards

Cross-curricular Activity Cards
• 1 Social Studies—Braille
• 2 Social Studies—The Manual Alphabet

Student Tool Cards
• Writer's Craft/Reading: Signal Words
  Showing Time and Order, 27
• Writer's Craft/Reading: Writing
  Paragraphs, 22

Independent Workshop

• Writer's Craft/Reading: Reading and
  Writing Biography and
  Autobiography, 8
• Writer's Craft/Reading: Giving
  Descriptions, 39
• Grammar, Mechanics, and Usage:
  Using Past-Tense Verbs, 64

FYI
Learning Framework Cards
• Independent Workshop, 5
• Reading Roundtable, 6
• Writing Seminar, 8

Teacher Tool Cards
• Writer's Craft/Reading: Indicators of
  Time and Order, 27
• Writer's Craft/Reading: Writing
  Paragraphs, 22
• Writer's Craft/Reading: Genre—
  Biography and Autobiography, 8
• Writer's Craft/Reading: Elaboration
  Through Providing Descriptions, 39
• Grammar, Mechanics, and Usage:
  Using Past-Tense Verbs, 64
• Classroom Supports: Question
  Board and Concept Board, 121

N O T E S

Asterisks (*) throughout the lesson indicate learning frameworks. Learning Framework Cards and Teacher Tool Cards can be found in the Teacher Toolbox.

- Have the students read the material in italics on page 30.
- You may also wish to share with students the information that follows about the story illustrations or about Laura Bridgman's connection with Helen Keller.

Background Information

The illustrations in this story show Laura Bridgman wearing a green ribbon around her eyes. We do not know why the Perkins Institute had its pupils wear such ribbons, perhaps because they thought the children would appear more attractive to visitors at the school. This is the way she and the other blind girls at the Perkins Institute are described by the English novelist Charles Dickens, who visited the school specifically to meet Laura Bridgman. The following passage appears in his *American Notes,* which was published in 1842:

> Her face was radiant with intelligence and pleasure. Her hair, braided by her own hands, was bound about a head whose intellectual capacity and development were beautifully expressed in its graceful outline, and its broad open brow; her dress, arranged by herself, was a pattern of neatness and simplicity; the work she had knitted lay beside her; her writing book was on the desk she leaned upon. . . . Like other inmates of that house, she had a green ribbon bound round her eyelids. A doll she had dressed lay near upon the ground. I took it up, and saw that she had made a green fillet such as she wore herself, and fastened it about its mimic eyes.

Although she never learned to speak, Laura Bridgman learned to read and to communicate by means of the manual alphabet. Helping teachers and working as a seamstress, Bridgman remained at the Perkins Institute until her death.

In 1887, Arthur and Kate Keller—whose daughter Helen, like Bridgman, had been blind and deaf from an early age—read about Bridgman's education in Dickens's *American Notes.* They asked the Perkins school to provide a teacher for their daughter. Bridgman, who by this time was over fifty, had recently befriended Anne Sullivan, the young woman the school chose for the job. Sullivan went to the Kellers' home carrying with her a doll dressed in clothing that Bridgman had made. This doll was a gift for Helen Keller from Laura Bridgman.

Anne Sullivan used the same methods Dr. Howe had used with Bridgman to teach Helen Keller. Shortly before Bridgman died, Sullivan took Keller to the Perkins Institute to meet Bridgman, and they communicated using the manual alphabet. Helen Keller eventually learned to read and write Braille and even to speak. She graduated from Radcliffe College with honors and became famous for her efforts to improve conditions for the blind.

About the Illustrations

Bridgman's Link to Helen Keller

*

COGNITIVE AND RESPONSIVE READING

Activating Prior Knowledge

Encourage students to share what they know about how blind people read or how deaf people communicate.

Setting Reading Goals and Expectations

Remind the students that they have learned a strategy for browsing fiction. Tell them that **good readers browse nonfiction differently from the way they browse fiction** because they are usually reading nonfiction in order to find information.

Explain that before they read they will **set reading goals and expectations.** To do this, they will **browse the selection** and **use the clues/problems/wondering procedure.** On the chalkboard under the headings clues, problems, and wonderings, write in brief note form the observations the students generate during browsing. For example, students might list the genre of the selection under *clues*; they might list unfamiliar words under *problems*; and they might note any questions that arise during browsing under *wonderings.* The students will return to these observations after reading.

For a review of **browsing**, see **Learning Framework Card 1A, Setting Reading Goals and Expectations.**

Recommendations for Reading the Selection

Allow the students time to decide how they would like to read the selection. "Into the Light of Day" is an expository piece that contains involved process descriptions. It is recommended that the students read the selection orally, or you might suggest they begin reading aloud and continue silently once they feel comfortable doing so.

If the students elect to **read orally,** you should **refer to the think-aloud prompts that are provided beneath the page miniatures.** Instead of or in addition to using these prompts, encourage the students to provide their own think-alouds. This would also be a good selection for **responding** to text **by expressing feelings** while reading aloud. Model this response, and then invite the students to respond.

If the students elect to **read silently,** have them **discuss problems, reactions,** and **strategies** after reading. Let the students know, however, that they can raise their hands anytime during reading to ask questions or to identify problems for discussion with the group.

About the Reading Strategies

"Into the Light of Day" describes the detailed process by which Laura Bridgman learned language. The selection also includes excerpts from actual progress reports about her. **Visualizing** is one strategy the students might find helpful if they are puzzled by what they read. Some students may also need to clarify unfamiliar words or confusing passages.

Introducing Visualizing

Good readers often see a picture in their minds of the people, scenes, and actions they read about. This ability to **visualize** helps them better understand and enjoy what they are reading. Encourage the students to discuss whether they have ever formed a picture in their minds to help them understand something they read or something someone said. If necessary, give an example of visualization. For example, you might say

If a friend of yours tells you that he doesn't like swimming in the ocean because of the water conditions, you might picture the ocean's crashing waves and the way icy cold water feels. You might think about the powerful pull of the undertow and the stinging taste of salt.

Visualizing these conditions helps you to understand why your friend doesn't like the ocean. When we visualize, we might imagine sights, sounds, tastes, and smells, as well as the way things feel.

Before the students read the selection, you might invite them to visualize the world that Laura Bridgman experienced, totally void of sight and sound.

Refer the students to the **reading strategy poster Responding to Text.** Point to and read aloud the part about **visualizing.** Discuss the strategy and have the questions read aloud. Remind the students to ask themselves these questions in order to use this strategy effectively. To review the strategy of **visualizing,** see **Learning Framework Card 1B, Responding to Text.**

Clarifying unfamiliar words and unclear passages requires that readers actively participate in reading by **identifying words and sentences that they do not understand.** Ask the students to explain how they usually go about clarifying things that are confusing to them in a text.

The students should understand that all readers, even good ones, get confused and occasionally need something clarified. Sometimes it's a single word. Sometimes it's a sentence or a paragraph. **Rereading the other words in a sentence or paragraph** will often clarify the meaning of an unfamiliar word. Sometimes the reader can ask a friend for help. Other times, a reader may look up an unfamiliar word in a dictionary.

Sometimes **putting a sentence into one's own words** will help to clarify it. Help students to understand, however, that they will not always be able to clarify a word or passage that confuses them. Sometimes they will have to keep the question of what the word or passage means in mind and look for the answer as they read on.

Before the students begin reading, point out the **strategy poster Clarifying Unfamiliar Words and Passages.** Read the poster together and discuss the questions. Remind the students to refer to and use this poster whenever they need to clarify. To review strategies for **clarifying unfamiliar words and passages,** see **Learning Framework Card 1D.**

Think-Aloud Prompts for Use in Oral Reading

Notice the think-aloud prompts with the page miniatures. These are simply suggestions for strategy use with this text. Remind the students that reading should make sense. If it doesn't, they should refer to the strategy posters for help with what to do next. Remind them also to share whatever strategies they use to solve a reading problem or to respond to the text in some way. Encourage the students to stop and ask for help if they are confused by something and to share any reactions they may have as they read. For a review of **modeling** and **generating think-alouds,** see **Teacher Tool Card 116.**

Reading Strategy Posters

Introducing Clarifying Unfamiliar Words and Passages

Reading Strategy Posters

THINK ALOUD PROMPTS

These prompts may be used as guides to promote cognitive and responsive reading.

1 If the students are confused about the boot in the cupboard, explain that before she went to school, Laura Bridgman spent much time with a family friend. He encouraged her to explore through her sense of touch the animals and objects on her family's farm and in the surrounding woods. She kept some items that she found —feathers, snail shells, etc.—in a large boot that she locked away in a cupboard.

INTO THE LIGHT OF DAY
from CHILD OF THE SILENT NIGHT
by Edith Fisher Hunter
illustrated by James Watling

When she was two years old, Laura Bridgman became very ill with scarlet fever and was left blind and deaf. Her parents were afraid that she would never be able to communicate with the people around her or to learn about the world. However, Dr. Samuel Gridley Howe, the director of the Perkins Institution for the Blind in Boston, wanted to try to teach her. Dr. Howe intended to first teach Laura the twenty-six letters of the alphabet and then help her to understand that people could share their thoughts by combining these letters into words.

When the first lesson began Laura was seated at a table across from Dr. Howe. Beside her sat Miss Drew, who was to be Laura's own special teacher. Miss Jeannette Howe sat watching nearby.

The doctor had arranged a row of objects on the table in front of him. There were a large key, a spoon, a knife, a fork, a book, a cup and a few other things with which he felt sure Laura would be familiar.

✣ 30 ✣

First Dr. Howe put the key into Laura's hand. It was a very large key. He let her handle it and feel it all over. She knew immediately what it was. The key at home with which she locked her boot in the cupboard was very much like this one—except for one thing. Her sensitive fingers paused as they felt the long key. There was something *on* this one.

Dr. Howe had fastened a paper label on the key. On the label the word *key* was written in a special kind of raised

1

lettering or embossing that was used at that time in writing for the blind. The Braille system, now so widely used, had not yet been adopted. Dr. Howe guided Laura's fingers over the raised lines of the letters several times. She had no idea, of course, what the letters were.

Then he took the key away from Laura and handed her a spoon. She took it, felt it and immediately recognized it as a spoon much like the ones with which she set the table at home. Again there was one important difference. Along the handle of the spoon Dr. Howe had pasted a label with the letters S-P-O-O-N written in raised type. Dr. Howe guided her fingers carefully over this word several times.

Now the doctor took away the spoon and gave the key back to Laura. He directed her fingers to the label on the key again. Then he gave her back the spoon and directed her fingers to the label on the spoon once more. He wanted Laura to feel that the shape of the lines on the key label and the shape of the lines on the spoon label were just as different from each other as the key and spoon themselves were different from one another.

Now the doctor did something else. He took away the key and the spoon and gave Laura just a piece of paper with some raised letters on it. The letters were K-E-Y again. Taking the key once more, Dr. Howe directed Laura's fingers to the label on it.

An expression on Laura's face made it quite clear that she recognized that the raised letters were the same on both papers, the one on the key and the separate label. Dr. Howe went through the same process with the spoon and a separate label that read S-P-O-O-N.

 32

The rest of that first lesson was spent letting Laura feel the remaining objects—cup, knife, book, and so forth—and the labels for these, both those pasted on the object and those that were separate. From that time on Laura had lessons every morning and afternoon. She seemed to enjoy them thoroughly and to consider them just a game, not work. It was difficult for Dr. Howe and Miss Drew to get her to stop "playing" this game.

By about the third day Dr. Howe and Miss Drew were delighted to see that Laura had grasped the important point that the separate label for *key* somehow went with the key and the label that was separate from the spoon went with the spoon. That she understood this was shown by the fact that

2 Some students may not understand the difference between embossed lettering and Braille letters. **Visualizing** may help them understand. You might explain that embossed letters are raised letters like the ones they would find on a coin. An explanation of Braille symbols is provided on Social Studies Activity Card 1.

she could take a separate label, such as the one spelling *book*, and feel about until she found a book without any label. Then she would place the label on the book.

3
In a very few days Laura could reverse this process. She could pick up an object, such as a spoon, search through a pile of loose labels on the table, feel them until she found the one that read S-P-O-O-N and then put it on a spoon. She could do this for any object for which she had been taught the feeling of the word.

Dr. Howe was greatly encouraged. He felt sure that he was going to succeed with Laura; his only question was how long it was going to take him. In a report that he once wrote about his work with her he said: "It sometimes occurred to me that she was like a person alone and helpless in a deep, dark, still pit, and that I was letting down a cord and dangling it about, in hopes she might find it, and that finally she would seize it by chance, and clinging to it, be drawn up by it into the light of day and into human society."

4
The lessons were going so well that Dr. Howe felt Laura was ready to take another important step forward. He had Miss Drew cut the labels for the words *key, spoon, knife*, and so forth, into separate letters. Up until this time Laura had seen words as wholes. Now he wanted her to learn that they are made up of parts—letters. Laura was allowed to follow closely, with her hands, all that Miss Drew did. After the words had been cut into separate letters, her hands followed Miss Drew's as she arranged the letters back into words.

In an astonishingly short time Laura had grasped the point of this new "game." If Miss Drew handed her the letters O, S,

🐚 34 🐚

N, O, P, in a flash Laura could arrange them in the correct order to spell S-P-O-O-N. If Miss Drew gave her Y, K, E, Laura arranged them into the word K-E-Y. O, K, O, B and I, K, E, N, F were equally simple for her. After a few more lessons Laura could do this with all the words in her vocabulary and soon after that she could take from a whole pile of loose letters whatever ones she wanted and spell correctly any word she wished of those she had been taught.

Dr. Howe thought it would be easier for Laura to arrange the letters if there were some kind of form into which they could be fitted. Therefore he had metal letters—types, he called them—made for her and a frame with grooves into which the letters could be fitted. He had four complete sets made of the twenty-six letters of the alphabet. Within a short time Laura was using the metal letters to build all the words she knew.

5
Two months had passed before Dr. Howe felt that Laura was ready to take the final step that he had planned for her. Miss Drew was sent to the home of a Mr. George Loring, who was deaf, to learn the manual alphabet. She learned it in one afternoon.

🐚 35 🐚

3 Since this is the end of the explanation of Laura's first lessons, students may want to check their understanding of what they have just read by **summing up** here. You might model checking your own understanding of Dr. Howe's teaching process by providing a summary that includes the following information:
- Dr. Howe gave Laura objects to feel that he knew she would recognize by touch.
- The objects were labeled with raised type, over which he guided her fingers several times.
- He also had her feel the embossed names of these objects on a separate piece of paper.
- Through this process, Laura learned to associate each object with a special set of embossed patterns, and after a few days she could match many different objects with their correct labels.

4 Dr. Howe's analogy may be unclear to some students. If you suspect some students may be confused, you might use a discussion starter such as the following: *That explanation was a little confusing to me. Is anyone else puzzled by what Dr. Howe wrote?*
The strategy of **visualizing** may help students understand this analogy. Ask them to imagine how eager they would be to be rescued from a dark pit, and how difficult it would be to find the rescue rope in such blackness, especially if they could not hear their rescuer guiding them to the rope that would save them. This visualization may help them to understand how it must have been for Laura to be rescued from her dark and silent world.

5 Before the students go on to the last step of Laura's learning process, they might want to stop and **sum up** to check their understanding. A good summary should be short and include only the important points.

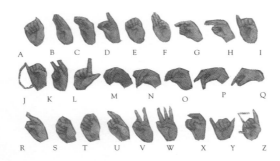

A B C D E F G H I
J K L M N O P Q
R S T U V W X Y Z

The manual alphabet is a way of forming the twenty-six letters of the alphabet with the hands. In the United States the one-handed manual alphabet is used. There is also a two-handed system used in some countries. In the one-handed system the letter *a*, for example, is formed by folding the four fingers over and keeping the thumb straight. *B* is formed by holding the fingers straight up with the thumb folded in. In only a few cases, as with *c* and *y*, for example, does the hand form a shape that very much resembles the shape of that letter as we write it.

A deaf person who has been "talking" with the manual alphabet for a long time can "say" with his hand as many as 130 words a minute. A deaf person who is skilled at watching another person "speak" with his hands can easily "read" 130 words a minute.

Laura, of course, would not be able to see the letters. Miss Drew would have to form them in Laura's hand so that she could feel them.

❧ 36 ❧

But how could she teach Laura that the various positions in which she held her fingers meant the letters of the alphabet that she had already learned with raised letters and metal types? This is how Miss Drew did it. She picked up the key and let Laura feel it. Then she took the letter K from the set of metal types and let Laura feel that. Then she shaped the letter *k* in the manual alphabet into Laura's hand, her first two fingers up and bent forward, the next two fingers folded down, and the thumb up. She made Laura feel the way her fingers were held. Then she let Laura feel the metal letter K again.

The same procedure was followed with the letter *e*. First Laura must feel the metal type of the E, then Miss Drew formed *e* in the manual alphabet, all the fingers folded over and the thumb folded down, and then back to the metal type again. Finally the letter Y was taken from the metal types and Laura allowed to feel it. The manual *y* is formed with thumb up, little finger up and other fingers all folded down. This one almost looks like a *y* as we write it. Now Miss Drew had set the metal types K-E-Y in the form.

She let Laura run her hand over the whole word. Then she formed again, in the manual alphabet, the letters *k-e-y* in Laura's hand and she placed the key itself in Laura's other hand. This was done with the spoon, the cup, and the key again.

And then it happened! For two months Laura had been "playing" these games with letters and words almost the way a trained dog performs certain tricks. Now, suddenly, it was different. Dr. Howe always said that he knew almost the exact moment when Laura's face showed that she at last

❧ 37 ❧

really understood what all this meant. Suddenly it seemed to become clear to her that every object had a name, that these names could be spelled by letters, either in raised letters, metal types or, most easily of all, by the manual alphabet.

In one of his yearly reports about his work with Laura Bridgman, Dr. Howe wrote: ". . . Now the truth began to flash upon her, her intellect began to work, she perceived that here was a way by which she could herself make up a sign of anything that was in her own mind, and show it to another mind, and at once her countenance lighted up with a human expression . . . I could almost fix upon the moment when this truth dawned upon her mind and spread its light to her <u>countenance</u>. . . ."

Laura had found the rope that Dr. Howe was dangling before her. She had caught hold of it at last and could be drawn up from the dark pit in which she lived into the light of day!

What a different world it was for Laura now!

Can you imagine what it must have been like for her? She had been alive for eight years and yet until this day she had never been able really to ask a single question! Now, suddenly, she could ask at least one enormous question: WHAT IS THE NAME OF THAT?

Of course she didn't know the words *what, is, the, name, of,* and *that,* but now by placing her hand on any object, she let her teacher know that she was asking for the name of that object.

And ask she did! At supper on the day she really understood that every object has a name, poor Miss Drew didn't

38

get a bite to eat. Laura wanted the name of everything and everybody. Usually at meals Miss Drew was expected to help not only Laura but several of the little blind girls. She cut their meat, buttered their bread and did anything else that needed doing. But tonight Laura demanded every single bit of Miss Drew's attention.

"I'll help with the other children," said Miss Jeannette. "This one meal we'll let Laura have you wholly to herself. It's a kind of birthday for her."

And so Laura began. She placed her hand on her napkin, and Miss Drew spelled "napkin" into Laura's hand. Then Laura spelled it into Miss Drew's hand. Then she asked the name of the tablecloth, the salt, the pepper, the sugar, the milk, and on and on and on. Miss Drew was thoroughly exhausted when she went to bed that night and the muscles of her spelling hand ached for hours.

6 Dr. Howe's description of the moment when Laura first understood language may be unclear to some students. You might suggest they first use context clues to **clarify** any **unfamiliar words,** such as *countenance*. If the passage is still confusing to some students, you might then suggest that they read further to see if the next paragraph helps them to **clarify** Dr. Howe's idea. There, the analogy which appears on page 34 is continued. The students might again use the strategy of **visualizing** to help them understand what is being described.

Discussing Strategy Use
Invite the students to share any difficulties they may have had while reading the selection and the strategies they used to help solve these problems. If students **visualized** periodically, have them discuss how this helped them better understand what they were reading. Encourage them also to discuss how they used the strategies for clarifying unfamiliar words or passages in the text.

Reflecting on the Selection
Whole-Group Discussion

∗ EXPLORING THROUGH DISCUSSION

The whole group discusses the selection and any **personal thoughts, reactions, problems,** or **questions** that it raises. During this time, students may also be invited to **return** to the **clues, problems, and wonderings** they noted on the chalkboard during browsing to determine whether the clues were borne out by the selection, whether and how their problems were solved, and whether their wonderings were answered or deserve further discussion and exploration. Avoid treating their ideas like a list to be discussed and eliminated in a linear fashion. Instead, let the **students decide which items deserve further discussion.** To stimulate discussion, the **students** can **ask** one another the kinds of **questions that good readers ask themselves** about a text: **What did I find interesting? What is important here? What was difficult to understand? Why would someone want to read this?** Your own participation in the discussion might take the form of expressing and modeling your reactions to characters or to other aspects of the story. It is important for the students to see you as a contributing member of the group.

To emphasize that you are part of the group, actively **participate in the handing-off process:** Raise your hand to be called on by the last speaker when you have a contribution to make. Point out unusual and interesting insights verbalized by the students so that these insights are recognized and discussed. As the year progresses, the **students will take more and more responsibility for the discussions** of the selections. The handing-off process is a good way to get them to take on this responsibility.

Assessment

In a successful discussion, it should not be necessary for you to ask questions to assess the students' understanding of the text. If necessary, however, engage in a discussion **to determine whether the students have grasped the following ideas:**
• the steps that led to Laura Bridgman's understanding of language
• the meaning of the title "Into the Light of Day"

Response Journal

If the students would like to remember any additional thoughts about the story, discuss the idea of their keeping a **personal response journal.** This journal could be a **section of their Writer's Notebook** in which they record thoughts, feelings, and reactions about and favorite passages or quotations from selections in *Collections for Young Scholars* or other reading. **Explain why they might want to keep such a journal:** writers keep journals as a source of ideas; readers keep journals to record what they liked about reading something; and anybody can keep a journal to express his or her feelings about events and experiences. Keeping a journal is similar to keeping a diary. To review information about the response journal, see **Teacher Tool Card 120, Writer's Notebook.**

TEACHING TIP In discussion of any selection, limit content questions from the teacher.

Introducing the Personal Response Journal

Exploring Concepts Within the Selection
Small-Group Discussion

Small groups discuss the relationship of the selection to learning. Circulate among the groups and observe the discussions. Refer the students to the Concept Board and the Question Board to keep them focused on their original ideas about learning and to see if those ideas have changed as a result of reading this selection.

ASSESSMENT TIP This may be a good opportunity to observe students working in groups and to mark observations in the Teacher's Observation Log.

Sharing Ideas About Explorable Concepts

Have the groups **report** their **ideas** and **discuss** them with the rest of the class. It is crucial that the students' ideas determine this discussion.
- The students may mention that most people learn language through hearing it. Laura Bridgman could only learn through her sense of touch.
- Some students could also comment that people usually learn to speak first, and then learn to read by seeing words that they have come to understand. Laura Bridgman learned to read without ever seeing words or hearing them spoken.
- The students may notice that Bridgman's understanding of the world was greatly enhanced by her learning to use language.

As these and other concepts are suggested or as questions are raised, have the students add them to the **Question Board** or **Concept Board.**

TIP FOR ENGLISH LANGUAGE LEARNERS

Encourage English Language Learners to express ideas that are important to them. They may have unique insights about learning to speak another language in order to communicate. Invite English Language Learners to discuss their ideas as they relate to the story, based on their own knowledge and experiences.

Exploring Concepts Across Selections

Ask the students how this selection reminds them of "The Library Card." They may make the following connections:
- The students may notice that when Rufus Moffat and Laura Bridgman began learning, neither understood much about the things they were being taught.
- The students could also mention that both Rufus and Laura had certain personality traits that helped them learn. Rufus was persistent and willing to cooperate with the library lady; Laura was enthusiastic about the tasks her teachers gave her and approached them as though she were playing a game.

VOCABULARY TIP Use important words related to learning during discussions with the students to model the utility of these words.

Recording Ideas

As students complete the above discussions, ask them how to **sum up what they have learned from their conversations and how they might use this information** in further explorations. Any special information or insights may be recorded on the **Concept Board.** Any further questions that they would like to think about, pursue, or investigate may be recorded on the **Question Board.** Students may want to discuss the progress that has been made on their questions. They may also want to cross out any questions that no longer warrant consideration.

Evaluating Discussions

▶ After discussion, the students should individually record their learning on page 4 of their Explorer's Notebook.

Recording Concept Information

As I read each selection, this is what I added to my understanding of learning.

"The Library Card" by Eleanor Estes

_____
_____
_____
_____
_____
_____
_____
_____
_____

"Into the Light of Day" by Edith Fisher Hunter

_____
_____
_____
_____
_____
_____
_____
_____
_____
_____
_____
_____

4 EN   Learning/Unit 1

Explorer's Notebook, page 4

2 READING WITH A WRITER'S EYE

MINILESSONS

Writer's Craft:
Indicators of
Time and Order

Understanding the passage of time and the order of events is important when reading both narrative and expository text. Ask the students to tell what they know about **how authors indicate time and order** and to cite any examples they can recall from their reading and writing. Students might remember that authors sometimes use specific words or phrases to signal to readers which events happen before or after others. Invite students to give examples of some of these clue words. If necessary, explain that words such as *yesterday, tomorrow, last month,* and *suddenly* are indicators of time. Other words, such as *first, next, after, last* and *then* are indicators of order.

Point out that Edith Fisher Hunter made the passage of time and the order of events in "Into the Light of Day" easy to follow by using such words and phrases. Provide a few examples from the story and explain them as necessary. Some examples include the following:

Indicators of Time

page 33, paragraph 2: "By about the third day"

page 34, paragraph 1: "In a very few days"

Indicators of Order
page 31, paragraph 1: "First Dr. Howe put the key into Laura's hand."
page 32, paragraph 1: "Then he took the key away"
page 32, paragraph 2: "Now the doctor took away the spoon"

Selective Reading:
Focus on Indicators of
Time and Order

Now have the students scan the selection for additional words and phrases that help them recognize the passage of time or understand the order of events. Invite volunteers to read aloud sentences or passages that include these indicators and to explain what each example tells them. Possible words and phrases include *now, next, soon after that, up until this time, after the words had been cut, the final step, finally, suddenly, at supper, on the day, usually, tonight.*

Selection-Based
Practice

Independent Practice:
Indicators of Time and
Order

➤ Use Reading/Writing Connection, page 4, for additional practice. Have students record other examples of words and phrases that indicate time and order. Provide time for them to share their findings and to explain how each word helps them follow events in the stories. **Make note of students who might need more help during Independent Workshop.**

Reading/Writing Connection, page 4

"Into the Light of Day"

Indicators of Time and Order

Find examples from "Into the Light of Day," "The Library Card," or other books you have read where the author uses words or phrases to indicate the passage of time and the order of events.

Title: _____ Author: _____
Words and phrases indicating time or order: _____
_____
_____
_____

How do these examples help you understand what you read?
_____
_____
_____
_____

Title: _____ Author: _____
Words and phrases indicating time or order: _____
_____
_____
_____

How do these examples help you understand what you read?
_____
_____
_____
_____

Name

Signal Words _____
4 R/WC   Learning/Unit 1

Writer's Craft:
Writing
Paragraphs

Point out that authors write in paragraphs; then ask the students to discuss what they know about paragraphs. Establish that **a paragraph is a group of two or more sentences that are related in some way, all telling about the same thing or idea.** Sometimes one of the sentences, often the first, provides the main idea of the paragraph. This is usually called a *topic sentence* or a *stated main idea.* Sometimes the main idea is not stated; then it is often called an *implied main idea* because the reader has to infer it.

In "Into the Light of Day," Edith Fisher Hunter uses many different kinds of paragraphs:

- page 30, paragraph 2: states an idea then lists examples. The topic sentence is the first one in the paragraph.
- page 31, paragraph 1: describes the related actions of a character. The main idea is implied: Dr. Howe began to teach Laura about language by first letting her feel a key.
- page 36, paragraph 1: is a description of something. The main idea is stated in the first sentence of the paragraph.
- page 37, paragraph 1: explains a series of steps. The main idea is implied: This is how Miss Drew taught Laura that the hand positions stood for the raised letters of the alphabet that she had already learned.

Selective Reading:
Focus on Writing
Paragraphs

Have the students examine the rest of the selection and tell how the sentences in other paragraphs are related, then decide whether the main idea is stated or implied. Students might mention some of the following paragraphs:

- page 33, paragraph 1: describes the related actions of a character. The main idea is implied: Laura continued her lessons and enjoyed them thoroughly.
- page 36, paragraph 2: describes something. The main idea is implied: Using this system, deaf people can communicate quickly.
- page 37, paragraph 2: explains a series of steps. The main idea is implied: Miss Drew taught Laura the last two letters of the word *key.*
- page 39, last paragraph: lists examples. The main idea is implied: Laura asked for the name of nearly everything in the room.

Selection-Based Practice

Independent Practice:
Writing Paragraphs

➤ Have the students use Reading/Writing Connection, pages 5–6, for additional practice.

WRITING

Linking Reading
to Writing

Have the students write paragraphs in which all the ideas are related. Encourage them to try writing the different types of paragraphs they discussed in the lesson, that is, paragraphs that describe something, list examples, give a series of steps, or tell the related actions of a character. Allow the students sufficient time to write, then invite volunteers to read their paragraphs aloud.

Worksheet (left page)

"Into the Light of Day"

Writing Paragraphs

Look back at "Into the Light of Day," "The Library Card," and other books. Locate and identify paragraphs that have different types of related ideas: a description of something, a series of steps, a main idea and a list of examples, or a series of actions by a character. Decide whether the main idea of each paragraph is stated or implied; then record that main idea.

Selection: _____ Author: _____
Page and paragraph: _____
How are the sentences related? _____
Is the main idea of the paragraph stated or implied? _____
What is the main idea? _____
_____

Selection: _____ Author: _____
Page and paragraph: _____
How are the sentences related? _____
Is the main idea of the paragraph stated or implied? _____
What is the main idea? _____
_____

Selection: _____ Author: _____
Page and paragraph: _____
How are the sentences related? _____
Is the main idea of the paragraph stated or implied? _____
What is the main idea? _____
_____

Writing Paragraphs
Unit 1/Learning   R/WC 5

Reading/Writing Connection, page 5

Worksheet (right page)

"Into the Light of Day"

Writing Paragraphs continued

Selection: _____ Author: _____
Page and paragraph: _____
How are the sentences related? _____
Is the main idea of the paragraph stated or implied? _____
What is the main idea? _____
_____

Selection: _____ Author: _____
Page and paragraph: _____
How are the sentences related? _____
Is the main idea of the paragraph stated or implied? _____
What is the main idea? _____
_____

Selection: _____ Author: _____
Page and paragraph: _____
How are the sentences related? _____
Is the main idea of the paragraph stated or implied? _____
What is the main idea? _____
_____

Selection: _____ Author: _____
Page and paragraph: _____
How are the sentences related? _____
Is the main idea of the paragraph stated or implied? _____
What is the main idea? _____
_____

Writing Paragraphs
6 R/WC   Learning/Unit 1

Reading/Writing Connection, page 6

★ Writing Process

Revising

Rethinking and Rewriting

If the students' personal narratives on learning are in rough-draft form, you can introduce the revising phase of the writing process. Remind the students that the purpose of revising is to make sure that their writing expresses their ideas clearly. As they work to make their writing better, they may need to move or change sentences, add new ideas or details, take out ideas or details that do not fit, or change words. If they notice spelling or grammar mistakes, they can correct them. However, they should not worry about correctness at this stage. Final corrections will be made at the next stage of the process.

Model revising for the students. Using a transparency, show your own rough draft of a narrative on learning. Be sure to include unclear and misplaced passages and incorrect word choices. Work quickly through your rough draft, thinking aloud as you revise. You might model comments such as

I think I should move this to the end.

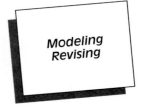

*Modeling
Revising*

I need a better word here.
This is good. I'll keep it like it is.
I should say more about this. I'll add more details to describe this.
Now this idea doesn't fit. I'll cross it out.

Demonstrate some shortcuts for revising. Make arrows to show how you want to move words or sentences. Write an asterisk or a number to indicate an insertion. Cross out words or sentences. Tell the students that you will worry about neatness and correctness later.

Elicit and discuss any suggestions from the students for further revisions. Make additional changes if necessary. Remind the students that during the revision process it is important to get feedback from others. Explain to them that they may do this more than once; writing is a recursive process.

Allow time for the students to revise their rough drafts. Have them work in pairs or small groups and **read their rough drafts to each other.** By sharing their stories with their peers, students will see whether their ideas are understandable and clearly presented or whether they are in need of further revision.

Getting Feedback

Remind the students that they can help each other become better writers by listening carefully and commenting in a helpful way on each other's writing. Suggest that they do the following after listening to a classmate's narrative:

- Retell the story in their own words. If they have trouble doing that, the writer will know some ideas need to be made clearer.
- Point out one thing they especially like about the narrative.
- Be specific about what they have trouble understanding or what they think could be improved.
- Make comments in a polite way, and show respect for the writer's feelings.

Stress that once a piece of writing has been critiqued and the writer has thought about the criticisms offered by his or her classmates, it is up to the writer to decide whether or not to make the suggested changes. To review information about **peer conferencing** during the writing process, see **Learning Framework Cards 7C** and **8, Revising** and **Writing Seminar.**

Peer Conferencing During Writing

Providing Feedback

During writing time and Independent Workshop, **conference briefly with individual students about their writing.**

- Have the student read the narrative aloud. Offer a specific comment.
- Encourage the student to think aloud about possible changes to the narrative.
- Ask questions that help the student clarify his or her thinking. To help with organization, for example, you might ask, What is most important about this experience? To help with other aspects of the narrative ask such questions as these: When did this happen? Where did this happen? Who were the people involved? What happened then? How did you feel about it at the time?

Some questions to ask *yourself* as you try to help the students become better writers are these:

- Does the beginning get my attention?
- Is this a good topic sentence?
- Is the ending conclusive?
- Is this related to the topic?
- Does sentence structure need to be varied by combining or shortening sentences?
- Is there a better word to express this?

For additional ideas on **teacher conferencing** during the writing process, see **Learning Framework Cards 7C** and **8, Revising** and **Writing Seminar.** To review information about the **writing process,** see **Learning Framework Card 7.**

> *Teacher Conferencing During Writing*
>
> **TEACHING TIP** Do not lead the student with content questions. Help her or him understand how to revise, not what to write.

VOCABULARY

Words the students might want to discuss and use in their explorations for this unit include the following:

Braille, manual, perceived

Remind students to add words and phrases to their personal dictionaries in their Writer's Notebook. Then provide an opportunity for volunteers to share words and phrases they've added and the reasons they chose them. Allow time for the students to complete Vocabulary Exploration forms, Reproducible Master 14, for those words they wish to learn or that are important to the unit concepts.

> *Adding to Personal Word Lists*

Professional Checkpoint: Reading with a Writer's Eye

Researchers and teachers are becoming more and more aware of the power of modeling: showing students how something is done, drawing their attention to the important features of what you're doing, and encouraging them to follow your lead. Modeling strategies can best be done through "thinking aloud" as you read or write. This way, you don't simply tell students what to do but give them a glimpse of what it's like to think while reading and writing.

Notes:

3 GUIDED AND INDEPENDENT EXPLORATION

EXPLORING CONCEPTS BEYOND THE TEXT

Guided Exploration

Students will select activities in which they explore the concept of learning. Refer them to the **Exploration Activities poster** and give them time to choose an activity and to discuss what they wish to explore and how they wish to go about it. If students need further help, here are some suggestions:

Encourage students to work together to make a list of things to find out about their neighborhood library in preparation for a class trip there. Remind them to include on their list a question about how biographies, autobiographies, and other nonfiction books are filed.

You may want to explain that libraries that use the Dewey Decimal System of Classification, including most school libraries, file biographies and autobiographies together in one part of the library. Within this section, books are filed alphabetically by the subject of the biography. The biography of Laura Bridgman by Edith Fisher Hunter, for example, would be filed under *B* for *Bridgman* rather than under *H* for *Hunter.*

In libraries that use the Library of Congress system, however, such books are filed with other nonfiction books according to subject. In a library with this system, *Child of the Silent Night* would be found with books about blindness or deafness or with books about educating people with disabilities.

➤ Some students may be interested in learning more about how libraries organize nonfiction books. These students can use page 10 of the Explorer's Notebook to compare the subject categories for the Dewey Decimal system with those for the Library of Congress. To check their understanding, they can answer the questions on page 11.

＊Exploring Through Reflective Activities

ASSESSMENT TIP This may be a good opportunity to observe students working in groups and to mark observations in the Teacher's Observation Log.

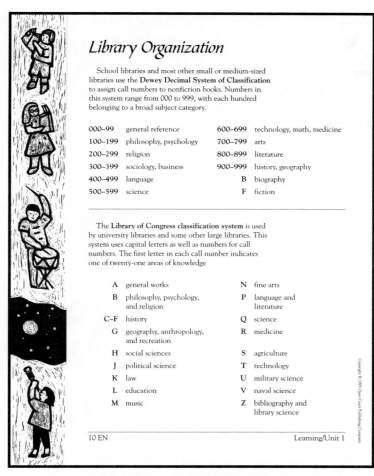

Library Organization

School libraries and most other small or medium-sized libraries use the **Dewey Decimal System of Classification** to assign call numbers to nonfiction books. Numbers in this system range from 000 to 999, with each hundred belonging to a broad subject category.

000–99	general reference	600–699	technology, math, medicine
100–199	philosophy, psychology	700–799	arts
200–299	religion	800–899	literature
300–399	sociology, business	900–999	history, geography
400–499	language	B	biography
500–599	science	F	fiction

The **Library of Congress classification system** is used by university libraries and some other large libraries. This system uses capital letters as well as numbers for call numbers. The first letter in each call number indicates one of twenty-one areas of knowledge

A	general works	N	fine arts
B	philosophy, psychology, and religion	P	language and literature
C–F	history	Q	science
G	geography, anthropology, and recreation	R	medicine
H	social sciences	S	agriculture
J	political science	T	technology
K	law	U	military science
L	education	V	naval science
M	music	Z	bibliography and library science

10 EN   Learning/Unit 1

Copyright © 1995 Open Court Publishing Company

Explorer's Notebook, page 10

Where would you expect to find each of these books? Write the numbers (Dewey Decimal System) and the letter (Library of Congress system) indicating the general location of the book in libraries using each of these systems. The first one is done for you.

Breakthrough: The True Story of Penicillin by Francine Jacobs 600s; R (medicine)

Drawing Life in Motion by Jim Aronsky _____

Galaxies by Seymour Simon _____

Incredible Journey of Lewis and Clark by Rhoda Blumberg _____

Ramona and Her Mother by Beverly Cleary _____

Young Writer's Handbook by Susan Tchudi _____

Choose three books from the unit bibliography. Write the titles. Then, using the charts on page 10, tell where you would look for each book on the library shelves.

_____
_____
_____
_____
_____
_____
_____
_____
_____
_____
_____
_____
_____
_____
_____
_____
_____

Copyright © 1995 Open Court Publishing Company

Unit 1/Learning   EN 11

Explorer's Notebook, page 11

Generating Questions to Explore

Have the students review the questions currently on the Question Board. If there are some that have been answered or need to be revised or rewritten, do that now. If the students have additional questions about learning or ideas for further exploration, remind them that this is a good time to post them on the Question Board with their name or initials. To review information about the **Question Board,** see **Teacher Tool Card 121.**

Using the Question Board

✳ INDEPENDENT WORKSHOP
Building a Community of Scholars

Student-Directed Reading, Writing, and Discussion

Remind the students that the first part of Independent Workshop will be spent working together on ideas for exploring learning. **Learning Framework Card 5** contains a complete discussion of conducting **Independent Workshop** and suggestions for helping English Language Learners during Workshop.

Additional Opportunities for Independent Reading, Writing, and Cross-curricular Activities

✻ Reading Roundtable

Some students may choose to read the book from which "Into the Light of Day" was taken, *Child of the Silent Night.* This book tells more about Laura Bridgman's life and education. For information about **Reading Roundtable**, see **Learning Framework Card 6.**

✻ Writing Seminar

Encourage the students to continue revising their personal narratives. For information about **Writing Seminar,** see **Learning Framework Card 8.**

Cross-curricular Activity Cards

Cross-curricular Activity Cards in the Student Toolbox that are appropriate for this selection include the following:
- 1 Social Studies—Braille
- 2 Social Studies—The Manual Alphabet

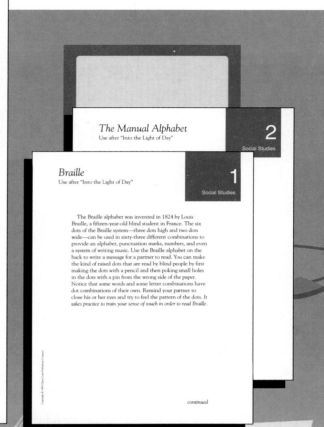

The Manual Alphabet
Use after "Into the Light of Day"

2
Social Studies

Braille
Use after "Into the Light of Day"

1
Social Studies

The Braille alphabet was invented in 1824 by Louis Braille, a fifteen-year-old blind student in France. The six dots of the Braille system—three dots high and two dots wide—can be used in sixty-three different combinations to provide an alphabet, punctuation marks, numbers, and even a system of writing music. Use the Braille alphabet on the back to write a message for a partner to read. You can make the kind of raised dots that are read by blind people by first making the dots with a pencil and then poking small holes in the dots with a pin from the wrong side of the paper. Notice that some words and some letter combinations have dot combinations of their own. Remind your partner to close his or her eyes and try to feel the pattern of the dots. *It takes practice to train your sense of touch in order to read Braille.*

continued

Additional Opportunities for Solving Learning Problems

Tutorial

Use this time to work with those students who need help in any area. Use peer tutoring when appropriate. Encourage the students to ask for help whenever they feel the need. The following teaching aids are available in the Teacher Toolbox for your convenience:
- Writer's Craft/Reading: Indicators of Time and Order, Teacher Tool Card 27
- Writer's Craft/Reading: Writing Paragraphs, Teacher Tool Card 22
- Writer's Craft/Reading: Genre—Biography and Autobiography, Teacher Tool Card 8
- Writer's Craft/Reading: Elaboration Through Providing Descriptions, Teacher Tool Card 39
- Grammar, Mechanics, and Usage: Using Past-Tense Verbs, Teacher Tool Card 64

On Your Own

Mukasa at School

1 READING THE SELECTION

INFORMATION FOR THE TEACHER

About the
Selection

Education is beyond the reach of most children in the African village where Mukasa lives. But because it was his mother's dream that her only child would go to school, she managed to raise the money for his fees and uniform. Now Mukasa is about to experience reading and writing for the first time. This quiet, serious story offers readers a glimpse of the experience of learning in a school that is probably very different from their own.

Link to the
Unit Concepts

Education is a privilege for Mukasa, and his delight in learning is obvious. The selection, which appears on pages 40–45, describes the thrill Mukasa experiences in learning how to put letters together to form words, and the pride he shares with his family as a result of his accomplishments.

About the
Author

"Mukasa at School" is an excerpt from John Nagenda's novel, *Mukasa.* Nagenda was born in Uganda in 1938 and attended a school like Mukasa's. He edited a literary magazine while in college and graduated with honors in English. Since 1966, the author has lived in England, where he has been a radio and magazine critic and a book editor. Nagenda's short stories, articles, and poetry have been published in Africa, Europe, and the United States. He writes in English but believes that African writers must begin to write in their own languages so that they can be better understood by other Africans. *Mukasa* is his first book for children.

Additional information about John Nagenda appears on page 45 of the student anthology.

LESSON OVERVIEW

"Mukasa at School" by John Nagenda, pages 40–45

READING THE SELECTION

Materials
Student anthology, pp. 40–45
Explorer's Notebook, p. 5
Assessment Masters 1–2
Map or globe

FYI
Learning Framework Cards
• Setting Reading Goals and
  Expectations, 1A

READING WITH A WRITER'S EYE

Minilesson
On Your Own

Materials
Reproducible Masters 14, 20–22
Home/School Connection 5

FYI
Learning Framework Cards
• Writing Process, 7
• Proofreading, 7D
• Publishing, 7E

Teacher Tool Card
• Spelling and Vocabulary: Building
  Vocabulary, 75

Options for Instruction
Writer's Craft: Characterization
Spelling and Vocabulary: Compound
  Words
(Use Teacher Tool Cards listed below.)

GUIDED AND INDEPENDENT EXPLORATION

Materials
Reproducible Master 23
Explorer's Notebook, pp. 12–15

Independent Workshop

**Optional Materials from
Student Toolbox**

Tradebook Connection Cards

Cross-curricular Activity Card
• 3 Social Studies—Uganda

Student Tool Cards
• Writer's Craft/Reading:
  Characterization, 13
• Spelling and Vocabulary: Compound
  Words, 79

FYI

Learning Framework Cards
• Independent Workshop, 5
• Reading Roundtable, 6
• Writing Seminar, 8

Teacher Tool Cards
• Writer's Craft/Reading:
  Characterization, 13
• Spelling and Vocabulary: Compound
  Words, 79

N O T E S

Asterisks (*) throughout the lesson indicate learning frameworks. Learning Framework Cards and Teacher Tool Cards can be found in the Teacher Toolbox.

INFORMATION FOR THE STUDENT

- Tell the students that the selection they are about to read is an excerpt from a book by John Nagenda. Share with them pertinent information about the author.
- You may also want to share with the students information about the setting of the story.
- After reading the selection, students should read and discuss the information about John Nagenda on page 45 of the student anthology.

Background Information

Uganda is a densely populated agricultural country with a diverse and scenic terrain. Magnificent national parks showcase snow-capped mountains, lush tropical forests, and numerous lakes. Most of Uganda's population work as herders and farmers, with women doing much of the farm work. Bananas, beans, cassava, corn, millet, and sweet potatoes are grown for food; coffee, cotton, tea, and sugar cane, for export.

Since the time when this story was set, the 1940s, Uganda has undergone much political upheaval. After gaining its independence from Great Britain in 1962, it suffered several violent changes in government. Many thousands of Ugandans were killed because they disagreed with the policies of dictator Idi Amin. The country's educational system declined sharply because of war and civil unrest.

Have the students locate Uganda on a globe, a world map, or a map of Africa.

Story Setting

*

COGNITIVE AND RESPONSIVE READING

Activating Prior Knowledge

Ask students to share what they remember about their first experiences with learning to read and to write their names.

Setting Reading Goals and Expectations

Explain to the students that before they will read they will **set reading goals and expectations.** To do this, they will **browse** the **first page** of the selection and **use the clues/problems/wondering procedure.** On the chalkboard under the headings clues, problems, and wonderings, write in brief note form the observations the children generate during browsing. For example, students might list the genre of the selection under *clues*; they might list unfamiliar words under *problems*; and they might note any questions that arise during browsing under *wonderings*. The children will return to these observations after reading.

For a review of **browsing,** see **Learning Framework Card 1A, Setting Reading Goals and Expectations.**

Recommendations for Reading the Selection

Tell the students that they will read "Mukasa at School" silently on their own. Encourage them to use any of the reading strategies that they have learned to help them read and understand the selection. Remind them to use the strategy posters if they encounter a reading problem or if they are unsure about how to use a strategy. You may want to briefly review the reading strategies already introduced in this unit.

TIP FOR ENGLISH LANGUAGE LEARNERS

English Language Learners may benefit from paired reading with above-average readers. With paired reading, English Language Learners may feel more relaxed about identifying problems and more apt to use the reading strategies to solve problems they are having with the text.

THINK ALOUD PROMPTS

To foster independence, think-aloud prompts are not provided for On Your Own lessons.

Uganda (yōō gan´ də)
Mukasa (mōō kä´ sə)
Nanteza (nan tē´ zə)
Kalanzi (kə lan´ zē)

MUKASA AT SCHOOL

from MUKASA by John Nagenda
illustrated by Tyrone Geter

Mukasa lives in a small village in Uganda in the 1940s and is the first of his family to go to school. Until his mother found a way to pay for his school fees and his uniform, Mukasa had assumed he would spend his life herding goats. Because reading and writing are almost unknown in his village, school has a special wonder for ten-year-old Mukasa.

Mukasa's teacher, Miss Nanteza, said, "How many of you know anything about reading and writing? Put up your hands."

Mukasa saw to his surprise that one of the boys put his hand up. He was the only one. Mukasa had not thought it was possible to learn these things before you came to school. The boy had a rather pleased look on his face which Mukasa found annoying. He also noticed that the boy's uniform looked smarter than his own.

Miss Nanteza said, "All right, Kalanzi. Anybody else?"

Later Mukasa found out that Kalanzi was Miss Nanteza's second cousin. Kalanzi's parents were the richest people for miles around, and in fact they had had Miss Nanteza give him lessons before he started school.

🐾 40 🐾

Miss Nanteza said, "If you all pay attention, most of you won't find it very difficult to follow what I am going to teach you."

Slates were passed around, together with funny-looking sticklike objects which left a mark when you scratched the slates with them.

Miss Nanteza started with the alphabet. She wrote a letter on the blackboard and said it out loud. The class said it after her and scratched its likeness on their slates. Then after about five letters, Miss Nanteza had everything wiped off. When that was done she wrote the letters down again and asked what each was.

Up went Kalanzi's hand immediately. After the second time she told him that until the rest of the class had caught up with him, she would not call on him to answer. The whole class laughed loudly at this, but Mukasa, although he too

laughed, felt a little sorry for Kalanzi; after all, it wasn't his fault that he already knew the answer.

As for himself, he was having a wonderful time. He had often wondered whether he would find it difficult to learn. At home if he was told something he always remembered it, indeed on some occasions he had annoyed his parents by remembering things which they would have preferred forgotten. But he had thought that school learning might be different. Now he discovered that once the teacher had written a letter and said it out loud, and once he had written it down himself, it seemed to stick in his mind. And what's more it seemed to make sense in itself so that the way it looked gave it a character of its own.

Before coming to school, Mukasa had from time to time seen old pieces of paper with writing on them; for example the shopkeeper sometimes used them for packaging. But every time Mukasa had looked closely at the writing, all he could think of were swarming little insects. Now it was as if Miss Nanteza gave sound and meaning to them.

Miss Nanteza filled the blackboard with more and more letters and then a few words, and it seemed to Mukasa as if a treasure chest were being opened up and offered to him. As if by magic, what had been an empty space on the wall was now covered, right before him, by all manner of exciting and mysterious things. If this was what learning was about, he was going to love it.

When Miss Nanteza rubbed the letters off, the dust of the chalk drifted over the whole class and to Mukasa even the somewhat biting sensation he felt in his nose was full of excitement.

42

He wished Miss Nanteza would move more quickly. By now he had almost forgotten about the others in the class. It was as if everything the teacher said was for him alone.

Every time Miss Nanteza asked a question, almost before she had completed it, Mukasa's hand shot up. But after a time he noticed that she would leave his hand up and look straight past him, and ask the question of someone who didn't even understand it, and in the meantime his own upraised arm would be getting unbearably heavy. He heard one or two sniggers from some of the class whenever this happened. On one occasion he caught Kalanzi openly laughing at him. Then finally just before the end of the day, when Mukasa stood up to answer yet another question, someone hit him on the back of the head with a piece of chalk.

"Who did that?" shouted the teacher.

Nobody answered. Mukasa had looked around quickly and he had seen who had thrown the chalk. Usually he wouldn't have told, but by now he was so fed up that before he knew it he had blurted out, "It was that nasty boy over there in the back row!"

"Come here, Mutahi," Miss Nanteza ordered.

The boy came forward slowly. Miss Nanteza reached out and like lightning slapped him twice, on either side of his face. The look Mutahi gave Mukasa as he walked back to his seat was <u>ferocious</u>.

After school Mukasa was walking past the staff room when he heard his teacher's voice. Something made him stop and listen.

He could hardly believe his ears: ". . . a real firecracker; his name is Mukasa, probably too good for his class!"

43

Mutahi (mōō tä´ hē)

Mukasa was still floating on air from that remark when he turned a corner. Mutahi was waiting.

It was only a brief fight before someone separated them, but it was long enough for Mukasa to know that he would have had no chance of winning it.

It didn't matter. There wasn't a thing on this wonderful evening that could for long <u>detract</u> from his happiness and he was almost singing as he ran home to tell his family all about it.

After the second day of classes he could write his name. When he had written it he looked at it for a long time and it seemed to be his name even more than ever before, and he thought it even looked like him.

He walked home with his name tucked away inside his exercise book.

"Look, look," he said, trying to appear calm and collected. "That's my name and I wrote it myself; with my own hand!"

He passed the book around.

"Now is not that something?" his mother exclaimed. She was looking at the writing as if she half expected it to come to life and shake her by the hand.

His grandparents were looking at it upside down.

It was while Mukasa was explaining how it all added up that his father came home.

"That's Mu and that's Ka and that's Sa. Mukasa," Mukasa said.

MEET JOHN NAGENDA, AUTHOR

Nagenda was born in Uganda in 1938, and Mukasa describes the way of life he knew there as a child. Nagenda explains:
"This story is set in the Uganda of the early 1940s. It takes place in a small village where most of the people are very poor in the money sense; they find it much more difficult to buy things, including education, than their fellows in towns or villages nearer to bigger towns. And of course they are far more tied to a traditional way of life.

"If you went to Mukasa's village today you would notice changes. For a start, the outside world has made more of an <u>impact</u> upon it. This is the result of better communications, and also because so many of the villagers have been to the towns, mainly to search for work. And of those who never left the village, quite a few possess radio sets and therefore know about other parts of the country and beyond.

"As for going to school, the chances are much better today, and in Mukasa's village there are fewer children who would now look forward only to a life of tending goats. But it is still true that many who go to school even today might go for just a couple of years before they are overtaken by lack of fees or classroom space.

"Perhaps the differences are not really as great as they seem, and it is truer to say that it is the <u>tempo</u> and flavor of village life that have changed. The steady rhythm of the village background has been drastically upset. At the same time the villagers lack the means of creating a worthwhile substitute. In other words, today Mukasa would find it easier to go to school, but unless he were very lucky, the horizons which schooling opened to him would remain as far off and <u>elusive</u> as ever."

 45

Discussing Strategy Use

Encourage the students to discuss any difficulties they had as they read and to explain how they used reading strategies to help them. Any students who have devised their own strategies should be encouraged to explain these strategies and their use to their classmates.

*

EXPLORING THROUGH DISCUSSION

Reflecting on the Selection
Whole-Group Discussion

The **whole group discusses** the selection and any **personal thoughts, reactions, problems,** or **questions** that it raises. During this time, students may also be invited to **return** to the **clues, problems, and wonderings** they noted during browsing to determine whether the clues were borne out by the selection, whether and how their problems were solved, and whether their wonderings were answered or deserve further discussion and exploration. Avoid treating their ideas as a list to be discussed and eliminated in a linear fashion. Instead, let the students decide which items deserve further discussion. To stimulate discussion, the **students** can **ask** one another the kinds of **questions that good readers ask themselves** about a text: **What did I [you] find interesting? What is important here? What was difficult to understand? Why would someone want to read this?** Your own participation in the discussion might take the form of expressing and modeling your reactions to characters or to other aspects of the story. It is important for the students to see you as a contributing member of the group.

To emphasize that you are part of the group, actively **participate in the handing-off process:** Raise your hand to be called on by the last speaker when you have a contribution to make. Point out unusual and interesting insights verbalized by the students so that these insights are recognized and discussed. As the year progresses, the **students will take more and more responsibility for discussion** of the selections. The handing-off process is a good way to get them to take on this responsibility.

Assessment

In a successful discussion, it should not be necessary for you to ask questions to assess the students' understanding of the text. If necessary, however, engage in a discussion to **determine whether the students have grasped the following idea:**
- why Mukasa feels as though a treasure chest is being opened up for him when he learns the letters of the alphabet.

TEACHING TIP Allow students to express their ideas without interruption.

Response Journal

Students may wish to record their personal responses to the selection.

Exploring Concepts Within the Selection
Small-Group Discussion

Have the students **form small collaborative groups and discuss** the relation of the selection to learning and the important concepts in the selection. Remind them to refer to the Concept Board and the Question Board to keep their discussions focused. Circulate among the groups and observe their discussions.

ASSESSMENT TIP This might be a good time to observe students working in groups and to mark observations in your Teacher's Observation Log.

Sharing Ideas About Explorable Concepts

Have the groups **report** and **discuss** their **ideas** with the rest of the class. It is crucial that the students' ideas determine this discussion.
- The students may notice that Mukasa understands that he is learning something very important and that it will change his life.
- Students may also suggest that Mukasa is excited about what he is learning, which helps him to learn.

As these ideas and others are stated, have the students **add them to the Question Board** or the **Concept Board.**

Exploring Concepts Across Selections

Ask the students whether this story reminds them of other selections they have read in the student anthology. If so, in what ways? Students may make the following connections:

- Students may notice that, like Rufus Moffat, Mukasa also learns to write his name.
- Students may notice that both Mukasa and Laura Bridgman are enthusiastic and eager to learn more.

Recording Ideas

As students complete the above discussions, ask them to **sum up what they have learned from their conversations and to tell how they might use this information** in further explorations. Any special information or insights may be recorded on the **Concept Board.** Any further questions that they would like to think about, pursue, or investigate may be recorded on the **Question Board.** Students may want to discuss the progress that has been made on their questions. They may also want to cross out any questions that no longer warrant consideration.

➤ After discussion, the students should individually record what they've learned on page 5 of their Explorer's Notebook.

Self-Assessment Questionnaire

➤ Distribute copies of Assessment Master 2, the Self-Assessment Questionnaire, which you will find in the booklet Masters for Continuous Assessment. Tell the students to answer the questionnaire after they have completed this lesson. Collect the completed questionnaires so that you can compare students' current assessments with later self-assessments when they again answer the same questionnaires. You might also examine their responses to see if the students' assessments of themselves are compatible with the assessments in your Teacher's Observation Log.

TIP FOR ENGLISH LANGUAGE LEARNERS

Provide time for informal conversational practice. Pair English Language Learners with native English-speaking students. Encourage partners to compare any two of the selections they have read so far.

Evaluating Discussions

"Mukasa at School" by John Nagenda
_____
_____
_____
_____
_____
_____
_____

"Do Bananas Chew Gum?" by Jamie Gilson
_____
_____
_____
_____
_____
_____

"Seventh Grade" by Gary Soto
_____
_____
_____
_____
_____
_____

Copyright © 1995 Open Court Publishing Company

Unit 1/Learning   EN 5

Explorer's Notebook, page 5

Self-Assessment Questionnaire

1. How would you rate this selection?
   ○ easy   ○ medium   ○ hard

2. If you checked **medium** or **hard**, answer these questions.
   • Which part of the selection did you find especially difficult?
   • What strategy did you use to try and understand it?
   _____
   _____

   • Were some of the words hard?
   • What did you do to figure out their meaning?
   _____
   _____

3. What do you feel you need to work on to make yourself a better reader?
   _____
   _____
   _____

4. Give an example of something you said in the group. Tell why you said it.
   _____
   _____
   _____

5. Give an example of something that people in the group helped you understand about the selection.
   _____
   _____
   _____

Date _____   Name _____   INDIVIDUAL   GROUP

Copyright © 1995 Open Court Publishing Company

Self-Assessment Questionnaire   Assessment Master 2

Assessment Master 2

---

2 READING WITH A WRITER'S EYE

MINILESSON

On Your Own

Remind the students that after reading each of the two previous selections they discussed something the author did especially well. For example, Eleanor Estes, the author of "The Library Card," used story structure effectively. Tell the students that since they read this selection on their own you would like them to identify something they think this author did especially well. Ask them to think back to any part of the story that they reacted to or particularly enjoyed. This might be a clue to especially good writing.

Allow time for the students to skim the story to refresh their memories. If they seem to be having difficulty expressing how they felt about the writing in this selection, **model a response** by talking about your own reactions to the story.

WRITING

Linking Reading to Writing

Encourage the students to use in their own writing any of Nagenda's writing techniques that they especially liked.

* Writing Process

Proofreading

Making Corrections

Remind students that they have practiced these parts of the writing process: prewriting, writing, and revising. Explain that once a piece of writing has been revised for content and style, the writer must read it carefully to make sure that

• punctuation, spelling, and capitalization are correct
• no words have been left out
• paragraphs are indented
• sentences are grammatically correct

➤ Distribute copies of Reproducible Master 20 and show students how to use these common proofreading symbols in correcting their papers. Ask students to keep this page in their Writer's Notebook.

➤ Sometimes a writer might ask another person to check a piece of writing for errors. Distribute copies of Reproducible Master 21 and ask students to keep this checklist in the Checking My Work section of their Writer's Notebook and use it as a reminder when proofreading their own work or someone else's.

Introducing Proofreading Marks

Reproducible Master 20

Proofreading Symbols

When you proofread your writing, you can use special marks that editors and proofreaders use to show where something needs to be changed. Here are some marks that you can use:

∧   This mark means insert something

ℓ   This mark means to remove something.

≡   this mark means to capitalize a letter.

/   This mark Means to make a small letter.

¶   This mark means to start a new paragraph.

∩   This means mark to switch letters or words.

Name

Reproducible Master 21

Proofreading Checklist

Read each sentence.

____ • Does each sentence begin with a capital letter and end with correct end punctuation?

____ • Do you notice any sentence fragments or run-on sentences?

____ • Are any words missing from the sentence?

____ • Is any punctuation or capitalization missing from within the sentence?

____ • Do you notice any incorrect grammar or incorrect word usage in the sentence?

____ • Do you notice any misspelled words in the sentence?

Look at the paragraphs.

____ • Are the paragraphs indented?

____ • Can very long paragraphs be broken into two paragraphs?

____ • Can very short paragraphs be combined into one paragraph?

Name

- Suggest that students use colored pencils to mark changes on their revised first drafts.
- Suggest that after they have proofread their own papers, they exchange papers with a partner. Have the partner use a different color to mark errors the writer may have missed.
- Writers should evaluate the corrections suggested by their partners and decide whether or not to accept them.
- When all corrections have been made, students should use their best handwriting to write their final drafts.

Preparing and Presenting Finished Work

Publishing

Remind students that once they have written, revised, proofread, and made final corrections in a piece of writing, they may want to share the completed work with others by publishing it. Writing can be published in different ways:

- It can be displayed on a bulletin board.
- It can be made into a book by putting the pages between covers.
- It can be collected with other pieces of writing and published in an anthology.
- It can be submitted for publication to a local newspaper or a national magazine.
- It can be published in a school newspaper.
- It can be read aloud to the class, to other classes, to younger students in the school, or to another group.

At this time, **provide materials for a publishing center** and explain their use to the students. A word processor or typewriter might be located in this center along with other tools for writing and illustrating books and for making covers.

Before students have made their final corrections, **have a brief publishing conference with each student.** At this time, help the student make any last-minute changes that are necessary before the piece can be published.

To review information about proofreading and publishing, see **Learning Framework Cards 7D and 7E.** To review information about the writing process, see **Learning Framework Card 7.**

❯ For this first published piece of writing, you might suggest that each student make an individual booklet that can be taken home and shared with families and then kept in the classroom library. Distribute Reproducible Master 22 and work through the steps for making a booklet. Then have students make corrected copies of their stories by writing on the booklet pages or by typing the story and pasting typewritten pages on the booklet pages.

❯ Since the stories are personal narratives, it might be appropriate for students to illustrate their stories with photographs that show them at the age they are in the story. If other family members figure in their stories, they might be shown as well. Distribute Home/School Connection 5, which provides information about the writing process and asks families to cooperate in providing family photographs. If photographs are not available, students might choose to make drawings that illustrate their stories.

VOCABULARY

Encourage the students to discuss words or phrases from the selection that they want to use in their speaking and writing or in their exploration for this unit. Words or phrases you might discuss include the following: **sniggers, blurted, ferocious, detract**

Remind students to add words and phrases to the Personal Dictionary section of their Writer's Notebook. Then provide an opportunity for students to fill out Vocabulary Exploration forms, Reproducible Master 14, for words they wish to learn or those that are important to the unit concepts. For additional opportunities to build vocabulary, see **Teacher Tool Card 75.**

Adding to Personal Word Lists

Reproducible Master 22

Making a Booklet

1. Cut two pieces of cardboard the same size.

2. Place cover material face down. Glue cardboard pieces to cover, leaving space between the two pieces.

3. Fold corners over and glue.

4. Fold sides in and glue.

5. Cut paper smaller than inside of open cover.

6. Fold pages.

7. Sew through all pages, placing knot at top of page on outside of fold and tying off thread at bottom of page on outside of fold.

8. Place sewed pages inside cover with stitches in space between cardboard pieces. Glue first and last pages to cover, making endpapers.

Name _____

RM 22   Writer's Notebook: Writing Ideas

Copyright © 1995 Open Court Publishing Company

Home/School Connection 5

"Mukasa at School"

A message from _____

Your child has completed work on a story about a personal experience and will be publishing this story in a booklet to be shared with you and with other students at the school. Can you provide your child with some photographs to illustrate this story? The photographs should be ones taken of your child or of any other family member mentioned around the time that the incident described in the story occurred.

From time to time your child may show you his or her writing assignments. The writing process has several phases, so you may see the same piece of writing at different stages of development.

- *Prewriting.* Your child makes notes and lists of ideas to write about.
- *Drafting.* He or she puts ideas down on paper. At this phase, the piece of writing may contain many unorganized ideas and many misspelled words, but this is not a matter for concern. Your child is trying to write down ideas as quickly as possible.
- *Revising.* At this phase, the writing will contain crossed-out words and sentences, added thoughts, and other changes. Your child is trying to make the writing better.
- *Proofreading.* Now your child is trying to correct spelling, grammar, capitalization, and punctuation.
- *Publishing.* The piece of writing is made final and ready to be shared with others.

Your child needs your support at every phase of this writing process. Please do not expect neatness or perfect spelling at early phases of the process. By the time a piece of writing is published, errors will have been corrected, ideas will be better organized, and your child will have the satisfaction of a job well done.

Encourage your child to share his or her writing with you.

Unit 1/Learning   H/SC 5

Copyright © 1995 Open Court Publishing Company

3 GUIDED AND INDEPENDENT EXPLORATION

EXPLORING CONCEPTS BEYOND THE TEXT

Guided Exploration

Students will select activities in which they explore the concept of learning. Refer them to the **Exploration Activities poster** and give them time to choose an activity and to discuss what they wish to explore and how they wish to go about it. If students need further help, here are some suggestions:

After reading this selection, some students may be interested in finding out more about education in other countries. The *Faces* magazine listed in the student bibliography includes articles on schools in India, France, and the Arab world. Library resources will suggest other countries to study. Students might consider writing about this or making a photo essay to present to the class. Allow students to work in pairs or in small groups based on shared interests.

➤ Students might interview people they know who moved to the United States from other countries. These may be students in their own or other grades, teachers, school staff members, family members, or neighbors. Have students think about how to learn more about what school was like for these people in other countries. Pages 12 and 13 in their Explorer's Notebook will help the students begin thinking about questions to ask during these interviews. Have the students work in small groups to complete the pages.

Generating Questions to Explore

Have the students review the questions currently on the Question Board. If some have been answered or need to be revised or rewritten, deal with them now. If the students have additional questions about learning, encourage them to post them on the Question Board. Remind them again to go to the board at any time during their exploration to add a question (being sure to sign their entry), discuss someone else's question, or simply check for ideas.

➤ Encourage the students to continue thinking about ideas for exploring learning. They may want to work in groups with others who have similar interests. Encourage them to use pages 14–15 of their Explorer's Notebook to plan and record plans for their exploration of learning.

---

* *Exploring Through Reflective Activities*

TIP FOR ENGLISH LANGUAGE LEARNERS

Provide an opportunity for English Language Learners to share their knowledge and experiences with the other students. If applicable, invite them to talk about school life in the countries where they lived. How is it the same? How is it different?

Conducting an Interview

- Always ask permission to interview the person. Be sure to tell him or her how much time you think you'll need.
- Decide ahead of time what you want to know.
- Think of questions that will help you get the information you need.
- Write your questions down in an organized order with space after each one for taking notes.
- Speak clearly and be polite.
- Take notes on the answers.
- Read over your notes immediately after you leave the interview, while the conversation is still fresh in your mind.
- If you use a tape or video recorder, ask permission to record the interview.

Make a list of some people you know who came to the United States from another country. Think about which of these people you would like to talk to about what it was like to go to school in that country. If some of these people went to schools in the United States as well, they might talk about the differences they found between schools in their homeland and schools in the United States. Which people do you think would agree to talk with you?

People I might interview: **Where they're from:**

Explorer's Notebook, page 12

Now think about questions that you might ask the person you interview. What do you especially want to know? Think about concepts related to learning. How will talking to this person help you learn more about learning? Write some questions that will help you find out about learning from the person you talk to. Discuss these questions with your classmates.

Explorer's Notebook, page 13

Planning Exploration

How can you explore learning further? Write down some questions about learning and some ideas you would like to explore.

As you begin your exploration of learning, you will want to keep a list of things you need to do. Check off each item as you complete it. Here is the start of a list of things you might want to remember to do. Add to it as you become more sure about what route your exploration will take.

Things to Do   **Completed**

talk to friends

talk to adults

find and use books from bibliographies

Explorer's Notebook, page 14

What ideas do you have for exploring and writing about learning? What ideas about learning would you like to explore further? Write your thoughts here. If you don't have many ideas right now, that's okay. You will probably think of more ideas as you read the rest of the selections in the unit. Add to this list each time you get a new idea.

If you decide to present your information, think of ways you might do this. Remember, you don't have to present a written report. You may choose to prepare a poster, a speech, a video, whatever you think would be the best way to present new information to your classmates. List your good ideas about how to present your information. Add to this list as you read and explore and come up with new ideas.

Explorer's Notebook, page 15

* INDEPENDENT WORKSHOP
Building a Community of Scholars

Student-Directed Reading, Writing, and Discussion

Remind the students to check the Concept Board and the Question Board for additional questions or ideas to aid them in their exploration.

At this time, the students may choose to complete any unfinished pages in their Explorer's Notebook or to discuss those pages with their classmates. **Learning Framework Card 5** contains a complete discussion of conducting **Independent Workshop** and suggestions for helping English Language Learners during Workshop.

WORKSHOP TIP

You may wish to have a tape recorder available for those students conducting interviews. Show the students how to take notes as they listen to their taped interviews. Have them write down important information and any direct quotations they wish to include in their final project.

Additional Opportunities for Independent Reading, Writing, and Cross-curricular Activities

✽ Reading Roundtable

Some students may choose to read and discuss *Mukasa,* the book from which the selection was taken. Suggest that, before the discussion, they write down a few good questions to ask each other. You could participate in this discussion yourself in order to model good discussion techniques. For a review of **Reading Roundtable,** see **Learning Framework Card 6.**

✽ Writing Seminar

Some students may want to continue working on their personal narratives about learning. Encourage them to continue with proofreading and publishing. Remind them to use the writing strategy posters whenever necessary.

Remind students to request a peer or teacher conference whenever they feel it would benefit their writing. For a review of information about **Writing Seminar,** see **Learning Framework Card 8.**

Portfolios

Ask students to think about putting their best work into their portfolios.

Cross-curricular Activity Cards

The following Cross-curricular Activity Card in the Student Toolbox is appropriate for this selection:

• 3 Social Studies—Uganda

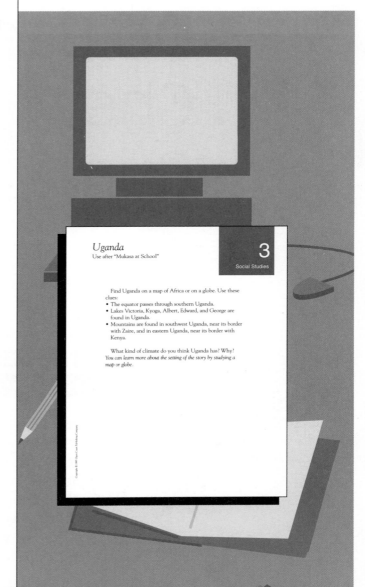

Uganda
Use after "Mukasa at School"

3
Social Studies

Find Uganda on a map of Africa or on a globe. Use these clues:
• The equator passes through southern Uganda.
• Lakes Victoria, Kyoga, Albert, Edward, and George are found in Uganda.
• Mountains are found in southwest Uganda, near its border with Zaire, and in eastern Uganda, near its border with Kenya.

What kind of climate do you think Uganda has? Why? You can learn more about the setting of the story by studying a map or globe.

Additional Opportunities for Solving Learning Problems

Tutorial

Use this time to work with those students who need help in any area. Remember to use peer tutoring with those for whom it would be appropriate. Encourage the students to ask for help whenever they feel the need. The following teaching aids are available in the Teacher Toolbox for your convenience:

• Writer's Craft/Reading: Characterization, Teacher Tool Card 13
• Spelling and Vocabulary: Compound Words, Teacher Tool Card 79

Do Bananas Chew Gum?

1 READING THE SELECTION

INFORMATION FOR THE TEACHER

About the Selection

Sam Mott is in the sixth grade but can barely read or write. In the past, he has tried to hide his disability and has acted the part of the class clown. Now, however, he has decided to talk to the learning disabilities teacher about his problems. Author Jamie Gilson is particularly good at reproducing the voice of a middle-grade child. In Sam Mott, she has created a sympathetic narrator who tells his story with a great deal of humor. The humor of the story helps to demystify learning disabilities and engages readers' sympathies for those who struggle with them.

Link to the Unit Concepts

"Do Bananas Chew Gum?" pages 46–59, dramatizes the frustration and shame often felt by people with learning disabilities. Through sessions with an optimistic teacher, Sam learns that people who have trouble learning one way can sometimes learn by using other methods, and that they can often call upon their strengths to overcome their weaknesses. Perhaps the most powerful message of the story is that each of us is ultimately responsible for his or her own learning.

About the Author

Before becoming a children's author, Jamie Gilson taught junior high school English and wrote for educational radio stations, Encyclopaedia Britannica filmstrips, and *Chicago* magazine. These experiences greatly influenced her style of writing. All of Gilson's books are written in the first person. "Before writing books for children," Gilson explains, "all of my professional writing had been for the voice—radio, TV, films—so that my books, too, are *told,* as a child would tell them. . . . When I started my first book, *Harvey, the Beer Can King,* it seemed best to take out the tape recorder to interview three neighbor boys who shared a formidable beer-can collection. I still read everything aloud after I write it." About

LESSON OVERVIEW

"Do Bananas Chew Gum?" by Jamie Gilson, pages 46–59

READING THE SELECTION

Materials
Student anthology, pp. 46–59
Explorer's Notebook, p. 5

FYI
Learning Framework Card
• Checking Understanding, 1C
Teacher Tool Card
• Classroom Supports: Modeling and Generating Think-Alouds, 116

N O T E S

READING WITH A WRITER'S EYE

Minilesson
Writer's Craft: First-Person Narrative
Writer's Craft: Informal Language

Materials
Reading/Writing Connection, pp. 7–8
Reproducible Master 14

FYI
Teacher Tool Card
• Spelling and Vocabulary: Building Vocabulary, 75

Options for Instruction
Writer's Craft: Figurative Language
Writer's Craft: Elaboration Through Providing Description
Grammar, Mechanics, and Usage: Complete and Incomplete Sentences
(Use Teacher Tool Cards listed below.)

GUIDED AND INDEPENDENT EXPLORATION

Materials
Explorer's Notebook, p. 16
Home/School Connection 6
Assessment Master 1

Optional Materials from Student Toolbox
Tradebook Connection Cards

Cross-curricular Activity Cards
• 2 Drama—Sam Mott at School
• 4 Social Studies—Conducting a Survey

Independent Workshop

Student Tool Cards
• Writer's Craft/Reading: Point of View, 12
• Writer's Craft/Reading: Differences Between Formal and Informal Writing, 18
• Writer's Craft/Reading: Figurative Language, 20
• Writer's Craft/Reading: Giving Descriptions, 39
• Grammar, Mechanics, and Usage: Complete and Incomplete Sentences, 46

FYI
Teacher Tool Cards
• Writer's Craft/Reading: Point of View, 12
• Writer's Craft/Reading: Formal Versus Informal Language, 18
• Writer's Craft/Reading: Figurative Language, 20
• Writer's Craft/Reading: Elaboration Through Providing Descriptions, 39
• Grammar, Mechanics, and Usage: Complete and Incomplete Sentences, 46

Asterisks (*) throughout the lesson indicate learning frameworks. Learning Framework Cards and Teacher Tool Cards can be found in the Teacher Toolbox.

her book *Do Bananas Chew Gum?*, Gilson said that she hoped children would find it "not only fun to read, but also revealing of the difficulties that a learning-disabled child faces."

INFORMATION FOR THE STUDENT

- Tell the students that this selection is an excerpt from a book of the same name written by Jamie Gilson.
- Share with them whatever information about the author you feel is appropriate. When discussing the use of a first-person narrator in Reading with a Writer's Eye, you might read the author's comments about her preference for that technique.
- Have the students read the italicized material that introduces the story.

Because the selection is from the last chapters of the book, there are several references to things that happened in previous chapters. If some students are familiar with the book, they can clarify these references as necessary. However, if neither you nor any of your students is familiar with the book, you will still understand the selection.

When the book begins, Sam Mott is new in school and is afraid that his classmates will find out that he can't read or write. He often writes words backwards and wears a dragon ring on his right hand to tell it from his left. Now his teacher, Mrs. Bird, and his parents have arranged for him to be tested by a learning disabilities specialist, and, at first, Sam is determined to avoid the tests. Recently, however, Sam has become interested in archaeology, and he wants very much to work on a science project related to this subject. At the last minute, Sam decides that he will forget the excuses he has prepared and will talk to Ms. Huggins, the learning disabilities teacher.

Story Background

COGNITIVE AND RESPONSIVE READING

Activating Prior Knowledge

In this selection, the main character takes diagnostic tests with a learning disabilities expert. Students may or may not be familiar with these types of tests.

Setting Reading Goals and Expectations

Have the students **browse** the **first page** of the selection using the clues/problems/wondering procedure. Students will return to these observations after reading.

Recommendations for Reading the Selection

Reading the story aloud will help students appreciate the author's technique of using a first-person narrator. For the scenes between Sam and the special education teacher, Ms. Huggins, you might suggest that one student read the part of the narrator and another read the part of Ms. Huggins, or you might read the part of Ms. Huggins yourself. Since the story is full of emotion, encourage expressive reading throughout.

During oral reading, use and encourage think-alouds. During silent reading, allow discussion as needed. Discuss problems, strategies, and reactions after reading. This would also be a good selection for **responding** to text **by expressing feelings** and **identifying with the characters** while reading aloud. Model this response, and then invite the students to respond.

About the Reading Strategies

The feelings of the main character in "Do Bananas Chew Gum?" and the reasons for his actions are not always explicit. Students will need to **interpret** as they read this selection.

Interpreting is something that good readers do often as they read and something that all of us do in a variety of everyday situations. The students will understand how often they interpret if they think about occasions when they have been able to tell how someone was feeling by the expression on his or her face or times when they have exchanged glances with a friend and known exactly what that friend was thinking. In situations like these, they are interpreting. Nothing is stated. No one says, "I'm angry" or "I'm bored," yet others are able to **interpret** these feelings by observing facial expressions, glances, tones of voice, or speech patterns.

When the students read about situations in which ideas or feelings are not stated in so many words, they may need to **interpret** what they read. They do this by making inferences, by connecting what they read to what they already know, or by making and applying generalizations. In short, the strategy of **interpreting** involves a combination of other strategies. It means reading between and beyond the lines and making judgments about what is found there.

Introducing Interpreting

Refer the students to the **strategy poster Checking Understanding,** and have a volunteer read aloud the portion about **interpreting.** Discuss the strategy together and remind the students to use this strategy and any others whenever they need help figuring out text.

For a review of the strategy of **interpreting,** see **Learning Framework Card 1C, Checking Understanding.**

Reading Strategy Posters

Think-Aloud Prompts for Use in Oral Reading

The think-aloud prompts are placed where students may encounter difficulties with the text. These are merely suggestions. Remind the students to refer to the strategy posters and to use any strategy they find helpful as they read. Encourage them also to stop and ask for clarification whenever necessary and to feel free to share their thoughts about and reactions to the story. For a review of **modeling** and **generating think-alouds,** see **Teacher Tool Card 116.**

THINK ALOUD PROMPTS

These prompts may be used as guides to promote cognitive and responsive reading.

DO BANANAS CHEW GUM?

from the book by Jamie Gilson
illustrated by Beth Roberge

Although Sam Mott is in sixth grade, he can barely read or write. His mother worries about his future. His father tries to help Sam by reading Sam's schoolbooks aloud to him each night and by doing most of Sam's homework. Now in a new town and a new school, Sam hides his disability by playing the part of the class clown. Eventually his classmates and his teacher catch on. In a class spelling bee, Sam is unable to spell the word "cute." Sam's teacher then arranges for him to take a series of tests with the school's learning disabilities specialist, Ms. Huggins.

I trudged down to room 102. It looked like a closet from the outside, mostly because it didn't have a window like the rest of the doors did. I knocked. Very lightly, so whoever was inside wouldn't hear.

"Come in. Come in," a voice called out.

I opened the door slowly and saw that it was a little room, not closet-sized, but little, painted green like the garbage room. There was a desk, a few chairs, and a crescent-shaped table, yellow-green like a slice of honeydew melon. The lady inside said hello. She was standing up and she was almost as tall as my dad. Her face was round and shiny and she had lots of curly dark hair.

"I know you," I told her, and without even checking my dragon ring, I stuck out my hand. She shook it with both of hers.

"My name is Ms. Huggins," she said.

I did know her. She was always stopping in our room and talking to kids or to Mrs. Bird. I didn't know she was the learning disabilities person, though. That really knocked me

🐚 46 🐚

out. I mean, she was at school *all* the time. That had to mean there were a *lot* of dumb kids like me. She let me sit down at the crescent table.

"Well, Sammy," she said, smiling, like she was tickled to death I'd decided to come.

"My name is Sam," I told her. Somehow I didn't want Ms. Huggins calling me the wrong name.

"OK, Sam," she said. "We've a job to do. I'm going to give you some tests today and again next Monday to find out how you learn best."

"That's what my dad said." I shrugged and stared down at the green floor. Green tile. It was very dull. "I don't know what else you need to know," I said, like I couldn't care less. I mean, she was nice and I really didn't want her to find out more about me.

"I expect you know more about yourself than anybody else," she said. "We can start there." She sat down in a chair across from me. "What do you do best, Sam?"

"Me?" I looked up. What a stupid question, I thought. Do *best?* "I don't know. Make people laugh at me, I guess. I'm good at that."

"You mean jokes? Like 'Why did the robber take a shower at the bank?' "

"Because he wanted to make a clean getaway," I flipped back. "No, mostly not jokes. Mostly *at* me." I shrugged again, like, of course, I didn't care.

"Come on, Sam. Mrs. Bird tells me you have a special ability in math. She says you're a bright boy."

"I light up the night."

🐚 *48* 🐚

"Ah, you're a sit-down comic. Then they *do* laugh because you want them to, sometimes. How about the math?"

"I know a few tricks with numbers, that's all. I'm mostly dumb."

She laughed. Laughed. I could have punched her. She wasn't so nice after all. "No, it can't be that easy," she went on, still looking much too cheerful. "You're not allowed in my door unless you're smart. Children with a low ability level don't come to me. There's another teacher who works with them."

She'd change her mind soon enough. I wasn't going to argue with her. I'd just let her start the tests. That'd show her. I stared out the window while she got some books and paper out, wondering just *how* smart people were different from me. I tried to imagine what was in their heads that wasn't in mine.

"I'm going to ask you some crazy questions, Sam," she said.

I looked up at her, wondering what she could ask that was crazy, and why.

"First," she said, "do bananas chew gum?"

I laughed out loud. "Are you kidding?"

"Not at all," she said. "Do clocks swim?"

"No, but time flies." Mom was always big on riddles. Were these riddles that I wasn't smart enough to figure out?

"Do babies cry?"

That wasn't a trick. "Sometimes."

🐚 *49* 🐚

1 Students may not understand why Sam gets angry when Ms. Huggins laughs. If necessary, help them **interpret** his feelings by helping them find in the text evidence that he likes Ms. Huggins. He says, however, that he doesn't want her to find out about him. He shrugs and makes jokes and acts as if he doesn't care when she asks him questions. Students can infer from what he does and from what he says that Sam fears that Ms. Huggins now thinks that he is stupid and is laughing at him.

If necessary, model **interpreting** by saying something like the following:

Sam makes jokes and acts as if he doesn't care when Ms. Huggins asks him questions, even though he thinks she's nice. I wonder why he's acting like this. He does say he doesn't want her to find out about him. Maybe he is afraid that he really is dumb and that Ms. Huggins now knows this and is laughing at him.

But then they started getting harder. After a while it was stuff like "Do <u>interpreters translate</u>?" Pretty soon the only word that made sense was "Do." I had to keep saying, "I don't know," and feeling like an idiot. But just when they were getting so hard I bet *she* didn't even know the answers, we started on something completely different.

Lots of pictures. You had to match them. Like this one I remember that had a baseball on one side of the page and on the other side pictures of a violin bow, a rake, and a baseball bat. Really simp stuff. But they got harder, too.

Pretty much every new part started out easy and got hard like that. There were lots of different kinds of things, like when Ms. Huggins laid these tiles down on a table and all the tiles had weird lines on them and squiggles and she'd say, "Which shape is different from the rest?" or she'd put up

another and say, "Find this shape. It's hidden in that picture." She was timing all this stuff with a stopwatch, and it was hard.

Then I was supposed to copy circles and arrows and boxes and stars and, boy, did I stink at that. So when we finally got to some math, it was like a vacation, or at least recess. It was real 2 plus 2 stuff to begin with. Then it got to be $5^1/3$ times $2^1/5$ equals, and then long division with decimals. She only gave me ten minutes to get it all done, but before the time was nearly up I got to these questions I didn't even know what they meant.

"That's OK," she said, "you won't learn how to do those problems until seventh grade. I knew we'd get to something you do really well. You were terrific at the math. Fast, accurate, all those good things. I doubt there's anyone in your class who could do so well."

"Alicia," I told her.

"Don't know her."

"You wouldn't."

"She pretty good at math?"

"She's good at everything. A brain." My stomach felt like lunchtime was getting close. I didn't want to start any more tests. I decided to stall. "Why is it easy for me to do math and not reading?" I asked her, even though I knew the answer. (*Dum-dum-dum.*)

She shook her head. "I'm not sure. Nobody's sure. Did you know some people can hardly do math at all? Some people just blink their eyes and shake their heads when you say that 4 plus 15 is 19. It's as if they've got a short <u>circuit</u> in their heads and they can't put numbers through their brain computer. If they're smart otherwise, that's a learning disability, too."

🐝 *51* 🐝

"Can they read?"

"Sometimes. Sometimes not. Learning disabilities come in all varieties."

"Like ice cream."

"More even than that." She smiled, like she knew I was stalling. "Ready for another test?"

"No," I said. "Is it hard?"

"I think so. Yes. This one's spelling."

"Yuck. Isn't it time for lunch?"

She checked her watch. "Eleven-ten. Not quite. Just this last one, OK? Then we'll break for lunch."

But geez, it was awful. After "dog" and "cat" and "hat" to make me feel like it wasn't going to be all that bad, it was word after word after word I couldn't spell and I knew I was guessing wrong. At least she didn't ask me to spell "cute."

"Try sounding it out," she'd say. "Try it out loud. Keep plugging." But how do you keep plugging on "similar" and "license" and "miracle" when you hardly know how to begin? I didn't care if I *ever* knew how to spell them. I mean, who cares, anyway? Every word more I sank lower and lower in the chair. My stomach growled like a mad dog.

After I guess she figured she'd tortured me enough, Ms. Huggins beamed out this huge smile even though I knew there wasn't anything to grin about. "Cheer up," she said. "It's chow time."

I didn't smile back.

"You're doing fine. I'm finding out a lot about how you can learn even better. And the math was fabulous."

"That's me, fabulous Sam." What a fake she is, I decided. Always smiling and saying "terrific" when what she means is

🌢 52 🐛

dumb. I get mad at Mom but at least she knows dumb when she sees it and doesn't lie about it.

"Do I have to come back?"

"Around one-thirty," she said, "we'll start afresh. Why don't you go early to the cafeteria and take a long lunch hour. I'll give you a note. I think I hear a hungry monster in your stomach."

It wasn't funny, so I didn't pretend it was. I just stared at her.

While she wrote out the pink permission slip I got up and hung around the door.

"See you at one-thirty," she said, holding out the paper. "Right after the party."

I started to bolt out the door. "Party?"

"Didn't Mrs. Bird say there'd be a party after lunch?"

"Oh, yeah," I said, remembering. "There'll be a bunch of bananas hanging around up there chewing gum and eating cupcakes." And I slammed the door on her silly smile. **2**

The lunch hour went on forever. We had pizza casserole. Not many kids like it so an awful lot got smashed up in the trash compacter. I threw away about half of mine, even though I'll eat almost anything.

After lunch I sat by myself, watched the first graders play, and then poked around in the grass with a stick, pretending to dig up treasures. All I found was a rusty nail and a few ants, who crawled all over a cookie crumb I fed them.

When the bell rang there wasn't anything to do but go back inside with the big stream of kids, like I was a fish on a hook. And there wasn't anything inside I wanted to do.

🌢 53 🐛

2 Some students may be unclear about why Sam is still acting upset. If necessary, help them **interpret** his behavior. Despite what Ms. Huggins has been telling him, Sam still believes he is dumb. Although he doesn't feel that Ms. Huggins is laughing at him any more, he does think she is insincere when she tells him his performance with the math problems was "fabulous."

Mrs. Bird's room was all laughs and giggles. It sounded so happy when I slammed my locker door I wondered if maybe it wouldn't be a great party after all. I was the last kid in, but Mrs. Bird hadn't gotten back from her lunch yet.

"Cutie," a girl yelled. "Did you see your cupcake yet?" I looked around the room, and on every desk was a cupcake, a napkin, and a paper cup with something in it. But kids were gathered around my desk like the ants on the crumb.

"Mine has AB on it for the birthday girl. What does it say on yours, Cutes?" a boy asked with a smirk.

"How do you *spell* it?" somebody giggled. They were really starting to laugh at me.

And I got mad. I got so mad I could have zapped them. I *know* getting mad makes it worse, but I could feel my face get red and I felt like I could level them all. I straight-armed the guy nearest me. Alicia just stood there by her desk and looked confused. It was like she knew she kept botching me up and didn't understand how.

The stupid cupcake sat there. SAM was on it with a red heart iced around the letters. I hadn't even noticed *that* before.

"What does it *say?*" somebody in the back asked. "Does it really say 'cute'?"

I picked up the cupcake and held it up high for them to see. I shouted so everyone could hear, "It says Sam. That's my name. I don't want to be called anything else. And don't you forget it." They looked at me with their mouths open and I stared them down, feeling tall like a statue.

I would have kept talking, too, but Mrs. Bird came back. She stood at the door of the silent room, trying to decide what was going on. Her eyes fixed on me.

🐦 54 🐦

"Sammy," she called out. I didn't move. I just got madder. "Sammy," she went on, "were you screaming? I could hear you down the hall."

"I was saying," I told her in less than a shout, "that my name is Sam. And I don't want to be called Sammy or New Kid or Metal Mouth or Dumbhead or—especially—Cutes. I don't want to be called anything but Sam Mott."

"That sounds reasonable to me," she said mildly. "Everybody agree to that?"

There was a kind of general mumbling and I sat down in my seat, feeling like a balloon somebody had let the air out of— like I had been all filled up with being mad and now it was gone I just felt bad. Mrs. Bird just didn't understand. I ate the top off the cupcake. The room was still very quiet.

🐦 55 🐦

3 If the students are confused, explain that the *A. B.* on the cupcake stands for Alicia Bliss, a girl in Sam's class who has told the other girls that she thinks he is "cute." She assigned him that word in a spelling bee and was distressed when he was unable to spell it.

"That was really something," Wally whispered.

I nodded, my mouth full of sweet stuff. Gulping it down, I said, "I was mad."

"Yeah," he said, "I could tell."

We all had to sing "Happy Birthday" to Alicia. And I sang it like almost everybody else did, "Happy birthday to you, you belong in a zoo. You look like a monkey, and you smell like one, too." I mean, that's the way we *always* sang it. There'd been about four birthdays since I'd been in this school and mostly everybody sang it that way. It wasn't being mean to Alicia, like name calling. After my big speech it worried me some. But I don't think it was. She didn't look mad.

After we finished eating the cupcakes and drinking lemonade, the Bird gave all the captains math problems to pass back. Then she stopped at my desk and leaned over. "Are you all right?" she asked and I nodded. "You may be excused, Sam," she said. "I would have called you Sam sooner if I'd known."

"Oh, it wasn't just you," I told her, and hurried out of the room while almost everybody else was groaning over the math.

I knocked on the door of room 102.

"Come in. Come in," Ms. Huggins called like before. When I opened it, she said, "You're back!" like she was surprised but glad. "How's the monster in your stomach?"

"Just fed him a cupcake and he's happy," I told her. I didn't know why I wasn't mad at her anymore.

We started out with easy stuff. Numbers.

"Repeat after me," she said, "17-1-4-42." Stuff like that. And it wasn't hard at all. A piece of cake. A piece of *cup*cake.

❦ 56 ❦

"Do you see?" she asked me when the test was over. "Do you see how much easier it is for you to learn from what you *hear* than from what you read? You remembered those so well."

The test had seemed easy. I did see, sort of.

"You don't have to read things to learn them," she went on. "Most people learn a lot by listening to other people, to movies, to television. You can even learn to *read* better by listening to *yourself*."

That sounded crazy. "How?"

"Just say there's a word you want to read . . ." she started.

"There *is*," I told her. "There is!" I'd stuck the archeology book Brenda had left for me in the orange crate with my good junk. I'd looked through it and even read a little bit of it. But I still couldn't figure out the word on the cover. I was sure it must be "archeology."

"Archeology," I said, almost begging. "That's the word I want to read. Can you teach me that one?"

"Good grief, you start at the top, don't you?" She wrote the word down for me on a piece of white paper, kind of splitting it up into parts—ARC-HE-OL-O-GY. "It isn't the easiest word to sound out, but . . ."

Then she took another piece of paper and tore a little square hole out of the middle. She put the hole on the word so I could just see the first three letters and she made me sound it out. Twice. And I did it. She moved the paper and I sounded out all the parts. Then she had me do that about ten times before she let me look at the word whole. And I could sound it out. Arc-he-ol-o-gy. Archeology. I kept looking at the word and saying it over. Out loud. Archeology. I was so excited I felt dizzy.

❦ 57 ❦

4 Some students may need help **interpreting** why Sam is no longer angry at Ms. Huggins. If necessary, you might model this strategy by saying something like the following:

It seems that yelling at his classmates has made Sam feel better. Also, now that he has thought about how he and the other students tease each other by changing the words to "Happy Birthday," I think he realizes that teasing is not always mean and that he has been oversensitive.

5 If necessary, explain that *Brenda* is Brenda Strawhacker, a graduate student of archeology. She identified some Native-American and nineteenth-century artifacts Sam dug up in a neighbor's yard and encouraged Sam in his interest in archeology.

"Can I have the paper with the hole?"

"My compliments. But it's not magic. You've got to do the work."

Then I looked at the paper and wondered how many words in the new book I could do that way by myself. But she kept after me. "Sam, that was terrific! The computer in your head sometimes gets confused by a lot of letters. If you just let it see a few at a time for a while, it'll help.

"There are so many things you can do, Sam. Have somebody record the pages you have to read, then listen to the tape as you read the words to yourself. Then try making a tape of your voice reading the words. Can you do that?"

"No kidding?" I asked her. "A tape recorder? It would be OK? My mom said it would be a crutch."

"Nothing's wrong with a crutch if you need one. If you had a broken leg she'd let you have a crutch. If you've got a tape recorder, put it on your desk to take notes for you. I'll talk to Mrs. Bird about it. Reporters take notes with tape recorders all the time."

"I'm earning the money for one right now!" I'd tell Mrs. Glass and she'd let me keep on baby-sitting. I was sure she would.

Then we started another test and I had to guess which of a list of words fit best into paragraphs that were hard to read and I felt awful again.

"This would be easy for Alicia and Wally," I told Ms. Huggins. "It's not fair."

"Right," she said, "it's not. Wouldn't be fair if you fell off your bike and broke your elbow either, but you'd have to deal with it, fair or not. You can either give up and just plug your

§ 58 ❦

head into a TV set or you can work like crazy. I can help. Your folks can help. A lot of people can help. But in the end it's got to be you."

Then she gave me another test. There was this one word at the top and five words listed under it. I was supposed to find the word that meant nearly the same as the word at the top. Like there'd be "nap" and under it would be "jump," "roll," "bad," and "sleep." Ms. Huggins said if I couldn't decide which word fit best to just go on to the next question. After the first four or five I was a disaster.

"You'll get there, Sam," she said when I started sagging down in my chair.

"Never," I groaned.

"Listen," she told me, still cheerful like I was winning the race, not crawling along on my knees, "Thomas Edison had a learning disability in school, and so did Hans Christian Andersen, and Vice President Rockefeller, and President Wilson. They didn't get famous by saying 'never.' They worked their way out of it. You can, too, but you have to do it a step at a time. Nobody's going to wave a wand."

When I left room 102 I felt better. Some. "We'll find out more about you next Monday, Sam Mott," she said. "After that we'll work together several times a week." It was like I'd just waded up to my ankles in cold Lake Michigan water knowing I had to swim across the lake and back again. **6**

§ 59 ❦

6 Students may need to **interpret** Sam's analogy at the end of the selection: Sam compares beginning to work on his learning problem to the situation of a swimmer getting ready to swim across Lake Michigan and back again. He understands that he has a great deal of work ahead of him.

Discussing Strategy Use

Encourage the students to discuss the strategies they used while reading the selection and to explain how these strategies helped them better understand what they read.

*

EXPLORING THROUGH DISCUSSION

Reflecting on the Selection
Whole-Group Discussion

The whole group discusses the selection and any personal thoughts, reactions, or questions that it raises. During this time, students also **return to the clues, problems, and wonderings** they noted on the chalkboard during browsing.

Assessment

To assess the students' understanding of the text, engage in a discussion to **determine whether the students have grasped the following ideas:**
- the kinds of problems Sam is having in school
- whether Ms. Huggins gave Sam good advice when she told him that it was up to him to work his way out of his difficulty

Response Journal

Students may wish to record their personal responses to the selection.

Exploring Concepts Within the Selection
Small-Group Discussion

Small groups discuss the relationship of the selection to learning. Circulate among the groups and observe the discussions. Refer the students to the Concept Board and the Question Board to keep them focused on their original ideas about learning and to see if those ideas have changed as a result of reading this selection.

Sharing Ideas About Explorable Concepts

Have the groups **report** and **discuss** their **ideas** with the rest of the class. It is crucial that the students' ideas determine this discussion.
- The students may mention that according to Ms. Huggins, Sam may be able to improve his reading by listening to himself read. Different people learn through different experiences.
- Some students may point out that, in order to learn more about archeology, Sam knows he must first improve his reading skills. Reading is not only essential for the learning that takes place in school, but necessary for learning more about personal interests as well.

As these ideas and others are stated, have the students **add them to** the **Question Board** or the **Concept Board.**

Have the students look at the fine-art pieces on pages 76–77 of the student anthology and briefly discuss the painting *The Music Lesson* by Johannes Vermeer. They may wish to express their thoughts and feelings about this particular work and point out any connections they think it has to the story they have just read. Students might compare or contrast the relationship of the teacher to the pupil in the painting with the relationship between the characters in the story.

Exploring Concepts Across Selections

Students may make connections with other selections in this unit.
- The students may recognize that Laura Bridgman had to overcome disabilities even greater than Sam's in order to learn to read and write.
- Some students may also suggest that both Sam and Mukasa were teased by people in their classes.

Fine Art

"Mukasa at School" by John Nagenda

_____
_____
_____
_____
_____
_____
_____

"Do Bananas Chew Gum?" by Jamie Gilson

_____
_____
_____
_____
_____
_____
_____
_____

"Seventh Grade" by Gary Soto

_____
_____
_____
_____
_____
_____
_____
_____

Unit 1/Learning   EN 5

Explorer's Notebook, page 5

Recording Ideas

As students complete the above discussions, ask them to **sum up what they have learned from their conversations and how they might use this information** in further explorations. Any special information or insights may be recorded on the **Concept Board.** Any further questions that they would like to think about, pursue, or investigate may be recorded on the **Question Board.** Students may want to discuss the progress that has been made on their questions. They may also want to cross out any questions that no longer warrant consideration.

➤ After discussion, the students should individually record their ideas on page 5 of their Explorer's Notebook.

Evaluating Discussions

Professional Checkpoint: Cognitive and Responsive Reading

Although there is a separate strategy called interpreting, readers are interpreting when they sum up or visualize as well. That is, it is the reader who decides what should be in a summary or a visualization of text and, thus, every summary and visualization is a personal perspective on the meaning of a text.

Notes:

2 READING WITH A WRITER'S EYE

MINILESSONS

Writer's Craft: First-Person Narrative

Explain to the students that one of the first things an author must do when writing a story is decide who will tell the story. Ask volunteers to share what they know about stories that are written in the first person. Establish that when one of the characters in a story tells what is happening, the author is using a writing technique called first-person narration. Readers can recognize this type of writing because the narrator uses first-person pronouns such as *I, me, we,* and *us.* In this kind of story, the narrator can describe her or his own experiences and thoughts and feelings, but cannot describe what is thought or felt by other characters. When a story is told by a narrator who is *not* a character in the story but instead an outside observer, we say that the story is written in third person. These stories use third-person pronouns such as *he, she,* and *they.* The third-person narrator can reveal how *all* of the characters in a story think and feel about story events, although many stories using a third-person narrator focus on only one main character, such as Rufus Moffat or Mukasa.

Invite the students to discuss why an author might choose to use a first-person narrator or a third-person narrator. Students might suggest that **authors write in first-person in order to bring readers closer to one particular character,** to see and experience the story from inside that character's mind. But if an author wants to "get inside the heads" of the other characters as well, he or she will write in the third person.

Ask the students whether Jamie Gilson used a first-person or a third-person narrator in this selection, and how they know. Students should recognize that the story was written in the first person—the narrator is a character in the story; the selection begins with the word *I.*

Selective Reading: Focus on First-Person Narrative

Have the students scan the story to see if they notice anything, in addition to the use of the pronoun *I,* that tells them that Gilson's story is written in the first person. Students might point out that the author uses words, expressions, and ways of speaking that the main character would use and might cite the following examples :

- The narrator uses the words *me, my, mine,* and *we.*
- Sam lets readers know what he is thinking and feeling; the intimate thoughts and feelings of the other characters in the story, however, are not revealed, although Sam does speculate about them.

Independent Practice: Focus on First-Person Narrative

➤ Have the students work in small groups, using Reading/Writing Connection, page 7, to extend their discussion of first-person narrative. After sufficient time, invite groups to share their observations.

Selection-Based Practice

"Do Bananas Chew Gum?"

Point of View

Look back at stories you have read and decide whether they were written as a first-person or a third-person narrative. From which point of view does the author tell the story? How do you know?

Story: _____ Author: _____

First-person or third-person narrative? _____

How do you know? _____

Why do you think the author chose to tell the story this way? _____

_____

Story: _____ Author: _____

First-person or third-person narrative? _____

How do you know? _____

Why do you think the author chose to tell the story this way? _____

_____

Story: _____ Author: _____

First-person or third-person narrative? _____

How do you know? _____

Why do you think the author chose to tell the story this way? _____

_____

Story: _____ Author: _____

First-person or third-person narrative? _____

How do you know? _____

Why do you think the author chose to tell the story this way? _____

_____

Name

Copyright © 1995 Open Court Publishing Company

Point of View

Unit 1/Learning R/WC 7

Reading/Writing Connection, page 7

**Writer's Craft:
Informal
Language**

Selection-Based Practice

Tell the students that Jamie Gilson does a good job of making her characters sound like real people when they talk and think. You might remind them that while preparing to write her first children's book, Gilson tape-recorded interviews with neighborhood boys. These recordings helped her learn the language of young people, and enabled her to make the story sound as if a child were telling it. Explain that writers often use informal language—vocabulary, expressions, and ways of speaking that may not follow standard rules, but may, in fact, more closely resemble a natural way of talking—in order to make their characters seem more like real people. Point out that although Gilson is an adult woman, *Do Bananas Chew Gum?* reads as if a young boy were telling the story. You might cite the following examples which illustrate how Gilson did this:

- page 47, paragraph 3: Sam notes that Ms. Huggins was "almost as tall as my dad." (child's point of view)
- page 47, paragraph 6: Sam says, "That really knocked me out." (an expression a young boy might use)
- page 48, top of page: Sam says "I mean" when he tries to explain himself. (a way of speaking)
- page 48, paragraph 4: Sam uses an incomplete sentence, "Green tile."

Selective Reading: Focus on Informal Language

Have the students scan the story to see if they can locate other words, expressions, or ways of speaking that make the narrator sound like a young boy. Invite volunteers to read these sentences or passages aloud:

- page 49, paragraph 10: "Mom was always big on riddles."
- page 50, paragraph 2: "Like this one I remember that had a baseball on one side of the page and on the other side pictures of a violin bow, a rake, and a baseball bat."
- page 52, paragraph 9: "But geez, it was awful."

Independent Practice: Informal Language

❯ To further their discussion of informal language, have the students use Reading/Writing Connection, page 8, to record words, expressions, or ways of speaking from this selection or others they have read, that make the characters seem more like real people.

WRITING

Linking Reading to Writing

Have the students consider using first- and third-person narrators and informal language in their stories. They might want to revise a few paragraphs from their own personal narratives by changing them from first-person to third-person or by having another person narrate the events described in the paragraphs. Or they might think about where and how to add particular words, expressions, or informal ways of speaking that can help their characters seem more like real people.

TEACHING TIP Reading is the ultimate source of good models for writing.

Reading/Writing Connection, page 8

"Do Bananas Chew Gum?"

Informal Language

Authors often use informal language to make the characters in their stories seem like real people. Look back at stories you have read and locate words, expressions, or ways of speaking that accomplish this. Write down examples you find and explain what the informal language shows about the characters.

Selection: _____

Examples of informal language: _____

What the language shows about the character: _____

Selection: _____

Examples of informal language: _____

What the language shows about the character: _____

Selection: _____

Examples of informal language: _____

What the language shows about the character: _____

Author's Style
8 R/WC   Learning/Unit 1

＊ Writing Process

Students who have finished proofreading and publishing their personal narratives may want to begin planning their second major writing assignment: a piece of realistic fiction. Remind them that they should plan the action of their stories before they begin. They may want to use a problem–solution structure, as in "The Library Card," and they may want to experiment with using the technique of a first-person narrator, such as was used in *Do Bananas Chew Gum?* Some students may want to use events from their classmates' personal narratives as starting places for planning the action of their stories.

VOCABULARY

Words and phrases the students might want to discuss and to use in their explorations for this unit include ***learning disability*** and ***archeology.***

Remind students to add words and phrases to the Personal Dictionary section of their Writer's Notebook. Then provide an opportunity for volunteers to share words and phrases they've added and tell why they chose them. Allow time for the students to complete Vocabulary Exploration forms, Reproducible Master 14, for those words they wish to learn or for those that are important to the unit concepts. For additional opportunities to build vocabulary, see **Teacher Tool Card 75.**

Adding to Personal Word Lists

3 GUIDED AND INDEPENDENT EXPLORATION
EXPLORING CONCEPTS BEYOND THE TEXT

Guided Exploration

Students will select activities in which they explore the concept of learning. Refer the students to the **Exploration Activities poster** and give them time to choose an activity, discuss what they wish to explore, and decide how they wish to go about it. If the students need further help, here are some suggestions:

Ms. Huggins tells Sam that the writer Hans Christian Andersen, the inventor Thomas Edison, Vice-President Nelson Rockefeller, and President Woodrow Wilson all had learning disabilities. Some other famous people with learning disabilities include Leonardo da Vinci, Albert Einstein, Agatha Christie, and Cher. Have interested students choose one of these people and find out more about him or her. After they have done some research, they might present a report on who this person is or was, why this person is famous, what problems this person had in school, and how this person overcame these problems.

＊ *Exploring Through Reflective Activities*

Library Research

▶ Have students form small groups and discuss different learning problems they might have had, including particular skills or subjects that were difficult for them to master. Have them use page 16 in their Explorer's Notebook to extend this discussion. Afterwards, have the

ASSESSMENT TIP This might be a good time to observe students working in groups and to mark observations in your Teacher's Observation Log.

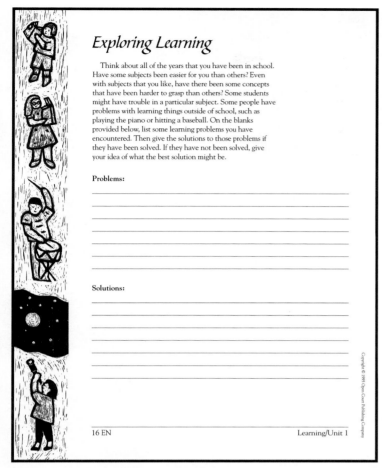

Exploring Learning

Think about all of the years that you have been in school. Have some subjects been easier for you than others? Even with subjects that you like, have there been some concepts that have been harder to grasp than others? Some students might have trouble in a particular subject. Some people have problems with learning things outside of school, such as playing the piano or hitting a baseball. On the blanks provided below, list some learning problems you have encountered. Then give the solutions to those problems if they have been solved. If they have not been solved, give your idea of what the best solution might be.

Problems:

_____

_____

_____

_____

_____

_____

Solutions:

_____

_____

_____

_____

_____

_____

_____

16 EN   Learning/Unit 1

Explorer's Notebook, page 16

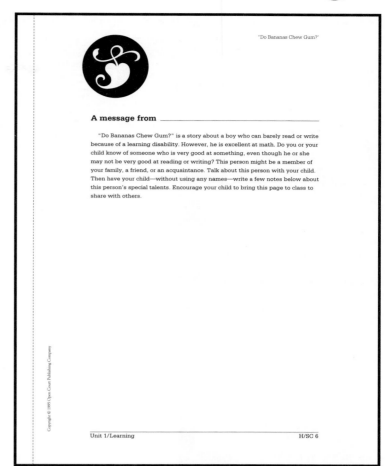

"Do Bananas Chew Gum?"

A message from _____

"Do Bananas Chew Gum?" is a story about a boy who can barely read or write because of a learning disability. However, he is excellent at math. Do you or your child know of someone who is very good at something, even though he or she may not be very good at reading or writing? This person might be a member of your family, a friend, or an acquaintance. Talk about this person with your child. Then have your child—without using any names—write a few notes below about this person's special talents. Encourage your child to bring this page to class to share with others.

Unit 1/Learning   H/SC 6

Home/School Connection 6

groups share their ideas and conclusions. Some students may want to write about this. Suggest that they frame their writing as a personal experience story.

➤ Distribute Home/School Connection 6. Encourage the students to discuss with adults at home the ways that people can compensate for limitations in one area by using skills they possess in other areas.

Continuing Exploration

Have the students review the questions on the Question Board and remove any that they no longer find interesting or appropriate.

Have students return to pages 14–15 in their Explorer's Notebook to continue planning and recording ideas for their exploration of learning. Remind them to add additional thoughts they might have about possible ideas to explore.

*INDEPENDENT WORKSHOP
Building a Community of Scholars

Student-Directed Reading, Writing, and Discussion

The students should spend the first part of Independent Workshop in their collaborative groups, working together on ideas for exploring the concepts related to learning. Remind them to use their bibliographies for ideas of books and resources to use as they explore.

If some students would like to present a unit project but have not yet decided what they want to do, suggest that they review the questions on the Question Board and indicate which ones are most interesting to them. They might then check with various collaborative groups to find one with common interests.

WORKSHOP TIP

Check to make sure that group members are working well together and that they understand the group's specific goals as well as their own personal goals.

Additional Opportunities for Independent Reading, Writing, and Cross-curricular Activities

* Reading Roundtable

Suggest to students who choose to read and discuss the book *Do Bananas Chew Gum?* that before their meeting they write a few good questions to ask each other about the book.

* Writing Seminar

Some students may still be publishing the final versions of their personal narratives about learning. Allow them time to work on those. Others may wish to begin work on the first drafts of their realistic fiction pieces. Remind them to refer to the writing strategy posters if they need help with their writing. Encourage them to begin new writing projects about learning at any time.

Cross-curricular Activity Cards

The following Cross-curricular Activity Cards in the Student Toolbox are appropriate for use with this selection:
- 2 Drama—Sam Mott at School
- 4 Social Studies—Conducting a Survey

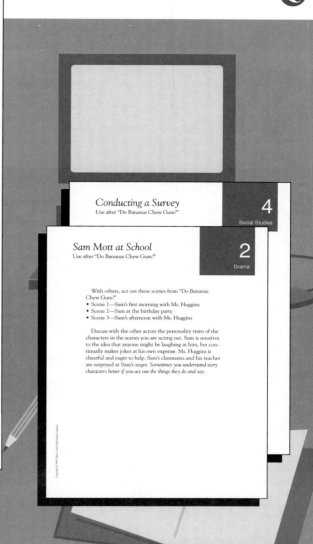

Additional Opportunities for Solving Learning Problems

Tutorial

Use this time to work with those students who need extra help. The following teaching aids are available in the Teacher Toolbox for your convenience:
- Writer's Craft/Reading: Point of View, Teacher Tool Card 12
- Writer's Craft/Reading: Formal Versus Informal Language, Teacher Tool Card 18
- Writer's Craft/Reading: Figurative Language, Teacher Tool Card 20
- Writer's Craft/Reading: Elaboration Through Providing Descriptions, Teacher Tool Card 39
- Grammar, Mechanics, and Usage: Complete and Incomplete Sentences, Teacher Tool Card 46

Seventh Grade

1

READING THE SELECTION

INFORMATION FOR THE TEACHER

About the Selection

It's the first day of school in Fresno, California, and seventh-grader Victor Rodriguez signs up for French because the girl he likes will be in that class. By the end of this funny short story, Victor has a good reason to work hard at learning French: he must keep up the pretense that he has known it all along. Calling on his own experience of growing up poor and Mexican-American in California's Central Valley, Gary Soto captures the language and culture of Latino children. However, people of all ages will enjoy and recognize themselves in this humorous scenario.

Link to the Unit Concepts

"Seventh Grade," pages 60–67, makes the point that people have different reasons for wanting to learn. The fact that Victor's French teacher doesn't reveal the truth about the boy's ignorance of the language suggests that what motivates people to learn may not always be that important, so long as the end result—learning—is achieved.

About the Author

"Seventh Grade" is an excerpt from *Baseball in April and Other Stories*, a collection of short stories by Gary Soto about young people in California. The book was an ALA Best Book for Young Adults, winner of the *Parenting Magazine* Reading Magic Award, and recipient of the 1990 John and Patricia Beatty Award. Soto has written numerous books for adults as well as for children, taking as his central theme ethnicity in America. "My target is Mexican children," the author explains. "It's really to make them feel that their story is as important as anyone else's story." In addition to writing, Soto, the son of an agricultural worker and a factory worker, is a professor of English and Chicano Studies at the University of California at Berkeley and a volunteer karate teacher at a local Boys' Club.

LESSON OVERVIEW

"Seventh Grade" by Gary Soto, pages 60–67

READING THE SELECTION

Materials
Student anthology, pp. 60–67
Explorer's Notebook, p. 5

FYI
Learning Framework Card
• Responding to Text, 1B

READING WITH A WRITER'S EYE

Minilesson
Writer's Craft: Setting

Materials
Reading/Writing Connection, p. 9
Reproducible Masters 14, 23

FYI
Teacher Tool Card
• Spelling and Vocabulary: Building Vocabulary, 75

Options for Instruction
Writer's Craft: Characterization
Writer's Craft: Dialogue
Grammar, Mechanics, and Usage: Adverbs
(Use Teacher Tool Cards listed below.)

GUIDED AND INDEPENDENT EXPLORATION

Materials
Explorer's Notebook, p. 17
Home/School Connection 7

Independent Workshop

Optional Materials from Student Toolbox
Tradebook Connection Cards

Cross-curricular Activity Card
• 5 Social Studies—France

Student Tool Cards
• Writer's Craft/Reading: Setting, 14
• Writer's Craft/Reading: Characterization, 13
• Writer's Craft/Reading: Using Dialogue in a Story, 19
• Grammar, Mechanics, and Usage: Using Adjectives and Adverbs, 68

FYI
Learning Framework Card
• Reading Roundtable, 6

Teacher Tool Cards
• Writer's Craft/Reading: Setting, 14
• Writer's Craft/Reading: Characterization, 13
• Writer's Craft/Reading: Using Dialogue in a Story, 19
• Grammar, Mechanics, and Usage: Using Adjectives and Adverbs, 68

NOTES

Asterisks (*) throughout the lesson indicate learning frameworks. Learning Framework Cards and Teacher Tool Cards can be found in the Teacher Toolbox.

INFORMATION FOR THE STUDENT

- Share with the students the title of the book this selection comes from. They may be interested in reading additional stories from this book or others by Gary Soto.
- Explain that Gary Soto grew up in Fresno, California, and uses that area of the country as the setting for many of his stories, including "Seventh Grade."
- Share any other information about the author that you think would interest the students.

COGNITIVE AND RESPONSIVE READING

Activating Prior Knowledge

In the story, the main character elects to study French, a language with which he is completely unfamiliar. Ask the students to share what they know about learning a foreign language.

Setting Reading Goals and Expectations

Have the students **browse** the **first page** of the selection, using the clues/problems/wondering procedure. Students will return to these observations after reading.

Recommendations for Reading the Selection

This story is short, and it includes both amusing dialogue and Spanish and French expressions. Most students would enjoy reading the selection aloud. During oral reading, use and encourage think-alouds. During silent reading, allow discussion as needed. Discuss problems, strategies, and reactions after reading. This would also be a good selection for **responding** to text **by visualizing** while reading aloud. Model this response, and then invite the students to respond.

About the Reading Strategies

"Seventh Grade" is about children close to the students' own age and about events with which they may readily identify; therefore, they will probably be able to **make connections** between information in the story and what they already know.

Ask the students how **making connections** between what they read and what they know helps them to better understand or appreciate a story. They should recognize that they do this in everyday life. For instance, if they are listening to someone tell a story about a camping trip, and they themselves have been camping, they will recognize the types of situations and problems a camper might have encountered. Good readers use **making connections** to help them understand how a character they are reading about feels or why the character does what he or she does.

Refer students to the **reading strategy poster Responding to Text** and read about the strategy of **making connections**. Discuss the strategy and have a volunteer read aloud the questions that accompany it. Encourage the students to make connections as they read by asking themselves such questions. Model relating the story to your own child-

TIP FOR ENGLISH LANGUAGE LEARNERS

Invite English Language Learners to share their experiences and knowledge about learning another language.

TIP FOR ENGLISH LANGUAGE LEARNERS

Give English Language Learners a chance to be a model for others. Invite the students who speak Spanish or French to read aloud the pages of the story that contain Spanish or French words. Praise their reading and pronunciation.

Introducing Making Connections

Reading Strategy Posters

hood experiences and then invite the students to make their own connections. To review the strategy of **making connections**, see **Learning Framework Card 1B, Responding to Text**.

The think-aloud prompts are placed where students may encounter difficulties with the text. These are merely suggestions. Remind the students to refer to the **reading strategy posters** and to use any strategy they find helpful.

Some of the Spanish and French expressions in the story may be familiar to students or may be understood from the context. Others may need to be translated. Encourage those students who speak either language to pronounce and explain the meanings of foreign words and phrases.

TEACHING TIP Observe students' nonverbal reactions as they read—a puzzled frown, a long pause, a look of surprise, a smile. When you see such reactions, ask students to share their questions or comments.

These prompts may be used as guides to promote cognitive and responsive reading.

raza (rä´ sä) -style: Spanish term for a kind of handshake popular among young Mexican-Americans

saludo de vato (sä lo͞o´ tho͞ dē vä´ tō): Spanish term for another kind of greeting popular among young people in California

ese (e´ sä): a Spanish interjection that is sometimes used for emphasis

GQ Gentlemen's Quarterly magazine

1 Some students may need to clarify the word *elective.* Encourage volunteers to suggest ways to clarify the term. They may be able to tell from **context** that it refers to a class that a student chooses, or elects, from among several alternatives.

2 Students might **visualize** in order to clarify the kind of faces Michael is making. The models in *GQ* magazine are sophisticated, well-dressed, adult men with unsmiling, rather arrogant expressions on their faces. Trying to imitate them, Michael probably looks sulky and pretentious.

SEVENTH GRADE
Gary Soto
illustrated by Andy San Diego

1 On the first day of school, Victor stood in line half an hour before he came to a wobbly card table. He was handed a packet of papers and a computer card on which he listed his one elective, French. He already spoke Spanish and English, but he thought some day he might travel to France, where it was cool; not like Fresno, where summer days reached 110 degrees in the shade. There were rivers in France, and huge churches, and fair-skinned people everywhere, the way there were brown people all around Victor.

Besides, Teresa, a girl he had liked since they were in <u>catechism</u> classes at Saint Theresa's, was taking French, too. With any luck they would be in the same class. Teresa is going to be my girl this year, he promised himself as he left the gym full of students in their new fall clothes. She was cute. And good at math, too, Victor thought as he walked down the hall to his homeroom. He ran into his friend, Michael Torres, by the water fountain that never turned off.

They shook hands, *raza*-style, and jerked their heads at one another in a *saludo de vato.* "How come you're making a face?" asked Victor.

"I ain't making a face, *ese.* This *is* my face." Michael said his face had changed during the summer. He had read a GQ magazine that his older brother borrowed from the Book Mobile

and noticed that the male models all had the same look on their faces. They would stand, one arm around a beautiful woman, and *scowl.* They would sit at a pool, their rippled stomachs dark with shadow, and *scowl.* They would sit at dinner tables, cool drinks in their hands, and *scowl.*

"I think it works," Michael said. He scowled and let his upper lip quiver. His teeth showed along with the <u>ferocity</u> of his soul. "Belinda Reyes walked by a while ago and looked at me," he said.

Victor didn't say anything, though he thought his friend looked pretty strange. They talked about recent movies, baseball, their parents, and the horrors of picking grapes in order to buy their fall clothes. Picking grapes was like living in Siberia, except hot and more boring.

"What classes are you taking?" Michael said, scowling.

"French. How 'bout you?"

"Spanish. I ain't so good at it, even if I'm Mexican."

"I'm not either, but I'm better at it than math, that's for sure."

A tinny, three-beat bell propelled students to their homerooms. The two friends socked each other in the arm and went their ways, Victor thinking, man, that's weird. Michael thinks making a face makes him handsome.

On the way to his homeroom, Victor tried a scowl. He felt foolish, until out of the corner of his eye he saw a girl looking at him. Umm, he thought, maybe it does work. He scowled with greater conviction.

In homeroom, roll was taken, emergency cards were passed out, and they were given a bulletin to take home to their parents. The principal, Mr. Belton, spoke over the crackling loudspeaker, welcoming the students to a new year, new experiences, and new friendships. The students squirmed in their chairs and ignored him. They were anxious to go to first period. Victor sat calmly, thinking of Teresa, who sat two rows away, reading a paperback novel. This would be his lucky year. She was in his homeroom, and would probably be in his English and math classes. And, of course, French.

The bell rang for first period, and the students herded noisily through the door. Only Teresa lingered, talking with the homeroom teacher.

"So you think I should talk to Mrs. Gaines?" she asked the teacher. "She would know about ballet?"

🌶 62 🌶

"She would be a good bet," the teacher said. Then added, "Or the gym teacher, Mrs. Garza."

Victor lingered, keeping his head down and staring at his desk. He wanted to leave when she did so he could bump into her and say something clever.

He watched her on the sly. As she turned to leave, he stood up and hurried to the door, where he managed to catch her eye. She smiled and said, "Hi, Victor."

He smiled back and said, "Yeah, that's me." His brown face blushed. Why hadn't he said, "Hi, Teresa," or "How was your summer?" or something nice?

As Teresa walked down the hall, Victor walked the other way, looking back, admiring how gracefully she walked, one foot in front of the other. So much for being in the same class, he thought. As he trudged to English, he practiced scowling.

In English they reviewed the parts of speech. Mr. Lucas, a portly man, waddled down the aisle, asking, "What is a noun?"

"A person, place, or thing," said the class in unison.

"Yes, now somebody give me an example of a person—you, Victor Rodriguez."

"Teresa," Victor said automatically. Some of the girls giggled. They knew he had a crush on Teresa. He felt himself blushing again.

"Correct," Mr. Lucas said. "Now provide me with a place."

Mr. Lucas called on a freckled kid who answered, "Teresa's house with a kitchen full of big brothers."

After English, Victor had math, his weakest subject. He sat in the back by the window, hoping that he would not be called on. Victor understood most of the problems, but some

🌶 63 🌶

---

3 Some students may need to clarify the word *conviction.* If no one is familiar with the word, encourage the students to suggest a clarification strategy, such as using the dictionary.

4 Some students may be reminded of an experience they have had. You might encourage them to **make a connection** by modeling your own reaction:

I can remember feeling this way and doing things like this when I was Victor's age.

of the stuff looked like the teacher made it up as she went along. It was confusing, like the inside of a watch.

After math he had a fifteen-minute break, then social studies, and, finally, lunch. He bought a tuna casserole with buttered rolls, some fruit cocktail, and milk. He sat with Michael, who practiced scowling between bites.

Girls walked by and looked at him.

"See what I mean, Vic?" Michael scowled. "They love it."

"Yeah, I guess so."

They ate slowly, Victor scanning the horizon for a glimpse of Teresa. He didn't see her. She must have brought lunch, he thought, and is eating outside. Victor scraped his plate and left Michael, who was busy scowling at a girl two tables away.

The small, triangle-shaped campus bustled with students talking about their new classes. Everyone was in a sunny mood. Victor hurried to the bag lunch area, where he sat down and opened his math book. He moved his lips as if he were reading, but his mind was somewhere else. He raised his eyes slowly and looked around. No Teresa.

He lowered his eyes, pretending to study, then looked slowly to the left. No Teresa. He turned a page in the book and stared at some math problems that scared him because he knew he would have to do them eventually. He looked to the right. Still no sign of her. He stretched out lazily in an attempt to disguise his snooping.

Then he saw her. She was sitting with a girlfriend under a plum tree. Victor moved to a table near her and daydreamed about taking her to a movie. When the bell sounded, Teresa looked up, and their eyes met. She smiled sweetly and gathered her books. Her next class was French, same as Victor's.

❦ 64 ❦

They were among the last students to arrive in class, so all the good desks in the back had already been taken. Victor was forced to sit near the front, a few desks away from Teresa, while Mr. Bueller wrote French words on the chalkboard. The bell rang, and Mr. Bueller wiped his hands, turned to the class, and said, *"Bonjour."*

"Bonjour," braved a few students.

"Bonjour," Victor whispered. He wondered if Teresa heard him.

Mr. Bueller said that if the students studied hard, at the end of the year they could go to France and be understood by the populace.

One kid raised his hand and asked, "What's 'populace'?"

"The people, the people of France."

Mr. Bueller asked if anyone knew French. Victor raised his hand, wanting to impress Teresa. The teacher beamed and said, *"Trés bien. Parlez-vous français?"*

Victor didn't know what to say. The teacher wet his lips and asked something else in French. The room grew silent. Victor felt all eyes staring at him. He tried to bluff his way out by making noises that sounded French.

"La me vava me con le grandma," he said uncertainly.

Mr. Bueller, wrinkling his face in curiosity, asked him to speak up.

Great rosebushes of red bloomed on Victor's cheeks. A river of nervous sweat ran down his palms. He felt awful. Teresa sat a few desks away, no doubt thinking he was a fool. Without looking at Mr. Bueller, Victor mumbled, "Frenchie oh wewe gee in September."

Mr. Bueller asked Victor to repeat what he had said.

❦ 65 ❦

Bonjour (bōn zhōōr): French expression meaning "Good day"

tres bien (trā byen): French; meaning "very good"

Parlez-vous francais? (pär lā vōō frän sā): French; meaning "Do you speak French?"

"Frenchie oh wewe gee in September," Victor repeated.

Mr. Bueller understood that the boy didn't know French and turned away. He walked to the blackboard and pointed to the words on the board with his steel-edged ruler.

"*Le bateau*," he sang.

"*Le bateau*," the students repeated.

"*Le bateau est sur l'eau*," he sang.

"*Le bateau est sur l'eau*."

Victor was too weak from failure to join the class. He stared at the board and wished he had taken Spanish, not French. Better yet, he wished he could start his life over. He had never been so embarrassed. He bit his thumb until he tore off a sliver of skin.

The bell sounded for fifth period, and Victor shot out of the room, avoiding the stares of the other kids, but had to return for his math book. He looked sheepishly at the teacher, who was erasing the board, then widened his eyes in terror

🎵 66 🎵

at Teresa who stood in front of him. "I didn't know you knew French," she said. "That was good."

Mr. Bueller looked at Victor, and Victor looked back. Oh please, don't say anything, Victor pleaded with his eyes. I'll wash your car, mow your lawn, walk your dog—anything! I'll be your best student, and I'll clean your erasers after school.

Mr. Bueller shuffled through the papers on his desk. He smiled and hummed as he sat down to work. He remembered his college years when he dated a girlfriend in borrowed cars. She thought he was rich because each time he picked her up he had a different car. It was fun until he had spent all his money on her and had to write home to his parents because he was broke.

Victor couldn't stand to look at Teresa. He was sweaty with shame. "Yeah, well, I picked up a few things from movies and books and stuff like that." They left the class together. Teresa asked him if he would help her with her French.

"Sure, anytime," Victor said.

"I won't be bothering you, will I?"

"Oh no, I like being bothered."

"*Bonjour*," Teresa said, leaving him outside her next class. She smiled and pushed wisps of hair from her face.

"Yeah, right, *bonjour*," Victor said. He turned and headed to his class. The rosebushes of shame on his face became bouquets of love. Teresa is a great girl, he thought. And Mr. Bueller is a good guy.

He raced to metal shop. After metal shop there was biology, and after biology a long sprint to the public library, where he checked out three French textbooks.

He was going to like seventh grade.

🎵 67 🎵

Le bateau est sur l'eau (lə ba tō ā sûr lō): French; meaning "The boat is on the water."

5 Students might **visualize** in order to clarify the author's description of Victor. The "rosebushes of shame" refer to Victor's blushes of embarrassment when he is sure he has made a fool of himself. The "bouquets of love" refer to Victor's blushes of happiness when Teresa asks him to help her with French.

Discussing Strategy Use

Invite volunteers to share ways in which they used the reading strategies as they read. You might ask them if the story reminded them of anything. Some of them may have made connections to something that happened in their own lives. Thinking about how they would feel in Victor's situation may help them to understand his behavior. As the students share their reactions, point out that when they do this they are using the reading strategy of **making connections**.

* ### EXPLORING THROUGH DISCUSSION

Reflecting on the Selection
Whole-Group Discussion

The whole group discusses the selection and any personal thoughts, reactions, or questions that it raises. During this time, students also **return to the clues, problems, and wonderings** they noted on the chalkboard during browsing.

Assessment

To assess the students' understanding of the text, engage in a discussion to **determine whether the students have grasped the following ideas:**
- whether Victor accomplishes what he wants by pretending to know French
- whether this experience will make Victor a better student, and why

Response Journal

Students may wish to record their personal responses to the selection.

Exploring Concepts Within the Selection
Small-Group Discussion

Small groups discuss the relationship of the selection to learning. Circulate among the groups and observe the discussions. Refer the students to the Concept Board and the Question Board to keep them focused on their original ideas about learning and to see if those ideas have changed as a result of reading this selection.

Sharing Ideas About Explorable Concepts

Have the groups **report** and **discuss** their **ideas** with the rest of the class. It is crucial that the students' ideas determine this discussion.
- Some students may think that Victor will become a better learner based on the events in the story.
- Students may also comment that people may have many different reasons for wanting to learn a subject.

As these ideas and others are stated, have the students **add them to** the **Question Board** or the **Concept Board.**

Exploring Concepts Across Selections

Ask the students how this story reminds them of other selections they have read.
- The students may remember that, like Victor Rodriguez, Rufus Moffat is willing to learn something in order to accomplish a personal goal: Rufus learns to write his name in order to check out a library book; Victor plans to learn French in order to win the admiration of Teresa.

Recording Ideas

As students complete the above discussions, ask them how to sum up what they have learned from their conversations and to tell how they might use this information in further explorations. Any special information or insights may be recorded on the **Concept Board.** Any further questions that they would like to think about, pursue, or investigate may be recorded on the **Question Board.** Students may want to discuss the progress that has been made on their questions. They may also want to cross out any questions that no longer warrant consideration.

TIP FOR ENGLISH LANGUAGE LEARNERS

Provide an opportunity for conversational practice. Pair English Language Learners with each other or with native English-speaking students. Have them share their ideas about how the selection relates to learning.

Evaluating Discussions

"Mukasa at School" by John Nagenda

_____
_____
_____
_____
_____
_____

"Do Bananas Chew Gum?" by Jamie Gilson

_____
_____
_____
_____
_____
_____

"Seventh Grade" by Gary Soto

_____
_____
_____
_____
_____
_____

Unit 1/Learning   EN 5

Explorer's Notebook, page 5

❯ After discussion, the students should individually record their ideas on page 5 of their Explorer's Notebook.

Professional Checkpoint: Cognitive and Responsive Reading

Discussing strategy use and evaluating class discussions as a group will help the students understand that they must remain aware of ways that help them make sense of what they read. Encourage each student to actively participate in these discussions.

Notes:

2 READING WITH A WRITER'S EYE

MINILESSON

Writer's Craft:
Setting

Ask the students to share what they know about the settings of stories. Remind them, if necessary, that *setting* is the time and place in which the events of a story occur. Explain that it is important for authors to provide vivid settings for their stories so that readers can picture what is taking place.

Point out that in "Seventh Grade" Soto does not simply describe the story's setting all at once, but instead **drops in details throughout the selection, to help readers visualize where the action is occurring.** Ask the students to identify when and where the selection takes place. Help them establish that the story is set in the present, as evidenced by details such as the mention of a computer card and the descriptions of the models in *GQ* magazine. Point out that the author gives not only some general information about the region in which Victor lives, but also specific details about the various rooms, hallways, and other areas of the school where the story's action takes place. As an example, share some of the following details:

- page 60, paragraph 1: "wobbly card table"; "Fresno, where summer days reached 110 degrees in the shade."
- page 60, paragraph 2: "the gym full of students in their new fall clothes."
- page 62, paragraph 5: "a tinny, three-beat bell"

Point out that Soto creates the setting by describing what Victor might see, hear, and feel. Realistic details about furniture, temperature, people, and sounds all help to make his story seem realistic and help readers make connections with the story. You might also point out that Soto includes some local language which helps make the setting seem more authentic.

Selective Reading:
Focus on Setting

Invite the students to locate details that describe other settings in the story. You might list these on the board in the form of a chart like the one pictured below.

Selection-Based Practice

Setting	Details That Describe Setting
hall	the water fountain that never turned off
homeroom	crackling loudspeaker
lunch area	small, triangular-shaped campus under a plum tree

Independent Practice:
Setting

> ➤ Use Reading/Writing Connection, page 9, to examine settings further. Have students record details from this selection or other stories that help them visualize where and when a story takes place.

Recording Examples
of Setting

Distribute copies of Reproducible Master 23 and have students insert these pages in the Story Elements section of their Writer's Notebook. Make available additional copies of this page so that the students can record examples of setting as the year goes on.

WRITING

Linking Reading
to Writing

Invite students to tell about a setting they would like to use in a story or in a personal narrative. This should be a place with which they are familiar. Encourage them to elaborate on what makes this setting interesting and how it might fit into a story.

✳ Writing Process

Have students continue the realistic fiction pieces they began in the previous lesson. As they develop and revise their stories, remind them to include details that will make their settings interesting. Students may want to note in list form some details of their settings.

TIP FOR ENGLISH LANGUAGE LEARNERS

English Language Learners may benefit from illustrating a setting they want to use in their writing to help clarify their ideas. Associating pictures with English concepts or words helps the students to think more in English.

Reading/Writing Connection, page 9

"Seventh Grade"

Setting

In order to help readers visualize what is happening in a story, authors often include information about the setting. Record any details from stories you have read that help you picture where and when the story takes place.

Story	Setting	Details That Describe the Setting
"Seventh Grade"	homeroom	crackling loudspeaker

Name

Copyright © 1995 Open Court Publishing Company

Unit 1/Learning

Story Elements
R/WC 9

Reproducible Master 23

Examples of Setting

Story/Author	Time	Place	Details of Setting

Name

Copyright © 1995 Open Court Publishing Company

Writer's Notebook: Story Elements

RM 23

VOCABULARY

Learning-related words the students might discuss include the following: **biology, campus, catechism, computer, elective, ferocity, herded, lingered, populace, portly, propelled, sprint, waddled**

Remind students to add words and phrases to the Personal Dictionary section of their Writer's Notebook. Then provide an opportunity for volunteers to share words and phrases they've added and tell why they chose them. Allow time for the students to complete Vocabulary Exploration forms, Reproducible Master 14, for those words they wish to learn or that are important to the unit concepts. For additional opportunities to build vocabulary, see **Teacher Tool Card 75.**

3 GUIDED AND INDEPENDENT EXPLORATION

EXPLORING CONCEPTS BEYOND THE TEXT

Guided Exploration

Students will select activities in which they explore the concept of learning. Refer them to the **Exploration Activities poster** and give them time to choose an activity, to discuss what they wish to explore, and to decide how they wish to go about it. If the students need further help, here are some suggestions:

❯ Some students might be interested in making a field trip to the junior high in their school district or, if seventh grade is in the same building as fifth grade, to a seventh-grade classroom. Have students use Explorer's Notebook, page 17, to organize questions they want to ask and information they collect on their field trip.

❯ Distribute copies of Home/School Connection 7 in order to involve the students' families in this investigation of schooling beyond fifth grade.

Continuing Exploration

As the students discuss and work on exploration activities, additional questions about learning may arise. Encourage them to add these questions to the **Question Board.**

* Exploring Through Reflective Activities

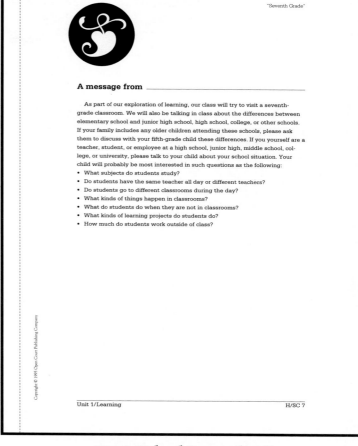

Visiting Seventh Grade

This is what I know about the seventh grade before visiting:

_____

_____

_____

_____

These are some things that I would like to find out about seventh grade:

_____

_____

_____

_____

These are things that I have learned about seventh grade:

_____

_____

_____

_____

These are things that I would like to know about high school, college, or another school:

_____

_____

_____

_____

Unit 1/Learning EN 17

Explorer's Notebook, page 17

"Seventh Grade"

A message from _____

As part of our exploration of learning, our class will try to visit a seventh-grade classroom. We will also be talking in class about the differences between elementary school and junior high school, high school, college, or other schools. If your family includes any older children attending these schools, please ask them to discuss with your fifth-grade child these differences. If you yourself are a teacher, student, or employee at a high school, junior high, middle school, college, or university, please talk to your child about your school situation. Your child will probably be most interested in such questions as the following:

- What subjects do students study?
- Do students have the same teacher all day or different teachers?
- Do students go to different classrooms during the day?
- What kinds of things happen in classrooms?
- What do students do when they are not in classrooms?
- What kinds of learning projects do students do?
- How much do students work outside of class?

Unit 1/Learning H/SC 7

Home/School Connection 7

*INDEPENDENT WORKSHOP
Building a Community of Scholars

Student-Directed Reading, Writing, and Discussion

Remind the students that, during the first part of Independent Workshop, they will work collaboratively in small groups to discuss their explorations. Remind them to make individual assignments within each group, if they wish, and then to come back together to share their findings.

Encourage them to check the Question Board and the Concept Board for new ideas relating to learning. New ideas about their questions may prompt them to explore new resources.

Additional Opportunities for Independent Reading, Writing, and Cross-curricular Activities

✳ Reading Roundtable
Encourage students to share with each other interesting reading they have been doing. For a review of **Reading Roundtable**, see **Learning Framework Card 6.**

✳ Writing Seminar
Remind the students that the writing process is recursive. They may need to revise some pieces more than once. They should use the process to help them develop and revise their fiction pieces to their satisfaction. If your class is using the optional Writer's Handbook, students doing peer tutoring might want to use it as a resource.

Portfolio
Remind students to think about which pieces of writing they might choose to put into their portfolios.

Cross-curricular Activity Cards
The following Cross-curricular Activity Card in the Student Toolbox is appropriate for this story:
• 5 Social Studies—France

Additional Opportunities for Solving Learning Problems

Tutorial
Use this time to help individuals or small groups who have exhibited a need in any area. Encourage students to discuss with you any areas in which they are having difficulties. The following teaching aids are available in the Teacher Toolbox for your convenience:
• Writer's Craft/Reading: Setting, Teacher Tool Card 14
• Writer's Craft/Reading: Characterization, Teacher Tool Card 13
• Writer's Craft/Reading: Using Dialogue in a Story, Teacher Tool Card 19
• Grammar, Mechanics, and Usage: Using Adjectives and Adverbs, Teacher Tool Card 68

The Struggle for an Education

1 READING THE SELECTION

About the Selection

This selection from Booker T. Washington's autobiography tells the inspiring story of how sixteen-year-old Washington set off on a five-hundred-mile journey to Hampton, Virginia with only a few dollars in his pocket. A school had recently been opened in Hampton to educate former slaves, and Washington was determined to go there. After many difficulties, he arrived, but he still had to pass the head teacher's unusual "entrance examination." Washington's serious, dignified tone conveys his sincere conviction that learning can give a person "a new life" and prepare him or her to "accomplish the most good in the world."

Link to the Unit Concepts

Improving oneself through education is an important theme in Washington's autobiography. In this selection, pages 68–75, readers will be impressed by young Washington's willingness to work hard and to endure cold, hunger, and exhaustion in order to have a chance at education.

About the Author

"The Struggle for an Education" is an excerpt from Booker T. Washington's *Up from Slavery: An Autobiography,* which was first published in 1901. In this book, which became a bestseller, Washington tells the story of his life from his birth as a slave to his emergence as a political leader.

Washington, who lived from 1856 to 1915, was the most influential African-American leader of his time. He gained prominence as the head of Tuskegee Normal and Industrial Institute, the vocational school for African Americans that he started in an old abandoned church and shack in 1881. The school trained teachers and taught trades such as carpentry, farming, and mechanics. After founding the school, Washington spent most of his time traveling around the country giving

LESSON OVERVIEW

"The Struggle for an Education" by Booker T. Washington, pages 68–75

READING THE SELECTION

Materials
Student anthology, pp. 68–75
Explorer's Notebook, p. 6

FYI
Learning Framework Cards
- Setting Reading Goals and Expectations, 1A
- Checking Understanding, 1C

READING WITH A WRITER'S EYE

Minilessons
Writer's Craft: Providing Specific Facts
Writer's Craft: Genre—Autobiography

Materials
Reading/Writing Connection, pp. 10–11
Reproducible Masters 14, 24

FYI
Teacher Tool Card
- Spelling and Vocabulary: Building Vocabulary, 75

Options for Instruction
Writer's Craft: Formal Versus Informal Language
Grammar, Mechanics, and Usage: Compound Sentences
Grammar, Mechanics, and Usage: Clauses and Phrases
(Use Teacher Tool Cards listed below.)

GUIDED AND INDEPENDENT EXPLORATION

Materials
Explorer's Notebook, pp. 14–15, 18
Home/School Connection 8

Optional Materials from Student Toolbox
Tradebook Connection Cards

Cross-curricular Activity Card
- 6 Social Studies—Washington's Journey

Student Tool Cards
- Writer's Craft/Reading: Telling Important Facts, 40
- Writer's Craft/Reading: Reading and Writing Biography and Autobiography, 8

Independent Workshop
- Writer's Craft/Reading: Differences Between Formal and Informal Language, 18
- Grammar, Mechanics, and Usage: Compound Sentences, 48
- Grammar, Mechanics, and Usage: Phrases, 49
- Grammar, Mechanics, and Usage: Clauses, 50

FYI
Teacher Tool Cards
- Writer's Craft/Reading: Elaboration Through Providing Specific Facts, 40
- Writer's Craft/Reading: Genre—Biography and Autobiography, 8
- Writer's Craft/Reading: Formal Versus Informal Writing, 18
- Grammar, Mechanics, and Usage: Compound Sentences, 48
- Grammar, Mechanics, and Usage: Phrases, 49
- Grammar, Mechanics, and Usage: Clauses, 50

NOTES

Asterisks (*) throughout the lesson indicate learning frameworks. Learning Framework Cards and Teacher Tool Cards can be found in the Teacher Toolbox.

speeches to raise money to support it. He stressed his belief that before they could hope to obtain political and social equality, African Americans needed to learn job skills, work hard, become property owners, and increase their economic power.

Washington became an advisor on racial problems to Presidents Theodore Roosevelt and William Howard Taft and influenced the appointment of several African Americans to federal office. He also owned or supported many African-American newspapers and founded the National Negro Business League to help African-American businesses. Washington secretly financed lawsuits that opposed segregation and that argued for the rights of African Americans to vote and to serve on juries. However, he never supported these causes publicly because he was not willing to alienate the white Southerners who contributed to his school.

INFORMATION FOR THE STUDENT

- Make sure that students understand that this selection is part of an **autobiography,** the story of a person's life written by that person.
- Before beginning the selection, have the students read the italicized paragraph that introduces it.
- Share any information about the author that you think will interest the students. They may be interested to learn that Washington became respected as a national leader in his lifetime.
- After they have read the selection, the students may be interested to know that once he was admitted as a student to Hampton Institute, Washington was given a job as school janitor, which enabled him to earn enough money for his room and board. Upon completing his studies, Washington became a teacher at the institute.

*   ## COGNITIVE AND RESPONSIVE READING

Activating Prior Knowledge

Ask the students to tell what they know about U.S. history just following the Civil War, in the period usually referred to as Reconstruction. Ask them what they know about educational opportunities for former slaves at that time.

Setting Reading Goals and Expectations

Have the students **browse the selection,** using the clues/problems/wondering procedure. Students will return to these observations after reading. For a review of **browsing,** see **Learning Framework Card 1A, Setting Reading Goals and Expectations.**

Recommendations for Reading the Selection

Since many of the sentences in "The Struggle for an Education" are long and difficult, most students would benefit from reading part or all of the selection aloud. During oral reading, use and encourage think-alouds. During silent reading, allow discussion as needed. Discuss problems, strategies, and reactions after reading. This would also be a good selection for **responding** to text by **expressing opinions** while reading aloud. Model this response, and then invite the students to respond.

TIP FOR ENGLISH LANGUAGE LEARNERS

Give English Language Learners a chance to build a broad base of knowledge and cultural understanding. Invite them to talk about anything they know about slavery, the Civil War, or the Reconstruction period in the United States.

About the
Reading
Strategies

Although his story is straightforward, Washington's style, with its long sentences and long words, is challenging. The students may find that the strategy of **asking questions** will help them understand the text.

The students should understand that good readers ask themselves questions while reading. This is a way of checking their understanding as new information is presented. Ask the students whether they ever ask themselves questions as they read. If so, how does this help them better understand what they are reading. Some students may be too busy trying to read words correctly to stop and ask themselves questions that will help them understand a text. They may not know that they should stop and ask a question, or they may not have enough experience to know what kinds of questions would help them.

Most students do have experience responding to teachers' questions. They can ask themselves similar questions and then find answers. By fifth grade, students should be asking questions—including some which require them to make inferences—about the central points of a text. Their questions should require more than a yes or no response and should lead to a discussion of the passage they have just read.

Direct the students' attention to the **reading strategy poster Checking Understanding**, and read the part about **asking questions.** Discuss the strategy and have a volunteer read aloud the questions that accompany it. Also remind the students that if they do not understand a sentence, they can read it aloud and try to put it into their own words.

For a review of the strategy of **asking questions** see **Learning Framework card 1C, Checking Understanding.**

Think-Aloud Prompts
for Use in Oral Reading

The think-aloud prompts are placed where students may encounter difficulties with the text. These are merely suggestions for ways in which the strategies may be used. Remind the students to refer to the **reading strategy posters** and to use any strategy they find helpful as they read.

Since Washington's book was published nearly one hundred years ago, students should expect to find some old-fashioned language and unfamiliar words as they read. During the early 1900s, British spellings were commonly used in American books; some students may notice that words such as *travelled*, *coloured*, and *favour* are spelled differently than they would be in a modern American book.

> *Introducing Asking Questions*

> *Reading Strategy Posters*

TEACHING TIP It is important for students to recognize that they may understand all the words in a sentence without understanding the sentence. Just as important, they may understand what the sentence as a whole means even if they are unclear about a certain word.

THINK ALOUD PROMPTS

These prompts may be used as guides to promote cognitive and responsive reading.

1 The old-fashioned language may be confusing for some students. If they ask for clarification of the first few sentences, invite volunteers to put each sentence into their own words. If necessary, model this strategy by paraphrasing the first sentence yourself.

2 The first pages contain a lot of information. To check their understanding of what they have read thus far, the students may find it helpful to **ask questions** like the following:

How did Washington get the money to go to the Hampton Institute?

Have the students check to make sure that the answers to their questions can be found in the text. Discuss whether their questions elicit the most important points in these paragraphs. If not, have the students continue to suggest questions until they arrive at some that do.

THE STRUGGLE FOR AN EDUCATION

from UP FROM SLAVERY:
AN AUTOBIOGRAPHY
by Booker T. Washington
illustrated by Marcy Ramsey

Booker T. Washington
as a young man.

Booker T. Washington was born a slave in Virginia in 1856. After being freed, he moved with his family to West Virginia. He taught himself how to read from an old spelling book that his mother found, and he went for lessons at a night school while working days at a salt refinery. Later, he worked at a coal mine. When he heard about a new school in Virginia for African Americans, the Hampton Normal and Agricultural Institute, he resolved to find a way to go there. In order to earn the money he needed, he took a job as a servant in the home of the mine owners, Mr. and Mrs. Ruffner, for a salary of five dollars a month.

❦ 68 ❦

Notwithstanding my success at Mrs. Ruffner's I did not give up the idea of going to the Hampton Institute. In the fall of 1872 I determined to make an effort to get there, although, as I have stated, I had no definite idea of the direction in which Hampton was, or of what it would cost to go there. I do not think that any one thoroughly sympathized with me in my ambition to go to Hampton unless it was my mother, and she was troubled with a grave fear that I was starting out on a "wild-goose chase." At any rate, I got only a half-hearted consent from her that I might start. The small amount of money that I had earned had been consumed by my stepfather and the remainder of the family, with the exception of a very few dollars, and so I had very little with which to buy clothes and pay my travelling expenses. My brother John helped me all that he could, but of course that was not a great deal, for his work was in the coal-mine, where he did not earn much, and most of what he did earn went in the direction of paying the household expenses.

Perhaps the thing that touched and pleased me most in connection with my starting for Hampton was the interest that many of the older coloured people took in the matter. They had spent the best days of their lives in slavery, and hardly expected to live to see the time when they would see a member of their race leave home to attend a boarding-school. Some of these older people would give me a nickel, others a quarter, or a handkerchief.

Finally the great day came, and I started for Hampton. I had only a small, cheap satchel that contained what few articles of clothing I could get. My mother at the time was rather weak and broken in health. I hardly expected to see her again,

❦ 69 ❦

and thus our parting was all the more sad. She, however, was very brave through it all. At that time there were no through trains connecting that part of West Virginia with eastern Virginia. Trains ran only a portion of the way, and the remainder of the distance was travelled by stage-coaches.

The distance from Malden to Hampton is about five hundred miles. I had not been away from home many hours before it began to grow painfully evident that I did not have enough money to pay my fare to Hampton. One experience I shall long remember. I had been travelling over the mountains most of the afternoon in an old-fashioned stage-coach, when, late in the evening, the coach stopped for the night at a common, unpainted house called a hotel.

All the other passengers except myself were whites. In my ignorance I supposed that the little hotel existed for the purpose of accommodating the passengers who travelled on the stage-coach. The difference that the colour of one's skin would make I had not thought anything about. After all the other passengers had been shown rooms and were getting ready for supper, I shyly presented myself before the man at the desk. It is true I had practically no money in my pocket with which to pay for bed or food, but I had hoped in some way to beg my way into the good graces of the landlord, for at that season in the mountains of Virginia the weather was cold, and I wanted to get indoors for the night. Without asking as to whether I had any money, the man at the desk firmly refused to even consider the matter of providing me with food or lodging. This was my first experience in finding out what the colour of my skin meant. In some way I managed to keep warm by walking about, and so got through the night.

My whole soul was so bent upon reaching Hampton that I did not have time to cherish any bitterness toward the hotel-keeper.

By walking, begging rides both in wagons and in the cars, in some way, after a number of days, I reached the city of Richmond, Virginia, about eighty-two miles from Hampton. When I reached there, tired, hungry, and dirty, it was late in the night. I had never been in a large city, and this rather added to my misery. When I reached Richmond, I was completely out of money. I had not a single acquaintance in the place, and, being unused to city ways, I did not know where to go. I applied at several places for lodging, but they all wanted money, and that was what I did not have. Knowing nothing else better to do, I walked the streets. In doing this I passed by many food-stands where fried chicken and half-moon apple pies were piled high and made to present a most tempting appearance. At that time it seemed to me that I would have promised all that I expected to possess in the future to have gotten hold of one of those chicken legs or one of those pies. But I could not get either of these, nor anything else to eat.

I must have walked the streets till after midnight. At last I became so exhausted that I could walk no longer. I was tired, I was hungry, I was everything but discouraged. Just about the time when I reached extreme physical exhaustion, I came upon a portion of a street where the board sidewalk was considerably elevated. I waited for a few minutes, till I was sure that no passers-by could see me, and then crept under the sidewalk and lay for the night upon the ground, with my satchel of clothing for a pillow. Nearly all night I could hear the tramp of feet over my head. The next morning I found

3 This paragraph tells why Washington spent a cold night outside instead of getting a room at the hotel. Some students may wish to check their understanding of how Washington felt about this situation. **Question asking** may help them do that. If necessary, have a volunteer ask a question that can be answered by reading the text.

myself somewhat refreshed, but I was extremely hungry, because it had been a long time since I had had sufficient food. As soon as it became light enough for me to see my surroundings I noticed that I was near a large ship, and that this ship seemed to be unloading a cargo of pig iron. I went at once to the vessel and asked the captain to permit me to help unload the vessel in order to get money for food. The captain, a white man, who seemed to be kindhearted, consented. I worked long enough to earn money for my breakfast, and it seems to me, as I remember it now, to have been about the best breakfast that I have ever eaten.

My work pleased the captain so well that he told me if I desired I could continue working for a small amount per day. This I was very glad to do. I continued working on this vessel for a number of days. After buying food with the small wages I received there was not much left to add to the amount I

must get to pay my way to Hampton. In order to economize in every way possible, so as to be sure to reach Hampton in a reasonable time, I continued to sleep under the same sidewalk that gave me shelter the first night I was in Richmond. Many years after that the coloured citizens of Richmond very kindly tendered me a reception at which there must have been two thousand people present. This reception was held not far from the spot where I slept the first night I spent in that city, and I must confess that my mind was more upon the sidewalk that first gave me shelter than upon the reception, agreeable and cordial as it was. **(4)**

When I had saved what I considered enough money with which to reach Hampton, I thanked the captain of the vessel for his kindness, and started again. Without any unusual occurrence I reached Hampton, with a surplus of exactly fifty cents with which to begin my education. To me it had been a long, eventful journey; but the first sight of the large, three-story, brick school building seemed to have rewarded me for all that I had undergone in order to reach the place. If the people who gave the money to provide that building could appreciate the influence the sight of it had upon me, as well as upon thousands of other youths, they would feel all the more encouraged to make such gifts. It seemed to me to be the largest and most beautiful building I had ever seen. The sight of it seemed to give me a new life. I felt that a new kind of existence had now begun—that life would now have a new meaning. I felt that I had reached the promised land, and I resolved to let no obstacle prevent me from putting forth the highest effort to fit myself to accomplish the most good in the world. **(5)**

73

---

(4) You might model thinking about the contrast that Washington sees between his experiences on his way to Hampton and his situation at the time of the reception. Washington is thinking about the period of his life when he was poor, tired, hungry, and friendless. By the time of the reception, he is so important that two thousand people want to meet him.

(5) To draw out the main point of this paragraph, students might **ask** a **question** such as this:

How does Washington feel at the end of his journey?

If necessary, explain that the expression "the promised land" is a reference to the biblical story of Moses, who led his people out of slavery in Egypt and through the wilderness to the land that their God had promised them. Many African-American spirituals from slavery times refer to this story.

As soon as possible after reaching the grounds of the Hampton Institute, I presented myself before the head teacher for assignment to a class. Having been so long without proper food, a bath and change of clothing, I did not, of course, make a very favourable impression upon her, and I could see at once that there were doubts in her mind about the wisdom of admitting me as a student. I felt that I could hardly blame her if she got the idea that I was a worthless loafer or tramp. For some time she did not refuse to admit me, neither did she decide in my favour, and I continued to linger about her, and to impress her in all the ways I could with my worthiness. In the meantime I saw her admitting other students, and that added greatly to my discomfort, for I felt, deep down in my heart, that I could do as well as they, if I could only get a chance to show what was in me.

After some hours had passed, the head teacher said to me: "The adjoining recitation-room needs sweeping. Take the broom and sweep it."

It occurred to me at once that here was my chance. Never did I receive an order with more delight. I knew that I could sweep, for Mrs. Ruffner had thoroughly taught me how to do that when I lived with her.

I swept the recitation-room three times. Then I got a dusting-cloth and I dusted it four times. All the woodwork around the walls, every bench, table, and desk, I went over four times with my dusting-cloth. Besides, every piece of furniture had been moved and every closet and corner in the room had been thoroughly cleaned. I had the feeling that in a large measure my future depended upon the impression I made upon the teacher in the cleaning of that room. When I was through, I reported to the head teacher. She was a "Yankee" woman who knew just where to look for dirt. She went into the room and inspected the floor and closets; then she took her handkerchief and rubbed it on the woodwork about the walls, and over the table and benches. When she was unable to find one bit of dirt on the floor, or a particle of dust on any of the furniture, she quietly remarked, "I guess you will do to enter this institution."

I was one of the happiest souls on earth. The sweeping of that room was my college examination, and never did any youth pass an examination for entrance into Harvard or Yale that gave him more genuine satisfaction. I have passed several examinations since then, but I have always felt that this was the best one I ever passed.

☙ 75 ❧

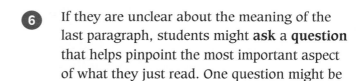 If they are unclear about the meaning of the last paragraph, students might **ask** a **question** that helps pinpoint the most important aspect of what they just read. One question might be

Why does Washington say that this was the best examination he ever passed?

Discussing Strategy Use
Discuss with the students the strategies they used to help them understand this selection. If they **asked questions** while reading, encourage the students to share how this strategy helped them to understand the text.

* | EXPLORING THROUGH DISCUSSION

Reflecting on the Selection
Whole-Group Discussion

The whole group discusses the selection and any personal thoughts, reactions, or questions that it raises. During this time, students also **return to the clues, problems, and wonderings** they noted on the chalkboard during browsing.

Assessment

To assess the students' understanding of the text, engage in a discussion to **determine whether they have grasped the following ideas:**
- what obstacles Washington had to overcome in order to attend school
- why Washington worked hard to gain entry to the Hampton Institute

Response Journal

Students may wish to record their personal responses to the selection.

Exploring Concepts Within the Selection
Small-Group Discussion

Small groups discuss the relationship of the selection to learning. Circulate among the groups and observe the discussions. Refer the students to the Concept Board and the Question Board to keep them focused on their original ideas about learning and to see if those ideas have changed as a result of reading this selection.

Sharing Ideas About Explorable Concepts

Have the groups **report** and **discuss** their **ideas** with the rest of the class. It is crucial that the students' ideas determine this discussion.
- The students may mention that Washington endured much discomfort and worked extremely hard in order to attend school.
- Some students may point out that Washington felt that having reached school, he had begun a new life.

As these ideas and others are stated, have the students **add them to** the **Question Board** or the **Concept Board.**

Have the students look at the fine-art pieces on pages 76–77 of the pupil anthology and briefly discuss *Tree of Knowledge* by Terry Chacon and Josefina Quezada and *The Library* by Jacob Lawrence. Students may wish to express their thoughts and feelings about these works and any connections they think the pieces might have to Washington's ideas about education.
- Students may notice that *The Tree of Knowledge* is painted on the outside wall of a public library in East Los Angeles and may comment on the symbolism of the tree, the books, and the rainbow in the mural.
- Students may be interested to learn that Jacob Lawrence, the painter of *The Library,* was himself much influenced by art and cultural programs at the 135th Street Library in New York City.

Exploring Concepts Across Selections

Ask the students how this selection reminds them of others they have read in this unit.
- Students may notice that Booker T. Washington and Dr. Samuel Gridley Howe (Laura Bridgman's teacher in "Into the Light of Day") used similar language when describing the effect of learning on

TIP FOR ENGLISH LANGUAGE LEARNERS

Encourage English Language Learners to participate in the whole-group discussion. Knowing that they will be heard and receive some response helps to build confidence in speaking.

Fine Art

Recording Concept Information continued

"The Struggle for an Education" by Booker T. Washington

_____

_____

_____

_____

_____

_____

_____

_____

_____

_____

"A Real Job" by Jean Little

_____

_____

_____

_____

_____

_____

_____

_____

_____

_____

_____

6 EN   Learning/Unit 1

Explorer's Notebook, page 6

people's lives: Washington wrote about arriving at Hampton Institute that "a new kind of existence had now begun . . . life would now have new meaning," and Dr. Howe wrote that learning to communicate with language brought Laura Bridgman "into the light of day and into human society."

Recording Ideas

As students complete the above discussions, ask them how to **sum up what they have learned from their conversations and to tell how they might use this information** in further explorations. Any special information or insights may be recorded on the **Concept Board**. Any further questions that they would like to think about, pursue, or investigate may be recorded on the **Question Board**. Students may want to discuss the progress that has been made on their questions. They may also want to cross out any questions that no longer warrant consideration.

➤ After discussion, the students should individually record their ideas on page 6 of their Explorer's Notebook.

Evaluating Discussion

Professional Checkpoint: Cognitive and Responsive Reading

Comprehension comes as a result of the blending of several things—ability to decode words, knowledge of word meaning, efficient use of context clues, prior knowledge of the subject or parts of the subject, and the ability to connect what is being read to other material one has read. The students' ability to participate in class discussion of the reading material is effective proof that all of these aspects of the reading process have, indeed, come together and resulted in thorough comprehension.

Notes:

2 READING WITH A WRITER'S EYE

MINILESSONS

Writer's Craft: Providing Specific Facts

Ask students to tell what it means to explain something. Remind them that **writers often use specific facts** to explain or expand on an idea. Point out that Booker T. Washington uses specific facts to help the reader understand some events in "The Struggle for an Education."

For example, in the first two paragraphs on page 70, Washington provides extra information about trains between Malden and Hampton so that readers will understand how difficult it was to travel between the two places. On page 71 Washington includes specific details about his first night in Richmond so that readers will understand just how desolate he felt on his first night in a large city.

Selective Reading: Focus on Specific Facts

Now have the students find other examples from the selection in which Washington uses specific facts to elaborate. Encourage volunteers to read each passage they find and to tell why Washington might have felt it important to provide further information for the reader. Students may mention the following passages:

- page 73, paragraph 1: Washington includes the information that Hampton Institute was a "large, three-story brick school building."
- page 75, paragraph 3: The author explains just how thoroughly he cleaned the recitation room.

Selection-Based Practice

Independent Practice: Specific Facts

➤ Have the students work in small collaborative groups, using Reading/Writing Connection, page 10, to extend their discussion of how writers use specific facts.

"The Struggle for an Education"

Telling Important Facts

Find examples from "The Struggle for an Education" or other selections in which the author uses specific facts to elaborate on an idea.

Selection: _____ Page: _____
What idea is being elaborated upon? _____
_____
What specific facts are provided? _____
_____
_____
_____
_____

Selection: _____ Page: _____
What idea is being elaborated upon? _____
_____
What specific facts are provided? _____
_____
_____
_____
_____

Selection: _____ Page: _____
What idea is being elaborated upon? _____
_____
What specific facts are provided? _____
_____
_____
_____
_____

Elaboration _____
10 R/WC   Learning/Unit 1

Reading/Writing Connection, page 10

Writer's Craft: Genre— Autobiography

Ask students to tell what they know about autobiographies. Explain that Booker T. Washington's *Up from Slavery,* from which "The Struggle for an Education" was excerpted, was a best-selling book when it was first published and is a well-crafted example of an autobiography. Students may find it easier to remember the meaning of the word *autobiography* if they understand that it is made up of the word parts *auto-,* meaning "self," *bio-,* meaning "life," and *graph-,* meaning "something written."

Briefly discuss the following elements of an autobiography:
- written by a person about his or her own life experiences
- usually written in the first person
- usually arranges events in chronological order
- includes specific dates and places
- can include photographs or illustrations
- includes descriptions of people and places, conversations, and other details to tell about incidents in the writer's life
- expresses the thoughts and feelings of the writer
- often written in a style that shows the personality of the writer
- often reflects what the writer believes to be important about his or her life

Elements of Autobiography

Selective Reading:
Focus on
Autobiography

Now have the students reread the selection in order to discuss elements of autobiography within the selection.

Students will notice that Washington's autobiography is written in the first person and includes events in his life arranged in chronological order. Some students may point out that Washington includes not only factual information about dates and places and what he said or did, but also tells what he thought and how he felt about the things that happened to him. Ask students to think about and discuss what the style of the selection shows about Washington's personality and how the selection shows what Washington considered most important about his experiences.

Selection-Based
Practice

Independent Practice:
Autobiography

▶ To continue their discussion of autobiography, have students use Reading/Writing Connection, page 11.

Reading/Writing Connection, page 11

"The Struggle for an Education"

Autobiography

In "The Struggle for an Education" or in other autobiographies you have read, find examples of different kinds of information provided by authors.

Selection: _____ Author: _____
Specific dates or places mentioned: _____
_____
_____

Thoughts and feelings expressed by the author: _____
_____
_____

What the author's way of writing shows about himself or herself: _____
_____
_____
_____

Selection: _____ Author: _____
Specific dates or places mentioned: _____
_____
_____

Thoughts and feelings expressed by the author: _____
_____
_____

What the author's way of writing shows about himself or herself: _____
_____
_____
_____

Genre
_____
Unit 1/Learning   R/WC 11

Name

Copyright © 1995 Open Court Publishing Company

WRITING

Linking Reading to Writing

Remind the students that it is very important for writers to make their ideas clear to their readers. Encourage them to look through their writing folders for paragraphs that could be improved by the addition of **specific facts.** When they have had sufficient time to choose and revise a paragraph, invite volunteers to read their original paragraphs and the rewritten versions.

∗ Writing Process

Some students may want to use Washington's "Struggle for an Education" as a model to plan a piece of **autobiographical writing.** Remind them to incorporate what they've learned about autobiographies. Students can begin their pieces at this time and continue them after reading the next selection, which is also an excerpt from an autobiography.

❯ Distribute Reproducible Master 24, Elements of an Autobiography, and ask the students to use this guide as they write their autobiographies. Remind them to add this page to the Genres section of their Writer's Notebook.

Writing an Autobiography or Biography

Other students may be interested in beginning work on a short **biography** of Booker T. Washington or of another person who interests them. Remind them that the author of "Into the Light of Day," Edith Fisher Hunter, did a great deal of research about Laura Bridgman before she began her biography and that they, like other biographers, should read as much as they can from as many different sources as possible before beginning to write about their subjects. Several biographies and autobiographies are included on student bibliographies for this unit.

Allow time for students to brainstorm about possible subjects for biographical pieces and to discuss research methods they might use to find out more about the people they choose to write about. The book *Learning About Biographies: A Reading and Writing Approach for Children*, which is included on the professional bibliography in the introduction to this unit, may provide you with some ideas about how to help the students write interesting biographies.

VOCABULARY

Encourage the students to discuss words or phrases from the selection that they want to use in their speaking and writing or in their exploration for this unit. Words or phrases related to learning include the following: **ambition, boarding school, institution, examination, wild goose chase, obstacle, worthiness, Yankee**

VOCABULARY TIP Words are sometimes made up of smaller words or units of meaning, such as affixes. Model for students how to use these word parts to help determine the meanings of unfamiliar words.

Remind students to add words and phrases to the Personal Dictionary section of their Writer's Notebook. Then provide an opportunity for students to fill out Vocabulary Exploration forms, Reproducible Master 14, for words they wish to learn or for those that are important to the unit concepts. For additional opportunities to build vocabulary, see **Teacher Tool Card 75.**

Elements of an Autobiography

- written by a person about his or her own life experiences

- usually written in the first person

- usually includes events arranged in chronological order

- can include photographs or illustrations

- includes descriptions of people and places, conversations, and other details to tell about incidents in the writer's life

- expresses the thoughts and feelings of the writer

- often written in a style that shows the personality of the writer

- often reflects what the writer believes to be important about his or her life

Name _____

Autobiographies I Have Read

RM 24   Writer's Notebook: Genres

Copyright © 1995 Open Court Publishing Company

Reproducible Master 24

3 GUIDED AND INDEPENDENT EXPLORATION

EXPLORING CONCEPTS BEYOND THE TEXT

Guided Exploration

Students will select activities to explore the concept of learning. Refer students to the **Exploration Activities poster** and give them time to choose an activity and to discuss what they wish to explore and how they wish to go about it. If students need further help, here are some suggestions:

Students might engage in a debate on one of the central themes of "The Struggle for an Education": Did Booker T. Washington's struggle to be admitted to the Hampton Institute make his education all the more precious to him? This question might be generalized into a statement such as the following: The fight to overcome obstacles in order to get an education makes that education more meaningful to the individual who has to struggle.

❯ To continue their exploration of individuals who have struggled for an education, have students complete page 18 in their Explorer's Notebook.

* Exploration Through Reflective Activities

Having a Debate

Obstacles to an Education

On the numbered lines below, list different obstacles that people must overcome to get an education.

1. _____
2. _____
3. _____
4. _____
5. _____
6. _____

What are some possible solutions to these problems? On the lines below, list some ways that people might overcome the obstacles that you have listed above.

_____
_____
_____
_____
_____
_____
_____
_____
_____
_____
_____
_____
_____
_____
_____

18 EN   Learning/Unit 1

Explorer's Notebook, page 18

A message from _____

"The Struggle for an Education," an excerpt from Booker T. Washington's autobiography, *Up From Slavery,* describes the obstacles Washington had to overcome in order to get an education. Many people have to overcome obstacles, although most of these are not as severe as those Washington overcame. Do you know someone who has had to struggle to get an education? This person might be you, a friend, a family member, or someone else. With your child, discuss how this person overcame the obstacles in his or her way. Then have your child write a few notes below about this person's achievement. Encourage your child to bring this page back to school to share with others.

Unit 1/Learning   H/SC 8

Home/School Connection 8

❯ Send home Home/School Connection 8. Encourage students to discuss with adults someone who has overcome obstacles in order to get an education.

Continuing Exploration

During Independent Workshop, students may work in their collaborative groups to continue exploring learning. Encourage them to use their notes on pages 14 and 15 in their Explorer's Notebook to organize their ideas.

As students discuss their ideas and perform their small group assignments, questions may come up that they would like to think more about. Encourage students to add such questions to the Question Board for later consideration.

∗ INDEPENDENT WORKSHOP
Building a Community of Scholars

Student-Directed Reading, Writing, and Discussion

The students may explore their ideas and questions by using information from their collaborative groups. They may use any sources available to them. Some students may need larger blocks of time to complete certain aspects of their exploration of the concepts surrounding learning. Some students may be well into the writing stage. Others may need a gentle reminder from you about organizing their time according to an approaching deadline.

FINE ART
LEARNING

Reading Le Figaro. 1883. Mary Cassatt.
Oil on canvas. Private collection. Photo: Bridgeman Art Library/Art Resource

Tree of Knowledge. 1978. Terry Chacon and Josefina Quezada.
Mural. Anthony Quinn Public Library, Los Angeles, California. Photo: © Michael Grecco/Sygma

❧ 76 ❧

The Music Lesson. c. 1665. Johannes Vermeer.
Oil on canvas. The Royal Collection, © 1993 Her Majesty Queen Elizabeth II

St. Gregory and the scribes. 10th century.
Carved ivory bookcover. Kunsthistorisches Museum, Vienna

The Library. 1960. Jacob Lawrence.
Tempera on fiberboard. Gift of S.C. Johnson & Son, Inc., National Museum of American Art, Smithsonian Institution, Washington, D.C. © 1993 Jacob Lawrence/VAGA, NY. Photo: Art Resource

she began traveling throughout Europe to study in the museums there. She eventually settled in Paris and was encouraged by the artist Edgar Degas to exhibit with the Impressionists, whose everyday subjects, bright light, and use of color were, as yet, unappreciated by the art critics or by the public.

Cassatt's art centered on the human figure. She was able to catch the fleeting expressions of her subjects and treated them with a tenderness that was uniquely her own. She is probably best known for her studies of women and children. She helped influence American taste by urging her friends to buy Impressionist art and was responsible for many of the Impressionist works that made their way into American collections and museums.

Reading Le Figaro is a portrait of Cassatt's mother, Katherine. Katherine Johnston Cassatt had read and spoken French since her childhood. After coming to live with her daughter Mary in Paris in 1877, Katherine Cassatt avidly read American newspapers sent from Philadelphia as well as the French newspapers, such as the Paris daily, *Le Figaro*. This painting is considered by many to be Mary Cassatt's finest portrait.

Tree of Knowledge. 1978.
Terry Chacon and Josefina Quezada. Mural (paint on plaster).

The mural art movement in East Los Angeles and Southern California is a continuation of the mural tradition in Mexico. Since the beginning of the twentieth century, murals have reflected the social and political realities of Mexico, as in the work of such artists as José Clemente Orozco, David Alfaro Siqueiros, and Diego Rivera. In East Los Angeles the mural movement was a part of the Chicano movement in the late 1960s. The murals relate to the issues and the people that are important to the Mexican-American communities of East Los Angeles and Southern California.

In the mural shown here, from the Anthony Quinn Public Library of Los Angeles County, the tree of knowledge branches out over everyone who reads and wants to learn. The images of books and the word *Read* represent the tools necessary for education. At the center of the mural, a rainbow symbolizes enlightenment and the gaining of knowledge.

The Music Lesson. c. 1665.
Johannes Vermeer. Oil on canvas.

Johannes (or Jan) Vermeer (1632–1675) was born in Delft, the Netherlands, and is considered one of the greatest Dutch artists of the seventeenth century. Although he was twice elected to head the painter's guild (which was similar in purpose and function to a trade union) in his native city, his art made little mark during his lifetime and was little known until the late 1800s. Most of his paintings are serene images of domestic life among the wealthier middle classes. The majority of his works contain one or two figures in a room, engaged in everyday tasks. His paintings are distinguished by his use of light and texture. The young woman in *The Music Lesson* is standing at a type of harpsichord, a keyboard instrument that was a forerunner of the piano. The Latin inscription on the lid translates as "Music is the companion of joy and the medicine of pain." A cello lies on the floor in the foreground. Learning to play a few pieces of music on one or two instruments would have been an important part of this lady's education, adding to her aura of elegance and refinement.

St. Gregory and the scribes. Tenth century.
Carved ivory book cover.

St. Gregory, called the Great, was born in Rome about A.D. 540. He was the son of a wealthy aristocratic family but chose for himself the life of a monk, founding several monasteries when he inherited his family's estates. In A.D. 590 he became Pope Gregory I. Remembered as a great teacher and writer, especially popular in northern Europe, St. Gregory was often depicted in tenth- and early eleventh-century German art as he is shown here: busy at his desk and in the company of scribes.

In the early Middle Ages, ivory was mainly used in the making of religious objects, such as altar fronts or book covers for inspirational works. During this period, most ivory was taken from the tusks of West African elephants, although walrus ivory (much of it imported by Vikings) was also used.

The Library. 1960.
Jacob Lawrence. Tempera on fiberboard.

Jacob Lawrence (1917–   ) spent his youth in Harlem, just after the peak of the Harlem Renaissance of the 1920s. He learned about African art and African-American history from the programs, exhibitions, and lectures sponsored by the 135th Street Library, which had extensive collections of African Art and historical materials. Ernestine Rose, the librarian at that time, believed that it was vital for all members of the community to be aware of their history and cultural heritage.

Through programs at the Harlem Art Workshop during the 1930s, Lawrence was exposed to the work of many artists and poets. Lawrence was also inspired by the forceful, socially aware art of Francisco Goya, Honoré Daumier, and José Clemente Orozco.

Lawrence's subjects are drawn from the everyday lives of African Americans as well as from their history. His works have included a number of series based on historical figures and occurrences. Among these are the *Toussaint L'Ouverture* series (1937–1938), chronicling the rebellion of Haitian slaves, led by Toussaint L'Ouverture, against the French in the late eighteenth and early nineteenth centuries, which resulted in the formation of the Republic of Haiti; the *Frederick Douglass* series (1938–1939), concerning the former slave who became a famous writer, lecturer, and abolitionist; the *Harriet Tubman* series (1939–1940), telling the story of the courageous woman, also a former slave, who led many of her people out of the South and out of slavery (see page 36 in volume 5, book 2, unit 4: The Civil War); and *The Migration of the Negro* series (1940–1941), relating the journey of many African Americans (including Lawrence's own family) from the Caribbean Islands and the South to the industrial North.

Assessment

A Real Job

1 READING THE SELECTION
INFORMATION FOR THE TEACHER

About the Selection

This selection from Jean Little's autobiography tells of the award-winning writer's first job as a teacher of handicapped students. Even more than the courses in special education and phonics that she takes to prepare for this job, the author's unsentimental acceptance of her own visual handicap prepares her to teach these children and to understand their need for books that realistically reflect their world.

Link to the Unit Concepts

"A Real Job," pages 78–83, describes how Little learned from the children she taught and stresses the importance of identifying with the characters one reads about.

About the Author

"A Real Job" comes from *Little by Little: A Writer's Education,* an autobiography by Jean Little. The book concentrates on Little's school years. Because she was cross-eyed and had very limited vision, Little was teased by other children and left out of many activities. She found comfort in reading and was encouraged in her efforts to write stories similar to those she liked to read.

Despite her poor vision, Little attended regular schools through college, where she earned a degree in English. She also participated in other activities and particularly enjoyed scouting and going to dances. During the summers of her college years, she worked as a counselor at a camp for children with physical handicaps.

In an autobiographical sketch written early in her career, Little tells about how she became a writer.

When we came to Canada and I began to attend public school, life became very difficult indeed. I was chased home from school and teased unmercifully. I had no armor at hand so I gave up the

LESSON OVERVIEW

"A Real Job" by Jean Little, pages 78–83

READING THE SELECTION

Materials
Student anthology, pp. 78–83
Explorer's Notebook, p. 6
Assessment Masters 1–3

	N O T E S

READING WITH A WRITER'S EYE

Minilesson
Assessment

Materials
Reproducible Master 14

FYI
Teacher Tool Cards
• Spelling and Vocabulary: Building Vocabulary, 75

GUIDED AND INDEPENDENT EXPLORATION

Materials
Home/School Connection 9

Independent Workshop

Optional Materials from Student Toolbox
Tradebook Connection Cards

FYI
Learning Framework Card
• Reading Roundtable, 6

Asterisks (*) throughout the lesson indicate learning frameworks. Learning Framework Cards and Teacher Tool Cards can be found in the Teacher Toolbox.

fight and retreated to the public library. The head librarian in our local children's library told me recently that as a child I literally read every book on the shelves. I read; I day-dreamed; and I lied prodigiously—so I prepared myself for becoming a writer.

I wrote for fun—and then discovered therein a new way to gain approval. From the first my Dad was my greatest critic and supporter. He plagued me to rewrite. He made me keep a diary. He insisted that I date each poem I wrote. He kept telling me I "had to get some conflict in!" and he scowled at my stories of elves and fairies. Each year he had me write, re-write and re-write a poem for our Christmas card. When I got to college he did research on every essay topic I had and insisted on tearing apart everything I wrote. He drove me crazy. Not until he died did I come to appreciate his unflagging zeal on my behalf.

In 1991, Little published a continuation of her autobiography titled *Stars Come Out Within.* This volume deals with the growth of her career as a writer, with her struggle to accept the blindness that overtook her in middle age, and with her eventual triumph over her disability. The **author profile** on **page 83** of the **student anthology** tells more about how and why Little became a writer.

INFORMATION FOR THE STUDENT

Have students read and discuss the information included on page 83 of the student anthology. Share any other information about the author that you think appropriate.

COGNITIVE AND RESPONSIVE READING

Activating Prior Knowledge

This selection tells about the author's first job as a teacher of children with physical handicaps. Encourage volunteers to share any information they might have about physical handicaps.

Setting Reading Goals and Expectations

Even though this selection has been designated as an Assessment selection, the class will proceed as usual with the setting of reading goals and expectations. To do this, have the students **browse the selection,** using the clues/problems/wondering procedure. Students will return to these observations after reading.

Recommendations for Reading the Selection

Explain to the students that they will read this selection to assess what they have learned about learning. Place the students in small groups. Tell them that they will decide in their small groups how they would like to read this selection. For example, the groups may choose to do one of the following:
- read silently but stay in groups, stopping to ask each other questions when they need help understanding
- alternate reading and summarizing one section at a time
- read silently on their own

Encourage the students to use the strategies that they think will best help them understand and appreciate the selection. They should feel free to **refer to the reading strategy posters** as needed. Encourage them to collaborate with others in their groups by asking questions when they encounter reading difficulties and by offering suggestions to others who need help.

➤ Distribute copies of Assessment Master 3, Concept Connections for unit 1, Learning, which you will find in the booklet *Masters for Continuous Assessment* in the Teacher Toolbox. Tell the students that after reading the selection in their small groups, they will write responses on the master independently. They will then regroup and share their findings, changing any ideas they wish.

As the students read the selection, circulate among the groups to observe their understanding of the concepts as well as their collaboration in solving difficulties in understanding the selection.

Assessment Master 3

Concept Connections

1. Explain what this selection is about. Write a short summary.

2. Tell what this selection has to do with learning.

3. Tell how this selection is like other selections you have read in this unit.

4. You have read many selections about learning. How did *this* selection change your ideas about learning?

Date

Name

Copyright © 1995 Open Court Publishing Company

Unit 1/Learning   Assessment Master 3

To foster independence, think-aloud prompts are not provided for Assessment lessons.

A REAL JOB

from LITTLE BY LITTLE:
A WRITER'S EDUCATION by Jean Little
illustrated by Ellen Beier

I wanted to be a writer. But I had been told over and over again that you could not make a living as a writer. You had to get a real job and write in your spare time.

But what real job could a legally blind girl with a B.A. in English do?

Then I learned that the Rotary Crippled Children's Centre planned to start a small class for handicapped children and would need a teacher for it. I had no teaching <u>qualifications</u>, but I had worked with children with <u>motor</u> handicaps for three summers at Woodeden Camp.

The Rotarians agreed to hire me if I would first go to Montreal for two weeks to take a course on educating children with motor handicaps. The course was taught by Ellen Thiel from the Institute for Special Education at the University of Utah in Salt Lake City. I was <u>intimidated</u> by the other students, most of whom were experienced teachers and, although I enjoyed the course itself, I decided I would have to give up the idea of being a teacher. They kept talking a language I did not understand. Phonics, for instance. It was clearly of <u>paramount</u> importance, and I did not know what it meant. When I went in for my final interview, I explained all this to Ellen.

🐚 78 🐚

She laughed. "Phonics <u>notwithstanding</u>, I think you just may be a born teacher. I'm about to give a six-week course in Salt Lake on teaching children with motor handicaps. How would you like to come home to Utah with me and we could find out if I'm right?"

I stared at her, not knowing for a second whether or not she was kidding. Then I saw her grin. It was very friendly and had in it the same challenge that Dad's had had so often.

"All right," I said dazedly. "Where's Utah?"

I called home half an hour later to tell Mother that I was coming home to pack tomorrow and, the day after, was meet-

🐚 79 🐚

ing this strange woman, Ellen Thiel, in Urbana and setting out for the American West.

"Wonderful," Mother said after only the shortest of <u>hesitations</u>. "I'll be there to meet you. You can tell me all about it while we pack."

At the end of that summer, I made a list in my diary of all the "new experiences" I had had since I left home. There are forty-nine items listed. I stopped only because I had filled the last page in that diary.

I did discover what Phonics meant, but I learned far more than that. The children in the demonstration class taught me a lot. So did Ellen's three children, Paula, Mary and Joe.

One evening I was reading *The Secret Garden* to the Thiel kids. Paula and Mary were <u>enthralled</u> by the story, but Joe kept fiddling with odds and ends on his bed and behaving as though he were extremely bored. When I closed the book, however, and started to shepherd the girls out of his room, he demanded that I give him the phone.

"Why?" I asked. "It's time you went to sleep. I read two extra chapters because the girls were so interested."

"I have to tell Mama something," Joe said.

Ellen was working late at the university. But I knew she was alone and besides, who was I to come between a boy and his mother?

I handed him the telephone on its long cord. Returning after tucking in the girls, I heard him say in a voice filled with wonder and delight, "Mum, they got into the garden!!!"

Never again did I make the mistake of thinking that a child who appeared inattentive was getting nothing out of a book.

🌱 80 🌿

His tone held exactly the joy Mary Lennox herself felt when she stepped through the ivy-covered green door.

At the end of the summer, Ellen wrote me a glowing letter of recommendation, and I went back to Guelph to start preparing for my teaching job at the Crippled Children's Centre.

I was not an ideal teacher. When your students continually correct your arithmetic, it keeps you humble. But I did one important thing well. I read to them.

I found that these were deprived children, not because they were not loved, but because they had largely been kept indoors due to their handicaps. Not one of them had ever seen a rainbow or been to a circus. They could not swim. They had not been taken to a zoo. Most of them had not ridden on a city bus. None had been on a train journey. Most had never eaten in a restaurant.

We did all these things, and Phonics, too.

🌱 81 🌿

Remembering how I had never found a cross-eyed heroine in a book, I decided to search for books about children with motor handicaps. I did not for one moment intend to limit my students to reading about crippled kids. I knew that they completely identified with Anne Shirley and Homer Price, that they actually became Bambi, Piglet and Wilbur. I did not think they needed a book to help them adjust. I did believe, however, that crippled children had a right to find themselves represented in fiction.

I began to search.

I found a book about a girl with polio. None of my students had polio. The Salk vaccine had already been discovered. I found several books that contained <u>invalid</u> children who completely recovered before the book ended. None of my students was ever going to recover completely.

I was looking for a book in which the child's handicap was present only in the background. The kids I taught were not conscious of their disabilities most of the time. They minded when people stared at them, or when their brothers and sisters got bicycles, of course. But usually they were too busy living to brood. Physio and occupational therapy were like arithmetic and reading, an accepted part of their days.

When we read *The Secret Garden*, Alec said, "What's the matter with Colin? Why doesn't he have therapy?"

"I guess it was written too long ago for them to know about therapy," I said weakly.

"What I can't figure out," Clifford complained, "is how he stood up for the first time in June and was well enough to beat Mary in a race by August. That's crazy."

🌱 82 🌿

The others loved the ending so much that they defended Colin's rapid recovery. But even they sounded a bit <u>dubious</u>.

We went through the same questions when we read *Heidi*. Clara got well even faster than Colin.

"Miss Little, what was wrong with Clara?"

It didn't say. I began to feel angry on their behalf.

Why couldn't there be a happy ending without a miracle cure? Why wasn't there a story with a child in it who resembled the kids I taught?

Somebody should write one, I thought.

It did not yet cross my mind that that somebody might be me.

MEET JEAN LITTLE, AUTHOR
Jean Little's mother taught her to read as a small child, and reading and writing remained the most important things in Little's life. She explains: "When I was a child, because of my limited vision and because my eyes looked peculiar, I was teased a lot and left out of games. I did not feel unloved though, because our family was a close one and because I found so many friends in the books I read. I went to the library every single day, unless I was sick in bed—and then I sent my mother.

"When I wasn't reading, I was making up a story in my head. . . . I was twelve when I began to write poems. My father gave me much criticism, attention, and praise. He . . . told me, in no uncertain terms, that I was going to be a writer."

🌱 83 🌿

*

Reflecting on the Selection

As you note their collaborative group discussions, mark your Teacher's Observation Log for the individuals in one or two groups. Take a moment to reflect on how each student is changing in her or his ability to use strategies to solve problems. Have the groups break while the students respond independently to Concept Connections, Assessment Master 3.

ASSESSMENT TIP This is an ideal time to mark observations in your Teacher's Observation Log.

Response Journal

Students may wish to record personal responses to the selection.

Exploring Concepts Within the Selection

Allow the students to regroup to compare and discuss their responses to Concept Connections. During these discussions you will have more opportunities to observe students and to mark your Teacher's Observation Log. Then gather the Concept Connections pages and continue with the lesson as usual.

ASSESSMENT TIP This is another ideal time to mark observations in the log.

Sharing Ideas About Explorable Concepts

Have the groups **report** and **discuss** their **ideas** with the rest of the class. It is crucial that the students' ideas determine this discussion.
- The students may notice that Little took classes in special education and in phonics in order to become certified as a teacher and generalize that learners often have a particular goal in mind when they set out to study something.
- Some students may mention that while attending school in Utah and while teaching, Little learned about how children experience books.
- Students may also mention that Little believed that handicapped children had a right to find children like themselves represented in fiction and implies that the desire to provide books with handicapped characters and realistic plots influenced her career as a writer.

TIP FOR ENGLISH LANGUAGE LEARNERS

Give English Language Learners an opportunity to speak with confidence. If the students do not share the opinions of others based on their own experiences and knowledge, invite English Language Learners to challenge opinions. Encourage them to express their reasons for their opinions.

As these ideas and others are stated, have the students **add them to** the **Question Board** or the **Concept Board.**

Exploring Concepts Across Selections

Encourage the students to discuss how this selection relates to others they have read so far in this unit. Students might make connections with other selections in the unit.
- The students may make the connection that Little learned from her students, just as Dr. Samuel Gridley Howe learned from teaching Laura Bridgman. Teacher-pupil relationships are also important in "The Library Card" and "Do Bananas Chew Gum?"

TEACHING TIP Ask other students for comments to new or unexpected ideas.

Recording Ideas

As students complete the above discussions, ask them to **sum up what they have learned from their conversations and how they might use this information** in further explorations. Any special information or insights may be recorded on the **Concept Board.** Any further questions that they would like to think about, pursue, or investigate may be recorded on the **Question Board.** They may want to discuss the

Evaluating Discussions

Explorer's Notebook, page 6

Recording Concept Information continued

"The Struggle for an Education" by Booker T. Washington

_____
_____
_____
_____
_____
_____
_____
_____
_____

"A Real Job" by Jean Little

_____
_____
_____
_____
_____
_____
_____
_____
_____
_____
_____

6 EN　　　　　　　　　　　　　　　　Learning/Unit 1

Assessment Master 2

Self-Assessment Questionnaire

1. How would you rate this selection?
   ○ easy　　　○ medium　　　○ hard

2. If you checked **medium** or **hard**, answer these questions.
   • Which part of the selection did you find especially difficult?
   • What strategy did you use to try and understand it?

   _____

   • Were some of the words hard?
   • What did you do to figure out their meaning?

   _____

3. What do you feel you need to work on to make yourself a better reader?

   _____

4. Give an example of something you said in the group.
   Tell why you said it.

   _____

5. Give an example of something that people in the group helped you understand about the selection.

   _____

Self-Assessment Questionnaire　　　　　　　　Assessment Master 2

---

progress that has been made on their questions. They may also want to cross out any questions that no longer warrant consideration.

➤ After discussion, the students should individually record their ideas on page 6 of their Explorer's Notebook.

Self-Assessment Questionnaire

➤ After all aspects of this lesson have been completed, you may wish to distribute copies of the Self-Assessment Questionnaire, Assessment Master 2, provided in the Teacher Toolbox. Allow plenty of time for the students to complete this important assessment piece.

2 READING WITH A WRITER'S EYE

MINILESSON

Assessment

Remind the students that in each selection they have read so far, you have discussed something the writer did particularly well. For example, Jamie Gilson, in *Do Bananas Chew Gum?* used informal language to make her characters more interesting and real.

Tell the students to work in small groups to identify something they think Jean Little did especially well. Is there something about the writing that they think stands out? Remind the students to think back to a portion of the story that they reacted to or particularly enjoyed. Their responses could be clues to especially good writing. Allow time for the students to skim the story, if necessary, to refresh their memories. If they seem to be having difficulty expressing what they admired about the writing in this selection, model a response for them by pointing out things you found noteworthy, such as Little's use of indicators of time and order.

WRITING

Linking Reading to Writing

Encourage the students to use in their own writing any of Little's writing techniques they especially liked. Invite them to go to their writing folders to find a piece of writing they might revise by adding indicators of time and order or by doing anything else they noticed was well done in this selection.

✱ Writing Process

Remind students who are working on biographies or autobiographies to use the writing process as they complete these pieces. Remind them to get input from their peers.

VOCABULARY

Encourage the students to discuss words or phrases from the selection that they might want to use in their speaking and writing. Words you might discuss that are related to the concept include the following:
intimidated, enthralled, inattentive, deprived, dubious

Have Vocabulary Exploration forms, Reproducible Master 14, available so that students can add their favorite words or phrases to the Personal Dictionary section of their Writer's Notebook. Some students may wish to share these additions and to tell why they chose them. For additional opportunities to build **vocabulary**, see **Teacher Tool Card 75.**

Adding to Personal Word Lists

3 GUIDED AND INDEPENDENT EXPLORATION

EXPLORING CONCEPTS BEYOND THE TEXT

Guided Exploration

Students will select activities in which they explore the concept of learning. Refer the students to the **Exploration Activities poster** and give them time to choose an activity and to discuss what they wish to explore and decide how they wish to go about it. If students need further help, here are some suggestions:

Remind them that in "A Real Job" Jean Little trains to teach handicapped children at the Rotary Crippled Children's Centre. Some students

✱ Exploring Through Reflective Activities

might be interested in discussing the once-common policy of providing special schools for physically handicapped, blind, or deaf children, as opposed to the current policy of having these children attend the same schools as other children. You might begin this discussion by asking the students to comment on Little's experiences as a partially-sighted child in a regular school.

❯ Distribute Home/School Connection 9. Encourage the students to discuss with their families someone they know who has had special training related to a job or profession.

Continuing Exploration

Students may want to add new information to the Concept Board or to check questions on the Question Board. Remind them to remove any questions that are no longer relevant.

Home/School Connection 9

✳ INDEPENDENT WORKSHOP
Building a Community of Scholars

Student-Directed Reading, Writing, and Discussion

Students should spend the first part of the Independent Workshop in their collaborative groups. Each group should conference together to make sure that all areas of their exploration have been considered. Some students may choose to complete any unfinished pages in their Explorer's Notebook and continue with their exploration.

Additional Opportunities for Reading, Writing, and Cross-curricular Activities

✱ Reading Roundtable

Some students may choose to read one of Little's two autobiographies—*Little by Little* or *Stars Come Out Within*—or one of the books mentioned in this selection—*The Secret Garden* or *Heidi*. For additional ideas for **Reading Roundtable**, see **Learning Framework Card 6**.

✱ Writing Seminar

Students may use this time to continue revising their biographies or autobiographies or any of their writing work in progress. Remind them to ask for peer input. Encourage them to refer to the writing strategy posters whenever they need help with their writing.

Additional Opportunities for Solving Learning Problems

Tutorial

Use this time to give extra help to individuals or small groups who need it. This is also a good time for peer tutoring. Have the students refer to the appropriate Student Toolbox Cards to guide their work together. Encourage them to discuss with you any questions they may have.

Storks

1 READING THE SELECTION

About the Selection

This selection tells the tender and delightful story of six schoolchildren in a Dutch fishing village who wonder why storks do not nest in their trees and on their roofs. Inspired by a classmate's essay, the children try to figure out why the storks no longer come to their village and what they can do to bring the storks back.

Link to the Unit Concepts

"Storks," pages 84–113, stresses the importance of wondering about one's own surroundings and of people working together to accomplish change. It shows schoolchildren, a "community of scholars," considering a problem and finding a solution. And it shows how ideas discussed in a classroom can influence the wider community beyond the school.

About the Author

Meindert DeJong was born in 1906 in Wierum, a small village in Holland, but moved with his parents to Grand Rapids, Michigan, when he was eight years old. He never forgot the village where he spent his earliest years, and many of his books for children are based on his childhood memories.

He said in a speech made in 1962,

I want to walk along the dike until I see again the tower of Wierum. The tower rises out of Wierum right beside the dike, but it also rises out of all my books about my childhood village; it rises out of my childhood soul. . . . Whatever the changes brought to my village by nearly a half century, the dike will still be there, and the tower. They will be there, because in the mind's eye, in the child's eye of an eight-year-old boy, they are there, strong and eternal, set forever.

LESSON OVERVIEW

"Storks" by Meindert DeJong, pages 84–113

READING THE SELECTION

Materials
Student anthology, pp. 84–113
Explorer's Notebook, p. 7
Assessment Master 1
Map or globe

FYI
Learning Framework Card
• Responding to Text, 1B

READING WITH A WRITER'S EYE

Minilessons
Writer's Craft: Characterization
Writer's Craft: Problems and Solutions

Materials
Reading/Writing Connection, pp. 12–13
Reproducible Masters 14, 25

Options for Instruction
Writer's Craft: Point of View
Writer's Craft: Setting
(Use Teacher Tool Cards listed below.)

GUIDED AND INDEPENDENT EXPLORATION

Materials
Explorer's Notebook, p. 19
Home/School Connection 10
Assessment Master 1

Independent Workshop

Optional Materials from Student Toolbox

Tradebook Connection Cards

Cross-curricular Activity Cards
• 2 Science—Ecology
• 7 Social Studies—The Netherlands

Student Tool Cards
• Writer's Craft/Reading: Characterization, 13
• Writer's Craft/Reading: Plot, 15
• Writer's Craft/Reading: Point of View, 12
• Writer's Craft/Reading: Setting, 14

FYI
Teacher Tool Cards
• Writer's Craft/Reading: Characterization, 13
• Writer's Craft/Reading: Plot, 15
• Writer's Craft/Reading: Point of View, 12
• Writer's Craft/Reading: Setting, 14

Asterisks (*) throughout the lesson indicate learning frameworks. Learning Framework Cards and Teacher Tool Cards can be found in the Teacher Toolbox.

DeJong wrote more than thirty books for children. The awards he won for his books include the following:

- two Newbery Honors in 1954 for *Hurry Home, Candy* and for *Shadrach*
- the Newbery Medal in 1955 for *The Wheel on the School*
- the Child Study Children's Book Committee at Bank Street College Award in 1956 for *A House of Sixty Fathers*
- a place on the International Board on Books for Young People Honor List in 1956 for *A House of Sixty Fathers*
- the Newbery Honor in 1957 for *A House of Sixty Fathers*
- the Newbery Honor in 1959 for *Along Came a Dog*
- the Hans Christian Andersen Award for the body of his work in 1962
- the National Book Award in 1969 for *Journey from Peppermint Street*

About the Illustrator

Maurice Sendak was born in 1928 in New York City. While in high school, he worked at illustrating comic books. After graduation, he worked for several years creating window displays and attended evening classes in drawing and painting. "It was the only kind of school I could endure, because it was freewheeling," said Sendak. "What you learned depended on what you wanted to learn."

In 1952, a book he had illustrated, *A Hole Is to Dig* by Ruth Krauss, was so successful that Sendak was able to quit his job decorating windows and work full time as an illustrator of children's books. He is best known for his books *Where the Wild Things Are, In the Night Kitchen,* and *Outside Over There,* and for his illustrations of the Grimms' stories *King Grisly Beard, The Juniper Tree,* and *Dear Mili.* He also illustrated eight books by Ruth Krauss and seven books by Meindert DeJong.

Sendak won the Caldecott Medal in 1964 for *Where the Wild Things Are* and the Caldecott Honor in 1982 for *Outside Over There.* In 1970, he was awarded the Hans Christian Andersen Medal for the body of his work, the first American artist to be so honored.

Sendak said about his work:

I really do these books for myself. It's something I have to do, and it's the only thing I want to do. Reaching the kids is important, but secondary. First, always, I have to reach and keep hold of the child in me.

INFORMATION FOR THE STUDENT

After reading the story, you may want to have the students discuss the information included in the paragraphs about Maurice Sendak in the student anthology. At that time, you may want to tell the students about other books Sendak has illustrated and written and about the life and work of Meindert DeJong.

Background Information

The fictional village of Shora is on the shore of the North Sea in Friesland, which is in the northeast corner of Holland. Holland is another name for the Netherlands. Approximately half of the land area of the

Netherlands was once covered by the North Sea. Since about 1300, the Dutch have been reclaiming land from the sea by building walls of earth or stone called *dikes* and by pumping out sea water from behind the dikes into canals that flow into the North Sea. Windmills were once used to power these pumps, which continue even today to drain the land behind the dikes.

Have the students locate the Netherlands, specifically this area of the Netherlands, on a globe, a world map, or map of Europe.

COGNITIVE AND RESPONSIVE READING

Activating Prior Knowledge

Encourage the students to discuss what they know about storks. You may want to share photographs of storks and of storks' nests so that they can get an idea of how large the birds are.

Setting Reading Goals and Expectations

Have the students **browse** the **first page** of the selection, using the clues/problems/wondering procedure. Students will return to these observations after reading.

Recommendations for Reading the Selection

Ask the students how they would like to read the selection. Although the selection is long, it is amusing and fun to read, and students may enjoy reading it aloud. During oral reading, use and encourage think-alouds. During silent reading, allow discussion as needed. Discuss problems, strategies, and reactions after reading.

This would also be a good selection for **responding** to text **by visualizing** and **giving opinions** while reading aloud. Model this response, and then invite the students to do the same.

Note: Notice that "Storks" has been divided into two parts in case the students don't finish reading the selection in one class period. The second part of the selection starts on page 103 and is designated by a large initial capital letter.

About the Reading Strategies

The teacher in the story encourages his class to wonder why there are no storks in the village and what might bring them back. Because this selection gives students a lot to think about, **wondering** is a reading strategy the students may find helpful. Students will have many opportunities to wonder about life in Holland and about storks.

It is important that the students feel free, at any time during reading, to **wonder** and ask questions about anything that makes them curious. This **selection provides many good models of wondering** as the teacher encourages his students to wonder about the storks. Wondering helps good readers think about what they are reading and ask questions that will help them understand and enjoy the text. Students can wonder about what they read as well as about things in their everyday lives.

Introducing Wondering

Direct the students' attention to the **strategy poster Responding to Text**, which should be displayed in a prominent place with the other **reading strategy posters.** Point to the poster and read the part about the strategy of **wondering.** Discuss the strategy and have a volunteer read aloud the questions that accompany it. Remind the students to use the strategy posters whenever they need help during reading. For a review of the strategy of **wondering**, see **Learning Framework Card 1B, Responding to Text.**

Reading Strategy Posters

Think-Aloud Prompts for Use in Oral Reading

Notice the suggested think-aloud prompts with the page miniatures. These are merely suggestions. Remind the students that reading should make sense. If they encounter difficulty while reading, they need to figure out a way to solve their problem. They should refer to the strategy posters for help. Review the other strategies they have learned. Encourage students to share with the class whatever strategies they use while reading.

1 It may help students to understand the setting of the story if they **visualize** the village of Shora. You might think aloud about your own visualization of Shora.

Students might **wonder** about what the author means by saying that the houses where old people and toddlers lived were not as important as the five houses where the six schoolchildren lived.

STORKS
from THE WHEEL ON THE SCHOOL
by Meindert DeJong
illustrated by Maurice Sendak

To start with there was Shora. Shora was a fishing village in Holland. It lay on the shore of the North Sea in Friesland, tight against the <u>dike</u>. Maybe that was why it was called Shora. It had some houses and a church and tower. In five of those houses lived the six school children of Shora, so that is important. There were a few more houses, but in those houses lived no children—just old people. They were, well, just old people, so they weren't too important. There were more children, too, but young children, toddlers, not school children—so that is not so important either.

🦢 84 🦢

The six children of Shora all went to the same little school. There was Jella; he was the biggest of the six. He was big and husky for his age. There was Eelka. He was slow and clumsy, except his mind; his mind was swift. There was Auka, and right here at the beginning there is nothing much to say about Auka—he was just a nice, everyday boy. You could have fun with him. There were Pier and Dirk; they were brothers. Pier and Dirk looked about as much alike as second cousins. But Pier liked what Dirk liked, and Dirk did what Pier did. They liked to be together. They were twins.

Then there was Lina. She was the only girl in the little Shora school. One girl with five boys. Of course, there was also a teacher, a man teacher.

Maybe to begin with, we really should have started with Lina. Not because she was the only schoolgirl in Shora, but because she wrote a story about storks. There were no storks in Shora. Lina had written this story about storks of her own accord—the teacher hadn't asked her to write it. In fact, until Lina read it out loud to the five boys and the teacher, nobody in school had even thought about storks.

But there one day, right in the middle of the arithmetic lesson, Lina raised her hand and asked, "Teacher, may I read a little story about storks? I wrote it all myself, and it's about storks."

Lina called it a story, but it was really an essay, a composition. The teacher was so pleased that Lina had written a little piece of her own accord, he stopped the arithmetic lesson right there and let Lina read her story. She began with the title and read on:

🦢 85 🦢

DO YOU KNOW ABOUT STORKS?

Do you know about storks? Storks on your roof bring all kinds of good luck. I know this about storks; they are big and white and have long yellow bills and tall yellow legs. They build great big messy nests, sometimes right on your roof. But when they build a nest on the roof of a house, they bring good luck to that house and to the whole village that that house stands in. Storks do not sing. They make a noise like you do when you clap your hands when you feel happy and good. I think storks clap their bills to make the happy sounds when they feel happy and good. They clap their bills almost all the time except when they are in the marshes and ditches hunting for frogs and little fishes and things. Then they are quiet. But on your roof they are noisy. But it is a happy noise, and I like happy noises.

🐦 86 🐦

That is all I know about storks; but my aunt in the village of Nes knows a lot about storks, because every year two big storks come to build their nest right on her roof. But I do not know much about storks, because storks never come to Shora. They go to all the villages all around, but they never come to Shora. That is the most that I know about storks, but if they came to Shora, I would know more about storks.

After Lina had finished reading her story, the room was quiet. The teacher stood there looking proud and pleased. Then he said, "That was a fine story, Lina. A very fine composition, and you know quite a lot about storks!" His eyes were pleased and bright. He turned to big Jella. "Jella," he said, "what do you know about storks?"

"About storks, Teacher?" Jella said slowly. "About storks—nothing." He looked surly and stubborn, because he felt stupid. He thought he ought to explain. "You see," he told the teacher, "I can't bring them down with my slingshot. I've tried and tried, but I just can't seem to do it."

The teacher looked startled. "But why would you want to shoot them down?"

"Oh, I don't know," Jella said. He wriggled a little in his seat. He looked unhappy. "Because they move, I guess."

"Oh," the teacher said. "Pier," he said then, "Dirk, what do you twins know about storks?"

"About storks?" Pier asked. "Nothing."

"Dirk," the teacher said.

"Just the same as Pier," Dirk said. "Nothing."

🐦 87 🐦

"Pier," the teacher said, "if I had asked Dirk first, what would have been your answer?"

"The same as Dirk's," Pier answered promptly. "Teacher, that's the trouble with being twins—if you don't know something, you don't know it double."

The teacher and the room liked that. It made everybody laugh. "Well, Auka," the teacher said, "how about you?"

Auka was still chuckling and feeling good about what Pier had said, but now he looked serious. "All I know is that if storks make happy noises with their bills like Lina said in her story, then I would like storks, too."

The teacher looked around and said: "Well, Eelka, there in the corner, that leaves only you."

Eelka thought awhile. "I'm like Lina, Teacher; I know little about storks. But if storks would come to Shora, then I think I would learn to know a lot about storks."

"Yes, that is true," the teacher said. "But now what do you think would happen if we all began to think a lot about storks? School's almost out for today, but if, from now until tomorrow morning when you come back to school, you thought and thought about storks, do you think things would begin to happen?"

They all sat still and thought that over. Eelka raised his hand. "But I'm afraid I can't think much about storks when I don't know much about storks. I'd be through in a minute."

Everybody laughed, but the teacher's eyes weren't pleased. "True, true," he said. "That's right, Eelka. We can't think much when we don't know much. But we can wonder! From now until tomorrow morning when you come to school again, will you do that? Will you wonder why and wonder why? Will

❦ 88 ❦

you wonder why storks don't come to Shora to build their nests on the roofs, the way they do in all the villages around? For sometimes when we wonder, we can make things begin to happen.

"If you'll do that—then school is out right now!"

There they were out in the schoolyard—free! Jella peered again over the roofs on the houses at the distant tower rising beside the dike. He couldn't believe it. But the big white face of the tower clock spelled out three—a little past three. "Boy," Jella said in wonderment, "he let us out almost a whole hour early, just because of storks." Jella was beginning to appreciate storks. "What'll we do?" he said eagerly to the other boys.

But Lina took charge. Since she had started it with her essay about storks, she felt responsible. It was a wonderful day, the sky was bright and blue, the dike was sunny. "Let's all go and sit on the dike and wonder why, just like the teacher said."

Nobody objected. They all dutifully set out for the dike, still feeling happy because of the hour of freedom that had so suddenly and unexpectedly come to them. Still grateful enough to the storks and Lina to be obedient to her and sit on the dike and think about storks. But Jella lagged behind, and that was unusual. Big Jella was generally in the lead. Going down the village street he stared at every house he passed as if they were something new in the new freedom. But he dutifully climbed the dike and dutifully sat down at the end of the row of boys. Lina sat at the other end.

They sat. Nobody seemed to know just how to begin to wonder without the teacher there to start them off. Jella stared up at the sky. There wasn't a cloud in the sky. There were no

❦ 89 ❦

2 Students might need to **summarize** the response of each of the five boys to the teacher's question about storks.

3 Students might need to clarify the fact that in the time in which the story is set children did not wear watches. Help them **visualize** a village like Shora where people told the time by looking at a town or village clock, usually situated on the church tower.

storks. There wasn't even a gull. Jella looked at the sea stretching empty before him—there wasn't a ship in the sea.

Jella looked along the quiet row. Everybody was just sitting, hugging his knees. Everybody looked quiet and awkward and uncomfortable. Suddenly Jella had had enough. He looked along the row of boys at Lina. "The teacher didn't say we had to sit in a row on the dike to wonder, did he?"

"No," Lina said, "but I thought, well, he's never given us a whole hour off from school before, and I thought . . ."

"Well, then," Jella said . . . It just didn't feel right to sit when you were free. But the quiet sea and the quiet sky suggested nothing to him. Then fortunately a slow canalboat came pushing around a faraway bend in the canal. The two men on deck lowered the sail and the mast, so the boat could slide under the low bridge. The men picked up poles to push the boat along under the bridge. Jella jumped up. Now he had an idea. "Hey, let's all go get our poles and go ditch jumping!"

〰 90 〰

All the boys, with the exception of Eelka, jumped up eagerly. Here was something to do—fun in the freedom.

"You, too, Eelka. Run and get your pole," Jella said. "And tell Auka to get mine, too. I'll wait here."

Lina stared at Jella in dismay. Even Eelka had to go. When it came to ditch jumping, Eelka generally was left out—he was too fat and slow and clumsy. "But I thought we were going to wonder why storks don't come to Shora?" Lina said. If even Eelka had to go along, she was going to be left behind all alone.

Lina glared down the dike after the running boys. "All right for you, Eelka," she yelled unhappily. She looked darkly at Jella. "Boy, if the teacher finds out that you . . ." She swallowed her words. It was a bitter, lost feeling to be left behind all alone in the surprise free hour.

Lina had a sudden hopeful thought. It must be that Jella wanted them all in on the ditch jumping, so that if the teacher found out, they'd all catch it together. Maybe he'd let her in on it, too! Maybe that was why he had stayed here with her on the dike. "Jella," Lina asked, "can I go, too? Why, if it wasn't for me, you'd be sitting in school right now. And I could get my mother's clothes pole. It's long and smooth and . . ."

"Naw," Jella said immediately. "Girls are no good at jumping. It's a boy's game."

"I'd be as good as Eelka. Better even," Lina said indignantly.

"Yeah, I guess so. But Eelka doesn't mind getting wet, but girls worry about wet feet and their dresses flying. And they squeal and scream, and then they get scared and go giggly."

〰 91 〰

Jella seemed to have thought a lot about it. Lina could see it was totally no use wheedling or arguing. She drew her wooden shoes primly up under her, hugged her knees, and stared wretchedly out at the sea. "Teacher said we were to wonder why the storks don't come. He even said if we wondered really hard things might begin to happen."

"We'll wonder while we jump ditches," Jella said shortly. He was a bit uneasy. But now the boys were coming back, Auka with two vaulting poles. Jella started to leave. "And we don't care if you do tell the teacher! He didn't say we were supposed to sit like dopes on the dike."

So Jella did care—he was even worried she would tell. She was no tattletale! Lina did not <u>deign</u> to turn around to answer. But she couldn't help looking down the dike when Eelka came dragging his long vaulting pole. "All right, for you, Eelka," she said stormily.

That was the trouble with being the only girl: you got left out of things. And if Eelka didn't also get left out, there was nothing for her to do but sit by herself or play with her little sister Linda and the other little children. What was the fun of that? Well, she'd show them. She'd sit right here and think and wonder really hard. Tomorrow morning when the teacher asked, up would go her hand, but there they'd all sit stupid and with their mouths full of teeth. It did not seem much of a threat. The excited voices of the boys came drifting back to her.

Lina fixed her eyes hard upon a distant hazy swirling far out above the sea, wanting it to be a stork but knowing all the time it was just a sea gull. She wouldn't play with Eelka again for a week! Maybe ten days even, maybe three weeks!

🐦 92 🐦

Even if in all that time Jella and the rest left Eelka out of every one of their games. She wouldn't bother with Eelka either. She just wouldn't bother!

She stared hard at the gull. It was still a gull; it wasn't a stork. Suppose a whole big flock of storks came flying up out of the sea. The boys, jumping ditches, wouldn't even see them. But Lina had to admit to herself it wouldn't make much difference if they saw the storks or not. The storks wouldn't stay in Shora, and the boys couldn't make them stay, so what was the difference. Lina sighed. It was hard being the only girl in Shora.

She took off one of her wooden shoes and sat staring moodily into it. She caught herself doing it. It was a lonely habit. She often sat staring into her shoe. It somehow made her feel better and seemed to help her to think better, but she didn't know why. She often wished she could wear her wooden shoes in the schoolroom instead of just socks. The wooden shoes had to be left out in the <u>portal</u>. Lina was sure it would help no end if she could pull off one of her shoes and stare and dream into it awhile—especially before doing an arithmetic problem. Lina sighed. You couldn't dream with arithmetic. With arithmetic you could only think. It made arithmetic sort of scary. Hard and scary and not very exciting.

Storks were exciting! "Wonder why? Wonder why?" Lina said quite hard into her wooden shoe. The words came bouncing back at her out of the hard wooden shell. She whispered it into the shoe; the words came whispering back. She sat dreaming, staring into the shoe. And the sea gull was swirling and sailing far out at sea.

🐦 93 🐦

4 A lot of information has been presented and students might need to **sum up** the events from the time of the children's early dismissal from school up to this point.

It might help students to **visualize** the game of ditch jumping. Point out that boats are pushed along the narrow canals by means of long poles and that these same poles could be used for vaulting. The game of ditch jumping is similar to the sport of pole-vaulting.

Still thinking and dreaming about storks, she got up in her nice hazy daze and wandered away from the dike, one shoe in her hand. She went slowly down the street, staring intently at the roofs of all the houses as if she'd never seen them before. The village street lay quiet and empty. Lina had it to herself all the way through the village to the little school. The school had the sharpest roof of all, Lina decided. All the roofs were sharp, but the school's was the sharpest.

A thin faraway shout and a shrill laugh came through to her. She turned. In the far, flat distance she could see the boys. Now big Jella, it must be Jella, went sailing high over a ditch. Hard behind him, first sprinting, then sailing high on their poles, came the other three boys. And then there came one more; it must be Eelka. But Eelka disappeared—he must have gone into the ditch. Now there was a lot of shouting and running. Lina caught herself waiting anxiously for Eelka to appear out of the ditch. Then she remembered that she wasn't going to play with Eelka for three weeks. She turned her back to the distant boys. "I hope he went in up to his neck," she heard herself saying half-aloud. It surprised her. For now it didn't matter whether or not Eelka went into the water up to his neck; it didn't matter that the boys were having fun. She knew why the storks didn't come to build their nests in Shora. The roofs were all too sharp! But not only did she know the reason why, she also knew what to do about it! They had to put a wagon wheel on top of one

94

of the roofs—a wagon wheel just like her aunt in Nes had on her roof. Tomorrow morning she would spring it on them in the schoolroom. They'd be surprised!

Lina started to hurry back to the village, almost as if she had to hurry to tell someone. She put her wooden shoe back on to hurry better. There wasn't anyone there, she knew. The boys were playing in the fields; the teacher had gone. She could go home and tell her mother, but she would tell her mother anyway. It just seemed to her there had to be somebody *new* to tell it to—she had that feeling. There wasn't anyone like that. The whole street lay empty. It made her hurrying suddenly seem senseless. Lina slowed herself by staring at a house.

Once more Lina dawdled down the street, once more she stood a dreamy while before each house. Her shoe came off again. She was staring up at the roof of Grandmother Sibble III's house when the old lady came out. It startled Lina.

"I know I'm a nosy old creature," Grandmother Sibble III said, "but there you stand again, staring. I've been watching you wandering from the dike to the school and back again like a little lost sheep."

Lina laughed a polite little laugh. "Oh, I'm not exactly wandering. I'm wondering."

"Oh," said the old lady, mystified. "Well, I guess wondering is always better than wandering. It makes more sense." She chuckled a nice little old lady's chuckle.

They looked at each other. And Lina thought how she had never talked much to Grandmother Sibble III except to say a polite "hello" as she walked by. Now she did not know just what to say to her.

95

5 Students might need to **interpret** Lina's feelings and thoughts after she is left alone by the boys.

The old lady was still looking at her curiously. "Is that why you have your shoe in your hand?" she said gently. "Because you were wondering so hard?"

In surprise Lina glanced down at her hand holding the wooden shoe. She reddened a little and hastily slipped it on her foot. What must Grandmother Sibble think—not that she was her grandmother, she was just the grandmother of the whole village, the oldest old lady. It certainly must have looked silly, her hobbling down the street on one shoe, carrying the other. No wonder Grandmother Sibble III had come out of the house!

"I . . ." Lina said, trying to explain. She giggled a little. "Oh, isn't it silly?" She fished in her mind for some sensible explanation. None would come. But Grandmother Sibble III wasn't standing there grinning in a superior, adult way. She just looked—well, mystified and <u>inquisitive</u>. Lina decided to tell her. "I guess it does look silly and odd, but it somehow

🐦 96 🐦

helps me think better to look into my shoe. Then when I get to thinking really hard, I forget to put it back on again," she said defensively.

"Why, yes," the old lady said immediately. "Isn't it funny how odd little things like that help? Now I can think much better by sort of rocking myself and sucking on a piece of candy, and I've done it ever since I was a little girl like you." She carefully settled herself on the top step of her brick stoop. She looked as if she was settling herself for a good, long chat. "Now of course, I've just got to know what it was you were thinking about so hard it made you forget your shoe." She chuckled her little old chuckle again. "And if you don't tell me, I won't sleep all night from trying to guess."

They laughed together. Grandmother Sibble patted the stoop next to her. "Why don't you come and sit down with me and tell me about it."

Lina eagerly sat down—close, exactly where the old lady had patted. Old Grandmother Sibble was nice, she thought to herself. It was a nice surprise. She didn't talk to you as if you were a tiny tot, almost a baby, and miles of years away, the way grownups usually did. She even understood silly girl things like looking into a wooden shoe. She understood it the way a girl friend—if you had a girl friend—would understand. A girl friend who also had silly tricks and secretly told you about them. Aloud Lina said, "I was thinking about storks, Grandmother Sibble. Why storks don't come and build their nests in Shora."

Grandmother Sibble looked thoughtful. "Well, that is a thing to ponder all right. No wonder you had your shoe off. We here in Shora always without storks."

🐦 97 🐦

"But I figured out why," Lina told the old lady proudly. "Our roofs are too sharp!"

"Well, yes . . . Yes, I guess so," the old lady said carefully, sensing Lina's sharp excitement. "But that could be remedied by putting a wagon wheel on the roof, couldn't it? The way they do in the other villages?"

"Yes, I'd thought of that," Lina said promptly. "My aunt in Nes has a wagon wheel on her roof, and storks nest on it every year."

"Ah, yes," the old lady said, "but doesn't your aunt's house have trees around it, too?"

"Yes, it has," Lina said, looking in surprise at the little old lady. Why, Grandmother Sibble must have been thinking about storks, too. It seemed amazing, the old, old lady thinking about storks. "I guess I never thought about trees. Well, just because there are no trees in Shora—so I didn't think about trees." Lina's voice faded away. Here was a whole new thing to think about.

"Would a stork think about trees?" the old lady wanted to know. "It seems to me a stork would think about trees. And it seems to me that in order to figure out what a stork would want, we should try to think the way a stork would think."

Lina sat bolt upright. What a wonderful thing to say! Lina fumbled for her shoe while she eagerly looked at the old lady.

"You see, if I were a stork, even if I had my nest on a roof, I think I would still like to hide myself in a tree now and then and settle down in the shade and rest my long legs. Not be on the bare peak of a roof for everybody to see me all the time."

🐦 98 🐦

Lina pulled her feet up under her and looked down confusedly at her wooden shoes. She really needed her wooden shoe right now. Her thoughts were racing.

"You see, years ago," Grandmother Sibble was explaining, "oh, years and years ago when I was the only girl in Shora, the way you are the only girl now, there were trees in Shora and there were storks! The only trees in Shora grew on my grandmother's place. My grandmother was then the only grandmother of Shora. She was Grandmother Sibble I, just like I am now Grandmother Sibble III and you would someday be Grandmother Sibble IV if your mother had named you Sibble instead of Lina. I asked her to! Oh, I had no business asking—we're not even related—but it just seems there should always be a Grandmother Sibble in Shora. But that's beside the point.

"The point is, my grandmother's little house stood exactly where your school stands now but, oh, so different from your little naked school. Really different! My grandmother's house was roofed with reeds and storks like reeds. And my grandmother's house was hidden in trees. And storks like trees. Weeping willow trees grew around the edge of a deep moat that went all around my grandmother's house. And in the shadowy water under the hanging willows, <u>pickerel</u> swam in the moat. And over the moat there was a little footbridge leading right to my grandmother's door. And in one of the willows there was always a stork nest, and there was another nest on the low reed roof of my grandmother's house. As a little girl I used to stand on the footbridge and think that I could almost reach up to the low roof of the little house and touch the storks, so close they seemed."

🐦 99 🐦

"Oh, I didn't know. I never knew," Lina said breathlessly.

Grandmother Sibble did not seem to hear. Her eyes were looking far, far back. She shook her head. "A storm came," she said. "As storms so often come to Shora. But this was a real storm. The wind and waves roared up the dike for longer than a week. For a whole week the water pounded and the salt spray flew. The air was full of salt; you even tasted the salt on your bread in your houses. And when it was all done, there were only three willows left at Sibble's Corner—that is what they called my grandmother's house, because everybody gathered there of a warm summer day to sit and chat and rest from work in the only shade in Shora, to talk and to lean their tired backs against the only trees. Then even those three left-over trees sickened and died. I guess their leaves had just taken in too much salt that long week of the storm.

"Later, after Grandmother Sibble I died, they came and tore down her house and chopped out the old rotted stumps of the willows and filled the moat with dirt. Then there was nothing for years and years, until they built your naked little school on the same spot. But the storks never came back."

Lina sat wide-eyed, hugging her knees, staring straight ahead, drinking it in, dreaming it over—the things the old lady had said—dreaming the picture. It sounded like a far-away tale, and yet it had been! Grandmother Sibble III had seen it! She had thought as a little girl that she could reach up and touch the storks, it had been so real and so close. Right in Shora!

"I never knew. I never knew," Lina whispered to herself. "And even a little footbridge," she told herself and hugged her knees.

🐦 100 🐦

Grandmother Sibble III roused herself. "So you see you mustn't think our sharp roofs is the whole story, must you?" she said softly. "We must think about other things, too. Like our lack of trees, our storms, our salt spray. We must think about everything. And to think it right, we must try to think the way a stork would think!"

Grandmother Sibble said "we"!

"Then have you been thinking about storks, too?" Lina asked in astonishment.

"Ever since I was a little girl. And ever since then I've wanted them back. They're lucky and cozy and friendly and, well, just right. It's never seemed right again—the village without storks. But nobody ever did anything about it."

"Teacher says," Lina told the old lady softly, "that maybe if we wonder and wonder, then things will begin to happen."

"Is that what he said? Ah, but that is so right," the old lady said. "But now you run in the house. There's a little tin on my kitchen shelf and in it there are wineballs. You get us each a wineball out of the tin. Then I'll sit on my stoop and you sit on yours, and we'll think about storks. But we'll think better each on his own stoop, because often thinking gets lost in talking. And maybe your teacher is right—that if we begin to think and wonder, somebody will begin to make things happen. But you go find the candy tin; I can think much better sucking on a wineball. And you take one, too. You watch if it doesn't work much better than looking inside an old wooden shoe."

Lina had never been in Grandmother Sibble III's house before, never in the neat kitchen. There was the shelf, and there was the candy tin. There were storks on the candy tin!

🐦 101 🐦

Pictures of storks in high sweeping trees were all around the four sides of the candy tin. On the lid was a village, and on every house there was a huge, <u>ramshackle</u> stork nest. In every nest tall storks stood as though making happy noises with their bills up into a happy blue sky.

Lina kept turning the candy tin to see the pictures again and again. Suddenly she woke up to the fact that she was staying in Grandmother Sibble's house a long, long time. Her first time in Grandmother Sibble's house, too! What would she think? She hastily shoved the candy tin back on its shelf and hurried to the stoop.

"Grandmother Sibble, storks on your candy tin! And on every roof a nest! Oh . . ." Suddenly Lina realized she'd forgotten the wineballs. She raced back. It was hard not to look at the storks, but she kept her face partly turned away and picked out two round, red wineballs. Then she ran back. "I forgot all about the wineballs," she apologized.

"Yes, I know," Grandmother Sibble said gently, for she saw that Lina—though looking straight at her while handing her her wineball—was not seeing her at all. Lina had dreams in her eyes. Lina was seeing storks on every roof in Shora. The old lady quietly let Lina wander off the stoop and to her own house. Lina had dreams in her eyes and would not hear words anyway.

On her own stoop Lina looked back for the first time. There sat Grandmother Sibble III rocking herself a little and sucking on her wineball. But the dream Lina was dreaming

🎵 *102* 🎵

was not just about storks—not directly. Later she would think about storks, try to think the way a stork would think, as Grandmother Sibble had said. But now she thought about Grandmother Sibble, who had a candy tin in her house with storks on it and who had known storks and who, when she was a little girl, had imagined she could reach up and almost touch the storks.

But that was not the wonder either, not quite. The real wonder was that, just as the teacher had said, things *had* begun to happen. Begin to wonder why, the teacher had said, and maybe things will begin to happen. And they had! For there sat Grandmother Sibble III on the stoop of her little house, and suddenly she had become important. She wasn't just an old person any more, miles of years away, she was a friend. A friend, like another girl, who also wondered about storks.

Lina looked again at the little old lady, sitting there on the stoop. She marveled; she sat feeling nice and warm about a little old lady who had become a friend. It was a lovely feeling, as sweet as a wineball, as sweet as a dream. Lina took one shoe off and peered into it. Why, storks did bring good luck! The storks had made a friend for her. Why, now when the boys left her out of their games, she could go to Grandmother Sibble, and they would sit and talk and chat. Lina looked up out of the shoe triumphantly. Why, yes!

In the morning it was school again. There they were in the schoolroom again, the five boys and Lina and the teacher. But this Saturday morning they did not start out by singing the old, old song about the country—"my lovely

🎵 *103* 🎵

---

6 **Summing up** the conversation between Lina and Grandmother Sibble may help students check their understanding of the story.

7 Encourage the students to make **predictions** about part 2 of the selection. Remind them that predictions are one way of setting a purpose for reading.

spot of ground, my fatherland, where once my cradle stood." No, they sat quietly as the teacher stood looking at each one of them in turn. And then he said, "Who wondered why? And where did it lead you?"

Lina's hand shot up. To her amazement every hand shot up with hers, even Jella's and Eelka's. The teacher looked so happy and pleased about it, it made Lina furious. "Why, Teacher, they never did! They went ditch jumping."

She clapped her hand to her mouth, but it was too late. She wasn't a tattletale. It was just that it had come boiling up out of her, because it had made her so furious. They were fooling the teacher, and it was making him happy.

The teacher looked at her a short moment. He seemed surprised. He turned away from her to Jella. Jella sat there in the front seat, big and stubborn and angry. He was really angry with her. But the teacher was saying, "Well, Jella, and what did you think was the reason why storks do not come to Shora?"

"Oh, I didn't think," Jella told the teacher honestly. "I asked my mother."

The teacher smiled. "Well, next to thinking, asking is the way to become wise. What did your mother say?"

"She said storks don't come to Shora because they never did. She said storks go back every year to the same nesting spots. So if they never came to Shora, they never will. So there's just nothing to be done about it, she said."

Lina sat in her seat, trembling with eagerness to tell them that storks had once come to Shora, to tell them what Grandmother Sibble had said. She wanted to wave her hand frantically. But all the boys were angry with her, and even

🐚 104 🐚

the teacher had been surprised and disappointed. It was a woebegone feeling, but still she had to do something. She quivered with eagerness. Then she *was* waving her hand, almost getting up out of her seat, but the teacher didn't take notice. She had to tell them! Lina heard herself saying out loud, "Oh, but storks did once upon a time come to Shora!"

They all turned to her, even the teacher. The next moment Lina was excitedly telling the room the story that Grandmother Sibble had told her about Sibble's Corner and the storks and the willow trees all around and the moat with the footbridge. About storks right here in the exact spot where the school now stood! She even told about the pickerel in the moat.

Jella in the front seat turned right around when he heard about the pickerel. He forgot he was angry with her; he forgot he was in school. He just said right out loud, without permission, "Oh, boy, pickerel! Were they big, Lina?"

All the boys had big excited eyes. They seemed to be much more interested in the pickerel than in the storks. All but Eelka. Eelka raised his hand, and now he was saying in his slow way, "What Lina said about trees. You know, Teacher, that is exactly what I thought when I wondered why. Storks don't come to Shora because we have no trees!"

Eelka's desk was next to Lina's. She twisted in her seat to stare at him. How did he dare? He'd wondered why! He'd gone jumping ditches!

It was as if Eelka knew what she was thinking, for he calmly told the teacher, "I don't suppose I would have thought of trees. It was really when I jumped right smack into the middle of a ditch and went under that I thought of it. I really got

🐚 105 🐚

8 Students may need to clarify the behavior of Lina when she tattles on the boys. Encourage the students to think about why the teacher is surprised at Lina.

soaked, and I wished there was a tree to hang my clothes on. But there aren't any trees, so I had to go home dripping wet. Boy, did I catch it from my mother!"

The teacher laughed as long and hard as the class. Even Lina had to laugh.

"Well, Eelka," the teacher said, "even though you had to do your thinking under water, it was still good thinking." His eyes were bright with laughter as he turned to the class. "All right, now. Does everyone agree with Eelka that the number one reason why storks do not come to Shora is because we have no trees?" He turned to the blackboard and wrote in big letters:

THE REASONS WHY STORKS
DO NOT COME TO SHORA

Under the words he put a big number one and waited.

"I still think the number one reason is what my mother said," Jella spoke up.

"Ah, but Lina has just told us that storks used to come to Shora. In fact, Jella, Grandmother Sibble III has seen storks nesting above the spot where you are sitting now. Where our school now stands. Imagine it!" said the teacher.

"I guess maybe my mother was wrong," Jella said slowly. He seemed to hate to have to admit it. He looked up at the ceiling in a troubled way.

Then Auka raised his hand and quietly said, "Then the number one reason is still NO TREES."

"That's what Grandmother Sibble thinks, too," Lina told the class honestly. "She says storks like shelter and trees and hiding and a shady place to rest their long legs. She said she

 106

would if she were a stork! And Grandmother Sibble told me the way to find out what a stork would want is to try to think like a stork."

The teacher stood looking at Lina. "Is that what Grandmother Sibble III told you? I think that is wonderful," he said. He turned back to the class. "Well, are we agreed then that the number one reason for no storks in Shora is no trees?" He turned toward the board with his chalk as if to write it down.

Lina frantically waved her hand to stop him. "Not trees—roofs!" she almost shouted when the teacher did not turn. "Teacher," she said desperately to the teacher's back, "even though Grandmother Sibble and everybody thinks it is trees, it has to be roofs. Storks don't just build nests in trees, they build their nests on roofs, too. But our roofs in Shora are too

107

sharp! Oh, it just has to be roofs," she pleaded. "Because we can put wheels on the roofs for storks to build their nests on, but we can't do anything soon about trees." Breathlessly she told the class about Grandmother Sibble's candy tin with the picture of a whole village on its lid and stork nests on every roof—because there was a wheel on every roof for the storks to build their nests on!

Pier and Dirk said almost together, "Oh, man, imagine a nest on every roof in Shora!"

"Even on the roof of our school!" Auka shouted.

"But that's just it. That's just it!" Lina all but shouted at them. "There's not a single wheel on any roof in Shora, because, just like Grandmother Sibble, everybody else must have figured it was no trees. So nobody ever put up a wheel. Nobody even tried! But how can we know if we don't try?"

Lina sat back waiting breathlessly, hopefully looking at the teacher. Oh, she had to be right! Teacher had to think it was right.

The teacher liked their excitement. He stood before the blackboard turning the piece of chalk in his hand in no hurry to write anything down. He looked at the boys who were still looking in surprise at Lina. He looked at Lina. "Aha," he said proudly. "Little Lina." And then he wrote on the blackboard Lina's reason in big white letters:

(9)

NO WHEELS ON OUR SHARP ROOFS

He turned back to the class. "Could it be?" he asked. "If we put wheels on our sharp roofs, could there be storks on every

🐸 108 🐸

roof in Shora, the way Lina saw it in the picture on the candy tin?"

"Aw, that was just a picture," Jella said, scornfully. "You can put anything in a picture. All that is is a dream."

"Ah, yes, that's all it is," the teacher said. "As yet! But there's where things have to start—with a dream. Of course, if you just go on dreaming, then it stays a dream and becomes stale and dead. But first to dream and then to do—isn't that the way to make a dream come true? Now sit for a moment, picture it for a moment: our Shora with trees and storks. Now Shora is bare, but try to see Shora with trees and storks and life. The blue sky above and the blue sea stretching behind the dike and storks flying over Shora. Do you see it?"

"Trees won't grow in Shora," Jella argued stubbornly. "It's the salt spray and the wind storms. There's only one tree in Shora, and that's a small cherry tree in the back yard of legless Janus. But the yard's got a high wall around it, so high you can hardly climb it. The cherry tree grows against the sunny wall of the house, and Janus pets it and guards it. He won't let a bird or a kid get even one cherry. Not one!"

(10)

"Well, but doesn't that show us something?" the teacher said. "That to raise trees in Shora we must perhaps protect them. And couldn't we raise trees that could withstand the storms and salt spray—stouter and stronger than willows? There must be trees that grow along the sea. Or maybe we would have to protect the willows with a windbreak of poplar trees. The point is, if trees once grew here, couldn't we make them do it again?"

🐸 109 🐸

(9) To check their understanding, students may want to **sum up** the class discussion about why storks do not come to Shora.

(10) If necessary, explain that legless Janus is a character who later becomes very important in the story. He is an old man who says that his legs were bitten off by a shark. He sits in a wheelchair in his yard and throws rocks at birds and at boys who try to steal cherries from his tree, the only tree in Shora.

"Oh, but that would take too long," Dirk said. "That would take years."

"Making dreams become real often takes long," the teacher said. "I don't mean that it should be done at once. Our first problem is how to make just one pair of storks come to nest in Shora. That is what we are trying to do right now by first thinking out the reasons why the storks don't nest in Shora. But after that . . . If trees once grew where our school now stands, wouldn't they grow there again? Think of it. Trees all around our school!"

"And a moat with pickerel in it," Jella promptly added. "We boys could even dig it ourselves, and Lina could make hot chocolate milk for the diggers."

"Yes, Jella, now you are getting into the spirit of it. For that matter, we could even plant our own little trees. But first, before we can even start to think of all that, what must we do?"

"Find a wheel to put on a roof," Lina promptly cried.

"Ah, hah," the teacher said. "Now we are getting to something that we can do. Now do you see? We wondered why and we reasoned it out. Now we must do. Now we must find a wagon wheel, and then we must put it up on a roof. But behind doing that lies the long dream—storks on every roof in Shora. Trees! Maybe even a moat around the school. Can you picture our Shora like that?"

Excitement was in his voice; excitement was in the whole room. Lina couldn't sit still. She squirmed and squirmed, and then her hand shot up. "And a footbridge leading right to the door! We'd go over the footbridge to school. Teacher," she pleaded. "Teacher, I could get Grandmother Sibble's candy

🐦 110 🐦

tin. Then we could all see what Shora would be like with storks and trees."

The teacher nodded. "Run then, Lina."

Grandmother Sibble III had no objections whatever to Lina's taking the candy tin to school. "Oh, no, child, keep it there as long as you like. Keep it until you get real storks in Shora." She opened the tin and took out a wineball. "Why, enough left for a wineball for each of you."

In the schoolroom they passed the candy tin around from hand to hand, and each one looked at all the pictures on the sides and on the lid. Each took out one wineball before reluctantly passing the tin on. The teacher took out the last wineball and then put the candy tin on the top ledge of the blackboard, on its side, so that the village with the trees and the storks on every roof could be seen from every point in the room. And underneath the tin, he wrote on the blackboard in big letters: "COULD IT BE?"

He turned back to the class. "Imagine a zebra in Shora," he said. "Imagine the long necks of two giraffes poking over the top of the dike. Imagine a giraffe running along our dike."

"Imagine a lion in Shora!" Auka said.

"Yes, Auka, even imagine a lion in Shora," the teacher surprisingly agreed. "A good lion, a gentle lion in our street. But isn't it almost like that with storks? Do you know where our storks come from—where they are when they aren't in Holland? Imagine the heart of Africa. The head of a big river deep in Africa, where it isn't a river any more but little <u>rivulets</u> and reedy swampland and marshes that go to make the beginnings of a big river. That's where our storks are now. Right there among the zebras and the herds of gazelles, among

🐦 111 🐦

the lions and the buffaloes. Do you see our stork? There's an old rhinoceros right behind him, <u>skulking</u> in the brush. Do you see the stork standing on the banks of the river where the river begins? Just beyond him in the swampy river is a herd of hippopotamuses, snorting and blowing in the deeper water. And the stork lives among them! Until a time comes and the big noble bird spreads his great wings, flaps his big wings, and comes out of the wilds of Africa to live among us. A great wild bird, yet tame and gentle, living among us in a village. Isn't it wonderful? And maybe, just maybe—It's still a dream. We haven't even a wheel as yet; we don't even know what roof we'll put it on."

"Oh, yes, we do! Oh, yes, we do!" the whole class shouted. "It's got to go right on the roof of our school."

"Why, yes," the teacher said. "Why, yes, class! Then who's going to look for a wagon wheel? Look for a wagon wheel where one is and where one isn't; where one could be and where one couldn't possibly be?"

They were all too breathless to say a word. But Jella hastily swallowed his wineball whole, then blurted it out for all of them. "We all are. From the moment school is out until we find one."

The teacher nodded and nodded. "That's how we'll begin to make a dream come true. We'll begin at noon. It's Saturday, and we

🖗 *112* 🖗

have our free afternoon before us. We'll have a whole afternoon to try to find a wagon wheel. We'll really work at it, because that is how to start to make a dream come true . . ."

MEET MAURICE SENDAK, ILLUSTRATOR

As a child, Maurice Sendak was not happy in school. He says, "In order to get there, I had to talk myself out of a state of panic nearly every day. I couldn't stand being [shut up] with other children—I never did like competition—and I was usually so embarrassed that I stammered."

Sendak did, however, come to appreciate books. He tells of the book he received on his ninth birthday: "Back in the thirties I didn't have any 'official' children's books. (I refer to the <u>classics</u>.) The only thing I can remember is cheap paperbacks, comic books . . . My sister bought me my first book, The Prince and the <u>Pauper</u>. A ritual began with that book which I recall very clearly. The first thing was to set it up on the table and stare at it for a long time. Not because I was impressed with Mark Twain; it was just such a beautiful object. Then came the smelling of it . . . it was printed on particularly fine paper, unlike the Disney books I had gotten previous to that, which were printed on very poor paper and smelled poor . . . It also had a shiny cover, a <u>laminated</u> cover. I flipped over that. And it was very solid. I mean, it was bound very tightly. I remember trying to bite into it, which I don't imagine is what my sister intended when she bought the book for me. But the last thing I did with the book was to read it. It was all right. But I think it started then, a passion for books and bookmaking. I wanted to be an illustrator very early in my life; to be involved in books in some way."

🖗 *113* 🖗

11 Students may need to clarify that the teacher describes Africa because that is where storks migrate to and from. They may notice that the teacher in the story asks the children in his class to **visualize** the things he describes.

Discussing Strategy Use
Encourage the students to discuss the strategies they used when they encountered difficulties while reading this story. Invite them to tell whether the strategy of **wondering** helped them better understand this story.

Reflecting on the Selection
Whole-Group Discussion

The whole group discusses the selection and any personal thoughts, reactions, or questions that it raises. During this time, students also **return to the clues, problems, and wonderings** they noted on the chalkboard during browsing.

Assessment

To assess the students' understanding of the text, engage in a discussion to **determine whether the students have grasped the following ideas**:
- how the Dutch children wonder and think in order to understand why there are no storks in their village and to come up with ways to bring them back
- how Lina's feelings about Grandmother Sibble III change after she has talked to her

Response Journal

Students may wish to record their personal responses to the selection.

Exploring Concepts Within the Selection
Small-Group Discussion

Small groups discuss the relationship of the selection to learning. Circulate among the groups and observe the discussions. Refer the students to the Concept Board and the Question Board to keep them focused on their original ideas about learning and to see if those ideas have changed as a result of reading this selection.

Sharing Ideas About Explorable Concepts

Have the groups **report** and **discuss** their **ideas** with the rest of the class. It is crucial that the students' ideas determine this discussion.
- Some students may mention that Lina's wondering about storks leads her to learn what Shora was like in the past.
- The students may notice that the children discuss the problem and decide on a plan to make their dream of storks in Shora come true.

As these ideas and others are stated, have the students **add them to the Question Board** or the **Concept Board.**

Exploring Concepts Across Selections

Ask the students whether this story reminds them of anything else they have read. They might make connections with other selections in the unit.
- Some students may notice that the children in Jean Little's classroom discuss the books they read much as the children in the schoolroom in Shora discuss their ideas about storks.

Recording Ideas

As students complete the above discussions, ask them to **sum up what they have learned from their conversations** and to tell **how they might use this information** in further explorations. Any special information or insights may be recorded on the **Concept Board.** Any further questions that they would like to think about, pursue, or investigate may be recorded on the **Question Board.** They may want to discuss the progress that has been made on their questions. They may also want to cross out any questions that no longer warrant consideration.

ASSESSMENT TIP This may be a good opportunity to observe the students working in groups and to mark observations in the Teacher's Observation Log.

TEACHING TIP Modeling should always be used to get the students started, but it should stop as soon as they think independently at the level you have demonstrated. Once you have turned the thinking aloud over to the students, your involvement should be limited to tactful shaping of their comments to improve their appropriateness.

Evaluating Discussions

"Storks" by Meindert DeJong

_____
_____
_____
_____
_____
_____
_____

"Sam at the Library" by Carol Combs Hole

_____
_____
_____
_____
_____
_____

"To Young Readers" by Gwendolyn Brooks

_____
_____
_____
_____
_____
_____
_____

Unit 1/Learning   EN 7

Explorer's Notebook, page 7

❯ The students should record their ideas and impressions about the selection on page 7 of their Explorer's Notebook.

Professional Checkpoint: Cognitive and Responsive Reading

Modeling cannot be totally effective if it remains solely in the hands of the teacher. Just as students can become dependent on teachers for answers, they can become dependent on a teacher for thinking. For students to fully understand and utilize thinking processes, it is crucial that they become responsible for thinking for themselves. Such independence cannot occur without careful teaching. In addition to modeling thinking, you must be willing and able to turn over the responsibility of thinking to the students.

Notes:

2 READING WITH A WRITER'S EYE

MINILESSONS

*Writer's Craft:
Characterization*

Ask the students to discuss the character of the school teacher. What kind of person do they think he is? They will very likely come to the conclusion that he is a kind and thoughtful man who cares about the children in his class and who wants them to wonder about the world around them and to learn to think for themselves.

After some discussion, point out that Meindert DeJong does not simply state that the teacher is a kind and thoughtful man. Instead, DeJong lets his readers learn about the teacher by showing what the teacher says and does and by showing what the children say and think about him. **Revealing what a character is like by the character's actions and words and by showing what others say and think about this character is** part of the writing technique of **characterization**.

There are several incidents that show that the teacher cares about his students and wants them to think for themselves.

- On page 85, the teacher allows Lina to interrupt the arithmetic lesson to read her essay about storks.
- On page 87, the teacher is startled when Jella says that he has tried to hit storks with his slingshot. He appears to be uncomfortable with the idea of trying to kill animals for no good reason. However, he does not scold Jella for shooting at the birds; instead, he moves on to the next student. He does not want to shame Jella in front of the class.

*Selective Reading:
Focus on
Characterization*

Have the students scan the story for examples of ways that Meindert DeJong reveals his characters. Encourage students to read aloud and explain the examples they find. Other examples include the following:

About Jella
- On page 90, he quickly becomes bored with sitting on the dike and wants to play.
- On page 91, he has someone else fetch his pole instead of getting it himself.
- On page 91, he won't let Lina play because she's a girl.

About Lina
- On page 93, she stares into her shoe when she thinks.
- On page 96, she is able to laugh at herself when she is caught staring into her shoe.
- On page 103, she thinks of Grandmother Sibble as a friend.
- On page 104, she feels bad about tattling on the boys for going ditch-jumping.

About Grandmother Sibble III
- On page 96, she doesn't think Lina is foolish for staring into her shoe.

*Selection-Based
Practice*

- On page 97, she doesn't talk to Lina as though she were a child.
- On page 98, she advises Lina to "think the way a stork would think."

➤ Distribute copies of Reproducible Master 25 and have students insert these pages in the Story Elements section of their Writer's Notebook. Make available additional copies of this page so that the students can record examples of characterization as the year goes on.

Recording Examples of Characterizations

**Independent Practice:
Characterization**

➤ Use Reading/Writing Connection, page 12, for additional practice in characterization. Have the students work in small groups to complete this page and discuss their answers.

**Writer's Craft:
Problems and
Solutions**

Ask students what they know about story plot. Remind them that **many stories are built around a problem that the main character must solve.** The events in the story are the steps that the character takes in order to solve the problem.

Because "Storks" is an excerpt from a longer book, the problem in this story is not solved by the end of the selection. However, DeJong does establish the problem in this selection. Lina's interest in storks is indicated in the first pages of the selection. The teacher, Grandmother Sibble III, and the boys in her class soon come to share her interest in storks. The question they must answer is why storks nest in all of the surrounding villages, but not in Shora. DeJong hints at how the problem will be solved by the title of his book, *The Wheel on the School.*

**Selective Reading:
Focus on Problems
and Solutions**

Have the students go back to "Storks" and find other clues from the story that show how Lina and the others will solve the problem. Encourage students to read aloud and explain what they find. Some clues to the problem and possible solutions include the following:

Selection-Based Practice

- On page 93, Lina admits to herself that even if she sees storks they won't stay in Shora.
- On pages 94 and 95, Lina decides that the way to attract storks is to put a wagon wheel on top of a sharp roof.
- On page 98, Grandmother Sibble suggests that storks like to hide in trees.
- On page 100, Grandmother Sibble explains why there are no trees in Shora.

**Independent Practice:
Problems and
Solutions**

➤ Have the students work independently or in small groups, using Reading/Writing Connection, page 13, to extend their discussion of how authors use problems and solutions in their writing. Encourage students to share their examples with the class.

WRITING

**Linking Reading
to Writing**

Remind the students that building a story around interesting characters is one way to make a story interesting. Good writers find ways to show their readers things about their characters rather than tell them.

Examples of Characterization

Story/Author	Character	What Character Says or Does

Name

Writer's Notebook: Story Elements

RM 25

Reproducible Master 25

"Storks"

Characterization

In "Storks," Meindert DeJong shows what the characters in his story are like by having them say or do different things. Look at other stories you have read. Write the title of the story, some things that a character in this story says or does, and what these things show about the character.

Story: _____

_____

What the character says or does: _____

_____

_____

What this shows about the character: _____

_____

_____

_____

Story: _____

What the character says or does: _____

_____

_____

What this shows about the character: _____

_____

_____

_____

Name

Story Elements

12 R/WC

Learning/Unit 1

Reading/Writing Connection, page 12

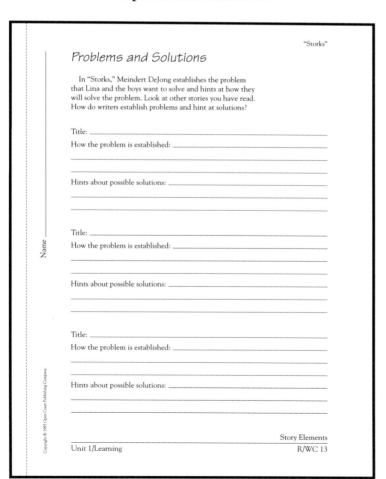

"Storks"

Problems and Solutions

In "Storks," Meindert DeJong establishes the problem that Lina and the boys want to solve and hints at how they will solve the problem. Look at other stories you have read. How do writers establish problems and hint at solutions?

Title: _____
How the problem is established: _____
_____
_____

Hints about possible solutions: _____
_____
_____

Title: _____
How the problem is established: _____
_____
_____

Hints about possible solutions: _____
_____
_____

Title: _____
How the problem is established: _____
_____
_____

Hints about possible solutions: _____
_____
_____

Name

Unit 1/Learning

Story Elements

R/WC 13

Reading/Writing Connection, page 13

Imagining an interesting problem for these characters to solve is another way to keep readers interested.

Encourage students to look through their writing folders for fiction pieces that could be made more interesting by changing the way that characters or plot are presented to readers. Have students share their original and revised versions with the class.

* Writing Process

Students may be interested in writing a brief essay about a subject they would like to know more about. Explain that an essay is a type of writing in which a writer gives information and expresses feelings about a subject. Ask volunteers to read aloud Lina's essay on pages 86 and 87 and to summarize the content of each of the two paragraphs in the essay. The first paragraph gives information about storks—what they look like, what noises they make, how they hunt for food in marshes, and that they bring good luck to the houses where they build their nests. This paragraph also tells how Lina feels about storks. The second paragraph tells about the storks that nest on Lina's aunt's house in the village of Nes and makes the point that storks come to all the nearby villages but not to Shora. The paragraph ends with the statement that Lina would know more about storks if they came to Shora.

Suggest that the students use Lina's essay as a model for a short essay of their own. Like Lina's, their essays should **summarize what they know and feel about a subject**. Their essays should be at least two paragraphs long, and, like Lina's, could begin with a question. The title could ask a question and the essay could answer the question. Have the students form small groups and brainstorm for subjects to write about.

Writing an Essay

VOCABULARY

Words connected to learning that the students may want to remember and use in their writing include the following:

essay, composition, wonderment, ponder, of her own accord, dike, lagged, dawdled, mystified, inquisitive, deign, woebegone, wheedling, ramshackle, skulk

Have Vocabulary Exploration forms, Reproducible Master 14, available for students who request them. Remind students to add words and phrases to the Personal Dictionary section of their Writer's Notebook. Then provide an opportunity for volunteers to share words and phrases they've added and tell why they chose them.

Adding to Personal Word Lists

3 GUIDED AND INDEPENDENT EXPLORATION

EXPLORING CONCEPTS BEYOND THE TEXT

Guided Exploration

Students will select activities in which they explore learning. Refer to the **Exploration Activities poster** and give them time to choose an activity and to discuss what they wish to explore and decide how they wish to go about it. If the students need further help, here are some suggestions:

- Students might consider making a picture or photo essay about storks. Allow the students to work in pairs or small groups.
- Remind the students that trees have a hard time growing in Shora because of the wind storms and the salt spray from the sea. Students may want to think about and discuss environmental conditions where they live in terms of problems, explanations, and possible solutions.

➤ Have students use Explorer's Notebook, page 19, to record their findings about local environmental problems and possible solutions.

➤ Distribute Home/School Connection 10. Encourage students to discuss with adults at home some animals (such as the storks in the story) that once lived in their area but are now rarely seen. Families will try to suggest possible reasons for this situation.

Continuing Exploration

Encourage students to discuss what they have learned about learning from their reading and other activities. If important concepts or ideas about learning are raised, be sure to have students add these to the Concept Board.

Exploring Through Reflective Activities

ASSESSMENT TIP This may be a good time to observe students working in groups and to mark observations in your Teacher's Observation Log.

Explorer's Notebook, page 19

Exploring the Environment

Look around the area where you live, whether it is a city block or a rural setting, and try to observe whether there are any environmental problems—for example, plants that have trouble growing. Talk to family and friends and ask them what the explanation might be for the problem. Then try to come up with a solution.

Description of the problem:

_____

_____

_____

_____

_____

Explanation for the problem:

_____

_____

_____

_____

_____

Possible solution to problem:

_____

_____

_____

_____

_____

Unit 1/Learning   EN 19

Home/School Connection 10

"Storks"

A message from _____

"Storks" tells the story of a group of children who try to find out why storks no longer come to their village. Is there some bird or other animal that was once common in your area that is now hard to find? You might ask older relatives or friends if they know of such animals. Discuss with your child any animals that are now rare. For each animal you can think of, try to give a reason why it might be more rare now. If you can't think of any animals, what about those that used to be rare where you live but are now making a comeback? For example, perhaps there are now fish in a lake or river near you because the water has been cleaned up.

Have your child list the animals you talk about with possible reasons for their disappearance or return.

Animal: _____

Reason: _____

_____

Animal: _____

Reason: _____

_____

Animal: _____

Reason: _____

_____

Animal: _____

Reason: _____

_____

Unit 1/Learning   H/SC 10

*INDEPENDENT WORKSHOP
Building a Community of Scholars

Student-Directed Reading, Writing, and Discussion

Students should be working in their collaborative groups to complete their exploration projects related to learning. Each group might conference together to make sure that all areas of their exploration have been considered. They should be considering whether they have any information to present to the rest of the class. Those groups that want to share their explorations should be preparing their information for presentation.

WORKSHOP TIP

Encourage students to take responsibility within the group. Give students time to work out group problems before offering advice.

Additional Opportunities for Independent Reading, Writing, and Cross-curricular Activities

✱ Reading Roundtable

Some students may choose to read *The Wheel on the School,* from which "Storks" was taken, and discuss it in a reading roundtable. Suggest to participants that before the meeting they write a few good questions to ask each other about the book.

✱ Writing Seminar

Remind the children to continue revising, proofreading, or publishing their autobiographies or biographies or to work on the first drafts of their essays. Students who are proofreading should be encouraged to use the proofreading marks on their copy of Reproducible Master 20 in their Writer's Notebook. You might also mention to the students that it is very hard to proofread one's own work. Encourage those students who are in the process of proofreading to exchange papers and proofread each other's writing.

Some students may want to read a piece of writing they are working on to a partner and then request feedback about what they have written.

Portfolio

Remind the students to think about pieces of writing that they might choose to put into their portfolios.

Cross-curricular Activity Cards

Cross-curricular Activity Cards in the Student Toolbox that are appropriate for this selection include:

- 2 Science—Ecology
- 7 Social Studies—The Netherlands

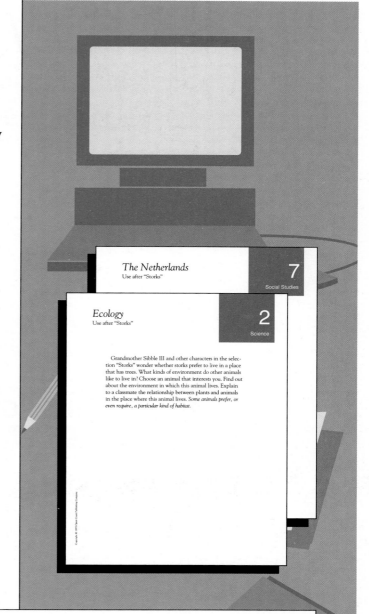

The Netherlands
Use after "Storks"

7

Social Studies

Ecology
Use after "Storks"

2

Science

Grandmother Sibble III and other characters in the selection "Storks" wonder whether storks prefer to live in a place that has trees. What kinds of environment do other animals like to live in? Choose an animal that interests you. Find out about the environment in which this animal lives. Explain to a classmate the relationship between plants and animals in the place where this animal lives. *Some animals prefer, or even require, a particular kind of habitat.*

Additional Opportunities for Solving Learning Problems

Tutorial

You may want to use this time to work with children who need help. The following teaching aids are available in the Teacher Toolbox for your convenience:

- Writer's Craft/Reading: Characterization, Teacher Tool Card 13
- Writer's Craft/Reading: Plot, Teacher Tool Card 15
- Writer's Craft/Reading: Point of View, Teacher Tool Card 12
- Writer's Craft/Reading: Setting, Teacher Tool Card 14

Poetry
Sam at the Library
To Young Readers

1 READING THE POEMS

INFORMATION FOR THE TEACHER

About the Poems

"Sam at the Library" is a funny narrative poem about how a boy learns to trust his own taste in choosing books to read. Students will enjoy the lively rhyme and rhythm of the poem. A very different mood is conveyed by "To Young Readers." Poet Gwendolyn Brooks delivers a serious message about the power of good books.

Link to the Unit Concepts

"Sam at the Library," pages 114–116, demonstrates in an amusing way that people have different tastes in books and like to learn about different things.

"To Young Readers," page 117, was commissioned by the Chicago Public Library. This poem tells students about the value of reading good books and the ways in which books can help people.

About the Poet

Gwendolyn Brooks was born in Topeka, Kansas, in 1917 and has lived most of her life in Chicago. At the age of thirteen, she published her first poem in a children's magazine. She won several awards for her first collection of poems, *A Street in Bronzeville.* In 1949 she won *Poetry* magazine's annual prize, and in 1950 she won the Pulitzer Prize for her second collection of poems, *Annie Allen.* She is poet laureate of Illinois.

Brooks has written only one book for children, *Bronzeville Boys and Girls.* This collection of poems about children living in the inner city was published in 1956. Each of these poems has as its title a child's name and is written in the voice of that child. The poems are concerned with children's inner lives—their wonderings, hurts, and sense of play.

LESSON OVERVIEW

"Sam at the Library" by Carol Combs Hole, pages 114–116
"To Young Readers" by Gwendolyn Brooks, page 117

READING THE SELECTION

Materials
Student anthology, pp. 114–117
Explorer's Notebook, p. 7

READING WITH A WRITER'S EYE

Minilesson
Writer's Craft: Sound and Meaning in Poetry

Materials
Reproducible Master 14

FYI
Teacher Tool Card
• Writer's Craft/Reading: Genre—Poetry, 10
(Use Teacher Tool Card listed below.)

GUIDED AND INDEPENDENT EXPLORATION

Independent Workshop

Optional Materials from Student Toolbox
Tradebook Connection Cards

Student Tool Card
• Writer's Craft/Reading: Reading and Writing Poetry, 10

FYI
Teacher Tool Card
• Writer's Craft/Reading: Genre—Poetry, 10

Asterisks (*) throughout the lesson indicate learning frameworks. Learning Framework Cards and Teacher Tool Cards can be found in the Teacher Toolbox.

INFORMATION FOR THE STUDENT

After reading and discussing the poems, share with the students any information about Gwendolyn Brooks that may interest them.

* COGNITIVE AND RESPONSIVE READING

Activating Prior Knowledge

The first poem is about a boy choosing books at a library. You might ask students to share what they know about different kinds of books people read for fun—mystery stories, fantasy, science fiction, etc.

Setting Reading Goals and Expectations

After the students have looked at and commented on the title, art-work, and length of each poem, have them talk briefly about poetry: What makes reading a poem different from reading a story or an article? What kinds of things does a reader find in a poem? Encourage students to share what they expect to find out about learning by reading the poems.

Recommen-dations for Reading the Poems

Have the students follow in the text as you read the poems aloud. Slightly emphasize the rhyming of words in "Sam at the Library": *me, three; third, word; bed, head, read.* Then stress the repetition of sounds within certain words of "To Young Readers"—*bandages, voyages, link-ages; hammers, redeemers; dials, bells, healing, hallelujah; Guest, Feast; lift, launch, applaud, world.*

Read the poems slowly two or three times, allowing students to stop you to clarify words or phrases. If necessary, model your reaction to some of the poem's statements or to combinations of words that you especially like.

During these readings, encourage the students to respond to the poems by connecting them to their own experiences.

* EXPLORING THROUGH DISCUSSION

Reflecting on the Poems

Have the students discuss each poem and any personal thoughts, reactions, or questions either one raised. Encourage them to think about how these poems add to what they know about learning. The students may notice that each poet has a definite attitude about books, and they may want to discuss these attitudes and how they relate to learning. Encourage the students to compare the poems to other selections in the unit, such as "The Library Card." Then have them add this information to the Concept Board.

> **TIP FOR ENGLISH LANGUAGE LEARNERS**
>
> Encourage English Language Learners to express what they think and understand. Take this opportunity to praise them for their use of language.

Response Journal

Poetry evokes very personal reactions. Students may wish to record their personal responses to the poems.

Recording Ideas

➤ Have the students sum up their discussions and record their ideas and impressions about the poems and the concepts on the Concept Board and in their Explorer's Notebook, page 7.

Evaluating Discussions

SAM AT THE LIBRARY

Carol Combs Hole
illustrated by Nelle Davis

My librarian
Said to me,
"This is the best book for grade three."
That was the year I was in third,
So I took the book
On her good word.
I hurried home, crawled into bed,
Pulled up the covers over my head,
And turned my flashlight on
And read.

But the book was awful
And icky and bad.
It wasn't funny;
It wasn't sad.
It wasn't scary or terribly tragic,
And it didn't have even an ounce of magic!

No prince,
No dragon,
No talking cat;
Not even a witch in a pointy hat.
Well!
What can you do with a book like that?

114

My librarian
Tried once more:
"This is the best book for grade four."
That was the year I was in fourth,
So I took her word
For what it was worth;
And I took the book back home to bed,
Draped the covers over my head
Turned my flashlight on,
And read.

But the book was dull as a Brussels sprout.
I couldn't care how the story came out.
It didn't have baseball
Or football or tennis,
It didn't have danger and lurking menace,
Or wicked kings like the ones in history,
And it didn't have even an ounce of mystery!
No midnight moan,
No deserted shack,
No great detective hot on the track,
Nobody tortured on the rack.
So naturally
I took it back.

My librarian
Used her head.
When I was in grade five, she said,
"Sam, it's silly to try to pretend
You like the books I recommend,

When it's perfectly,
Patently,
Plain to see—
Your taste and mine will never agree.
You like sports books—
I can't stand them.
I don't like mysteries—
You demand them.
You think fairy tales are for babies.
You hate dog stories worse than rabies.
You're not me,
And I'm not you.
We're as different as pickles and stew.
So from now on, Sam,
You go to the shelf,
And pick out the books you want,
Yourself."

And ever since then
We get along fine.
She reads her books;
I read mine.
And if we choose to converse together,
We smile—
And talk about the weather.

TO YOUNG READERS

Gwendolyn Brooks
illustrated by Nelle Davis

Good books are
bandages
and voyages
and linkages to Light;

are keys and hammers,
ripe redeemers,
dials and bells and
healing hallelujah.

Good books are good
nutrition.
A reader is a Guest
nourished, by riches of the
Feast,
to lift, to launch, and to
applaud the world.

117

"Storks" by Meindert DeJong

_____
_____
_____
_____
_____
_____

"Sam at the Library" by Carol Combs Hole

_____
_____
_____
_____
_____

"To Young Readers" by Gwendolyn Brooks

_____
_____
_____
_____
_____
_____

Unit 1/Learning   EN 7

Explorer's Notebook, page 7

2 READING WITH A WRITER'S EYE

MINILESSON

Writer's Craft:
Sound and
Meaning in
Poetry

Ask the students if there was anything about the poems that they especially enjoyed. Remind them that in poetry sound and rhythm are important. Poetry is often read aloud so that the listener can hear and enjoy the sound and rhythm of the words and phrases. These elements help create the mood of a poem.

Tell the students that the sound of the words the poet chooses is often as important as their meaning. Many poems have **rhyming** lines. Have volunteers read "Sam at the Library" and identify the rhyming words.

Tell the students that even when lines do not rhyme, poets use words that **repeat** the **sounds** of other words in the poem. For example, a poet might use a series of words beginning with the letter *m* or a series of words that have the long *o* sound. Although it might not always be obvious to the readers, poets put words together so that sounds echo from one word to another. Have volunteers read "To Young Readers" and find the sounds that are repeated (for example, *bandages, voyages, linkages; hammers, redeemers; dials, bells*).

Tell students that besides being concerned with the sound of words, poets are concerned with the feelings that certain words evoke. Ask volunteers to tell how, in the third stanza of "To Young Readers," the phrase "riches of the Feast" gives listeners a different feeling than would the phrase "elegant food at the banquet."

WRITING

Linking Reading to Writing

* Writing Process

Invite volunteers to share with the group instances of how they or other writers have used rhyme or repeated sounds in poetry.

If students are working on poems, encourage them to improve the poems by choosing words that convey feelings appropriate to the meanings of their poems and that echo the sounds of other words.

For more information about reading and writing **poetry**, see **Teacher Tool Card 10.**

VOCABULARY

Words that students might discuss and record in the Personal Dictionary section of their Writer's Notebook include the following:
patently, converse, redeemers, hallelujah, nourished, launch

Allow time for the students to complete Vocabulary Exploration forms, Reproducible Master 14, for words they wish to learn and remember.

3 GUIDED AND INDEPENDENT EXPLORATION

EXPLORING CONCEPTS BEYOND THE TEXT

Guided Exploration

Students will select activities in which they explore learning. Refer them to the **Exploration Activities poster** and give them time to choose an activity and to discuss what they wish to explore and how they wish to go about it. If the children need further help, here is a suggestion:
• Students might like to invite the school librarian to speak to the class about choosing books to read for personal enjoyment.

Presenting Exploration Results

If any of the collaborative groups have information to present to the rest of the class, allow sufficient time for them to do so. Encourage the students to take their time and make their presentations as interesting to their audience as possible. Be sure that any audiovisual equipment the students need has been provided.

After each presentation, encourage classmates to respond to the presentation. What did they enjoy most about the presentation? Which ideas were the most interesting? What new facts did they learn? Can they link information from the presentation with something they have learned during the course of the unit?

TIP FOR ENGLISH LANGUAGE LEARNERS

Invite English Language Learners to say a rhyming poem or a poem that contains repeated sounds in their primary language to help them feel more relaxed about using language. Listening to other languages provides an opportunity for native English-speaking students to learn about languages and cultures other than their own.

* INDEPENDENT WORKSHOP
Building a Community of Scholars

Student-Directed Reading, Writing, and Discussion

Collaborative groups should be bringing their exploration of learning to closure. Suggest that they think about whether they have any special ideas to share with the rest of the class. They should discuss how they want to present their ideas.

If any of the students have become very involved in a research project and are not yet ready to present their findings, allow as much time as they need. As students progress into the next unit provide time for these students to present their findings.

Additional Opportunities for Independent Reading, Writing, and Cross-curricular Activities

✱ Reading Roundtable

Students might enjoy reading or listening to more poetry about books. *Good Books! Good Times!* by Lee Bennett Hopkins contains a collection of poems on this subject. Encourage the students to practice reading some of these poems themselves.

✱ Writing Seminar

Encourage students to look through their writing folders to determine if there are any pieces they would like to prepare for publishing. Remind them to proofread carefully before they publish.

Portfolio

Remind students to think about which pieces of writing they will put into their portfolios.

Additional Opportunities for Solving Learning Problems

Tutorial

You may want to use this time to work with students who need extra help. For your convenience, the following teaching aid is available in the Teacher Toolbox:

- Writer's Craft/Reading: Genre—Poetry, Teacher Tool Card 10

Unit Wrap-up

UNIT DISCUSSION

Initiate a general class discussion on the unit. Remind the students to think about previous discussions on ideas from the Concept Board and to refer to page 3 of their Explorer's Notebook to remind themselves of what their ideas about learning were when the unit began and of what they expected to learn from the unit. Ask them what new ideas they have acquired and what new information they have learned. The discussion may be extended to include

- an evaluation of the unit selections. Which selections did the students find the most interesting? Which were the least interesting?
- an evaluation of the unit activities. Which activities did the students find the most enjoyable or informative? Which did not seem interesting or valuable?
- an evaluation of the overall unit. How well did the unit cover concepts related to learning? Was learning a worthwhile subject to examine? Why?
- suggestions of ideas related to learning that are worth further exploration, possibly beginning with any questions left on the Question Board.

Small-Group Discussion

As an alternative, you might have the students work in small groups to discuss the unit. Then have the groups share with classmates important points and conclusions from their discussions.

ASSESSMENT

Informal Assessment

❯ Give the students the opportunity to make individual evaluations of their learning experiences during this unit by completing Explorer's Notebook pages 20–21. You may want to conference individually with each student to discuss each evaluation.

End-of-Unit Assessment

At this point, you might wish to carry out end-of-unit assessments for unit 1, Learning. You will find the following end-of-unit assessment booklets in the Teacher's Toolbox:

Comprehension Assessment
- Understanding the Selection
- Making Connections Across Selections
- Checking Skills
- Multiple-Choice Option

Essay and Writing Assessment

You may pick and choose among the various assessment components to find the right mix for assessing areas you want to stress. See *Formative Assessment: A Teacher's Guide* for specific suggestions on how to use these assessment materials.

UNIT CELEBRATION

Encourage the students to suggest how they might celebrate the completion of this unit. Suggestions might include ideas similar to the following:

- Invite other classes or family members in for a classroom tour. The students can act as tour guides, pointing out projects and explaining their significance and explaining concepts from the Concept Board.
- Create a learning mural. In small groups the students could plan and draw scenes from the selections in this unit, or they could depict scenes from their own experiences. Each student should be encouraged to contribute to the mural.

Explorer's Notebook, page 20

Unit Wrap-up

How did you feel about this unit?
☐ I enjoyed it very much. ☐ I liked it.
☐ I liked some of it. ☐ I didn't like it.

How would you rate the difficulty of the unit?
☐ easy ☐ medium ☐ hard

How would you rate your performance during this unit?
☐ I learned a lot about learning.
☐ I learned some new things about learning.
☐ I didn't learn much about learning.

Why did you choose this rating?
_____
_____
_____
_____

What was the most interesting thing you learned about learning?
_____
_____
_____
_____

Is there anything else about learning that you would like to learn? What?
_____
_____
_____
_____

20 EN   Learning/Unit 1

Explorer's Notebook, page 21

What did you learn about learning that you didn't know before?
_____
_____
_____
_____

What did you learn about yourself as a learner?
_____
_____
_____
_____

As a learner, what do you need to work on?
_____
_____
_____
_____

What resources (books, films, magazines, interviews, tool cards, other) did you use on your own during this unit? Which of these were the most helpful? Why?
_____
_____
_____
_____
_____
_____

Unit 1/Learning   EN 21

Astronomy

UNIT INTRODUCTION

BACKGROUND INFORMATION FOR THE TEACHER

Explorable
Concepts

Although by fifth grade most students have learned that the earth is round and that it goes around the sun, studies have shown that they are often very unclear about this, and that they harbor serious doubts about the "official" story. In this unit they will learn that all over the world, and for centuries, people have wondered about many of the same things—how it is that the sun can disappear each night in the west and reappear each morning in the east, why we do not fall off the earth, whether there is an end to time or space, and so on.

Accordingly, the emphasis throughout this unit will be on spelling out what students really do think, about the earth, the moon, the sun, and the universe; developing those ideas; and relating them to the different concepts they read about.

In this process, it is important that the students' own conceptions be the focus of attention and classroom discourse, and that students not feel constrained to recite what they may know to be the "correct" theory. After all, scientists themselves are not in agreement about the ultimately "correct" theory—though they do agree about many of its necessary ingredients and about which facts it needs to explain. Present-day theories of the universe are highly mathematical and are inseparable from the most basic theories of physics. Only a few thousand astronomers, physicists, mathematicians, astrophysicists, and philosophers fully

understand these theories; to reach such understanding took each of them decades of study. What is more, these theories are extremely puzzling and do not seem to correspond at all to our everyday ideas about cause and effect—so in a sense, *no one* understands them.

But that does not mean that students should not be encouraged to wrestle with the fundamental problems just as the pre-Socratic philosophers did. Knowledge has progressed, to be sure, but many of the basic questions about the universe raised by the ancient Greeks are still in dispute among physicists and philosophers, and may never yield final answers.

As do other units, this one raises a broad range of questions. But in this case, it is important that you and your students not avoid some of the basic conceptual issues that are at the core of the history of speculation about the universe. Examples of questions along those lines are:

- If you lived thousands of years ago, or hadn't read about it in books, would you be able to tell whether the earth is flat, and whether the earth revolves around the sun or vice versa?
- What has the telescope been able to show us about the universe that we would not have known without it?
- Have ancient myths and stories about the stars and planets lost their value?

- What can ancient sites like Stonehenge or Bighorn Medicine Wheel tell us about what people long ago knew about the sun and stars?

Resources

Among the following resources are **professional reference books and magazines and audiovisual materials.** The professional reference materials are intended to help you develop the topic and organize information to share with the students in whatever way you choose. Among the audiovisual materials are some that only you will be able to obtain and others that will be available to both you and the students. For a complete list of audiovisual resources, see page 567.

In addition to the resources listed here, **bibliographies for the students** appear in the student anthology, on **Reproducible Masters 26–31,** and on **Home/School Connections 11–12, 16, and 17.** Encourage the students to use these bibliographies as they explore astronomy.

Professional Reference Books and Magazines

Abell, George O.; Morrison, David; and Wolf, Sidney C. *Exploration of the Universe.* Saunders College Publishing, 1993. This beginning college text will help you to guide students' explorations.

Asimov, Isaac. *Guide to Earth and Space.* Random House, 1991. Asimov answers many of the questions about the universe that beginning astronomers want to know.

Boorstin, Daniel J. *The Discoverers: A History of Man's Search to Know His World and Himself.* Random House, 1983. This readable account includes chapters on the development of the calendar and on pioneering astronomers.

Carlson, John B. "America's Ancient Skywatchers." *National Geographic,* March 1990. An archaeoastronomer discusses calendar markers left by Native Americans.

Davidson, Norman. *Sky Phenomena.* Lindisfarne Press, 1993. This resource for teachers includes sky charts, experiments, poetry and myths about astronomical phenomena, and other enrichments.

Davies, Paul. *Superforce: The Search for a Grand Unified Theory of Nature.* Touchstone Books, 1985. This book gives a somewhat different point of view from Hawking's or Gribbin's (see entries below) on many of the same subjects. It's a little easier to understand than Hawking's, a little more detailed than Gribbin's.

Degani, Meir. *Astronomy Made Simple.* Doubleday, 1976. This simple guide to the basic principles of astronomy contains information about the earth, moon, sun, and stars.

Goldsmith, Donald. *The Astronomers.* St. Martin's Press, 1991. This book looks at the most important astronomical discoveries of the century.

Gribbin, John. *In Search of the Big Bang: Quantum Physics and Cosmology.* Bantam, 1986. Gribbin's popular book is an introduction to the current state of research in cosmology—the structure and history of the universe.

Hawking, Stephen. *A Brief History of Time: From the Big Bang to Black Holes.* Bantam, 1988. Stephen Hawking is one of the best known and most widely respected of present-day physicists. He has spent most of his professional life disabled by a crippling disease and is not even able to speak with his own voice anymore. However, through a digitally-assisted voice mechanism, he was able to dictate this world-wide best-seller about the basic questions of the universe.

Kuhn, Thomas. *The Copernican Revolution.* Harvard University Press, 1957. This classic, by one of the best known philosophers and historians of science, tells the story of the replacement of the earth-centered picture of the universe by Copernicus's sun-centered picture in the sixteenth and seventeenth centuries.

Simon, Sheridan. *Stephen Hawking: Unlocking the Universe.* Dillon Press, Inc., 1991. This book comments on Hawking's ideas about the universe.

Smith, Bradford A. "New Eyes on the Universe." *National Geographic,* January 1994. This article describes new techniques for exploring the sky.

Sobol, Dava. "The Last World." *Discover,* May 1993. NASA scientists are preparing a tiny spacecraft for a long, cold trip to our only unexplored planet: weird little Pluto.

Audiovisual Materials

Earth Colonies in Space. Lucerne Media, 1986. This videocassette explores what life in a space colony might be like, with particular focus on the physical and psychological changes space pioneers will face. 20 minutes; film and videocassette.

Our Solar System: The Search for Other Life. Lucerne Media, 1986. This film speculates on the existence of life elsewhere in the universe and discusses the technologies that may help in the discovery. 20 minutes; film and videocassette.

Starting with Stars. Pyramid Film & Video, 1992. This film takes the viewer on a journey to the sun and to the second-nearest star, Alpha Centauri. It also contains a discussion of what has been seen through telescopes. 14 minutes; videocassette.

What Makes the World Go Around? Lucerne Media, 1991. The mysteries of gravity and its effect on objects in our solar system are discussed. 9 minutes; film and videocassette.

Community/School

Other resources that may be helpful in working with explorable concepts involving astronomy include the following:

- Local observatory or planetarium personnel
- Instructors of astronomy from local universities

Concept Board

Remind the students that they will be organizing a **Concept Board** for astronomy where they will **display important ideas, observations, writings, and artwork** as they proceed through the unit.

Using the Concept Board

Question Board

Designate an area of the classroom for the **Question Board. Remind the students to post any concept-related questions they have as they proceed through the unit.** You and the students should review the questions periodically and add or remove questions as necessary.

For a review of information about the **Concept Board** and the **Question Board,** see **Teacher Tool Card 121.**

Using the Question Board

UNIT PREVIEW BY THE STUDENTS.

Activating Prior Knowledge

Have the students discuss what they already know about astronomy. If any of them have visited planetariums or used telescopes or binoculars to examine the night sky, encourage them to tell what they have learned. Add this information to the **Concept Board.**

Setting Reading Goals and Expectations

- Have the students examine the photograph on pages 120–121 and share their ideas about it. The streak of light across the Milky Way was made by an orbiting satellite.
- Have the students spend a few minutes **browsing the selections** in the unit. Encourage them to list on the chalkboard the subjects and the people they think they will be reading about in the Astronomy unit.
- Tell the students that this unit has been designated as a research unit. Astronomy is a subject for which there is abundant factual material and one that might naturally arouse intellectual problems or arouse curiosity. The Research Cycle will provide a systematic, scientific framework for inquiry that is driven by the students' wonderings and conjectures. Display the Research Cycle poster for use throughout the unit. It might be helpful to post notes on the poster showing where each group is in the cycle as it proceeds in its exploration.

For information about **browsing** the unit, see **Learning Framework Card 1A, Setting Reading Goals and Expectations.**

For information about the **Research Cycle,** see **Learning Framework Card 4.**

❯ Have the students complete page 22 in their Explorer's Notebook and share their responses. Have them suggest and record on the **Question Board** any questions they want to pursue in their reading of the unit.

Explorer's Notebook, page 22

Knowledge About Astronomy

This is what I know about astronomy before reading the unit.

_____
_____
_____
_____
_____
_____
_____
_____
_____
_____

These are some things I would like to know about astronomy.

_____
_____
_____
_____
_____
_____
_____
_____
_____
_____
_____
_____

Reminder: I should read this page again when I get to the end of the unit to see how much I've learned about astronomy.

22 EN

Astronomy/Unit 2

Learning Unit: Astronomy

SELECTION	LINK TO THE UNIT CONCEPTS
● ▲ **How Did We Find Out the Earth Is Round?** pages 202–227 nonfiction by Isaac Asimov, illustrated by Stephen Marchesi	Through logic and careful observation, early Greek thinkers developed accurate theories about the shape of the earth.
● ■ **The Heavenly Zoo**, pages 228–245 legends from the book by Alison Lurie, illustrated by Monika Beisner	Lacking any scientific knowledge of the stars, ancient peoples created myths to give meaning to these phenomena.
Circles, Squares and Daggers: How Native Americans Watched the Skies, pages 246–263 informational article by Elsa Marston	Early Native Americans built elaborate observations to track the movement of the sun and stars, and thus chart the passage of time.
● **Sun and Star Calendars**, pages 264–281 nonfiction from *Skywatchers of Ages Past* by Malcolm E. Weiss, illustrated by David Rickman SLJ Best Books, 1983; Outstanding Science Trade Books for Children, 1982	Astronomers of the ancient Mayan civilization created a written calendar, basing it upon the movements of the sun and certain planets.
ON YOUR OWN ● **Galileo**, pages 282–297 biography from *Pioneer Astronomers* by Navin Sullivan	When Galileo became the first scientist to train a telescope on the heavens, he opened up a brand new world of knowledge.
● **Telescopes**, pages 298–309 nonfiction from *The Way Things Work* written and illustrated by David Macaulay Times Educational Supplement Information Book Awards, 1989; Science Book Prize, 1989; American Institute of Physics, Children's Science Writing Award, 1990	Telescopes—the basic tools of astronomy since the seventeenth century—have grown increasingly powerful and sophisticated.
FINE ART pages 310–313 *Cosmic Universe*, Natalie Goncharova; *The Starry Night*, Vincent van Gogh; **The constellation of Leo; Astronomers working in an Istanbul observatory**, Turkish miniature; **Tycho Brahe pictured at Uranienborg**	Artists express their visions of the heavens and ideas about astronomy.
● **Voyager to the Planets**, pages 314–335 nonfiction from the book by Necia Apfel ALA Notable Book, 1991; NCTE Outstanding Nonfiction, 1991; Best Science Books for Children, 1991	Modern technology, as implemented in the Voyager space probes, has vastly expanded our knowledge of the outer planets.
● **A Meeting in Space**, pages 336–359 science fiction from *Barbary* by Vonda N. McIntyre, illustrated by Mary Beth Schwark and Bob Kuester	Might the future of astronomy include human-inhabited space stations and, perhaps, contact with alien life forms?
ASSESSMENT ● ▲ **Stars**, pages 360–373 nonfiction by Seymour Simon	We now know what stars are made of, and how they are born and die.

● Award-winning authors and/or illustrators　　▲ Full-length trade books　　■ Dramatized on audiocassette

Exploration Through Research

SELECTION-BASED MINILESSONS		RESEARCH
TEACHER'S GUIDE	**TEACHER TOOLBOX**	
Questions and Conjectures, Parts of a Book	Causal Indicators, Providing Concept Information	Problem Phase 1 Stargazing Experiments in astronomy
Writing Paragraphs Using the Card Catalog	Using Dialogue, Adjectives and Adverbs, Synonyms and Antonyms	Problem Phase 2 Constellation myths Identifying constellations
Using Headings and Captions	Comparison and Contrast, Compound Words	Conjecture Phase Early observatories Native-American beliefs about astronomy
Strong Topic Sentences	Subject/Verb Agreement	Needs and Plans Phase 1 Early calendars Astronomy time chart
Students choose a writer's craft to focus on.	Biography, Providing Concept Information	Needs and Plans Phase 2 Famous astronomers Astronomy time chart
Paraphrasing Understanding Diagrams	Expository Text, Using Headings and Captions	Research Cycle Visiting an observatory Types of telescopes
Elaboration Through Providing Specific Facts Organizing Information in a Chart	Comparison and Contrast, Pronoun/Antecedent Agreement	Research Cycle Researching space probes Observing planets
Genre—Science Fiction Dialogue	Setting, Using and Punctuating Dialogue	Research Cycle Discussing science fiction
Choosing a writer's craft to study is part of assessment.		Research Cycle

Assessment available for this unit includes: Teacher's Observation Log, Self-Assessment Questionnaire, Concept Connections, Portfolios, and separate Comprehension, Essay and Writing, and Research assessments.

Learning Unit: Astronomy

SELECTION	LINK TO THE UNIT CONCEPTS

Despite our ever-increasing knowledge of the universe, it still holds many mysteries.

● Award-winning authors and/or illustrators

Exploration Through Research

SELECTION-BASED MINILESSONS		RESEARCH
TEACHER'S GUIDE	**TEACHER TOOLBOX**	
Discussing Poetry		Research Cycle
		Discussing the mysteries of space
		Sharing of group knowledge, insights, and ideas

Assessment available for this unit includes: Teacher's Observation Log, Self-Assessment Questionnaire, Concept Connections, Portfolios, and separate Comprehension, Essay and Writing, and Research assessments.

How Did We Find Out the Earth Is Round?

1 READING THE SELECTION

About the Selection

Some students may believe that Christopher Columbus was the first person to realize that the earth is not flat. Actually, certain Greek scholars preceded him by thousands of years. In this selection, noted author Isaac Asimov explains carefully and clearly how early scholars such as Anaximander used their powers of observation to deduce that the earth is round. Drawings and diagrams by Stephen Marchesi illuminate the text.

Link to the Unit Concepts

How Did We Find Out the Earth Is Round?, pages 122–139, summarizes how early thinkers came to conclude that the earth is a sphere and how they came to understand the earth's relation to the heavenly bodies. In this selection, early myths about the universe are contrasted with some of the first examples of scientific thinking about the universe, as represented by the Greek scholars Anaximander and Philolaus, who lived approximately twenty-five hundred years ago.

Some of the ideas that the ancients developed about the universe led to the development of other ideas. Knowledge about the moon and its phases, for example, led to knowledge about the earth's shape.

After reading this selection, students may find themselves asking whether, without prior knowledge about the universe or the benefit of technology, they could have discovered that the earth is round.

About the Author

The author, Isaac Asimov, was three years old when his family emigrated from Russia to the United States, where he grew up in a neighborhood of impoverished Jews and Italians in Brooklyn. He earned advanced degrees in chemistry from Columbia University.

LESSON OVERVIEW

How Did We Find Out the Earth Is Round? by Isaac Asimov, pages 122–139

READING THE SELECTION

Materials

Student anthology, pp. 122–139
Explorer's Notebook, p. 23

FYI

Learning Framework Cards
- Setting Reading Goals and Expectations, 1A

- Responding to Text, 1B
- Checking Understanding, 1C

Teacher Tool Card
- Classroom Supports: Modeling and Generating Think-Alouds, 116

READING WITH A WRITER'S EYE

Minilesson

Writer's Craft: Questions and Conjectures

Materials

Reading/Writing Connection, p. 14
Reproducible Master 14

Options for Instruction

Writer's Craft: Causal Indicators
Writer's Craft: Elaboration Through Providing Concept Information
(Use Teacher Tool Cards listed below.)

GUIDED AND INDEPENDENT EXPLORATION

Minilesson

Research Aid: Parts of a Book

Materials

Explorer's Notebook, pp. 28–30
Home/School Connection 11–12
Reproducible Masters 26–31

FYI

Learning Framework Cards
- Research Cycle, 4
- Problem Phase 1 and 2, 4A
- Writing Seminar, 8

Optional Materials from Student Toolbox

Tradebook Connection Cards

Cross-curricular Activity Cards
- 3 Science—Lunar Log
- 1 Math—Counting the Stars

Independent Workshop

Student Tool Cards
- Writer's Craft/Reading: Writing Questions and Conjectures, 45
- Writer's Craft/Reading: Showing Cause and Effect, 31
- Writer's Craft/Reading: Giving Concept Information, 43
- Study and Research: Parts of a Book, 98

FYI

Teacher Tool Cards
- Writer's Craft/Reading: Elaboration Through Forming Questions and Conjectures, 45
- Writer's Craft/Reading: Causal Indicators, 31
- Writer's Craft/Reading: Elaboration Through Providing Concept Information, 43
- Study and Research: Parts of a Book, 98

N O T E S

Asterisks (*) throughout the lesson indicate learning frameworks. Learning Framework Cards and Teacher Tool Cards can be found in the Teacher Toolbox.

Asimov is best known for his science-fiction stories and novels; however, he also wrote mysteries and books about the Bible, Shakespeare, physics, chemistry, biology, astronomy, and ancient and modern history.

Asimov was a man who truly enjoyed writing. In 1984, he told an interviewer, "Writing is more fun than ever. The longer I write, the easier it gets." He wrote every day, sometimes using as many as seven typewriters to work on manuscripts for seven different books in various stages of progress. A quick mind and a strict regimen enabled Asimov to write almost five hundred books before his death in 1992.

INFORMATION FOR THE STUDENT

Students who are unfamiliar with his writings may be interested in knowing that Isaac Asimov wrote many books and articles about astronomy. Students who found *How Did We Find Out the Earth Is Round?* informative might look for other books and articles by Asimov that will help them in their research on astronomy.

COGNITIVE AND RESPONSIVE READING

Activating Prior Knowledge

Ask the students what they can tell you about how people found out that the earth is round. They are probably aware that people used to think the earth was flat, but they may not know when and where thinkers began to theorize that the earth is round. Before reading the selection, allow time for students to tell what they know concerning early theories about the shape of the earth and how these theories gave way to scientific fact.

Setting Reading Goals and Expectations

Remind the students that the strategy they will use before they read is **setting reading goals and expectations.** To do this, they will **browse the selection** and **use the clues/problems/wondering procedure.** On the chalkboard under the headings clues, problems, and wonderings, write in brief note form the observations the students generate during browsing. For example, students might list the genre of the selection under *clues*; they might list unfamiliar words under *problems*; and they might note any questions that arise during browsing under *wonderings.* The students will return to these observations after reading.

For a review of **browsing,** see **Learning Framework Card 1A.**

Recommendations for Reading the Selection

Ask the students how they would like to read the text. Notice that because of its length *How Did We Find Out the Earth Is Round?* has been divided into two parts. The second part begins on page 132 and is indicated by a large initial capital letter. The selection also contains unfamiliar words and much new information. Students may want to begin the selection by reading aloud and then continue silently when they are sure that they can handle the vocabulary and content.

If the students elect to **read orally,** you should **refer to the think-aloud prompts that are provided beneath the page miniatures.**

Instead of or in addition to using these prompts, encourage the students to provide their own think-alouds while reading.

This would also be a good selection for **responding** to text **by wondering** while reading aloud. Model this response, and then invite the students to respond.

If they elect to **read silently,** have the students **discuss problems, reactions,** and **strategies** after reading. Let them know, however, that they can raise their hands anytime during reading to ask questions or to identify problems for discussion with the group.

About the Reading Strategies

How Did We Find Out the Earth Is Round? contains many descriptions of what early Greek scholars and other ancient peoples observed about the earth, the moon, the sun, and the stars. Students may comprehend some parts of the text more fully by employing the strategy of **visualizing**—that is, picturing in their minds what the author is describing or explaining in the text. Visualizing is one way to help clarify meaning.

When visualizing, it often helps to ask questions like

- Can I picture what the author is describing?
- What knowledge or experience do I have that will help me visualize what is happening in the text?
- Does the piece contain illustrations or diagrams that will help me visualize what is being described?

Because this selection is long and contains many facts, the students may also benefit from pausing occasionally to **sum up.** To review the strategies of **visualizing** and **summing up,** see **Learning Framework Cards 1B and 1C.**

Think-Aloud Prompts for Use in Oral Reading

Notice the suggested think-aloud prompts with the page miniatures. Remind the students that what they read should make sense to them. If it does not, they should refer to the strategy posters for help in deciding which reading strategies to use to help them unlock the meaning of the text. Explain to the students that occasionally you will model out loud the strategies that you use when you have difficulty or when you want to get more meaning out of the text. They may also share the strategies they use to solve a reading problem or to enhance their understanding of the text. Remind them to stop and ask for help or clarification if anything in the story puzzles them. They should also feel free to stop and share important thoughts as they read.

Model whenever necessary, using the think-aloud method. Encourage the students to take over the process as soon as possible. For a review of **modeling** and **generating think-alouds,** see **Teacher Tool Card 116.**

TEACHING TIP When a reading problem arises for one or more students, use the problem as a discussion topic, and let the class seek a solution.

THINK ALOUD PROMPTS

These prompts may be used as guides to promote cognitive and responsive reading.

HOW DID WE FIND OUT THE EARTH IS ROUND?

from the book by Isaac Asimov
illustrated by Stephen Marchesi

IS THE EARTH FLAT?

Far back in ancient times, everybody thought the earth was flat. This is because it looks flat.

If you are in a boat way out in the middle of the ocean, the top of the water looks flat in every direction and the sky seems to fit over it like an upside-down bowl. The line where the sky and water meet is called the "horizon." The horizon looks like a circle with you yourself at the center.

If you are on land, the land stretches out to a horizon also. The horizon on land, however, is not even. It goes up and down because of houses, trees, hills, and other things.

Some ancient people suspected the earth went on forever. They thought it might be a huge flat piece of land and sea with no end at all.

122

But if this were the case, then what about the sun? The sun rose in the east in the morning. It traveled across the sky and set in the west in the evening. Then the next morning, it rose again in the east.

Some ancient people tried to explain this by saying that every morning a brand-new sun was <u>manufactured</u> and rose. When it set, it was destroyed.

Others said that the sun set in the ocean to the west. Then during the night, it was put in a boat and rowed to the east. By morning, it was ready to rise again.

Still others thought the sun was a golden, flaming chariot pulled by magic horses that could fly through the air. In the morning, the sun-god would get into the chariot in the east. Then he and his horses would climb through the air, reaching the top of the sky at noon. They would race downward, reaching the far western ground in the evening. Somehow the sun-god would get back to the east during the night when his golden, flaming chariot gave out no light.

Stars that were very far from the North Star moved in such big circles that those circles dipped below the horizon. Those stars rose in the east and set in the west.

The moon also traveled across the sky from east to west. So did the stars. These things had to be explained also. The ancient explanations just didn't make sense.

Suppose we have a flat earth stretching out in every direction. How deep is it? Suppose you begin to dig a hole. Can you keep on digging forever, going down and down without end?

Or is the earth just a slab of material, maybe a mile thick—or ten miles—or fifty miles? If it is just a slab of material, what keeps it from falling down?

123

The people who lived in India in ancient times decided the earth didn't fall because it was resting on huge elephants.

But what were the elephants standing on? They said all the elephants were standing on the back of a gigantic turtle.

And what was the turtle standing on? They said it was swimming in a tremendous ocean.

Well, then, did the ocean stretch all the way down? There was no answer to that.

1 So you see, while the earth *looks* flat, it may not be safe to decide that it *is* flat. There are problems to the flatness.

The first people who thought about the problems of the flat earth were certain Greeks who lived about twenty-five hundred years ago on what is now the western coast of the nation of Turkey.

One of them was a man named Anaximander. He wasn't satisfied with the tales of sun-gods and flaming chariots and flying horses. Instead, he looked at the night sky and asked himself what he really saw.

On a clear night, he saw the stars. During the night, they seemed to travel across the sky.

One star, however, didn't move. It was the North Star. It stayed in the same place in the northern sky all night long. It stayed there night after night. The stars near it moved in a circle around it. If the stars were very near it, they moved in small circles. If they were farther away, they moved in bigger circles.

The most important thing about the night sky to Anaximander was that the stars traveled in patterns. They weren't like a swarm of bees, in which each bee moves its own way.

 124

The flat earth under the bowl of the sky.

The sun being rowed to the east during the night.

The sun god in his chariot by day.

The Indian belief.

The sphere of the sky around a central axis.

1 Students may wish to stop here to **sum up** Asimov's introduction. Encourage a volunteer to explain in his or her own words what, according to the introduction, the focus of this article will be. A good summary should mention the main problem (some people are no longer certain the earth is flat) and the reason for the problem (people have observed some things that may contradict the theory of the earth's flatness).

If the students have difficulty **summing up**, model the strategy for them. **Visualizing** may help students better comprehend why the question of how the sun got back to the eastern horizon was so puzzling to the ancients. Picturing the earth as a flat slab of land, and then imagining the sun rising in the east, traveling over the slab from above, and setting in the west may help the students understand why some ancient Greeks concluded that the sun could not possibly show up each morning on the east side of a flat earth.

Instead, all the stars moved together.

Anaximander decided that the sky was a huge hollow ball, or "sphere." The sphere of the sky turned around on an invisible line or "axis." One end of the axis stuck through the sky where the North Star was situated. The other end was at the opposite side of the sphere where he couldn't see it.

Every day the sphere of the sky turned around, or "rotated." The stars were all stuck to the sky and turned with it. That's why they kept the same pattern. The sun and moon were stuck to the sky, too, and that's why they rose and set.

Even though the sky was a sphere, it was still possible for the earth to be flat. Anaximander thought it was a flat slab that stretched across the sphere of the sky at its center.

As the sphere of the sky turned, the sun rose in the east, traveled across the sky, and set in the west. The turning sky carried it along. Then as the sky kept turning, the sun was carried to the bottom part of the sphere. When the sun shone on the bottom side of the slab of the earth, it was night. When the turning sky carried the sun around to the east, it rose and it was day again. The moon and the stars also moved in this way. Anaximander's idea made more sense than the ideas of earlier thinkers. The sun was not destroyed each night nor was it rowed from west to east. Yet Anaximander wasn't satisfied. He kept on thinking.

THE DISAPPEARING STARS

If the earth were a flat slab that fitted tightly across the middle of the sphere of the sky, we could travel to the place where the earth and sky met. We could reach the place where

❀ 126 ❀

the sun rose in the east and we could reach out and touch it (unless its heat killed us).

If we traveled far enough to the west, we could reach the place where the sun set.

Some people, centuries ago, really thought that could be done. They even drew pictures showing a man coming to the place where the sky touched the earth. The man could stick his head through the sky and see the machinery that kept the sphere of the sky turning.

The ancient Greek thinkers, however, didn't really believe that. After all, no matter how far to the east or west people traveled, they never seemed to get any closer to the sun, the moon, or the stars.

Perhaps, then, the earth didn't stretch from one side of the sky to the other. Perhaps our eyes only fooled us when they showed the sky touching the earth at the horizon.

Maybe the earth was a flat disc that was quite large but was far smaller than the sphere of the sky. If this were the case, the sun, the moon, and the stars would be far away from the edge of the earth. No one on earth would be able to reach them or even get particularly close to them.

But if the earth were a flat disc in the center of the sphere of the sky, with the sky far away on all sides, then why didn't travelers reach the end of the earth?

Perhaps because the land portion of the earth was in the middle of the flat disc and was surrounded by water. Travelers always reached the ocean if they traveled far enough. It was the ocean, then, that stretched out to the end of the earth. People, in ancient times, didn't travel far out of sight of the land. Maybe that was why they never came to the end of the earth.

❀ 127 ❀

2 **Visualizing** Anaximander's ideas about the earth and sky is one way to comprehend the text better. The illustration on page 125 is useful, but it may not help students visualize the way the sky moved in Anaximander's theory. Invite students to describe the earth and sky according to Anaximander's beliefs. How does he explain sunrise and sunset? If the students have problems, suggest that volunteers draw on the chalkboard a diagram of Anaximander's version of sunrise and sunset.

A lot of information has been presented so far. To check their understanding of the text, students may wish to **sum up** the first portion of Asimov's article. They should note the transition from making up stories to explain mysterious phenomena to examining problems in a scientific way.

3 In order to understand the idea described here, students may need to **visualize** it. If some students need help, ask a volunteer to draw a diagram on the chalkboard.

4 Students may understand this idea better if they **visualize** it. If some students continue to have trouble, ask a volunteer to diagram the idea on the chalkboard.

The earth as a shallow bowl.

But then why didn't the water of the ocean spill off the end of the earth?

Maybe the end of the earth was turned up at every side, so that the water was held in. Maybe the earth wasn't exactly a flat slab, but was a shallow bowl.

In that case, why didn't the whole earth simply fall?

It was still hard to consider the earth as flat, even if the sky was a huge sphere and the problem of sunrise and sunset was explained.

If the earth isn't flat, what other shape can it be?

Suppose we look at the sky again. In the sky, there are many shining objects, but most of them are stars. Stars are just little points of light to the eye and the ancient thinkers couldn't tell anything about them.

Two objects in the sky are different, however. They are the sun and the moon.

The sun is a circle of light at all times, but the moon isn't. Sometimes it *is* a circle of light, but sometimes it is only half

❧ 128 ❧

a circle. Sometimes it is in between a whole circle and half a circle. Sometimes it is just a thin curve of light called a "crescent."

The Greeks who watched the moon, night after night, noticed that it changed its position in respect to the sun. They noticed that as it changed its position, it also changed its shape.

When the moon and sun were on opposite sides of the earth, the moon was always a full circle of light. The sun shone past the earth onto the moon. It lit up the whole side of the moon.

When the moon and sun were on the same side of the earth, they couldn't see the moon at all. The sun shone on the other side of the moon, the side they couldn't see. The side they could see received no sunlight and it was dark.

The ancient scholars who observed this decided the sun had light of its own and the moon didn't. The moon shone only because it was lit up by the sun. The moon shone by "reflected light."

The ancient Greeks had begun to work out the study of "geometry," which deals with the shapes of objects. They considered the different shapes of the lighted part of the moon. They considered the half-moons, the crescent-moons, and other types. They could easily show that in order for the lighted part of the moon to take on the shapes it did, the moon had to be a round ball, or sphere.

Then what about the shape of the sun? It shone on the moon and it did so equally well from all angles. Whether the moon and sun were on opposite sides of the earth, or on the same side, or anything in between, the moon received the

❧ 129 ❧

5 This passage contains many important ideas that may be new to the students. They may wish to pause to **sum up** early ideas about the earth and the sky, giving the reason that each idea was rejected by Greek scholars.

6 To understand the preceding passage, students may need to visualize the movements of the moon in relation to the earth. If they express difficulty, engage them in a problem-solving discussion. You might say something like, *I am not sure that I understand what happens to produce a full moon or what happens to make the moon disappear from the sky during an eclipse. Is anyone else having trouble visualizing these situations? Let's find a way to understand these occurrences so that we can picture them in our minds.*

same kind of light on the side that faced the sun. This could only have happened if the sun were a sphere.

7 With all this in mind, Anaximander could see that there were three objects in the sky that had a particular shape. There was the sun, the moon, and the whole sky itself. All three were spheres.

Did that mean the earth was also a sphere? Did that mean the earth was round instead of flat?

Not necessarily. Maybe the rules were different for the sky and earth. Just because the sky and a few objects in the sky were spheres didn't mean that the earth had to be a sphere. After all, the sun was hot and blazing but the earth wasn't. The moon moved through the sky, but the earth didn't seem to. The sky itself was full of stars but the earth wasn't.

No, in order to decide upon the shape of the earth, people had to consider the earth itself, and not other objects.

So let's go back to the earth and ask ourselves the following question: Would we see the stars differently from different parts of the earth?

We wouldn't if the earth were flat. Suppose we looked at the sky at night. We would see all the stars in the sky above us if the night were clear. If we were anywhere else on a flat earth, we would still see those same stars.

But that is not the way things really are!

There were many people, in ancient times, who had to travel. People who traveled north would notice that the sky at night seemed a little different. Some stars that they used to see near the southern horizon when they were at home couldn't be seen at all when they went northward. Then,

130

when they returned home, those stars they hadn't been able to see showed up again just above the southern horizon.

People who traveled southward found things just the opposite. When they went south, they could make out stars just above the southern horizon that they never saw at home. When they returned, those stars disappeared again.

This was true of the northern horizon, too. At home, some stars dipped just a little below the northern horizon as they turned with the sky. If one traveled north, those stars stayed just a little above it. If one traveled south, stars that stayed a little above the northern horizon when one was at home began to dip below it.

The fact of the matter was that the stars were not seen from all parts of the earth, so the earth could not be flat.

The changing position of the stars.

131

7 In this portion of the text, Anaximander concludes that the sun, the moon, and the sky are spheres. Some students may want to **summarize** the sequence of ideas that led Greek thinkers like Anaximander to this conclusion.

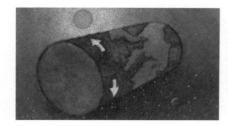

The earth as a cylinder.

Maybe the earth was shaped like a tin can, or "cylinder." This is exactly how Anaximander thought the earth might be shaped. He thought it was a cylinder lying in the center of the sphere of the sky. When you went north, you traveled along the curve of the cylinder. When you looked back, the curve hid some of the stars to the south. If you went south, you also traveled along the curve of the cylinder. When you looked back, the curve hid some of the stars to the north.

That explained the difference in the appearance of the sky as you went from place to place.

THE DISAPPEARING SHIPS

Anaximander's theory of a cylindrical earth raises some questions.

First, if the earth is <u>cylindrical</u>, why does it look flat?

That's not hard to answer. The earth is so large and we're so small that we can only see a tiny part of it as we look around.

❧ 132 ❧

The curve is so slight on a very tiny part of the earth that the surface looks flat.

To see this, imagine a large balloon blown up until it is a couple of feet across. Imagine a tiny circle on the balloon $1/8$ of an inch across. If a tiny insect could see only that much of the balloon, the surface of the balloon would appear flat.

A tiny circle on a sphere looks flat.

Here is a second question that's harder to answer. If you are traveling down a curve when you go northward or southward, why don't you feel as though you are walking downhill? Why don't you start to slide?

You might think that the ground is so rough that it prevents you from sliding. But what if you're not traveling over rough ground? What if you travel by ship northward or southward over the smooth ocean? Why doesn't the ship start sliding forward? In fact, why doesn't the whole ocean just slide downward and all its water pour right off the earth?

Anaximander didn't have a good answer for that. He just felt that there was no other way to explain the appearance of the night sky than to suppose the earth had a cylindrical shape.

Why does the earth curve only if we go north and south? Suppose we go east and west. Does the appearance of the stars change? Do stars disappear behind the western horizon if we go east? Do they disappear behind the eastern horizon if we go west?

That's hard to tell. Since the sky turns, stars are always appearing at the eastern horizon and disappearing at the western horizon. Traveling east and west doesn't change that.

❧ 133 ❧

8 Understanding how the stars appear and disappear is necessary to the students' understanding of why the earth cannot be flat and why, therefore, it must be curved. If students are confused about the ideas in this passage, **visualizing** may help them.

Note: This is a good place to stop reading if you and your class feel that you cannot finish the selection during this class period.

If the sky stopped rotating, it would be possible to tell whether stars were appearing and disappearing in the east and west. But the sky never stops rotating for even a moment, so that's no help.

But it's not very good to make a decision just because you have no evidence. To prove something, you need evidence.

Perhaps there's some other way of getting information about the shape of the earth, some way that doesn't involve the sky and the way it turns.

That kind of information can be obtained on the seashore and does not involve the sky.

If the earth were flat, a ship would get smaller and smaller as it sailed farther and farther away from shore. Finally, it would become a dot and disappear.

This, however, is not what happens. To begin with, someone watching a ship sail away can see the whole ship. He or she sees the wooden hull of the ship below and the sails above. After a while, however, the hull disappears. The water seems to reach above it and all that is left are the sails. Then only the top of the sails. Then the whole ship disappears.

Can it be that the ship is sinking? Is the water rising higher and higher, covering first the hull and then the sails?

That can't be, since it happens to every ship that sails away and most of them return safely. When a ship returned in ancient times, the sailors swore that at no time did the water rise above the hull.

How else could this be explained?

There was one way. Suppose the earth's surface curved. The ship would then sail away over that curve and would gradually

 134

A ship disappearing over the horizon.

disappear behind it. Naturally, the bottom part would disappear first.

The ships were hidden by the curve of the earth, just as the stars near the horizon would disappear first.

But there was one great difference. You could see the stars disappear behind the curve of the earth only if you traveled north and south. In other directions, the turning of the sky spoiled things.

The ships, on the other hand, disappeared bottom-first, in *whatever* direction they went. They disappeared bottom-first, whether they went north, south, east, west, or any direction in between.

What's more, it always looked as though they disappeared at about the same rate. If they were two miles away, a certain amount of the hull was hidden, no matter in what direction they were sailing.

It looked as though the earth curved in *every* direction, and by the same amount in every direction.

But the *only* shape that curves by the same amount in every direction is a sphere. If you make a point on a large ball and

135

draw a line away from that point in any direction, you will see that all the lines will curve in the same way.

Judging by what happens to ships, the earth is not a cylinder, but a sphere. It is a large sphere in the center of the much larger sphere of the sky. If the earth is a large sphere, then the tiny bit we can see at any one time looks flat.

A sphere curves equally in all directions.

But that still leaves us with the question of why we don't slip off the earth when we move around and why the air and ocean don't slip off. Is there something else that can give us proof of the earth's shape? There is something, but for that we have to go back to the sky again.

9

THE EARTH'S SHADOW

Every once in a while, the moon loses its light. A black shadow moves across it until all one can see is a dim red glow. After a while, the shadow moves away and the moon is back again, shining as brightly as ever.

When this happens, the moon is said to be "eclipsed."

In ancient times, an eclipse of the moon frightened people. They thought the moon might remain dark forever and they did not want to lose the moon's helpful light at night.

Those who studied the sky carefully were sure this would not happen. They noticed, for instance, that an eclipse took place only at the time of the full moon. It never took place at any other time. What's more it only took place during certain full moons.

🌿 136 🌿

The ancient Greeks who studied the sky knew that when the moon was full, it was on the opposite side of the earth from the sun. The sun shone past the earth onto the moon. The sun lit up the entire side facing them and that is why the Greeks saw the moon as a full, round circle of light.

Suppose, however, that the earth was *exactly* in between the moon and sun. Then the sunlight would have to go through the earth to reach the moon. It couldn't do that, of course, so no light would reach the moon.

Another way of saying this is that the earth casts a shadow. During an eclipse, the earth's shadow falls on the moon and darkens it. Every once in a while, at the time of the full moon, the earth is exactly in between the moon and the sun, and at those times there is an eclipse.

When the earth casts a shadow on the moon, we can find out something about the shape of the earth. The first thing we notice is that the edge of its shadow is a curve that looks exactly like part of a circle.

The Greeks watched eclipses of the moon that took place in different parts of the sky. They watched eclipses when the moon was high in the sky, or low, or at the horizon. When the

The shadow of the earth on the moon.

🌿 137 🌿

9 Understanding the way in which ships disappear from view as they travel away from shore is the key to understanding this passage.

Some students may need to clarify why it is that a ship passing from view bottom-first would lead observers to believe the earth was curved rather than flat. Students may want to **visualize** how a ship would disappear from view if the earth were flat instead of round. The illustrations on page 135 may help them understand and **visualize** how a ship sinks from view bottom-first.

moon was in different positions during an eclipse, the sunlight struck the earth from different angles. The shape of the shadow never changed. No matter where the moon was during the eclipse, the earth's shadow, as it moved across the moon, always looked like part of a circle.

This meant that the earth had a shape that cast a circular shadow in every possible direction. There is only one shape that does that, and that shape is a sphere.

About 450 B.C., a Greek scholar named Philolaus, who lived in southern Italy, was finally convinced.

He put all the evidence together. The change in the stars, the way in which ships disappeared as they moved away, and the shadow of the earth during an eclipse of the moon led him to one conclusion: The earth was a sphere located in the center of the much larger sphere of the sky.

So far as we know, Philolaus was the first man ever to say that the earth was a sphere.

But that still left questions. If the earth were a sphere and we were all living on top of it, why didn't we slide off as soon as we moved away from the top? Why didn't the ocean drip off and all the air drift away?

Let's think about this a little. Things fall downward. If we drop something, down it goes. But what do we mean by "down"? If the earth is a sphere and something falls down, it is falling toward the center of the earth.

This is true for every person on earth, no matter where he is standing. A person may be on one side of the sphere of the earth, or on the opposite side, or anywhere in between. Wherever he is, he and everything else about him are attracted to the center of the earth. Wherever he is standing, the

❧ 138 ❧

center is always in the direction of his feet, so that his feet seem to be "down" and his head "up."

About 350 B.C., the Greek scholar Aristotle pointed this out clearly.

Aristotle's view that everything was attracted toward the center of the earth meant that the earth *had* to be a sphere.

This explains why the oceans and air stay on the spherical earth, and don't slide **10** or drop off. Wherever they are, they are pulled "down" toward the center.

Down is toward the center of the earth.

MEET ISAAC ASIMOV, AUTHOR

While Isaac Asimov was growing up, he worked after school in his father's candy store. He was not allowed to read most of the magazines in the store, but because the magazine Science Wonder Stories *had the word science in the title, Asimov's father made an exception to his rule. When he was eighteen, Asimov had his first science-fiction story published in the magazine* Amazing Stories.

While working on advanced degrees in chemistry, Asimov continued writing stories. Later, when he worked as a teacher and researcher in biochemistry at Boston University, Asimov wrote a biochemistry book for students. He found that he enjoyed writing nonfiction even more than doing research. He continued to work as both a chemist and a writer until he decided to make his living as a full-time writer. Besides science fiction and nonfiction, Asimov wrote joke books, murder mysteries, explanations of history, and books about words, over four hundred books and a thousand articles in all. Astronomer Carl Sagan called him "the great explainer of the age." Asimov was a writer and a scientist who helped millions to understand the past, present, and future of our world and our universe.

❧ 139 ❧

10 Students might collaborate in **summing up** this final passage. Encourage students to help one another **visualize** the sun casting its light on the earth and the earth casting circular patterns of shadow on the moon. Visualizing this image will help them clarify how the Greeks finally concluded that the earth is round.

Some students may note that the belief in a spherical earth led to the development of the theory of gravity.

Discussing Strategy Use
Encourage the students to share the strategies they used while reading the selection. Have volunteers point out challenging passages and name the strategies that helped them understand the text.

*

EXPLORING THROUGH DISCUSSION

Reflecting on the Selection
Whole-Group Discussion

The whole group discusses the selection and any **personal thoughts, reactions, problems,** or **questions** that it raises. During this time, the students may also be invited to return to the **clues, problems,** and **wonderings** they noted on the board during browsing to determine whether the clues were borne out by the selection, whether and how their problems were solved, and whether their wonderings were answered or deserve further discussion and exploration. Avoid treating their ideas like a list to be discussed and eliminated in a linear fashion. Instead, let the **students decide which items deserve further discussion.** To stimulate discussion, the students can ask one another the kinds of **questions that good readers ask themselves about a text: What did I find interesting? What is important here? What was difficult to understand? Why would someone want to read this?** Your own participation in the discussion might take the form of expressing and modeling your reaction to characters or to some other aspect of the story. It is important for the students to see you as a contributing member of the group.

To emphasize that you are part of the group, actively **participate in the handing-off process:** When you have a contribution to make, raise your hand to be called on by the last speaker. Point out unusual and interesting insights verbalized by the students so that these insights can be recognized and discussed. As the year progresses, the **students will take more and more responsibility for the discussions** of the selections. The handing-off process is a good way to get them to take on this responsibility.

Assessment

In a successful discussion, it should not be necessary for you to ask questions to assess the students' understanding of the text. If necessary, however, engage in a discussion to **determine whether students have grasped the following ideas:**

- how all of the ancient scholars' observations and conclusions about the ships, the stars, and the lunar phases fit together
- why the earth looks flat even though it is round
- what reasons existed to convince people that the earth is round before there was technology to prove it

TEACHING TIP Emphasize that overall understanding of the text is more important than simply finding answers to specific questions.

Response Journal

Students may wish to record their personal responses to the selection.

Exploring Concepts Within the Selection
Small-Group Discussion

While the small groups discuss the relationship of the selection to astronomy, circulate and observe the discussions. Remind the students to refer to the Concept Board and the Question Board to help keep their discussions focused.

Sharing Ideas About Explorable Concepts

Have the groups **report their ideas** and **share** them with the rest of the class. It is crucial that the students' ideas determine this discussion.

- The students may point out that myths about the universe did not satisfy ancient scholars like Anaximander and Philolaus. Instead, these

TEACHING TIP Encourage the students to comment on one another's ideas.

early astronomers employed a pattern of questioning, observing, and reasoning to explain phenomena. They were interested in uncovering facts, not in creating fictions.

- Some students may notice that many of the initial observations and discoveries that the Greeks made about the earth, the sun, and the moon led to additional discoveries and theories.

As these ideas and others are stated, add them to the **Question Board** or **Concept Board.**

Exploring Concepts Across Selections

Students may **make connections with other selections in the student anthology.**

- Some students may compare this selection with "The Wheel on the School," in the Learning unit, in which a group of schoolchildren gradually pieced together various items of knowledge in order to understand why storks did not nest in their town. Students may point out similarities between the observation and reasoning processes used by the Greeks and those used by the schoolchildren.

Recording Ideas

As they complete the above discussions, ask the students to **sum up what they have learned from their conversations** and to tell how they might use this information in further explorations. Any special information or insights may be recorded on the **Concept Board.** Any further questions that they would like to think about, pursue, or investigate may be recorded on the **Question Board.** The students may want to discuss the progress that has been made on their questions. They may also want to cross out any questions that no longer warrant consideration.

➤ Encourage the students to record their findings on page 23 in the **Explorer's Notebook.**

Connections Across Units

TIP FOR ENGLISH LANGUAGE LEARNERS

Provide opportunities for conversations about how humans have learned about astronomy. Encourage English Language Learners to discuss with a partner how testing theories through experiments and revising theories based on the results of experiments relates to the selection.

Professional Checkpoint: Cognitive and Responsive Reading

As they read, good readers envision the action being described in a text. This process heightens their enjoyment of the text but also improves comprehension and long-term memory. Many elementary readers do not visualize sufficiently. As a result, their comprehension suffers. The mental images created while visualizing are a form of interpretation. They reflect the interaction between what the reader receives from the text and what he or she brings to the reading of the text. These images are a type of nonverbal coding that is deeper and more meaningful than the verbal coding that follows from reading words of the text.

Notes:

Recording Concept Information

As I read each selection, I learned these new things about astronomy.

How Did We Find Out the Earth Is Round? by Isaac Asimov

_____
_____
_____
_____
_____
_____
_____

"The Heavenly Zoo" by Alison Lurie

_____
_____
_____
_____
_____
_____
_____
_____

"Circles, Squares, and Daggers" by Elsa Marston

_____
_____
_____
_____
_____
_____
_____

Copyright © 1995 Open Court Publishing Company

Unit 2/Astronomy   EN 23

Explorer's Notebook, page 23

2 READING WITH A WRITER'S EYE

MINILESSON

Writer's Craft:
Questions and
Conjectures

Have students **discuss why the writer of an article will sometimes ask a question and then immediately answer it.** Some students may understand that the writer foresees a question that the reader might have about something he or she has written. In order **to make sure that the reader does not get confused, the writer asks the question and answers it.**

Point out that, in writing, questions can serve other purposes. **A writer may ask questions in an article to make his or her readers think along certain lines.** For example, in *How Did We Find Out the Earth Is Round?,* Isaac Asimov uses questions and conjectures to illustrate how scientists decided that the earth is round.

Asimov tells his readers things that early scientists observed about the earth, the sun, and the stars. Then he asks his readers the questions that these scientists asked themselves about their observations. Asimov explains how these observers tried to answer their questions with conjectures. Then he points out new questions that arose from each conjecture and new conjectures that were offered to answer the questions. By following several series of questions and conjectures, Asimov is able to show how some theories were abandoned when important questions could not be answered and how scientists eventually arrived at the explanations that we accept today.

On page 124, Asimov begins by describing a series of questions and conjectures that show how one mythical concept of the earth developed in ancient India. The original conjecture was that the earth was a flat slab that rested on the backs of huge elephants.

This raised the question, "Where were the elephants standing?"

". . . on the back of a gigantic turtle."
"And what was the turtle standing on?"
". . . it was swimming in a tremendous ocean."
"Did the ocean stretch all the way down?"

Asimov says that, because there was no answer for the last question, people had to look for other explanations of what the earth was like.

Selective Reading:
Focus on Questions
and Conjectures

Have students go back to *How Did We Find Out the Earth Is Round?* and find other examples of how Asimov uses a series of questions and conjectures to explain the thinking of scientists as they tried to determine the shape of the earth. Encourage volunteers to read aloud and explain the examples they find.

Other **examples of Asimov's use of questions and conjectures** in the article **include**
- page 127: the Greeks' conjecture that the earth was a flat disc
- page 132: Anaximander's conjecture that the earth was shaped like a cylinder
- page 134: the explanation of why ships seem to sink as they sail away from the viewer
- page 138: the explanation of why people and ships and the ocean do not fall off the earth

Independent Practice:
Questions and
Conjectures

➤ To provide additional practice for recognizing how questions and conjectures can be used to guide readers' thinking, have the students work in small groups to discuss and complete Reading/Writing Connection 14. Make a note of **students who might need help during Independent Workshop.**

WRITING

Linking Reading
to Writing

Remind the students that sometimes they can explain things more clearly to their readers by using questions and conjectures to show how they arrived at their ideas.

Encourage students to look through their writings for ideas that are not as clear as they would like them to be. Suggest that they use a question-and-conjecture format to help them explain the ideas.

∗ Writing Process

If they have elected to begin a new piece, encourage the students to make brief notes on ideas that they might want to incorporate into their

Selection-Based Practice

Reading/Writing Connection 14

writing. If necessary, have the students meet with their classmates to generate prewriting ideas. If they are involved in writing the essay they began after reading "Storks," suggest that they be alert for places in which they can use questions or conjectures to explain their ideas.

VOCABULARY

Concept-related words from the selection that the students may want to remember and use include the following:

horizon, sphere, spherical, axis, rotated, eclipse, cylinder, geometry, crescents

Have Vocabulary Exploration forms, Reproducible Master 14, available for students who request them.

VOCABULARY TIP The Vocabulary Exploration forms allow the students to use new words in a variety of ways and to relate new words to what they already know to improve their vocabularies.

3 GUIDED AND INDEPENDENT EXPLORATION

EXPLORING CONCEPTS BEYOND THE TEXT

Guided Exploration

The following activities do not have to be completed within the days devoted to this lesson.

• Tell the students that they might combine traditional library research with other forms of research. They might engage in firsthand experimentation or make firsthand observations of an astronomical phenomenon, much as the early Greeks did in Isaac Asimov's selection.

- Students might study the night sky to identify particular constellations or to observe the phases of the moon.
- Individually, in small groups, or as a class, students might conduct simple experiments from books like Janice VanCleave's *Astronomy for Every Kid* (see the unit bibliography, pages 242–243 of the student anthology) or they might devise experiments of their own. For example, a globe and a tiny sailboat could be used to demonstrate how sails disappear on the horizon; a light bulb and two balls could be used to demonstrate the phases of the moon and how eclipses occur.

TIP FOR ENGLISH LANGUAGE LEARNERS

Give English Language Learners a chance to participate and succeed in the learning process. Encourage them to work in cooperative/collaborative groups with students who share their interest in conducting experiments.

To find answers to their questions, early astronomers observed carefully and kept notes on important observations. Tell the students that in the course of their research, whether they are reading information or making firsthand observations, they should keep notes on important information and ideas they discover. They can write their notes on blank sheets of notebook paper and store these sheets in their Explorer's Notebook. They will gather at certain times during their research activities to share what they have observed and learned.

➤ Distribute Home/School Connection 11–12 to **introduce the students' families or adults at home to the explorable concepts** and to encourage them to join with the students in exploring astronomy.

➤ Distribute copies of Reproducible Masters 26–31 so that the students will have this **bibliography** available when they begin their research. Remind them also to consult the bibliography on student anthology pages 242–243. Students should **examine the bibliographies for subjects they might choose as research topics.**

Research Cycle: Problem Phase 1

➤ **Outline the research-project schedule for the students:** how long the project in the Astronomy unit is expected to take, how much time will be available for research, when the first presentation will be due. This schedule will partly determine the dimensions of the problems that students should be encouraged to work on. Most projects should be completed at the time you finish the unit. Inform the students, however, that some projects may take longer. Additional information on pacing is provided on **Learning Framework Card 4.** Have the students enter key dates on the calendar in their Explorer's Notebook, pages 28–29. Encourage them to make note of their accomplishments each day. This will help them monitor their progress and will enable you to help them manage their time. Explain to the students that the type of research they will conduct will take several weeks and will require them to make important decisions about managing their time. Suggest that they record dates on the calendar in pencil, since schedules often need to be revised.

Have the students **examine their original questions and ideas about astronomy** on the Question Board and the Concept Board. Encourage them to **use these initial questions and theories about the explorable concepts to suggest research ideas.**

✱ Exploring Through Research

How Did We Find Out the Earth Is Round?

A message from _____

The unit we are now reading is about astronomy. Astronomy is the study of the stars, planets, and other objects that make up the universe. Like the astronomers and astronauts, students will be exploring the universe—learning about the stars, planets, sun, moon, space travel, and much more.

They will begin their explorations by considering how early thinkers concluded that the earth is round. They will go on to read about myths and legends associated with the stars, early calendars, Galileo, telescopes, the Voyager explorations, and current investigations into such phenomena as black holes and quasars.

You can help in this exploration by reading books, observing the night sky, performing experiments, or visiting a planetarium with your child.

The following books and articles may help you and your child as you begin to explore the universe together.

"America's Ancient Skywatchers" by John B. Carlson. *National Geographic,* March 1990. This article tells about calendar markers left by ancient Americans.

A Field Guide to the Stars and Planets by Donald H. Menzel and J. M. Pasachoff. This all purpose guide contains sky maps and other aids for amateur astronomers.

How the Earth Works: 100 Ways Parents and Kids Can Share the Secrets of the Earth by John Farndon. You and your child may enjoy performing the experiments within the section entitled Planet Earth—all of which relate to the spinning earth.

"New Eyes on the Universe" by Bradford A. Smith. *National Geographic,* January 1994. This article describes new techniques for exploring the sky.

continued

Unit 2/Astronomy   H/SC 11

Home/School Connection 11

How Did We Find Out the Earth Is Round?

continued

The Night Sky: An Introduction to Star Watching by Dennis Mammana. This book gives directions on identifying constellations, as well as information on binoculars and simple telescopes.

Our Solar System by Seymour Simon. This book contains beautiful four-color photographs and fascinating information about the planets, moons, asteroids, meteoroids, and comets that travel around our sun.

Whitney's Star Finder by Charles Allen Whitney. This wheel-shaped device will help you to find constellations at different times of the year.

Other books and magazines can be found on bibliographies your child can share with you.

Unit 2/Astronomy   H/SC 12

Home/School Connection 12

BIBLIOGRAPHY

Ancient Astronomy by Isaac Asimov. This book from the series Isaac Asimov's Library of the Universe briefly describes the history of astronomy from prehistoric times until the time of Galileo.

Anno's Medieval World by Mitsumasa Anno. How did the discoveries of Galileo and Columbus change ways of thinking about the world and the universe? Beautiful illustrations help to tell the story.

Astronomy for Every Kid: 101 Easy Experiments that Really Work by Janice VanCleave. Have fun while you learn the basic concepts of astronomy.

The First Travel Guide to the Moon: What to Pack, How to Go, and What to See When You Get There by Rhoda Blumberg. Take a trip to the moon with this imaginative guidebook.

❧ *242* ❧

The Nova Space Explorer's Guide: Where to Go and What to See by Richard Maurer. Explore the moon, the planets, and beyond with this book based on the popular television series.

Sky Above and Worlds Beyond by Judith Herbst. This introduction to studying the stars includes information about the astronomy of ancient Britons, Mayas, Egyptians, and Native Americans.

To Space & Back by Sally Ride with Susan Okie. An astronaut tells what it's like to live on a space shuttle.

A Wrinkle in Time by Madeleine L'Engle. In this popular book, L'Engle describes a trip through space and time.

❧ *243* ❧

Bibliography

Books and magazines related to astronomy are listed below. You may use these as references along with other books and magazine articles you find that are related to the explorable concepts.

Notes

The Asteroids by Isaac Asimov. From Asimov's Library of the Universe series, this book tells of the 3,000 or more "flying mountains" found in the asteroid belt between the orbits of Jupiter and Mars.

Calendar Art by Leonard Everett Fisher. This fascinating picture book describes the history and function of thirteen different calendars, from the very first one developed by the Sumerians almost 5,000 years ago, to the Gregorian calendar used in most parts of the world today.

Calendars by Necia H. Apfel. In ancient times people looked to the sun, moon, and stars to help them chart the passing of time and the changing of the seasons. Find out how these early skywatchers used their observations to create the first calendars, and how our modern calendar evolved from the calendars of the ancients.

Comets and Meteors by Isaac Asimov. In this volume from his Library of the Universe series, Asimov tells us what comets and meteors are made of, what a "shooting star" really is, what causes meteor showers, and much more.

Name

RM 26   Unit 2/Astronomy

Reproducible Master 26

Bibliography *continued*

Notes

The Donkey Planet by Scott Corbett. Two young space scientists from Earth secretly visit the planet Vanaris to exchange metal samples with a Vanarian scientist. But Vanarian Isolationists, led by the tyrannical Commander Gru, are violently opposed to contact with other planets. What happens when Gru discovers the scientists?

Galaxies by Seymour Simon. Learn about different types of galaxies, such as spiral and dwarf galaxies. Look deep into the past via infrared telescope photos of distant galaxies, whose light traveled for millions of years before it reached us!

The Green Book by Jill Paton Walsh. After a four-year journey from the dying planet Earth, young Pattie and her fellow refugees land safely on a beautiful distant planet. But life on the planet Shine proves perilous. Will the colony of Earthlings survive?

Jupiter by Seymour Simon. Read about the many fascinating features of Jupiter, the largest planet in our solar system, and enjoy amazing *Voyager* photographs of this stormy planet and its four Galilean moons.

Look to the Night Sky: An Introduction to Star Watching by Seymour Simon. This book explains how to observe the moon, stars, and planets using only your own eyes. Included is a guide to locating the major constellations and every planet visible to the naked eye.

The Magic Schoolbus Lost in the Solar System by Joanna Cole. A class field trip turns into a funny yet informative trip through space.

Name

Unit 2/Astronomy   RM 27

Reproducible Master 27

Bibliography *continued*

Notes

Mercury by Seymour Simon. See Mercury for yourself through photographs from the *Mariner 10* expeditions, and find out what we have learned about the fascinating environment of the planet closest to the sun.

The Moon by Seymour Simon. In the strange, dead atmosphere of the moon, not even a spaceship's rockets can create a sound. Enjoy haunting photographs from the *Apollo* landings while reading about our nearest neighbor in space.

Moon-Whales and Other Moon Poems by Ted Hughes. Imagine a moon-nasturtium, seething with green caterpillars the size of anacondas. These and other bizarre and deadly creatures inhabit the moon of Ted Hughes's imagination. Read about them in this delightfully chilling collection of poems.

Neptune by Seymour Simon. Discover what we've learned about the turbulent environment of this distant planet, where winds can reach speeds of 700 miles per hour and gigantic tropical hurricanes rage constantly.

Odyssey magazine. Published monthly by AstroMedia Corporation, this magazine is for beginning astronomers and often includes sky games and activities.

Our Solar System by Seymour Simon. Visit the nine planets, many moons, and thousands of comets, asteroids, and meteoroids that revolve around our sun. This journey through our solar system is illustrated with many stunning full-color photographs.

Name

RM 28   Unit 2/Astronomy

Reproducible Master 28

Bibliography *continued*

Notes

Quasars, Pulsars and Black Holes by Isaac Asimov. This volume from the Library of the Universe series tells about some of the most interesting and mysterious astronomical discoveries made during the past fifty years.

Rooftop Astronomer: A Story about Maria Mitchell by Stephanie Sammartino McPherson. This biography tells the story of Maria Mitchell, the first woman acknowledged as an astronomer in the United States.

Saturn: The Spectacular Planet by Franklyn M. Branley. Drawing on information and photographs gathered by the spacecrafts *Voyager 1* and *Voyager 2*, Branley discusses Saturn's size, shape, temperature, atmosphere, satellites, and remarkable rings.

Seeing Earth from Space by Patricia Lauber. View our world as the astronauts have! Illustrated with photographs and satellite images of Earth as it appears from space, this book explains how remote sensing devices are used from spacecraft to teach us more about our planet.

Sky Dragons and Flaming Swords by Marietta Moskin. Solar eclipses, some of our early ancestors believed, were caused by monsters eating the sun. Comets were thought to foretell plagues. Find out more about how early skywatchers interpreted astronomical phenomena, as well as why such events *really* happen and what modern astronomers have learned from them.

Name

Unit 2/Astronomy   RM 29

Reproducible Master 29

Bibliography *continued*

Notes

Small Worlds: Sixty Moons of Our Solar System by Joseph W. Kelch. Seven of the nine planets in the solar system are circled by at least one moon—Saturn may have as many as twenty-three! This book identifies and describes each known moon and even suggests which moons might most easily be colonized by humans.

The Solar System: Opposing Viewpoints by Peter and Connie Roop. Have you ever wondered where the solar system came from or what comets really are? Read about these and other mysteries that have puzzled experts for years.

Sun Dogs and Shooting Stars: A Skywatcher's Calendar by Franklyn M. Branley. This book provides aspiring stargazers with a guide to the most interesting sights to look out for each month and season, as well as instructions for making your own basic starwatching tools.

Think about Space: Where Have We Been? Where Are We Going? by Isaac Asimov and Frank White. This book traces the history and politics of humankind in space—focusing on the U.S.-Soviet "space race" of the 1950s and '60s—and poses some challenging questions about the planning and goals of future space missions.

Truth on Trial: The Story of Galileo Galilei by Vicki Cobb. In 1633, Italian astronomer Galileo Galilei was sentenced to life imprisonment for supporting the then-radical theory that the earth revolves around the sun. Read about his trial and the brilliant career that led up to it in this intriguing biography.

Name

RM 30 — Unit 2/Astronomy

Reproducible Master 30

Bibliography *continued*

Notes

Uranus: The Seventh Planet by Franklyn M. Branley. A two-year-old Uranian would be 168 years old on Earth! Find out more about this cold and distant planet.

Venus: A Shrouded Mystery by Isaac Asimov. Years ago, some scientists imagined Venus as a tropical world of warm oceans and abundant plant and animal life. Find out what we now know about our nearest planetary neighbor in this fact-filled volume from Asimov's Library of the Universe series.

What Are You Figuring Now? A Story about Benjamin Bannekar by Jeri Ferris. This African American published the first American almanac, a listing of astronomical events.

What Makes the Sun Shine? by Isaac Asimov. This book explains how the sun manufactures energy.

Add books and articles you find.

- _____
  _____
- _____
  _____
- _____
  _____
- _____
  _____
- _____
  _____

Name

Unit 2/Astronomy — RM 31

Reproducible Master 31

Project Planning

Use the calendar to help schedule your astronomy unit project. Fill in the dates. Make sure that you mark any days you know you will not be able to work on the project. Then choose the date on which you will start and the

Sunday	Monday	Tuesday	Wednesday

28 EN — Astronomy/Unit 2

Explorer's Notebook, *page 28*

date on which you hope to finish. You may also find it helpful to mark the dates by which you hope to complete different parts of the project. Record what you accomplish each day.

Thursday	Friday	Saturday

Unit 2/Astronomy — EN 29

Explorer's Notebook, *page 29*

Have them **post on the Question Board any additional questions** raised by *How Did We Find Out the Earth Is Round?* Remind them that they can post questions at any time throughout the unit. Encourage them to consult the board periodically to **answer posted questions, to look for ideas for exploration, or to find out who has similar interests so that they can exchange ideas and information.** Remember to post your own questions from time to time as well.

The selections in this unit introduce only some of the important people who worked as astronomers and helped solve some of the mysteries of the universe. Encourage the students to explore the different theories of other scientists and thinkers who labored to explain the workings of the stars and planets. Encourage them to think about the contributions made by these individuals and about the difficulties they may have faced.

To start the Problem Phase of the Research Cycle, conduct a **free-floating discussion of problems and questions that interest the students.** Explain to the students that a good research problem or question will not only require them to consult multiple sources, but will add to the group's knowledge of astronomy, be engaging, and generate further questions. Explain that a research problem is different from a research topic.

To help the students understand the difference between a research topic and a research problem, you might have them consider the difference between the topic "California" and the problem "Why do so many people move to California?" Explain that if they choose to research the topic "California," everything they look up under the subject heading or index entry *California* will be related in some way to their topic. They will have difficulty choosing what information to record. This excess of information will also create problems for them in organizing their research. Clearly then, this topic is too broad and general. Choosing a specific question or problem relating to the topic, one that particularly interests them, will help them narrow their exploration and advance their understanding. Explain that the question "Why do so many people move to California?" is easier to research. Many sources will contribute to an answer to the question, and all the information located can be easily evaluated in terms of its usefulness in answering the question.

❯ Help the students think about problems related to astronomy that they might like to research. Generate a list of these on the chalkboard. Model for the students how to turn their research ideas into good research problems, especially if their initial responses are topics rather than problems. For additional information on modeling the formation of good research problems or questions, see **Learning Framework Card 4A.** When the discussion is completed, assign page 30 of their Explorer's Notebook to be completed during Independent Workshop.

Research Aid:
Parts of a Book
Guided Practice:
Parts of a Book

Have the students use the student anthology and other books to review the parts of a book:

- title page
- copyright page
- table of contents
- glossary
- bibliography
- index (The student anthology does not include an index.)

Call on a volunteer to look in the student anthology for the year of publication. You might need to direct the student to the copyright page.

Independent Practice:
Parts of a Book

Divide the students into small groups, and have each group look at a different part of the student anthology or other books. Encourage the students to find some interesting fact in a table of contents, a glossary, a bibliography, or an index and share it with the rest of the class.

Explorer's Notebook, page 30

Research Cycle: Problem Phase 1

A good problem to research:

_____
_____
_____
_____
_____
_____

Why this is an interesting research problem:

_____
_____
_____
_____
_____
_____

Some other questions about this problem:

_____
_____
_____
_____
_____
_____

30 EN   Astronomy/Unit 2

✳ INDEPENDENT WORKSHOP
Building a Community of Scholars

Student-Directed Reading, Writing, and Discussion

Tell the students that they will devote the first part of each day's Independent Workshop to **collaborative work with peers on their unit projects.** They can spend the remainder of Independent Workshop time on options of their own choosing.

WORKSHOP TIP

Students should be sharing information freely. They should be encouraged to use the Concept Board and the Question Board often. In their Explorer's Notebook they should write questions, notes, or information from either board that they think will be useful. It is important that they share with their classmates the ideas and information that they record in their Explorer's Notebook.

Research Cycle: Problem Phase 1 Students should complete the Problem Phase 1 page in their Explorer's Notebook. Ask them to elaborate on their reasons for wanting to research their stated problems. They should go beyond simple expressions of interest or liking and indicate what is puzzling, important, potentially informative, and so forth, about their chosen problem. If the students are having difficulties generating problems or questions for research, have them browse the Cross-curricular Activity Cards in the Student Toolbox for ideas. If the students are having trouble turning their ideas into questions or problems to research, see **Learning Framework Card 4A** for helpful hints on focusing their ideas.

Resources The students will need as many resources as possible to help them choose their research problems. Provide as many of the suggested resources as you can.

Additional Opportunities for Independent Reading, Writing, and Cross-curricular Activities

✷ Reading Roundtable

Remind the students that the **Tradebook Connection Cards** in the Student Toolbox are always a good resource for Reading Roundtable books. Encourage the students to recommend and share other books they have read about astronomy.

✷ Writing Seminar

Encourage the students to use writing process activities as they begin new pieces or work on existing pieces from their writing folders. For a review of Writing Seminar, see **Learning Framework Card 8.**

Cross-curricular Activity Cards

Encourage the students to look through the Cross-curricular Activity Cards. The cards are interesting and informative and may provide some ideas for areas to research. The following Activity Cards in the Student Toolbox are appropriate for this selection:

- 3 Science—Lunar Log
- 1 Math—Counting the Stars

Counting the Stars
Use after *How Did We Find Out the Earth Is Round?*

1
Math

Lunar Log
Use after *How Did We Find Out the Earth Is Round?*

3
Science

Astronomers observe the sky and keep detailed notes about their observations. Take a sheet of unlined paper and draw a line down the center of the page. At the top of the left-hand column, write: My Observations. In the middle of the right-hand column, trace a circle around an object, such as a jar lid or a soda can. Under the circle, write:
Date:_____ Time:_____
Photocopy the page fifteen times. On another unlined sheet of paper write: Lunar Log by (your name). Staple the sheets together down the left margin.

Remember that the moon rises in the east and sets in the west, but it does so at different times each day. When the moon is full it will rise in the east at about the same time that the sun sets in the west. When it is **waning** (getting smaller), it will rise before the sun does and so is best seen during the daytime to the west of the sun. When it is **waxing** (getting larger), it will set after the sun does and so is best seen in the early evening.

Every other night or day for thirty nights, observe the moon. Write your observations down. You might notice weather conditions, the moon's color, its brightness, its movement in the sky, and, of course, its shape. Darken the area of the circle that can't be seen so that the unshaded area represents the shape of the moon on that particular night. At the end of the thirty days, you can flip through the log pages from front to back to see the phases of the moon pass quickly before your eyes. *Firsthand observation is the primary way scientists learn about the universe.*

Additional Opportunities for Solving Learning Problems

Tutorial

Use this time to assist **students who could use extra help.** Invite students to discuss with you any subject or area in which they need extra help. Some students may benefit from giving or receiving peer tutoring. Have tutoring pairs refer to the appropriate Student Tool Cards to guide their work.

Work with individuals or small groups who need help in a particular area. The following teaching aids are available in the Teacher Toolbox:

- Writer's Craft/Reading: Elaboration Through Forming Questions and Conjectures, Teacher Tool Card 45
- Writer's Craft/Reading: Causal Indicators, Teacher Tool Card 31
- Writer's Craft/Reading: Elaboration Through Providing Concept Information, Teacher Tool Card 43
- Study and Research: Parts of a Book, Teacher Tool Card 98

The Heavenly Zoo

1 READING THE SELECTION

INFORMATION FOR THE TEACHER

About the Selection

Thousands of years ago, people gazed at the night sky and saw men, women, and beasts in the stars. They invented engaging and fanciful tales to explain how these creatures came to live in the sky. This selection offers a brief sampling of the hundreds of existing constellation myths. Readers will enjoy the stories of a loyal prince and a heroic scorpion while learning something about the beliefs and values of the ancient Indian and Greek cultures.

Link to the Unit Concepts

This pair of myths, one Indian and one Greek, illustrates how early people attempted to make sense of a mysterious universe. By studying star patterns, recognizing familiar objects in the patterns, and creating stories about them, the ancients could attribute meaning to a phenomenon—stars—about which they had no technical knowledge. Creating myths like those of "The Great Dog" and "The Scorpion" helped make the unknown familiar.

Further, the stories presented in "The Heavenly Zoo," pages 140–145, tell us something about the beliefs and values of the people who created the stories. For instance, "The Great Dog," written more than two thousand years ago, conveys the ancient Indians' love of animals, their belief in life after death, and the value they placed on love and wisdom over power, beauty, and self-gratification.

Likewise, the myth of "The Scorpion" tells a good deal about the values and beliefs of the ancient Greeks. The story warns against the dangers of vanity and the abuse of power, rewards good behavior over bad, and promises life after death.

LESSON OVERVIEW

"The Heavenly Zoo," retold by Alison Lurie, pages 140–145

READING THE SELECTION

Materials
Student anthology, pp. 140–145
Explorer's Notebook, p. 23

FYI
Learning Framework Card
• Setting Reading Goals and Expectations, 1A

Teacher Tool Cards
• Classroom Supports: Modeling and Generating Think-Alouds, 116
• Classroom Supports: Question Board and Concept Board, 121

READING WITH A WRITER'S EYE

Minilesson
Writer's Craft: Writing Paragraphs

Materials
Reading/Writing Connection, p. 15
Reproducible Master 14

FYI
Teacher Tool Card
• Spelling and Vocabulary: Building Vocabulary, 75

Options for Instruction
Grammar, Mechanics, and Usage: Adjectives and Adverbs
Grammar, Mechanics, and Usage: Using Dialogue
Spelling and Vocabulary: Synonyms and Antonyms
(Use Teacher Tool Cards listed below.)

GUIDED AND INDEPENDENT EXPLORATION

Minilesson
Research Aid: Using the Card Catalog

Materials
Explorer's Notebook, pp. 27, 31
Home/School Connection 13

FYI
Learning Framework Cards
• Problem Phase 1 and 2, 4A
• Reading Roundtable, 6

Optional Materials from Student Toolbox
Audiocassette

Tradebook Connection Cards

Cross-curricular Activity Card
• 4 Science—Creating the Constellations

Independent Workshop

Student Tool Cards
• Writer's Craft/Reading: Writing Paragraphs, 22
• Grammar, Mechanics, and Usage: Using Adjectives and Adverbs, 68
• Grammar, Mechanics, and Usage: Using and Punctuating Dialogue, 70
• Spelling and Vocabulary: Synonyms and Antonyms, 78
• Study and Research:Using the Card Catalog, 99

FYI
Teacher Tool Cards
• Writer's Craft/Reading: Writing Paragraphs, 22
• Grammar, Mechanics, and Usage: Using Adjectives and Adverbs, 68
• Grammar, Mechanics, and Usage: Using and Punctuating Dialogue, 70
• Spelling and Vocabulary: Synonyms and Antonyms, 78
• Study and Research: Using the Card Catalogue, 99

N O T E S

Asterisks (*) throughout the lesson indicate learning frameworks. Learning Framework Cards and Teacher Tool Cards can be found in the Teacher Toolbox.

Similarities between the myths in "The Heavenly Zoo" suggest that love, compassion, justice, loyalty, and respect for all living beings were important values to both cultures.

Note: "The Great Dog" is an excerpt from the *Mahabharata* (mə hä´ bär´ə tə), one of two classical Sanskrit epics of ancient India. The *Mahabharata* is a legend by definition, but portions of it are mythical. Since "The Great Dog" exhibits some mythical qualities, it is treated as a myth in this lesson.

About the
Author

Alison Lurie is a professor of English at Cornell University, where she teaches creative writing, folklore, and children's literature. She is also an author and literary critic. Lurie won the Pulitzer Prize for fiction in 1985 for her novel *Foreign Affairs.* Some of her other books are *Imaginary Friends, Real People, The War Between the Tates, Clever Gretchen and Other Forgotten Folktales,* and *Don't Tell the Grown-ups,* a collection of essays that explores the subversion of adult values in children's literature.

Alison Lurie's writing successes have been hard won. Juggling the responsibilities of wife and mother with that of writer was difficult for Lurie. At the beginning of her career, she was discouraged from writing by both friends and family. Add to this the difficulties of getting published, and it is not hard to understand why Lurie twice attempted to give up writing. But her passion for writing prevailed.

Lurie once described a futile attempt to give up writing. She had taken her baby down to the river to give him some fresh air. She "parked the carriage beside a bench and sat down on the grassy, sloping riverbank. The sun shimmered on the flowing water, and a white fishnet of cloud slid up behind the trees on the other shore. The words 'fishnet' and 'slid' crossed my mind, but I didn't try to stop them or scribble them down on the back of an envelope as I would have before, when I was a writer. There was no point in saving ingredients for new spells; I wouldn't need them anymore. Two people strolled by along the path: an oddly assorted couple, one very tall, taking long strides; the other much shorter and hop-skipping to keep up. I didn't speculate about them; I deliberately inhibited myself from imagining who they were or what their relationship was. You needn't bother; you are free of all that now, I told myself. You are normal, you are happy.

"I sat there by the water waiting to experience my new condition, to feel my freedom and normality and happiness, to be filled with it, to flow naturally as the river flowed and enter fully into Being, but instead another sensation, very much stronger, came over me. It was a sensation of intense boredom. Now that I wasn't a writer the world looked flat and vacant, emptied of possibility and meaning; the spring day had become a kind of glossy, banal calendar photograph: View of the Charles River. 'This is stupid,' I said aloud. I stood up and pushed the baby home and changed him and nursed him and put him down for a nap—and went back to the typewriter."

She has been there ever since.

About the
Illustrator

Monika Beisner has written and illustrated a number of intriguing books for children. Her distinctive style has been called sleek, sophisticated, mystical, and quaint, depending on who is critiquing her work. Alison Lurie's *The Heavenly Zoo: Legends and Tales of the Stars,* from which "The Heavenly Zoo" is taken, is a collection of stories about the origins of "animal" constellations. The stories come from Greece, Babylon, Egypt, Sumeria, the Bible, Norway, the Balkans, Indonesia, and Native America. Beisner's brilliant and finely detailed illustrations provide unity to the book and give it an almost mystical quality.

Monika Beisner has also collaborated with Alison Lurie on another children's book called *Fabulous Beasts.* In addition, she has written and illustrated *Catch That Cat!: A Picture Book of Rhymes and Puzzles, Topsy Turvy, Monika Beisner's Book of Riddles,* and *Secret Spells and Curious Charms.*

Beisner lives in London, and spends part of each year at her home on the island of Gozo in Malta.

INFORMATION FOR THE STUDENT

Your students may be interested in learning about the background of "The Great Dog." This constellation myth is excerpted from an Indian epic called the *Mahabharata.* Its title translates from the Sanskrit as *Great Tale of the Descendents of Bharata.* The central story of the Mahabharata tells of a great battle between two related families, the evil Kauravas and the five noble Pandava brothers. The story is thought to be based on actual events that took place between 1400 B.C. and 1000 B.C. The *Mahabharata* was written by several unknown bards, philosophers, and Hindu priests from about 400 B.C. through A.D. 400 and is the longest poem in the world (about eight times as long as the *Iliad* and *The Odyssey* combined). The poem's numerous episodes tell stories of war, politics, ethics, religion, mythology, folklore, heroic adventures, and love.

Share with the students information about the books on which the author and the illustrator have collaborated.

*

COGNITIVE AND RESPONSIVE READING

Activating Prior
Knowledge

Encourage the students to share any stories they have read or heard about the constellations. If some students have heard "The Scorpion" and "The Great Dog" before, remind them not to give away the plots.

Setting Reading
Goals and
Expectations

Have the students browse the first page of the selection and use the **clues/problems/wondering procedure.** Students will return to these observations after reading.

For a review of **browsing,** see **Learning Framework Card 1A, Setting Reading Goals and Expectations.**

Recommendations for Reading the Selection

Ask the students how they would like to read "The Heavenly Zoo." The myths in the selection are dramatic and contain some interesting imagery. For these reasons, the students may enjoy reading the selection aloud.

During oral reading, use and encourage think-alouds. During silent reading, allow discussion as needed. Discuss problems, strategies, and reactions after reading.

This would also be a good selection for **responding** to text by **visualizing** while reading aloud. Model this response, and then invite the students to do the same.

The selection contains several proper nouns that may be unfamiliar to the students. While these proper nouns are not listed in the glossary, they are listed and "pronounced" for you in the miniatures of the selection. Encourage students who are reading silently to check the glossary or a dictionary to find the pronunciation of other unfamiliar words. You may have to help students pronounce some words during oral reading.

About the Reading Strategies

Remind the students that what they read should make sense. If they encounter difficulty while reading, they should figure out a way to solve the problem. They should refer to the strategy posters if they need ideas for solving a reading problem. Students should also feel free to share with the group whatever strategies they use to help solve problems. Explain that occasionally you will model the strategies you use to understand challenging passages or to get more meaning out of the text. Since both myths include plot twists and other elements of suspense, students may benefit from pausing occasionally to **sum up** the action and **predict** what will happen next.

Think-Aloud Prompts for Use in Oral Reading

The think-aloud prompts with the page miniatures are merely suggestions. Remind the students to use any strategies they need to help them understand the text. Refer them to the **reading strategy posters** if necessary. For a review of **modeling** and generating **think-alouds,** see **Teacher Tool Card 116.**

TEACHING TIP Invite students to share their thinking aloud with the group.

THINK ALOUD PROMPTS

These prompts may be used as guides to promote cognitive and responsive reading.

1 The introduction to "The Heavenly Zoo" establishes what the selection will be about. The first paragraph confirms what the students have learned about how some ancient cultures dealt with the mysteries of the universe. Students may want to **sum up** the author's opening remarks.

2 Students may need help pronouncing the following names:

Yudistira (yoo di´ shti rə)
Sahadeva (sə hə da´ va)
Nakula (nə koo´ lə)
Arjuna (är´ jə nə)
Bhima (bē´ mə)

THE HEAVENLY ZOO

retold by Alison Lurie
illustrated by Monika Beisner

1 From the earliest times people have looked at the night sky and tried to understand what they saw there. Long before anyone knew that the stars were great burning globes of gas many millions of miles from the earth and from one another, men and women saw the sky as full of magical pictures outlined with points of light.

What shapes ancient people saw in the sky depended on who and where they were. Thus the group of stars that we call the Big Dipper, which is part of the Great Bear, was known to the Egyptians as the Car of Osiris, to the Norse as Odin's Wagon, and in Britain first as King Arthur's Chariot and later as the Plough. Many of the pictures that we see today are very old. The constellation we call the Great Dog was first known as a dog five thousand years ago in Sumeria; Taurus the Bull was already a bull in Babylon and Egypt.

Our ancestors saw all sorts of things in the stars: men and women, gods and demons, rivers and ships. But what they saw most often were beasts, birds, and fish. And for most of these creatures there was a legend of how they came to be there.

140

THE GREAT DOG

This story is from the Mahabharata, which was written in India. Parts of this collection of stories were written more than two thousand years ago.

Once upon a time in India there were five princes who left their kingdom to seek the kingdom of heaven. With them they took only food and drink for the journey; and the prince Yudistira brought his dog Svana.

Now besides Yudistira, who was the eldest, the brothers were Sahadeva the all-wise, who was <u>learned</u> beyond other men; Nakula the all-handsome, famed for his grace and beauty; Arjuna the all-powerful, who had never been defeated in any contest of arms; and Bhima the all-joyful, known far and wide for his good temper and love of pleasure.

2 So they set forth, and journeyed many days and many nights. Presently they came to a fair, where music was playing and people were drinking and dancing and feasting. Some of them saw Bhima the all-joyful, and called out for him to come and join them. Bhima said to himself, "I will rest here today and be happy, and seek the kingdom of heaven tomorrow." So he entered into the dance. And Yudistira and his brothers Sahadeva and Nakula and Arjuna and his dog Svana went on without him.

They traveled for many days and many nights, till they came to a broad plain where a great army was drawn up in ranks facing the enemy. When the soldiers saw Arjuna the all-powerful they shouted out, summoning him to come and lead them into battle. Arjuna said to himself, "I will fight today for my country, and seek the kingdom of heaven tomorrow." So

141

he joined the soldiers; and Yudistira and his brothers Sahadeva and Nakula and his dog Svana went on without him.

So they traveled for many days and nights, till they came to a magnificent palace surrounded by a garden full of flowers and fountains; and in this garden a beautiful princess was walking with her attendants. When she saw Nakula the all-handsome she was seized with love and longing, and she cried out for him to come nearer. Nakula too was struck with love, and said to himself, "I will stay with this princess today, and seek the kingdom of heaven tomorrow." So he went into the garden, and Yudistira and his brother Sahadeva and his dog Svana went on without him.

They journeyed on for many weary days and nights, until they came to a great temple. When the holy men who lived there saw Sahadeva the all-wise they ran out, inviting him to come and join them in prayer and study. And Sahadeva said to himself, "I will stay here today, and seek the kingdom of heaven tomorrow." So he went into the temple, and Yudistira and his dog Svana went on without him.

At last Yudistira came to Mount Meru, which is the doorway to heaven. And Indra the Lord of Past and Present appeared before him, and invited him to <u>ascend</u>. Yudistira bowed low and replied, "Very willingly I will do so, if I may bring my dog Svana with me."

"That may not be," said Indra. "There is no place in heaven for dogs. Cast off this beast, and enter into <u>eternal</u> happiness."

"I cannot do that," said Yudistira. "I do not wish for any happiness for which I must cast off so dear a companion."

"You traveled on without your four brothers," said Indra. "Why will you not ascend to heaven without this dog?"

❧ 142 ❧

"My lord," replied Yudistira, "my brothers left me to follow the desires of their hearts. But Svana has given his heart to me; rather than <u>renounce</u> him I must renounce heaven."

"You have spoken well," said Indra. "Come in, and bring your dog with you." So Yudistira and Svana ascended into paradise; and Indra, in recognition of their devotion to each other, set in the sky the constellation of the *Great Dog*, whose central star Sirius is the brightest of all in the heavens.

❧ 143 ❧

3 Students have begun to learn what the brothers are like. Call on volunteers to **sum up** what they have read so far. Remind them to focus on the important aspects of the story.

After students have summed up the story, ask for a volunteer to **predict** what may happen next. Students should have little trouble predicting that Nakula will remain at the palace with the princess.

Encourage them to **predict** beyond the upcoming scene. Some students will realize that Sahadeva also has been given a label (the all-wise) that describes a particular talent or passion and therefore he is the likelier to get sidetracked from his journey to heaven.

4 Yudistra has finally reached the doorway to kingdom of heaven. Call on students who wish to **predict** how the story will end.

5 Now that they've finished reading "The Great Dog," students should **check their predictions** and **sum up** the whole story.

THE SCORPION

This story was told in ancient Greece.

Orion was one of the greatest of the Greek giants. Because he was the son of Poseidon, the god of the sea, he was as much at home in the water as on land. When he wished to get from one island to another he walked across on the bottom of the ocean; he was so tall that his head was always above the waves, and so large and broad that his travels caused high tides.

From childhood on Orion was famous for his beauty and his tremendous strength. He grew up to be a great hunter, able to track and slay all kinds of beasts with the help of his giant hound Sirius. When the island of Chios was oppressed and terrified by lions and wolves, Orion came to its assistance. He tracked down and destroyed every one, so that the people and their flocks could live in safety.

By the time Orion came to the large island of Crete, his fame was so great that Artemis, the goddess of the moon, invited him to go hunting with her. All went well until Orion, who had become vain of his skill, began to boast that he would soon have killed all the wild animals in Crete. Now the scorpion, who was listening, said to himself that this must not be. So he lay in wait for Orion, and stung him to death with his poisoned tail.

But Orion's spirit did not have to go down to dwell in the Underworld with the souls of ordinary mortals. The gods, who loved him, transported him instead to the sky, where he can be seen in his golden armor and sword-belt, holding up his golden shield, with his faithful dog Sirius at his heel. The scorpion who saved the wild animals of Crete was also raised into the heavens, and became a constellation in the southern sky.

6 Every night, as the *Scorpion* rises, Orion fades and vanishes.

144

6 Students may want to **ask questions** to help each other clarify any confusion they have regarding "The Scorpion." Some students may not understand that the constellation Orion actually does disappear from view as Scorpius rises. Finally, ask a volunteer to briefly **sum up** the story.

Orion (ô rī´ ən)
Chios (kī´ os)
Artemis (är´ tə mis)

Discussing Strategy Use
Encourage the students to tell about any problems they encountered while reading "The Heavenly Zoo" and which strategies they employed to solve the problems. Invite them to share any predictions they made while reading and to explain the reasoning behind their predictions.

* **EXPLORING THROUGH DISCUSSION**

Reflecting on the Selection
Whole-Group Discussion

The whole group discusses the selection and any personal thoughts or questions that it raises. During this time, students also **return to the clues, problems, and wonderings** they noted on the board during browsing.

Assessment

To assess the students' understanding of the text, engage them in a discussion to **determine whether they understand**
- how Yudistira was different than his brothers
- why he refused to leave his dog behind even to enter heaven
- why the Scorpion killed Orion

Response Journal

Students may have been reminded by "The Great Dog" of their own pets. They may wish to record their personal responses to the selection.

Exploring Concepts Within the Selection
Small-Group Discussion

Remind the students to check the Concept Board and the Question Board to determine whether their original perceptions about astronomy have changed as a result of this selection. Circulate among the groups to see if any of the groups have difficulty connecting this selection to the unit concepts.

> **TIP FOR ENGLISH LANGUAGE LEARNERS**
>
> Give English Language Learners an opportunity to be leaders. Encourage them to restate the group's opinions and discuss them with other groups.

Sharing Ideas About Explorable Concepts

Have the groups **report** and **discuss** their **ideas** with the rest of the class. It is crucial that the students' ideas determine this discussion.
- The students may point out that while myths such as "The Great Dog" and "The Scorpion" are no longer taken seriously as explanations for natural phenomena, many such myths have been preserved for thousands of years. Encourage the students to share their opinions about why this is so.
- Students may note that, although constellation myths sound silly to modern people, the creators of the myths had only their naked eyes with which to observe and study the stars. Perhaps their stories made as much sense as any other explanation could have at that time.
- Some students may realize that the myths not only explained how the stars came to be, but also helped the ancients remember, locate, and identify certain stars.

As these ideas and others are stated, have the students **add them to the Question Board** or the **Concept Board.** For a review of the Question Board and the Concept Board, see **Teacher Tool Card 119.**

Encourage the students to examine the fine-art piece depicting the constellation Leo, on the top of page 181 in the student anthology. In this work, created circa 1500, students will find another example of how people long ago saw pictures in the stars. Some students may know that the lion is one of the signs of the zodiac, the band of twelve constellations in the northern hemisphere that were once believed to govern the destinies of people born under them. Some students may even know the

Fine Art

Recording Concept Information

As I read each selection, I learned these new things about astronomy.

How Did We Find Out the Earth Is Round? by Isaac Asimov

_____
_____
_____
_____
_____
_____

"The Heavenly Zoo" by Alison Lurie

_____
_____
_____
_____
_____
_____

"Circles, Squares, and Daggers" by Elsa Marston

_____
_____
_____
_____
_____

Unit 2/Astronomy   EN 23

Explorer's Notebook, page 23

story of the Nemean lion, who fell from the moon to Nemea, in Greece, and was eventually slain by the hero Hercules.

Exploring Concepts Across Selections

Ask the students if this selection reminds them of anything else they have read. They may **make connections with other selections in this unit.**

- Students might compare the theories of the Greek scholars in *How Did We Find Out the Earth Is Round?* to the constellation myths told by the ancients in "The Heavenly Zoo."

Recording Ideas

As students complete the above discussion, ask them to **sum up what they have learned from their conversations and to tell how they might use this information in further explorations.** Any special information or insights may be recorded on the **Concept Board.** Any further questions that they would like to think about, pursue, or investigate may be recorded on the **Question Board.** They may want to discuss the progress that has been made on their questions. They may also want to cross out any questions that no longer warrant consideration.

➤ Allow time for the students to record new information in the Explorer's Notebook, page 23.

TEACHING TIP Ask content-free questions as often as possible so that the students can apply them to many different selections.

Evaluating Discussions

Professional Checkpoint: Cognitive and Responsive Reading

A good reader knows when and where to use familiar strategies. Students can become autonomous in their use of strategies only by being given years of encouragement in choosing appropriate strategies. Thus, you should not tell the students when to predict or when to summarize. Rather, you should prompt students who are not using strategies to check the strategy posters and choose a strategy that helps them make sense of what they are reading.

Notes:

2 READING WITH A WRITER'S EYE

MINILESSON

Writer's Craft:
Writing
Paragraphs

Ask the students to discuss paragraphs. They should understand that **a paragraph is one or more sentences that tell about one main idea.** Most paragraphs, however, include at least two sentences. They should also know that **often one sentence in the paragraph, the topic sentence, will tell what the main idea is.** Students might also mention the use of paragraphs in writing dialogue to show that different characters are speaking.

Remind them that there are **two ways that paragraphs are set off from each other.** Either the first sentence of the paragraph is indented, or an extra line space is inserted between paragraphs.

Point out that in "The Heavenly Zoo" Alison Lurie switches from expository writing on page 140 to fiction writing on pages 141 through 144. The expository paragraphs on page 141 are used to introduce the stories which follow. The first paragraph says that our ancestors tried to explain the stars in the sky as magical pictures. The second paragraph explains that the pictures that the people saw depended on where they lived and who they were. The third paragraph says that most of the pictures were of animals and that legends often explained how the animals came to be placed in the heavens.

Direct the students' attention to the third paragraph on page 141. Point out that although Bhima speaks here, there is no new paragraph. Explain that this is because only one person is speaking, so there is no dialogue between characters.

Selective Reading:
Focus on Writing
Paragraphs

Have the students go back to "The Heavenly Zoo" to see how the focus of ideas changes from one paragraph to the next or how a change in speaker or speakers generates a new paragraph. **Encourage volunteers to read aloud and to explain the examples that they find.**

Most paragraphs will, of course, reveal a change in the focus of ideas or a change in speakers from the previous paragraph.

Selection-Based Practice

Writing Paragraphs

In "The Heavenly Zoo," Alison Lurie begins new paragraphs whenever she moves from one main idea to another or shifts from one speaker to another. Look at other selections you have read to see how writers use paragraphs to indicate such changes. Write the title of the selection, the page number, and the reason that the writer begins a new paragraph in each case (new main idea, different speaker).

Selection: _____

Page: _____ Reason for new paragraph: _____
_____

Selection: _____

Page: _____ Reason for new paragraph: _____
_____

Selection: _____

Page: _____ Reason for new paragraph: _____
_____

Selection: _____

Page: _____ Reason for new paragraph: _____
_____

Selection: _____

Page: _____ Reason for new paragraph: _____
_____

Look back at this page for examples when you need help in deciding where to begin new paragraphs.

Writing Paragraphs

Unit 2/Astronomy   R/WC 15

Name

Reading/Writing Connection, page 15

Independent Practice: Writing Paragraphs

❯ For additional practice in understanding paragraphs, have the students work in small groups to discuss and complete Reading/Writing Connection, page 15.

WRITING

Linking Reading to Writing

Remind the students that writers use paragraphs to organize their ideas when they are writing. Each paragraph should be about a single main idea with no unrelated thoughts that might confuse a reader. **Encourage students to look through their writing folders for pieces that could be improved by revising paragraphs that don't have clear main ideas.** After sufficient time has passed for students to select and revise a piece of their writing, **invite volunteers to read** their **original passages** and their **rewritten passages** and to **explain how the revisions improved their writing.**

* Writing Process

Although no specific writing assignment is recommended here, students may concentrate on an appropriate phase in the writing process with any writing on which they are currently working.

VOCABULARY

Concept-**related words** from the selection which may come up in discussion or that students may wish to remember include the following: **constellation, heavens, feasting, attendants, ascend, renounce**

Have Vocabulary Exploration forms, Reproducible Master 14, available for students who need them. Remind the students to add these or any other words and phrases from the story to the Personal Dictionary section of their Writer's Notebook. Some students may wish to share these additions with the class. For additional ideas on how to build vocabulary, see **Teacher Tool Card 75.**

VOCABULARY TIP Encouraging the students to use new vocabulary in speech and writing by praising their efforts is an effective method for improving vocabulary and increasing the students' comprehension of text. Post-reading discussions are an appropriate time to encourage the students to use the new vocabulary they have learned.

3 GUIDED AND INDEPENDENT EXPLORATION

EXPLORING CONCEPTS BEYOND THE TEXT

Guided
Exploration

The following activities do not have to be completed within the days devoted to this lesson.

* Some students may be interested in learning how to identify constellations in the night sky. They may have noticed in reading the selection that the bright star Sirius, which is the central star of the Great Dog constellation (Canis Major), can be found close to the constellation of Orion. The photograph on page 228 of the student anthology shows Sirius and several bright stars in the constellation of Orion. Books on the unit bibliographies will provide more information about Orion, Canis Major, Scorpius, and other constellations.
* "The Great Dog" and "The Scorpion" are stories about how three constellations originated. The students may be interested in reading stories about the origins of other constellations. They can find other myths about constellations in the library. In fact, Alison Lurie's *The Heavenly Zoo: Legends and Tales of the Stars* is a good source. In addition to "The Great Dog" and "The Scorpion," it contains stories about the origins of fourteen other constellations.

❯ Distribute Home/School Connection 13. It explains that myths like "The Great Dog" and "The Scorpion" were written to explain the origin of constellations. It also **encourages families or adults at home to read with the students** about other constellations and to locate the constellations in the evening sky.

✳ Exploring Through Research

Research Cycle:
Problem Phase 2

By this point each student should have completed the Problem Phase page in their Explorer's Notebook. The next step is for students to **discuss one another's proposed problems**, which will lead to the **creation of research groups to work on selected problems.**

Have students present their proposed problems, along with reasons, allowing open discussion of how promising and interesting various pro-

"The Heavenly Zoo"

A message from _____

Our class has just finished reading "The Great Dog" and "The Scorpion," which are myths about how three constellations—The Great Dog, the Scorpion, and Orion—came to be. The stories were written by the ancient peoples of India and Greece long before any facts were known about the stars or other heavenly bodies. The ancients wrote stories to help make sense of those phenomena about which they knew little.

You and your child may want to read about other constellations and look for them in the evening sky. Use the bottom of this sheet to list the constellations that you and your child read about and/or locate in the sky. Then have your child bring the list back to class to share with his or her classmates.

Constellation	Name of Myth and Country of Origin	When Observed	Comments

Unit 2/Astronomy   H/SC 13

Home/School Connection 13

Research Cycle: Problem Phase 2

My research group's problem:

_____

What our research will contribute to the rest of the class:

_____

Some other questions about this problem:

_____

Unit 2/Astronomy   EN 31

Explorer's Notebook, page 31

posed problems are. To aid the formation of groups, students may record their problems on the chalkboard. During the discussion, arrows may be drawn to link related problems. Final groups should be constituted in the way you find best for your class—by self-selection, by assignment on the basis of common interests, or by some combination of methods.

For more information on Problem Phase 2 of the Research Cycle, see **Learning Framework Card 4A.**

❯ Assign the next steps for students to carry out during Independent Workshop: **Each group will meet to agree on and state the problem that it will be working on** and what working on that problem will contribute to the class's knowledge. Have them record this in their Explorer's Notebook, page 31.

MINILESSON

Research Aid:
Using the
Card Catalog

Remind students that most libraries have a card catalog that provides an alphabetical listing of books. Encourage them to **share what they know about the card catalog system** and how it works. If necessary, remind them that each book is listed three ways: **by author's name, by the title** of the book, and **by the subject** of the book. Many libraries have their card catalogs on computers.

Using the Card Catalog

J
QB
802.R47

CONSTELLATIONS

Rey, H. A.
Find the Constellations
written and illustrated by H. A. Rey.
—Boston, MA: Houghton Mifflin, 1992.
72 p.: col. ill.

Summary: A method for recognizing the
stars and finding constellations is described.

Copy information from a subject card for a book you find about stars.

Unit 2/Astronomy   EN 27

Explorer's Notebook, page 27

Call on a volunteer to tell where one would look in the card catalog to locate books about constellations—groups of stars that have been named—such as Orion. If necessary, explain that one would look in the subject-card section of the card catalog. Most people would not know names of books or authors who have written books about constellations. For example, one could look up *Orion* or *constellation* in the card catalog to find books that deal with the Orion constellation in particular or with other groups of named stars.

Guided Practice: Using the Card Catalog

➤ Ask the students to turn to page 27 of the Explorer's Notebook and explain that this is a sample subject card of a book on constellations. Point out the following information:

subject listing: CONSTELLATIONS
call number: J QB 802.R47
author's name: Rey, H. A.
title of book: Find the Constellations
publisher: Houghton Mifflin
place and date of publication: Boston, 1992
number of pages: 72
summary: see card

Explain that the *J* in the call number is a clue to the researcher indicating the section of the library in which the book can be found. This letter may differ depending on the library. Some libraries use *C* for Children's, *Y* for Youth, or *J* for Juvenile.

Independent Practice: Using the Card Catalog

Using the blank card at the bottom of Explorer's Notebook, page 27, students should work independently in the school library to find one book about stars that really interests them and copy the card onto their papers. Suggest that they may wish to incorporate into their research information they find in the books on this topic that are in their library. Have the students share any information that they found using the suggested headings, or information that they located on their own.

*INDEPENDENT WORKSHOP
Building a Community of Scholars

Student-Directed Reading, Writing, and Discussion

Research Cycle: Problem Phase 2 Each newly formed research group should meet to agree on a precise statement of its research problem, the nature of the expected research contributions, and a list of related questions (which may help later in assigning individual roles). These should be entered in their Explorer's Notebook, page 31.

Additional Opportunities for Independent Reading, Writing, and Cross-curricular Activities

✳ Reading Roundtable

Encourage students to recommend and share other myths or legends they have read, or other books about the constellations. For additional ideas for Reading Roundtable, see **Learning Framework Card 6.**

✳ Writing Seminar

Encourage students who are beginning new writing pieces to collaborate with their classmates in brainstorming for ideas.

Cross-curricular Activity Cards

The following Cross-curricular Activity Card in the Student Toolbox is appropriate for this selection:
- 4 Science—Creating the Constellations

Creating the Constellations
Use after "The Heavenly Zoo"

4 Science

You can project a constellation onto the ceiling of a darkened room just as they do on the ceiling of a planetarium—by placing a light source behind a pattern of holes that represent the shape of the constellation.

Materials you will need: a piece of dark construction paper; a powerful flashlight; a cardboard tube (the narrower the tube, the brighter will be the image projected); and four straight pins.
- Draw the pattern of stars in a particular constellation on a piece of paper.
- Prick a hole through each star in the constellation. Some stars are brighter than others in a constellation, so you'll need to make larger holes for the brighter stars.
- Pin your star map to the end of a cardboard tube. The best way is to lay the paper flat on the end of the tube and drive the pins down through the paper into the rim of the tube.
- Turn off the lights in the room and draw the blinds or curtains so that the room is completely dark.
- Turn on the flashlight and place it inside the open end of the cardboard tube. The light shines through the holes and projects the constellation onto the ceiling of the darkened room.

You can draw several constellations, each on its own sheet of paper. *Learning the shapes of constellations can help you locate them in the evening sky.*

Additional Opportunities for Solving Learning Problems

Tutorial

You might want to use this time to work with students who need extra help. Some students may benefit from peer tutoring. Have tutoring pairs refer to the appropriate **Student Tool Cards** to guide their work. The following **Teacher Tool Cards** are available in the Teacher Toolbox to aid you:
- Writer's Craft/Reading: Writing Paragraphs, Teacher Tool Card 22
- Grammar, Mechanics, and Usage: Using Adjectives and Adverbs, Teacher Tool Card 68
- Grammar, Mechanics, and Usage: Using and Punctuating Dialogue, Teacher Tool Card 70
- Spelling and Vocabulary: Synonyms and Antonyms, Teacher Tool Card 78
- Study and Research: Using the Card Catalog, Teacher Tool Card 99

Circles, Squares, and Daggers

1 READING THE SELECTION

About the Selection

Lacking calendars and clocks, early Native Americans relied on the sun and stars to tell them when to plant crops, prepare for winter, or hold ceremonies. This selection introduces readers to the field of archaeoastronomy as it describes the workings of four sophisticated early observatories erected by Native Americans to help them track—with amazing accuracy—of the passing of time and the changing of the seasons.

Link to the Unit Concepts

Even before people knew much about the sun, they were aware of its influence over their lives. The Native-American cultures described in "Circles, Squares, and Daggers," pages 146–155, had no knowledge about what the sun and other stars were made of or how they came to be, but they could and did observe the movement of the sun and stars over long periods of time. They noticed that certain weather and temperature conditions repeated in cycles and that they could clock these cycles according to the movements of the sun. So careful were their observations that they were able to determine on which days the sun's position signified the end of one cycle and the beginning of another. Without having any scientific knowledge of the sun and stars, Native-American tribes like the Ponca, Mississippian, and Anasazi were able to use them to measure time.

About the Author

Elsa Marston's writing career began in 1981 with the publication of *The Cliffs of Cairo*, in which an American teenager becomes entangled in a mystery involving the art and history of medieval Cairo. This novel was followed by other juvenile and young adult books. Marston has also written articles for *Highlights for Children, Odyssey, Calliope, Faces,* and *Hopscotch* magazines.

LESSON OVERVIEW

"Circles, Squares, and Daggers: How Native Americans Watched the Skies"
by Elsa Marston, pages 146–155

READING THE SELECTION

Materials
Student anthology, pp. 146–155
Explorer's Notebook, p. 23
U.S. map

FYI
Learning Framework Card
• Responding to Text, 1B

READING WITH A WRITER'S EYE

Minilesson
Writer's Craft: Using Headings and
Captions

Materials
Reading/Writing Connection, p. 16
Reproducible Master 14

FYI
Learning Framework Card
• Writing Process, 7

Teacher Tool Card
• Spelling and Vocabulary: Building
Vocabulary, 75

Options for Instruction
Writer's Craft: Comparison and
Contrast
Grammar, Mechanics, and Usage:
Compound Sentences
Study and Research: Using Maps
(Use Teacher Tool Cards listed below.)

GUIDED AND INDEPENDENT EXPLORATION

Materials
Home/School Connection 14
Explorer's Notebook, p. 32
Assessment Master 1

FYI
Learning Framework Card
• Conjecture Phase, 4B

Independent Workshop

**Optional Materials from
Student Toolbox**
Tradebook Connection Cards

Cross-curricular Activity Cards
• 5 Science—Create an Observatory
• 6 Science—Measuring Time on a Dial

Student Tool Cards
• Writer's Craft/Reading: Using
Headings and Captions, 35
• Writer's Craft/Reading: Comparing
and Contrasting, 36
• Grammar, Mechanics, and Usage:
Compound Sentences, 48
• Study and Research: Using Maps, 104

FYI
Teacher Tool Cards
• Writer's Craft/Reading: Using
Headings and Captions, 35
• Writer's Craft/Reading: Elaboration
Through Providing Comparison and
Contrast, 36
• Grammar, Mechanics, and Usage:
Compound Sentences, 48
• Study and Research: Using Maps, 104

Asterisks (*) throughout the lesson indicate learning frameworks. Learning Framework Cards and Teacher Tool Cards can be found in the Teacher Toolbox.

Marston enjoys art, history, and archaeology and incorporates these subjects into her works. "In my books I try to combine the present with the past, the contemporary American character with the foreign. Their settings are places where I have lived or visited: Cairo, Carthage, Lebanon, the Greek Islands, a historic seacoast town in Massachusetts. I hope that by presenting characters a young reader can identify with, in an unfamiliar but attractive setting, I can encourage an awareness of the world beyond here and now."

INFORMATION FOR THE STUDENT

Students may not be familiar with the term *observatory* as it is used in this selection and in the selection that follows, "Sun and Star Calendars." Although it usually means, as their glossary says, "a place that is designed for astronomers to study the stars," in these selections it means "a calendar-keeping device." Tell the students that this selection is about ancient structures used by Native Americans to track the movement of the sun and certain stars and thus keep track of time. Although these structures were made centuries ago, it is only recently that scientists have begun to understand their purpose.

COGNITIVE AND RESPONSIVE READING

Activating Prior Knowledge

Invite the students to discuss anything they might know about how people measured time before calendars and clocks were invented.

Setting Reading Goals and Expectations

Have the students **browse the selection** using the clues/problems/wonderings procedure. The students will return to these observations after reading.

Recommendations for Reading the Selection

Ask the students how they would like to read the selection. Students may benefit from reading this selection aloud because of its vocabulary and challenging content. An oral reading will allow students to assist one another in pronouncing and defining vocabulary, and in clarifying important parts of the text.

During **oral reading, use and encourage think-alouds**. During **silent reading**, allow discussion as needed. Discuss problems, strategies, and reactions after reading.

This would also be a good selection for students to **respond to text** by **wondering** as they read aloud. Model this response, and then invite the students to do the same.

Before they read about each Native-American observatory in "Circles, Squares, and Daggers," have the students find the site of the observatory on a map of the United States. This exercise will help students better remember what they learn about each particular observatory.

TEACHING TIP After students have browsed expository text, ask them what they expect to learn and what they would like to find out from reading the selection.

Map Reading

About the
Reading
Strategies

When we read about ancient civilizations that grasped the workings of the universe without benefit of scientific knowledge or modern tools, it often makes us wonder about them. Who were these people who could chart so precisely the movement of stars and sun just by observing? When did they first realize that the seasons of the year are cyclical and that each cycle is of precise duration? How did they become aware of the solstices and equinoxes—those four days of the year that mark each new season? How did they know it was possible to construct devices for predicting the movement of the sun and stars?

We can answer some questions we wonder about by reading the selection or by doing outside research about the topic. Other questions may have no definite answer. We are left with our own imaginings about those things or people who pique our curiosity.

As the students read the selection, they, too, may wonder about the people and information in the text. **Wondering** is something good readers do: They react to what they are reading by asking themselves questions and by thinking beyond the information so as to gain greater meaning from the text. In "The Wheel on the School" in unit 1, the students learned about the importance of wondering—sometimes when we wonder we can make things begin to happen. To review the strategy of **wondering,** see **Learning Framework Card 1B**, **Responding to Text**.

Think-Aloud Prompts
for Use in Oral Reading

Notice the suggested think-aloud prompts with the page miniatures. Model whenever necessary—particularly when introducing a new reading strategy—using the think-aloud method. Remind the students that what they read should make sense to them. If it doesn't, they should refer to the **reading strategy posters** if they need ideas for solving a reading problem. Students should also feel free to share with the group whatever strategies they use to help solve problems. Explain that occasionally you will model the strategies you use to understand difficult passages or to get more meaning out of the text.

THINK ALOUD PROMPTS

These prompts may be used as guides to promote cognitive and responsive reading.

1 The selection mentions the body of science called archaeology during its discussion of archaeoastronomy. Students may need to **ask questions** to clarify for themselves what archaeology is so that *archaeoastronomy* makes sense to them. Understanding this new field of study is key to understanding and appreciating Marston's article.

2 The word *medicine* in Bighorn Medicine Wheel means holy or supernatural, but the text does not elaborate here about what connection there might be between religion and an astronomical observatory. (The connection will become apparent at the end of the article.) Students may **wonder** about how the observatory got this name and what it means.

CIRCLES, SQUARES, AND DAGGERS:
HOW NATIVE AMERICANS WATCHED THE SKIES
by Elsa Marston

You have probably heard about stargazers of the past such as the ancient Egyptians, the builders of <u>Stonehenge</u>, and the Mayas. Did you know that Native Americans, too, made <u>astronomical</u> <u>observatories</u>—long before Europeans arrived?

The study of these ancient observatories is called *archaeoastronomy*. By combining <u>astronomy</u> with <u>archaeology</u>, we are beginning to understand how people of the past observed the skies.

1 Archaeoastronomy is a very new field. The Native American observatories have been discovered—or their purposes understood—only recently. Most of the sites had been abandoned centuries ago, and their original uses had been forgotten.

Let's look at some of the different ways Native Americans devised to follow the movements of the sun and, in certain cases, the stars.

❦ *146* ❦

MEDICINE WHEELS

One of the most dramatic observatories lies on a windswept <u>plateau</u> high in the Bighorn Mountains of Wyoming. It is simply a circle of stones that looks something like a wheel, 80 feet across. In fact, it's called the Bighorn Medicine Wheel ("medicine" means holy or supernatural).

2

In the center of the wheel is a large pile of stones called a <u>cairn</u>. Twenty-eight lines of stones lead like spokes from the "hub" to the rim. Just outside the circle stand six smaller cairns.

Though the wheel had been known for about a hundred years, it was not until the early 1970s that its secrets began to come clear. An astronomer, John Eddy, discovered how the wheel "works."

The Bighorn Medicine Wheel. The diagram shows cairns marking sunrise and sunset on the summer solstice and the rising of the bright stars Aldebaran, Rigel, Sirius, and Fomalhaut.
© Dewey Vanderhoff

If you stand at a particular small cairn on the day of the summer <u>solstice</u> (usually June 21st), you will see the sun rise directly over the large cairn in the center of the wheel. At the end of the day, standing at a different pile, you'll see the setting sun line up with the center cairn. The medicine wheel tells almost exactly when the longest day of the year has arrived, the day we say summer begins.

The wheel shows other <u>alignments</u> as well. Pairs of small cairns were found to point to bright stars that shone briefly on the horizon on certain days before and after the summer solstice. These stars appeared roughly 28 days apart. Possibly the 28 "spokes" were supposed to help keep track of these intervals.

The Bighorn Medicine Wheel was probably built around 1700. The Ponca tribe claims that its ancestors constructed the original wheel. Other tribes probably added to it after moving into the area.

There is a similar medicine wheel in Saskatchewan, Canada. The Moose Mountain Medicine Wheel has cairns placed

Fieldworkers at Moose Mountain. The diagram shows cairns marking sunrise on the summer solstice and the rising of the bright stars Capella, Aldebaran, Sirius, and Fomalhaut.
© Thomas F. Kehoe

like those of the Bighorn Wheel. This gave a clue to its age. The point on the horizon where a star rises changes slightly over time. The wheel was dated by figuring out when bright stars rose closest to the points shown by the cairns. The <u>calculations</u> agreed with carbon dating for the site. The Moose Mountain Medicine Wheel was probably built around 2000 years ago!

CIRCLES AND SQUARES

At Cahokia, a major Native American site in western Illinois near St. Louis, archaeologists discovered traces of four large circles of wooden posts. They reconstructed part of one of these circles.

Seen from the center at dawn, the sun lines up with certain posts at the summer solstice and winter solstice (the shortest day of the year, usually December 21st). A third post is <u>aligned</u> with the rising sun at the spring and fall <u>equinoxes</u> (usually

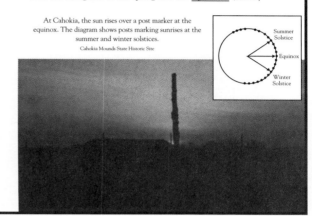

At Cahokia, the sun rises over a post marker at the equinox. The diagram shows posts marking sunrises at the summer and winter solstices.
Cahokia Mounds State Historic Site

3 It may not be immediately clear to some students that the summer solstice is the longest day of the year, because the text does not explicitly say so. If the students seem confused, you may want to model **clarifying** at this point. You might use a discussion starter such as

This paragraph says that the medicine wheel tells when the longest day of the year has arrived. It also says that the sun rises and sets directly over the center cairn at the summer solstice.

4 A reference to carbon dating appears in this paragraph, but the process is not explained. Curious students might wish to clarify this term by **checking the glossary or a dictionary.**

March 21st and September 21st, when day and night are of equal length).

Another observatory was discovered near Kansas City, Missouri, in the early 1980s. Again, traces of posts were found, but this time in the shape of a square. About 35 feet long on each side, the square suggested a building such as a fort—except that the corners were open. A triangle of posts had stood in the center, and on the south side of the square was a double row of post marks.

A local astronomy society made a simple reconstruction of the square. They found that on the summer solstice, a person standing a certain distance from the center posts could see the sun rise and set through two of the open corners. The other two corners framed the sunrise and sunset at the winter solstice. On the equinoxes, the sun shone directly between the double lines of posts. Both observatories were made by Native Americans of the Mississippian culture, probably about a thousand years ago.

SUN DAGGERS

The Anasazi—a name that means simply "ancient ones"—lived in the beautiful but dry country of northern New Mexico, Colorado, Utah, and Arizona around 900 years ago. In Chaco Canyon, New Mexico, they designed an especially clever kind of observatory. It was discovered in 1977 by an artist, Anna Sofaer, who was examining rock carvings.

Near the top of Fajada Butte, a high rock that rises from the canyon floor, three large slabs of stone lean against a vertical rock face. About 9 feet long, they stand on end only a

150

Fall equinox.

Winter solstice.

The solar marker in Chaco Canyon at noon on the summer solstice.

Spring equinox.

few inches apart, their narrow sides against the rock. On the shadowed rock behind them, two spirals have been cut.

At noon on the summer solstice, a tiny shaft of sunlight falls between two of the slabs. It makes a spot that looks like a dagger—cutting right through the middle of the larger spiral.

151

As the weeks pass, the "dagger" of sunlight moves to the right. Meanwhile, a second vertical streak of light appears. At the fall equinox, it cuts through the smaller spiral. By the winter solstice, the two "daggers" rest on the edges of the larger spiral. It's as though the spiral, now empty of sunlight, is a symbol of winter when the world is cold. Gradually, then, the sun daggers move to the left until, on the longest day of the year, the first one again strikes the center of the larger spiral.

All over the Southwest there are many such figures, called petroglyphs, cut in the rock. Spirals, crosses, rough outlines of humans, lizards, birds—all had meanings.

At many sites, the petroglyphs are touched by spots of sunlight, usually falling between two large rocks. Astronomer Robert Preston and his wife Ann, an artist, discovered many of these sites in Arizona. Light strikes the rock carving at the solstices, the equinoxes, or, in some cases, a point halfway between the fall equinox and the winter solstice.

⑤

"SUN ROOMS"

The Anasazi thought of other ways to observe the travels of the sun. Between Tucson and Phoenix, Arizona, rises a three-story <u>adobe</u> building known as Casa Grande ("Great House"). At dawn, a person standing inside this ancient structure will see the sun shining through a small hole high in the east wall. The spot of light strikes the opposite wall, moves toward a small hole in that wall, and disappears into it. The spot of sunlight hits this bull's-eye only on the days close to the spring and fall equinoxes.

〰 152 〰

Casa Grande a little after dawn, at the time of the spring equinox. Sunlight passes through holes in two different walls, one behind the other.
© Jerry Jacka

There is a different type of Anasazi "sun room" at Hovenweep National Monument in Utah. Attached to a large stone structure called Hovenweep Castle is a tower-like room. At sunset on the solstices and equinoxes, the sun's rays enter small holes and a door, shine through the room, and strike

〰 153 〰

⑤ Observant readers may notice that observatories of the Anasazi seem more sophisticated than those mentioned earlier in the article. They may **wonder** about these ancient people and what the petroglyphs that appear on their observatories tell us about them. You might stimulate a discussion by saying something such as

Reading about the Anasazi's observatories makes me wonder about them. There's something about them that makes them seem different from other Native Americans we've read about so far. Could their petroglyphs be a form of written language? Have any of you wondered about the Anasazi? What do you wonder about them?

Hovenweep Castle.
© Jerry Brody

doorways in the inside walls. The archaeoastronomer who studied Hovenweep Castle, Ray Williamson, determined that the beams of sunlight could not enter the room in this way merely by chance.

6

WHY?

All over this country, Native Americans came up with <u>ingenious</u> ways to observe the skies. But *why* did they study astronomy?

🌿 *154* 🌿

The skies were the Native Americans' calendar. They had no fixed, written calendar as we do today. They relied on what nature would tell them about the changing times of the year. Important solar events such as the solstices and the equinoxes helped them know when to plant their crops, when to start preparing for the winter, when to move from one place to another.

The sun and stars told Native Americans when important ceremonies were supposed to take place. These ceremonies were usually concerned with the "return" of the sun and start of a new year, and with planting, harvesting, and hunting.

Other special occasions might have been for social purposes such as tribal <u>rituals</u>, gatherings of tribes, trade, or payment of <u>tribute</u>. For example, the most likely function of the Bighorn Medicine Wheel was to keep a calendar so large groups could assemble in summer for trading fairs.

It's probable that only special persons knew how to use the observatories and make the announcements awaited by the people. The observatories must have strengthened the power of the chiefs and religious leaders.

There is a deep religious meaning in Native American astronomy. The sun is a vital symbol in the beliefs of many Native American cultures. And something equally important: Native Americans' understanding of the heavens helped them feel in harmony with the universe—for in many Native American religions, human beings are only one small part of the world, living in peace with the rest of nature.

Today we are coming to recognize Native Americans' achievements in astronomical knowledge—and to appreciate the ways in which they used that understanding.

7

🌿 *155* 🌿

6 After reading about the sun rooms, students may **wonder** more about the Anasazi and how they accomplished what they did. Encourage your students to wonder about the different groups of Native Americans mentioned in the article, particularly about why they built their observatories. **Wondering** often leads to further research and learning.

7 The last section of the article explains why the Native Americans constructed their observatories. **Summing up** here may help the students check their understanding of the text. A good summary should note the sun's religious meaning to the Native Americans.

Discussing Strategy Use
After reading a selection, encourage open discussion of any difficulties students encountered. What did they learn from these reading problems?

*

EXPLORING THROUGH DISCUSSION

Reflecting on the Selection
Whole-Group Discussion

The whole group discusses the selection and any thoughts, reactions, or questions that it raises. During this time, students also **return to the clues, problems, and wonderings** they noted on the board during browsing.

Assessment

To assess the students' understanding of the text, engage in a discussion to **determine whether they understand**
- how each observatory in the selection looked and functioned, and why observatories were important to cultures like the Ponca, Mississippian, and Anasazi

Response Journal

Allow time for the students to record their personal responses to the selection.

Exploring Concepts Within the Selection
Small-Group Discussion

Small groups discuss the relationship of the selection to the explorable concepts. Circulate among the groups and observe the discussions. Refer the students to the Concept Board and the Question Board to keep them focused on their original ideas about astronomy.

Sharing Ideas About Explorable Concepts

Have the groups **report** and **discuss** their **ideas** with the rest of the class. It is crucial that the students' ideas determine this discussion.
- Students may recognize that studying the astronomical records and observatories of past civilizations can help us find out not only what those civilizations knew about astronomy, but also something about what was important to them and how they lived.
- Some students may point out that there are many reasons to note the movement of the sun and stars, and that people all over the world, at widely varying times, devised methods for doing so.
- Students may notice that the behavior of the sun has remained the same throughout history. We can still count on the solstices to occur twice a year, six months apart, just as they did 2,000 years ago when the Moose Mountain Medicine Wheel was built. Some students may recognize that it is the predictability of the sun's and the earth's behavior that allows us to measure time with clocks and calendars.

As these ideas and others are stated, have the students **add them to the Question Board or the Concept Board.**

Exploring Concepts Across Selections

Students might make connections with previous selections.
- The students may point out that, like the Greeks in *How Did We Find Out the Earth Is Round?,* early Native Americans were amazingly astute observers of the sun and stars. Though neither the Greeks nor the Native Americans had tools such as telescopes and computers, both were able to devise clever and complicated methods for observing and recording the movements of the heavenly bodies.
- The students may mention that both the Greeks in *How Did We Find Out the Earth Is Round?* and the various Native-American groups

---

TIP FOR ENGLISH LANGUAGE LEARNERS

Provide conversational opportunities for English Language Learners. Encourage a discussion about the selection's photographs and illustrations and how they match the text. Praise students' efforts in using language.

TIP FOR ENGLISH LANGUAGE LEARNERS

Provide explanations when discussing difficult concepts with English Language Learners. Discuss how applying scientific principles promotes understanding. Identify examples from the selections to support your explanations.

discussed in this selection made good practical use of their astronomical observations.

Recording Ideas

As students complete the above discussions, ask them to **sum up what they have learned from their conversations and to tell how they might use this information in further explorations**. Any special information or insights may be recorded on the **Concept Board**. Any further questions that they would like to think about, pursue, or investigate may be recorded on the **Question Board**. They may want to discuss the progress that has been made on their questions. They may also want to cross out any questions that no longer warrant consideration.

➤ Ask the students to record their findings in the Explorer's Notebook, page 23.

Evaluating Discussions

Explorer's Notebook, page 23

Recording Concept Information

As I read each selection, I learned these new things about astronomy.

How Did We Find Out the Earth Is Round? by Isaac Asimov

"The Heavenly Zoo" by Alison Lurie

"Circles, Squares, and Daggers" by Elsa Marston

Unit 2/Astronomy   EN 23

2 READING WITH A WRITER'S EYE

**Writer's Craft:
Using Headings
and Captions**

Ask students to discuss what they know about the use of headings and captions in expository or nonfiction writing. They should already know that **captions are used to explain photographs, illustrations, diagrams, or other visual aids in an article.** Discussion should lead to the understanding that headings are used when a longer piece of expository writing can be divided into sections. **A heading lets the reader know the kind of information that is in the section that follows it.** Headings also are a way of organizing information while the writer is writing an article. Creating headings helps a writer decide what information to include in each section of an article.

Point out that Elsa Marston uses both captions and headings in her article, "Circles, Squares, and Daggers." For example, on page 147 Marston starts to discuss medicine wheels and she gives this section that heading. On the same page she shows a picture of one medicine wheel and a diagram that explains how the wheel functions. A caption explains the illustrations.

**Selective Reading:
Focus on Using
Headings and Captions**

Have the students go back to "Circles, Squares, and Daggers" and look for other headings and captions. Encourage volunteers to read aloud and explain the examples they find.

Other headings and captions in "Circles, Squares, and Daggers" include

- page 148: a caption for an illustration and diagram describing the Moose Mountain Medicine Wheel
- page 149: the heading, "Circles and Squares" and a caption for an illustration and diagram describing the Cahokia archeological site
- page 150: the heading "Sun Daggers"

*Selection-Based
Practice*

**Independent Practice:
Using Headings and
Captions**

❯ For additional practice in recognizing how headings and captions help to organize expository articles, have the students work in small groups to discuss and complete Reading/Writing Connection, page 16.

**Linking Reading
to Writing**

Remind the students that headings are used to tell readers what kind of information can be found in the sections they precede. They also help writers organize information. Mention also that articles can be made clearer through the use of illustrations or other graphics and that captions are used to explain these.

Then **encourage the students to look through their writing folders for any pieces of their own expository or nonfiction writing which they think could benefit from the addition of headings.** Suggest that, if they decide to include headings, they should also determine whether

---

"Circles, Squares, and Daggers"

Using Headings and Captions

Elsa Marston uses headings and captions to organize her ideas in "Circles, Squares, and Daggers." Look at other articles you have read for more examples of ways writers use headings and captions. Write the title of the article, two examples of headings or captions from the article, and the pages on which the examples occur.

Title: _____

First example: _____

_____ Page: _____

Second example: _____

_____ Page: _____

Title: _____

First example: _____

_____ Page: _____

Second example: _____

_____ Page: _____

Title: _____

First example: _____

_____ Page: _____

Second example: _____

_____ Page: _____

Look back at this page for examples when you need help using headings and captions.

Name

Headings and Captions
16 R/WC   Astronomy/Unit 2

Reading/Writing Connection, page 16

all the information below each heading belongs in that section or whether it might fit better in another section of the piece.

It is unlikely that students will have illustrations for any of the writing they have done so far. Suggest that they look for places where a picture would be helpful in making an idea easier to understand and then write a short description of what the illustration should contain. Explain that doing this helps writers remember where to place illustrations when they do the final drafts of their work and also reminds them of exactly what they want the illustrations to show.

Students might like to spend some time making or collecting drawings or photographs that would add or clarify information related to their research projects or to other pieces of writing related to astronomy.

∗ Writing Process

If students are ready to begin new writing projects, suggest that they try writing expository pieces on topics related to astronomy that interest them personally. The **Concept Board** and the **Question Board** could provide ideas for topics, or students could form **small groups** to **brainstorm for ideas**. As they begin prewriting activities, urge them to keep in mind the techniques they have learned in this unit, such as using headings and captions and providing questions and conjectures. For a review of the **Writing Process**, see **Learning Framework Card 7.**

TIP FOR ENGLISH LANGUAGE LEARNERS

Encourage English Language Learners to discuss their ideas for adding illustrations to their writing and to talk about how the pictures match their text.

VOCABULARY

Concept-related words from the selection that the students may want to discuss or remember and use include the following:

stargazers, observatories, archaeoastronomy, solstice, alignments, equinoxes, petroglyphs, cairns, ingenious, rituals, tribute

Have Vocabulary Exploration forms, Reproducible Master 14, available for students who request them. Remind the students to add these or any other words and phrases from the story to the **Personal Dictionary** section of their **Writer's Notebook**. Some students may wish to share these additions with the class. For additional opportunities to build vocabulary, see **Teacher Tool Card 75.**

VOCABULARY TIP Encourage the students to make webs for any new words recorded on the Concept Board. Use the webs to show relationships among these words.

3 GUIDED AND INDEPENDENT EXPLORATION

Guided Exploration

EXPLORING CONCEPTS BEYOND THE TEXT

The following activities do not have to be completed within the days devoted to this lesson.

- "Circles, Squares, and Daggers" describes several astronomical observatories built by Native Americans. Students may be interested in learning more about other Native-American observatories or similar observatories in other areas of the world. They can find more information about observatories in their school and community libraries. If the natural history museum in your community features Native-American cultures, it may contain information or an exhibit about astronomical observatories.
- Students may also be interested in reading about the ideas and beliefs of various Native-American groups regarding the universe and their place in the universe.

➤ Distribute Home/School Connection 14. It tells families about the observatories discussed in "Circles, Squares, and Daggers" and encourages them to make observations of the sun's movements with students.

Research Cycle: Conjecture Phase

➤ Explain to the students that a conjecture is a kind of educated guess, an explanation that we suggest for something before we have a great deal of evidence. Conjectures may be proved right, proved wrong, or modified in some way by the evidence. Students should work on the Conjecture Phase of the Research Cycle on page 32 in their Explorer's Notebook. If they are unsure of themselves, it will be helpful to have **group discussion featuring modeling of conjectures.** For this, you might choose a problem that has already been suggested for research but that has not been chosen by any group. Using such a problem, the whole class can engage in conjecturing without taking anything away from an

* Exploring Through Research

"Circles, Squares, and Daggers"

A message from _____

In "Circles, Squares, and Daggers" your child learned about some ancient observatories that were built by the Ponca, Mississippian, and Anasazi cultures. These observatories tracked the days and seasons of the year before there were such things as printed calendars and almanacs. These Native-American societies planned the events of their lives and grew their crops according to the passage of the seasons. Ask your child to share information with you about these observatories.

Other ancient cultures, like the Aztecs, Mayas, Egyptians, and Britons, constructed observatories of their own. Help your child extend his or her knowledge by reading about the observatories built by these and other ancient civilizations. Your child may want to create an observatory at home by following the instructions on Science Activity Card 5 of the program. If so, assist your child in this activity. During the month that you observe the sun's movements, you and your child might keep a diary about your observations, thoughts, and impressions. Your child can then bring it and the markings of the sun's movements to class and share the experience with his or her classmates.

Copyright © 1995 Open Court Publishing Company

Unit 2/Astronomy

H/SC 14

Home/School Connection 14

individual group's project. (The problems and conjectures will be useful in a later lesson, so you may want to record them.) As the students share their conjectures, record them on the chalkboard. Explain that they need not come to a consensus at this point. As they begin their research, they will revisit their conjectures and revise them based on new information. If necessary, explain to the students that the phases of the Research Cycle are recursive, therefore students will continually return to the previous phases of the cycle and assess how their problems and the conjectures have changed and what new information they need.

If the students are comfortable with the conjecture phase of the Research Cycle, they can go directly to work on their research problems during Independent Workshop. If they are having difficulties with forming conjectures, refer to **Learning Framework Card 4B** for ideas. Encourage the students to record their own ideas, even if these ideas are vague or limited. The important thing is that the students progress toward more sophisticated conjectures in subsequent cycles.

ASSESSMENT TIP This may be a good opportunity to observe students working in groups and to mark observations in the Teacher's Observation Log.

Planning My Research: Conjecture Phase

Our problem:

_____
_____
_____
_____
_____
_____
_____

Conjecture (my first theory or explanation):

_____
_____
_____
_____
_____
_____
_____
_____
_____
_____
_____
_____
_____
_____

As you collect information, your conjecture will change.
Return to this page to record your new theories or
explanations about your research problem.

32 EN   Astronomy/Unit 2

Explorer's Notebook, page 32

Professional Checkpoint: Guided and Independent Exploration

You should spend some time in individual conferences with students during Independent Workshop to help them with their writing and research projects. Here are a few specific pointers for conferencing:

- Focus first on the student's stated problem. Determine whether there is a problem or the student just needs reassurance from you.
- If there is a problem, determine the student's approach. If that approach isn't working, discuss alternative approaches.
- Review peer feedback.
- Determine with the student the next step or goal.
- Refer the student to any helpful resources, such as the Writer's Handbook and the Student Tool Cards in the Student Toolbox.

Notes:

✳ INDEPENDENT WORKSHOP
Building a Community of Scholars

Student-Directed Reading, Writing, and Discussion

Research Cycle: Conjecture Phase Each student should develop his or her own conjectures regarding the research problem of his or her group and enter them in the Explorer's Notebook, page 32. Then groups should meet to discuss their conjectures.

As you observe the groups discussing their conjectures, encourage them to record each group member's ideas. Explain that they can refine their conjectures as they collect information. Remind them that the purpose of their research is to improve their conjectures. Rephrasing the students' conjectures will help you elicit additional information from the groups and will help them clarify and refine their ideas. Remind the students that they will return to this page later in their research.

WORKSHOP TIP

Remind the students to check the Concept Board and the Question Board for additional questions or ideas to aid them in their exploration.

Additional Opportunities for Independent Reading, Writing, and Cross-curricular Activities

* Reading Roundtable

Students should look forward to this period of the day when they can discuss with their classmates the books they have most enjoyed reading. If students particularly enjoyed reading about Native-American observatories, they might read other books or articles about early observatories and share them during Reading Roundtable.

Portfolio

Remind the students to think about which pieces of writing they might choose to put into their portfolios.

Cross-curricular Activity Cards

The following Cross-curricular Activity Cards from the Student Toolbox are appropriate for this selection:

- 5 Science—Create an Observatory
- 6 Science—Measuring Time on a Dial

Measuring Time on a Dial
Use after "Circles, Squares, and Daggers"

6
Science

Create an Observatory
Use after "Circles, Squares, and Daggers"

5
Science

You learned in "Circles, Squares, and Daggers" how some ancient cultures constructed observatories to track the movement of the sun. Now you can create your own observatory with just a few simple materials.

You will need a piece of clear plastic wrap, tape, a dark felt-tipped pen or marker, and a window with a clear view of the western horizon.

What to do: Attach the piece of plastic to the window with tape. The plastic should cover the full width of the window. Choose a time in the early evening when the sun is setting. Find some object on the horizon, like a tree or rooftop. Draw an outline around the object. This will be your reference point for observing the sun. If you stand so that the outline is in place each time you observe, your record of the sun's movement will be more precise.

Now draw a circle around the sun. Write the date above the circle. Do this every two or three days for a period of one month. The sun should be the same distance from the top of the window each time you record its position in the sky. During the fall months, the sun will reach this position earlier each evening because the days are getting shorter; the sun is setting earlier each day.

After one month's time you will have a record of the sun's movements. Have you by chance captured the sun's position during an important solar event, such as the fall equinox or the winter solstice! Creating your own observatory helps you to understand how the ancient observatories worked.

Additional Opportunities for Solving Learning Problems

Tutorial

Use this time to help **individuals or small groups who have exhibited a need in any area.** Encourage students to ask for help whenever they need it. The following teaching aids are available in the Teacher Toolbox for your convenience:

- Writer's Craft/Reading: Using Headings and Captions, Teacher Tool Card 35
- Writer's Craft/Reading: Elaboration Through Providing Comparison and Contrast, Teacher Tool Card 36
- Grammar, Mechanics, and Usage: Compound Sentences, Teacher Tool Card 48
- Study and Research: Using Maps, Teacher Tool Card 104

Sun and Star Calendars

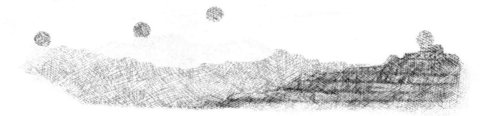

1 READING THE SELECTION

INFORMATION FOR THE TEACHER

About the Selection

From the book *Skywatchers of Ages Past,* this selection tells the fascinating story of how some of the world's first calendars were developed and of how, over the course of several generations, the ancient astronomers of the Yucatán meticulously tracked and recorded the movements of the sun, moon, and planets.

Link to the Unit Concepts

Though they lacked sophisticated tools to aid their observations, ancient astronomers around the world performed careful and accurate studies of the movements of the heavenly bodies, using natural landmarks or ingeniously designed, manmade observatories as their guides. The information they gathered led them to further discoveries and a better understanding of the workings of their world.

Focusing particularly on the Mayas and Egyptians, "Sun and Star Calendars," pages 156–165, explains how the skywatchers of several ancient civilizations accomplished their meticulous observations, and how they applied their expanding knowledge of the world in a number of useful and important ways.

About the Author

Malcom E. Weiss was born in Philadelphia, Pennsylvania. He studied chemical engineering at the University of Wisconsin, English literature at the University of Chicago, and psychology at City College in New York. He worked for several years as an associate editor of *Science World* at Scholastic Magazines, Inc. He left the magazine to become a full-time writer. Since that time, he has written several nonfiction books for both young and adult readers and has written for magazines, such as *Science World* and *Cricket.*

LESSON OVERVIEW

"Sun and Star Calendars" by Malcolm Weiss, pages 156–165

READING THE SELECTION

Materials
Student anthology, pp. 156–165
Explorer's Notebook, p. 24

FYI
Learning Framework Card
• Checking Understanding, 1C

READING WITH A WRITER'S EYE

Minilesson
Writer's Craft: Strong Topic Sentences

Materials
Reading/Writing Connection, p. 17
Reproducible Master 14

FYI
Teacher Tool Card
• Spelling and Vocabulary: Building Vocabulary, 75

Option for Instruction
Grammar, Mechanics, and Usage: Subject/Verb Agreement
(Use Teacher Tool Card listed below.)

GUIDED AND INDEPENDENT EXPLORATION

Materials
Explorer's Notebook, pp. 33–35
Home/School Connection 15

Independent Workshop

Optional Materials from Student Toolbox
Tradebook Connection Cards

Cross-curricular Activity Card
• 2 Math—Astronomy Word Problems

Student Tool Cards
• Writer's Craft/Reading: Strong Topic Sentences, 23
• Grammar, Mechanics, and Usage: Making Subject and Verb Agree, 67

FYI
Learning Framework Cards
• Needs and Plans Phase 1 and 2, 4C
• Writing Seminar, 8

Teacher Tool Cards
• Writer's Craft/Reading: Strong Topic Sentences, 23
• Grammar, Mechanics, and Usage: Subject/Verb Agreement, 67

NOTES

Asterisks (*) throughout the lesson indicate learning frameworks. Learning Framework Cards and Teacher Tool Cards can be found in the Teacher Toolbox.

Four of Weiss's books have been cited as Outstanding Science Trade Books for Children by the National Science Teachers Association and the Children's Book Council. He was also the recipient of the Distinguished Achievement Award in 1972 from *Science World* magazine and has received numerous awards for his articles in *Science World*.

Weiss has always been fascinated with astronomy and with the ancient peoples who had only the simplest tools with which to study the sun, moon, and stars. "Though we now know the universe is far vaster, older, and more complex than ancient sky watchers could have imagined, we, like them, are driven by curiosity and a search for order and beauty to probe even deeper."

About the Illustrator

David Rickman was born in 1953. A member of a Navy family, he lived in many places as a child, but spent most of his growing-up years in the San Francisco Bay area. He now lives in Wilmington, Delaware.

Rickman attended the University of California at Berkeley, earning a B.A. in history and anthropology. He began his illustrating career by drawing coloring books that featured Native Americans and the West. He credits his eye for detail and his curiosity about historic periods with making his illustrations authentic and exciting.

". . . [We] tend to have set ideas of how things looked in the past, and I think the most exciting part about doing research is discovering that . . . the past was very different from [what we expect]." Rickman has learned such things as "how the pyramids were made, . . . that they were built of raw stone with no mortar and yet they were so carefully fitted that you couldn't slip a piece of paper between the stones."

Rickman's knowledge of pyramids influenced his rendering of the Mayan pyramid that appears on page 158 of the student anthology.

INFORMATION FOR THE STUDENT

You may want to share with the students some information about the author and the illustrator.

COGNITIVE AND RESPONSIVE READING

Activating Prior Knowledge

Ask the students to share anything they know about what the sun and stars have to do with calendars. Tell the students that this selection will explain how the Mayas and the ancient Egyptians devised calendars. Invite the students to tell what they know about those early civilizations.

Setting Reading Goals and Expectations

Have the students **browse the selection,** using the clues/problems/wonderings procedure. Students will return to these observations after reading.

Recommendations for Reading the Selection

Ask the students how they want to read the selection. Some of the information and vocabulary in "Sun and Star Calendars" may be challenging to students during a first reading. An oral reading would allow the students to discuss, explain, ask questions, and clarify information as they read.

During **oral reading, use and encourage think-alouds.** During silent reading, allow discussion as needed. Discuss problems, strategies, and reactions after reading.

This would also be a good selection for **responding** to text **by visualizing** while reading aloud. Model this response, and then invite the students to do the same.

About the Reading Strategies

Remind the students that what they read should make sense. If they encounter difficulties while reading, they should figure out a way to solve the problems. They should refer to the strategy posters if they need ideas for solving a reading problem. Students should also feel free to share with the group whatever strategies they use to help solve problems. Explain that occasionally you will model the strategies you use to understand difficult passages or to get more meaning out of the text. This selection tells about several groups of people, and presents some very complicated information. **Summing up** and **asking questions** are two strategies that might prove useful. To review **summing up** and **question asking,** see **Learning Framework Card 1C, Checking Understanding.**

Think-Aloud Prompts for Use in Oral Reading

The think-aloud prompts that appear with the page miniatures are merely suggestions. Encourage the students to use whichever strategies will most increase their comprehension of the text. Invite them to share the strategies they use as they read.

TEACHING TIP Before assigning a reading selection, skim the text for difficulties that you want to discuss before, during, and after reading.

THINK ALOUD PROMPTS

These prompts may be used as guides to promote cognitive and responsive reading.

SUN AND STAR CALENDARS
from Sky Watchers of Ages Past
by Malcolm E. Weiss
illustrated by David Rickman

Using only the simplest of tools, ancient people kept track of the movements of the sun, moon, and stars. This selection describes sun calendars that were kept by the ancient Mayas and star calendars that were kept by the ancient Egyptians.

Where the horizon is hilly and uneven, it can be used as a sun calendar. A Native American group, the Hopi, use such a horizon calendar. Observing from the same place each day, the Hopi take note of where the sun rises and sets on important days. Each important day has the peak of a hill or the notch of a valley named after it—the peak or notch where the sun rises or sets on that day. The sun-watcher looks for the first glimpse of the sun in the morning, and for the sun's last gleam in the evening. He numbers the days with notches on a wooden stick, and warns the people when an important day is coming. The time for planting corn or beans, the time for the flute dance, the main harvest, and the winter-solstice ceremony—all are marked on the distant horizon.

156

Hopi horizon calendar showing sunsets from October 24 to December 21. Notice that on October 24, about the time for the Hopi corn harvest, the sun sets over a peak far to the right. By December 21, the time for the winter solstice ceremony, the sun sets over a peak far to the left. Ceremonies taking place near the end of winter were also marked by sunsets over peaks on the right. Ceremonies taking place in the summer were marked by sunsets over peaks even further to the right.

Halfway around the world, Russian peasants track the sun in the same way as the Hopi. In the Caucasus Mountains, village chiefs choose an old man to watch for sunset each day. He sits on a bench and watches the sun disappear behind the jagged mountain peaks. Using landmarks on the horizon to keep track of the year is a very old practice used by people everywhere.

This method could be used in early times because it was so simple. Nothing had to be built. All that was needed was a good view of the horizon, with natural landmarks and a place to stand while watching the sunrise and sunset.

But what if there is no clear view of the horizon? At Uaxactún, in the Mexican state of Yucatán, for example, the horizon is tree-covered and there are no landmarks to pinpoint the sun's position. There, in about A.D. 300, the Maya Indians used other means to measure the year. In a sense they built their own horizon, complete with landmarks.

157

Mayan observatory at Uaxactún.

The Mayas developed a mighty <u>civilization</u> in Central America. Mayan civilization reached its peak between A.D. 100 and A.D. 900. Then, about a thousand years ago, the classic Mayan civilization collapsed. No one really knows why or how that happened.

At Uaxactún, the Mayas built a large pyramid. East of the pyramid, on a platform, they built three small temples. These temples were lined up with the pyramid, to fix the dates of the spring and fall <u>equinoxes</u> and the summer and winter solstices.

A priest stood on the steps of the pyramid, facing the middle temple. He sighted over the top of a stone column, to the center of the temple roof. At the equinoxes, the sun rose over the center of this roof.

Standing on the same spot at the time of the summer solstice, the priest could see the sun rise over the corner of the temple to his left—the northern temple. And at the winter

158

solstice, the sun rose over the corner of the temple to the right—the southern temple.

Throughout their empire, the Mayas used similar means to <u>plot</u> the motions of the sun. And they did much more. They mapped the motions of the moon. They learned to predict <u>eclipses</u> of the sun and moon. They plotted the movements of the planet Venus with almost as much <u>accuracy</u> as do modern astronomers.

To do all this took careful observations over a period of several lifetimes. The Mayas had a written language that helped them pass along knowledge from one generation to the next. Most of that language is still a mystery to us. We have only decoded the signs for numbers and dates. These were the signs they used in making their calendars and <u>astronomical</u> tables. The signs included brilliantly colored pictures of gods, strange drawings of human and animal heads and skulls, and bars and dots.

These records were set down in "books" made of paper from the bark of the wild fig tree. A strip of paper making up a book was about eight inches high and several yards long.

Both sides were written on. The "pages" were separated from each other by painted lines. When the book was complete, the entire strip was folded up accordion-like along the lines that marked the pages.

These ancient picture books are now called codices. *Codices* is a Latin word, the plural of *codex*, meaning a book in manuscript form. Thousands of these codices were drawn and painted by the Mayas, and by the people of other Indian civilizations in Central America.

159

1 The students have had a lot of information to digest about the observatories of the Hopis, the Russians, and the Mayas. If students are confused about some of the details, it may help them to study the illustrations and captions on pages 157 and 158. Students may wish to **sum up** the information in their own words and clarify any facts about which they are confused.

"Picture book" does not really do justice to the codices. Even the simplest-appearing pictures in the codices are more than pictures. They are words and often whole phrases or ideas in picture form. Simple symbols merge into not-so-simple ones, sometimes in a striking way. A wagging tongue, for example, means "talking." A wagging tongue surrounded by flowers means "singing."

Of the thousands of codices that once existed, only seventeen are left. The others were burned by the Spanish, who conquered the Mayan lands between 1519 and 1521. The high civilization of the Mayas had collapsed centuries before the Spanish arrived. But the descendants of the Mayas still lived according to the old traditions, and the ancient language was still spoken.

Many of the books were burned by Spanish soldiers. The remainder were destroyed by missionaries. Bishop Diego de Landa, of Merida, capital of the Spanish province of Yucatán, summed up the reasons for the burning: "We found a larger number of books . . . and as they contained nothing but superstitions and lies of the devil, we burned them all, which the Indians regretted to an amazing degree, and which caused them great anguish."

Yet Bishop de Landa knew that the books contained more than mere superstition. He wrote: "These people [the Mayas] also made use of certain characters or letters, with which they wrote in their books their ancient affairs and their science, and with these and drawings, and with certain signs in these drawings, they understood their affairs and made others understand them and taught them."

🌿 *160* 🌿

Eclipse tables from the
Dresden codex.
Sächsische Landesbibliothek
Dresden/Deutsche Fotothek

De Landa learned to speak the Mayan language. He discovered that large parts of certain codices were about astronomy and the Mayan calendar. In later years, he wrote down what he knew of the written language of the Mayas—largely how they wrote numbers and dates, and how they recorded national holidays, festivals, and astronomical events.

One reason the Mayas kept such careful count of days was that they believed the past foretold the future. As far as predicting the motions of the sun, moon, and planets is concerned, this is very nearly true. Their movements through the sky are repeated in regular cycles. Some of the cycles are simple; some are complicated. But by patient observing, Mayan astronomers found the patterns of many of these movements.

Some of the patterns are recorded in the Dresden Codex, which is now housed in a museum in Dresden, in Germany. The Dresden Codex is a collection of tables on the motions of the moon and the planet Venus. It is also a kind of horoscope, since the Mayas thought that the motions of heavenly bodies affected the fates of people on earth.

🌿 *161* 🌿

The Dresden Codex records the movements of Venus for over three hundred years. The Mayas calculated that the time it takes Venus to get back to the same point in the sky is 584 days. Using modern telescopes and observatory instruments, present-day astronomers have calculated the time as 583.92 stars.

In the tables about the moon, the Mayas used the number 6585. As modern astronomers know, this is the period of time it takes for a series of eclipses of the sun and moon to repeat itself. The ancient Babylonians, who lived on the other side of the globe from the Mayas, also discovered and used this figure.

The Mayas did not use fractions or decimals, as the Babylonians did and as present-day astronomers do. They did learn to use whole numbers to express fractions very exactly, however.

For example, in the Dresden Codex the Mayas wrote that there are 405 moons (the time from new moon to new moon) in 11,958 days. If we divide 11,958 days by 405 moons, we get the length of one moon, or lunar month—29.52593 days. Modern astronomers use the figure of 29.5306 days.

In other words, the ancient astronomers of the Yucatán made an error of about seven minutes out of some twenty-nine days!

To keep watch on the stars, people invented what are probably the most ancient tools of astronomy—constellations, or sky pictures.

The constellations are star-finding tools. Most of us know that the pointer stars of the Big Dipper show the way to the North Star. We may recognize a few other easily seen sky groups such as Orion. Orion and the Big Dipper are bright enough to be visible even in the city, where skies are never

162

completely dark. At best, not more than a few hundred stars are visible in city skies.

On a clear, moonless night in the country, far from city lights, you can see some three thousand stars, however. The bare outlines of familiar constellations are lost to us in the glow of unfamiliar stars. There is no shape or pattern to the thousands of sparkling points of light.

But if you look at the sky for a while, you will begin to see patterns and shapes. You will find yourself making up your own star pictures. This is what prehistoric peoples did from the earliest times.

In one group of stars, the Eskimos saw kayaks, and steps cut into the sides of a steep snowbank so hunters could climb to the top. In that same group of stars, the Egyptians saw a hippopotamus in the Nile River. The Blackfoot Indians of North America saw the arrowhead of a great hunter there. And the Cherokees saw three magicians. We know these stars as the Belt of Orion, the mighty hunter. That is how the ancient Greeks and Romans saw them.

Stories about the constellations were handed down by word of mouth for thousands of years. When people do not have a written language, such stories are more than entertainment. They are like star maps. They record where a constellation is in the sky, and what position it is in during each season. Early sky watchers found, as they had with the sun, regular patterns in the way the stars moved. This cycle of the stars, like the yearly cycle of the sun, allowed astronomers to measure the year.

Naturally, sky watchers could not fix the exact date when a star rose and set with the sun. For a good many days before

163

2 This passage contains a lot of details. Some students may need to **clarify** the significance of the Dresden Codex. It's not necessary for students to remember the figures from the Dresden Codex in the tables for Venus and the moon. They should, however, understand that the Mayas, like the ancient Babylonians on the other side of the world, thought the earth stood still and all heavenly bodies revolved around it.

Students will also understand this passage better if they understand what an eclipse is. They should remember discussing the lunar eclipse in *How Did We Find Out the Earth Is Round?* Encourage them to **connect** this passage with previous reading about eclipses.

If students are confused about some of the concepts and main points in this passage, **asking questions** and **summing up** are two strategies that may help.

This detail of a calendar from the tomb of a pharaoh shows the months as Egyptian gods.
© Robert Lackenbach/Black Star

and after that date, the star would be invisible all night long. Its rising and setting would be hidden in the glare of sunrise and sunset.

But the ancient astronomers found a way around that difficulty. They watched for the *last* evening when a certain star was visible in the evening twilight in the west. Then, some weeks later, they looked for the exact date when that same star was *first* visible in the east in the morning twilight. This first appearance of the star before dawn is the heliacal rising of the star. The ancient astronomers discovered that the amount of time between two *heliacal* risings of a star was one year. So the first heliacal rising of a particular star before dawn was often used by ancient people to mark important dates. Around the world, stars were used to mark times of the year for hunting, fishing, and planting; to mark the times of great cold or heat, the rainy season, and the dry season.

3 Some four thousand years ago, the Egyptians used the rising of Sirius—the brightest star in the sky—to mark the yearly flooding of the Nile River in July. This was the start of the Egyptians' calendar year. Their year had 365 days and 12 months. That was the amount of time the Egyptians counted between two heliacal risings of Sirius.

But as time passed, the Egyptians realized that something was wrong with their calendar. After only forty years, the heliacal rising of Sirius was ten days late, according to their cal-

🌿 164 🌿

culations. After 730 years, it was half a year late. Not until 1460 years had passed were Sirius and the Egyptian calendar back in step. The Egyptians called this 1460-year cycle the *Sothic* cycle. Sothic was their name for Sirius.

The Egyptians realized that it was the calendar, not the star, that was out of step. If Sirius seemed late, this meant that the calendar year was shorter than the true year. So they began the practice of adding an extra day every four years. They passed this idea along to the Romans in the time of Julius Caesar. In 46 B.C., Caesar reformed the Roman calendar, adopting the Egyptian leap year.

That made the calendar 365 1/4 days long. This was quite accurate—just eleven minutes and four seconds longer than the true cycle of the seasons.

But it was still not accurate enough to keep the calendar in line with the seasons over very long periods of time. By 1582, the date of the spring equinox had slipped back to March 11. At that time, ten days were dropped from the calendar. The rules about leap years were changed, too. Only those century years—years ending in two zeroes—that were divisible by 400 would be leap years.

That meant that 1800 and 1900 were not leap years. But 2000 will be. The next century leap year after that will be 2400. With this correction, it will take the calendar 1,000 years to gain three days over the true year.

The reformed calendar of 1582 was proclaimed by Pope Gregory XIII, on the advice of the Jesuit astronomer Christopher Clavius. And neither Clavius nor the pope ever knew that more than eight hundred years earlier, Mayan astronomers had produced a calendar even more accurate than theirs. **4**

🌿 165 🌿

3 This passage explains that the ancient Egyptians used the heliacal rising of the bright star Sirius in midsummer to mark the beginning of their calendar year. *Heliacal* means "with the sun." Some students may need to **ask questions** to determine why the stars sweep across the sky from east to west each night or why, as the year progresses, Sirius rises a few minutes earlier each night. You might assist them by modeling a question or two of your own. Remind them of how the earth turns on its axis each day and how it travels around the sun each year.

4 Students may need to **ask a question** in order to understand why the Romans had to adjust the Julian calendar. They may not remember immediately that the spring equinox should fall on March 21, not March 11.

Note: Be sure that students who **sum up** the information in this passage understand the author's main point: The inaccuracies in the Egyptian and Roman calendars were not due to any change in the movement of stars; they were due to the way the calendar year was calculated mathematically.

A leap year has 366 days. Every year whose last two digits are divisible by 4 and every century year that is divisible by 400 is a leap year. Leap years contain a February 29.

Discussing Strategy Use

Encourage volunteers to discuss the strategies they used while reading the selection.

*

EXPLORING THROUGH DISCUSSION

Reflecting on the Selection
Whole-Group Discussion

The whole group discusses the selection and any thoughts, reactions, or questions that it raises. During this time, students also **return to the clues, problems, and wonderings** they noted on the board during browsing.

TEACHING TIP Whenever possible, encourage students to generate and direct discussion and to take over the process of instruction.

Assessment

To assess the students' understanding of the text, engage in a discussion to determine whether the students understand
• how the Mayan system of observing the sun differed from that of the Hopi and the Russian peasants
• how the Mayan calendar compared to the Egyptian and Roman calendars
• how written calendars relate to the movements of the sun

Response Journal

Invite students to record their personal responses to the selection.

Exploring Concepts Within the Selection
Small-Group Discussion

Small groups discuss the relationship of the selection to the explorable concepts. Circulate among the groups and observe the discussions. Refer the students to the Concept Board and the Question Board to keep them focused on their original ideas about astronomy.

TIP FOR ENGLISH LANGUAGE LEARNERS

Take this opportunity to praise English Language Learners for listening and discussing what they think about the concepts.

Sharing Ideas About Explorable Concepts

Have the groups **report** and **discuss** their **ideas** with the rest of the class. It is crucial that the students' ideas determine this discussion.
• The students may note that sometimes seemingly irrational beliefs can actually lead to practical knowledge—the idea that events of the past can be used to foretell the future led the Mayas to plot their calendar with extreme care.
• The students may point out that people's knowledge expanded as they developed new methods for exploring the universe. Uncovering recognizable patterns, or constellations, in the stars helped early astronomers to locate and remember certain stars and to track the movements of those stars.
• Some students may note that, as ancient astronomers learned about the movements of the sun, moon, and stars, they began to figure out important practical information about living on earth; for example, their awareness of the yearly cycle of the sun or of the cycle of a star allowed early astronomers to calculate the length of the year.

As these ideas and others are stated, have the students add them to the **Question Board** or **Concept Board.**

Invite the students to look at and discuss the Turkish miniature reproduced on page 181 of the student anthology. This piece depicts astronomers at work in yet another early observatory.

Fine Art

Recording Concept Information continued

"Sun and Star Calendars" by Malcolm Weiss

_____
_____
_____
_____
_____
_____
_____

"Galileo" by Navin Sullivan

_____
_____
_____
_____
_____
_____
_____

"Telescopes" by David Macaulay

_____
_____
_____
_____
_____
_____
_____

24 EN   Astronomy/Unit 2

Explorer's Notebook, page 24

Exploring Concepts Across Selections

Students may **make connections with selections in this and other units.** For example, the students may point out that, like the Native Americans discussed in "Circles, Squares, and Daggers," the people discussed in "Sun and Star Calendars" relied on astronomical observations to help them chart the passing of time and mark the arrival of new seasons and other important events in their lives.

Recording Ideas

As students complete the above discussions, ask them to **sum up what they have learned from their conversations and to tell how they might use this information** in further explorations. Any special information or insights may be recorded on the **Concept Board.** Any further questions that they would like to think about, pursue, or investigate may be recorded on the **Question Board.** They may want to discuss the progress that has been made on their questions. They may also want to cross out any questions that no longer warrant consideration.

➤ The students should note new observations and insights on page 24 of their Explorer's Notebook.

Evaluating Discussions

Professional Checkpoint: Cognitive and Responsive Reading

Students need to be informed that one-time reading almost never leads to deep understanding and that it is natural *not* to understand everything in the first reading of a selection. Rather, good readers reread. One signal that suggests the necessity of rereading is the feeling that one does not fully comprehend the meaning of the text. Good readers think about text for a long time and build multiple reactions to it. Recognizing one's own confusion is a mature response and shows an awareness of the process of comprehension. Rereading or searching for clues to meaning as part of clarifying is even more mature and something that the very best readers do routinely.

Notes:

2 READING WITH A WRITER'S EYE

MINILESSON

Writer's Craft: Strong Topic Sentences

Ask the students to **review what they have learned about paragraphs.** They should understand that a paragraph consists of two or more sentences that tell about the same thing; that a paragraph has a topic sentence—that is, a sentence that implies or states the main idea of the paragraph; that paragraphs are set off from each other by indenting the first sentence of a new paragraph or by skipping one line space between paragraphs; and that when authors write dialogue, they begin a new paragraph whenever they change speakers.

Remind the students that **paragraphs help a writer organize his or her ideas.** Because each paragraph contains only one main idea, the writer can more easily "string" ideas together clearly and sequentially. This is especially useful in writing expository pieces. Because this type of writing relies so much on including necessary information in proper sequence, **nonfiction writers must be careful to write paragraphs that present their ideas clearly.** Malcom Weiss does this especially well in "Sun and Star Calendars."

For instance, on page 156, he begins by saying that the horizon can be used as a calendar. Then he elaborates on this idea by explaining how this is done by the Hopi Indians. The next paragraph at the top of page 157 explains that this method of keeping track of time is very old and that people all over the world have used it. As an example, the paragraph states that peasants in Russian villages also keep track of the days of the year by watching where the sun rises and sets on the horizon. The third paragraph explains that using the horizon as a calendar is such a widespread method because no special tools are needed—only a visible horizon with natural landmarks and a place to stand.

Selective Reading:
Strong Topic
Sentences

Have the students go back to the selection and look for other examples of how Weiss uses paragraphs to help him present his ideas. Encourage volunteers to explain how Weiss's ideas progress from one paragraph to the next.

Almost every paragraph can be used as an example of how ideas progress from paragraph to paragraph.

Selection-Based Practice

Independent Practice:
Strong Topic
Sentences

▶ For additional practice in recognizing how writers construct paragraphs and use them to organize the presentation of their ideas, have the students work in small groups to discuss and complete Reading/Writing Connection, page 17.

WRITING

Linking Reading
to Writing

Encourage the students to look through their writing folders for pieces with paragraphs that contain vague main ideas or for a series of paragraphs that do not move logically from one idea to the next. Suggest that they revise those paragraphs to make their ideas clearer. Invite volunteers to read both versions to the class and explain how they think the revisions improved the original paragraphs.

Reading/Writing Connection, page 17

"Sun and Star Calendars"

Strong Topic Sentences

In "Sun and Star Calendars," Malcolm Weiss uses paragraphs with clearly stated main ideas in order to organize information and to indicate how ideas are related. Look at other selections you have read to find pairs of well-written paragraphs that show a clear transition from one idea to another. Write the title of the selection the two paragraphs appear in, the main idea of each paragraph, and the page on which the first paragraph begins.

Title: _____

Main idea of first paragraph: _____
_____

Main idea of second paragraph: _____
_____ Page: _____

Title: _____

Main idea of first paragraph: _____
_____

Main idea of second paragraph: _____
_____ Page: _____

Title: _____

Main idea of first paragraph: _____
_____

Main idea of second paragraph: _____
_____ Page: _____

Look back at this page for examples when you need help in writing strong topic sentences to present your ideas clearly.

Name

_____   Writing Paragraphs

Unit 2/Astronomy   R/WC 17

* Writing Process

If the students began prewriting activities for expository articles after the last selection, encourage them to keep going with the writing process. They may want to continue to develop the ideas they want to include in their articles or they may want to begin their first drafts. Again, **urge them to keep in mind the techniques that they have learned in this unit,** such as providing questions and conjectures, using headings to organize sections of the article, thinking of illustrations and captions that would make their ideas clearer, and writing in clear, concise paragraphs.

VOCABULARY

Concept-related words from the selection that students may wish to discuss or remember include the following:

cycle, heliaca, codices, codex, manuscript, missionaries, horoscope, reformed

Have Vocabulary Exploration forms, Reproducible Master 14, available for students who need them. Remind the students to add these or any other words and phrases from the article to the Personal Dictionary section of their Writer's Notebook. Some students may wish to share these additions with the class. For additional opportunities to build vocabulary, see **Teacher Tool Card 75.**

Adding to Personal Word Lists

3 GUIDED AND INDEPENDENT EXPLORATION

EXPLORING CONCEPTS BEYOND THE TEXT

Guided Exploration

The following activities do not all have to be completed within the time allotted for this lesson.

- In "Sun and Star Calendars," the students learned a little bit about the Mayan, Egyptian, Julian, and Gregorian calendars and how these calendars were created and perfected. Students may be interested in learning more about how these and other calendars came to be. For instance, how were the Chinese and Babylonian calendars created? How does their history compare with that of the Egyptian and Roman calendars? Did these cultures calculate the year in similar ways, or not?

➤ By now the students have read about many ancient cultures and what they knew about astronomy. They will continue to read about the history of astronomy in the selections that follow in the unit, moving from early to contemporary times. Students may enjoy placing in a time chart the various peoples about whom they've read, the eras in which they lived, some of their ideas about astronomy, and, if pertinent, the tools they used to learn about the sun, moon, stars, and planets. Explorer's Notebook pages 34–35 are designed to help students with this exercise. Students should continue to fill out this chart as they read the remaining selections in the unit.

TIP FOR ENGLISH LANGUAGE LEARNERS

Build cultural understanding and appreciation for contributions of ancient cultures. English Language Learners may want to know more about the accomplishments and outstanding contributions of groups or individuals from different countries. Encourage English Language Learners in their research and invite them to share their research with the class.

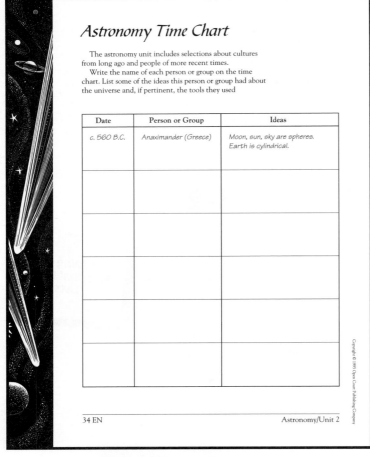

Astronomy Time Chart

The astronomy unit includes selections about cultures from long ago and people of more recent times.
Write the name of each person or group on the time chart. List some of the ideas this person or group had about the universe and, if pertinent, the tools they used

Date	Person or Group	Ideas
c. 560 B.C.	Anaximander (Greece)	Moon, sun, sky are spheres. Earth is cylindrical.

34 EN   Astronomy/Unit 2

Explorer's Notebook, page 34

to learn about the sun, moon, stars, and planets. List also any important discoveries or inventions they made. You may have to do some research to determine the correct time periods. Add the names of other people and groups as you read the remaining selections in the unit.

Discoveries or Inventions	Tools

Unit 2/Astronomy   EN 35

Explorer's Notebook, page 35

▶ Send home the Home/School Connection 15, which encourages the students and their families to do some research on ancient calendars and to write a brief summary of their findings. Allow time for students to read and discuss their reports when they return them to class.

Research Cycle: Needs and Plans Phase 1

The students should already have produced individual conjectures regarding their chosen research problems and discussed them in their research groups. A whole-class discussion of these may now be conducted, in which problems and conjectures are briefly presented and all students have a chance to contribute suggestions, criticisms, and questions. These ideas should help the research groups as they enter the next phase, Needs and Plans.

Remind the students that *needs* refers to **things they need to find out or understand.** To help groups get started in identifying knowledge needs related to their problems, you might focus on one of the conjectures that came out of Guided Exploration during the previous lesson. Relevant questions are, *What facts will we need to help us decide whether this conjecture is right? Where can we look for these facts? What would an expert on this problem know that we do not know?*

* Exploring Through Research

TEACHING TIP Handing-off is a useful procedure in research discussions as well as text discussions because it encourages the students to talk to one another rather than to you.

A message from _____

"Sun and Star Calendars"

In "Sun and Star Calendars" your child learned about the horizon calendar of the Hopi and the elaborate observatory of the Mayas, which consisted of a pyramid and three temples. Your child also learned how early civilizations, like the Mayas, Egyptians, and Romans, created written calendars based on their observations of the sun and stars as they passed through the sky during the year. Your child learned how these people calculated the true year and how they made sure that their calendars would be accurate from one year to the next. Ask your child to share with you what he or she learned in "Sun and Star Calendars."

With your child, choose one of the ancient cultures from the selection—the Mayas, Egyptians, or Babylonians—and learn more about how their calendars came to be and how the calendar influenced their lives. There are books in the library about the history of calendars and about the customs and beliefs of these ancient societies. The book *Calendars* by Necia Apfel will provide you with some solid information about calendars and how they are calculated. After you and your child have completed your research, write a brief summary of your findings so that your child may share the information with her or his classmates.

Copyright © 1995 Open Court Publishing Company

Unit 2/Astronomy　　　　H/SC 15

Home/School Connection 15

Research Cycle: Needs and Plans Phase 1

My group's problem:

_____
_____
_____
_____
_____
_____

Knowledge Needs—Information I need to find or figure out in order to explore the problem:

A. _____
B. _____
C. _____
D. _____
E. _____

Source	Useful?	How?
Encyclopedias		
Books		
Magazines		
Newspapers		
Videotapes, filmstrips, etc.		
TV		
Interviews, observations		
Museums		
Other		

Copyright © 1995 Open Court Publishing Company

Unit 2/Astronomy　　　　EN 33

Explorer's Notebook, page 33

❯ Have the students examine the resources listed on Explorer's Notebook, page 33. If they are unfamiliar with any of these resources, briefly explain the purpose of each and where it can be found. The students may be unaware of alternate sources of information, such as interviews, films, and primary sources materials. Highlight these sources of information and have the students discuss how each might be useful to their research. Remind them to review the annotations on the unit bibliographies. Explain to them that these annotations will help them narrow their search for information by letting them know whether the book deals with their research problem. Tell the students that the manner in which they want to present their research might also affect the resources they use. For example, a student who decides to make a poster might want to collect photographs and illustrations from magazines to place on the poster. Encourage the students to begin thinking of interesting ways to present the information they collect. These presentations might include reports, posters, dioramas, video presentations, plays, or a combination of two or more methods. If necessary, remind the students that the Cross-curricular Activity Cards in the Student Toolbox can provide them with ideas.

Following this discussion, assign page 33 in their Explorer's Notebook, which calls for **listing knowledge needs and possible sources of information.**

∗INDEPENDENT WORKSHOP
Building a Community of Scholars

Student-Directed Reading, Writing, and Discussion

Research Cycle: Needs and Plans Phase 1 Working individually, students can list knowledge needs and resources on page 33 of their Explorer's Notebook. Then they can discuss their lists in their research groups, adding to their individual notebooks any items that arise from the discussion. To review information about Needs and Plans, see Learning Framework Card 4C.

Resources Provide additional library time and assistance for students locating resources for their research.

WORKSHOP TIP

Provide time to discuss research topics with students. Assist them in narrowing the focus of their research and in locating resources.

Additional Opportunities for Independent Reading, Writing, and Cross-curricular Activities

✻ Reading Roundtable

If students enjoyed reading "Sun and Star Calendars," they may wish to read other science books or articles by Malcolm E. Weiss.

✻ Writing Seminar

Have the students continue to apply the writing process to any writing pieces they are drafting or revising. For more information about Writing Seminar, see **Learning Framework Card 8.**

Portfolio

Remind the students to think about which pieces of writing they might choose to put into their portfolios.

Cross-curricular Activity Cards

The following Cross-curricular Activity Card from the Student Toolbox is appropriate for this selection:

- 2 Math—Astronomy Word Problems

Astronomy Word Problems
Use after "Sun and Star Calendars"

2 Math

The Mayas, Egyptians, and Romans in this selection made calculations based on the movement of the sun and stars to create and perfect their calendars. See how well you can calculate the following word problems.

There are about 365.25 days in one year. How many leap years will there be in the period 1999 to 2050? Remember the rules about leap years: they are those years whose last two digits are divisible by 4 and only those century years that are divisible by 400.

Our calendar would be off by how many days if, for a period of 50 years, we didn't count that .25 day at the end of the year?

There are 29.53 days in a lunar month. How many days are there in a lunar year? How many more days are there in a solar year than in a lunar year?

The sun is much larger than the earth. If the sun were hollow, more than a million earths could fit inside it. The sun also has much greater mass than the earth. This means that there is a much greater gravitational pull on the sun than on the earth and, therefore, things weigh much more on the sun. If someone weighed 85 pounds on earth, he or she would weigh 2,380 pounds on the sun. How much is one earth pound on the sun? Figure out how much you would weigh on the sun.

Because astronomers make many calculations about the earth, planets, and other heavenly bodies they study, good math skills are a necessary part of being an astronomer.

Answers appear on the back.

Additional Opportunities for Solving Learning Problems

Tutorial

You might use this time to **help individuals or small groups of students who have exhibited a need in any area.** Encourage students to ask for help whenever they need it. The following teaching aids are available in the Teacher Toolbox for your convenience:

- Writer's Craft/Reading: Strong Topic Sentences, Teacher Tool Card 23
- Grammar, Mechanics, and Usage: Subject/Verb Agreement, Teacher Tool Card 67

On Your Own

Galileo

1 READING THE SELECTION

About the
Selection

In this selection, readers will meet a pioneer astronomer whose work opened up amazing new worlds in the field of astronomy. Galileo Galilei (1564–1642) was the first person ever to view the night sky through a telescope and one of only a few scientists of his time who were willing to defy authority by publicly asserting that the earth is not the center of the universe. Navin Sullivan's friendly, conversational style brings the scholar and his work to life.

Link to the
Unit Concepts

The events of "Galileo," pages 166–175, illustrate the enormous importance of tools and technology in expanding people's knowledge of the universe. During the fourth century B.C., the Greek philosopher Aristotle (upon whose ideas Ptolemy based his system) pronounced the heavenly bodies to be perfect—that is, perfectly smooth and spherical—an idea that was more or less accepted for the next two thousand years. Yet when he trained his telescope on the moon and saw for the first time its mountains and valleys, Galileo was able to dispense with Aristotle's notion in the span of a few moments. Indeed, Galileo learned more about our solar system with his telescope than earlier sky watchers had discerned over thousands of years of observing the heavens with the naked eye.

The telescope enabled astronomers like Galileo to amass new information not only about individual bodies in the solar system but also about the workings of the system as a whole. Not until astronomers had telescopes with which to observe such phenomena as the phases of Venus could they *prove* that our solar system is heliocentric (sun-centered) rather than geocentric (earth-centered) and really begin to understand and calculate correctly the motions of the planets.

LESSON OVERVIEW

"Galileo" by Navin Sullivan, pages 166–175

READING THE SELECTION

Materials
Student anthology, pp. 166–175
Explorer's Notebook, p. 24
Assessment Masters 1–2

FYI
Learning Framework Card
• Setting Reading Goals and
  Expectations, 1A

READING WITH A WRITER'S EYE

Minilesson
On Your Own

Materials
Reproducible Master 14

FYI
Learning Framework Card
• Writing Process, 7

Teacher Tool Card
• Spelling and Vocabulary: Building
  Vocabulary, 75

Options for Instruction
Writer's Craft: Genre—Biography
Writer's Craft: Elaboration Through
  Providing Concept Information
(Use Teacher Tool Cards listed below.)

GUIDED AND INDEPENDENT EXPLORATION

Materials
Home/School Connection 16
Explorer's Notebook, p. 38
Assessment Master 1

Independent Workshop

**Optional Materials from
Student Toolbox**
Tradebook Connection Cards

Cross-curricular Activity Card
• 3 Drama—Writing and Acting Out a
  Conversation

Student Tool Cards
• Writer's Craft/Reading: Reading and
  Writing Biography and
  Autobiography, 8
• Writer's Craft/Reading: Giving
  Concept Information, 43

FYI
Learning Framework Card
• Needs and Plans Phase 1 and 2, 4C

Teacher Tool Cards
• Writer's Craft/Reading: Genre—
  Biography and Autobiography, 8
• Writer's Craft/Reading: Elaboration
  Through Providing Concept
  Information, 43

NOTES

Asterisks (*) throughout the lesson indicate learning frameworks. Learning Framework Cards and Teacher Tool Cards can be found in the Teacher Toolbox.

About the Author

"Galileo" is excerpted from *Pioneer Astronomers* by British author Navin Sullivan. In this book, published in 1964, Sullivan traces the development of the science of astronomy by profiling the works of groundbreaking astronomers. Each chapter is devoted to a different astronomer, beginning with Copernicus (1473–1543) and finishing with the twentieth-century team of Graham Smith and Walter Baade.

Sullivan has had a lifelong interest in various fields of science. He has written many science books for children, including the award-winning *Pioneer Germ Fighters.* He has also published numerous fictional stories for children, in both English and American magazines.

INFORMATION FOR THE STUDENT

- Tell the class that the selection that they are about to read was excerpted from *Pioneer Astronomers,* Navin Sullivan's book about important astronomers.
- After they have read the selection, you may want to share with the students some of the following background information about Galileo, Ptolemy, Copernicus, and seventeenth-century Rome.

Astronomer, physicist, and mathematician, Galileo Galilei was born in Pisa—a city in what is now Italy—in 1564. While he did not invent the refracting telescope, he was able to build his own telescopes after hearing from a friend about this amazing new invention. In 1609 he became the first scientist to use a telescope to study the heavens.

For many years prior to his first observations with the refracting telescope, Galileo worked as a professor of mathematics. Through his teaching he became familiar with the theories of the Greek astronomer Ptolemy (second century A.D.), who had held that the sun and the planets orbited a stationary earth. Galileo's research into the Ptolemaic system eventually convinced him that Ptolemy's theories were in error.

The Polish astronomer Nicolaus Copernicus (1473–1543) had advanced the radical and widely scorned theory that the earth and the rest of the planets orbit the sun. Galileo knew of Copernicus's theories, and by 1609 he was convinced that Copernicus had been right.

Galileo's telescopes enabled him to discover many new facts about the heavenly bodies and were a great help in his defense of the Copernican system. For instance, the telescope allowed Galileo to observe that Venus has phases like those of Earth's moon—a phenomenon that would not be possible unless Venus was traveling around the sun. Galileo first published his findings in 1610, and in 1632 completed his *Dialogue on the Great World Systems,* in which he asserted the logical superiority of the Copernican system over the Ptolemaic system. (What Galileo referred to as a world system is what we now refer to as a solar system. The term *solar system* means "sun-centered system" and thus, of course, was not used in Galileo's day.)

In Galileo's time the Roman Catholic Church was not only the highest religious authority but was also the political ruler over much of what is

The Historical Figure

now Italy. The Church, which taught that the earth was the center of the universe, considered Galileo's teachings heresy. Galileo was eventually silenced by the Inquisition—the Church's powerful court in Rome—but his findings later provided the foundation for the work of other important scientists such as Sir Isaac Newton (1642–1727).

The telescope Galileo created was a type of *refracting* telescope. It consisted of a tube with a convex (curving outward) lens at one end and a concave (curving inward) eyepiece lens at the other end. Light striking the convex lens was bent, or refracted, to a focal point near the bottom of the tube. When he talks about telescopes with magnifications of three, ten, or thirty, Galileo means that these telescopes make the stars and planets appear to be three, ten, and thirty times closer than they really are.

Galileo's Tools

* ## COGNITIVE AND RESPONSIVE READING

Activating Prior Knowledge

Invite the students to discuss anything they know about using telescopes to observe the night sky.

Setting Reading Goals and Expectations

This selection has been designated as an On Your Own selection. Have the students **read** the selection **independently**. Encourage them to use the strategies they have learned when they are confronted with difficulties in the text.

Before they read the selection independently, have the students **browse** the selection using the **clues/problems/wonderings procedure**. For a review of browsing, see **Learning Framework Card 1A, Setting Reading Goals and Expectations**. Following the reading of the selection, the students will complete a Self-Assessment Questionnaire.

ASSESSMENT TIP This may be a good opportunity to observe students working in groups and to mark observations in the Teacher's Observation Log.

THINK ALOUD PROMPTS

To foster independence, think-aloud prompts are not provided for On Your Own lessons.

GALILEO
from PIONEER
ASTRONOMERS
by Navin Sullivan

Portrait of Galileo. Ottavio Leoni.
Date unknown.
Biblioteca Marucelliana. Photo: SCALA/Art Resource

One May evening in 1609, a carriage rattled briskly through the streets of Padua, in Italy. In it was Galileo Galilei, professor of mathematics, returning from a trip to Venice. While he was there, he had received news from a former pupil named Jacques Badovere—news that had sent him hurrying home.

"A marvelous tube is on sale here," wrote Badovere, who was now living in Paris. "This tube makes distant objects appear close. A man two miles away can be seen distinctly. People call these tubes 'Dutch perspectives' or 'Dutch cylinders.' Some say that they were invented by Hans Lippershey, an obscure maker of eyeglasses in Middleburg, Holland. What is sure is that they employ two lenses, one convex and the other concave."

The carriage turned into the Borgo dei Vignali and stopped outside Galileo's house. Pausing only to glance at his garden, Galileo hurried indoors and went to his study.

"One convex and one concave," he repeated as though in a trance. He drew writing paper toward him, dipped a sharpened quill in the ink, and began to draw.

"Suppose the convex lens is placed in front, to gather the light," he muttered. "Then if the concave lens is placed the right distance behind, it should magnify the gathered light."

He only had to figure the distance and he would be able to make one of these marvelous "Dutch perspectives" for himself! He had already taken the precaution of bringing a good assortment of eyeglass lenses from Venice.

By the time that Galileo went to bed he felt fairly sure that he had solved the problem. Early the next morning he hurried to his workshop. The place was filled with gadgets he had already invented, including an apparatus for indicating temperature and another for timing the pulse of a patient. Now he would make a tube to demolish distance.

Seizing a handy piece of lead tubing, he cut it down to the length he wanted. Then he took a convex lens and placed it in one end, and placed a concave lens in the other. Excitedly, he held the tube to his eye and peered through. Immediately he gave a cry of delight. It worked! The church tower several streets away might have been just outside.

How much did his tube magnify? Galileo cut different-sized circles of paper and pinned them up on a wall. When he found that his tube made a small circle look the size of a larger one seen with the naked eye, he could figure the magnification by comparing the actual sizes of the circles. In this

166

167

Two of Galileo's telescopes on display at a museum in Florence, Italy.

Museum of the History of Science, Florence.
Photo: SCALA/Art Resource

way he found that his telescope magnified three times.

Proudly he sat down and wrote to his friends in Venice telling them of his success. Then, after getting the lenses mounted in a more imposing tube made of wood, he hurried back to Venice himself. The Venetians were famous as sailors and navigators. This tube would show them ships out at sea long before they could be seen with the naked eye. Surely, thought Galileo, the nobles of Venice would pay well for such a device.

His thinking was right. On August 8, 1609, even the aged members of the Venetian Senate clambered painfully up to the very top of the tower of St. Mark's Cathedral, the highest building in Venice. There they gazed out to sea through Galileo's primitive telescope and, to their delight, found that they could see ships sailing toward them a good two hours before they were visible with the naked eye. They promptly doubled Galileo's salary as professor of mathematics which, although he was at the University of Padua, was controlled by them.

Galileo returned triumphantly to Padua and disappeared into his workshop. Already he was planning better lenses

🌿 *168* 🌿

and longer tubes. He intended to teach himself lens grinding. He dreamed of magnifications of 8, 20, even 30!

And when he had made these telescopes, he was going to use them to look not at the sea but the sky. Five years earlier, all Padua had seen an extraordinary happening: a new star had appeared in the sky. (The astronomer Johannes Kepler had seen it too, and had pointed out that evidently the stars were not unchanging, as people then believed.) Like everyone else, Galileo had been surprised and puzzled by the new star. Now he promised himself that he was going to look more closely at the heavens.

It was four days after new moon. Galileo's newest telescope, magnifying 30 times, was resting in its cradle on a tripod stand. He squinted through it at the bright crescent, then drew what he saw by the light of a flickering candle.

The moon was, he knew, lit from one side by the sun. He noticed that the boundary between light and dark on the moon's surface was wavy and uneven. Also, he saw bright spots of light dotted over the dark area. What could they be?

He puzzled over them for a while, and then he made a bold deduction.

"These spots of light are mountain peaks just catching the sunlight," he decided. "And the wavy line at the boundary between light and dark exists because there are mountains there, too. It is sunrise up there and, just as on earth at dawn, the mountain peaks are bathed in sunlight while the valleys are still dark." It seemed incredible. Yet it must be true. There were mountains on the moon, as there were on earth!

🌿 *169* 🌿

Until then no one had seriously supposed that the moon might be something like the earth. People had thought of the moon and planets as heavenly bodies, things quite different in kind from the earth.

How high were the mountains? Galileo could not measure them directly, but he devised a way of comparing them with the diameter of the moon, which was fairly accurately known. When he had worked out the figures, he could hardly believe them. The moon mountains proved to be enormous, much higher than earthly mountains: up to four miles high.

It was a whole new world that Galileo was looking at. But was it full of living creatures or was it dead? He wondered if there was air on it, and shuddered at the idea that it might be cold and silent, a dead world forever circling the earth.

Then he began to explore the sky. Night after night he gazed upward, and what he found was a revelation. With the naked eye only about 2,000 stars are visible at any one time. Even with his relatively low-power telescope, Galileo found myriads more than that.

He examined the belt and sword of Orion: instead of the usual nine stars he found 89! The constellation of the Pleiades, in which sharp-eyed observers could only see seven stars, became a swarm of 43. As for the Milky Way—it was impossible to think of counting the stars in it. Wherever Galileo looked, his telescope showed crowded clusters of stars.

"Many of them are tolerably large and extremely bright," he noted, "but the number of small ones is quite beyond determination."

🌿 *170* 🌿

On January 7, 1610, while he was gazing at the sky an hour after sunset, he noticed that the planet Jupiter was visible. Immediately he turned his telescope onto it, eager to examine one of the planets for the first time.

He saw that it was a small, round disk that did not sparkle like a star. Peering more closely, he saw something else: three bright little points of light were grouped near it, two to the east of Jupiter, one to the west:

(East)  (West)

At first he told himself that these bright points must be three fixed stars. But the next night, to his astonishment, they were differently grouped: all three were to the west of Jupiter.

(East)  (West)

"Can Jupiter have moved past them?" Galileo asked himself in bewilderment. "If so, it is not traveling the way astronomers have always said it does."

He waited impatiently to look again the next night, but to his disappointment the sky was cloudy. However, the following night was clear. He rushed to his telescope and

🌿 *171* 🌿

turned it with trembling hands toward Jupiter. This is what he saw:

(East)   (West)

For a moment he wondered if he were going crazy. Now there were only two points of light, and both were to the east of Jupiter.

"Is Jupiter moving back and forth like a pendulum?" he muttered.

He searched the sky nearby, checking to see if Jupiter had moved in this way against the background of the fixed stars. It had not; it was on the course that astronomers had always charted for it.

"If Jupiter is not swinging to and fro, then the little points of light are," reasoned Galileo. "And since one of them has disappeared tonight, it is probably hidden by Jupiter—it has probably gone behind the planet. It looks as if these points of light are swinging *around* Jupiter!"

This meant that the points of light could not be stars. To make sure that they were swinging around Jupiter, Galileo began a methodical series of observations.

On the next night, January 11th, he still saw only two of them, but now they had moved farther away from the planet. On the 12th they were closer again, and a third had appeared on the west of the planet. On the 13th, he had another surprise: there were four points of light.

❧ *172* ❧

(East)      (West)

He doubted no longer. "These are not fixed stars, but bodies belonging to Jupiter and going around it in various orbits," he decided. "Jupiter has four satellite moons of its own, just as the Earth has one!"

Full of excitement, he settled down to write a short account of all that he had discovered with his telescope. Two months later this was published in Venice, under the title *Messenger from the Stars*. His discoveries amazed the whole of Europe. Soon they were even being discussed in faraway Peking (now Beijing).

Galileo had opened up a new vision of the heavens. He had shown that the moon is a rocky, mountainous globe, that the earth is not unique in having a satellite moon, and that millions upon millions of stars exist. Soon he went further and discovered that Venus appears first as a crescent, then full, then dark, as it circles the sun and reflects light at different angles. He even traced the movement of mysterious spots across the face of the sun. The fact that the sun has spots shocked some people, who felt that a celestial object ought to be without blemish. Galileo, however, was very interested, for the movement of the spots, in one direction, indicated that the sun, like the earth, was spinning round on its axis.

❧ *173* ❧

To many people this probing of the skies was exciting. They realized that for the first time people had a means of exploring space. But to others it was unsettling, even dangerous. This was because, although they were living 70 years after Copernicus, they still believed that the earth did not move and was the center of the universe. The Church of Rome officially agreed with this belief, although some of its members did not.

Until now Galileo had not dared to defy the Church openly and declare that the earth moved round the sun.

"I would certainly dare to publish my ideas at once if more people like you existed," he had once written to Kepler. "Since they don't, I shall refrain from doing so."

However, his discoveries made Galileo a much more important man. He decided, finally, that the Church would not dare to curb him, and he began to state publicly that the earth circled the sun.

"Let them try to prove me wrong!" he exclaimed.

For some years the Roman Catholic Church let Galileo talk freely, only warning him from time to time, but many high officials of the Church remained unconvinced. And in fact, whatever Galileo said, he could not *prove* that the earth goes round the sun; he could only say, with Copernicus, that it seemed likely. (It was not until 1728 that conclusive proof was given by James Bradley, Third Astronomer Royal of England.)

In 1623 a new Pope was elected and the Church hardened against Galileo. He received more severe warnings than before, but would not give way. In 1632 he published a

🌱 *174* 🌱

brilliant argument in favor of his beliefs, entitled *Dialogue on the Great World Systems.*

This was open defiance of the Church, and Galileo was summoned to appear before the Inquisition in Rome. Interrogation began on April 12, 1633. Galileo was asked to declare that he was wrong and that the earth stood still. The questioning continued for a month.

The great astronomer was now seventy years old, and he was worn out by fatigue and by fear of the Inquisition. In the end, Galileo did as he was told. Never again did he say in public that the earth moved.

Aristotle, Ptolemy, and Copernicus are shown on the cover of Galileo's book *Dialogue on the Great World Systems.*
The Bettmann Archive

Discussing Strategy Use

Invite volunteers to tell which strategies they used while reading "Galileo," how they used each strategy, and how the strategies helped them.

* EXPLORING THROUGH DISCUSSION

Reflecting on the Selection
Whole-Group Discussion

The whole group discusses the selection and any thoughts, reactions, or questions that it raises. During this time, students also **return** to the **clues, problems, and wonderings** they noted on the board during browsing.

Assessment

To assess their understanding of the text, engage the students in a discussion **to determine whether they have grasped the following ideas:**
- how the telescope made a difference in Galileo's investigations
- the way in which Galileo's findings about the heavenly bodies differed from what people had imagined about them

Response Journal

Encourage the students to record their personal thoughts and ideas about the selection.

Exploring Concepts Within the Selection
Small-Group Discussion

Small groups discuss the selection's relationship to the concepts. Circulate among the groups. If any of the groups need assistance, refer them to the **Question Board** and the **Concept Board** for discussion ideas.

Sharing Ideas About Explorable Concepts

Have the groups report and discuss their ideas with the rest of the class. It is crucial that the students' ideas determine this discussion.
- The students may recognize that the invention of the telescope made possible an enormous leap forward in people's ability to learn about the universe. They may point out that the telescope enabled astronomers to substantiate or disprove very quickly ideas that earlier scientists had spent years developing and debating.
- The students may wonder and theorize about why Galileo was so harshly punished for supporting an idea that is now routinely accepted as correct.

As these ideas and others are stated, have the students add them to the **Question Board** or the **Concept Board.**

Ask the students to examine and discuss the fine-art piece on page 181 of the student anthology that illustrates Dutch astronomer Tycho Brahe at work. Brahe was an immediate predecessor of Galileo.

Exploring Concepts Across Selections

Students may make connections with selections in this or other units.
- The students may compare Galileo's methods of inquiry with those of Anaximander, Philolaus, and other early Greeks in *How Did We Find Out the Earth Is Round?* They may notice that both Galileo and the early Greeks formed their hypotheses about the solar system on the basis of careful observation.

TEACHING TIP Whenever possible, allow students to generate and direct discussion.

TEACHING TIP As in actual conversation, build on students' comments and questions; that is, do not become locked into a preplanned sequence for discussion.

Fine Art

Evaluating
Discussions

Recording Ideas

As they complete their discussions, ask the students to sum up what they have learned from their conversations and to tell how they might use this information in further explorations. Any special information or insights may be recorded on the Concept Board. Any further questions that they would like to think about, pursue, or investigate may be recorded on the Question Board. They may want to discuss the progress that has been made on the questions. They may also want to cross out any questions that no longer warrant consideration.

➤ Encourage the students to record their findings in the Explorer's Notebook, page 24.

Self-Assessment Questionnaire

➤ Distribute copies of Assessment Master 2, Self-Assessment Questionnaire, which you will find in the booklet Masters for Continuous Assessment. Tell the students to answer the questionnaires after they have finished this lesson. Collect the completed questionnaires so that you can compare the students' current self-assessments with later self-assessments when they again answer the same questionnaires. You might also examine their responses to see whether the students' assessments of themselves are compatible with your assessments of them in your Teacher's Observation Log.

Explorer's Notebook, page 24

Recording Concept Information continued

"Sun and Star Calendars" by Malcolm Weiss

_____
_____
_____
_____
_____

"Galileo" by Navin Sullivan

_____
_____
_____
_____
_____

"Telescopes" by David Macaulay

_____
_____
_____
_____
_____

24 EN   Astronomy/Unit 2

Assessment Master 2

Self-Assessment Questionnaire

Date

1. How would you rate this selection?
   ○ easy   ○ medium   ○ hard

2. If you checked **medium** or **hard**, answer these questions.
   • Which part of the selection did you find especially difficult?
   • What strategy did you use to try to understand it?

   _____

   • Were some of the words hard?
   • What did you do to figure out their meaning?

   _____

INDIVIDUAL

3. What do you feel you need to work on to make yourself a better reader?

   _____
   _____
   _____

Name

4. Give an example of something you said in the group. Tell why you said it.

   _____
   _____

5. Give an example of something that people in the group helped you understand about the selection.

   _____
   _____

GROUP

Self-Assessment Questionnaire   Assessment Master 2

2 READING WITH A WRITER'S EYE

On Your Own

Remind the students that **in each selection they have read, they have discussed something that the writer did particularly well.** For example, in "Circles, Squares, and Daggers," they discussed Elsa Marston's use of headings and captions to organize her information and to explain illustrations to her readers. Review also the discussions about writing paragraphs that the class had after reading "The Heavenly Zoo" and "Sun and Star Calendars."

Tell the students that since they have read "Galileo" on their own, you would like them to try to identify something that Navin Sullivan did especially well. Does something about the writing stand out? They might think back to a portion of the selection that they reacted to or particularly enjoyed. Their reactions may be a clue to especially good writing.

Allow time, if necessary, for the students to skim the selection to refresh their memory. If they have difficulty expressing their feelings about the writing in this selection, model a response for them by pointing out things that you felt were noteworthy.

For example, you may wish to point out that Sullivan's diagrams make it easier to understand events that are described in the selection. On pages 171, 172, and 173, the diagrams help the reader "see" what Galileo saw through his telescope. Words describe what Galileo saw, but the diagrams make certain that the reader understands what the words say.

WRITING

Linking Reading to Writing

Encourage the students to **use in their own writing anything that they particularly enjoyed about Sullivan's writing.** Invite them to look in their writing folders for a piece of writing they could revise by including some element that the author used effectively in this selection.

* Writing Process

Although no specific writing assignment is recommended here, the students may concentrate on the appropriate phase of the writing process for any writing on which they are currently working. For a review of the **writing process,** see **Learning Framework Card 7.**

VOCABULARY

Concept-related words and phrases from "Galileo" that the students may want to discuss or remember and use include the following:
satellite moon, celestial objects, magnification, concave, convex, revelation, tolerably

Have Vocabulary Exploration forms, Reproducible Master 14, available for students who request them.

TIP FOR ENGLISH LANGUAGE LEARNERS

Provide an opportunity for English Language Learners to contribute to explaining the concept-related vocabulary. Encourage them to illustrate a word or a phrase from the story.

Remind the students to add these or any other words and phrases from the story to the Personal Dictionary section in their Writer's Notebook. Some students may wish to share these additions with the class. For additional ideas on how to build vocabulary, see **Teacher Tool Card 75.**

VOCABULARY TIP During discussions with the students, use important words related to the explorable concepts in order to model the utility of these words.

Professional Checkpoint: Reading with a Writer's Eye

If the students are having trouble thinking of what to write about, this is usually a symptom of other difficulties. This checklist may help you pin down a particular student's problem.

- Is the student trying to write on a different topic every time? Help the students develop personally meaningful and longer pieces that will occupy them for several days.
- Does the student avoid rewriting? Try to get a commitment during Independent Workshop. Prompt group interest in a revised version.
- Does the student treat writing as a chore? Use conferences to express genuine interest in what the student has to say.
- Is the student overly dependent on teacher guidance? Assign a peer helper or a small group to ease the student away from dependence on you.
- Has everything else failed? Suggest specific topics on the basis of the student's interests and previous writing successes.

Notes:

3 GUIDED AND INDEPENDENT EXPLORATION

EXPLORING CONCEPTS BEYOND THE TEXT

Guided
Exploration

The following activities do not have to be completed within the days devoted to this lesson.

➤ This is a good time to distribute Home/School Connection 16. Students can collaborate with their families or adults at home in locating and reading books about Galileo and other famous astronomers.

In the selection, the astronomers Johannes Kepler and Nicolaus Copernicus are mentioned briefly. Tycho Brache is the subject of the illustration on page 181. Isaac Newton is another extremely important early astronomer. Have interested students use an encyclopedia or other books to find out more about these people. Have them add these astronomers to their astronomy time chart, Explorer's Notebook, pages 34–35. Provide time for students to share this information with the rest of the class.

Research Cycle:
Needs and Plans
Phase 2

Before the research groups meet to settle on definite research plans, whole-class discussion will be important to accomplish the following goals:

* **Help students who are having trouble identifying knowledge needs related to their conjectures.** It is important for students to recognize what knowledge they will need before they embark on gathering information; otherwise their research is liable to proceed aimlessly.
* **Remind research groups that they can still change their research problems.** By this time some groups may have discovered that their problem is not very promising. A group may choose to keep the same general problem but to formulate the problem more precisely. (It is also possible that some students will want to change groups because they have become more interested in the problem of another group.)
* Provide any other needed discussion or guidance before students embark on formulating and carrying out their research plans.

➤ Assign page 38 of the Explorer's Notebook to be completed after each planning group has agreed on a final statement of its problem, its knowledge needs, and its individual job assignments. As you observe the groups making their job assignments, encourage the students to take on tasks that are related to their strengths and likings. For example, a student who loves to draw might particularly enjoy planning and making the visual portion of the research project, or examining photographs, illustrations, and diagrams for useful information. A student with good verbal skills might benefit from conducting interviews, while a less verbal student might primarily contribute information located in books, magazines, and other references. Whatever the job assignment, it is

✱ Exploring Through Research

important that each student have a significant role in the group and be able to provide valuable information to help the group in its investigation and to add to its increasing understanding of astronomy. For more information on the Needs and Plans phase of the Research Cycle, see **Learning Framework Card 4C.**

Home/School Connection 16

"Galileo"

A message from _____

Our class has just finished reading "Galileo." In this selection we learned about the Italian astronomer Galileo Galilei, who in 1609 became the first astronomer to explore the night sky with a telescope. We read about some of the amazing discoveries Galileo made with his telescope. We also learned how Galileo defended the idea that the earth and planets revolve around the sun. During Galileo's time, many important people still believed that the earth was the center of the universe. Galileo's ideas got him in serious trouble. Ask your child to share with you what he or she learned about Galileo's work.

Galileo had a long and fascinating career, which included many accomplishments not discussed in the selection. You and your child may enjoy reading more about Galileo's life and work, or you may wish to select another famous astronomer to research. Record anything that interests you about the person you and your child choose, but be sure to note such information as when and where the astronomer lived, her or his most important contributions to the science of astronomy, and how his or her work has influenced the work of later scientists. When you and your child have completed your research, write a brief summary of your findings for your child to share with the class.

The following titles may help you to choose and research a famous astronomer.

Astronomy by Dennis B. Fradin. A comprehensive work covering the birth of astronomy through the search for alien radio signals, this fact-filled book contains a great deal of information on important astronomers of yesterday and today.

Pioneer Astronomers by Navin Sullivan. In this book, from which "Galileo" was excerpted, Sullivan tells the history of the study of astronomy through profiles of several ground-breaking astronomers.

Truth on Trial: The Story of Galileo by Vicki Cobb. This brief biography of Galileo focuses on his support of the Copernican world system and his subsequent battle with the Roman Catholic Church.

Explorer's Notebook, page 38

Research Cycle: Needs and Plans Phase 2

Our problem:
_____
_____
_____
_____
_____

Knowledge Needs—Information we need to find or figure out to explore the problem:

A. _____
B. _____
C. _____
D. _____
E. _____
F. _____

Group Members	Main Jobs

Hint: To save rewriting Knowledge Needs in the Main Jobs section, put in the capital letter marking the Knowledge Needs line.

✳ INDEPENDENT WORKSHOP
Building a Community of Scholars

Student-Directed Reading, Writing, and Discussion

Research Cycle: Needs and Plans Phase 2 Students should work together in their research groups to complete their group plan in their Explorer's Notebook, page 38. Group members should agree on each item so that their plans are all the same. It is important that each member have a copy of the plan for future reference. Have the students examine their planning calendars. Assist them in allotting enough time to conduct their research and complete their research projects before the ending date. It may be helpful to record on the research cycle poster, using self-stick notes, where each group is in the cycle. Provide additional library time, if possible.

Resources If needed, provide students with additional library time to look for research sources. You may want to designate an area of the classroom for the sharing and the storage of resource materials.

WORKSHOP TIP

Assessment This may be a good opportunity to observe students working in groups and to mark observations in your Teacher's Observation Log.

Additional Opportunities for Independent Reading, Writing, and Cross-curricular Activities

Portfolio

Remind the students to think about choosing pieces of writing to put into their portfolios.

Cross-curricular Activity Card

The following Cross-curricular Activity Card in the Student Toolbox is appropriate for this selection:

- 3 Drama—Writing and Acting Out a Conversation

Writing and Acting Out a Conversation
Use after "Galileo"

3
Drama

Visit your school library. Use the card catalog or an encyclopedia to find some information about one or more of the following astronomers: Aristotle, Ptolemy, Tycho Brahe, Nicolaus Copernicus, or Johannes Kepler. Find out what each astronomer you chose thought the moon looked like or what each thought about the earth's position in the universe. Did the astronomer think the earth revolved around the sun, or vice versa? How did he support his claims?

When your research is complete, write a conversation between Galileo and the astronomer or astronomers you chose. Use the information you found to imagine what these people might say to one another. When you finish writing the conversation, find a partner or partners to help you dramatize the conversation for the class. *Dramatizing a conversation between scientists of the past will help you to understand the history of science.*

Additional Opportunities for Solving Learning Problems

Tutorial

Use this time to work with individuals or small groups of students who need help in any area. Encourage students to ask for help whenever they need it. The following aids in the Teacher Toolbox are available for your convenience:

- Writer's Craft/Reading: Genre—Biography and Autobiography, Teacher Tool Card 8
- Writer's Craft/Reading: Elaboration Through Providing Concept Information, Teacher Tool Card 42

Telescopes

1 READING THE SELECTION

About the Selection

In this selection, excerpted from his award-winning book *The Way Things Work,* respected children's nonfiction author David Macaulay uses thoroughly detailed diagrams and clear, concise prose to explain the workings of astronomers' most important tools.

Link to the Unit Concepts

The advent of the telescope as an astronomer's tool might be considered the birth of modern astronomy. Since the days when Galileo trained his first small telescope on the heavens, telescopes and other tools of astronomy have become increasingly sophisticated, bringing us ever greater knowledge of the universe.

"Telescopes," pages 176–179, explains the basic structure of the refracting and reflecting telescopes, the tools used by astronomers since Galileo's time. Then it describes two very modern astronomers' tools, the radio telescope and the Hubble space telescope.

About the Author

David Macaulay was born in England and moved to the United States when he was eleven years old. He studied architecture at the Rhode Island School of Design. Although he never worked as an architect, he says his study of architecture "fueled and educated" his desire to understand how things work.

Macaulay began writing books for children because he decided that he wanted to be an illustrator of books and he could not find any texts that he wanted to illustrate.

Macaulay worked for three years researching and making drawings for *The Way Things Work.* In this book he explains and illustrates hundreds of machines and inventions and the scientific principles behind them. Interspersed with the serious drawings and explanations of air-

LESSON OVERVIEW

"Telescopes" by David Macaulay, pages 176–179

READING THE SELECTION

Materials
Student anthology, pp. 176–179
Explorer's Notebook, p. 24

READING WITH A WRITER'S EYE

Minilesson
Paraphrasing

Materials
Reproducible Master 14

FYI
Teacher Tool Card
• Spelling and Vocabulary: Building
  Vocabulary, 75

Options for Instruction
Writer's Craft: Genre—Expository Text
Writer's Craft: Using Headings and
  Captions
(Use Teacher Tool Cards listed below.)

GUIDED AND INDEPENDENT EXPLORATION

Minilesson
Research Aid: Understanding Diagrams

Independent Workshop

**Optional Materials from
Student Toolbox**

Tradebook Connection Cards

Cross-curricular Activity Card
• 7 Science—Making a Telescope

Student Tool Cards
• Writer's Craft/Reading: Reading and
  Writing Expository Text, 9
• Writer's Craft/Reading: Using
  Headings and Captions, 35
• Study and Research: Using and
  Understanding Diagrams, 114

FYI
Learning Framework Cards
• Reading Roundtable, 6
• Writing Seminar, 8
Teacher Tool Cards
• Writer's Craft/Reading: Genre—
  Expository Text, 9
• Writer's Craft/Reading: Using
  Headings and Captions, 35
• Study and Research: Using and
  Understanding Diagrams, 114

```
N O T E S
```

Asterisks (*) throughout the lesson indicate learning frameworks. Learning Framework Cards and Teacher Tool Cards can be found in the Teacher Toolbox.

planes, zippers, televisions, computers, toilet tanks, cameras, sewing machines, atomic power plants, internal combustion engines, and so forth, are funny pictures and amusing stories.

INFORMATION FOR THE STUDENT

Share some information about the author with the students. After students have read the selection, share the following information:

Soon after the Hubble space telescope was launched in 1990, scientists realized that its primary mirror was deformed, making the instrument "nearsighted." Although computer manipulations of the Hubble's images enabled scientists to see many things that could not be seen from earth, the orbiting telescope's usefulness as a scientific instrument fell far short of expectations. A repair mission in 1993 provided "eyeglasses" in the form of ten corrective mirrors. The project cost about 100 million dollars and involved seven astronauts working for several days.

About the Hubble Telescope

* COGNITIVE AND RESPONSIVE READING

Activating Prior Knowledge

Invite the students to talk about telescopes and how they are used in astronomy.

Setting Reading Goals and Expectations

Have the students **browse** the selection, using the clues/problems/wondering procedure. The students will return to these observations after reading.

Recommen-dations for Reading the Selection

Ask the students how they want to read the selection. They may prefer to read the text and study the diagrams in small groups.

During oral reading, use and encourage think-alouds. During silent reading, allow discussion as needed. Discuss problems, strategies, and reactions after reading.

This would also be a good selection for **responding** to text **by wondering** while reading aloud. Model this response, and then invite the students to respond similarly.

TEACHING TIP Before the class reads an expository selection with a clear title, ask students what they already know about the subject.

About the Reading Strategies

Students may have difficulty understanding the diagrams. **Question-asking** is one strategy that may help them. Also, you may want to explain the difference between a cross-section diagram, which shows an object as though it had been cut in half, and a cutaway diagram, which shows an object with part of its outside covering removed.

Think-Aloud Prompts for Use in Oral Reading

The think-aloud prompts are placed where students may encounter difficulties with the text. Encourage them to use whatever reading strategies they need in order to understand what they read.

THINK ALOUD PROMPTS

These prompts may be used as guides to promote cognitive and responsive reading.

1 At this point, some students may be confused by the two kinds of telescopes they have just read about. They may suggest **summing up** what they have read about each type of telescope.

TELESCOPES
from THE WAY THINGS WORK
by David Macaulay

TELESCOPES

A telescope gives a close-up view of a distant object, which, in the case of an <u>astronomical</u> telescope viewing a far-off planet or galaxy, is very distant indeed. Most telescopes work in the same basic way, which is to produce a real image of the object inside the telescope tube. The eyepiece lens then views this image in the same way as a magnifying glass. The viewer looks at a very close real image, which therefore appears large. The degree of <u>magnification</u> depends mainly on the power of the eyepiece lens.

REFRACTING TELESCOPE

In a <u>refracting</u> telescope, an objective lens forms the real image that is viewed by the eyepiece lens. The image is upside down, but this is not important in astronomy.

REFLECTING TELESCOPE

In a reflecting telescope, a large <u>concave</u> primary mirror forms the real image that is then viewed by an eyepiece lens. Usually, a secondary mirror reflects the rays from the primary mirror so that the real image forms beneath the mirror or to the side. This is more convenient for viewing.

🌿 *176* 🌿

Reflecting telescopes are important in astronomy because the primary mirror can be very wide. This enables it to collect a lot of light, making faint objects visible. Collecting light from an object is often more important than magnifying it because distant stars do not appear bigger even when magnified. **1**

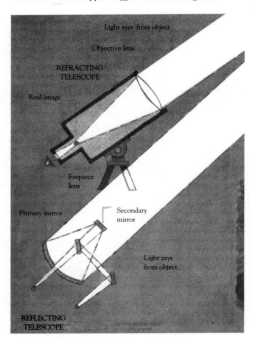

RADIO TELESCOPE

Many objects in the universe send out radio waves, and a radio telescope can be used to detect them. A large curved metal dish collects the radio waves and reflects them to a focus point above the center of the dish, rather as the curved mirror of a reflecting telescope gathers light waves from space. At this point, an antenna intercepts the radio waves and turns them into a weak electric signal. The signal goes to a computer. Radio telescopes detect very weak waves, and can also communicate with spacecraft.

By detecting radio waves coming from galaxies and other objects in space, radio telescopes have discovered the existence of many previously unknown bodies. It is possible to make visible images of radio sources by scanning the telescope or a group of telescopes across the source. This yields a sequence of signals from different parts of the source, which the computer can process to form an image. Differences in frequency of the signals give information about the composition and motion of the radio source.

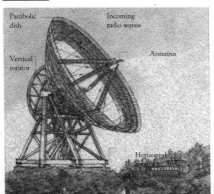

Parabolic dish
Incoming radio waves
Vertical rotator
Antenna
Horizontal rotator

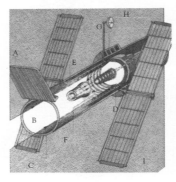

A. Aperture door

B. Light rays from star or galaxy

C. Telescope tube. The main body of the telescope is 43 feet long and 14 feet across.

D. Primary mirror. The space telescope is a reflecting telescope with a main mirror 8 feet in diameter.

E. Secondary mirror

F. Baffles. These ridges reduce the reflection of stray light from surfaces in the tube.

G. Equipment section. Light detectors change the visual images produced by the mirrors into television signals. The space telescope also contains scientific instruments.

H. Radio dish. The dish sends telescope images and measurements from instruments back by radio to ground stations below.

I. Solar panels. The pair of panels provides electricity to work the instruments aboard the space telescope.

SPACE TELESCOPE

The Hubble space telescope is part optical telescope and part satellite. It promises to revolutionize astronomy because it operates outside the atmosphere, which hampers any observations made from the ground. The space telescope orbits the earth, observing distant stars and galaxies in the total clarity of space. It can peer seven times further into the universe than we can see from the ground, and can also detect very faint objects. The telescope may be able to "see" far back in time by observing ancient light waves from the most distant galaxies. Among these may be light waves produced just after the big bang that blew the universe into existence some 15 billion years ago. **2**

🌀 *179* 🌱

2 If students are having difficulty understanding what they just read, they may remember that **asking questions** about the text is often a helpful way of organizing facts and understanding ideas. Have a volunteer ask a question that is answered in the text.

Discussing Strategy Use
Encourage the students to discuss any difficulties they experienced while reading "Telescopes" and to share the strategies they used to overcome these difficulties.

*

Reflecting on the Selection
Whole-Group Discussion

The whole group discusses the selection and any thoughts, reactions, or questions that it raises. During this time, students also **return to the clues, problems, and wonderings** they noted on the board during browsing.

Assessment

To assess the students' understanding of the text, engage in a discussion to determine whether the students have grasped the following ideas:

- the difference between a reflecting and a refracting telescope
- some types of information radio telescopes bring us
- what makes the Hubble space telescope different from other powerful telescopes

TIP FOR ENGLISH LANGUAGE LEARNERS

When discussing difficult concepts with English Language Learners, provide expansions, restatements, and explanations.

Response Journal

Provide time for students to record their personal responses to the selection.

Exploring Concepts Within the Selection
Small-Group Discussion

While the small groups discuss the relationship of the selection to astronomy, circulate and observe the discussions. Remind the students to refer to the Concept Board and the Question Board to help keep their discussions focused.

Sharing Ideas About Explorable Concepts

Have the groups **report** and **discuss** their **ideas** with the rest of the class. It is crucial that the students' ideas determine this discussion.

- The students may mention that there are many objects in the universe that people could never have seen or learned more about without the use of modern technology.
- The students may note that technology has allowed modern astronomers to find out what the sun, moon, and stars really are—their sizes, compositions, and approximate ages—and how they may have come to exist, rather than simply observing their movements as early astronomers did.
- Some students may point out that tools such as the Hubble telescope, which can detect light waves from galaxies billions of light years away, may help scientists to learn more about how the universe began.

As these ideas and others are stated, have the students **add them to** the **Question Board** or **Concept Board**.

Exploring Concepts Across Selections

Ask the students whether this selection reminds them of anything else they have read. They may make connections with selections in this and other units.

- Students may comment on how astronomers' knowledge of the universe has expanded since the advent of the telescope, as discussed in "Galileo."

Recording Ideas

As students complete the above discussions, ask them to **sum up what they have learned from their conversations and to tell how they might use this information** in further explorations. Any special information or insights may be recorded on the **Concept Board.** Any further questions that they would like to think about, pursue, or investigate may be recorded on the **Question Board.** They may want to discuss the progress that has been made on their questions. They may also want to cross out any questions that no longer warrant consideration.

❯ Provide time for the students to record their findings on page 24 in their Explorer's Notebook.

Evaluating Discussions

Explorer's Notebook, page 24

Recording Concept Information continued

"Sun and Star Calendars" by Malcolm Weiss

_____
_____
_____
_____
_____
_____
_____

"Galileo" by Navin Sullivan

_____
_____
_____
_____
_____
_____
_____

"Telescopes" by David Macaulay

_____
_____
_____
_____
_____
_____
_____
_____

24 EN   Astronomy/Unit 2

2 READING WITH A WRITER'S EYE

Writer's Craft: Paraphrasing

Because this selection contains a great deal of challenging information, students may wish to reread the entire selection. They will benefit from concentrating on those passages they find particularly interesting or important and then paraphrasing them in writing. Have the students discuss the passages they chose to paraphrase and clarify any differences of opinion as to the meaning of the passages.

TIP FOR ENGLISH LANGUAGE LEARNERS

Encourage English Language Learners to paraphrase a passage first to themselves to help them clarify its meaning and to make sure they have included the most important ideas in their paraphrasing.

WRITING

Linking Reading to Writing

Have the students summarize, in writing, the most difficult or important parts of "Telescopes." Students need not summarize only challenging passages from the text of "Telescopes"; they may also write summaries explaining any difficult information that was presented in diagram form in the selection. Allow time for volunteers to share their summaries with the class. Encourage them to explain how they decided which parts of the text to summarize and what information to include in their summaries.

✷ Writing Process

No specific writing assignment is recommended here. Encourage the students to keep the writing process in mind as they begin new pieces and revise works in progress.

WRITER'S NOTEBOOK TIP

Ask the students to review all sections of their Writer's Notebook. Encourage them to update or complete any unfinished pieces.

VOCABULARY

Concept-related words and phrases from "Telescopes" that the students may want to discuss and add to their Writer's Notebook include the following:

galaxies, refracting, universe, solar, primary mirror, secondary mirror, optical, baffles, revolutionize

Adding to Personal Word Lists

Provide Vocabulary Exploration forms, Reproducible Master 14, so that the students can add these or any other words from the selection to their Writer's Notebook. For additional opportunities to build vocabulary, see **Teacher Tool Card 75.**

3 GUIDED AND INDEPENDENT EXPLORATION

Guided Exploration

The following activities do not have to be completed within the days devoted to this lesson.

- If there is an astronomical observatory in your area, students might visit it as a class or with their families to view the different telescopes the observatory uses.
- Students might be interested in learning more about one of the different kinds of telescopes described in the selection. If so, they can find more information in their school or community library.

Research Cycle

Invite each **research group** to present its **plan for discussion and possible refinement.** From this point onward, there will be no specific suggestions for Guided Exploration in the Research Cycle. Meet with the whole class as needed for the following purposes:

- to arrange schedules and update calendars
- to discuss problems that students are encountering with their research
- to hear preliminary presentations and discussions of interesting findings
- to arrange more formal presentations of students' research
- to provide guidance to ensure that groups progress through phases of the Research Cycle—obtaining information; revising problems, conjectures, needs, and plans (perhaps with input resulting from a presentation to the class); and proceeding to a further cycle of problem, conjecture, and so forth

Exploring Through Research

MINILESSON

Research Aid: Understanding Diagrams

Guided Practice: Understanding Diagrams

Remind students that **diagrams are drawings that show the parts of something.** Diagrams can show

- how something is put together
- how something is arranged
- how something works
- where parts are located in relation to other parts
- how things are joined together
- what parts are larger than others
- the names of the parts

Have the students discuss these elements in relation to the diagrams of a reflecting and a refracting telescope on page 177 of the student anthology. Call on a volunteer to tell which telescope has an objective lens. Invite another volunteer to tell which has a secondary mirror.

Independent Practice:
Understanding
Diagrams

Divide the students into three groups and have each group look at one of the three diagrams in the selection. **Encourage each group to prepare a brief summary** of how the telescope in their diagram functions and then **have each group share its summary with the rest of the class.**

TIP FOR ENGLISH LANGUAGE LEARNERS

Give English Language Learners a chance to be leaders. Encourage them to share the group's summary with the class.

Professional Checkpoint: Guided and Independent Exploration

Provide plenty of opportunity for individuals, research groups, and the whole class to consider possible revisions of their work. During discussions regarding revisions, most of the real thinking and knowledge building occurs. Knowledge does not come simply from the acquisition of new information, but from reconsidering current beliefs and conjectures in the light of new information and trying to make sense of them in combination. The principles for successful revision are the same as those for discussions in general: constructive commenting, handing-off, refocusing, and participant modeling.

Notes:

* INDEPENDENT WORKSHOP
Building a Community of Scholars

Student-Directed Reading, Writing, and Discussion

Research Cycle The students may explore their ideas and questions by using information from their collaborative groups. They may use any sources available to them. Remind them to check the **Question Board** and **Concept Board** for new ideas relating to astronomy. New ideas about their questions may prompt them to explore new resources.

Provide additional library time and assistance for students who are locating resources for their research. Encourage them to use sources other than books and encyclopedias. Remind them that many of the Student Tool Cards, such as Parts of a Book or Using the Card Catalog, can assist them in using resources and collecting information. Provide a space in the classroom in which sources can be stored and shared. In order to keep the research focused, you might take the opportunity during individual conferences to ask the students questions such as, *What did you look up? What are you finding out? What else might you need to find out? Can you give me more details about that fact or idea? How does this information help you? What does this information tell you that you didn't already know?*

Additional Opportunities for Independent Reading, Writing, and Cross-curricular Activities

✱ Reading Roundtable

Remind the students that the **Tradebook Connection Cards** contain activities connected to many well-known trade books. Encourage students to read other books by David Macaulay and share them with their classmates. For additional information about Reading Roundtable, see **Learning Framework Card 6**.

✱ Writing Seminar

When revising and proofreading, provide time for students to meet and read each other's written work. Encourage the students to use a thesaurus when revising. For a review of Writing Seminar, see **Learning Framework Card 8**.

Portfolio

Remind the students to think about which pieces of writing they might choose to put into their portfolios.

Cross-curricular Activity Cards

The following Cross-curricular Activity Card from the Student Toolbox is appropriate for this selection:

• 7 Science—Making a Telescope

Making a Telescope
Use after "Telescopes"

7
Science

Make a telescope from two magnifying glasses and two cardboard tubes. For the body of the telescope, use mailing tubes or other cardboard tubes. One tube must fit snugly inside the other. Use two lenses from two different-sized magnifying glasses. Attach a lens to the outside of each tube with tape or glue. Look through the smaller end of the telescope. Slide the tubes in or out until the object comes into focus. The telescope, like an astronomer's refracting telescope, will make objects appear upside down. (Warning: Do not aim your telescope at the sun. It is very dangerous to look directly at the sun.) *Making a telescope can help you to appreciate astronomers' work and tools.*

Additional Opportunities for Solving Learning Problems

Tutorial

You might use this time to **help individuals or small groups of students who have exhibited a need** in any area. The following Teacher Tool Cards are available in the Teacher Toolbox for your convenience:

• Writer's Craft/Reading: Genre—Expository Text, Teacher Tool Card 9
• Writer's Craft/Reading: Using Headings and Captions, Teacher Tool Card 35
• Study and Research: Using and Understanding Diagrams, Teacher Tool Card 114

Fine Art

DISCUSSING FINE ART

Included here is some background information about the pieces of fine art shown on pages 180–181 of the student anthology. Share with the students whatever you feel is appropriate. Some works may be familiar to them. Encourage them to express their reactions to each piece—for example, what the piece has to do with astronomy, whether they think it is related to this unit, and why. Encourage them to find out more about artists or artistic styles that interest them. For additional information on discussing fine art, refer to **Teacher Tool Card 123**.

Cosmic Universe. c. 1957.
Natalia Goncharova. Watercolor on paper.

Natalia Goncharova (1881–1962) was a Russian painter, graphic artist, and designer. In 1892, she left her home in central Russia to take advantage of the new access to higher education for women by studying history and science in Moscow. She later enrolled at the Moscow School of Painting, Sculpture, and Architecture, completing her education in 1903. Goncharova was influenced in her work by the major art movements of her time, including, among others, Impressionism and Cubism. She was deeply interested in Russian peasant art and in icons, which are images of saints painted on wooden panels. She incorporated much of the vivid expression and color of icons into her work. Goncharova left Russia in 1915, living in Switzerland, Spain, and Italy, before settling permanently in Paris four years later. There she designed sets and costumes for the theatre, as well as continuing with her painting. Her designs for the Russian ballet producer Diaghilev and the Ballets Russes are considered to be among her best works.

During her last years, Goncharova was inspired by themes of resurrection and by the exploration of space. After the Soviet launching of *Sputnik* (the first of a series of earth-orbiting satellites) in 1957, she

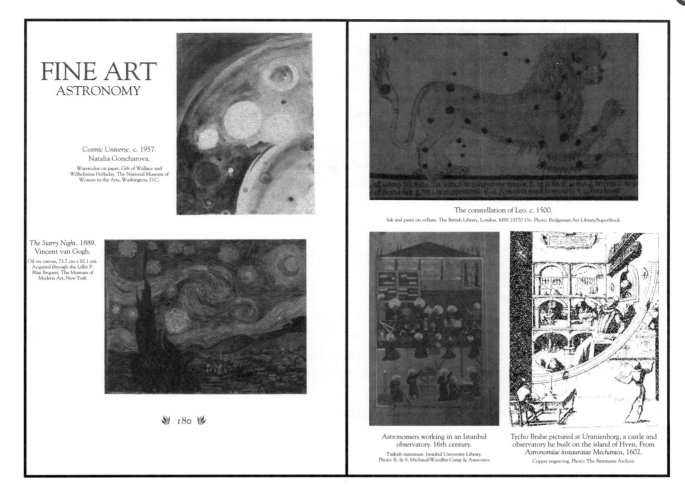

FINE ART
ASTRONOMY

Cosmic Universe. c. 1957.
Natalia Goncharova.
Watercolor on paper. Gift of Wallace and
Wilhelmina Holladay, The National Museum of
Women in the Arts, Washington, D.C.

The Starry Night. 1889.
Vincent van Gogh.
Oil on canvas, 73.7 cm x 92.1 cm.
Acquired through the Lillie P.
Bliss Bequest, The Museum of
Modern Art, New York

180

The constellation of Leo. c. 1500.
Ink and paint on vellum. The British Library, London. MSS 23770 13v. Photo: Bridgeman Art Library/SuperStock

Astronomers working in an Istanbul
observatory. 16th century.
Turkish miniature. Istanbul University Library.
Photo: R. & S. Michaud/Woodfin Camp & Associates

Tycho Brahe pictured at Uranienborg, a castle and
observatory he built on the island of Hven. From
Astronomiae instauratae Mechanica, 1602.
Copper engraving. Photo: The Bettmann Archive

exhibited a group of works relating to images of the universe. *Cosmic Universe* may be a continuation of those works, a reference to a mythic place made real through human effort.

The Starry Night. 1889.
Vincent van Gogh. Oil on canvas.

Vincent van Gogh (1853–1890) was born in Groot-Zundert, the Netherlands. He spent many years searching for a profession that would allow him to help others. In 1880 van Gogh realized that art would be the means by which he could reach out to others. From 1881 to 1885, van Gogh's paintings portrayed peasants and workers. It was during this time that he painted one of his most famous pieces, *The Potato Eaters* (1885). In February of 1886 van Gogh moved to Paris, and his ideas about his work changed drastically.

Instead of painting realistic images, van Gogh now expressed his ideas through colors. "Instead of trying to reproduce exactly what I have before my eyes," he wrote to his brother Theo, "I use color . . . so as to express myself (with more force)."

In May of 1889, van Gogh placed himself in a mental hospital near Arles in France for treatment of what may have been manic depression, an illness in which extreme enthusiasm alternates with severe depression. His stay in the hospital lasted a year, but that did not keep him from creating; besides drawings, van Gogh completed one hundred and fifty paintings, of which *The Starry Night* is one.

The Starry Night is filled with energy. The moon and stars shimmer as they are caught in the swift, swirling tide of night. In the foreground, the cypress trees dance like dark flames. Van Gogh's color and brush strokes vividly convey the force of the natural world and the disturbance in his own mind.

Van Gogh once said that cypress trees "were always occupying my thoughts—it astonishes me that they have never been done as I see them . . . a splash of *black* in a sunny landscape."

Although he sold only one painting during his lifetime, van Gogh is now regarded as one of the greatest modern artists, one who, in the last five years of his life alone, produced more than eight hundred paintings.

The constellation of Leo. c. 1500.
Ink and paint on vellum.

A constellation is a particular group of stars. Early civilizations named the constellations for animals or for characters in their myths. The constellation of Leo is named for the lion, as shown in the illustration pictured. Leo is the fifth sign of the zodiac and is regarded as a fire sign ruled by the sun. The zodiac is a band of twelve constellations in the northern hemisphere. Since to ancient peoples the sun, moon, and planets appeared to travel through these constellations, it was thought that the zodiac influenced the change of seasons. In time, some people came to believe that the zodiac also influenced people's lives. Astrologers are people who try to predict events on earth on the basis of the movements of the planets. They differ from astronomers, who seek scientific knowledge about the universe.

In Western scientific thought, astrology and astronomy have not always been at odds. Until the sixteenth century, astrology and astronomy were studied from the same principles. Then, in the 1500s and 1600s several different astronomers, including Tycho Brahe and Galileo Galilei, made discoveries that conflicted with the principles of astrology. Since then, the two fields have differed in their principles and purposes.

Astronomers working in an Istanbul observatory. 16th century.
Turkish miniature.

The people called the Turks were originally nomads, who in the tenth century began to migrate from central Russia and northern Mongolia to Anatolia, an area which lies between the Black Sea and the Mediterranean. In the 1300s a Turkish chieftain named Osman began the career of conquest that would lead to the founding of the Ottoman Empire. At its height in the sixteenth century, the empire extended from the Danube to the Nile and from the Euphrates almost to Gibraltar.

The observatory depicted in the miniature shown was established in 1577 by the sultan Murad III for his court astronomer, the former clock-maker Taki al-Din. The observatory was as advanced as that of the Danish astronomer Tycho Brahe, which was then the most modern in Europe. In fact, several of the instruments created at Islamic observatories appeared at Brahe's Uranienborg and Stjerneborg observatories, and, in turn, Taki al-Din used clocks imported from Europe as models for some of his own instruments.

Taki al-Din's observatory was built for astrological as well as astronomical purposes; as in Europe, the study of astronomy was pursued partly because of its relevance to astrology. A group of *ulema,* the Ottoman officials who were the heads of law and religion, opposed astronomy and astrology as irreligious interests, like fortune-telling.

During an outbreak of plague, these *ulema* told the sultan that the epidemic had been caused by the efforts of astronomers and astrologers to learn secrets of the heavens that mortals were not meant to have. The sultan heeded the warning, and in 1580 the observatory was destroyed.

Tycho Brahe pictured at Uranienborg, a castle and observatory he built on the island of Hven. From *Astronomiae instauratae Mechanica,* 1602. Copper engraving.

Tycho Brahe (1546–1601) was a Danish astronomer who pioneered the art of accurate observation. While making his observations of planetary motion, Brahe had to rely on his eyesight and on such instruments as astrolabes (used to determine the position of the sun and the stars) and sextants (used to find latitude and longitude by measuring angular distances) because telescopes had not yet been invented. However, because he made observations regularly, his observations were more accurate than those of earlier astronomers.

On November 11, 1572, Brahe discovered a supernova in the constellation Cassiopeia. He published a report on his observations of the supernova, and his work became famous. As a result, the king of Denmark gave Brahe the island of Hven (now called Ven), where he built Uranienborg castle. The castle contained two observatories. When he ran out of room at Uranienborg, Brahe built a new observatory, called Stjerneborg, just south of the castle. Stjerneborg consisted of five underground chambers; the middle room was Brahe's study, and each of the other rooms held one of his four large astronomical instruments. The individual roofs of the chambers could be made to slide open. In the engraving shown here, Brahe is seen seated behind his giant quadrant, which was used to measure the altitude of the stars and the planets.

Voyager to the Planets

1 READING THE SELECTION

INFORMATION FOR THE TEACHER

About the
Selection

This selection tells the stranger-than-fiction story of the space probe Voyager 2 and its epic journey to the edge of the solar system and beyond. Stunning photographs of the planets and their moons, taken by the Voyager spacecraft, help to emphasize how much astronomers have learned about the solar system as a result of Voyager's twelve-year journey from Earth to Neptune.

Link to the
Unit Concepts

"Voyager to the Planets," pages 182–199, is the first selection in the unit to deal with explorations of space in modern times. It demonstrates dramatically the increase in information about the solar system made possible by modern technology. Until rocket technology and other technologies made space probes possible, the only information astronomers had about the planets and their moons came from observations made on Earth with telescopes.

About the
Author

Necia Apfel worked at the Adler Planetarium in Chicago until 1979, when she became a full-time writer. Among Apfel's books are two college textbooks and several books for children. These include *It's All Relative: Einstein's Theory of Relativity; Stars and Galaxies; The Moon and Its Exploration; Astronomy and Planetology; It's All Elementary: From Atoms to the Quantum World of Quarks, Leptons, and Gluons; Calendars; Space Station; Astronomy Projects for Young Scientists;* and *Nebulae: The Birth and Death of Stars.*

INFORMATION FOR THE STUDENT

- Before reading the selection have the students read the material in italics on page 183 of the student anthology.

LESSON OVERVIEW

"Voyager to the Planets" by Necia H. Apfel, pages 182–199

READING THE SELECTION

Materials

Student anthology, pp. 182–199
Explorer's Notebook, p. 25

NOTES

READING WITH A WRITER'S EYE

Minilesson

Writer's Craft: Elaboration Through
Providing Specific Facts

Materials

Reading/Writing Connection, p. 18
Reproducible Master 14

Options for Instruction

Writer's Craft: Comparison and Contrast
Grammar, Mechanics, and Usage:
Pronoun/Antecedent Agreement
(Use Teacher Tool Cards listed below.)

GUIDED AND INDEPENDENT EXPLORATION

Minilesson

Research Aid: Organizing Information
in a Chart

Materials

Explorer's Notebook, pp. 36–37
Assessment Master 1

FYI

Learning Framework Card
• Needs and Plans Phase 1 and 2, 4C

Independent Workshop

**Optional Materials from
Student Toolbox**

Tradebook Connection Cards

Cross-curricular Activity Cards
• 8 Social Studies—Planets and Days of
the Week
• 8 Science—The Solar System

Student Tool Cards
• Writer's Craft/Reading: Telling
Important Facts, 40
• Writer's Craft/Reading: Comparing
and Contrasting, 36
• Grammar, Mechanics, and Usage:
Using the Right Pronoun for the
Right Noun, 61
• Study and Research: Organizing
Information in a Chart, 112

FYI

Teacher Tool Cards
• Writer's Craft/Reading: Elaboration
Through Providing Specific Facts, 40
• Writer's Craft/Reading: Elaboration
Through Providing Comparison and
Contrast, 36
• Grammar, Mechanics, and Usage:
Pronoun/Antecedent Agreement,
61
• Study and Research: Organizing
Information in a Chart, 112

Asterisks (*) throughout the lesson indicate learning frameworks. Learning Framework Cards and Teacher Tool Cards can be found in the Teacher Toolbox.

- After reading the selection, students may be interested in some of the information below.
- Information about Necia Apfel is found on page 199 of the student anthology.

In the 1960s, scientists began to send rockets into space, and astronomers began making plans to explore the planets and moons of our solar system by means of cameras and other instruments put into space.

In 1962, the remote-control space probe Mariner II passed within twenty-two thousand miles of Venus and reported information to scientists on Earth. Since then, several other space probes have investigated Venus, Mars, and Mercury; and in 1976, Viking I and Viking II actually landed on Mars and sent back information.

Scientists wanted to find out more about the outer planets of the solar system. However, because of the enormous distances, it would take about two years for a space probe to reach Jupiter, and unless scientists could find a way to greatly increase the speed of the space probe, it would take thirty years more to reach Neptune.

Astronomers had observed that asteroids or comets that passed close to Jupiter or one of the other planets got a boost in speed from the planet's gravity and then shot off quickly in a new direction. They thought it might be possible to make use of this phenomenon to boost the speed of a space probe. In 1973, scientists sent Mariner X first to Venus, where it received a boost in speed from Venus's gravity, and then on to Mercury.

Scientists decided to use this boosting technique again when all of the outer planets would be on the same side of the sun in the late 1970s. Since it takes the most distant planets over one hundred Earth-years to orbit the sun, such an alignment is a rare event, one that had not occurred for 175 years and would not occur again for another 175 years. Scientists thought that if they aimed it carefully, they could send a space probe first to Jupiter, use Jupiter's gravity to boost it on in the direction of Saturn, then use Saturn's gravity to boost and redirect it to Uranus, and so on to Neptune and Pluto. With these boosts in speed, a space probe could travel to the outer planets in about twelve years instead of thirty. In 1970, the National Aeronautics and Space Administration (NASA) decided that one probe, Voyager 1, would go to Jupiter and Saturn—flying especially close to Saturn's large moon, Titan—then leave the solar system. A second probe, Voyager 2, would go to Jupiter, Saturn, Uranus, and Neptune. Neither probe would go to Pluto.

NASA asked scientists from different fields to submit ideas for experiments that might be undertaken with the space probes and for information that might be gathered by them. Scientists decided to concentrate on four areas of research with respect to the planets: their atmospheres, their magnetic fields, their rings, and their moons.

The probes would carry infrared radiation detectors, ultraviolet spectrometers, photopolarimeters, radio-astronomy sensing equipment, magnetometers, and television cameras. The power source for the equipment on the probes would be batteries that used plutonium to generate electricity. Each space probe would also have three on-board computers to

A History of the Voyager Mission

TEACHING TIP Offer interesting facts about the selection to generate or enliven discussion, but avoid giving minilectures.

tell it where to go and what to do. Some of the programming of the computers would be done on Earth; other programming would be transmitted over radio systems.

*

COGNITIVE AND RESPONSIVE READING

Activating Prior Knowledge

Ask volunteers to tell what they know about the outer planets of our solar system. Using a model or a drawing of the solar system, review with students the order of the planets from the sun. The illustration on page 183 of the student anthology may be helpful; however it does not show the planets Mercury, Venus, Mars, or Pluto.

Setting Reading Goals and Expectations

Have the students **browse the selection,** using the clues/problems/wondering procedure. Students will return to these observations after reading.

Recommendations for Reading the Selection

Ask the students how they would like to read the selection. "Voyager to the Planets" contains a lot of information, much of which may be new to the students. For this reason, students may prefer reading it aloud so that they can ask one another questions and help one another clarify the meaning of some passages.

During oral reading, use and encourage think-alouds. During silent reading, allow discussion as needed. Discuss problems, strategies, and reactions after reading. This would be a good selection for **responding to text** by **visualizing while reading aloud.** Model this response, and then invite the students to respond.

Note: Because it may be too long to read in one class period, this selection has been divided into two parts. The second part starts on page 189 and is designated by a large initial capital letter.

About the Reading Strategies

This article contains so much information that students may have difficulty deciding what is most important. The **summing up** and **question-asking** strategies may help them. You may want to model the use of these strategies at the beginning of the selection and gradually turn over to the students the responsibility for using them.

Remind the students that the purpose of the **question-asking** strategy is to ask questions about important points in the text. The questions should be about things that can be answered by reading the text.

Think-Aloud Prompts for Use in Oral Reading

The think-aloud prompts are placed where the students may want to check their understanding of the text. The prompts are merely suggestions. Remind the students to refer to the **reading strategy posters** and use any strategy that will help them make sense of the text.

TEACHING TIP When you think aloud, be sure to demonstrate how you solved a problem or arrived at an idea.

THINK ALOUD PROMPTS

These prompts may be used as guides to promote cognitive and responsive reading.

VOYAGER TO THE PLANETS
from the book by Necia H. Apfel

Voyagers 1 and 2 are space probes, spacecraft sent to explore other planets. Space probes carry instruments that collect information and send photographs and other data back to earth. Before the Voyagers, space probes had been sent to gather information from Mars, Venus, Jupiter, Saturn, and Mercury. Voyager 1 flew by Jupiter and Saturn. Voyager 2, however, was the first space probe to go on a "grand tour" of several planets. This selection follows the long journey of Voyager 2 from the time it left Earth.

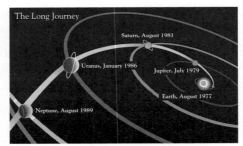

Diagram of Voyager 2's twelve-year journey to Jupiter, Saturn, Uranus, and Neptune.

On August 20, 1977, Voyager 2 was placed atop a Titan 3-E/Centaur rocket at the United States launching site on Cape Canaveral in Florida. The rocket blasted off and rose majestically into the clear blue sky.

182

183

All was well. But now the real countdown began. Voyager would take two years to reach its first destination—the giant planet Jupiter.

Voyager is a strange-looking machine with tubes and box-like structures sticking out all over it. These contain its many instruments, including cameras, radio receivers, and ultra-violet and infrared sensors. The instruments were designed to collect data from places Voyager would visit and to send this information back to Earth, where scientists and engineers were eagerly awaiting the reports.

Sometimes instructions had to be sent from stations on Earth to Voyager, telling it when to change its position, what data to record, or which instruments to use. Voyager was equipped with a big umbrella-shaped antenna to receive these directions.

In designing Voyager, the engineers tried very hard to anticipate any problems or emergencies that might arise on its

The Voyager spacecraft.
Jet Propulsion Laboratory

long journey. But the first difficulty occurred much sooner than they expected. Only eight months after Voyager was launched, its primary radio system stopped working and the backup radio receiver developed a short circuit. These defects drastically reduced Voyager's ability to receive instructions from the scientists. New computer programs had to be sent to Voyager so that it could respond to future commands. The scientists could only hope that the defective radio system would last for the entire journey. Otherwise, there would be no way for them to communicate with Voyager.

With its faulty radio operating weakly, Voyager kept sailing farther into space. After two years it finally arrived at the colorfully banded planet Jupiter, passing closest to it on July 9, 1979.

Jupiter is so big that more than 1,300 Earths could fit inside of it. It has more material in it than all the other planets in the solar system combined. It is truly a giant planet.

Following commands from programmers on Earth, Voyager took pictures of Jupiter's clouds, recorded their temperatures and speeds, and analyzed their composition. The spacecraft found that it is very cold out there, a half-billion miles from the sun. Jupiter receives only one twenty-fifth the sunlight we receive on Earth. Its pretty clouds have temperatures of about -230° F. Deep inside Jupiter it is much warmer, and at the planet's center the temperature rises to 54,000° F. That's around five times as hot as the surface of the sun.

This great heat rising from the interior would make Jupiter's cloud tops look like a multicolored bubbling mixture if the planet were not turning around rapidly on its axis. But Jupiter rotates very fast. A day on Jupiter lasts only ten hours.

185

① Students may want to **sum up** the information in the preceding paragraphs before reading more about Voyager. If they have difficulty focusing on the main points, you might model, using a discussion starter such as the following:

The Voyager spacecraft was equipped with many cameras, radio receivers, and other instruments. The instruments would serve three major functions . . .

Encourage the students to **ask questions** about the text that will help check their under-standing. A good question about Voyager's equipment might be, *What was Voyager equipped to do?*

If necessary, model such a question for the students.

② The preceding paragraph tells about the first problem Voyager faced in space. You might model **questions,** such as,

What was the first problem that arose on Voyager 2's journey, and how did scientists solve it?

The planet Jupiter. The Great Red Spot is just below the planet's equator.
NASA

This rapid rotation causes the clouds to be pulled out into a series of colored bands. Different substances in the clouds give them their varied colors.

The bands of clouds circling Jupiter are not smooth or featureless. Within them are huge, <u>turbulent</u> storms, whirlpools, and other disturbances. Weather on this giant planet is extremely violent and forceful. The most noticeable storm is called the Great Red Spot. It is so big that it can be observed through telescopes on Earth and has been seen for at least three hundred years.

Long before Voyager was launched, astronomers knew that the Great Red Spot was a giant storm, towering 10 miles

186

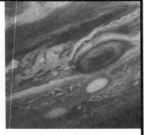

A closeup of the Great Red Spot surrounded by turbulent cloud formations.
NASA

above the rest of the clouds that swirl around it. Through their telescopes, they had seen the Red Spot change in size and in brightness, although it never seemed to vanish completely. Voyager's pictures showed the Red Spot to be about the size of Earth, but at other times it was known to be three times the size of Earth. Its color also varied from bright cherry red to very faint reddish <u>hues</u>. Astronomers aren't sure why the Great Red Spot appears red or why it has lasted such a long time.

Although the Great Red Spot drifts around the planet, it is always about the same distance below Jupiter's equator. As it drifts, it also rotates, taking about six days to turn around once. This rotation and drifting cause the gases around the Red Spot to <u>eddy</u> and swirl, somewhat like the way rocks and other barriers cause a rapidly rushing stream of water to froth and foam into small whirlpools and eddies. The photographs taken by Voyager show these eddies and swirls in great detail. **③**

Jupiter is the center of its own <u>miniature solar system</u>. It has at least sixteen moons, three of which were discovered by Voyager. Four of Jupiter's moons are very large, with diameters of several thousands of miles. The other twelve moons are no bigger than a few hundred miles across, and many are much smaller.

We now know that all four of the planets visited by Voyager have ring systems. Saturn's magnificent ring system was

187

③ The students have read many facts about Jupiter and its Great Red Spot. They may want to **sum up** this information before they continue reading. A good summary will include information about Jupiter's size, its temperature, and the nature of its clouds.

Students who are having difficulty sorting through the information may benefit from **asking** themselves **questions** about the points that confuse them.

Some students may **wonder** why the interior of Jupiter is so hot, since the text does not explain.

discovered about 1610 by Galileo. In 1977, more than 350 years later, faint rings around the planet Uranus were detected through powerful telescopes. Astronomers started theorizing that perhaps Jupiter and Neptune also had ring systems. Voyager proved them right when it discovered rings around both planets.

From afar, all these ring systems appear solid, but they are actually composed of thousands of individual chunks of ice, all following similar orbits around a planet. Saturn's rings are the most spectacular, but all four ring systems are fascinating in different ways.

Voyager found that Jupiter's ring system is just a single ring consisting of several parts with no gaps between them. The brightest part is the outer edge, but even this section is too faint to be detected from Earth. Just outside this edge Voyager found two very small moons. Both moons race rapidly around Jupiter, taking only about seven hours to complete their orbits. By contrast, our moon takes twenty-nine and one-half days to orbit Earth, which is a much smaller planet.

By moving so quickly, these tiny moons prevent any ring particles from straying beyond the ring's outer edge, farther out into space. Astronomers call such moons shepherd satellites because, like sheep dogs with sheep, they keep ring particles confined within certain regions.

4 Because no shepherd satellites control the inner particles of Jupiter's ring system, they have spread out very thinly, reaching all the way to Jupiter's cloud tops. Only when Voyager was very close to Jupiter could it detect this faint, wispy diffusion of tiny particles.

❧ 188 ❧

Leaving Jupiter, Voyager headed farther into the frigid emptiness of space. For two more years it traveled outward another half-billion miles, reaching the ringed planet Saturn in August 1981.

Saturn's rapid rotation, like Jupiter's, causes its clouds to appear as colorful bands. But Saturn has no giant storms like Jupiter's Great Red Spot. It has much smaller storms that look brown and white in Voyager's photographs.

Saturn also has much less material in it than Jupiter. In fact, although it is the second largest planet and has a diameter ten times that of Earth, it is a lightweight planet. Saturn is so light that it would actually float on water if it were put into a swimming pool large enough to hold it.

The planet Saturn.
Jet Propulsion Laboratory

4 Students may want to **sum up** the information about Jupiter before moving on. Encourage volunteers to reiterate the most important facts about the moons and rings of Jupiter.

Students who feel confused about this passage might **ask themselves or one another questions** like these: *Why did scientists think that Jupiter might have a ring system? What are shepherd satellites?*
Invite the students to ask questions about anything that puzzles them. Model a good question if necessary.

Note: This is a good place to stop reading if you and your class feel that you cannot finish the selection during this class period.

The many rings of Saturn. Differences in the color of the rings indicate different chemical compositions.
Jet Propulsion Laboratory

A thick layer of haze covers Saturn, making its atmospheric markings look much more muted than Jupiter's. Its clouds appear in different shades of butterscotch rather than bright orange, yellow, and white.

Nothing obscures Saturn's magnificent rings. Billions of icy particles orbit the planet in a flat sheet, extending outward more than 45,000 miles. But the thickness of this sheet is only about one hundred yards, the length of a football field. The rings cast shadows on Saturn's clouds but are thin enough for stars to be seen through them, even from Earth. As Voyager had found at Jupiter, shepherd satellites help herd the tiny particles of Saturn's rings into confined orbits.

Saturn, like Jupiter, has its own solar system, with at least eighteen moons. But Saturn has only one large moon, Titan. The rest are quite small. Eight of these have been called "moonlets" or "the Rocks" because they are very tiny, irregular chunks of rocky material. Some of them are shepherd satellites.

Titan, on the other hand, is bigger than the planet Mercury. It is also the only moon in the solar system that has a thick atmosphere. This atmosphere is so thick, in fact, that Voyager couldn't see Titan's surface at all. Titan's atmosphere is mainly nitrogen, much like Earth's atmosphere, which also

190

contains oxygen. Titan lacks oxygen, the element so vital to life on Earth.

Beneath its thick, smoglike clouds, Titan's surface must be a dark, gloomy place, much like the depths of an ocean on Earth. Because of its nitrogen atmosphere, Titan may be the way Earth was billions of years ago. Of course, Titan is much colder than Earth ever was. Its surface temperature is around −296° F.

Voyager had been carefully aimed so that Saturn could give it a gravity-assist change of direction toward Uranus. Before Voyager 2 reached Uranus, however, the engineers found that the spacecraft had lost much of the lubricant needed to keep its scanning platform operating. Without the ability to turn easily, the cameras mounted on this platform could not be aimed properly. Instead, the entire spacecraft would have to be rotated, a much more difficult maneuver. Also, Voyager's computer software, especially those commands controlling Voyager's stabilization and photographing instructions, had to be redesigned.

The engineers knew that whereas Voyager had been able to spend several days at Jupiter and Saturn, it would have only about six hours at Uranus. And because Uranus is so much farther from the sun than either Jupiter or Saturn, much, much less sunlight reaches it. Taking a picture at Uranus has been compared to photographing a ball park at night by the light of a single candle.

The engineers calculated that Voyager would be moving at about 12 miles per second when it went past Uranus. This meant that in 10 seconds it would move 120 miles. So Voyager's camera had to be moved backward at just the right

191

(5) Students have read many facts about Saturn in the preceding passage. They might check their understanding of the information by **asking questions** and **summing up** what they have read. Students may ask two important questions:

What are some things that scientists know about Saturn? What are the weather conditions on Titan?

Invite volunteers to summarize the passage in their own words, reminding them to include only main points.

Note: Students may be confused by the difference between the way the author compares Jupiter to Earth in terms of *volume* ("1,300 Earths could fit inside of it") but compares Saturn to Earth in terms of *diameter* ("ten times that of Earth"). Students may make the mistake of thinking that Jupiter is 1,300 times as large as Earth and Saturn is only ten times as large as Earth. In fact, Saturn is only 17 percent smaller than Jupiter and over 700 Earths could fit inside it.

speed to compensate for this rapid forward motion. All these commands had to be sent to Voyager almost three hours beforehand, because that's how long it takes light or radio waves, traveling at the speed of light, to reach the planet from Earth.

Also, because of the increased distance, Voyager's radio signals back to Earth became much weaker. The engineers had to expand the Deep Space Network that tracked and communicated with Voyager. To do this, they started using powerful radio telescopes, such as the Very Large Array (VLA) in New Mexico and a similar one in Australia. These large series of connected radio telescopes act as one huge telescope, detecting radio waves too faint for a single receiver to pick up. Once again, when Voyager had in effect radioed home for help, the engineers were able to devise new and brilliant solutions. Voyager's engineers were the real heroes of this story.

All these preparations took place while Voyager silently traveled onward. On January 24, 1986, after four and a half long years, the sturdy spacecraft came within about 50,000 miles of Uranus. It was only 10 miles off the desired point after having traveled 2 billion miles from Earth.

Uranus was discovered during the time of the American Revolutionary War. In 1781, the English astronomer Sir William Herschel realized that what previously had been recorded as a star was actually the seventh planet in our solar system. Many years later, five moons were found orbiting Uranus, and then in 1977 Uranus's ring system was detected.

Uranus's main peculiarity, however, was known long before Voyager's journey. It is not the planet's rings or its moons that are unique. It is the planet itself. Unlike other planets, which

॰ *192* ॰

rotate in an upright position, Uranus rolls along in its orbit like a top spinning on its side. As a result, during half of its eighty-four-year orbit Uranus's north pole faces the sun, and during the other half its south pole is sunlit. Uranus's moons and rings also follow this strange orientation because they all have orbits directly above Uranus's equator.

Astronomers were disappointed at how few features Voyager was able to detect in Uranus's clouds. Layers of thick haze hang over most of the upper clouds, obscuring any details that may exist below. A small amount of methane gas in the haze and clouds gives the planet its soft blue-green color.

Although Voyager found Uranus almost featureless, the visit was not in vain. Besides discovering ten new Uranian

The planet Uranus. One of Uranus's moons, Miranda, is shown in the foreground.
NASA

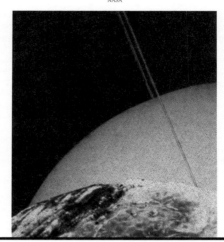

6 Students may benefit from **summing up** the information about the spacecraft's faulty scanning platform and how ground engineers solved the problem.

moons and obtaining close-up photographs of the five known ones, Voyager was able to distinguish ten very narrow rings of particles in Uranus's ring system. The rings are widely separated by several shepherd satellites that were among the ten new moons found by Voyager.

Particles in the rings are made of ice but are covered with sootlike material, which makes them appear very dark. Most of the particles are about the size of a fist or bigger. One would expect to find smaller particles as well, possibly as small as dust. Astronomers theorize that some process must be sweeping the rings clear, leaving only the larger chunks.

The astronomers would have liked Voyager to linger longer at Uranus. But even as the spacecraft approached Uranus, they were preparing speed and direction commands to be radioed to it. With a gravity-assist from Uranus, Voyager would head toward Neptune.

By the time Voyager arrived at Neptune, the engineers were already jokingly describing the spacecraft as being hard of hearing with a touch of <u>arthritis</u> and a slight loss of memory. Voyager was a very old spacecraft indeed.

However, Voyager came closer to Neptune than it did to any other object in its long journey. It passed 2,700 miles above the cloud tops over Neptune's north pole. That was on August 25, 1989, twelve years after its launch. Voyager was now $2\,3/4$ billion miles from Earth. The spacecraft was so far from the people who sent commands to it that it would have to operate at the very limit of its capability to hear their directions.

Neptune is too far away from us to be seen without a telescope. Sunlight reaching Uranus is very dim, but it is two and a half times as much as the amount of light reaching Neptune.

❦ 194 ❦

Neptune receives only one-thousandth the amount of light we receive on Earth.

Astronomers thought that Neptune would be featureless like Uranus. They were delightfully surprised. Neptune is about the same size as Uranus and shares the same blue-green color because of a small amount of methane in its clouds. But heat rising from Neptune's hot interior keeps its cloud top temperatures similar to Uranus's temperatures, even though Neptune is more than a billion miles farther away from the sun.

This rising heat drives fierce winds, creating huge storms in Neptune's atmosphere, much like those found on Jupiter. Instead of finding a peaceful-looking planet, Voyager found active cloud structures in a turbulent state.

The planet Neptune. The Great Dark Spot is at the equator, just above the white cloud.
NASA

7 After reading about Uranus, students may **ask questions** like these:

What is unique about Uranus? What did Voyager 2 discover when it reached Uranus?

If the students choose to **sum up** information about Uranus, their summaries should include the most important facts about its discovery and its moons, rings, and rotation.

Some students may need to **clarify** how Uranus's rotation differs from that of Earth and the other planets. Drawing a diagram on the board may help students **visualize** this phenomenon.

Neptune's biggest feature is called the Great Dark Spot, which is a huge rotating storm about the size of Earth. Unlike Jupiter's Great Red Spot, the Great Dark Spot is a hole or depression in the clouds. It lets us look deep into Neptune's atmosphere, although all we see is darker shades of Neptune's blue-green methane covering.

About 30 miles above the atmosphere, white cirruslike clouds form and <u>dissipate</u> around the Great Dark Spot, similar to the way clouds form on mountainsides on Earth. White wispy clouds are also found near a small triangular-shaped storm, which moves around the planet faster than the Great Dark Spot and has therefore been dubbed Scooter. Another storm, Dark Spot Two, is smaller than the Great Dark Spot and is <u>oval</u> in shape. It has a white cloud hovering above its center.

The thick blue-green clouds covering Uranus and Neptune make up only about 10 to 20 percent of the planets' mass. The rest is rock and ice beneath the clouds. Uranus and Neptune are not true gas planets like Jupiter and Saturn. Scientists believe that they may be the <u>accumulation</u> of thousands of huge boulders that crashed together and formed planets early in the solar system's history.

8 After Voyager confirmed that both Jupiter and Uranus had ring systems, astronomers were fairly sure that Neptune would have one, too. They were, therefore, not surprised when Voyager detected it. When the spacecraft was still far away from Neptune, the pictures it sent back to Earth showed only sections of rings. Not until Voyager was much closer could the rest of the rings be observed. The brighter sections seen at first were found simply to have more material in them, making them more visible. And once again, Voyager detected shepherd

≫ *196* ≪

satellites confining two of the first three rings it discovered into very narrow areas. The third ring is much more spread out. Later, after studying Voyager's photographs more closely, astronomers discovered a fourth and fifth ring.

Voyager also found six new moons orbiting Neptune, raising the total number known to eight. But most amazing was what Voyager discovered about Triton, Neptune's largest moon. Although Triton had been observed from Earth many years before, little was known about it other than that it was one of the largest satellites in the solar system. Triton orbits Neptune in a retrograde motion, which means that it goes

A portion of Neptune's largest moon, Triton. Seasonal changes cause melting and collapsing of its icy surface. *Inset:* A detail of Triton's south pole shows what may be ice volcanoes.
NASA

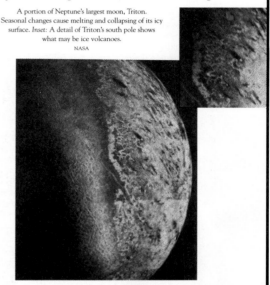

8 Students may ask these key **questions** before **summing up** information about Neptune:

Why were scientists surprised by the data they received from Neptune? What is Neptune made of?

A **summing up** of this passage should include information about Neptune's storm systems, the material of which Neptune is composed, and scientists' theories about how Neptune was formed.

around Neptune in the direction opposite to Neptune's spin. It is the only major moon in the solar system to have this characteristic, although some of the smaller moons of Jupiter have retrograde motion.

The surface of Triton, as revealed by Voyager, is fascinating. Bright snowfalls only a few decades old contrast with craters billions of years old. In general, however, craters are very scarce on Triton, indicating that its crust is quite young and is constantly changing.

Voyager found several active volcanoes on Triton. The material coming from them is not molten rock like the hot lava that comes out of volcanoes on Earth. Instead, water mixed with other substances is spewed out, making the volcanoes more like geysers.

Voyager also photographed dark plumes of dust-filled nitrogen gas erupting from beneath Triton's surface. The gas rises some 5 miles into the thin atmosphere before being blown more than 150 miles across the moon. The dark plumes are seen as streaks of black on the much lighter landscape.

9 After Voyager 2 passed Neptune, its program was given a new name—Voyager Interstellar Mission (VIM)—because now it is headed out of the solar system, out to the stars.

Very little will change on Voyager as it sails on through outer space. Eventually its electrical power will be used up and its instruments will cease to function, but there is nothing in space that will stop Voyager from traveling

One of Voyager's last pictures of Neptune and Triton. NASA

farther and farther from us. Only when it comes close enough to be affected by another star's gravitational attraction will its path be altered. Astronomers have calculated that that won't happen for at least twenty-seven thousand years!

We don't know if there are any intelligent beings elsewhere in the universe, but if there are—and if they find either of the two Voyagers wandering out in space—they will discover, in addition to all the instruments, a very special gold-plated record on the side of each spacecraft. On each record is a recorded greeting from the people on Earth in fifty-five languages as well as many sounds that are common on Earth. These include the roar of a jet plane, the crying of babies, the chirping of crickets, and ninety minutes of a variety of music. Covering this precious record is a diagram showing what Earth people look like and where Earth is in the solar system. The story of Voyager will be an ancient legend before any alien being can possibly find the spacecraft. But maybe, many thousands of years from now . . .   **10**

MEET NECIA APFEL, AUTHOR
Necia Apfel's childhood interest in astronomy was discouraged. "Women don't become astronomers," she was told. Her interest was renewed when her husband gave her a telescope for her birthday, and she began graduate study of astronomy at Northwestern University. As a graduate research assistant, she coauthored a college textbook on astronomy. Since that time she has written several books for children and teenagers about astronomy. She has also lectured for children at the Adler Planetarium in Chicago and written a monthly column in Odyssey magazine answering readers' questions about astronomy. "Only children can think up the kinds of questions I receive," she said. "They are marvelous."

 199

9 To aid in **summing up** information about Neptune's rings and satellites, students might **ask** themselves such **questions** as these:

What did Voyager discover about Neptune's rings? What features did Voyager find on Triton, Neptune's largest moon?

Some students may need to **clarify** the meaning of the term *retrograde motion.* **Visualizing** Triton in motion may help them to do so.

10 Students may **sum up** the concluding paragraphs of the article something like this:

After leaving Neptune, Voyager 2's mission was renamed Voyager Interstellar Mission because it was headed out toward the stars. It will continue on its present course for at least 27,000 years. It will take that long for it to approach close enough to a star that its path will be altered. If intelligent beings from another solar system ever find one of the two

Voyagers now traveling through space, they will find on its side a phonograph record including greetings from Earth and diagrams of what Earth people look like and of Earth's position in the solar system.

Students may need to **clarify** how Voyager will be able to continue on its journey for thousands of years. Remind them that in space there is nothing to alter the direction or speed of a moving object. Also, Voyager does not require fuel. Once it left Earth's atmosphere, Voyager needed energy only to change its course and to operate its instruments.

Discussing Strategy Use
Encourage the students to share any problems that they had while reading "Voyager to the Planets." If they used the summing-up or question-asking strategy while reading, ask them to share how they decided where to sum up or what questions to ask.

* **EXPLORING THROUGH DISCUSSION**

Reflecting on the Selection
Whole-Group Discussion

The whole group discusses the selection and any thoughts, reactions, or questions that it raises. During this time, students also return to the **clues, problems, and wonderings** that they noted on the board during browsing.

Assessment

To assess their understanding of the text, engage the students in a discussion to determine whether they have grasped the following ideas:

- the way scientists on Earth communicated with and received information from Voyager 2
- new facts scientists discovered about each of the planets that the Voyagers visited

Response Journal

Allow time for students to record their personal responses to the selection.

Exploring Concepts Within the Selection
Small-Group Discussion

Remind the students to check the Question Board and the Concept Board to determine whether their original perceptions about astronomy have changed as a result of this selection. Circulate among the groups to see whether any of the groups are having difficulty connecting this selection to the unit concepts.

Sharing Ideas About Explorable Concepts

Have the groups **report** their **ideas** and **discuss** them with the rest of the class. It is crucial that the students' ideas determine this discussion.

- Students may recognize that technology has advanced enormously since the days of Galileo and his telescopes and that our knowledge of the universe has increased accordingly.

As these ideas and others are stated, have the students **add them to the Question Board** or the **Concept Board**.

Exploring Concepts Across Selections

Students may make connections with other selections in the unit.

- Students may point out that even ancient astronomers, such as the Mayas, kept track of the movements of some of the planets.
- Students may notice that the Voyager probes expanded on discoveries made by earlier scientists, such as Galileo.

Ask the students to examine the fine-art piece *Cosmic Universe* on page 180 in the student anthology. Encourage them to share their reactions to the piece and discuss its connection to the selection they just read.

Recording Ideas

As students complete the above discussions, ask them to **sum up what they have learned from their conversations and to tell how they might use this information** in further explorations. Any special information or insights may be recorded on the **Concept Board**. Any further questions that they would like to think about, pursue, or investigate may be recorded on the **Question Board**. They may want to discuss

TEACHING TIP Encourage students to ask questions about what they read.

TIP FOR ENGLISH LANGUAGE LEARNERS
Give English Language Learners a chance to practice using the vocabulary associated with the selection. Have them reread some of the passages in the selection with native English-speaking partners. Encourage partners to discuss the meaning of the passages as they relate to astronomy.

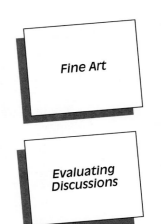

Fine Art

Evaluating Discussions

"Voyager to the Planets" by Necia Apfel

_____
_____
_____
_____
_____
_____

"A Meeting in Space" by Vonda N. McIntyre

_____
_____
_____
_____
_____
_____

Stars by Seymour Simon

_____
_____
_____
_____
_____
_____

Unit 2/Astronomy   EN 25

Explorer's Notebook, page 25

the progress that has been made on their questions. They may also want to cross out any questions that no longer warrant consideration.

❯ Have the students record their findings on page 25 in the **Explorer's Notebook.**

Professional Checkpoint: Cognitive and Responsive Reading

Summing up serves to refocus the students' attention on the selection after a break for clarifying or predicting, or after a change of readers. It is not an end in itself, but a springboard back into the selection. At the lowest grades, it involves a simple retelling of what has gone just before. By fifth grade, the students briefly sum up only the main gist of the selection in their own words.

It is important that summing up not become intrusive. Therefore, it should be done quickly, and only a few times in the course of active reading. The summing up at the end of a selection can be a more complete recounting of the main thread of the whole selection.

Notes:

2 READING WITH A WRITER'S EYE

MINILESSON

Elaboration Through Providing Specific Facts

Ask students to discuss the meaning of the term *nonfiction.* They should understand that **nonfiction** is an account of **something that is true or something that really happened.** Readers expect the information in nonfiction writing to be true. They expect to find **facts that back up what the writer says**. Guide discussion to the understanding that sometimes facts are presented in story form, as in biographies like "Galileo," and that sometimes facts are presented as an explanation, as in articles like "Telescopes." A good writer presents facts in a way that makes his or her article interesting as well as informative.

In "Voyager to the Planets," Necia Apfel presents her facts in an interesting way. For example, on page 185, she describes conditions on Jupiter: "Its pretty clouds have temperatures of about $-230°$ F. Deep inside Jupiter it is much warmer, and at the planet's center the temperature rises to $54,000°$ F."

Selective Reading: Focus on Providing Specific Facts

Have the students go back to "Voyager to the Planets" and look for other examples of how Apfel provided specific facts for her readers. Encourage volunteers to read aloud the examples that they find.

Other passages in which the author provides specific facts include the following:

- page 190: the description of Saturn's rings
- pages 191 and 192: the description of the procedure used to photograph Uranus
- pages 195 and 196: the description of Neptune's surface
- pages 197 and 198: the description of the moon Triton

Selection-Based Practice

Independent Practice: Providing Specific Facts

➤ To provide additional practice in recognizing how writers provide specific facts, have the students work in small groups to discuss and complete Reading/Writing Connection, page 18.

WRITING

Linking Reading to Writing

Remind the students that a good writer can present facts in a way that holds the reader's interest. Encourage the students to look through their writing folders for articles they have written in which they do not provide specific facts to back up what they say or in which they might present their facts in a more interesting manner. After sufficient time has passed to allow students to select and revise a piece of writing, invite volunteers to read their original passages and the revised versions and to explain how the changes improved their articles.

TIP FOR ENGLISH LANGUAGE LEARNERS

Peer tutoring and collaborative group work are ways to increase the English input that English Language Learners receive. Have English Language Learners work with native English-speaking peers to brainstorm ideas.

∗ Writing Process

If students have elected to publish any previously written, revised, and proofread pieces, encourage them to place the pieces in the classroom library to share with the rest of the class.

"Voyager to the Planets"

Telling Specific Facts

In "Voyager to the Planets," Necia Apfel provides many specific facts to support important ideas. Look back at "Voyager to the Planets" or other articles you have read in which writers present their facts well. Write the title of the article, the facts that interested you, the idea the facts support, and the page numbers on which the facts appear.

Title: _____

Interesting facts: _____

_____

Idea the facts support: _____

_____ Page: _____

Title: _____

Interesting facts: _____

_____

Idea the facts support: _____

_____ Page: _____

Title: _____

Interesting facts: _____

_____

Idea the facts support: _____

_____ Page: _____

Look back at the pages you noted for examples when you are looking for ways to present facts in your own writing.

Elaboration

18 R/WC   Astronomy/Unit 2

Name

Copyright © 1995 Open Court Publishing Company

Reading/Writing Connection, page 18

Concept-related words and phrases from the selection that students may want to discuss or remember and use include the following: **shepherd satellites, atmospheric, space probe, composition, turbulent, theorizing, orientation**

Have Vocabulary Exploration forms, Reproducible Master 14, available for students who request them.

Adding to Personal Word Lists

3 GUIDED AND INDEPENDENT EXPLORATION

EXPLORING CONCEPTS BEYOND THE TEXT

Guided Exploration

The following activities do not have to be completed within the days devoted to this lesson.

- Students who would like to learn more about the Voyager space probes might look at Necia H. Apfel's book *Voyager to the Planets,* from which this excerpt is taken.
- Students can watch the night sky to see whether they can observe any of the planets mentioned in this selection.

- Suggest that interested students use unit bibliographies and library resources to find further information on the planets and their moons.

Research Cycle

Meet with the whole class as needed for the following purposes:
- to arrange schedules and update calendars
- to discuss problems that students are encountering with their research
- to hear preliminary presentations and discussions of interesting findings
- to arrange more formal presentations of students' research
- to provide guidance to ensure that groups progress through phases of the Research Cycle—obtaining information; revising problems, conjectures, needs, and plans (perhaps with input resulting from a presentation to the class); and proceeding to a further cycle of problem, conjecture, and so forth

* Exploring Through Research

For additional ideas for informal presentations, see **Learning Framework Card 4C, Needs and Plans Phase 1 and 2.** A few presentation ideas include the following:
- Mini-debate: Group members who have opposing conjectures present them, along with evidence and arguments, for the rest of the class to react to.
- Problem presentations: Groups who are stuck, not able to find relevant material, or who are finding something puzzling or inconsistent, present their problem for suggestions from their peers.
- Poster session: When not enough time is available, groups put up small displays (including posters, graphs, and summaries) of any kind showing their preliminary findings. The students examine these displays during Independent Workshop and give feedback to their peers.

TEACHING TIP These informal presentations should take some of the emphasis off the final research product and give the students a better sense of research as a continuous process.

MINILESSON

Research Aid: Organizing Information in a Chart

Remind the students that "Voyager to the Planets" contained much information about each of the planets Voyager visited. By doing research in resources listed in the bibliography and in other library resources, they will be able to find more detailed information on these planets. They will be able to find even more information on Earth's neighbors, Venus and Mars, than on the outer planets.

Ask the students to **suggest a graphic organizer that they could use to record information** about each planet. The organizer should help them **compare certain kinds of information** about different planets.

Guided Practice: Organizing Information in a Chart

One kind of organizer students might make is **a chart with a section for each planet in the solar system or for each of the planets visited by Voyager.** Each section should have places for particular kinds of information—information about moons, rings, distance from the sun, and so forth.
- Have a volunteer begin this chart by writing the planet names **Jupiter, Saturn, Uranus,** and **Neptune** across the top of a large section of the chalkboard or on butcher's paper fastened to a wall.

- Ask the students to look again at the information given about each planet in the selection and to suggest types of information that could go on the chart.
- Point out that Apfel provides information about the following: (1) the size of each planet; (2) its composition; (3) its distance from the sun; (4) its atmosphere; (5) its ring system; and (6) its moons. Because Apfel also provides other miscellaneous information about each planet, including historical information about what scientists of the past knew about the planet or moon, you might suggest that students include space for miscellaneous information (7) as well.

Using the seven categories of information listed above, students would write the following information about Jupiter:

(1) 1,300 Earths could fit inside it; (2) gas (page 196); (3) 500 million miles; (4) clouds in colored bands with storm systems, including Great Red Spot; (5) a single ring with no gaps, confined at outer edge by shepherd satellites; (6) at least 16 moons, 4 of which are very large. Miscellaneous information (7) might include the following: Cloud temperatures, –230°F; temperature at core, 54,000°F; receives 1/25 as much sunlight as Earth; day is 10 hours long; shepherd satellites orbit planet in 7 hours.

Independent Practice: Organizing Information in a Chart

Have students **complete the chart by finding the same kind of information they recorded for Jupiter for each of the other planets visited by Voyager.**

This information is not given in the same order for each planet, and information for some planets is more complete than for others. However, with some looking, students will be able to find all of the information listed below in the selection. Other sources will give more complete information.

In each of the seven categories, **students should write the following information about Saturn:** (1) diameter 10 times that of Earth; (2) gas; (3) 1 billion miles; (4) clouds in brown and white bands, with no giant storm systems; (5) first seen by Galileo in 1610 (page 188), icy particles in sheet 45,000 miles wide but only 100 yards thick, confined by shepherd satellites; (6) at least 18 moons, of which only Titan is large. Miscellaneous information (7) might include the following: second largest planet, but so light that it could float in water; rapid rotation like Jupiter's.

The chart should have the following information about Uranus: (1) no information in text; (2) rock and ice (page 196); (3) 2 billion miles; (4) layers of thick blue-green haze, containing small amount of methane and making up 10–20 percent of planet's mass; (5) discovered in 1977, 10 rings of large, soot-covered ice particles, widely separated by shepherd satellites; (6) at least 15 moons. Miscellaneous information (7) might include the following: discovered in 1781 by English astronomer Herschel; takes 84 Earth years to orbit the sun; rotates on its side rather than in upright position; receives very little sunlight.

The chart should have the following information about Neptune: (1) about the same size as Uranus; (2) same as Uranus; (3) 2.75 billion

ASSESSMENT TIP This may be a good opportunity to observe students working in groups and to mark observations in the Teacher's Observation Log.

miles; (4) similar to Uranus but has storm systems including Great Dark Spot, Scooter, and Dark Spot Two; (5) 5 rings, separated by shepherd satellites; (6) at least 8 moons. Miscellaneous information (7) might include the following: can be seen from Earth only with a telescope; receives only 1/1000 as much sunlight as Earth.

➤ Apfel's book and other books about planets and moons include much information about moons that is not found in this selection but that might be added to a chart such as the one on Explorer's Notebook pages 36–37. The text includes much information on Titan's size (larger than Mercury), atmosphere (thick clouds composed mostly of nitrogen), and surface temperature (around –296°F).

The text also includes the following information on Neptune's large moon Triton: only large moon that orbits in retrograde motion; constantly changing surface; several active ice volcanoes; dark plumes of nitrogen gas erupting from within and rising 5 miles into atmosphere.

Explorer's Notebook, page 36

Moons of the Planets

Find out more about the moons of Jupiter, Saturn, Uranus, and Neptune. Then fill in some of the spaces on the chart below.

	Size	Atmosphere	Surface
Moons of Jupiter			
Moons of Saturn Titan			
Moons of Uranus			
Moons of Neptune Triton			

Explorer's Notebook, page 37

Other Features	Miscellaneous Information

* INDEPENDENT WORKSHOP
Building a Community of Scholars

Student-Directed Reading, Writing, and Discussion

Research Cycle Meet with the whole class as needed to assess the progress of each research group. If the students have not already done so, have them select an organized way to store their research information. Remind them, if necessary, that the unit will soon come to a close. Some research groups should be ready to make plans for their final projects.

Students will begin presenting their final research project during the class period in which they read *Stars.* They will finish presenting their projects during the class period in which they read "Sun" and "Secrets."

Additional Opportunities for Independent Reading, Writing, and Cross-curricular Activities

* Writing Seminar

Some students may want to work on writing projects in their writing folders. Encourage them to work with partners, making comments and suggestions about each other's work.

Portfolio

Remind the students to think about pieces of writing they might choose to put into their portfolios.

Cross-curricular Activity Cards

The following Cross-curricular Activity Cards in the Student Toolbox are appropriate for this selection:

- 8 Social Studies—Planets and Days of the Week
- 8 Science—The Solar System

The Solar System
Use after "Voyager to the Planets"

8
Science

Planets and Days of the Week
Use after "Voyager to the Planets"

8
Social Studies

Use an encyclopedia or a book about calendars to find out about the days of the week. Try to answer some of the questions below. If you find enough information, organize it into a chart with space for each weekday and for information about this day in different cultures.

- How many days of the week did people in the ancient Middle East—the Egyptians, the Babylonians, and the Hebrews—have?
- Which heavenly body was each day named after in Roman times?
- Why did ancient people consider the Sun and the Moon to be planets along with Mars, Mercury, Jupiter, Venus, and Saturn?
- Which German gods are associated with the days Tuesday, Wednesday, Thursday, and Friday?
- What are the names of the days of the week in one of these languages: Spanish, French, or Italian?

The names of many everyday things, such as the days of the week and the planets, have their origins in ancient times.

Additional Opportunities for Solving Learning Problems

Tutorial

Use this time to **work with individuals or small groups who need help in any area**. Encourage students to ask for help whenever they need it. The following aids are available in the Teacher Toolbox for your convenience:

- Writer's Craft/Reading: Elaboration Through Providing Specific Facts, Teacher Tool Card 40
- Writer's Craft/Reading: Elaboration Through Providing Comparison and Contrast, Teacher Tool Card 36
- Grammar, Mechanics, and Usage: Pronoun/Antecedent Agreement, Teacher Tool Card 61
- Study and Research: Organizing Information in a Chart, Teacher Tool Card 112

A Meeting in Space

1 READING THE SELECTION

INFORMATION FOR THE TEACHER

About the
Selection

This selection is excerpted from *Barbary,* the first children's book by award-winning science-fiction author Vonda N. McIntyre. "A Meeting in Space" takes readers on a thrilling ride through space as young protagonists Barbary and Heather attempt to rescue Barbary's runaway cat while avoiding both Heather's worried father and the mysterious alien spaceship that lurks near the space station they call home. Unlike much science fiction for children, this exciting, suspenseful story does not present scientifically impossible situations. Instead, it will stimulate readers to wonder about worlds beyond our solar system and the life that may inhabit them.

Link to the
Unit Concepts

In reading "A Meeting in Space," pages 200–227, students are encouraged to wonder about how people of the future will learn about the universe. Space-research stations such as Atlantis are likely to add greatly to their knowledge of astronomy. Contact with intelligent life from elsewhere in the universe would also increase future people's knowledge.

About the
Author

Vonda N. McIntyre was born in Louisville, Kentucky, in 1948 and lives in Seattle, Washington. Her novelette "Of Mist, and Grass, and Sand" won the Nebula Award from Science Fiction Writers of America in 1974, and her book *Dreamsnake* won the Nebula Award, the Hugo Award from the World Science Fiction Convention, and a nomination for the American Book Award in 1980. She wrote the novel versions of the screenplays for *Star Trek II: The Wrath of Khan, Star Trek III: The Search for Spock,* and *Star Trek IV: The Voyage Home.* She also wrote another novel about *Star Trek* characters, *Enterprise: The First Adventure. Barbary* is her first book for younger readers.

LESSON OVERVIEW

"A Meeting in Space" by Vonda N. McIntyre, pages 200–227

READING THE SELECTION

Materials
Student anthology, pp. 200–227
Explorer's Notebook, p. 25

FYI
Learning Framework Card
• Responding to Text, 1B

READING WITH A WRITER'S EYE

Minilessons
Writer's Craft: Genre—Science Fiction
Writer's Craft: Dialogue

Materials
Reading/Writing Connection, pp. 19–20
Reproducible Masters 14, 32

FYI
Teacher Tool Card
• Spelling and Vocabulary: Building
  Vocabulary, 75

Options for Instruction
Writer's Craft: Setting
Grammar, Mechanics, and Usage: Using
  and Punctuating Dialogue
(Use Teacher Tool Cards listed below.)

GUIDED AND INDEPENDENT EXPLORATION

Independent Workshop

**Optional Materials from
Student Toolbox**
Tradebook Connection Cards

Cross-curricular Activity Card
• 2 Art—Making Sets for a Puppet Show

Student Tool Cards
• Writer's Craft/Reading: Reading and
  Writing Science Fiction, 6
• Writer's Craft/Reading: Using
  Dialogue in a Story, 19
• Writer's Craft/Reading: Setting, 14
• Grammar, Mechanics, and Usage:
  Using and Punctuating Dialogue, 70

FYI
Teacher Tool Cards
• Writer's Craft/Reading: Genre—
  Science Fiction, 6
• Writer's Craft/Reading: Using
  Dialogue in a Story, 19
• Writer's Craft/Reading: Setting, 14
• Grammar, Mechanics, and Usage:
  Using and Punctuating Dialogue, 70

NOTES

Asterisks (*) throughout the lesson indicate learning frameworks. Learning Framework Cards and Teacher Tool Cards can be found in the Teacher Toolbox.

McIntyre says, "I write science fiction because its boundaries are the only ones wide enough for me to explore experiences people have not had—*yet*; and because it allows my characters to develop as far as their ability will take them, unlimited by the crippling demands and unambitious expectations our society puts on us."

INFORMATION FOR THE STUDENT

Share with the students some information about Vonda N. McIntyre, including her comment on why she writes science fiction.

When they have finished reading the story, especially during their discussion of science fiction, students may be interested in some of the information below.

Many astronomers working today first became interested in learning about the universe through science fiction. Students may be interested in learning more about this popular genre.

Scientific fiction began in the late nineteenth century with the French writer Jules Verne. In his books *Journey to the Center of the Earth, Around the World in Eighty Days, Twenty Thousand Leagues Under the Sea, From the Earth to the Moon,* and *Round the Moon,* Verne used the science of his day to make predictions about the future. Many things that he predicted, including the submarine, electric lights, and the Atlantic cable, were invented soon after his books were written.

Although science fiction for children is often more concerned with space monsters and time travel than with science, the best science fiction is scientifically accurate. Robert A. Heinlein, a well-known writer of science fiction for both children and adults, says that the author of science fiction must always stick to the truth of "the real world as we know it, including all established facts and natural laws. The result can be extremely fantastic in content, but it is not fantasy; it is legitimate—and often very tightly reasoned—speculation about the possibilities of the real world."

Often science-fiction stories involve characters voyaging out into space and encountering dangers and adventures of all kinds. Sometimes, however, science-fiction stories are set on the earth in the future and deal with experiences that future people may have. These stories are often about something people are currently doing that may cause problems in the future. For example, a science-fiction story may contain descriptions of an earth ravaged by nuclear war or having lost its ozone layer.

The predictions made by science-fiction writers are usually based on the scientific work being done at the time the story is written. Writers in the nineteenth and early twentieth centuries had not had experience with computers, rockets, space stations, or many other scientific and technological advances of the late twentieth century, and so they could not have imagined many of the events described in "A Meeting in Space." Science-fiction writers in future centuries will write about many inventions and scientific discoveries that we cannot now imagine.

Science Fiction

COGNITIVE AND RESPONSIVE READING

*

Activating Prior Knowledge

Tell the students that this selection involves a young girl's journey through space to rescue her pet. Encourage them to discuss anything they have heard or read about space travel. Invite them also to share their previous experiences with the genre of science fiction.

Setting Reading Goals and Expectations

Have the students **browse** the **first page** of the selection, using the clues/problems/wondering procedure. Students will return to these observations after reading.

Recommendations for Reading the Selection

Ask the students how they wish to read the selection. Since "A Meeting in Space" is suspenseful and exciting, the students may prefer to read it silently and without interruptions.

During oral reading, use and encourage think-alouds. During silent reading, allow discussion as needed. Discuss problems, strategies, and reactions after reading.

This would also be a good selection for **responding** to text **by making connections** while reading aloud. Model this response, and then invite the students to do the same. For a review of making connections, see **Learning Framework Card 1B, Responding to Text.**

Note: Notice that "A Meeting in Space" has been broken into two parts in case students don't finish the selection in one class period. The second part begins on page 216 and is indicated by a large initial capital letter.

About the Reading Strategies

Because this selection is long and suspenseful, students may find themselves using **summing up** and **predicting** strategies to review and predict story events.

Think-Aloud Prompts for Use in Oral Reading

The think-aloud prompts with the page miniatures are placed where students may want to check their understanding of the text. These prompts are merely suggestions. Remind the students to refer to the **reading strategy posters** and to use any strategy they feel is appropriate as they read.

STEPS TOWARD INDEPEND-ENCE During browsing, students should be noticing different text types.

A MEETING IN SPACE

from BARBARY by Vonda N. McIntyre
*illustrated by Mary Beth Schwark
and Bob Kuester*

*Orphaned Barbary and her cat Mick have come to the space
research station Atlantis to live with her mother's old friend
Yoshi and his daughter Heather, who has a serious heart
condition. Barbary arrives at an exciting time. An alien
spacecraft has entered Earth's solar system. Yoshi's friend Thea,
an astronomer, plans to send a probe with a camera to learn
more about the alien craft. But when the probe is launched,
Barbary finds that Mick is aboard it. In trying to rescue him she
herself will play a role in the first meeting between the
aliens and Earth people.*

Barbary entered the launch chamber. Heather's raft sat
on its tracks, waiting to go out again. Barbary floated to
it, opened its door, and slid into the seat.

She stared at the controls. She thought she remembered
what Heather had done, but she was not certain. She was not
even sure she could figure out in which direction to go to find
the alien ship, and Mick's raft. Away from the sun, she guessed.
But there was an awful lot of nothing out there, and rafts were
awfully small.

Heather said the computer could drive the raft —
She turned it on.

"Can you hear me?"

"I can hear you."

"Do you know where the raft with the transmitter is?"

"Yes."

"I want to go there."

"Please wait."

The kaleidoscope patterns appeared. Barbary gritted her
teeth. Computers were supposed to know everything instantly.

But if it knew the location of Mick's raft, why was it making
her wait? The only reason she could think of was that it was
reporting her.

🌿 200 🌿

🌿 201 🌿

She slapped the switch that turned off the computer. She did not know if that would keep it from reporting her—if that was what it was doing—but it was the only thing she could think of. She would have to find Mick herself. She pulled down the door and sealed it and tried to remember what control Heather had used first.

"Open up!"

Barbary started at the muffled voice and the rap on the transparent roof.

Heather stared in at her. She looked furious.

Barbary opened the hatch.

"Move over!"

"Heather, they're going to shoot Thea's contraption, and Mick's inside it. I have to stop them—"

"Move over!"

Barbary obeyed.

Heather swung in, slammed the hatch shut, and fastened her seat belt.

"Your computer told me part of it, and I figured out the rest." She took over the controls.

"Thea tried to make her camera come back, but it wouldn't."

"Mick probably knocked loose some of the connections."

Their raft slid into the airlock. The hatch closed.

"I just hope I got here soon enough to get us out," Heather said. "I bet they'll freeze all the hatches in about two seconds, if they haven't already—"

The outer door slid open.

Heather made a sound of triumph and slammed on the power. The acceleration pushed them both back into their seats.

1

⚜ 202 ⚜

With the raft accelerating and the station growing smaller behind them, Heather glared at Barbary.

"Now," she said. "Why didn't you wake me up?"

"There wasn't time," Barbary said.

"Oh." Heather's scowl softened. "That's a good point."

Barbary squinted into starry space. "How do you know where to go?"

"It's not that hard. From where the station is now, and the direction and speed the ship's approaching, it has to be lined up with Betelgeuse, if Atlantis is directly behind us."

2

Barbary tried to imagine the geometry of the arrangement Heather described, with all the elements moving independently of one another, and came to the conclusion that it *was* hard, even if Heather was so used to it that she didn't know it.

She peered into the blackness, unable to make out anything but the bright multicolored points of stars.

Heather drew a piece of equipment from the control panel. It looked like a face mask attached to a corrugated rubber pipe. Heather fiddled with a control.

"Here," she said, and pushed the mask toward Barbary. "You can focus with this knob if you need to."

The image of the alien ship floated before her, a sharp, clear three-dimensional miniature, a jumble of spheres and cylinders, panels, struts, and irregularities, some with the hard-edged gleam of metal, some with the softer gloss of plastic, some with a rough and organic appearance, like tree bark. But for all Barbary knew, alien plastic looked like tree bark and their trees looked like steel. If they had trees, or plastic, or steel.

3

"Can you make it show Mick's raft?"

⚜ 203 ⚜

1 Since "A Meeting in Space" is an excerpt from the last part of the novel *Barbary,* students may be confused about the relationships between the characters or about other aspects of the story. They may want to stop at the end of page 202 and **sum up** Barbary's situation.

Students should **clarify** anything they didn't understand about the situation. They may not understand, for example, that the reason Barbary "floats" to the raft is that there is no gravity in the launch chamber. Encourage the students to ask questions about anything that confuses them.

2 If students are confused by the scene described here, they may want to **visualize** these objects in space: the sun, the earth, the moon, the space station. The illustrations on pages 204 and 205 may help them.

Students may need to **clarify** that Betelgeuse is a very bright star in the constellation of Orion.

3 Barbary reflects that on the aliens' planet plastic may look like tree bark and trees may look like steel. Encourage students to **wonder** about the various conditions under which life might exist on planets in other solar systems.

"That's harder," Heather said, "since I don't know what course Thea used. But I'll try." She bent over the mask, fiddling. "Hey, Barbary," she said.

"Yeah?"

"Were you really going to come out here all by yourself?"

"I guess so. I couldn't think of anything else to do."

"That was brave."

"Dumb, though," Barbary said. She never would have remembered the right controls, and she would have headed off in the wrong direction. "I guess you would have had to come out and get me and Mick both."

"Still, it was brave."

"Did you find Mick yet?" Barbary asked, embarrassed.

"Unh-uh, not yet."

204

"Can we use his transmitter?"

Heather glanced up, frowning.

"We could," she said, "but we can't, if you see what I mean. We'd have to use the computer, and if we turn it on it would probably lock our controls and take us home. But we'll find him, don't worry."

"Okay," Barbary said. "How long before we catch up to him, do you think?"

"It sort of depends on how fast the raft went out and how rapidly it was accelerating. Which I don't know. But it couldn't have been too fast, or it would use up all its fuel before it got to the ship. Then it wouldn't be able to maneuver, so it would just fly by very fast. Without much time to take pictures. So it has to be going slowly, instead. Anyway,

205

4

we ought to catch up within a couple of hours. I don't want *us* to run out of fuel—and I don't want to get going so fast that we go right past without seeing Mick."

The raft hummed through silent space. Barbary kept expecting the stars to change, to appear to grow closer as the raft traveled toward them. But the stars were so distant that she would have to travel for years and years before even a few of them looked any closer or appeared to move, and even then they would still be an enormous distance away.

"Heather . . . "

"Yeah?"

"Thanks for coming with me," she said.

"Hey," Heather said, her cheerfulness touched with bravado. "What are sisters for?"

A red light on the control panel blinked on.

"Uh-oh," Heather said.

"What is it?"

"Radio transmission. Somebody from the station calling us. With orders to come back, probably."

They stared at the light. Heather reached for the radio headset.

Barbary grabbed Heather's hand. "If you answer them, they'll just try to persuade us to turn around."

"But we ought to at least tell them that it's us out here," Heather said.

"They probably already know. If they don't, maybe we ought to wait until they figure it out."

"Yoshi will be worried," Heather said sadly, "when he comes home, and he can't find us."

206

"We're going to have to transmit a message to the aliens anyway," Barbary said. "To tell them we don't mean to bother them, but Mick is in the first raft and we're coming out to rescue him. When we do that, they'll hear us back in Atlantis."

"Uh-huh." Heather gazed into the scanner. "I wonder why they don't want us to come near them? I wonder what they do when somebody does?"

"I guess they could blow us up with death-rays," Barbary said. "But that doesn't seem too civilized."

"And how are we going to explain cats to them? I wonder if they have pets? I wonder what they look like?"

"Maybe they're big cats themselves, like the aliens in *Jenny and the Spaceship*," Barbary said. "Did you read that?"

"Big *cats?*" Heather said. "That's silly, Barbary. The aliens come from some other star system. They evolved on a whole different planet. They probably don't even have the same chemistry we do. They might breathe cyanide or methane or something. Big *cats?*"

"Okay, okay, forget it," Barbary said. "It was just a book."

The radio light continued to glow. To Barbary, it seemed to be getting brighter and brighter, more and more insistent.

Heather finally put on the headset. When she turned on the radio, she spoke before a transmission from Atlantis could come through.

"Raft to alien ship, raft to alien ship. Um . . . hi. My sister Barbary and I—I'm Heather—are trying to rescue a . . . a sort of friend of ours who got stuck in the first raft by mistake. Now we can't make the raft turn around, so we have to catch up to it to get him." She hesitated. "Please don't be mad or anything. Over and out."

207

4 Students might want to stop at this point and **make predictions** about what might happen next in the story. Remind them that any predictions should be based on evidence in the part of the story they have already read.

In the instant between the time Heather stopped transmitting and turned off the radio, the receiver burst into noise.

"—do you hear me? You girls get back here right now, or—"

Barbary recognized the voice of the vice president.

Heather clicked off the radio.

"He sounded pretty mad," she said. "I guess now they'll tell Yoshi where we are."

"Heather, what if the aliens try to call us? We won't be able to hear them, if we don't leave the radio turned on."

Heather raised one eyebrow and flicked the switch again.

"—return immediately, and you won't be punished. But if—"

She turned it off.

She shrugged cheerfully. "We wouldn't be able to hear the aliens anyway, with Atlantis broadcasting nonstop at us, unless the aliens just blasted through their signal. I'll try later—maybe the vice president will get tired of yelling at us."

"What do we do now?"

"We just wait," Heather said. "I'll keep looking for Mickey's raft. When we find it we'll know better what we need to do and how long it'll take."

"Let me help look," Barbary said.

"Okay."

Heather showed her how to search the star-field for anomalies. At first glance, they looked like stars. But if one looked at an anomaly at two different times, the bright speck would have moved in relation to the real stars. The scanner could save an image and display it alternately with a later view of the same area. An anomaly would blink from one

place on the image to another, and the human eye could see the difference. A computer could, too, but it took processing time or a lot of memory, or both, to do what a person could do in an instant.

"Astronomers used to discover new planets and comets and things this way," Heather said. "You can also search by turning up the magnification, but that means you can only see a little bit of space at once. So unless you got really lucky, you'd spend days and days trying to find what you were looking for."

Barbary scanned for the alien ship. When she finally found it she felt pleased with herself, until she remembered how easily Heather had done the same thing.

"Shouldn't Mick's raft be right in between us and the alien ship?" Barbary asked.

"It could be," Heather said. "But it isn't. Nothing moves in straight lines in space, not when there are gravity fields to affect your course. Besides, I'm sure Thea didn't send her camera on a direct line to where the ship is now. She probably planned to arc around it. I mean, she wouldn't want to run into it. There's no way to tell exactly what course she chose. We could call and ask her—"

"As if she'd tell us—"

"She would. But I don't think the VIPs would let her."

"So we just keep looking?"

"Yeah."

Barbary let Heather have the scanner. She knew Heather could find Mick about a hundred times faster than she could.

"What's it like back on earth?" Heather said abruptly, without looking up. "What's it like to visit a farm, or camp out in the wilderness?" She waited quite a while, as Barbary tried to

figure out how to answer her. Finally Heather said in a small voice, "Never mind. I didn't mean to pry."

"It's okay," Barbary said. "It isn't that. It's just a hard question to answer. There are so many different places and different things to see—only I haven't seen most of them. It's hard to get a permit to go out in the wilderness, and you need a lot of equipment, and that costs money. Nobody I knew ever did it."

"What about farms? Did you see cows and horses and stuff?"

"I've never been on a farm, either. There weren't any near where I lived, and they aren't like in movies. They're all automated. Big machines run them. Some of them are covered with plastic to keep the water and the heat in. A couple years ago I snuck off to a zoo. I saw a cow then. It looked kind of bored and dumb. Horses are prettier, but hardly anybody on farms has them anymore. Mostly, rich people keep them to ride."

"How about an ocean?"

"I never saw that, either."

"Oh."

"I wish I could tell you . . ."

"That's all right. I've talked to other people about it, and I've seen pictures and tapes. But I can't figure out what it would be like to see it myself."

"You know, Heather," Barbary said, "an awful lot of people talk about going to the mountains, or going to the ocean, but hardly anybody ever did it. Not anybody I knew, anyway."

"But they could have gone if they wanted."

"Yeah. They could have."

"I usually don't care. But sometimes I wish I could go see the mountains or the ocean, or blue sky."

"Your sky is prettier."

"I bet a blue one would be easier to find a raft in." Heather raised her head from the scanner. She looked exhausted. She had dark circles under her eyes. Barbary felt afraid for her.

"Want me to look?" Barbary asked.

"I'll do it a while longer, then it'll be your turn," Heather said. She stretched, and hunched and relaxed her shoulders a couple of times. "I don't suppose you brought along any sandwiches or anything, did you?"

"No," Barbary said. "I didn't even think of it."

"Oh, well. There are some rations in the survival ball. But they're pretty boring. Probably we should wait till we're really hungry before we use them."

Barbary thought she would get sick if she tried to eat. She felt empty and scared.

Heather bent over the scanner once more. "Hey! Look at this!"

Barbary peered into the scanner.

"I just see stars."

"Keep looking." Heather touched the blink control.

In the center of the picture, one of the bright points jumped.

"Is that Mick?"

"Has to be," Heather said.

Barbary flashed the control again; again the image jumped.

"Now zoom in."

Barbary did so. The raft appeared. The airless distance of space transmitted details sharp and clear, but all she could find was the silver and plastic shape of the raft, and the shadows of Thea's contraption inside. Nothing moved.

"There it is!" she said. She magnified it even more. "I don't see Mick though."

"Let me look."

Heather teased the scanner controls.

"Can you see him?"

"Umm . . . no," Heather said. "I can't. But there's a lot of stuff in there. He'd practically have to sit on top of it for me to find him."

"He's probably sitting under it," Barbary said. "Yowling. Or growling like a wildcat."

Heather laughed. "I bet you're right."

Barbary felt both overjoyed and terrified. Heather had found Mick—but Barbary would not be able to stop worrying till she saw for herself that he was all right.

"Where is he?" she asked. "Right in front of us?"

"No, he's kind of over to the side." Heather pointed. "Thea must have planned to circle all the way around the alien ship, then follow it as far as she could. I'm going to have to turn us pretty hard. Are you strapped in?"

"Uh-huh. How long will it take to get there?"

"A couple of hours, maybe. I'm just guessing, though."

"How do we get him when we get there?"

"We can't. There's no safe way to open a raft in space unless everybody inside is in a space suit or a survival ball, and Mick couldn't get in one by himself. So we'll stick out our claws and grab his raft and turn us both around, and go back."

"Oh," Barbary said. She had been hoping there was some way of getting from one raft to another. But at least she would be able to look inside and see Mick.

"Hang on."

The raft plunged into free fall as Heather cut the acceleration. Barbary flung her hands out before her, for it really did

213

feel as if she were falling. The steering rocket flared on, the stars swung, and the rocket on the other side counteracted their spin. Now, Barbary knew, they were traveling in the same direction as before, but Heather had turned the raft a few degrees to the left.

Heather applied some thrust to the raft. The new acceleration would add to their previous velocity, changing their direction and speed so they would be heading more nearly toward Mickey.

Getting to the right spot in space took a lot of care and calculation. It would have been much easier if they could have flown the raft like an airplane, or like a spaceship in a movie, banking into turns and *swooshing* from place to place. But in a vacuum, without any air, ships could not bank into turns or *swoosh*.

⑤ "I don't want to kill any more velocity than I have to," Heather said. "It takes too much fuel. So I'll probably have to correct our course a bunch of times. But for now we're sort of heading for where Mick ought to be when we get there."

Barbary tried to figure out how that worked. It sounded suspiciously like a math word problem, which she had never been very good at. She had never seen the point of figuring out when two trains would pass each other when the only trains left were tourist attractions that she had never ridden anyway. But being able to figure out in her head how to meet another raft in space would be useful. She wished she had paid more attention to word problems in school, and she wondered if it was too late for her to learn how to do what Heather could do.

🌾 214 🌾

"Hey, Heather—Heather!"

Heather jerked up from the scanner, blinking and confused.

"Huh? What? I'm awake!" She stopped, abashed.

"No, you're not," Barbary said. "You fell asleep sitting up! Heather . . . look . . . maybe . . ." With a shock, she realized how much danger she and Mick had put Heather in.

"Oh, no!" Heather said. "Don't even say it! We're not turning around and going back like we just came out here to make trouble and then lost our nerve!"

Barbary hunched in her seat. She felt miserable.

"I'm afraid you're going to get sick," she said.

"I'm okay! I'm just a little tired!" Heather snapped. Her expression softened. "Look," she said. "I don't have to do anything for a while. I could take a nap, and you could keep an eye on the scanner. I'll set it so the image of Mick's raft will get closer and closer to the center till we intercept it. If it goes past the center of the focus, wake me up to correct the course." She showed Barbary the faint band of color outlining a square in the center of the scanner. The other raft lay at the left edge of the screen; it moved, almost imperceptibly, centerward.

"That sounds easy enough," Barbary said.

Heather grinned. "It's a lot easier than trying to sleep in a raft, that's for sure." She squirmed around, trying to get comfortable.

"Lie down crosswise and put your head in my lap," Barbary said. "I'll try not to bonk you with the scanner."

"Okay."

🌾 215 🌾

⑤ Students may want to **clarify** some of the scientific information in this part of the story: why stars are so bright away from the earth's atmosphere, why nothing moves in a straight line in space, why Barbary and Heather can't get out of their raft in space. Encourage the students to **wonder** about these things, and suggest sources of information if they want to find out more.

Barbary took off her jacket and tucked it around Heather's shoulders. Heather curled up under it, hiding her eyes from the light of the control panel. Her position still did not look very comfortable, but within a few minutes she was fast asleep.

6

Barbary looked around. Far behind her, spinning, lit from behind, the station grew smaller. The earth and the moon each showed only a slender crescent of light, for Barbary was on their night sides. The raft's automatic shield hid the sun and prevented it from blinding her.

Even in the observation bubble of the transport ship, she had never felt so alone and so remote. Beauty surrounded her, a beauty too distant and too enormous for her ever to reach or comprehend. She gazed out at the stars for a very long time, till she realized how long she had been staring. She quickly grabbed the scanner. To her relief, the other raft still lay within the field, halfway to the center of the focus.

Barbary increased the magnification, but that sent the raft all the way off the screen. If she moved the focus, she might not get it back to the place where Heather had aimed it. That also meant she could not use the scanner to find the alien ship, to see if it was doing anything threatening or even simply different.

Heather slept on. The radio receiver's light never flickered from its brilliant red. Trying to keep her attention on the scanner, Barbary forced herself to remain calm. But worry raced through her mind. She began to wonder if perhaps the aliens, and not the space station, might be trying to

216

call the raft: to tell her they understood, everything was all right; to tell her they did not understand, please try to explain more clearly; or to tell her they understood, but they did not believe her and did not trust her and did not care anyway, and were going to shoot both rafts with death-rays.

She put on the headset and turned on the radio and the transmitter.

"This is the second raft calling, in case you didn't hear us before." She whispered, trying not to wake Heather. "We're coming out to rescue the first raft so it won't bother you. It's a mistake that it's out here, and we're really sorry. We're trying to fix things."

She turned off the transmitter, leaving the channel open for just a moment.

"Barbary!" Yoshi said. "Is Heather all right?"

"You two turn around and—"

The vice president's voice faded as Barbary cut the power to the radio without replying. She would have liked to reassure Yoshi, but she was afraid to get into a fight with any of the adults, especially Yoshi. Yoshi could say things that would make her want to turn around and go back, so he would not be so disappointed with her.

She glanced behind the raft. The science station was a bright turning toy, part lit, part shadowed, spinning between the more distant crescents of the earth and the moon.

Before her, space lay beautiful but still. Somehow the stars reminded her of snow early in the morning, before dawn, in a quiet, windless winter. She peered into the scanner to reassure herself that the other raft was still there. She squinted, search-

217

6 If your class stopped reading here and is now about to begin again, invite volunteers to **sum up** what has happened up to this point in the story before the class reads the remainder of the selection.

ing for any sign of Mick. But his raft drifted onward, showing no signs of life.

She yawned, then shook her head to wake herself up. She could not go to sleep, though Heather's steady breathing in the silence of the little ship had a <u>hypnotic</u> effect. She yawned again. She pinched herself, hard.

A glimmer of light on metal caught her gaze.

Off to the left, far away but as clear as a close-up model, Mick's raft crept along. Now that she had found it, Barbary did not understand how she could have failed to see it for so long. She could tell it was in motion; she could tell her own raft was approaching it, slowly and at a tangent. In the scanner, the image had touched the outer edge of the focus square.

She started to touch Heather's shoulder, but decided against waking her yet. They still had quite a way to go before their raft intercepted Mick's, and Heather needed the rest.

Still careful not to change the direction of the scanner, Barbary increased the magnification. Now she could see part of the raft in the center of the frame. But the transparent roof had not yet come into view. Barbary stared at the image, willing it to move faster so she could look inside. It crept onto the screen, appearing to move sideways because of its <u>orientation</u> and because she was approaching it from behind and to one side. She wished she could see its front. Often, when Mick had ridden in a car, he crouched up front looking through the windshield. But she supposed he would have trouble crouching on the dashboard of a raft, without any gravity.

Something glided through the picture.

Her heart pounding with excitement, Barbary bent closer over the scanner.

❧ 218 ❧

"Mick," she whispered, "hey, come past again, okay?" The portion of the image taken up by transparent raft roof increased. She held her breath.

As if he knew she was coming after him, Mick brought himself up short against the plastic and peered directly at her. He opened his mouth wide. If they had not been separated by the vacuum of space, she would have heard his plaintive yowl.

"Okay," she said, laughing with relief. "I'm coming to get you, you dumb cat."

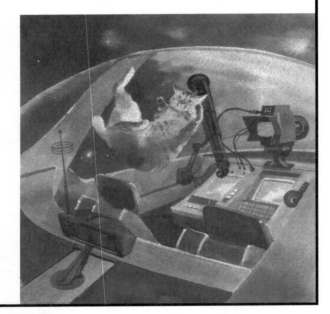

The scanner grew foggy. She had come so close to crying that she had misted up the mask. She sat up and reached into it to rub away the condensation with her sleeve. She glanced outside to check the position of Mick's raft.

To her shock, it—and Mick, looking at her—lay no more than twenty meters away. She was gaining on it.

"Heather!" she cried.

She pushed the scanner out of the way and pulled her jacket off Heather's shoulders. She shook her, but Heather remained sound asleep.

"Heather, come on!"

Barbary did not intend to come this far and lose Mick. She did not know if they could turn around and come back for him if they passed his raft. She jammed her hands into the grasps of the claw controls. She reached out; the grapples extended from beneath the raft. She opened her fingers and closed them; the claws followed her motion.

The distance between the rafts diminished to ten meters, then to five.

Barbary reminded herself again and again that the key to doing anything in space was to do it calmly and smoothly. She did not feel calm. She felt terrified and ignorant. Sweat rolled into her eyes. She could not take her hands from the grasps, and she was afraid to take her gaze off the other raft long enough to lean down and rub her forehead on her sleeve.

"Heather—!"

Even if Heather woke now, there was no time for her to take over the controls. As her raft approached Mick's, so much faster than it had seemed to be moving when they were far away, Barbary grabbed for it.

❧ 220 ❧

As she clenched her fingers in the grappler controls, the two rafts came together with a tremendous, wrenching *clang*. Barbary gasped, fearing she had rammed hard enough to breach the hull of Mick's raft or her own. The ships began a slow tumble. Around them, the stars spun. Barbary squeezed her eyes tight shut. That was even worse. She opened her eyes again. The claws kept the two vehicles clamped tight together. She could no longer see Mick, for he was underneath her. But as the reverberations of the crash faded, she heard, transmitted through the hulls, Mick's angry, objecting howl.

She laughed with relief. The motion of the rafts was beginning to make her dizzy, though, and the rafts would continue to tumble till someone used the steering rockets to counteract the spiraling twist. Heather would know how to do it.

"Hey, Heather—"

Usually when Heather wanted to sleep some more, she muttered and pulled her blanket over her head. This time, she lay still.

"Heather?"

Heather's hands felt cold as ice and her skin was very pale. Frightened, Barbary leaned down and put her ear to her sister's chest. Her heartbeat sounded weak and irregular. Barbary wished she knew what it was supposed to sound like, or what it usually sounded like.

Afraid to try to wake her again, Barbary covered her with her jacket and pillowed Heather's head in her lap.

"It's okay," she said. "I got Mick, I can get us back." She studied the controls. She would have to figure out how to make the ship stop tumbling, then turn it around. She wished she did not feel so dizzy—

❧ 221 ❧

Then she thought, You dummy! If you turn on the radio and the computer, back at Atlantis they'll send out the signal to bring us back. It's what they've wanted all along!

She threw the two switches, and got ready to be bawled out. The radio remained silent.

As the raft rotated, an enormous shape slid past the roof.

The rotation of the raft slowed, though Barbary felt no vibration from the steering rockets.

The huge shape slid into view again, the rotation stopped, and Barbary found herself gazing through the roof at the looming alien ship.

Barbary put her arms across Heather as if she could protect her.

7 Slowly, the raft moved toward the irregular, multicolored hull.

The alien ship drew the raft closer, growing larger and larger till its expanse of incomprehensible shapes stretched as far as Barbary could see.

Trembling, she hugged Heather closer. She wrapped her jacket closer around her sister's shoulders, trying to keep her warm. The raft slid between two irregular projections from the alien ship's hull: a <u>spire</u> taller than any building on earth, covered with delicate strands and symbols, and a wavy, faceted shape resembling the crystals that form around a string suspended in a supersaturated solution of sugar and water.

Roof first, Barbary's raft floated toward a wide black slash in the ship's hull. If she did not keep telling herself she was going "up," she felt as if she were falling, upside down and in slow motion.

Intense darkness closed in around her.

The raft's control panel spread a ghostly light on Heather's pale face and Barbary's hands. She heard the echo of Mick's plaintive <u>miaow</u>, and the feathery whisper of Heather's breath.

A faint chime rang, growing louder and closer. Barbary blinked, trying to figure out if she only imagined light outside

222

7 Some students may need to **clarify** why the rafts would tumble in space until corrected by rockets or some other force. If necessary, remind them that, in space, there is no gravity to stop the ships from tumbling.

Because so much happened in the previous passage, students may want to **sum up** the action and predict what will happen to Barbary, Heather, and Mick now. Remind the students to check their earlier predictions to see if they were correct.

the raft, or if she were seeing a glow as gentle as dawn. The ringing reached a pleasant level and remained there, while the light brightened till Barbary could see. She had weight as well, but she had not noticed when the gravity appeared. She felt as if she weighed as much as she did on earth, and this increased her concern for Heather.

Her raft hung in a round room whose surface glistened like mother-of-pearl. The columns supporting the ceiling looked like frozen waterfalls or translucent pillars of melted glass. She searched for the opening that had let her in, but it had closed or sealed itself up. From the wind-chime sound transmitted to her through the raft's body, she decided she must be surrounded by an atmosphere, but she did not know if it was oxygen or—as Heather had speculated—methane or cyanide. She had no way to tell whether it was safe to breathe, or poisonous.

Mick miaowed again, louder.

"It's okay, Mick," she said. She swallowed hard, trying to steady her voice. "It's going to be okay."

"Do you hear us?"

The radio spoke with the beautiful voice of the alien's first message to Atlantis.

"Yes," she whispered, her throat dry. "Can you hear me?"

"We sense you. Will you meet us?"

"I want to. I really do," Barbary said. "But I have to get Heather into zero gravity and back to the space

224

station. She's sick and I can't wake her up. The gravity's too strong for her here. Besides, all the important people are waiting to meet you, and they'll be really angry if I see you first."

"But," the voice said, "you have already seen us."

Barbary stared around the chamber, looking for creatures, great ugly things like the aliens in old movies, or small furry things like the aliens in books. They must be hiding behind the tall glass pillars.

The gravity faded till it was barely enough to give Barbary's surroundings a "down" and an "up."

"Is this gravity more comfortable for you?"

"Yes," Barbary said. "Thanks."

"We believed we calibrated your gravity correctly."

"You did," Barbary said. "At least it felt okay to me. But Heather . . . Heather has to live in lower gravity. Won't you let us go? She's sick! Anyway, I can't see you—" She stopped, amazed.

Though she had not seen them move, the crystal columns had come closer. They clustered around her. Their rigid forms remained upright, yet they gave the impression of bending down like a group of worried aunts or friendly trees. A long row of crystalline fibers grew along the side of each column. The fibers quivered rapidly, vibrating against and stroking the main body of each being, producing the wind-chime voices.

"Oh," she said. "Oh. I do see you. You're beautiful!"

"We will loose your craft if you wish," the voice on the radio said. "But our ship will reach your habitat before your vessel could fly to it, and here the gravity can be controlled."

"Can you hurry? I'm really worried about Heather."

"We will hurry."

225

Barbary listened to Heather's rapid, irregular heartbeat.

"Can't you help her?" she said to the aliens. She remembered all the movies she had seen where people got hurt and aliens healed them. "Can't you make her well? Aliens are supposed to be able to make people well!"

"But we have only just met you," one of the aliens said, perplexed and regretful. "We know little of your physiology. Perhaps in a few decades, if you wish us to study you . . ."

Barbary thought she should have learned by now not to expect anything to work the way it did in books or movies. She leaned over Heather again, willing her to awaken.

Heather's eyelids fluttered.

"Barbary . . . ?"

Heather opened her eyes. She sounded weak, confused, and tired.

"It's okay, Heather. Anyway, I think it is—what about you?"

"I feel kind of awful. What happened?"

"We're on the alien ship."

A spark of excitement brought some of the color back to her sister's cheeks. She struggled to a sitting position.

"Are there aliens?" Heather whispered. She was shivering. Barbary chafed her cold hands and helped her put on the jacket.

"There are other beings," the gentle voice said. "We hope not to be alien, one to the other, for very long. Will you meet us?"

"Can we breathe your air?" Heather hugged the jacket around her.

 226

"It is not our air. We do not use air. It is your air. You should find it life-sustaining, uninfectious, and sufficiently warm to maintain you."

Barbary gingerly cracked the seal of the roof-hatch. Warm, fresh air filled the raft. Heather took a deep breath. Her shivering eased.

"If you join us," a voice said, no longer from the radio but from one of the crystalline beings, "then we may rotate your vehicles and release the small person in the lower craft. It does not respond to our communications in an intelligible fashion, and it appears to be quite perturbed."

Barbary could not help it: she laughed. Heather managed to smile. Barbary picked her up—her weight was insignificant in this gravity—and carried her from the raft. The aliens made a spot among them for her; they slid across the mother-of-pearl floor as if, like starfish, they had thousands of tiny sucker-feet at their bases. The floor gave off a comforting warmth. Barbary laid Heather on the yielding surface.

"I'm okay, I really am," Heather said. She tried to sit up, but she was still weak. Barbary helped her, letting Heather lean back against her. Heather gazed at the aliens. "Holy cow."

Mick's furry form hurtled across the space between the rafts and Barbary. He landed against her with all four feet extended and stopped himself by hooking his claws into her shirt. Somehow he managed to do it without touching her skin with his claws. He burrowed his head against her, and she wrapped her arms around him and laid her cheek against his soft fur.

"Boy, Mick," she whispered, "did you cause a lot of trouble." **8**

227

---

8 Students might want to **sum up** the final part of the selection and **notice whether predictions they made were correct.**

Students may understand this scene better if they **visualize** it.

Students might also comment on the way the aliens speak to Barbary and Heather. Their English is very formal and each word seems to have a very specific meaning. You might encourage students to **wonder** about the aliens' language and about how they learned English.

Discussing Strategy Use

Encourage the students to share any problems they had while reading "A Meeting in Space." If they used the **summing-up, predicting,** or **visualizing** strategies while reading, ask them to share how these strategies helped them to understand or enjoy the story.

* EXPLORING THROUGH DISCUSSION

Reflecting on the Selection
Whole-Group Discussion

The whole group discusses the selection and any personal thoughts, reactions, or questions that it raises. During this time, students also **return to the clues, problems, and wonderings** they noted on the board during browsing.

TEACHING TIP As students learn more about how to read, class discussion should be more and more student-directed and less and less teacher-directed.

Assessment

To assess the students' understanding of the text, engage them in a discussion to determine whether they have grasped the following ideas:
- why Barbary found it difficult to pilot the space raft
- how Barbary's preconceived ideas about the aliens compared with what the aliens were really like
- how the "future" earth that Barbary described is different from earth as we know it today

Response Journal

Students may wish to record their personal responses to the selection.

Exploring Concepts Within the Selection
Small-Group Discussion

Small groups discuss the relationship of the selection to the explorable concepts. Circulate among the groups and observe the discussions. Refer the students to the Concept Board and the Question Board to keep them focused on their original ideas about astronomy.

Sharing Ideas About Explorable Concepts

Have the groups **report** and **discuss** their **ideas** with the rest of the class. It is crucial that the students' ideas determine this discussion.
- Students may point out that space-research stations such as Atlantis would add greatly to our knowledge of astronomy.
- Students may acknowledge that life forms from another planet would not necessarily resemble earth life in any way.
- Students may notice that for human beings to live somewhere other than earth would require a great many physical adjustments.

TIP FOR ENGLISH LANGUAGE LEARNERS

To clarify their understanding of the selection, encourage English Language Learners to explain or sum up the main ideas of the selection to themselves and then to their classmates.

As these ideas and others are stated, have the students **add them to** the **Question Board** or the **Concept Board**.

Exploring Concepts Across Selections

Students may **make connections with other selections** in this unit.
- The students may notice that Barbary's raft operates on much the same principle as the Voyager space probes do.
- The students may point out that Barbary was willing to face grave danger to rescue her cat, just as Yudistira in "The Great Dog" chose to renounce heaven rather than betray his dog.

Recording Ideas

As students complete the above discussions, ask them to **sum up what they have learned from their conversations and to tell how they might use this information** in further explorations. Any special information or insights may be recorded on the **Concept Board**. Any further questions that they would like to think about, pursue, or investigate may be recorded on the **Question Board**. They may want to discuss

Evaluating Discussions

"Voyager to the Planets" by Necia Apfel

"A Meeting in Space" by Vonda N. McIntyre

Stars by Seymour Simon

Unit 2/Astronomy   EN 25

Explorer's Notebook, page 25

the progress that has been made on their questions. They may also want to cross out any questions that no longer warrant consideration.

❯ Encourage the students to record their findings on page 25 of the Explorer's Notebook.

2 READING WITH A WRITER'S EYE

MINILESSONS

Writer's Craft: Genre—Science Fiction

Ask the students to discuss what they know about science fiction. They should know at least that **science fiction stories include events that are not possible in our world today.** They should also understand that **science fiction** is different from other types of fantasy because it **suggests** that as science advances, the **things which are impossible today could become possible in the future.**

Really good writers of science fiction can make their readers believe that their stories could actually happen someday. There are rules that science-fiction writers follow to help their readers believe. One of the most important rules is that, for the most part, **the story should seem consistent with the real world.** This means that the writer doesn't include unrealistic concepts without offering a plausible explanation for them. Another way to help the reader believe that the ideas in the story could someday be possible is to **describe future technological procedures realistically.**

Vonda McIntyre follows all of these rules in "A Meeting in Space." Although there are no space stations orbiting earth today, most readers can easily picture one in the future. And with the billions of stars in the universe, it is easy to imagine other beings coming to visit our earth. **This makes her story consistent with the real world.**

McIntyre also **describes technical procedures realistically.** On **page 203** she describes the procedures that Barbary's friend, Heather, uses to guide their launch to the probe. Although the geometry is not easy to picture, **the explanation seems reasonable, and this adds to the realism of the story.**

Selective Reading: Focus on Genre— Science Fiction

Have the students go back to "A Meeting in Space" and look for other instances in which McIntyre makes her science fiction believable for her readers. Encourage volunteers to read aloud and explain the examples that they find. Other examples include the following:

- page 203: the operation of the telescopic device
- page 205: the realistic explanation of why the first raft would not have been traveling too fast
- page 208: the description of the procedure for using "anomalies" to locate objects in space
- page 210: Barbary's description of zoos and farms on earth
- page 214: the description of how spacecraft had to be maneuvered outside of gravity and atmosphere

Independent Practice: Genre—Science Fiction

➤ Have the students work in small groups to discuss and complete Reading/Writing Connection, page 19. Distribute Reproducible Master 32, listing characteristics of science fiction, and have the students insert it in the Genres section of their Writer's Notebook.

Writer's Craft: Dialogue

Have the students discuss how writers use dialogue in stories. They should understand that dialogue serves several purposes in writing. By **using dialogue, a writer makes his or her readers feel as though they are witnessing a story as it happens** rather than hearing about it afterwards. For example, when Barbary talks to the computer the reader gets a feeling that he or she is in the raft with Barbary.

Dialogue can be used to move the action of a story along quickly. For example, on page 202, when Heather joins Barbary in the raft, their conversation explains how Heather found out that Barbary was about to take off in the raft ("Your computer told me part of it, and I figured out the rest"), and it offers an explanation of why the probe with the camera doesn't respond to remote commands from the spaceship ("Mick probably knocked loose some of the connections").

Finally, **dialogue helps the writer reveal things about the characters** who are speaking as well as the characters or things that they are talking about. For example, in the discussion on page 204, Heather tells

Selection-Based Practice

"A Meeting in Space"

Science Fiction

In "A Meeting in Space," Vonda McIntyre makes her story more believable by keeping story events consistent with the way things happen in the real world and by describing future technology in a realistic manner. Think about other science fiction stories you have read. How did the writers of these stories make you believe that the events they describe could happen someday? Write the title of a story, tell why it could not happen today, and describe one way the writer makes you believe it could happen someday.

Title: _____

Why the story couldn't happen today: _____

_____

How the writer makes the story seem possible someday: _____

_____

_____

Title: _____

Why the story couldn't happen today: _____

_____

How the writer makes the story seem possible someday: _____

_____

_____

Title: _____

Why the story couldn't happen today: _____

_____

How the writer makes the story seem possible someday: _____

_____

_____

Unit 2/Astronomy

Genre

R/WC 19

Reading/Writing Connection, page 19

Genre—Science Fiction

Characteristics of science fiction:
- The plot concerns events, conditions, or discoveries that are not possible in the real world today.
- The plot suggests that scientific or technological advancements could make such things possible in the future.

Some rules for writing good science fiction:
- Make the plot, setting, and characters believable, and keep them believable and consistent throughout the story.
- Describe future scientific and technological advancements realistically—be sure they do not defy known scientific facts or laws of nature.
- Provide logical explanations for all new ideas and events presented in the story.

Here are some of my own thoughts and observations about science fiction:

_____

_____

_____

_____

_____

_____

_____

_____

_____

_____

_____

_____

_____

_____

_____

RM 32

Writer's Notebook: Genres

Reproducible Master 32

Barbary that she is brave because she was willing to go out alone after Mick. This indicates not only that Barbary is brave, but also that Heather admires Barbary. The reader learns something about both girls. When Barbary admits that the idea was dumb, the reader learns that she is able to view herself objectively.

Selective Reading: Focus on Dialogue

Have the students go back to "A Meeting in Space" and find other examples of how McIntyre uses dialogue. Encourage volunteers to read and explain the examples they find.

Dialogue for characterization
- page 207: This exchange shows that Heather has a more practical idea of what the aliens might look like than does Barbary.
- page 215: This exchange shows that Barbary worries about Heather and that Heather is not one to give up on something she has started even if it is dangerous for her.
- page 224: The first words from the aliens indicate that they are friendly.

Dialogue for plot development
- page 211: The girls finally spot the raft with Mick aboard.
- page 214: Heather explains how she directed the girls' raft toward the raft that carries Mick.

Selection-Based Practice

- page 225: The aliens indicate that their ship is en route to the space station.

Independent Practice: Dialogue

❯ Have the students work in small groups to discuss and complete Reading/Writing Connection, page 20.

WRITING

Linking Reading to Writing

Encourage students to look through their writing folders for pieces of fiction that could be improved by the addition of dialogue. Invite volunteers to read the original and the revised versions to the rest of the class and to explain why they think the dialogue improved the piece.

✱ Writing Process

After reading "A Meeting in Space," some students may want to start their own science fiction pieces. Allow time for them to form small groups and brainstorm for prewriting ideas.

TIP FOR ENGLISH LANGUAGE LEARNERS

Encourage English Language Learners to try out their dialogue. Listening to an audience respond helps develop the capacity to revise as students work toward a more finished version.

Reading/Writing Connection, page 20

"A Meeting in Space"

Dialogue

In "A Meeting in Space," Vonda McIntyre uses dialogue to make readers feel as if they are present as the story unfolds, to reveal things about the character who is talking, or to move the plot along. Look back at other stories that you have read that contain dialogue. Write the title of the story, the pages on which the dialogue appears, and the purpose the dialogue serves.

Story title: _____
Purpose the dialogue serves: _____
_____
_____ Page: _____

Story title: _____
Purpose the dialogue serves: _____
_____
_____ Page: _____

Story title: _____
Purpose the dialogue serves: _____
_____
_____ Page: _____

Story title: _____
Purpose the dialogue serves: _____
_____
_____ Page: _____

Look back at this page for examples when you need help using dialogue in your writing.

Name

Dialogue
20 R/WC   Astronomy/Unit 2

VOCABULARY

Concept-related words in this selection include the following: **maneuver, rotation, velocity, contraption, kaleidoscope, corrugated, three-dimensional, supersaturated, anomalies, reverberations, physiology**

Have **Vocabulary Exploration forms, Reproducible Master 14,** available for students who request them. For additional opportunities to build vocabulary, see **Teacher Tool Card 75.**

VOCABULARY TIP Getting the students to use new words in speech and in writing is a goal of vocabulary instruction. Noticing students' efforts in speaking and writing helps build a classroom environment conducive to vocabulary development.

3 GUIDED AND INDEPENDENT EXPLORATION

EXPLORING CONCEPTS BEYOND THE TEXT

Guided Exploration

The following activities do not have to be completed within the days devoted to this lesson.

Invite the students to discuss other works of science fiction they have read. Some students may wish to evaluate their previous science-fiction reading according to criteria given in the minilesson. Interested students can compile a bibliography of their favorite science-fiction novels and stories to share with the class. Encourage them to post the bibliography on the **Concept Board.**

Research Cycle

Meet with the whole class as needed for the following purposes:
- to arrange schedules and update calendars
- to discuss problems that students are encountering with their research
- to hear preliminary presentations and discussions of interesting findings
- to arrange more formal presentations of students' research
- to provide guidance to ensure that groups progress through phases of the Research Cycle—obtaining information; revising problems, conjectures, needs, and plans (perhaps with input resulting from a presentation to the class); and proceeding to a further cycle of problem, conjecture, and so forth

✱Exploring Through Research

*INDEPENDENT WORKSHOP
Building a Community of Scholars

Student-Directed Reading, Writing, and Discussion

Research Cycle Meet with the whole class, as needed, to assess the progress of each research group. By this time, most groups should be revising any written work they intend to present.

Additional Opportunities for Independent Reading, Writing, and Cross-curricular Activities

✱ Reading Roundtable

Some students may choose to read *Barbary,* the book from which "A Meeting in Space" was taken, or other books of science fiction. In their discussions of these books, remind them to use the criteria for science fiction that they have formulated.

✱ Writing Seminar

If your class is using the optional Writer's Handbook, students should be encouraged to use it to help them as they write their science fiction stories or other pieces.

Cross-curricular Activity

The following Cross-curricular Activity Card in the Student Toolbox is appropriate for this selection:

• 2 Art—Making Sets for a Puppet Show

Making Sets for a Puppet Show
Use after "A Meeting in Space"

2
Art

Build a puppet theater with sets for acting out science-fiction stories. Library books will give you ideas for many different types of puppet theaters and puppets. For acting out the scenes from "A Meeting in Space," build the space raft and the alien ship.

Make puppets for Barbary, Heather, Mick, and the aliens. Act out all of the parts yourself, using different voices for each character, or have a partner help you to present your show.

Make modifications in the sets and the puppets to act out other science-fiction stories from books, films, or television programs. Or write your own science-fiction play and use puppets to present it. *In designing sets for a science-fiction play, you must use your imagination as well as information about science and technology.*

Additional Opportunities for Solving Learning Problems

Tutorial

You might use this time to help individuals or small groups who have exhibited a need in any area. Encourage students to ask for help whenever they need it. The following aids are available in the Teacher Toolbox for your convenience.

• Writer's Craft/Reading: Genre—Science Fiction, Teacher Tool Card 6
• Writer's Craft/Reading: Using Dialogue in a Story, Teacher Tool Card 19
• Writer's Craft/Reading: Setting, Teacher Tool Card 14
• Grammar, Mechanics, and Usage: Using and Punctuating Dialogue, Teacher Tool Card 70

Assessment

Stars

1 READING THE SELECTION

INFORMATION FOR THE TEACHER

About the Selection

Beautiful photographs of nebulas, quasars, supernovas, and other stellar phenomena illuminate this exceptionally lucid text. Award-winning children's nonfiction author Seymour Simon presents a great deal of sophisticated and fascinating information in clear, simple language.

Link to the Unit Concepts

In *Stars,* pages 228–237, the importance of sophisticated tools in learning about the universe is underscored. Galileo's simple telescopes showed him that there are many, many more stars in the sky than can be seen with the naked eye. With the aid of high-powered telescopes, scientists have discovered not only what a mind-boggling number of stars there really are but also what stars are made of, how stars are born and how they die, and much more. Radio telescopes, like those the students read about in "Telescopes," have alerted astronomers to the existence of such stellar phenomena as pulsars and quasars. And photographs like those that accompany the text of *Stars* have been made possible by the use of cameras attached to high-powered telescopes. In fact, almost none of the information presented in *Stars* could have been discovered without the help of extremely sophisticated equipment.

In this selection author Seymour Simon also demonstrates how discovering and learning about one phenomenon can lead to further discoveries. The information that scientists have gathered in studying the stars is helping them learn more about how the universe itself began and developed. Most quasars, for instance, are so far away from earth that their light must travel for 10–15 billion years before it reaches us. In studying objects such as quasars, scientists get a glimpse of the universe as it was in its earliest stages.

LESSON OVERVIEW

Stars by Seymour Simon, pages 228–237

READING THE SELECTION

Materials
Student anthology, pp. 228–237
Explorer's Notebook, p. 25
Assessment Masters 1–2, 4

FYI
Learning Framework Card
- Setting Reading Goals and Expectations, 1A

READING WITH A WRITER'S EYE

Minilesson
Assessment

Materials
Reproducible Master 14

FYI
Teacher Tool Card
- Spelling and Vocabulary: Building Vocabulary, 75

GUIDED AND INDEPENDENT EXPLORATION

Materials
Home/School Connection 17

Independent Workshop

Optional Materials from Student Toolbox
Tradebook Connection Cards

Cross-curricular Activity Cards
- 3 Art—Drawing the Stars
- 9 Science—Understanding How Black Holes Form

NOTES

Asterisks (*) throughout the lesson indicate learning frameworks. Learning Framework Cards and Teacher Tool Cards can be found in the Teacher Toolbox.

About the
Author

Seymour Simon, who spent twenty years teaching science in New York City public schools, has written over one hundred science books for children. His interest in astronomy began during his childhood, when he was an amateur astronomer and the president of the Junior Astronomy Club at the Museum of Natural History in New York City.

Simon believes that it is important for children to begin reading about science at an early age: "If we want a literate citizenry, we have to start children on science books when they're young. They have no fear at a young age, and they will stay familiar with science all of their lives."

Stars is one of a series of photo-illustrated astronomy books that Simon has written for children. Some of the books are about individual planets; the final book in the series is about our solar system as a whole. Simon has also written a very useful manual on amateur stargazing. Students who enjoy *Stars* will probably appreciate Simon's other astronomy books. (Several books from the series appear in the bibliographies for this unit.)

INFORMATION FOR THE STUDENT

Tell the students that the selection they are about to read was written by Seymour Simon, and share some of the information and the quotation in About the Author.

* COGNITIVE AND RESPONSIVE READING

Activating Prior
Knowledge

Encourage the students to discuss anything they already know about stars.

Setting Reading
Goals and
Expectations

Even though this selection has been designated as an Assessment selection, the class will proceed as usual with the setting of reading goals and expectations: they will **browse** the selection and **use the clues/problems/wondering procedure.** For a review of the **browsing** procedure, see **Learning Framework Card 1A, Setting Reading Goals and Expectations.**

Recommen-
dations for
Reading the
Selection

Explain to the students that **they will read this selection to assess what they have learned about astronomy.** Place the students in small groups. Tell them that they will decide in their small groups how they would like to read this selection. For example, the groups may choose to
- read silently but stay in groups, stopping to ask each other questions when they need help understanding
- alternate reading and summarizing a section at a time
- read silently on their own

Encourage the students to use the strategies that they think will best help them understand and appreciate the selection. They should feel free to refer to the **reading strategy posters** as needed. Encourage them to collaborate with others in their groups by asking questions when they

TEACHING TIP Ask students to demonstrate their own reading strategies.

encounter reading difficulties and by offering suggestions to others who need help.

➤ Distribute copies of Assessment Master 4, Concept Connections for unit 2, Astronomy, which you will find in the booklet Masters for Continuous Assessment. Tell the students that after reading the selection in their small groups, they will write responses on the master independently. They will then regroup and share their findings, changing any ideas they wish.

Assessment Master 4

Concept Connections

1. Explain what this selection is about. Write a short summary.

Date _____

2. Tell what this selection has to do with astronomy.

3. Tell how this selection is like other selections you have read in this unit.

Name _____

4. You have read many selections about astronomy. How did *this* selection change your ideas about astronomy?

Unit 2/Astronomy   Assessment Master 4

THINK
ALOUD
PROMPTS

To foster independence,
think-aloud prompts are not provided
for Assessment lessons.

STARS
Seymour Simon

Stars are huge balls of hot, glowing gases. Our sun is a star. It is just an ordinary star, not the biggest nor the brightest. But the sun is the star that is nearest to our planet Earth. Earth is part of the sun's family of planets, moons, and comets called the Solar System. All of the other stars that we see in the sky are much farther away from Earth. The stars are so far away from us that even through powerful telescopes they look like small points of light.

People long ago gave names to the brighter stars and learned where and when to look for them. They also gave names to the constellations, groups of stars that seem to form patterns in the sky. Usually these constellations were named after gods, heroes, or animals.

The photograph shows the constellation of Orion, the Hunter. Orion is visible during winter evenings. Look for the three bright stars in a row that form the belt of Orion. The bright red star in the upper left of Orion is named Betelgeuse (most people call it "beetle juice"). The brilliant

Betelgeuse

Sirius   Rigel

Kyle Cudworth, Yerkes Observatory

 228

blue-white star in the lower right is named Rigel. The brightest star in the sky is Sirius, the Dog Star. It is just to the lower left of Orion in the constellation of Canis Major, the Big Dog.

Thousands of years ago Orion looked different than it does today. And thousands of years in the future it will look different than it does now. That's because stars move in space. They move very rapidly, ten or more miles per second. But the stars are so far away from us that we do not notice their motion in our lifetimes.

Imagine traveling in a spaceship going ten miles a second. Even at that speed, it would still take you about three and a half months to reach the sun. But it would take more than seventy thousand *years* to reach the next nearest star, Alpha Centauri.

Alpha Centauri is about twenty-five trillion miles away. There are other stars *millions* of trillions of miles away. These numbers are so big that they are hard to understand. Measuring the distance between the stars in miles is like measuring the distance around the world in inches.

Because of the great distances between stars, scientists measure with the light-year instead of the mile. Light travels at a speed of about 186,000 miles every second. A light-year is the distance that light travels in one year: a bit less than six trillion miles. Alpha Centauri is a little more than four light-years away. The stars shown in this giant cloud of gas in the constellation of Orion are fifteen hundred light-years away.

NOAO

How many stars do you think you can see on a clear, dark night? Can you see thousands, millions, countless numbers? You may be surprised that in most places only about two thousand stars are visible without a telescope.

When the great scientist Galileo looked through his low-power telescope in the year 1610, he saw thousands and thousands of stars that no one on earth had ever seen before. As more powerful telescopes were made, millions and millions of other stars were seen.

What looks like clouds in the photograph of the Milky Way galaxy below are really millions of stars too far away to be seen as separate points of light. With powerful telescopes we can see that the stars are as many as the grains of sand on an ocean beach.

Stars are born in giant clouds of gas and dust called nebulas. Most of the gas is hydrogen with a small amount of helium. Over millions of years, gravity pulls the gas and dust

NOAO

particles together and squeezes them so that they heat up. When the gas gets hot enough, it sets off a <u>nuclear reaction</u> like that of a super hydrogen bomb and a star is born. This computer-colored photograph shows a newborn

NASA

star (*arrow*) in the cloud of gas and dust known as Barnard 5.

Stars change as they grow older. For example, young stars (10 to 200 million years old) are very hot—with surface temperatures of more than 12,000 degrees (F)—and are usually blue or blue-white in color. Middle-aged stars like our sun are yellow and not as hot—10,000 degrees (F).

After about ten billion years stars begin to run out of their hydrogen fuel. Most of these old stars collapse upon themselves and they get hotter and hotter. Then, like a piece of popcorn when it "pops," the stars balloon out and become hundreds of times larger. They become what are known as red giant stars.

A red giant star may be 40 or 50 million miles across. Some are even larger. Betelgeuse is a red supergiant star 250 million miles across. If Betelgeuse were put in place of our sun in the center of the Solar System, it would swallow up Mercury, Venus, Earth, and Mars.

Some older stars go through a stage where they keep growing and then shrinking. These stars are called variable stars because at times they appear bright and at other times they are dim.

❧ 231 ❧

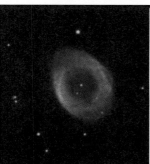

NASA

Other older stars shoot out a large cloud of gas into space. These stars are called planetary nebulas because through low-power telescopes they look like round planets. This photograph taken with a high-power telescope shows the real nature of a planetary nebula. This is the Ring Nebula in the constellation Lyra.

Finally, older stars cool and start collapsing. They shrink down to about the size of a small planet and are called white dwarf stars. As the white dwarfs slowly cool off they become black dwarf stars. And then the stars are dead.

Sometimes a star, usually a white dwarf, suddenly explodes and becomes much brighter. To people long ago it looked like a new bright star had appeared in the sky. They called the star a nova (*nova* means "new"). Even though most novas are too far away for us to see, scientists think that two or three dozen novas appear in the Milky Way every year.

Much rarer are the gigantic explosions known as supernovas. A supernova star flares up and becomes millions of times brighter than normal.

A supernova may appear only once every few hundred years. In the year 1054, Chinese astronomers saw a supernova in the constellation of Taurus. Today we can see the gaseous remains of that exploding star. We call it the Crab Nebula.

❧ 232 ❧

NASA

Some supernovas shatter completely, leaving behind only the wispy gases of a nebula. But a few supernovas leave a small, tightly packed ball of particles called a neutron star. A tiny drop of a neutron star would weigh a billion tons on earth.

The sudden collapse of a supernova causes a neutron star to spin very rapidly and give off a beam of X-ray radiation. Like the beam from a lighthouse, we can detect the X rays as a pulse. So a <u>rotating</u> neutron star is called a pulsar.

This X-ray photograph shows a pulsar in the middle of the Crab Nebula. The X rays from the pulsar in the Crab blink on and off thirty times every second. The star is visible when the X rays are "on" and invisible when the X rays are "off."

Some stars are much larger than the average star. When such a massive star cools and collapses, it becomes

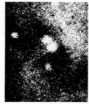

NOAO

something very special. The star is crushed together by the huge weight of the collapsing gases. Gravity keeps squeezing and squeezing until the star seems to disappear. The star has become a black hole.

Anything passing too close to a black hole will be pulled into it and never get out again. Even light is pulled in and cannot escape, so a black hole is invisible. Yet, scientists think they have located several black holes.

❧ 233 ❧

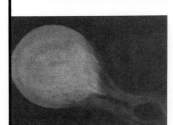

This drawing is of a double star called Cygnus X-1. Only one of the stars is visible: a hot, blue giant star. Near it is a black hole that pulls gases from its neighbor. As the gases are sucked in they become so hot that they give off huge amounts of X rays. Some scientists think that there are many such black holes scattered throughout space.

Our sun is an unusual star. It does not have any nearby stars circling it. Most stars have one or more companion stars and they revolve around each other. The star groups are so far from us that most look like single points of light to our eyes.

About half of all the stars we can see are double, or binary, stars. There are also many groups with three, four, a dozen, or even more stars in them. These groups of stars move through space together like flocks of birds in flight. Scientists think that the stars in such a group were all formed at the same time.

Very large groups of stars are called star clusters. This is a photograph of the Pleiades, an open cluster of stars. It contains several hundred stars that form a loose group with no special shape. These are young stars and they are surrounded by clouds of gas and dust.

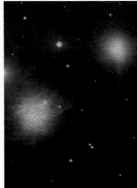

NOAO

NASA

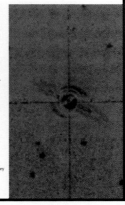

Here is a different kind of star cluster called a globular cluster. A globular cluster contains many thousands, or even millions, of stars very close together.

This is the great globular cluster known as M.13 in the constellation of Hercules. It is visible just as a dot of light to the naked eye. But through a telescope we can see that it has at least a million stars. Most of these stars are very old and they have stayed together throughout their lifetime.

The biggest star clusters of all are called galaxies. Galaxies are the largest kind of star systems. Our sun and its planets are a member of a galaxy called the Milky Way. There are more than one hundred billion stars in the Milky Way galaxy.

The sun is located almost out on the edges of the Milky Way. All the stars in the Milky Way whirl around the center of the galaxy, each at its own speed. The sun along with the Solar System moves at about 150 miles a second around the center of the galaxy. But the galaxy is so big that the sun takes about 225 million years to go around once.

Are there planets circling other stars in our galaxy? The answer is almost definitely yes. This picture shows a ring of material surrounding the star Beta Pictoris. This material is thought to be a young solar system in the making.

🌿 235 🌿

Jet Propulsion Laboratory

Planets form at the same time and from the same gases as do stars. So scientists think it is likely that some or even many stars have planets circling them. If even a tiny percentage of these planets are similar to Earth, then there may be millions of Earth-like planets in the galaxy.

Do any of these planets have life on them? No one knows. But scientists are using radio telescopes to listen for signals of intelligent life in outer space. They think the signals will come in the form of radio waves much like those of our own radios and televisions. So far scientists have not found anything, but they are not discouraged. Until they have examined every star that may have planets they won't know for sure.

The Milky Way is only one galaxy among millions of others in the universe. Galaxies — large and small, single or in groups and clusters, and in many different shapes — are found in every direction.

The Andromeda galaxy, shown here, is a spiral galaxy with almost twice as many stars as there are in the Milky Way. The Andromeda galaxy lies in far distant space, almost twelve quintillion miles away. That's 12,000,000,000,000,000,000! Light from this galaxy has been traveling for more than two million years by the time we see it in our telescopes.

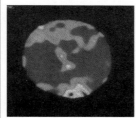

NOAO

🌿 236 🌿

How many galaxies are there in the universe? No one knows. But scientists think that there are about one hundred billion other galaxies. And each one of these galaxies contains hundreds of thousands of millions of stars.

Many mysteries confront us in the distant reaches of space. Beyond most of the galaxies that we can see with our largest telescopes are bright starlike objects called quasars. Each quasar gives off more than one hundred times the energy of all the stars in the Milky Way galaxy put together.

This is a computer-colored photo of a quasar-galaxy pair. Scientists think that quasars may be the centers of young galaxies that are just forming. Light from most quasars has been traveling for ten to fifteen billion years by the time it reaches Earth. That means that we are viewing quasars as they were ten to fifteen billion years ago, just after the universe began.

This photograph of Betelgeuse is the first ever to show the surface of a star other than the sun. Powerful telescopes orbiting above Earth's atmosphere may soon show us the very edges of the universe and the beginning of time itself. Will all our questions about stars then be answered? It's not likely. Each mystery that we solve about space seems to lead to many more unsolved questions about the nature of the universe.

NOAO

*

EXPLORING THROUGH DISCUSSION

Reflecting on the Selection

As the students read the selection, circulate among the groups to observe their understanding of the concepts as well as their collaboration in solving difficulties in understanding the selection.

As you note their **collaborative group discussions,** mark your **Teacher's Observation Log** for the individuals in one or two groups. Take a moment to reflect on how each student is changing from unit to unit in his or her ability to use strategies to solve reading problems.

Have the groups break while the students respond independently to the Concept Connections on Assessment Master 4.

ASSESSMENT TIP This is an ideal time to mark observations in your Teacher's Observation Log.

Exploring Concepts Within the Selection

Allow the students to regroup to **compare** and **discuss** their **responses to the Concept Connections.** During these discussions you will have more opportunities to observe students and mark your Teacher's Observation Log. Then gather the **Concept Connections** page and continue with the lesson as usual.

ASSESSMENT TIP This is another ideal time to mark observations in the log.

Sharing Ideas About Explorable Concepts

Have the groups **report** their **ideas** and **discuss them** with the rest of the class. It is crucial that the students' ideas determine this discussion.

- Students may note how enormously our knowledge of the stars has increased since the days when stories like "The Great Dog" and "The Scorpion" were created—and even since the days when Galileo first began to view the stars through his telescopes.
- The students may point out that most of the information presented in this selection applies to our own sun as well as to the stars we see at night.
- Some students may comment on the likelihood that other stars, like our sun, are orbited by planets, forming solar systems that may house intelligent life forms.
- Students may point out that the distances between objects in space are so vast as to be almost incomprehensible—so vast that the possibility of locating and exploring another solar system seems dubious at present.
- Students may comment on the disparity between what stars look like to the naked eye and what they are really like.

As these ideas and others are stated, have the students **add them to the Question Board** or the **Concept Board.**

Invite the students to enjoy Vincent van Gogh's famous painting, *The Starry Night,* reproduced on page 180 of the student anthology. Allow time for the students to comment on the work.

Fine Art

Exploring Concepts Across Selections

Students may make connections between this selection and others they have read.

- The students may point out that people have learned from the stars since the earliest recorded times. In *How Did We Find Out the Earth Is*

Round? the ancient Greeks studied the stars to figure out the shape of the earth; in "Sun and Star Calendars," early Egyptians, Native Americans, and others kept track of the seasons by charting the positions of certain stars and constellations; now, modern scientists are studying the stars to learn more about how the universe itself began.

Recording Ideas

As students complete the above discussions, ask them to **sum up what they have learned from their conversations and to tell how they might use this information** in further explorations. Any special information or insights may be recorded on the **Concept Board**. Any further questions that they would like to think about, pursue, or investigate may be recorded on the **Question Board**. They may want to discuss the progress that has been made on their questions and to cross out any questions that no longer warrant consideration.

➤ Remind them to note new information in their Explorer's Notebook, page 25.

Self-Assessment Questionnaire

➤ After these aspects of the lesson have been completed, you may wish to distribute a Self-Assessment Questionnaire, Assessment Master 2, which you will find in the Teacher Toolbox. Allow plenty of time for the students to complete this important assessment piece.

Evaluating Discussions

Explorer's Notebook, page 25

"Voyager to the Planets" by Necia Apfel

_____
_____
_____
_____
_____
_____
_____

"A Meeting in Space" by Vonda N. McIntyre

_____
_____
_____
_____
_____
_____
_____

Stars by Seymour Simon

_____
_____
_____
_____
_____
_____

Unit 2/Astronomy   EN 25

Assessment Master 2

Self-Assessment Questionnaire

1. How would you rate this selection?
   ○ easy   ○ medium   ○ hard

2. If you checked **medium** or **hard**, answer these questions.
   • Which part of the selection did you find especially difficult?
   • What strategy did you use to try to understand it?
   _____
   _____

   • Were some of the words hard?
   • What did you do to figure out their meaning?
   _____
   _____

3. What do you feel you need to work on to make yourself a better reader?
   _____
   _____
   _____

4. Give an example of something you said in the group. Tell why you said it.
   _____
   _____
   _____

5. Give an example of something that people in the group helped you understand about the selection.
   _____
   _____
   _____

Self-Assessment Questionnaire   Assessment Master 2

2 READING WITH A WRITER'S EYE

Assessment

Remind the students that in **each selection they have read, you have discussed something the writer did particularly well.** For example, in "A Meeting in Space" Vonda McIntyre used dialogue to move her story along. In the article "Voyager to the Planets," Necia Apfel provided facts in a way that holds her readers' attention.

Tell the students that since they have read *Stars* on their own, you would like them to **try to identify something that Seymour Simon did especially well.** Does something about the writing stand out? They might think back to a section of the article that they reacted to or particularly enjoyed. Their **reaction** might be a **clue** to especially good writing.

Allow time, if necessary, for the students to **skim** the article to refresh their memories. If they have difficulty expressing their feelings about the writing in this selection, **model a response** for them by pointing out things that you found noteworthy.

You may wish to point out that Simon **provides definitions** for many different kinds of stars. He also **explains extremely large numbers** in a way that gives them meaning to his readers. He tells his readers that stars travel around ten miles per second, a speed that readers can grasp by using their imaginations. Then he tells them that even at this tremendous speed, it would take a spacecraft three and a half months to get from the earth to the sun and more than seventy thousand years to get to the next nearest star.

Later Simon describes the size of the supergiant red star, Betelgeuse, which is 250 million miles in diameter. The gigantic size of the star is unpicturable until he tells his readers that if it replaced our sun, Betelgeuse would swallow up Mercury, Venus, Earth, and Mars.

WRITING

Linking Reading to Writing

Encourage the students to **use in their own writing anything that they particularly enjoyed about Seymour Simon's writing.** Invite them to look in their writing folders for a piece of writing that they might revise by including something that they noticed was done well in this story.

＊ Writing Process

Although no specific writing assignment is recommended here, the students may concentrate on an appropriate phase of the writing process for any writing on which they are currently working. Students who began science-fiction stories might work at revising and proofreading them.

VOCABULARY

Concept-related words and phrases from the selection that the students may want to discuss and record in their Writer's Notebook include the following:

nebula, red giant star, variable stars, white dwarf stars, nova, black hole, binary stars, star clusters, globular clusters, quasars, gaseous, nuclear reaction

Have Vocabulary Exploration forms, Reproducible Master 14, available for students who request them.

For additional opportunities to build vocabulary, see **Teacher Tool Card 75.**

VOCABULARY TIP Students need multiple exposures to new vocabulary words. Encourage them to read other books about astronomy.

Professional Checkpoint: Reading with a Writer's Eye

Proofreading sessions allow the students time to apply grammar, usage, and mechanics skills to their own writing. Because you have a large sample of every student's writing, you know where the written language problems of each lie. Sometimes these problems are persistent. Proofreading deals with these problems in a constructive way.

Notes:

3 GUIDED AND INDEPENDENT EXPLORATION

EXPLORING CONCEPTS BEYOND THE TEXT

Guided Exploration

The following activity does not have to be completed within the days devoted to this lesson.

❯ Distribute Home/School Connection 17. Students and their families can learn more about stars.

Research Cycle

Meet with the whole class as needed for the following purposes:

* to arrange schedules and update calendars
* to discuss problems that students are encountering with their research
* to hear preliminary presentations and discussions of findings
* to arrange more formal presentations of students' research
* to provide guidance to ensure that groups progress through phases of the Research Cycle—obtaining information; revising problems, conjectures, needs, and plans (perhaps with input resulting from a presentation to the class); and proceeding to a further cycle of problem, conjecture, and so forth.

Allow time for groups to present their research projects. Have the students add information to the Concept Board.

✳ Exploring Through Research

Home/School Connection 17

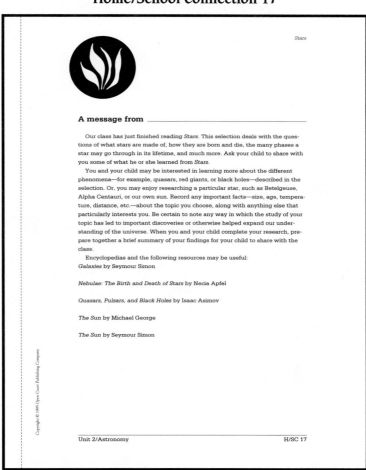

Stars

A message from _____

Our class has just finished reading *Stars*. This selection deals with the questions of what stars are made of, how they are born and die, the many phases a star may go through in its lifetime, and much more. Ask your child to share with you some of what he or she learned from *Stars*.

You and your child may be interested in learning more about the different phenomena—for example, quasars, red giants, or black holes—described in the selection. Or, you may enjoy researching a particular star, such as Betelgeuse, Alpha Centauri, or our own sun. Record any important facts—size, age, temperature, distance, etc.—about the topic you choose, along with anything else that particularly interests you. Be certain to note any way in which the study of your topic has led to important discoveries or otherwise helped expand our understanding of the universe. When you and your child complete your research, prepare together a brief summary of your findings for your child to share with the class.

Encyclopedias and the following resources may be useful:
Galaxies by Seymour Simon

Nebulae: The Birth and Death of Stars by Necia Apfel

Quasars, Pulsars, and Black Holes by Isaac Asimov

The Sun by Michael George

The Sun by Seymour Simon

Unit 2/Astronomy   H/SC 17

✻ INDEPENDENT WORKSHOP
Building a Community of Scholars

Student-Directed Reading, Writing, and Discussion

Research Cycle Meet with the whole class as needed to assess the progress of each research group. Remind the students that the next selection ends the unit. By this point, all groups intending to present written work should be revising their work.

Additional Opportunities for Independent Reading, Writing, and Cross-curricular Activities

✱ Writing Seminar

When they are revising and proofreading, provide time for the students to meet and read each other's written work. If your class is using the optional Writer's Handbook, encourage students to use it when revising.

Portfolio

Remind the students to think about choosing pieces of writing to put into their portfolios. These pieces can be examples of the students' best work. They might also be pieces of special significance to the students. Have the students include a short note with each piece, explaining why it was chosen.

Cross-curricular Activity Cards

The following Cross-curricular Activity Cards in the Student Toolbox are appropriate for this selection:

- 3 Art—Drawing the Stars
- 9 Science—Understanding How Black Holes Form

Understanding How Black Holes Form
Use after *Stars*

9
Science

Drawing the Stars
Use after *Stars*

3
Art

Select one of the constellations that have been discussed in your reading for the astronomy unit. Use an encyclopedia or a book about stars to find out about some of the major stars and other objects in your constellation. Write a brief description of each object, then illustrate your work using materials of your choice. You may enjoy working with a partner or partners to make a star mural. *Studying and drawing the stars can help you learn more about them and about the universe.*

Additional Opportunities for Solving Learning Problems

Tutorial

Use this time to **work with individuals or small groups who need help** in any area. Encourage students to ask for help whenever they need it.

Poetry
Sun
Secrets

1 READING THE POEMS

INFORMATION FOR THE TEACHER

About the Poems

In these evocative poems, award-winning author Myra Cohn Livingston ponders the mystery and enormity of space. Paintings by Leonard Everett Fisher enhance the sense of wonder and awe evoked in the poems.

Link to the Unit Concepts

"Sun," page 239, may cause students to ask wondering questions about how the sun creates energy. "Secrets," page 241, reinforces the idea of the vastness of space and of the many questions scientists ask about the universe.

About the Poet

Myra Cohn Livingston was born in 1926 in Omaha, Nebraska, and now lives in southern California. She says this about poetry:

> It is difficult to define why poetry is important to the individual. Poetry is, after all, a personal thing; its meaning to each human being is private. It invades the innermost thoughts; it clings to and bolsters the inner life. . . . The degree to which the reader is pro-voked to find the part, the fraction that is missing or not under-stood, is [a] measure of a poem's worth.

About the Illustrator

Leonard Everett Fisher was born in 1924 in New York. He has written books on Colonial crafts and trades, nineteenth-century trades, the Great Wall of China, the Tower of London, and the pyramids of Teotihucan. He has illustrated more than 150 books for children. The acrylic paintings he created for the several books on which he collaborated with Myra Cohn Livingston have been especially praised by critics.

LESSON OVERVIEW

"Sun" and "Secrets" by Myra Cohn Livingston, pages 238–241

READING THE SELECTION

Materials

Student anthology, pp. 238–241

Explorer's Notebook, p. 26

READING WITH A WRITER'S EYE

Minilesson

Discussing Poetry

Materials

Reproducible Master 14

FYI

Teacher Tool Card

• Spelling and Vocabulary: Building
  Vocabulary, 75

GUIDED AND INDEPENDENT EXPLORATION

Independent Workshop

Optional Materials from Student Toolbox

Tradebook Connection Cards

Student Tool Card

• Writer's Craft/Reading: Reading and
  Writing Poetry, 10

FYI

Teacher Tool Card

• Writer's Craft/Reading: Genre—
  Poetry, 10

Asterisks (*) throughout the lesson indicate learning frameworks. Learning Framework Cards and Teacher Tool Cards can be found in the Teacher Toolbox.

Tell the students that both poems come from a book titled *Space Songs,* and that the poet and painter collaborated to produce the book. Share some information about Livingston and Fisher.

COGNITIVE AND RESPONSIVE READING

Activating Prior Knowledge

Ask the students to discuss what the term *secrets* might mean in relation to astronomy.

Setting Reading Goals and Expectations

Ask the students to look at the title and length of each poem and the artwork that accompanies the poems. **Engage the students in a brief discussion of poetry.** What makes reading a poem different from reading a story or an article? What kinds of things does a reader find in a poem? Encourage them to share what ideas about astronomy they expect to find in the poems.

Recommendations for Reading the Poems

Read each poem aloud and have students follow in the text as you read, or select volunteers to do the reading. Emphasize the repetition of sounds within certain words of each poem—for example, the /b/ and /l/ sounds in "Sun" or the /s/ sound in "Secrets." Pause at the end of each line of the poem. Pause longer at the end of each sentence. Allow the students to stop you to clarify words or phrases, if necessary. This would be a good opportunity for students to **respond to text** by **visualizing** and **telling feelings.**

When you have read both poems aloud, select volunteers to reread them, reminding the volunteers to read aloud with expression.

EXPLORING THROUGH DISCUSSION

Reflecting on the Poems

Have the students **discuss each poem** and any **personal thoughts, reactions,** or **questions** it raised. Invite them to **discuss** what these **poems added to their exploration of the concepts** in the Astronomy unit. The students may note that even today people have many unanswered questions about the universe. Encourage the students to compare the poems to the myths they read earlier in the unit. Some students may point out that the heavenly bodies continue to fascinate and awe modern people, despite our increased technical knowledge of them. Have them add information to the **Concept Board.**

❯ Provide time for them to add new information about the concepts to page 26 of the Explorer's Notebook.

Response Journal

Poetry evokes highly personal reactions. Students who are keeping a personal response journal should be given time to record their thoughts and feelings about these poems.

TEACHING TIP Watch for new or unexpected student comments.

TIP FOR ENGLISH LANGUAGE LEARNERS

Creating mental images helps to clarify ideas or feelings. English Language Learners may benefit from illustrating how each poem makes them feel.

SUN

Myra Cohn Livingston

illustrated by
Leonard Everett Fisher

Space
is afire
with bursts of bubbling gas,

colliding atoms,
boiling wells
and solar flares

spewing

from a burning star, the sun.

Ninety-three million miles away

this mass,
quaking inferno,
pluming arcs and bridges

roars;

a giant bomb
exploding
hydrogen.

239

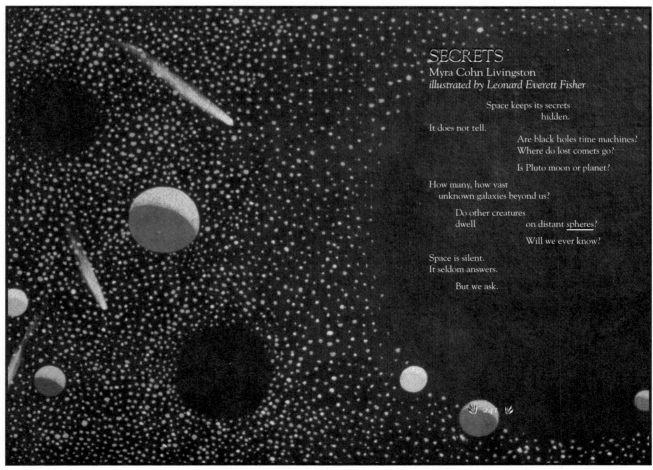

SECRETS

Myra Cohn Livingston
illustrated by Leonard Everett Fisher

Space keeps its secrets
hidden.

It does not tell.

Are black holes time machines?
Where do lost comets go?

Is Pluto moon or planet?

How many, how vast
unknown galaxies beyond us?

Do other creatures
dwell   on distant spheres?

Will we ever know?

Space is silent.
It seldom answers.

But we ask.

241

Recording Concept Information continued

"Sun" by Myra Cohn Livingston

_____

_____

_____

_____

_____

_____

_____

_____

_____

_____

_____

_____

_____

"Secrets" by Myra Cohn Livingston

_____

_____

_____

_____

_____

_____

_____

_____

_____

_____

_____

_____

_____

_____

26 EN   Astronomy/Unit 2

Explorer's Notebook, page 26

2 READING WITH A WRITER'S EYE

MINILESSON

Discussing
Poetry

Ask the students if there was anything about the poems that they especially enjoyed. Remind them that the **sound and rhythm** of a poem are important. Poetry is often read aloud so that the listener can hear and enjoy the **sounds and patterns** of the **words, phrases, and stanzas.** Often these sounds and patterns help to create the poem's effect on the reader. Encourage the students to share what emotions these poems have elicited and how the author's choice of **words, rhythm, rhyme, and stanza structure** help to create the mood of each poem.

WRITING

Linking Reading
to Writing

Encourage the students to use any of the writing techniques discussed in their own poetry writing.

✱ Writing Process

Encourage those students who have decided to write poetry to use the writing process as needed in developing their poems. Students may prefer to work in pairs or small groups while generating ideas.

VOCABULARY

Words and phrases related to astronomy that you might want to discuss include the following:

solar flares, hydrogen, spheres, quaking, inferno, pluming

Have Vocabulary Exploration forms, Reproducible Master 14, available for those students who need them. For additional opportunities to build vocabulary, see **Teacher Tool Card 75.**

VOCABULARY TIP Examine the students' writing for their usage of new words learned during this unit. Record your observations in the Teacher's Observation Log.

3 GUIDED AND INDEPENDENT EXPLORATION

EXPLORING CONCEPTS BEYOND THE TEXT

Guided Exploration

The following activities do not have to be completed within the days devoted to this lesson.

- Ask the students to tell something they wonder about concerning the sun or the subjects mentioned in "Secrets": black holes, Pluto, and extra-terrestrial life. Have them write some of their questions on the Question Board. Discuss which of these questions could be answered by research and where they might begin such research. Remind them to look at the unit bibliographies for books about these subjects.

Research Cycle

Meet with the whole class as needed for the following purposes:

- to arrange schedules and update calendars
- to discuss problems that students are encountering with their research
- to hear preliminary presentations and discussions of interesting findings
- to arrange more formal presentations of students' research
- to provide guidance to ensure that groups progress through phases of the Research Cycle—obtaining information; revising problems, conjectures, needs, and plans (perhaps with input resulting from a presentation to the class); and proceeding to a further cycle of problem, conjecture, and so forth

* Exploring Through Research

Continue to schedule time for groups to present their projects. Encourage the students to add to the Concept Board new information from the presentations. Remind interested students to continue researching and learning about their problems.

❋ INDEPENDENT WORKSHOP
Building a Community of Scholars

Student-Directed Reading, Writing, and Discussion

Research Cycle Meet with the whole class, as needed, to assess the progress of each research group. Students should continue to present their research projects.

Additional Opportunities for Independent Reading, Writing, and Cross-curricular Activities

✱ Reading Roundtable

The students might enjoy listening to other poems from the collection *Space Songs.* Encourage them to practice reading some of these poems themselves.

✱ Writing Seminar

Remind the students to use the phases of the writing process as they work on new writing pieces or revise pieces from their folders.

Portfolio

Remind the students to think about which pieces of writing they might choose to put into their portfolios.

Additional Opportunities for Solving Learning Problems

Tutorial

Use this time to help individuals or small groups who exhibit a need in any area. Encourage students to ask for help whenever they need it. The following aid is available in the Teacher Toolbox for your convenience:

• Writer's Craft/Reading: Genre—Poetry, Teacher Tool Card 10

Unit Wrap-up

After the students have completed their presentations, initiate a general class discussion on the unit. Remind them to think about previous discussions of ideas from the Concept Board. You might encourage them to refer to page 22 of their Explorer's Notebook to remind themselves of what their ideas about astronomy were when the unit began and what they expected to learn from the unit. Ask them what new ideas they have acquired and what new information they have learned.

The discussion may be extended to include

- an evaluation of the unit selections. Which selections did students find most interesting? Which were the least interesting?
- an evaluation of the unit activities. Which activities did students find most enjoyable or informative?
- an evaluation of the overall unit. How well did the unit cover the explorable concepts? Was astronomy a worthwhile subject to examine? Why or why not?
- suggestions of ideas related to astronomy that are worth further exploration, possibly beginning with any questions left on the Question Board.

Small-Group Discussion

As an alternative, have the students work in small groups to discuss the unit. Encourage the group participants to refer to the Concept Board, browse the student anthology selections, and review their Explorer's Notebook pages for the Astronomy unit to refresh their memories of important ideas raised in the unit. Then have the groups share with classmates important points and conclusions from their discussions.

ASSESSMENT

Informal Assessment

❯ Give the students the opportunity to make individual evaluations of their learning experiences during this unit by completing Explorer's Notebook, pages 39–40. You may want to meet individually with the students to discuss their evaluations.

End-of-Unit Assessment

At this point, you might wish to carry out end-of-unit assessment for unit 2, Astronomy. You will find the following end-of-unit assessment booklets in the Teacher's Toolbox:

Comprehension Assessment

- Understanding the Selection
- Making Connections Across Selections
- Checking Skills
- Multiple-Choice Option

Essay and Writing Assessment

Research Assessment

You may pick and choose among the various assessment components to find the right mix for assessing areas you want to stress. See *Formative Assessment: A Teacher's Guide* for specific suggestions on how to use these assessment materials.

UNIT CELEBRATION

Have the students suggest how they might celebrate their completion of this unit. They may offer such ideas as these:

- Create a classroom gallery of pictures of those involved in astronomy, past and present, and information about their contributions.
- Invite other classes or family members in for a classroom "tour." The students can act as tour guides, pointing out projects, explaining their significance, and explaining concepts from the Concept Board.
- Write questions about astronomy on notecards. Use these questions in a quiz-show format to review information learned in the unit.

Explorer's Notebook, page 39

Explorer's Notebook, page 40

Unit Wrap-up

How did you feel about this unit?

☐ I enjoyed it very much.   ☐ I liked it.

☐ I liked some of it.   ☐ I didn't like it.

How would you rate the difficulty of the unit?

☐ easy   ☐ medium   ☐ hard

How would you rate your performance during this unit?

☐ I learned a lot about astronomy.

☐ I learned some new things about astronomy.

☐ I didn't learn much about astronomy.

Why did you choose this rating?

_____

_____

_____

_____

_____

What was the most interesting thing that you learned about astronomy?

_____

_____

_____

_____

_____

_____

_____

Unit Wrap-up continued

What did you learn about astronomy that you didn't know before?

_____

_____

_____

_____

What did you learn about yourself as a learner?

_____

_____

_____

_____

What do you need to work on as a learner?

_____

_____

_____

_____

What resources (books, films, magazines, interviews, tool cards, other) did you use on your own during this unit? Which of these were the most helpful? Why?

_____

_____

_____

_____

_____

_____

_____

_____

Family
Heritage

UNIT INTRODUCTION

Explorable
Concepts

The family is the basic unit of social organization almost everywhere. But what exactly is a family? There is a huge variety of family forms even within the United States. Some people are worried that the bonds of the family are weakening. But what does it mean for a family to be "weak" or "strong"? And what exactly are those politically controversial "family values"? Clearly, these questions are central to our lives, and are worth thinking about, reading about, and discussing. But it can be difficult for fifth graders to do these things because they take the idea of the family so much for granted. The selections in this unit are chosen to make this reflection process easier by **showing the students a variety of family forms and values,** some of which will be very different from their own.

The study of family forms has been a long-standing preoccupation of the social sciences; sociologists, anthropologists, demographers, historians, and economists have studied many different aspects of the family, why it takes the forms it does in different societies, and how it has evolved over the centuries. None of these approaches has found "the answer" about the family, however; you can give free rein to the speculations of your students. The important thing is to make sure that wherever their ideas begin, the students broaden and deepen their understanding by becoming aware of some of the approaches various writers

FAMILY
HERITAGE

(literary as well as scientific) have taken to the family. What this unit is about can be summed up by considering how to answer questions such as these:

- In some cultures, the emphasis is on the extended family (grandparents, aunts, uncles, cousins, etc.) rather than on the "nuclear" family (parents and children). Why is the nuclear family usually the basic unit in the United States? Has it always been?
- Who are your closest relatives?
- How would our culture be affected by different ways of defining kinship?
- What makes your family different from others?
- Are the roles of men and women within the family changing?

Note: A discussion of the word *heritage* may be necessary. Have the students define the term in their own words or refer to the dictionary definition. Explain that a family heritage can include a variety of influences from a variety of sources. For example, a person's great-grandparents may have come from Europe or Asia, but each one could have come from a different place, with different traditions, languages, etc.
Be sensitive to students such as adopted or foster children who don't know about their "roots." In activities involving exploration or

discussion of their own families, these students will need encouragement to build on what they do know or to **focus on the heritage of their adoptive or foster families.**

Resources

Among the following resources are professional reference books, read-alouds, and audiovisual materials. The reference books are intended to help you develop the concepts and organize information to share with the students in whatever way you choose. The read-alouds are books that may be too challenging for many students of this age to read independently but that fit the concepts well and are quality literature. Among the audiovisual materials are some that only you will be able to obtain and others that will be available to both you and the students. For a complete list of audiovisual resources, see page 567.

In addition to the books listed here, **bibliographies for the students** appear in the student anthology, on **Reproducible Masters 33–37,** and on **Home School Connection 18–19.** Encourage the students to use these bibliographies as they explore family heritage. You should also choose and read books from the students' bibliographies. Reading books about family heritage written for children will help you see and understand the students' point of view.

Professional Reference Books

Harris, Violet J., ed. *Teaching Multicultural Literature in Grades K–8.* Christopher-Gordon, 1992. This book includes essays about Asian, African, Native-American, Puerto Rican, and Mexican-American literature for children.

Kolb, Frances. *Portraits of Our Mothers.* The Network, 1989. This handbook tells how teachers and students used oral history to learn about women in their families and community. The book includes activities, materials, and resources and can be used as a guide for projects on oral history.

Rochman, Hazel. *Against Borders: Promoting Books for a Multicultural World.* American Library Association, 1993. This book includes a collection of essays and bibliographies organized around themes such as "Outsiders" and "Family Matters."

Rossel, Seymour. *Family.* Franklin Watts, 1980. The author examines the family as a social unit from ancient to modern times.

Wolfman, Ira. *Do People Grow on Family Trees?* Workman, 1991. This book includes stories and photos of immigrants arriving at Ellis Island, information on the history and meaning of family names, and sources to investigate for information about one's family history.

Zimmerman, William. *How to Tape Instant Oral Biographies.* Guarionex Press Ltd., 1981. This handbook for preserving life stories includes suggestions on how to conduct an interview and how to record responses.

Read-Alouds

Field, Edward, translator and editor. *Eskimo Songs and Stories.* Dell, 1973. Poems based on songs and stories of the Netsilik people reflect their daily life.

Hamilton, Virginia. *The People Could Fly: American Black Folktales.* Knopf, 1985. This book includes African-American folktales that range from fantastic, funny, and supernatural stories, to history and personal narratives.

Pomerantz, Charlotte. *If I Had a Paka: Poems in Eleven Languages.* Greenwillow, 1982. This book includes Swahili, Serbo-Croatian, Samoan, Dutch, Vietnamese, Japanese, Indonesian, Spanish, Yiddish, and Native-American poems.

Sneve, Virginia Driving Hawk. *Dancing Teepees: Poems of American Indian Youth.* Holiday House, 1989. This book is a collection of tribal songs, prayers, and short poems by contemporary, Native-American poets.

Audiovisual Materials

African Journey. Public Media Video, 1992. When Luke spends the summer with his father, who has recently been transferred to southeast Africa, he learns to respect the African culture. 165 minutes; videocassette.

American Eyes. Cynthia A. Cherbak Productions, 1991, The Media Guild. In this CBS Schoolbreak Special, a Korean teenager becomes the target of racial prejudice, prompting his older Caucasian brother to fight on his behalf. 30 minutes; videocassette.

Many Voices. TVOntario, 1991. This video consists of nine short dramas with multicultural themes. In "Positively Native," ten-year-old Martin gets fed up with being teased about his Iroquois heritage, so he videotapes his family in Toronto as well as his relatives who have remained on a reservation. Nine programs, each 15 minutes; videocassette.

Molly's Pilgrim. Phoenix/BFA, 1985. Based on the book by Barbara Cohen, this is the story of a Russian immigrant child who is at first ostracized for being different and then wins acceptance. 24 minutes; videocassette.

Suemi's Story: My Modern Mayan Home. Little Fort Media, 1991, United Learning, Inc. A girl from a village in the Yucatan is proud of her home, school, market, and an ancient Mayan site near her home. 25 minutes; videocassette.

Victor. Barr Films, 1989. A young immigrant boy adjusts to a new life in the United States, yet remains proud of his Mexican heritage. 26 minutes; film or videocassette.

Community/School
- Neighborhood and school libraries
- Local historical societies
- Community centers

It would be useful to have in the classroom a large map of the world or a globe on which the students could locate the countries of the families featured in the selections or the places that have been important in their own family histories.

Concept Board

Designate an area of the classroom for the **Concept Board**. Remind the students that, as in previous units, the class will keep a Concept Board to record any information about family heritage that they gather and wish to share with their classmates. This information can include writing by the students, letters they receive as a result of investigations into their own heritage, drawings, photographs, and articles from newspapers or magazines. Information collected might relate to the heritage of the families in the selections, the heritage of the students' own families, or the heritage of any group the students are interested in.

Using the Concept Board

Question Board

Designate another area for the **Question Board**. Remind the students to post any questions they have about family heritage as they proceed through the unit. Take time to review these questions periodically so that students can add new questions or remove old questions when they no longer warrant consideration.

For a review of information about the **Concept Board** and the **Question Board**, see **Teacher Tool Card 121**.

Using the Question Board

UNIT PREVIEW BY THE STUDENTS

Activating Prior Knowledge

Be sure the students realize that throughout this unit they will have opportunities to share information about their own family heritage or another heritage they are familiar with.

Setting Reading Goals and Expectations

- Have the students examine the illustration and unit title that appear on pages 244–245. The illustration shows several generations of a family at a picnic or, perhaps, a family reunion.
- Have the students spend a few minutes browsing the selections.
- Encourage them to share and discuss anything in the text, photographs, or illustrations that catches their attention.
- Explain to the students that throughout this unit they will be participating in activities that will extend their experiences and deepen and expand their knowledge of family heritage. These **exploratory activities** may include writing, drama, art, interviews, debates, and panel

discussions. The students will be allowed ample opportunity to reflect on and discuss the activities they complete. **Some selections** in this unit **may** raise questions or **present problems that the students would like to research.** Encourage interested students to pursue research projects.

For a review of information about **browsing,** see **Learning Framework Card 1A, Setting Reading Goals and Expectations.**

❯ Have the students complete page 41 in their Explorer's Notebook and share their responses. Have them suggest and record on the Question Board questions they would like to pursue in their reading of the unit.

Explorer's Notebook, page 41

Knowledge About Family Heritage

This is what I know about family heritage before reading the unit.

_____
_____
_____
_____
_____
_____
_____
_____
_____

These are some things about family heritage that I would like to talk about and understand better.

_____
_____
_____
_____
_____
_____
_____
_____
_____

Reminder: I should read this page again when I get to the end of the unit to see whether my ideas about family heritage have changed.

Unit 3/Family Heritage

EN 41

Learning Unit: Family Heritage

SELECTION	LINK TO THE UNIT CONCEPTS

● Award-winning authors and/or illustrators   ■ Dramatized on audiocassette

Exploration Through Reflective Activities

SELECTION-BASED MINILESSONS		REFLECTIVE ACTIVITIES
TEACHER'S GUIDE	**TEACHER TOOLBOX**	
Elaboration Comparison	Genre—Expository Text, Writing Paragraphs, Elaboration Through Providing Background	Interviewing a family member Planning a photo essay
Discussing a Song		Comparing information about cultures
Indicators of Time and Order Characterization	Point of View, Compound Sentences	Group discussion
Students choose a writer's craft to focus on.	Characterization, Setting, Using Possessive Pronouns	Interviewing someone who emigrated from another country Comparing aspects of cultures
Sensory Details	Characterization, Using Dialogue in a Story, Figurative Language	Literature search—folk tales
Figurative Language in Poetry		Panel discussion
Suspense Dialogue	Genre—Adventure, Characterization, Using and Punctuating Dialogue	Letter writing
Choice of a writer's craft to study is part of assessment.		Dramatizing a reading selection
Elaboration	Elaboration Through Providing Reasons or Causes, Elaboration Through Providing Descriptions, Capitalization	Completing a family tree
		Sharing of group knowledge, insights, and ideas

Assessment available for this unit includes Teacher's Observation Log, Self-Assessment Questionnaire, Concept Connections, Portfolios, and separate Comprehension, Essay, and Writing assessments.

In Two Worlds: A Yup'ik Eskimo Family

1 READING THE SELECTION

INFORMATION FOR THE TEACHER

About the Selection

This vivid photographic portrait features a family living in Alaska on the coast of the Bering Sea. **Three generations tell about their lives and customs,** and about how they strive to adopt **the best of modern ways without abandoning their traditional values**.

"In Two Worlds," pages 246–265, includes several chapters from a book by the same name; other chapters in the book describe family activities such as fishing, seal hunting, berry picking, home life, and school life. The book also includes an excellent bibliography of books, periodicals, and films about the native peoples of the Arctic.

Link to the Unit Concepts

For generations of Yup'iks, life was difficult, yet people shared with each other and kept traditions alive. Today, the Rivers family keeps some of the old ways, but it must also deal with changes brought about by contact with the modern world.

Note: The Yup'iks are one major group of the Eskimo peoples. Native Alaskans who were questioned about the use of the term *Eskimo* said that it was commonly used among the native peoples and that it was not considered offensive. However, they appreciated being called by the name of their specific Alaskan cultures, such as Inuit or Yup'ik.

About the Authors

Aylette Jenness has written several photo documentaries about families and their special heritage. These include *Along the Niger River, A Life of Their Own: An Indian Family in Latin America,* and *Families.* In *Families,* Jenness focuses on seventeen young people with varying family and cultural backgrounds, including adopted children, foster children, and a Cuban-American child with sixty-two relatives.

While she was working on her two previous books about life in Alaska, *Gussuk Boy* and *Dwellers of the Tundra,* Jenness lived in

LESSON OVERVIEW

"In Two Worlds" by Aylette Jenness and Alice Rivers, pages 246–265

READING THE SELECTION

Materials
Student anthology, pp. 246–265
Explorer's Notebook, p. 42
Assessment Master 1
Globe or map of North America

FYI
Learning Framework Card
• Setting Reading Goals and Expectations, 1A

READING WITH A WRITER'S EYE

Minilesson
Writer's Craft: Elaboration
Writer's Craft: Comparison

Materials
Reading/Writing Connection, pp. 21–22
Reproducible Master 14

Teacher Tool Card
• Spelling and Vocabulary: Building Vocabulary, 75

Options for Instruction
Writer's Craft: Genre—Expository Text
Writer's Craft: Writing Paragraphs
Writer's Craft: Elaboration Through Providing Background
(Use Teacher Tool Cards listed below.)

GUIDED AND INDEPENDENT EXPLORATION

Materials
Explorer's Notebook, pages 12, 45–47
Home/School Connection 18–19
Reproducible Masters 33–37

FYI
Learning Framework Cards
• Independent Workshop, 5
• Reading Roundtable, 6
• Writing Seminar, 8

Optional Materials from Student Toolbox
Tradebook Connection Cards
• *In the Year of the Boar and Jackie Robinson* by Bette Bao Lord
• *The Land I Lost* by Huynh Quang Nhuong

Cross-curricular Activity Card
• 9 Social Studies—Steps into Statehood

Student Tool Cards
• Writer's Craft/Reading: Giving Examples, 38
• Writer's Craft/Reading: Telling Important Facts, 40

Independent Workshop

• Writer's Craft/Reading: Comparing and Contrasting, 36
• Writer's Craft/Reading: Reading and Writing Expository Text, 9
• Writer's Craft/Reading: Writing Paragraphs, 22
• Writer's Craft/Reading: Giving Background, 41
• Study and Research: Interviewing, 110

FYI
Teacher Tool Cards
• Writer's Craft/Reading: Elaboration Through Providing Examples, 38
• Writer's Craft/Reading: Elaboration Through Providing Specific Facts, 40

• Writer's Craft/Reading: Elaboration Through Providing Comparison and Contrast, 36
• Writer's Craft/Reading: Genre—Expository Text, 9
• Writer's Craft/Reading: Writing Paragraphs, 22
• Writer's Craft/Reading: Elaboration Through Providing Background, 41
• Study and Research: Interviewing, 110
• Classroom Supports: Question Board and Concept Board, 121

Asterisks (*) throughout the lesson indicate learning frameworks. Learning Framework Cards and Teacher Tool Cards can be found in the Teacher Toolbox.

Scammon Bay. At the time, Alice Rivers was a teenager and worked for Jenness as a baby-sitter. The two women became friends and, twenty-five years later, decided to collaborate on a book showing how Scammon Bay had changed over the years. Jenness took the photographs and wrote the accounts of changes in Scammon Bay. Rivers provided a first-person account of growing up in Scammon Bay and of her life today. Rivers also encouraged her mother, sister, husband, and children to contribute to the book.

When the authors were asked about their purposes for writing *In Two Worlds,* Rivers said that she wanted the book to be a record for her children and their children, and Jenness said that she wanted people outside Alaska to learn how Yup'ik families live today.

INFORMATION FOR THE STUDENT

- A small map showing Alaska, the Bering Sea, and Scammon Bay can be found on page 248 of the selection. You might also help students to identify Alaska and the Bering Sea on a large map or globe.
- Information on how Jenness and Rivers met and how they later decided to collaborate appears on page 265 of the student book. The students may read and discuss this material before or after reading the selection. You may want to share other information about the authors.

*   ## COGNITIVE AND RESPONSIVE READING

Activating Prior Knowledge

Encourage students to share what they already know about Alaska and about the people who live there.

Setting Reading Goals and Expectations

Remind the students that before they read they will **set reading goals and expectations.** To do this, they will **browse the selection** and **use the clues/problems/wondering procedure.** On the chalkboard under the headings clues, problems, and wonderings, write in brief note form the observations the students generate during browsing. For example, students might list the genre of the selection under *clues*; they might list unfamiliar words under *problems*; and they might note any questions that arise during browsing under *wonderings.* The students will return to these observations after reading.

For a review of **browsing, see Learning Framework Card 1A, Setting Reading Goals and Expectations.**

STEPS TOWARD INDEPENDENCE During browsing, students should be noticing headings.

Recommendations for Reading the Selection

Ask the students how they would like to read the selection. The first few pages of the selection contain some unfamiliar vocabulary and some difficult ideas. Students might benefit by reading them aloud. The remainder of the selection consists mainly of first-person accounts, and students may enjoy reading these aloud also.

If the students elect to **read orally,** you should **refer to the think-aloud prompts that are provided beneath the page miniatures.** Instead of or in addition to using these prompts, encourage the students to provide their own think-alouds while reading.

This would also be a good selection for **responding** to text **by visualizing** while reading aloud. Model this response, and then invite the students to respond.

If the students elect to **read silently,** have them **discuss problems, reactions,** and **strategies** after reading. Let them know, however, that they can raise their hands anytime during reading to ask questions or to identify problems for discussion with the group.

About the Reading Strategies

Because of the unfamiliar subject matter of this selection, students may need to stop and summarize at several points in the text. Remind them that good readers clarify unclear passages as they go along and **sum up in order to better understand and remember** what they have read.

Note: "In Two Worlds" is a long selection. If the students need a break, the suggested second part of the selection begins on page 257 and is indicated by a large initial capital letter.

Think-Aloud Prompts for Use in Oral Reading

The think-aloud prompts are placed where students may encounter difficulties with the text. These are merely suggestions for ways to deal with the text. Remind the students to refer to the **reading strategy posters** and to use any strategy they feel they need to help make sense of what they are reading. Encourage the students to collaborate with classmates when confronted with difficulties while reading.

TEACHING TIP Accept students' comments as they are given without turning them into what you have in mind. It is the students' thinking that you should be trying to encourage and develop. If a comment seems irrelevant, ask the student to explain further. If a comment seems incomplete, ask the student to add more or call on other students to add to it.

THINK ALOUD PROMPTS

These prompts may be used as guides to promote cognitive and responsive reading.

Alice and Billy Rivers and their children.

246

IN TWO WORLDS:
A YUP'IK ESKIMO FAMILY
from the book by
Aylette Jenness and Alice Rivers
photographs by Aylette Jenness

THE PAST

Long Ago

Alice and Billy Rivers live with their children in the small town of Scammon Bay, Alaska, on the coast of the Bering Sea. They are Yup'ik Eskimos. Their story really begins long, long ago.

Alice and Billy's parents, grandparents, great-grandparents, great-great-grandparents—all their ancestors for several thousand years—have always lived here. They were part of a small group of Yup'ik Eskimos whose home was this vast area of tidal flats bordering the sea, with, inland, marshes, ponds, creeks, and rivers lacing the flat treeless tundra, broken only by occasional masses of low hills.

Each year, as the northern part of the earth tilted toward the sun, the long hours of sunlight here melted the snow, melted the sea ice, melted the rivers, melted, even, the frozen land down to the depth of a foot or so. Briefly, for a few months, birds came from the south to lay their eggs and raise

247

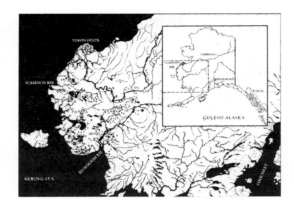

their young. The fish spawned, plants grew, berries ripened. And then the earth tilted away from the sun. Days grew shorter, the sun weaker, temperatures fell. The rain turned to snow, plants withered, birds flew south. Ponds, creeks, rivers, and finally even the Bering Sea froze, and layers of snow covered the whole landscape. Fish, sea mammals, and land animals all moved beneath thick blankets of ice and snow.

The small, scattered groups of Yup'ik Eskimos knew exactly how to survive here. Living as single families, or in small groups of relatives, they moved with the seasons to catch each kind of fish, bird, or mammal when and where each was most easily available. They harpooned the whales that migrated

248

north along the coast in spring and south in the fall. They shot and snared birds nesting on the tundra, and they gathered the birds' eggs. They netted saltwater fish coming to lay their eggs in the rivers and creeks, and they caught freshwater fish moving beneath the ice of inland creeks. They trapped small mammals on the land for meat and for fur clothing. They knew where to find and how to catch dozens of different fish and animals for food, for clothing, even for light and heat for their small homes.

They had fire, but they didn't know how to use it to make metal. Everything they had they made themselves, with their hands, with stone, bone, or ivory tools—their many intricate snares and nets and traps, their boats and sleds, their homes and their clothing. Life was hard and precarious. Nothing was wasted.

Their mark on the land was light. Today their old sites are nearly part of the earth, not easy to see. These Yup'ik Eskimos didn't build monuments to gods or leaders. They believed that animals had spirits, and that the spirits survived the animals' death to inhabit other animals. After killing a seal, they put water in its mouth to show their caring and respect for it and to ensure that its spirit would return in the form of another seal another time. They made up stories and dances of awe, fear, and pleasure in the animals they knew so well.

They shared with each other, and no one was much better or worse off than anyone else. Families, or groups of families, had rights to certain places for hunting or fishing, but no one owned the land or its resources.

They knew no outsiders, no one different from themselves. During those hundreds and hundreds of years, their way of life

249

1 Some students may need clarification on how lands near the North Pole tilt toward the sun for part of the year and away from the sun for the rest of the year. Students will remember from their discussions while reading the Astronomy unit that the earth's axis is tilted.

2 Students may not have heard the word *precarious* used this way before. You might model the strategy of using **context clues** for clarifying a word that is used in an unfamiliar way by saying something like the following:

I've heard this word used to describe something that was unsteady or dangerous. But here the author says that life was precarious. I think the author must mean that survival for the Yup'iks depended on what they found to eat and whether they could stay warm. Since finding food and staying warm were often very difficult, life was precarious.

changed very little. People followed in the footsteps of their ancestors, children learning from their parents the vast body of knowledge necessary for survival in this environment.

But during the last fifty years, their lives have changed enormously. And these changes are within the memory of the older people living here now.

3 Listen to Alice Rivers's mother, Mary Ann, describe her childhood. She speaks in Yup'ik, and one of her daughters, Leota, translates into English.

Mary Ann Remembers

"I was born, as I was told, in the late fall. My mother delivered me outside in the tundra, out in the open. My mother told me that after I was born I clutched some tundra moss and grass in my hand. I do not know why I was born outside, but it must have been because my mother was out in the tundra.

"When I was first aware of my surroundings, we lived on the other side of the mountains of Scammon Bay. The name of the place where I was born is called Ingeluk, and I think it's called this name because we are surrounded by small hills. We were the only people living in that area. We were <u>secluded</u> away from other people. There was my father, my mother, my two older sisters, and one older brother, and I am the youngest in the family.

"We lived in a sod house. The insides of our house had braided grass hanging on the walls as paneling. We had only one window, which was made out of dried seal guts, and it made a lot of noise when it was windy. Our floor was plain, hard, dried mud. Our beds were dried grass, piled high to keep us warm. We had no blankets. We mostly did with what we had at hand, and we used our parkas to keep us warm. I remember we had one kettle, a small half kerosene tank for our cooking pot, and the plates we had were carved from wood by my father.

"For light, we used seal oil when we had the oil, and it smoked a lot. Other times we had no light because we had no oil. I remember my mother cooked whitefish, and she carefully skimmed off the oil from the pot we had, and what she took out of the cooking pot we used in our oil lamp. The oil from the fish made pretty good light; it never smoked like the seal oil did. There were lots of stories being told, that's what we did during the evenings.

"Our main diet was fish, caught in my father's traps. There were times that we were really hungry. We were very poor. Sometimes when we woke up in the morning, we had nothing at all to eat.

🌀 *251* 🌀

3 This is a good point to **sum up,** since the expository section ends here and there is a shift to first-person narrative.

"We didn't have any kind of bread. We did not know what coffee and tea were.

"I saw my first white man when we were traveling by our skin boat. I did not know who he was, but later on I was told that the white man was trading goods for fur or skins. Maybe I was fifteen years old when I saw an airplane.

"I liked the life we used to live a long time ago, but we were always in need of something. I would say we live in comfort now. I don't go in hunger now. I say both lives I led were good, and I like both."

Mary Ann grew up and married a man who lived nearby, Teddy Sundown. They began to raise their family in Keggat-miut, as Scammon Bay is known in Yup'ik. It was a good site, and a number of families settled there. They built their small log houses on the lower slope of a range of hills that rose out of the flat tundra. A clear stream, racing down the hillside, flowed into the river that wound along the base of the hills, and finally emptied into a wide, shallow bay of the Bering Sea. Mary Ann and Teddy still moved to seasonal camps to fish, trap, and hunt, but as the village grew, they began to spend more and more of the year there.

The United States government set up a school in Scammon Bay and hired a Yup'ik teacher. All of the children were expected to attend school.

4 Missionaries had come to convert the people from their traditional religion, and the village was divided between Catholics and Protestants. Two churches were built.

Alice was the fourth child born to Mary Ann and Teddy. She is shown at the age of ten, standing on the far right of her family. She speaks of growing up in Scammon Bay.

◎ 252 ◎

Gonzaga Collection, Yugtarvik Museum, Bethel, Alaska

Alice Remembers

"Our home was a one-room building. Our beds were together—Mom and Dad's bed and our bed. All of us kids slept together in one bed. No table—the tables came later on. We used to eat sitting on the floor, Eskimo way. Mom used to cook bread on top of the stove, 'cause there was no oven. To me it used to be the best bread I've eaten. Then as I grew older, we got a stove and oven, and she started baking bread.

"We ate bread, birds, dried herrings, clams, mussels, fish—boiled and frozen—seals, mink, muskrats. There were two stores. We bought shortening, flour, tea, coffee—just what we needed.

◎ 253 ◎

4 Students may want to **sum up** what the text tells about changes in the Yup'iks' life-style. Instead of living in single families, as Mary Ann did when she was a child, and instead of moving to follow the animals they hunted, as Arctic people had always done, the Yup'iks began to settle and spend most of the year in villages like Scammon Bay.

A school was set up in Scammon Bay and missionaries made converts and built churches. These also were changes from traditional ways. In the past, children had learned the many skills they needed to survive from their parents, and Yup'iks had practiced a religion based on honoring the spirits of the animals they killed.

Jonathan Jenness

"We were always together. We'd go to church every morning. Mom would wake us up early, we'd go to mass. We never used to be lazy, we used to just go, get up and go, get up to a real cold morning, and by the time we were home, the house would be nice and warm.

"Right after church we used to go straight to school, all of us. I remember that learning to write my name was the hardest thing. I was maybe about six. We had Eskimo teachers. It was one room, and everything was there.

"After school, we'd have lots of things to do—bringing some wood in, dishes to wash, house to clean, babies to watch, water to pack. We had aluminum pails with handles. We used to run over to the stream and pack water until we

254

had what we needed. In the winter we had to keep one hole in the ice open the whole winter. This was one of the things I used to do with my sisters, not only me.

"Planes came in maybe once a week with mail. We didn't know about telephones. We had a radio, just for listening. I think we listened to one station all the time. No TV.

"The teachers had a short-wave radio. If someone got sick, they would report us to the hospital. They would give us medication or send us to the hospital in Bethel." **5**

Alice Grown Up

By the time Alice was an adult, Scammon Bay was a village of a hundred and fifty people, with twenty-five log and frame homes. For transportation, each family had a dog sled and team, and a boat for use in summer.

The government began to take a larger role in the Yup'ik villages. A new school was built, with living quarters for non-Eskimo teachers from outside of Alaska. Children were taught a standard public elementary school curriculum, which had little reference either to their own lives or to what they knew and didn't know about life outside Scammon Bay. They were forbidden to speak Yup'ik in school, in the belief that this would help them to learn English, and that learning English was very important.

A postmaster was hired from among the village men, and a custodian for the school. A health aide

Jonathan Jenness

255

5 Students might want to **sum up** the differences between Alice's way of life when she was a child and her mother's way of life when she was a child. These differences include the following: Alice lived in a one-room log building instead of in a sod house. Her family slept on beds and cooked on a stove instead of sleeping on dried grass and cooking everything in one pot. (Alice's family still did not have a table or an oven.) The family ate bread and drank tea and coffee instead of eating just fish and meat, and they bought a few things from a store. The family attended church together, and the children attended school. They were connected to the outside world by a short-wave radio and a plane that flew into the village about once a week.

was trained, and a small clinic built and stocked. More planes came to Scammon Bay, and it became easier to fly someone needing hospital care out—as long as the weather was good.

Government money became available for low-income families and for the elderly and disabled. There were few opportunities to earn cash, but almost all of the men in Scammon Bay were able to earn some money by hunting or trapping seals, mink, muskrats, and beaver and selling the skins to be made into luxury fur coats outside of Alaska. In summer they netted salmon in the river mouths north of Scammon Bay and sold this valuable fish to processors, who marketed it throughout the United States as smoked fish, or lox.

Each summer a freighter came up the coast from Seattle, Washington, with supplies for the villages. Everyone began to buy more factory-made goods. Some families bought stoves that burned fuel oil instead of relying on brush wood they cut nearby. Some bought windmills, which produced enough electricity for one or two light bulbs in their homes. Some

256

bought snowmobiles, which enabled them to travel farther than they could by dog team to hunt and trap, but which, unlike dogs, required money for fuel and new parts.

And for the first time in the long history of the Yup'ik Eskimos, some people began to travel away from their homeland. Some teenagers went to boarding school in the state of Washington. Some men went to National Guard training, and some families moved away permanently, settling in Alaskan towns and cities, or even as far away as Oregon and California.

But most remained in Scammon Bay, and some new Yup'ik people came to live there from other towns.

6

NOW

Alice's life today is both very similar to that of her mother at the same age—and very different. Scammon Bay has grown and changed in many ways.

There are three hundred and fifty people in Scammon Bay now, living in fifty-six houses. Most of the old log homes are now used for storage, and many people, like the Riverses, have new houses provided by the government at low cost. A dish antenna relays television to all the homes. Satellite transmission enables families to make telephone calls anywhere in the world. Huge storage tanks hold fuel to run an electric generator that provides enough power for each home to have all the lights that people want. A water and sewage disposal system required building a water treatment plant and a lagoon on the tundra for waste water. The dump, full of cans, plastic, fuel drums, and broken machinery, is a reminder of the difficulty of disposing of modern trash.

7

257

6 Students might want to **sum up** the differences between Alice's way of life as a child and her way of life as a young adult (about 1970). These differences include the following: when she was a young adult, the village was larger; non-Eskimo teachers at a new school taught a standard curriculum in English instead of in Yup'ik; a clinic had been opened; money was used more, since some people got money from the government and most people sold fish or animal skins for money. People used stoves that burned fuel oil instead of burning wood, and their community made use of windmills that produced electricity. Some had snowmobiles instead of dog teams. For the first time, people left the village to go to school or to serve in the armed forces.

7 Students will notice that the text now concerns the present. Ask them to continue to look for similarities and differences between the past and the present as they read the rest of the article. Differences include new homes, telephones, more electricity, water-treatment and sewage-disposal systems, a garbage dump, an airstrip, a high school, more consumer goods, a community center, and television.

For some years the state government made a great deal of money from taxes on oil found in Alaska, and this money paid for many of the modern conveniences in Scammon Bay and other rural towns. An airstrip was built so that planes could land more easily at all times of the year; it is regularly plowed in winter. Three small planes a day fly into Scammon Bay, bringing everything from cases of soft drinks to boxes of disposable diapers and, of course, the mail. A huge new gym has been built, and a new clinic, a preschool center, town offices, and a post office. The school is now run by the state, not the federal government, and goes all the way through the twelfth grade.

In spite of the changes, the traditional pattern of living from the land is still powerful. This can be seen most clearly as people move to seasonal camps during the summer months.

Fish Camp

On rocky Bering Sea beaches south of the village, herring come in immense schools to lay their eggs, and many families move there to fish for several weeks. Alice and Billy leave Scammon Bay with the children as soon as school is out for the summer.

Alice says, "Billy goes first and sets up our camp—tent, blankets, bed, clothes, pots and pans for cooking, and our grub. Then we go, maybe the third week in May. We pick spring greens, go hunting, take walks. We eat fish and fresh geese. It never gets dark when we're out camping, and it's fun."

Billy and other fishermen catch the herring in gill nets, both for their own use and to sell. Here the old ways and the

258

new meet; Yup'ik Eskimos have been catching herring and drying them for winter food for hundreds of years, but it is only recently that they have been able to sell them for cash.

Billy sells his catch—as much as twenty thousand pounds of herring in a good year—to huge Japanese fish processing boats that wait out to sea. Prevented by law from fishing close to the coast of the United States, the Japanese buy the catch of Americans. The herring eggs are a great delicacy for the Japanese, who will pay very high prices for this special-occasion food. Most of the rest of the fish is ground up to make fertilizer.

Scammon Bay people still dry large numbers of herring for the winter, just as they have for hundreds of years. Split open, cleaned, and hung up to dry, the fish become a good-tasting, chewy, oily, protein-rich food that can last all winter. The fish that aren't caught in the nets lay their eggs on seaweed along the shores. The seaweed, dried, is also a traditional favorite food of Scammon Bay people. Soaked in water during the winter, it tastes fresh at a time when no fresh vegetables are available.

Jonathan Jenness

When the herring run is finished, people get ready to go north up the coast to the mouths of the rivers where salmon enter to lay their eggs. This is another chance to earn money. And Alice will dry a lot of salmon for the family's own use.

On the Weekends

During the school year, traditional ways of life are practiced mostly on the weekends. The end of each school week marks the beginning of two days of hunting and fishing for the whole Rivers family.

Alice says, "On the weekends, we get to go traveling with Billy. Usually we decide what we're going to do ahead of time, what's going to happen. Like if we want to go fishing, we go fishing, or hunting ptarmigans. We're out most of the day Saturday doing this and that."

This is where Billy becomes the teacher, training the kids in both the oldest methods of hunting and fishing, and the newest. Since the children spend so much time in school, this is an important time for them to learn how to survive as Eskimos.

"I teach my boys the way I've been taught, the way my dad taught me. What I think that's wrong, I try to do it better than my dad. And when I make a mistake, I try to correct it to my boys, so they'll do it better than I did.

"I start taking them out as soon as they're old enough—like in the boat, when they're old enough to sit down and take care of themselves. I tell them little things like taking the anchor out, putting the anchor back up. As soon as they understand our words, we teach them from there. If they show you something that they know, you'll know they learned it—and then they can start doing it by themselves.

"Each one of them that goes with me, I talk to them, I tell them about little things—what's dangerous, what's not dangerous. I tell them about melting ice—even though it looks good on the surface, some places you can't see when it's covered with snow, it's thin. That's where they fall through. I

261

teach them what thin ice looks like, and how it looks when it's safe.

"Oscar's been going with me first, 'cause he's the oldest one, then Jacob. One of them will know more, the one that pays attention more, just like in school. The one that doesn't listen, or doesn't pay attention, he'll make more mistakes or get more scolding.

"Oscar was about seven or eight when I first let him shoot a gun. He got his first seal when he was maybe eight or nine. In the boat I did the driving, and I had him do the shooting. He got a young mukluk that was a baby in springtime. He shot it, and after he shot it, he looked at me, looked back, and he smiled. 'I catch it.' "

Oscar remembers this very clearly. He says, "My grandpa divided the seal up in circles and gave it to the old people." This is the traditional Yup'ik way of sharing a boy's first catch with the elders, still carried on, though motorboats have replaced kayaks, and rifles are used in place of thrown harpoons.

THE FUTURE

Alice and Billy know very well that life is changing fast here in Scammon Bay, and they want their children to be prepared for this.

Alice says, "When I was a kid, I used to do things with my mom. I used to watch her sew. Now I try to have Mattie knit, crochet, make things, but she thinks it's too boring. She knows how to do it, but she can't sit and look at one thing for a long time. I can't even teach her how to sew a skin. She doesn't have any patience.

"Now there's so many other things going on. In our time there was no basketball, no Igloo [community center], hardly any dances."

Billy says, "When I was Billy Junior's age, I used to run maybe twenty or thirty times around a pond with my little wooden boat. Just run around, play with it, put mud inside of it, and run around. I'd never think of TV, it wasn't in my mind.

263

"Everything is not the same here in Alaska, not like before. Things are changing. Things are getting more expensive. Most of the people are depending on more jobs. I mean working, you have to have a job.

"I talk to the kids, I just say what we'd like them to do. I tell them, 'If you go to school, and be smart over there, and try to learn what you're taught, you guys will have good jobs, and good-paying jobs. I want you to have good-paying jobs, so we'll have the things that we need, anything we need'; like this I talk to them.

"I'd be happy to have them travel to see other countries, to have them learning something that's Outside—*if* they have a job. 'Cause Outside there's many people without jobs, no home. Here it's okay, as we help each other here in the villages.

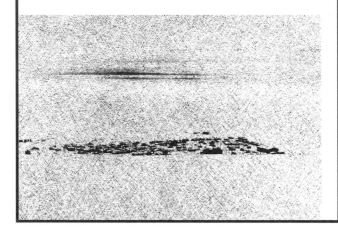

"We get after the kids for not doing their homework. We want them to be more educated, more than us. I mean, learn more. I only went up to the fifth grade."

Alice agrees. She adds "I want them to learn other ways—Outside ways. And I want them to learn our ways, too—hunting for our kind of foods. We can't have store-bought food all the time. I want them to learn both ways."

Looking down on Scammon Bay from the hill, it seems like a very small settlement, nearly lost in the huge expanse of tundra around it. From this distance it doesn't look so different from the Scammon Bay of Alice's childhood. Yet it is invisibly connected to the whole world now. And so is the Rivers family.

MEET AYLETTE JENNESS AND ALICE RIVERS, AUTHORS
Photographer and writer Aylette Jenness met Alice Rivers when Jenness lived in Scammon Bay, Alaska, during the 1960s. Jenness first came to Alaska to work on her books Gussuk Boy *and* Dwellers of the Tundra, *both of which were about the people of Scammon Bay. When Jenness returned to Alaska for a visit more than twenty years later, the two friends decided to work together on the story of how Rivers's family has grown and changed and how the little community on the Bering Sea has changed as well. Rivers's mother, Mary Ann Sundown, also contributed to the book by telling about the way people lived during the years she grew up near Scammon Bay.*

265

8 Students may need to **interpret** what Billy Rivers means when he says that families help each other in the villages. They may remember that on page 249 the author says that Yup'ik families traditionally shared their resources and that no one was much better or much worse off than anyone else.

9 Encourage students to **interpret** the statement that Scammon Bay is now "invisibly connected to the whole world," particularly the meaning here of *invisibly*.

Discussing Strategy Use
Encourage the students to discuss how they used the visualizing and summing up strategies as they read the selection. Were they able to use descriptions in the text to make pictures in their minds? In summarizing, did they use subheadings and other clues in the text to help them?

EXPLORING THROUGH DISCUSSION

Reflecting on the Selection
Whole-Group Discussion

The **whole group discusses** the selection and any **personal thoughts, reactions, problems,** or **questions** that it raises. During this time, students may also be invited to **return** to the **clues, problems, and wonderings** they noted on the board during browsing to determine whether the clues were borne out by the selection, whether and how their problems were solved, and whether their wonderings were answered or deserve further discussion and exploration. Avoid treating their ideas like a list to be discussed and eliminated in a linear fashion. Instead, let the **students decide which items deserve further discussion.** To stimulate discussion, the **students** can **ask one another** the kinds of **questions that good readers ask themselves** about a text: **What did I find interesting? What is important here? What was difficult to understand? Why would someone want to read this?** Your own participation in the discussion might take the form of expressing and modeling your reactions to characters or to other aspects of the story. It is important for the students to see you as a contributing member of the group.

To emphasize that you are part of the group, actively **participate in the handing-off process**: Raise your hand to be called on by the last speaker when you have a contribution to make. Point out unusual and interesting insights verbalized by the students so that these insights are recognized and discussed. As the year progresses, the students will take more and more responsibility for the discussions of the selections. The handing-off process is a good way to get them to take on this responsibility.

Assessment

In a successful discussion, it should not be necessary for you to ask questions to assess the students' understanding of the text. If necessary, however, engage in a discussion to **determine whether students have grasped the following ideas**:

- what influence the Yup'iks' unique physical environment had on their culture
- which things are still almost the same for the Yup'iks as they were in the past and which things are different
- how many of the changes that have taken place in the Yup'iks' way of life have occurred within the last fifty years

Response Journal

Students may wish to record their personal responses to the selection.

Exploring Concepts Within the Selection
Small-Group Discussion

Have the **students form small collaborative groups** and spend a few minutes **discussing whether this story gave them any new ideas about family heritage.** Remind them to include in their discussions ideas about family heritage that have come from their own experiences as well as from experiences they have heard or read about in other books. Have them refer to the **Concept Board and the Question Board.** If they discussed their ideas about family heritage before they began the unit and posted these on either board, be sure that they review those ideas now and consider how they have been affected by this story.

TIP FOR ENGLISH LANGUAGE LEARNERS

English Language Learners may have unique insights about the main ideas presented in the story. Encourage them to share their knowledge and experiences as they relate to the ideas of the story.

ASSESSMENT TIP This may be a good opportunity to observe students working in groups and to mark observations in the Teacher's Observation Log.

Sharing Ideas
About Explorable
Concepts

Have the groups **report** and **discuss** their **ideas** with the rest of the class. It is crucial that the students' ideas determine this discussion.

- Students might discuss the idea that Alice and Billy Rivers want their children to learn both the new ways and the old ways.
- The students might conclude that this hope that future generations will continue to value their cultural traditions is similar to that of parents in other cultures.

As these ideas and others are stated, have the students **add them to** the **Question Board** or the **Concept Board.**

Recording Ideas

As students complete the above discussions, ask them to **sum up what they have learned from their conversations and to tell how they might use this information** in further explorations. Any special information or insights may be recorded on the **Concept Board.** Any further questions that they would like to think about, pursue, or investigate may be recorded on the **Question Board.** They may want to discuss the progress that has been made on their questions. They may also want to cross out any questions that no longer warrant consideration.

❯ After discussion, the students should individually record their ideas on page 42 of their Explorer's Notebook.

TIP FOR ENGLISH LANGUAGE LEARNERS

Invite English Language Learners to model for others. Have them share their knowledge and experiences. If applicable, encourage them to discuss what is the same and what is different about living in this country compared to living in their native country.

Evaluating Discussion

Explorer's Notebook, page 42

Recording Concept Information

As I read each selection, this is what I added to my understanding of family heritage.

"In Two Worlds: A Yup'ik Eskimo Family" by Aylette Jenness and Alice Rivers

_____
_____
_____
_____
_____
_____

"The History of the Tunrit," translated by Edward Field

_____
_____
_____
_____
_____
_____
_____

"The Night We Started Dancing" by Ann Cameron

_____
_____
_____
_____
_____
_____
_____

42 EN   Family Heritage/Unit 3

Professional Checkpoint: Cognitive and Responsive Reading

Try to find out what students know about something before telling them what you know. Get their ideas first. They may have more knowledge than you think. If they have no ideas at all, help them rather than letting them make random guesses. But always get their ideas first.

Notes:

2 READING WITH A WRITER'S EYE

MINILESSONS

Writer's Craft: Elaboration

Remind the students that good writers organize their information into paragraphs. Often, the most important idea in the paragraph is stated at the beginning. **The rest of the paragraph provides details that support or elaborate on the main idea.** Ask students to tell what they know about using elaboration.

In this selection students will see two different kinds of elaboration used in paragraphs: **elaboration by examples** and **elaboration by details.**

Have a volunteer read the first sentences of the paragraph beginning on page 248. The **important idea** of this paragraph is stated in **the first two sentences**: "The small, scattered groups of Yup'ik Eskimos knew exactly how to survive here. Living as single families, or in small groups of relatives, they moved with the seasons to catch each kind of fish, bird, or mammal when and where each was most easily available."

Ask students to tell what **examples** the author provides to elaborate on this idea in the remaining sentences in the paragraph. In the **third** sentence, she talks about harpooning whales; in the **fourth,** about trapping and shooting birds and gathering birds' eggs; in the **fifth,** about catching fish; in the **sixth,** about trapping small mammals. The **last** sentence is a **restatement of the main idea of the paragraph**: "They knew where to find and how to catch dozens of different fish and animals for food, for clothing, even for light and heat for their small homes."

Have a volunteer read the first sentences of the second paragraph on page 251. The **important idea** of this paragraph is stated in the **first sentence**: "We lived in a sod house." Ask students to tell what **details** are provided in the remaining sentences in the paragraph to elaborate on this idea. The **second** sentence tells about the braided grass on the walls of the house; the **third,** about the window; the **fourth,** about the floor; the **fifth, sixth, and seventh** about the family's beds and how they stayed warm in them; the **last,** about cooking and eating utensils.

Selective Reading:
Focus on Elaboration

Have the students look through the selection for other paragraphs in which a **general statement** is **followed by specific examples or details.** Other paragraphs in which main ideas are elaborated by details or examples include the following:

- page 247, third paragraph: details about seasons in the Arctic
- page 249, second paragraph: details about Yup'ik life in the past
- page 253, first paragraph: details about the furnishings of Alice's home

Independent Practice:
Elaboration

Have students complete Reading/Writing Connection, page 21, individually or in small groups. If they work individually, have them share their work in small groups when they complete the page.

Writer's Craft:
Comparison

Tell the students that in "In Two Worlds," Jenness and Rivers provide the reader with many comparisons. Ask them to talk about anything they have learned about using comparisons and to describe any examples they can remember from their reading and writing. Explain that the **authors made use of comparisons in order to make clear the differences between the past and the present.** Provide the following examples to illustrate comparisons:

- page 252: "I liked the life we used to live a long time ago, but we were always in need of something. I would say we live in comfort now. I don't go in hunger now. I say both lives I led were good, and I like both."
- page 253: "No table—the tables came later. Mom used to cook bread on top of the stove, 'cause there was no oven. . . . Then as I grew older, we got a stove and oven, and she started baking bread."
- pages 256–257: "Some families bought stoves that burned fuel oil instead of relying on brush wood they cut nearby. . . . Some bought snowmobiles, which enabled them to travel farther than they could by dog team to hunt and trap, but which, unlike dogs, required money for fuel and new parts."

Selective Reading:
Focus on Comparison

Have the students look through the selection for other places in which the present is compared to the past. Other places in the text where the past and the present are compared include the following:

- page 262: motorboats and rifles versus kayaks and harpoons
- page 263: Alice and Billy on their children's activities compared to their own as children
- page 264: on economic changes in Alaska

Independent Practice:
Comparison

Have students complete Reading/Writing Connection, page 22, individually or in small groups. If they work individually, have them share their work in small groups when they complete the page.

WRITING

Linking Reading
to Writing

Have students look through their writing folders for paragraphs that can be improved by elaboration or for places where they might provide

"In Two Worlds"

Elaboration

Choose four paragraphs from "In Two Worlds." Write
the page number on which each paragraph appears. Write
the important idea in each paragraph. Then list the
examples or details that are used to elaborate on each
important idea.

Page: _____ Important idea: _____
_____
Examples or details: _____
_____
_____

Page: _____ Important idea: _____
_____
Examples or details: _____
_____
_____

Page: _____ Important idea: _____
_____
Examples or details: _____
_____
_____

Page: _____ Important idea: _____
_____
Examples or details: _____
_____
_____

Name

Copyright © 1995 Open Court Publishing Company

Unit 3/Family Heritage
Elaboration
R/WC 21

Reading/Writing Connection, page 21

"In Two Worlds"

Comparing

Choose comparisons from "In Two Worlds" or from
another selection you have read. Write the page where
each comparison appears. Write the things being
compared. Then list the details that are used to elaborate
on each comparison.

Page: _____ Things compared: _____
_____
Details: _____
_____

Page: _____ Things compared: _____
_____
Details: _____
_____

Page: _____ Things compared: _____
_____
Details: _____
_____

Page: _____ Things compared: _____
_____
Details: _____
_____

Page: _____ Things compared: _____
_____
Details: _____
_____

Name

Copyright © 1995 Open Court Publishing Company

Elaboration
22 R/WC
Family Heritage/Unit 3

Reading/Writing Connection, page 22

comparisons. Have them work together to think of examples or details
that will improve these pieces.

✱ Writing Process

Students might want to begin a new piece of writing at this time. You
might suggest that they write several paragraphs that compare situations. They might **compare some aspect of life in the past with a situation in the present,** as did the authors of the selection they just read.
Or they might **compare certain aspects of life in different places,** for
example, Scammon Bay and their own communities.

Spend some time brainstorming about situations they might write
about. Use the selection for ideas, if necessary. Remind students to limit
their comparisons to one or two aspects of life. As they make notes of
ideas to write about or begin their first drafts, **remind them to include
enough examples and details to make their paragraphs interesting
and to support their main ideas.**

VOCABULARY

Encourage the students to discuss words or phrases from the selection
that they want to use in their speaking and writing or in their exploration for this unit. Words or phrases you might discuss that are related
to the concept include the following:

heritage, secluded, migrated, intricate, resources, ancestors, survival

VOCABULARY TIP Use important words related to family
heritage during discussions
with the students to model
the utility of these words.

Vocabulary Exploration

Word: _____

Why you chose this word: _____
_____

Definition as used in the selection: _____
_____

Other meanings: _____
_____

Any antonyms you can think of: _____
_____

Any synonyms you can think of: _____
_____

Where else have you found this word? _____

How might you use this word in your writing? _____
_____

Your sentence using the word: _____
_____

Remember to use this word in speaking as well as in writing.

RM 14   Writer's Notebook: Personal Dictionary

Reproducible Master 14

Provide an opportunity for students to fill out Vocabulary Exploration forms, Reproducible Master 14, for words they wish to learn or those that are important to the unit concepts. Remind them to add these words or any other words and phrases from the story to the Personal Dictionary section of their Writer's Notebook. For additional opportunities to build vocabulary, see **Teacher Tool Card 75**.

Adding to Personal Word Lists

3 GUIDED AND INDEPENDENT EXPLORATION

EXPLORING CONCEPTS BEYOND THE TEXT

Guided Exploration

Students will engage in **activities of their own choosing** that allow them to explore family heritage more deeply and to use the questions they have raised to do so. These explorations may relate to the current selection or to a number of selections, but they must revolve around family heritage. The following is a **menu of possible activities** from which the students may choose:

*Exploring Through Reflective Activities

- A literature search to pursue a question or a problem. Discussion or writing may follow.
- An original play or puppet show based on family-related situations.
- A role–playing game to work out a problem about a family situation.
- A panel discussion with audience participation on a question or a problem. (This discussion would have a leader and could be videotaped.)

- A debate on an issue related to family heritage. (Debaters would form teams. They would be required to follow some basic rules of debate, providing reasoned support for their side of the issue.)
- An advice column dealing with family-related problems.
- A personal experience story related to family heritage.
- An interview with someone on a subject related to family heritage.
- A survey on an issue or question related to family heritage.
- The questioning of a visiting expert about family heritage.
- A picture or photo essay about family heritage.

Display the **Exploration Activities poster** listing the activities above so that in future lessons the students may readily select from them.

Students may **work** on these activities **alone, in pairs,** or in **small groups,** with an option to write about them or to present them to the group.

If the students need help in deciding on an activity, here are some suggestions to get them started:

The best way for students to explore their own heritage is to talk to family members or close family friends. Let the students tell what they know about interviewing. Remind them that interviewing involves making certain arrangements—such as contacting in advance the person to be interviewed, preparing questions to ask, and listing subjects to discuss. Explorer's Notebook, page 12, lists some guidelines for conducting interviews.

For a review of information about **interviewing**, see **Teacher Tool Card 110.**

> Explorer's Notebook, page 45, has space for students to write some preliminary questions to use in these interviews. Interviews can be recorded on audiotape or videotape or in the form of written notes, which can be recorded on Explorer's Notebook, page 46. Some students might want to take photographs of people they interview.

> Distribute Home/School Connection 18–19 to enlist students' families in their explorations of family heritage.

Some students might be interested in planning a photo essay about a family or about a neighborhood in which many families of a particular culture live. Suggest that they examine the selection again in order to consider how the text and photographs complement each other and what information is conveyed in each photograph. Bibliographies for the unit will provide other examples of photo essays. See especially *Joel: Growing Up a Farm Man, Pueblo Storyteller,* and *Making a New Home in America.*

Generating Questions to Explore

Have the students continue their discussion of family heritage, raising any new questions that they wish to explore. Tell them that as they read further, they may come up with a variety of ideas for ways to explore.

Tell the students that this is a good time to post on the Question Board any new questions they may have about family heritage. Be sure

Interviewing a Family Member

Photo Essay

Using the Question Board

they include their names or initials so that they can find out who has similar interests in order to exchange ideas. Point out that they may post a question on the board at any time during the course of their exploration—after they have read a selection in the anthology or after they have done some reading on their own. They should feel free to write an answer or a note on someone else's question or to consult the board for ideas for their own exploration. Remember that you are a part of the group and therefore should feel free to post your own questions from time to time as well.

To review information about the Question Board, see Teacher Tool Card 121.

▶ Distribute the bibliography for family heritage, Reproducible Masters 33–37, so that students will have it available as they begin to explore. Remind them also to use the bibliography on pages 354–355 of their student anthology. Also encourage the reading of any other books or magazines about the explorable concepts. Remind the students to keep track of the books they examine, recording the titles, authors, and other pertinent information that might be useful to them as they work on unit activities.

▶ Have the students use Explorer's Notebook, page 47, to help them start thinking about questions related to family heritage.

Explorer's Notebook, page 45

Conducting an Interview

Think about questions that you might ask the person you interview. What do you especially want to know? How will talking to this person help you learn more about your family heritage? Write some questions that will help you find out what you want to know. Discuss these questions with your classmates.

Questions about where my ancestors were born:

_____
_____
_____
_____
_____

Questions about languages that my ancestors spoke:

_____
_____
_____
_____
_____

Questions about traditions that have been passed down in my family:

_____
_____
_____
_____
_____

Explorer's Notebook, page 46

Conducting an Interview *continued*

Now organize the information you got from your interview.

Information about where my ancestors were born:

_____
_____
_____

Information about languages that my ancestors spoke:

_____
_____
_____

Information about traditions that have been passed down in my family:

_____
_____
_____

Other information:

_____
_____
_____

A message from _____

Our new reading anthology unit deals with concepts related to family heritage. Your child will be exploring the heritage of many different families from around the world.

You and your child might enjoy finding out more about your family history together. Encourage your child to share this information with the rest of the class. Here are some questions to guide your exploration:

- Where were some of our ancestors born?
- Did any of our ancestors speak other languages? What languages?
- Are there any traditions that have been passed down from generation to generation in our family?
- How can we learn more about our family's heritage?

Listed below are some books about family heritage that you might like to read with your child. Most should be available at your public library. Add to this list other books that you and your child find together.

Beauties and Beasts by Betsy Hearne. This book is a collection of international versions of well-known folk tales. With each story there are notes about the tale's origin and culture.

Goodbye, My Island by Jean Rogers. In this book based on a true story, an Eskimo girl tells of the last winter her people spent on King Island, Alaska, in 1964.

How My Family Lives in America by Susan Kuklin. African-American, Asian-American, and Hispanic-American children describe ways their family heritage and cultural traditions are passed on through language, stories, songs, games, special food, language, and special celebrations.

If Your Name Was Changed at Ellis Island by Ellen Levine. In question-and-answer format, this book explains the migration of immigrants to the United States from the 1800s to 1914, and features quotes from children and adults who passed through New York's Ellis Island.

continued

Unit 3/Family Heritage　　　　H/SC 18

Home/School Connection 18

continued

Letters From Rifka by Karen Hesse. In letters to her cousin back "home" in Russia, a twelve-year-old Jewish girl tells of her dangerous and difficult journey to America in 1919. This book is based on a true story.

The Lost Garden by Lawrence Yep. Growing up in San Francisco during the 1950s, Lawrence Yep thought of himself as a typical American boy—a boy who played sports, ate with a fork, and spoke English. Read how Yep's dual heritage helped him become the award-winning author that he is today.

Now Is Your Time! The African-American Struggle for Freedom by Walter Dean Myers. This book presents the stories of several African-American people whose lives made a difference.

The Strength of the Hills: A Portrait of a Family Farm by Nancy Price Graff. A family of six live and work on a small farm in Vermont that has been in their family for generations. This book offers a look into a way of life that is fast disappearing from the American landscape.

You might also enjoy watching with your child the following movies related to family heritage.

The Karate Kid. Columbia Tristar Home Video, 1984. In order to defend himself against a bully, a boy turns to a Japanese karate master and learns self-confidence as well as physical skills. 126 minutes, videocassette.

Roots. Warner Home Videos, 1977. This television series was based on Alex Haley's best-selling novel that followed an African-American man's search for his heritage. 6 volumes, 90 minutes each, videocassette.

Unit 3/Family Heritage　　　　H/SC 19

Home/School Connection 19

BIBLIOGRAPHY

Going Home by Nicholasa Mohr. Eleven-year-old Felita, a New Yorker, spends the summer with relatives in Puerto Rico.

Grandparents' Houses: Poems about Grandparents, selected by Corrine Streich. You'll enjoy the poems in this book and the illustrations by Lillian Hoban that go with them.

The Great Ancestor Hunt: The Fun of Finding Out Who You Are by Lila Perl. This book might help you start your search for your roots.

Homesick: My Own Story by Jean Fritz. Growing up in China, Jean Fritz was intensely aware of her American heritage.

Immigrant Kids by Russell Freedman. Photographs from the early 1900s help tell about the experience of immigrants from Europe.

A Jar of Dreams by Yoshiko Uchida. A Japanese-American girl growing up in California in the 1930s comes to appreciate her heritage when her aunt visits from Japan.

Joel: Growing Up a Farm Man by Patricia Demuth. Thirteen-year-old Joel is already working at the job he hopes to do all of his life: caring for crops and animals, and managing the business of farming.

Pueblo Storyteller by Diane Hoyt-Goldsmith. A young Native-American girl living in the Cochiti Pueblo near Santa Fe, New México, tells about her people's customs and about the storyteller dolls her grandmother makes.

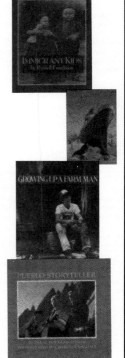

Bibliography

Books and magazines related to family heritage are listed below. Add other books and magazine articles you find.

Notes

Alice Yazzie's Year by Ramona Maher. In these poems, Maher describes events in the life of a modern-day Navaho girl.

The American Family Farm: A Photo Essay by George Ancona, with text by Joan Anderson. Three farm families continue to work with one another despite hardships and unpredictable disasters.

Appalachia: The Voices of Sleeping Birds by Cynthia Rylant. This book gives the reader a sense of Appalachia and the people who live there.

Ashanti to Zulu: African Traditions by Margaret Musgrove. The author describes ceremonies, celebrations, and day-to-day customs of twenty-six African tribes, with names beginning with letters A through Z.

Black Americans: A History in their Own Words by Milton Meltzer. This book is a history of African Americans told through letters, speeches, articles, eyewitness reports, and other documents.

The Book of Festivals and Holidays the World Over by Marguerite Ickis. This book may inspire you to celebrate some of these traditions in your own home.

The Call of the Running Tide: A Portrait of an Island Family by Nancy Graff Price. The author provides a picture of a unique life style.

Name

Reproducible Master 33

Bibliography *continued*

Notes

Child of the Owl by Laurence Yep. Casey Young learns to appreciate her Chinese heritage.

Childtimes: A Three-Generation Memoir by Eloise Greenfield and Lessie Jones Little. Three generations of women in an African-American family tell about their childhoods.

Cinderella, edited by Judy Sierra. This book includes various versions of the Cinderella story as it is told around the world.

Cobblestone magazine, March 1991 and November 1991. These issues feature articles on Ellis Island and immigration to the United States.

El Chino by Allen Say. This is the true story of the very first Chinese bullfighter.

Everybody Cooks Rice by Norah Dooley. A young girl learns about a variety of cultures as she observes the many different ways rice is prepared in the different homes she visits in her neighborhood.

Hello, My Name Is Scrambled Eggs by Jamie Gilson. When his parents host a Vietnamese family that has come to settle in their town, Harvey tries to Americanize twelve-year-old Tuan.

Holiday Cooking Around the World by Robert L. Wolfe and Diane Wolfe. Create an international meal for your family or friends with the help of this book of recipes from fifteen different countries.

Name

Reproducible Master 34

Bibliography *continued*

Notes

How Juan Got Home by Peggy Mann. A Puerto Rican boy finds friends in New York.

In Two Worlds by Aylette Jenness and Alice Rivers. In this book, Jenness and Rivers tell about the many changes in the way of life of a Yup'ik family in Alaska.

The Invisible Thread by Yoshiko Uchida. In this autobiography, the author describes her childhood in California as a second-generation Japanese American, her family's imprisonment during World War II, and her great sense of pride in her heritage.

Kids Explore America's Hispanic Heritage by Westridge Young Writer's Workshop. Students describe Hispanic-American culture, including its history, art, songs, dances, cooking, games, and jokes.

Magdalena by Louisa Shotwell. A Puerto Rican girl and her very traditional grandmother disagree about whether Magdalena should cut her hair.

My Grandmother's Stories by Adele Geras. A grandmother tells stories from her Russian-Jewish heritage.

My Place by Nadia Wheatly. Beginning in 1988, the author takes us on a journey into Australia's past, ten years at a time, back to 1788. On each page a different child tells about her or his life.

The New Americans: Changing Patterns in U.S. Immigration. This book offers a look at today's immigrants, including refugees and illegal aliens.

Name

Reproducible Master 35

Bibliography *continued*

Notes

The Night Journey by Kathryn Lasky. A Jewish girl learns to appreciate her family heritage.

Pacific Crossing by Gary Soto. Lincoln Mendoza goes to Japan to continue his martial-arts training. His hosts are as eager to learn about the United States as Lincoln is to learn about Japan.

The Sacred Harvest: Ojibway Wild Rice Gathering by Gordon Regguinti. Wild rice is more than just a food to the Ojibway Indians of northern Minnesota; this grain has also played a role in their religion and history.

Sign of the Chrysanthemum by Katherine Paterson. Set in the twelfth century, this story is about a boy who searches for his father, whom he believes to be a samurai warrior.

The Talking Earth by Jean Craighead George. A Seminole girl learns to appreciate the wisdom found in the legends of her people.

Where Did You Get Those Eyes? by Kay Cooper. Have you ever wondered whether you look like one of your ancestors? Cooper will show you how much fun it is to research your family's past.

Whirling Rainbows by Susan Terris. By birth Leah is part Polish and part Chippewa Indian, but she has spent all of her thirteen years with her Jewish adoptive parents. At summer camp she decides to search for her roots.

Name

Reproducible Master 36

Bibliography *continued*

Notes

Yang the Youngest and His Terrible Ear by Lensey
Namioka. Newly arrived in Seattle from Shanghai,
Yingtao Yang would rather practice baseball than
the violin, much to his father's disapproval.

Add books and articles you find.

- _____
- _____
- _____
- _____
- _____
- _____
- _____
- _____
- _____
- _____

Name _____

Unit 3/Family Heritage   RM 37

Reproducible Master 37

Planning Exploration

How can you explore the concept of family heritage
further? Write down some questions and some ideas you
would like to explore.

_____
_____
_____
_____
_____

As you begin your exploration of family heritage, you
will want to keep a list of things you need to do. Check off
each item as you complete it.

_____
_____
_____
_____
_____

If you decide to present your information, think of ways
you might do this. Add to this list as you read and explore
and come up with new ideas.

_____
_____
_____
_____
_____

Unit 3/Family Heritage   EN 47

Explorer's Notebook, page 47

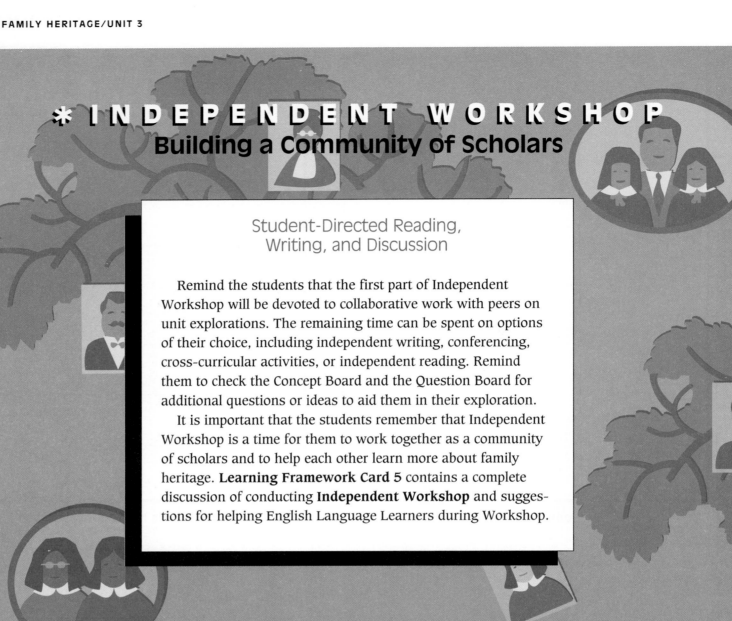

* INDEPENDENT WORKSHOP
Building a Community of Scholars

Student-Directed Reading, Writing, and Discussion

Remind the students that the first part of Independent Workshop will be devoted to collaborative work with peers on unit explorations. The remaining time can be spent on options of their choice, including independent writing, conferencing, cross-curricular activities, or independent reading. Remind them to check the Concept Board and the Question Board for additional questions or ideas to aid them in their exploration.

It is important that the students remember that Independent Workshop is a time for them to work together as a community of scholars and to help each other learn more about family heritage. **Learning Framework Card 5** contains a complete discussion of conducting **Independent Workshop** and suggestions for helping English Language Learners during Workshop.

Additional Opportunities for
Independent Reading, Writing, and
Cross-curricular Activities

✷ Reading Roundtable

Encourage the students to read *In Two Worlds,* books listed in the bibliographies, or any other books having to do with family heritage. Students can share what they read by telling about the books or by writing brief summaries of them. Summaries can be either posted or filed in a box that other students can refer to. For additional ideas for **Reading Roundtable,** see **Learning Framework Card 6.**

Tradebook Connection

Remind the students that the Tradebook Connection Cards are a good resource for ideas about what to read. Two books that are particularly appropriate for this unit are *In the Year of the Boar and Jackie Robinson* by Bette Bao Lord and *The Land I Lost* by Huynh Quang Nhuong.

✷ Writing Seminar

Students might continue work on writing first drafts or revisions of the paragraphs they began on comparing situations. Remind students to seek and provide feedback for their own and other's writing. For a review of **Writing Seminar,** see **Learning Framework Card 8.**

Cross-curricular Activity Cards

The students can refer to these cards for interesting activities and for ideas about areas to explore. The following card is particularly relevant to this selection:

• 9 Social Studies—Steps to Statehood

Steps to Statehood
Use after "In Two Worlds"

9
Social Studies

For many years the United States consisted of forty-eight states. In 1959, Alaska became the forty-ninth state. That same year, Hawaii became the fiftieth.
On your own or with a partner, do some research to find out about Alaska's statehood. Make a chart or a time line to show some important events. You may include all or some of the following years on your time line: 1799, 1867, 1899, 1903, 1906, 1912, 1959, 1980. *Studying history can help you to understand things that are happening now.*

Additional Opportunities for
Solving Learning Problems

Tutorial

Work with individuals or small groups who need help in any area. The following Teacher Tool Cards are available for your convenience:

• Writer's Craft/Reading: Elaboration Through Providing Examples, Teacher Tool Card 38
• Writer's Craft/Reading: Elaboration Through Providing Specific Facts, Teacher Tool Card 40
• Writer's Craft/Reading: Elaboration Through Providing Comparison and Contrast, Teacher Tool Card 36
• Writer's Craft/Reading: Genre—Expository Text, Teacher Tool Card 9
• Writer's Craft/Reading: Writing Paragraphs, Teacher Tool Card 22
• Writer's Craft/Reading: Elaboration Through Providing Background, Teacher Tool Card 41
• Study and Research: Interviewing, Teacher Tool Card 110

Song
History of the Tunrit

1 READING THE SONG

About the Song

    On the famous Fifth Thule Expedition across the Arctic regions of North America, explorer Knud Rasmussen recorded the legends and songs of the Netsilik, a remote people among whom he lived for three years. By sharing their rugged life, Rasmussen hoped to learn not only how they survived, but how they understood the universe. "History of the Tunrit" tells the story of the Tunrit, a strong, rugged people who lived in their "difficult country" before the Netsilik arrived and who taught the Netsilik how to survive there. The legend, which is typically chanted as a song, tells how the Tunrit left the land they shared with the Netsilik and about the heritage they left to them.

Link to the Unit Concepts

    "History of the Tunrit," pages 266–267, is from *Eskimo Songs and Stories,* a book of material collected by Rasmussen and selected and translated by Edward Field. The legend, which is typically chanted as a song, illustrates that people's ways of life are influenced by others who live among them as well as by their environment.

About the Editor/Translator

    Edward Field has published books of his own poetry and has written the narration for an award-winning documentary, *To Be Alive.* As editor of *Eskimo Songs and Stories,* he selected and retold material from the literal records of Rasmussen's expedition. He said, "Rasmussen wrote down everything just as the Netsilik Eskimos told it to him. . . . When you talk you tell a lot by gestures, facial expressions, and the way you use your voice. . . . I tried to put all that life back in, so that the reader would sense a real person in the words. . . ."

About the Artist

    Pudlo belongs to a group of native artists in the West Baffin Eskimo Cooperative. The cooperative is situated at Cape Dorset on West Baffin Island, just south of the Arctic Circle. The people of the community have

LESSON OVERVIEW

"History of the Tunrit," translated by Edward Field, pages 266–267

READING THE SELECTION

Materials

Student anthology, pp. 266–267

Explorer's Notebook, p. 42

READING WITH A WRITER'S EYE

Minilesson

Discussing a Song

Materials

Reproducible Master 14

GUIDED AND INDEPENDENT EXPLORATION

Materials

Explorer's Notebook, pp. 48–49

Independent Workshop

Optional Materials from Student Toolbox

Audiocassette

Tradebook Connection Cards

NOTES

Asterisks (*) throughout the lesson indicate learning frameworks. Learning Framework Cards and Teacher Tool Cards can be found in the Teacher Toolbox.

a long tradition of carving and craftsmanship and are recognized world-wide for their stencils and stone cuts. Like much of Pudlo's work, the picture on page 267, "Perils of the Hunter," depicts the world of the spirits, the magic that links the hunter with the animals he kills.

INFORMATION FOR THE STUDENT

The song comes from *Eskimo Songs and Stories,* a book based on material gathered by the explorer Knud Rasmussen. Rasmussen was a member of an Arctic expedition made during the years 1921 to 1924. He was part Eskimo and had grown up in Greenland speaking an Eskimo language.

From Greenland to Alaska, the languages spoken by peoples who live in the Arctic are similar. Rasmussen found that songs and stories told by various Arctic peoples were also very similar, even though the groups lived thousands of miles apart. Eventually, Rasmussen sought out the Netsilik, who lived along the North American coast above the Arctic Circle.

The Netsilik did not have a written language. The songs that they sang and the stories that they told were part of an oral tradition, remembered and passed down from one generation to the next. This song is about the Tunrit, a group who once shared the Netsilik's lands.

✳ COGNITIVE AND RESPONSIVE READING

Activating Prior Knowledge

Ask the students to review what they learned about Yup'ik ways of life by reading "In Two Worlds."

Setting Reading Goals and Expectations

After the students have looked at and commented on the title of the song and the art that accompanies it, have them talk about what they expect it will be about.

Recommendations for Reading the Song

Read the song aloud for students at least twice. Then allow interested students to practice reading it aloud to each other. Remind the students that when reading a song or poem aloud they should continue reading until they come to a punctuation mark.

✳ EXPLORING THROUGH DISCUSSION

Reflecting on the Song

Have the **students discuss the song** and any **thoughts, reactions,** or **questions** it raises. Encourage them to think about how the song adds to their understanding of family heritage.

- Students will probably conclude that the Netsilik admired the Tunrit and that the speaker feels sad that the Tunrit, who were so strong and so brave, left the lands they once shared.
- Students might discuss the idea that the Tunrit contributed to the heritage of the Netsilik.
- Students will notice that the Netsilik and the Tunrit share many ways of life with the Yup'iks.

TIP FOR ENGLISH LANGUAGE LEARNERS

Provide opportunities for English Language Learners to share their knowledge. Invite them to tell any familiar stories, poems, or songs.

HISTORY OF THE TUNRIT
traditional Netsilik Eskimo legend
translated by Edward Field
illustrated by Pudlo

When our forefathers came to these hunting grounds
the Tunrit people already lived here.
It was the Tunrit who first learned
how to survive in this difficult country.
They showed us the caribou crossing places
and taught us the special way to fish in the rivers.

Our people came from inland
so we love <u>caribou</u> hunting more than anything else,
but the Tunrit were sea people
and preferred to hunt seal.
They actually went out on the salt sea in their <u>kayaks</u>,
hunting seal in open water. That takes nerve.
We only hunt them through the ice at their breathing holes.
They also caught whales and walruses as they swam by:
The bones of these creatures are still lying around
in the wrecks of the Tunrit houses.
And they hunted bear and wore their skins for clothes.
We wear caribou.

266

The Tunrit were strong, but easily frightened.
In a fight they would rather run than kill. Anyway,
you never heard of them killing anyone.
And we lived among the Tunrit in those days peacefully,
for they let us come and share their land:
Until once by accident some of them killed one of our dogs
and ran away scared, leaving their homeland.

All of the Tunrit fled from their villages here finally,
although we cannot remember why anymore:
They just ran away or the land was taken from them.
And on leaving us they cried:
"We followed the caribou and hunted them down,
now it is your turn to follow them and do the hunting."

And so we do to this day.

Have the students look at the fine-art pieces on pages 313–314 of the student anthology and discuss the stone carving *Family Greeting* by Eli Tikeayak. They may wish to express their thoughts and feelings about this work and any connections they think it has to the song they have just read.

Fine Art

- Some students may remember that people who live in Arctic regions, such as the Yup'iks, the Netsilik, the Tunrit, and the Inuit, tend to live in widely-scattered family groups.
- They may speculate about whom the family shown in the sculpture is greeting. Another member of their own family? A family member who is, perhaps, returning from a hunting expedition? Another family? A family of friends or relatives whom they have not seen for many months? Or perhaps a family of strangers who has recently moved nearby, as the Netsilik moved near the Tunrit?

Response Journal

Students may wish to record their personal responses to the song.

Recording Ideas

➤ Have the students sum up their discussions and record their ideas and impressions about the song and the concepts on the Concept Board and in their Explorer's Notebook, page 42.

Evaluating Discussions

Recording Concept Information

As I read each selection, this is what I added to my understanding of family heritage.

"In Two Worlds: A Yup'ik Eskimo Family" by Aylette Jenness and Alice Rivers

_____
_____
_____
_____
_____
_____

"The History of the Tunrit," translated by Edward Field

_____
_____
_____
_____
_____
_____

"The Night We Started Dancing" by Ann Cameron

_____
_____
_____
_____
_____
_____
_____

42 EN   Family Heritage/Unit 3

Explorer's Notebook, page 42

2 READING WITH A WRITER'S EYE

MINILESSON

Discussing a Song

Ask the students if there was anything about the song that they particularly enjoyed. Encourage the students to discuss specific information about the Tunrits and the Netsilik that the song provides.

WRITING

Linking Reading to Writing

Invite volunteers to share with the group instances of how they or other writers have used songs or poems to tell stories.

✷ Writing Process

If any students are interested in writing songs or poems that tell stories, encourage them to include specific, concise details about events or settings that will help to tell their stories in just a few lines.

VOCABULARY

Words and phrases students might discuss and record in the Personal Dictionary section of their Writer's Notebook include the following:
forefathers, caribou, inland, homeland

Provide Vocabulary Exploration forms, Reproducible Master 14, for students who want to complete them.

3 GUIDED AND INDEPENDENT EXPLORATION

EXPLORING CONCEPTS BEYOND THE TEXT

Guided Exploration

Students will select activities in which they explore learning. Refer them to the **Exploration Activities poster** and give them time to choose an activity and to discuss what they wish to explore and how they wish to go about it. If the students need further help, here is a suggestion:

Remind the students that **one way to keep track of information is to organize it on a chart.** Ask them to share what they know about using charts to organize information. Remind them that the form of the chart they use depends on the kind of information they want to organize. For example, to organize information about how the Netsilik, the Yup'iks, and other Eskimo peoples lived in the past compared to how they live now, they might make a chart such as the one on Explorer's Notebook pages 48–49. Encourage students to complete this chart using information about the way Arctic peoples lived in the past from "The History of the Tunrit" and from pages 247–250 of "In Two Worlds," and about the way Yup'iks live now from the last sections of "In Two Worlds."

* Exploring Through Reflective Activities

Explorer's Notebook, page 48

Comparison Chart

You have read about different Arctic peoples: the Tunrit, the Netsilik, Yup'iks of ancient and recent times, and Yup'iks of today. Think about how these peoples are similar and how they are different. Then fill in some of the spaces on the chart below.

	Tunrit	Netsilik	Yup'iks of Long Ago
Homes			
Food			
Clothing			
Transportation			
Education			
Community Life			

Explorer's Notebook, page 49

Yup'iks of 50 Years Ago	Yup'iks of 25 Years Ago	Yup'iks of Today

* INDEPENDENT WORKSHOP
Building a Community of Scholars

Student-Directed Reading, Writing, and Discussion

The students should work in collaborative groups during the first part of Independent Workshop to share ideas for exploring family heritage. Provide time for individuals or small groups to use the library as needed to locate reference materials and information. Have them work with their groups to share and evaluate the resources they have found.

Additional Opportunities for Independent Reading, Writing, and Cross-curricular Activities

✱ Reading Roundtable

Students might enjoy reading or listening to more selections from *Eskimo Songs and Stories.* Encourage them to practice reading some of these aloud.

✱ Writing Seminar

Encourage students to revise, proofread, and publish their pieces comparing and contrasting situations. Remind them to use the Writing Strategy Posters whenever necessary.

Additional Opportunities for Solving Learning Problems

Tutorial

Use the time to work with those students who need help in any area. Remember to use peer tutoring with those for whom it would be appropriate. If your class is using the optional Writer's Handbook, students doing peer tutoring might want to use it to help them.

The Night We Started Dancing

1 READING THE SELECTION

INFORMATION FOR THE TEACHER

About the
Selection

Eight-year-old Luisito lives in Guatemala with his grandparents and other family members. In a very authentic voice, he tells the story of what has happened to him and his family in the last few years and, especially, of what happened on last Christmas Eve, the night they started dancing. He speaks of his town and of the achievements of his Mayan ancestors, of the accident that killed his parents and of the bad dreams he still has about it, and, especially, of his grandfather, who continues to grieve for his dead son.

Link to the
Unit Concepts

"The Night We Started Dancing," pages 268–283, tells about an extended family that remains close despite the death of two of its members.

About the
Author

Ann Cameron is known primarily for her popular *Julian* books. *The Stories Julian Tells* was an American Library Association Notable Book and won a Parent's Choice award. She writes about children from cultures that are not part of her own family heritage—the *Julian* stories are set in South Africa, and *The Most Beautiful Place in the World,* in Guatemala. Cameron disagrees with people who believe that authors cannot write authentically about cultures that are not their own:

What entitles any writer to draw the portrait of a culture or cultures? What qualifies a reader to judge that portrait? For me, the answer in both cases is the same—knowledge, imagination, and sympathy. Our license to create and to judge is not a particular experience, a particular racial or national background. It is our humanness. . . . Among many Americans, old style racism and

LESSON OVERVIEW

"The Night We Started Dancing" by Ann Cameron, pages 268–283

READING THE SELECTION

Materials

Student anthology, pp. 268–283
Explorer's Notebook, p. 42

READING WITH A WRITER'S EYE

Minilessons

Writer's Craft: Indicators of Time and Order
Writer's Craft: Characterization

Materials

Reading/Writing Connection, pp. 23–24
Reproducible Masters 14, 25

FYI

Teacher Tool Card
• Spelling and Vocabulary: Building Vocabulary, 75

Options for Instruction

Writer's Craft: Point of View
Grammar, Mechanics, and Usage: Compound Sentences
(Use Teacher Tool Cards listed below.)

GUIDED AND INDEPENDENT EXPLORATION

Materials

Home/School Connection 20

Independent Workshop

Optional Materials from Student Toolbox

Tradebook Connection Cards

Cross-curricular Activity Cards
• 1 Music—Songs of Latin America
• 10 Science—Making Traditional Foods
• 10 Social Studies—Cultures of Middle America

Student Tool Cards
• Writer's Craft/Reading: Signal Words Showing Time and Order, 27
• Writer's Craft/Reading: Characterization, 13
• Writer's Craft/Reading: Point of View, 12
• Grammar, Mechanics, and Usage: Compound Sentences, 48

FYI

Teacher Tool Cards
• Writer's Craft/Reading: Indicators of Time and Order, 27
• Writer's Craft/Reading: Characterization, 13
• Writer's Craft/Reading: Point of View, 12
• Grammar, Mechanics, and Usage: Compound Sentences, 48

N O T E S

Asterisks (*) throughout the lesson indicate learning frameworks. Learning Framework Cards and Teacher Tool Cards can be found in the Teacher Toolbox.

ethnocentricity is dead. But there are new misunderstandings about ethnicity and identity. Many of us assume that our ethnicity is a simple thing. Many of us assume that it divides the world into air-tight racial compartments. Some of us believe that only such compartments offer authentic windows on life, and our only license to comment on it. . . .

We forget that identity is not only what we come from, it is what we reach toward . . . . All of us are born incomplete, desperate to become larger, to know a wider world. For each of us, all kinds of people from all kinds of places can contribute to our wholeness. In the end, for each of us, what wholeness means will be an individual thing.

What is central to us, however, should include the recognition of shared humanity—the importance of being human. Being human includes competence and learning, friendship and loyalty, knowing what we stand for and what we stand against. Being human includes knowing what cruelty is—and being able to recognize it and oppose it even when we find it in ourselves. That is what our best children's books, multicultural or otherwise, teach.

INFORMATION FOR THE STUDENT

- "The Night We Started Dancing" is a **realistic story** about a family living in Santa Cruz, Guatemala, in Central America. It is told through the eyes of the youngest member of the family, an eight-year-old boy.
- Ann Cameron lives in Guatemala and got the idea for "The Night We Started Dancing" from a Christmas Eve celebration at the home of Guatemalan friends.
- Some students may be interested in knowing that Cameron is the author of the *Julian* books.

COGNITIVE AND RESPONSIVE READING

Activating Prior Knowledge

Ask students to think about special family times around holidays and any special holidays that their families celebrate.

Setting Reading Goals and Expectations

Have the students **browse** the **first page** of the selection, using the clues/problems/wondering procedure. Students will return to these observations after reading.

Recommendations for Reading the Selection

Ask the students how they would like to read the selection. The simple, expressive voice of the narrator and the animated conversations among the characters make this story a good choice for reading aloud.

During oral reading, use and encourage think-alouds. During silent reading, allow discussion as needed. Discuss problems, strategies, and reactions after reading.

TIP FOR ENGLISH LANGUAGE LEARNERS

Invite English Language Learners to describe special holidays.

This would also be a good selection for **responding** to text **by making connections** and **expressing feelings** while reading aloud. Model this response, and then invite the students to respond similarly.

About the Reading Strategies

This selection is written in **nonchronological order**. That is, the narrator often goes back in time to tell about a past event and then returns to the present. Students may need to **ask questions** and **sum up** in order to clarify these shifts in time. They may also **make predictions** about the outcome of the story.

Think-Aloud Prompts for Use in Oral Reading

The think-aloud prompts are placed where students may encounter difficulties with the text. These are merely suggestions. Remind the students to refer to the **reading strategy posters** and to use any strategy they feel they need to help make sense of what they are reading. Encourage the students to collaborate with classmates when confronted with difficulties while reading.

Reading Strategy Poster

THINK ALOUD PROMPTS

These prompts may be used as guides to promote cognitive and responsive reading.

1 The students might want to **sum up,** since these first paragraphs have provided much information. Summaries should include the following:
- The story is set in modern times, in Guatemala.
- Luisito lives with his extended family.
- The boy's parents were missing from the list of family members with whom he is living.
- Luisito is interested in the history of his people.

2 Students may notice that the narrator switches from the present to the past tense. Also, he introduces this episode by saying, "Once, when I was six."

THE NIGHT WE STARTED DANCING

Ann Cameron
illustrated by Gonzalez Vicente

I am named after my dad, Luis, but everybody calls me Luisito. I live with my grandfather and grandmother; my four uncles; my two aunts; my cousin, Diego; a girl named Maria who helps my grandmother; our two dogs, Chubby and Pilot; our two cats, Stripes and Hunter; and our big green parrot, Bright Star, that my grandmother always says she is going to bake and serve for dinner someday.

We live in a town called Santa Cruz, in Guatemala, Central America. Santa Cruz has a park where there are great band concerts, free, every week. It has a public school, and a big college for army cadets, and it has an electronics store where you could special-order a computer, but it doesn't have paved streets, it has only dirt streets that turn to dust in the winter when it's dry, and to mud in the summer when it rains.

I like dirt streets. It goes with the special thing about Santa Cruz, which is that it's a very old town. It was a town before Columbus discovered America, and before the Spaniards

268

came from Spain to steal our land and our gold and make slaves of people, because they said their religion was the true one, and God liked them better than us.

On the edge of Santa Cruz there is a high hill covered with old pine trees and the ruins of pyramids and an ancient fortress. That's where the headquarters of our people was, the headquarters of the kingdom of the Quichés, where our ancestors fought the Spaniards harder than anybody in Guatemala, before they lost for good. **1**

Once, when I was six, a real Spaniard from Spain came to our house for dinner. He was going to do some business with my grandfather, so my grandmother invited him. **2**

The whole dinner I kept watching my grandfather and the Spaniard all the time, and looking at my grandfather's big machete knife that he keeps by the front door.

Finally, I couldn't stand it, I said, "*Con permiso,* excuse me," and got up from the table and followed my grandmother into the kitchen when she went to get more food, and I even ducked under Bright Star's perch to get there faster.

"When?" I asked my grandmother. "When is he going to do it?"

"Who?" my grandmother said. "Do what?"

"When is Grandpa going to kill the Spaniard?" I whispered, and Bright Star hissed in his loudest voice, "Kill the Spaniard!" and the Spaniard looked around fast and dropped his fork.

My grandfather stopped munching his tortilla. "Don't be concerned," he said to the Spaniard, "we just have a crazy parrot," and my grandmother said, "One day I am going to bake you, Bright Star!"

Then she took me into one of the bedrooms and closed the door.

"What is this all about?" she said. "Why would Grandpa kill the Spaniard?"

"For being a Spaniard," I said.

"Are you crazy?" my grandmother said. "How can the Spaniard help being a Spaniard? He was born one, just like you were born a Guatemalan and a Quiché. Don't you know the battles with the Spaniards were over hundreds of years ago? We have to judge people by what they do, not by where they come from. And we have to fight our own battles, too, not the ones our ancestors fought."

So that was when I first found out that we'd never get our kingdom back—at least not the way it used to be.

270

My grandfather was born poor, and he never went to school. He worked from the time he was six years old, out in the wheat fields and the cornfields, hoeing. Every day when he finished work and went home, he would pass by his own dad in the street, drinking and spending all the family money. My great-granddad never helped my granddad at all. But my granddad just kept working, and when he was twenty, he started buying land—pieces nobody thought were good for anything—and on the land he planted apple orchards, and when the apples grew all over, big and beautiful, he got rich. He built a big house for my grandmother and our family, with five big bedrooms, and a patio in the middle full of flowers, and a living room where he and my grandmother put up all the pictures of both their families, except my grandfather never put up a picture of his dad. Then, last year, he must have finally started feeling sorry for his father, because he got his picture out of a drawer, and dusted it off, and put it up in the living room, only not with the rest of the pictures. So now my great-grandfather is staring out at the rest of the family, kind of ashamed-looking, from behind a fern.

My grandmother only learned to read four years ago, but she made my aunts and uncles study hard in school, and now she's making me do it, too. When I asked her why I had to study so hard, she said, "So that you aren't working with a hoe in the fields all your life, with the sun beating down on your head like a hammer."

When my grandparents' kids got to be old enough to study in the capital, my grandparents bought a house there for them to live in. So most of the year my aunts and uncles are there,

271

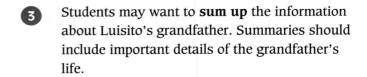 Students may want to **sum up** the information about Luisito's grandfather. Summaries should include important details of the grandfather's life.

studying architecture, and economics, and dentistry, and law, and accounting, and psychology. Only my youngest aunt, Celia, who is sixteen, is still living in Santa Cruz all the time. But next year she's going to the capital, too. She says she's going to study to be a doctor. My grandparents are very proud of all their children. The sad thing is, their oldest son, the only one who was studying agriculture and who loved the land the way my grandfather does, was my father, and he died. My mother died with him.

My mother was teaching grade school and my dad was in the last year of his agriculture studies when they died. I was four years old.

It happened four years ago, when my mom and dad and I and Uncle Ricardo were taking a bus from the capital to go back to my grandparents' house for Christmas. The bus terminal was full of dust and people trying to sell ice cream and coconuts and last-minute Christmas presents. Lots of people were going back to their hometowns for the holidays, and there weren't enough buses. Everybody was pushing and shoving to get on the ones there were.

My mom had a suitcase, and my dad had me on his back because he figured I couldn't run fast enough, and Uncle Ricardo was staring toward the sun with his hand shading his eyes, trying to see the bus that goes to Santa Cruz.

"Santa Cruz! That's it! Run!" he shouted, and my mom and dad raced for the front door of the bus, and Uncle Ricardo raced for the back, and they did flying dives over the top of a bunch of other people. My mom and dad got seats right behind the driver, and I sat on my mom's lap. Uncle Ricardo got stuck at the back, standing up.

272

Everybody pushed the windows down to get more air, and the driver put the bus in gear, but it didn't move, and his helper, the ticket taker, got out a hammer and a wrench and raised the hood on the bus and hammered on something for a while, and then the driver tried to move the bus again, and it went, and Uncle Ricardo heard my mother say, "A miracle! What a miraculous miracle!" and the ticket taker ran after the moving bus and jumped in the open door with the hammer and the wrench in his hand, and we were off.

Uncle Ricardo settled in and tried to take his elbow out of the stomach of the person on his right, and get his feet out from under the feet of the person on his left. My mom and dad were probably about the only ones who could see out the window, and who knew how the driver was driving.

The bus didn't go very fast, because it couldn't with so many people on it, but after a while Uncle Ricardo felt the bus lurch, and he heard my dad say to the driver, "Be careful, brother!" so he figured that the bus driver must have been taking a chance passing on a mountain curve.

4 Students may need to **sum up** what they know about Luisito and his family so far.

If students wonder how Luisito's parents died, encourage them to **ask a question** about their deaths and to read to find the answer.

A little while later he felt the bus twist again, and he heard my father say to the driver, "A man who foresees trouble and prevents it, is worth two men." But it seemed like the driver didn't feel like listening, because a little while later Uncle Ricardo heard my father say, "No matter where you are going, you don't have to get there first. The thing is, to get there."

And after that he heard my mother say, "Driver, there is more time than life."

And that was all he heard, except for my mother's voice just once more, shouting, "Luisito!" just before my father grabbed me with one hand and threw me out the window.

The bus driver went head-on into another bus. And my mother was right, because time just keeps going on and on and on, but she and my dad and the bus driver and the ticket taker and a lot of other people ran out of life completely.

⑤ Uncle Ricardo was okay because he was at the back, and I was okay.

The only part I remember begins with the grip of my father's hand, and how it hurt when he shoved me through the window frame. But I don't like to remember. I like to think about daytime things, my aunts and uncles, and things that are happening now.

But sometimes I still dream about it, being thrown out the window. In the dream I am little again, the same age I was then, and I land down a hillside in a freshly hoed field, just the way I really landed, but it is not daytime, it is almost completely dark, and I get up and go back to the wrecked bus, to find my mom and dad, but it gets darker and darker, and I never can find them.

274

Uncle Ricardo says one day I won't have the dream anymore. He says that my parents loved me a lot, and that I will always have them in my heart. He says one day my dream self will understand that, too. It will know that my parents are always with me when I remember them. It won't have to go back to the wrecked bus to look for them anymore.

And really I am okay, and Uncle Ricardo is okay, and my grandmother also is okay, because she loves all her children very much, but equally. The only one who has not been okay is my grandfather, because he loved my dad more than anybody. My dad wasn't only his son, he was his best friend.

The first Christmas after the accident we didn't celebrate, because nobody wanted to. But the next Christmas we didn't celebrate either, because Grandpa didn't want to. On the anniversary of the accident, he cut a lot of white roses and put them in front of my parents' wedding picture that hangs in the living room, and we visited their graves at the cemetery, so that was all there was of Christmas that year, too.

And from the beginning my grandmother said we shouldn't mention my mom and dad in front of my grandfather because it might upset him too much. She said we should just wait, and in time he would get better.

But it got to be September of the third year after my father died, and my grandfather still wasn't any better. My aunt Patricia, who had been leaving my cousin Diego with us a lot in Santa Cruz, decided to take Diego to the city. She said it was because she didn't have so many courses and she would have more time to spend with him, but Uncle Ricardo told me it was really because she thought it was too gloomy for Diego around our house.

275

⑤ Luisito has now told the story of his parents' deaths. If necessary, have the students stop and **sum up** the story of the bus trip. They should note:

- Luisito was four years old at the time of the accident and is now eight.
- His Uncle Ricardo was also on the bus but survived.
- Luisito's father saved his son's life by throwing Luisito off the bus.

The only reason I liked being in the house is that I like my grandmother and Celia a lot, my grandmother because she never yells at anybody, and Celia because she treats me like a grown-up. She got me to help her with a lot of projects, especially her Laugh Development Project, in which she said she needed the opinion of a man.

She wanted to develop four new laughs, even though my grandmother said it was a waste of time, and she couldn't see what was wrong with the laugh Celia was born with.

Celia said these are modern times, and a person should have five of everything. She said her original laugh was for when she really felt like laughing, and the other four would be for when she couldn't afford to be serious. She wanted my opinion because she wanted to make sure the four new laughs would be good enough to impress boyfriends.

So when Grandpa wasn't around, she practiced in front of the big cracked mirror on the patio.

"Ha, ha, HAH, HAH, hah," went the first laugh, which is a rapid one where she tosses her long black hair back behind her shoulders. That is her Rio de Janeiro laugh.

"Ho ho ho," she laughs slowly, and rubs her chin thoughtfully with the finger of one hand. That's her Paris laugh.

"Hee hee hee," she giggles, and covers her eyes with her hands. That's her Tahiti laugh.

"Hoo, hoo, hoo, hoo," she laughs, and raises her eyebrows very high. That's her Mexico City laugh.

276

She got all the ideas for the laughs from TV and from fashion magazines. After she got them all worked out, I told her they were all good, except the Tahiti laugh, which looked like she was just waking up in the morning, so she decided to rename it a waking-up laugh, to throw a stretch into it.

So she did. But just when she had them all perfect, Bright Star got them perfect, too. He sang them all off in a row, and then he said, in my voice, "Laugh Development Project."

"Now I can't bring any boyfriend home!" Celia said. "Either I can't bring one home, or I can't use my laughs."

"Not only that," I said, "Grandpa is going to know about this for sure."

Celia shrugged. "Maybe he'll borrow a laugh," she said. "He doesn't seem to have one of his own. Anyway, what more can he do? We already don't have Christmas anymore."

Sure enough, when Grandpa came home, Bright Star talked. He laughed all four laughs, and then imitated me, saying "Laugh Development Project."

It happened at dinner. My grandfather looked at Bright Star, and he looked at Celia, and he looked at me, but all he said was, "After school tomorrow, I want to take you out to the orchards, Luisito."

So I said okay, and the next afternoon we hiked out to the orchards.

"You are around your Aunt Celia too much," my grandfather said, but not unkindly. "You need the influence of a man."

"I am a man," I said.

"You are?" my grandfather said. "How do you know?"

"Celia said so."

277

6 Students might need to **interpret** Celia's remark about her father and the laugh-development project.
- Other family members have recovered from the death of Luisito's parents, but the grandfather has not.
- Some family members are drifting away because of the grandfather's attitude.
- The grandfather doesn't seem to like people to laugh around him.

He looked at me and said it took more than Celia's saying so to make somebody a man, and then he started telling me about the trees, and what you had to do to take care of them, and how many different kinds of apples there were, and how you could tell them apart.

But a bad thing happened, because the orchards are right next to the pyramids and the forts of the old kingdom, and I kept thinking about them and wanting to go over there, instead of listening to my grandfather.

"Luisito," he said suddenly, "how many kinds of apples do I have?"

And I couldn't tell him.

"You're not listening! Your father understood and remembered everything when he was your age!" he shouted. "Go on home to your grandmother!"

So I left, and instead of going straight home, I went over to the pyramids and ran up to the top of the biggest and stood there listening to the branches of the pine trees in the wind. It didn't help anything. And then I walked home alone.

When I told my grandma what happened, she said, "Your dad did understand and remember very well when he was your age. But when he was your age, he also played with matches once and set a whole cornfield on fire. It took us, the neighbors and the whole fire department to put it out."

"Tell Grandpa that!" I said. "Remind him about it!"

"I will sometime," my grandmother said, "but not now."

"When?" I asked. "You said Grandpa would get better and we just had to be patient. He used to make jokes, Celia says. He used to take everybody on trips. Now he never does, and he never gets any better."

"You are right," my grandmother said.

"Besides," I said, "Christmas is coming, and I am tired of not having Christmas, and so is Celia."

"You're probably right," my grandmother said. "We should celebrate Christmas."

And she actually used the telephone, which she never uses, to call up Ricardo and talk to him about it.

And that night at dinner, she told my grandfather, "It's time we started to celebrate Christmas again."

"I would rather not," my grandfather said.

"The children say they won't come home for Christmas, unless we celebrate, like the old days. Luis and Celia say they would rather go into the city to be with Ricardo and everybody if we don't celebrate Christmas."

"Um," my grandfather said.

279

"I might go, too," my grandmother said.

"*You* might go?" my grandfather said.

"Yes, I probably will go," my grandmother said.

"You would *leave* me?" my grandfather said.

"Just for Christmas," my grandmother said.

"It wouldn't be good," my grandfather said. "We've been together thirty-one years. You've never been away. Not one day!"

"Times change," my grandmother said.

"Well," my grandfather said, "we had better celebrate Christmas. But I won't dance."

7 "You don't have to dance," my grandmother said. "Nobody has to dance. But at least we will have dance music, anyway."

Celia and I made a beautiful golden Christmas tree out of corn husks that we cut to fasten on wires and make the shape of branches. When we were done, the tree went all the way to the ceiling, and we draped it with red chains of tinsel. And

⚘ 280 ⚘

my grandmother stood in front of the stove all Christmas Eve day making the tamales for the midnight dinner—corn stuffed with chicken and meat and olives and raisins and hot chili sauce, and wrapped in banana leaves to cook. And everybody arrived from the city about six-thirty at night, just in time for the supper we were going to have to tide us over to the real dinner at midnight.

Uncle Ricardo brought Diego and me about sixty fire-crackers to set off at midnight, when all the kids in town go outside to set off firecrackers, so we were feeling good. And my grandfather had dressed up in his best and happiest clothes, new pants, and a cap that makes him look as young as my uncles.

Everybody hugged, and we all sat down to eat, but nobody talked much until we were almost finished, when Aunt Patricia said, "All the same, it's sad anyway."

And my Uncle Pedro, who had been an exchange student in the U.S. for one year of high school, said, "If the roads had shoulders, the way the highways do in the U.S., they never would have died."

And Celia said, "So in the great U.S.A. there are no traffic accidents?"

And before Pedro could answer her, my grandfather got up out of his chair and went out on the patio, and we all stopped talking.

"Luisito," my grandmother said, "go be with your grand-father."

So I went out on the patio and stood by my grandfather, who was looking up at the sky and wouldn't look down.

I just stood there by him, looking up, too.

⚘ 281 ⚘

7 Students may want to **sum up** the events leading to the decision to celebrate Christmas again.

Students may be able to **predict** the outcome of the story from its title.

There was a full moon, shining down on the patio and on the papery violet leaves of the bougainvillea, and my grandfather spoke, in a choked voice.

"See the leaves? There are so many you can't see the branch, and all different.

"And we are like them, all different, but holding on to an invisible branch—but two of us are missing!

"Why do they have to talk about it? Don't they know I've cried enough? What do they think I do out in the orchard, but cry?"

"You should cry with us," I said, and I saw my grandfather's eyes drop tears, and we stood there a long time.

Everybody else had gone into the living room, and while we were standing there, the dance music started, very slowly, low music, soft like smoke, winding into the moonlight.

"Oh, Luisito," my grandfather said. "What can we do? What can anybody do? Luisito, we should dance."

And so my granddad and I danced, around the cage of Bright Star, who was sleeping under a new Christmas blanket, and past the cracked mirror and the bougainvillea vine, and then, very slowly, into the living room. And then I danced with Celia, and my grandfather put his arms around my grandmother and danced with her, and everybody danced with everybody, straight through until midnight when the fireworks started going off in huge booms all over town, and we all held hands, and every one of us kissed every other one, and I noticed for the first time in a long time that in the photo of my mom and dad, above Grandpa's white roses, they were smiling.

⊚ 282 ⊚

8 If students have difficulty understanding the reference to the bougainvillea vines, invite volunteers to **interpret** the analogy.

Discussing Strategy Use
Encourage the students to discuss how they used the summing-up, question-asking, and predicting strategies as they read the selection.

* **EXPLORING THROUGH DISCUSSION**

Reflecting on the Selection
Whole-Group Discussion

The whole group discusses the selection and any personal thoughts, reactions, or questions that it raises. During this time, students also **return to the clues, problems, and wonderings** they noted on the board during browsing.

Assessment

To assess the students' understanding of the text, engage in a discussion to determine whether the students have grasped the following idea:
- how Luisito's grandfather comes to the decision that he will celebrate life with the rest of his family

Response Journal

Students may wish to record their personal responses to the selection.

Exploring Concepts Within the Selection
Small-Group Discussion

Small groups discuss the relationship of the selection to family heritage. Circulate among the groups and observe the discussions. Refer the students to the Concept Board and the Question Board to keep them focused on their original ideas about family heritage and to see if those ideas have changed as a result of reading this selection.

Sharing Ideas About Explorable Concepts

Have the groups **report** and **discuss** their **ideas** with the rest of the class. It is crucial that the students' ideas determine this discussion.
- Students may notice Luisito's interest in the history of his people, the Quichés.
- Students may discuss the importance of holiday traditions in Luisito's family and conclude that such celebrations are important to families in many different cultures.
- Students may discuss the closeness of Luisito's extended family—grandparents, uncles, aunts, and cousins—and the idea that the great-grandparents and Luisito's parents are also present at family gatherings because their photographs hang in the living room.
- Students might discuss the significance of the analogy Luisito's grandfather makes between the leaves of the bougainvillea plant and the various members of the family.

As these ideas and others are stated, have the students **add them to** the **Question Board** or **Concept Board.**

Have the students look at the fine-art pieces on pages 312–313 of the student anthology and discuss the Japanese woodblock print of an Ainu family. They may wish to express their thoughts and feelings about this work and any connections they think it has to the selection they have just read. The scroll depicts a family eating a meal together. Students may connect this with the scenes in "The Night We Started Dancing" in which Luisito's family eats together and generalize that mealtime is an important time for families to be together.

TEACHING TIP Encourage natural conversation—between student and student and between student and teacher—in a class discussion.

TIP FOR ENGLISH LANGUAGE LEARNERS

Encourage English Language Learners to use creative language to express their thoughts. Invite them to discuss the main ideas in the story and to relate the ideas to their own knowledge and experiences.

Fine Art

Exploring
Concepts Across
Selections

Students might make connections with other selections in the student anthology.

- They might remember that, just as Luisito's grandfather had wanted his son to carry on the family orchards, the parents of the family in "In Two Worlds" wanted their children to learn about their ways of life.
- Students might remember that the Mayas, the people who built the pyramids that interest Luisito, were discussed in "Sun and Star Calendars" in unit 2.

*Connections
Across Units*

Recording Ideas

As students complete the above discussions, ask them to **sum up what they have learned from their conversations and to tell how they might use this information** in further explorations. Any special information or insights may be recorded on the **Concept Board.** Any further questions that they would like to think about, pursue, or investigate may be recorded on the **Question Board.** They may want to discuss the progress that has been made on their questions. They may also want to cross out any questions that no longer warrant consideration.

❯ After discussion, the students should individually record their ideas on page 42 of their Explorer's Notebook.

Explorer's Notebook, page 42

Recording Concept Information

As I read each selection, this is what I added to my understanding of family heritage.

"In Two Worlds: A Yup'ik Eskimo Family" by Aylette Jenness and Alice Rivers

_____
_____
_____
_____
_____
_____

"The History of the Tunrit," translated by Edward Field

_____
_____
_____
_____
_____
_____

"The Night We Started Dancing" by Ann Cameron

_____
_____
_____
_____
_____
_____

42 EN   Family Heritage/Unit 3

2 READING WITH A WRITER'S EYE

**Writer's Craft:
Indicators of
Time and Order**

Have the students discuss how they were able to keep track of the order of the events that Luisito describes in "The Night We Started Dancing." Remind them that in telling his story, Luisito moves back and forth in time, and that the beginning of the story provides a background for the events he describes in the last part of the story. Point out that **Ann Cameron had Luisito use certain words and phrases that made it clear when things happened.** For example, the first phrase in paragraph 2 on page 269, "Once, when I was six," signals that Luisito will tell about something that happened previously.

**Selective Reading:
Focus on Indicators of
Time and Order**

Have volunteers point out some words or phrases that Luisito uses to tell the reader when different events in the story occurred. Tell the students that although they may not always see an exact reference to time, they will usually be able to **figure out when something happened by using clues provided by the author**. Students may mention some of the following clues:

- page 271: "My grandfather was born poor"; "Then, last year"
- page 271: "So now"; "four years ago"; "When my grandparents' kids got old enough to study in the capital"
- page 275: "The first Christmas after the accident, we didn't celebrate"; "But it got to be September of the third year after my father died"
- page 282: "and while we were standing there, the dance music started" (Explain that **words indicating concurrence are also clues to time and order.**)

**Independent Practice:
Indicators of Time
and Order**

➤ To focus on some differences between a chronological sequence and the sequence Luisito uses to tell his story, have students retell the events of the story in chronological order using Reading/Writing Connection, page 23. (Even though the time of some events may be only approximate, students should be able to get most of the events in order.)

Then have them discuss whether they think the author's way of ordering events is more interesting than it would have been had she begun her story with the accident and moved forward in time from there.

**Writer's Craft:
Characterization**

Have the students talk about ways that authors tell about their characters. The most obvious way, of course, is simply to describe the character. It is easy to state flatly that a character is tall or foolish or young. But **good writers let their readers discover such things for themselves by having the character say or think or do something**. Ann Cameron reveals many things about her characters in this way.

For example, on page 276 Cameron has Luisito tell about Celia's Laugh Development Project. "Celia said these are modern times, and a person should have five of everything. She said her original laugh was for when she really felt like laughing, and the other four would be for

*Selection-Based
Practice*

when she couldn't afford to be serious. She wanted my opinion because she wanted to make sure the four new laughs would be good enough to impress boyfriends." Although Cameron never actually uses adjectives to describe Celia's personality, the reader learns more about Celia in this short passage than a list of adjectives could show.

Selective Reading: Focus on Characterization

Have the students go back to "The Night We Started Dancing," and find other examples of ways that Cameron tells her readers about the characters in her story. Encourage volunteers to read and explain the examples they find. Remind them to consider how Cameron lets readers know about the character of Luisito himself.

Examples of characterization in the selection include the following:

- page 271, Luisito describes his grandfather: "My grandfather was born poor, and he never went to school. He worked from the time he was six years old, out in the wheat fields and cornfields, hoeing." (He has been ambitious and hard-working all of his life.)
- page 271, Luisito describes his grandmother: "My grandmother only learned to read four years ago, but she made my aunts and uncles study hard in school, and now she's making me do it, too." (She is ambitious for her children and grandchildren, and she is not afraid to take on a difficult task such as learning to read.)
- page 275, Luisito tells something about himself and about Uncle Ricardo: "Uncle Ricardo says one day I won't have the dream anymore. He says that my parents loved me a lot, and that I will always have them in my heart. He says one day my dream self will understand that, too. It will know that my parents are always with me when I remember them. I won't have to go back to the wrecked bus to look for them anymore." (Luisito has accepted his parents' death; Uncle Ricardo is kind and understanding.)

Independent Practice: Characterization

➤ Have students work together in small groups, using Reading/Writing Connection, page 24, to extend their discussion of characterization in the story. Provide time for the groups to share their ideas.

Recording Examples of Characterization

Have students turn to the Story Elements section of their Writer's Notebook and record examples of characterization on a copy of Reproducible Master 25. Distribute additional copies if necessary.

WRITING

Linking Reading to Writing

Remind students that by creating characters who seem real, writers make their stories more readable and that **characters seem more real when they are described in some detail.** Point out that **good writers can reveal what their characters are like by what they have the characters do or say.** To provide opportunities for students to practice describing characters in their stories, have them look through their writing folders for pieces in which characters are not well-defined and encourage them to elaborate on these characterizations. Then have them

Selection-Based Practice

TIP FOR ENGLISH LANGUAGE LEARNERS

Encourage English Language Learners to share their writing with native English speakers. Have them exchange ideas about ways to develop stronger characters in their writing.

"The Night We Started Dancing"

Time and Order

Retell the events of "The Night We Started Dancing" in the order in which they actually happened.

_____
_____
_____
_____
_____
_____
_____
_____
_____
_____

Now list some words and phrases indicating time or order that the author uses to make clear when things happen.

_____
_____
_____
_____
_____
_____
_____
_____

Signal Words

Unit 3/Family Heritage   R/WC 23

Reading/Writing Connection, page 23

"The Night We Started Dancing"

Characterization

Choose a character from "The Night We Started Dancing" or from another selection you have read. Write some things you know about this character and how you know each thing. Include things the character says, things he or she does, and things other characters say about this character. Write the page where you find each piece of information about the character.

Character: _____

Things the character says:

_____ Page: _____
_____ Page: _____
_____ Page: _____

Things the character does:

_____ Page: _____
_____ Page: _____
_____ Page: _____

Things other characters say about the character:

_____ Page: _____
_____ Page: _____
_____ Page: _____

What do these things tell you about the character?

_____
_____
_____
_____

Story Elements

24 R/WC   Family Heritage/Unit 3

Reading/Writing Connection, page 24

---

look to see if there are pieces in which something can be made clearer by adding indicators of time or order.

* Writing Process

Encourage students to begin writing a piece of **realistic fiction.** Have them brainstorm in small groups to come up with ideas about plot, setting, and characterization. Suggest that they consider creative ways of indicating time and order as they work on developing their plot lines.

VOCABULARY

Concept-related words from the selection that the students may want to remember and use include the following:

celebrate, ancestors, anniversary, pyramids, bougainvillea, orchard, dream self

Adding to Personal Word Lists

Have Vocabulary Exploration forms, Reproducible Master 14, available for students who request them. Remind the students to add these or any other words and phrases from the story to the Personal Dictionary section in their Writer's Notebook. Some students may wish to share these additions with the class. For additional opportunities to build vocabulary, see **Teacher Tool Card, 75.**

3 GUIDED AND INDEPENDENT EXPLORATION

EXPLORING CONCEPTS BEYOND THE TEXT

Guided
Exploration

Students will select activities in which they explore family heritage. Refer them to the **Exploration Activities poster** and give them time to choose an activity. If the students need further help, here is a suggestion:

Ask the students to turn to page 250 and reread the sentences about the Yup'iks of the past following in the footsteps of their ancestors. Then remind them that Luisito's grandfather had hoped that his son would take over the management of the family's apple orchards.

❯ Have the students discuss ways that family members share skills related to providing food or to other work. Then ask students to fill out Home/School Connection 20 at home and to bring it back for sharing.

Students might be interested in discussing what happens to a family when its younger generation chooses not to follow in the footsteps of the parents or grandparents. For example, some younger Yup'iks left to live in cities. Ask students to think about how making choices different from one's parents' could affect future generations of a family.

✱ Exploring Through Reflective Activities

Home/School Connection 20

"The Night We Started Dancing"

A message from _____

Your child has been discussing ways that family members pass down skills and information about jobs, trades, and professions from one generation to another. Discuss the following questions with your child and encourage him or her to share this information with the class.

Did any members of our family learn about their jobs or trades from older relatives? If so, what kinds of things did they learn? _____

_____
_____

If I choose the same career as that of another family member, what kinds of skills will I need? _____

_____

What schooling will I need? _____

_____

What can I do now to start preparing for that kind of work? _____

_____
_____

What are some other kinds of work I might like to do? _____

_____
_____
_____

Unit 3/Family Heritage   H/SC 20

Copyright © 1995 Open Court Publishing Company

* INDEPENDENT WORKSHOP
Building a Community of Scholars

Student-Directed Reading, Writing, and Discussion

The students may explore their ideas and questions by using information from their collaborative groups. They may use any sources available to them. Remind them to check the Question Board and the Concept Board for new ideas related to family heritage. New ideas about their questions may prompt them to explore new resources.

Additional Opportunities for Independent Reading, Writing, and Cross-curricular Activities

✶ Reading Roundtable

Students may be interested in discussing books from the unit bibliographies that describe families living in other countries.

✶ Writing Seminar

Encourage students to continue working on planning and drafting their realistic-fiction pieces. Remind them to work quietly on their own during the drafting stage.

Portfolio

Have the students spend some time considering which pieces of writing they might choose to put into their portfolios.

Cross-curricular Activity Cards

Cross-curricular Activity Cards in the Student Toolbox that are appropriate for this selection include the following:

- 1 Music—Songs of Latin America
- 10 Science—Making Traditional Foods
- 10 Social Studies—Cultures of Middle America

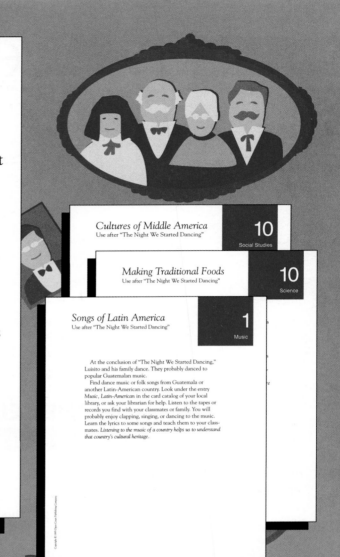

Additional Opportunities for Solving Learning Problems

Tutorial

The following Teacher Toolbox Cards are available for your convenience:

- Writer's Craft/Reading: Indicators of Time and Order, Teacher Tool Card 27
- Writer's Craft/Reading: Characterization, Teacher Tool Card 13
- Writer's Craft/Reading: Point of View, Teacher Tool Card 12
- Grammar, Mechanics, and Usage: Compound Sentences, Teacher Tool Card 48

On Your Own

The West Side

1 READING THE SELECTION

INFORMATION FOR THE TEACHER

About the
Selection

Juan Morales wants to go home to Puerto Rico. Although he likes his uncle's comfortable New York apartment, he despairs of ever finding friends. None of the boys in the East Side neighborhood where his uncle lives speak Spanish. Then, on a search for Puerto Rican food, he goes to the West Side. Here he finds some reminders of Puerto Rico, and here, for the first time, he makes friends with a New Yorker. Colorful dialogue and vivid settings help make this selection fun to read.

Link to the
Unit Concepts

"The West Side," pages 284–295, is from the final chapters of *How Juan Got Home* by Peggy Mann. The selection illustrates that family heritage need not be left behind when one leaves one's homeland.

About the
Author

Peggy Mann was fortunate and talented enough to achieve success as a writer at an early age. When she was seventeen, some articles she sent to magazines were published. She went on to write more articles, scripts for television, and books for adults and children. *How Juan Got Home* is one of several books based on the experiences of Mann's family after they had bought, renovated, and moved into a home in a poor neighborhood in New York's Upper West Side in the 1960s. The first of these books, *The Street of Flower Boxes,* was made into a TV film and won a Peabody Award. Carlos, a character in "The West Side," also appears in these books. Another of Mann's books, *My Dad Lives in a Downtown Hotel,* which deals with the effects of his parents' divorce on a young boy, was adapted for an ABC Afterschool Special.

LESSON OVERVIEW

"The West Side" by Peggy Mann, pages 284–295

READING THE SELECTION

Materials
Student anthology, pp. 284–295
Explorer's Notebook, p. 43
Assessment Masters 1–2

FYI
Learning Framework Card
• Setting Reading Goals and Expectations, 1A

READING WITH A WRITER'S EYE

Minilesson
On Your Own

Materials
Reproducible Master 14

FYI
Teacher Tool Card
• Spelling and Vocabulary: Building Vocabulary, 75

Options for Instruction
Writer's Craft: Characterization
Writer's Craft: Setting
Grammar, Mechanics, and Usage: Using Possessive Pronouns
(Use Teacher Tool Cards listed below.)

GUIDED AND INDEPENDENT EXPLORATION

Materials
Explorer's Notebook, pp. 50–51
Home/School Connection 21

Independent Workshop

Optional Materials from Student Toolbox
Tradebook Connection Cards
• *In the Year of the Boar and Jackie Robinson* by Bette Bao Lord

Cross-curricular Activity Cards
• 11 Social Studies—Imports and Exports
• 12 Social Studies—Community Resources

Student Tool Cards
• Writer's Craft/Reading: Characterization, 13
• Writer's Craft/Reading: Setting, 14
• Grammar, Mechanics, and Usage: Using Possessive Pronouns, 60

FYI
Learning Framework Card
• Reading Roundtable, 6

Teacher Tool Cards
• Writer's Craft/Reading: Characterization, 13
• Writer's Craft/Reading: Setting, 14
• Grammar, Mechanics, and Usage: Using Possessive Pronouns, 60

NOTES

Asterisks (*) throughout the lesson indicate learning frameworks. Learning Framework Cards and Teacher Tool Cards can be found in the Teacher Toolbox.

INFORMATION FOR THE STUDENT

- You may want to share the information above about how Mann's inspiration for *How Juan Got Home* came from living and raising her family in a neighborhood like the one Juan finds on the West Side of New York City.
- Have students read the introduction to the selection in the student book.

COGNITIVE AND RESPONSIVE READING

Activating Prior Knowledge

Have the students tell what they know about being far away from home in a strange place.

Setting Reading Goals and Expectations

Before students read the selection independently, have them **browse** the **first page** of the story, using the clues/problems/wondering procedure. For a review of **browsing,** see **Learning Framework Card 1A.** Following the reading of the selection, the students will complete a Self-Assessment Questionnaire.

Recommen-dations for Reading the Selection

This story has been designated as an On Your Own selection. Have the students read the selection independently. Encourage them to use the strategies they have learned when confronted with difficulties in the text.

Note: Although there are a number of Spanish words that may be unfamiliar to students, most of these words are made clear by their context. Pronunciations and definitions of these words are printed with the miniature pages. Of necessity, the pronunciations are only approximations written in English respellings. If you have Spanish-speaking students in your class, you might ask them to pronounce the words for their classmates after the story has been read.

TIP FOR ENGLISH LANGUAGE LEARNERS

Give English Language Learners a chance to share their unique experiences as travelers.

ASSESSMENT TIP This may be a good opportunity to observe students working in groups and to mark observations in the Teacher's Observation Log.

THINK ALOUD PROMPTS

To foster independence, think-aloud prompts are not provided for On Your Own lessons.

Bodega Rivera (bō de´ gä rē ve´ rä) Rivera's Grocery

THE WEST SIDE
from HOW JUAN GOT HOME
by Peggy Mann
illustrated by Karin Lidbeck

Juan Morales has come from Puerto Rico to New York to live with his Uncle Esteban. Juan's mother believes that he will receive a better education in New York than in Puerto Rico. When the plane lands and his uncle's arrival at the airport is delayed, Juan is told that the airline will give him a free flight back to Puerto Rico if his uncle does not arrive to pick him up. Juan misunderstands and believes he will be able to return to Puerto Rico any time he decides to do so. After a few days in his uncle's apartment and some unsuccessful attempts to make friends with the English-speaking boys who live on his street, Juan is unhappy and is determined to return to Puerto Rico. In the meantime, however, he agrees to go on a shopping expedition for Puerto Rican food in a neighborhood on the West Side of New York.

Juan stepped off the bus at Columbus Avenue. It was as though he had stepped off the bus into Puerto Rico. The street was alive with children and Spanish music. Some of the children, barefoot and wet, played around the water gushing from a fire hydrant, ran in and out screaming laughter and Spanish words. Latin music came blaring from radios on windowsills . . . from a young man who sat on a box in front of Bodega Rivera strumming a guitar and singing a Spanish love

284

song . . . from a bongo band on the corner playing hard rock with a loud Latin beat.

Women leaned out of windows shrilling in Spanish to children on the sidewalk. A group of men sat around a bridge table on the sidewalk, playing dominoes. Women in bright cotton dresses sat on the front steps gossiping in Spanish. And the stores! At home the stores often had *americano* names: the Blue Moon Bar Restaurant . . . Joe's Shop . . . the Cooperative . . . Mercado's Barbershop . . . But here: everything Spanish! Farmacia Flores . . . Tienda La Favorita . . . Zapatería El Quijote . . . Repostería Borinquén. . . .

All crowded together like this, the store signs, the music, the look and the sound of the Spanish people, it seemed somehow *more* Puerto Rican than anything he had seen in Puerto Rico. He was no longer a stranger. He didn't even need to ask directions. With a smile on his face he strode into Bodega Rivera.

He *was* home. The small crowded grocery store was just like the one on his street in Barranquitas. The same small, sweet *niños* bananas hung in clumps in the dusty window; and the long, green *plátanos* hung next to them on iron hooks. The same bins of tropical fruits and vegetables. The same cans and bottles on the shelves: guava juice, papaya juice, *asopao de jueyes*, red beans, pink beans, white beans, pinto beans, chick peas, *Doraditos*, *Florecitas*, *coco rico* and *chinita*. Even the same penny candy machine. And the same packets of ladies' panty hose on the rack behind the counter.

The shopkeeper, who wore a large black mustache and a dirty white apron, was arguing with a customer about the price of his *batatas*. Loudly Señor Rivera informed her that

286

he had to import the *batatas* from the island. If she could not pay for special Spanish food she should eat American.

When, grumbling, she counted out her money, and left, a boy about Juan's age stood on tiptoe in front of the counter and asked in a loud voice whether Señor Rivera would sell him some boxes.

"Boxes of *what*?" Señor Rivera said.

"Empty boxes," the boy said. "We're having a stickball game on the street tomorrow afternoon and we already sold twenty box seats to people who want to watch from the sidewalk. Now we gotta get the boxes."

"Get out of here, Carlos," Señor Rivera said. "I'm busy."

"But Señor Rivera!" Carlos persisted. "I'm willing to pay for the boxes. Usually you give them out free to customers. I'm going to *pay*!"

"Yes?" Señor Rivera said. "And how are my customers going to carry home their groceries if I got no more boxes?"

"Listen," Carlos said, "I'll make you a deal. If you let us have the boxes, I'll let your son Willie umpire the game."

Señor Rivera said nothing. He scowled.

"As you know," Carlos said, "your boy Willie is kind of a pain-in-the-neck kid. That's why he gets beat up so much. But nobody beats up an umpire. You got to respect an umpire."

"How much did you sell the box seats for?" said Señor Rivera.

"Five cents a box for cardboard, ten cents for wood. I told them they could take the seats home with them."

"And how much are you planning to pay me, Carlos, for every box I give you?"

287

americano (ä meʹ rē käʹ nō) American

Farmacia Flores (fär mäʹ syä flōʹ res) Flores Pharmacy

Tienda La Favorita (tyenʹ dä lä fäʹ vō rēʹ tä) The Favorite Store

Zapatería El Quijote (sä pä te rēʹ ä el kē hōʹ te) Quijote's Shoe Store

Reposotería Borinquén (re pōʹ sō te rēʹ ä bō rēn känʹ) Puerto Rican Pastry Shop

niños (nēʹ nyōs) a kind of banana

plátanos (pläʹ tä nōs) plantain bananas (usually prepared cooked)

asopao de jueyes (äʹ sō päʹ ō dä hwäʹ yes) kind of thick vegetable soup or stew

Doraditos (dōʹ rä dēʹ tōs) a fried chip

Florecitas (flōʹ rä sēʹ täs) a candy from Puerto Rico

coco rico (kōʹ kō rēʹ kō) a beverage made with coconut

chinita (chē nēʹtä) an orange

batatas (bä täʹ täs) sweet potatoes

Señor (sen yorʹ) term of respect, like Mister

"Well," Carlos said, "a penny for cardboard. Two cents for wood."

Señor Rivera laughed. "Carlos," he said, "you're going to grow up to be the president of the First National Bank. Listen," he added, "go down in my cellar and haul yourself up twenty boxes. You can have them for free."

Carlos grinned and started for the flight of steps leading down to the cellar.

"Save a box seat for me," Señor Rivera called after him. "I want to come watch my son Willie be umpire."

Juan then stood on tiptoe in front of the greasy glass counter. He ordered twelve *plátanos verdes*, two pounds of *gandules* and one ounce of *ajíes*. But when he paid his money, and held the three paper bags in his hands, he still did not want to leave.

If only his uncle had the job of maintenance engineer on Columbus Avenue! Then he, Juan, might not even want to go home. If he lived over here, then he could go to school over here. Maybe here they even had Spanish schools and he'd never need to learn English at all!

But Uncle Esteban had explained that a boy must go to school in the district where he lived. He would have to go to school on the rich East Side of Manhattan; a school which would, no doubt, be filled up tight with *americanos*.

He noticed the boy called Carlos who came staggering up from the cellar with an armload of cardboard boxes. "Hey!" He walked over to Carlos. "You want me to help you carry those boxes to wherever you're going?"

"Sure," Carlos said in English. "Matter of fact, I was going to ask you to give me a hand." He smiled.

🌀 288 🌀

Juan didn't understand the English, but a smile was the same in any language.

He smiled back.

They made two trips from the Bodega Rivera to the basement of the brownstone rooming house where Carlos lived. Juan kept talking almost nonstop all the way. He had so much talk inside him it seemed he just couldn't get it all said.

Carlos spoke very little. When they had finished piling the boxes in a corner of the basement, Carlos explained why he always answered Juan in such short sentences. He knew very little Spanish.

Juan stared at him through the basement gloom, astounded. A *puertorriqueño* who didn't know Spanish?

Carlos shrugged and explained that they'd come from the mainland when he was three years old to live with his grandmother. He'd been brought up on English, in the streets and in school. In fact, the only Spanish he knew came from talking to his grandmother.

Juan nodded. He felt he had found a friend—only to lose him. What was worse, he felt like a fool. Here he'd been jabbering away to this boy all about Barranquitas and his house and his mother and sisters and friends and his miniature car collection and the Piñonas River and his school and the TV programs he watched at home. And all the time Carlos had hardly understood a single word!

"As a matter of fact," Carlos said in English as he started up the basement stairs, "you'll find that most of the Spanish kids on this street don't speak Spanish. At least, their Spanish is nothing to speak of!" Then, having made a kind of <u>pun</u>, Carlos laughed.

🌀 289 🌀

plátanos verdes (plä´ tä nōs vâr´ dās) green plantains

gandules (gän dōō´ les) peas with a small black dot (pigeon peas)

ajíes (ä hē´ es) chili peppers

puertoriqueño (pwär´ tō rē ken´ yō) Puerto Rican

Barranquitas (bä´ rän kē´ täs)

Piñonas (pēn yō´ näs)

But Juan trudging up the stairs behind him did not laugh. He had not understood a word Carlos said.

Carlos turned then and repeated the sentences in a stiff and inaccurate Spanish.

Juan nodded glumly. He felt betrayed. Even if he took the bus over here every day to play with the *puertorriqueño* kids on Columbus Avenue, it would be no good. He would still be a stranger—among his own people. Only they weren't his own people anymore. They were *americanos*.

When they reached the street Carlos said, in Spanish, "Well, thanks for helping me out."

And, in Spanish, Juan replied. "That's okay." Then he added, "I better say good-bye now. I'll be going back home at the end of the week."

"To the island?" Carlos said, in some surprise.

Juan nodded.

"You must be pretty rich," Carlos said, "to come hopping all the way over here just for one week. How much is the plane fare?"

Juan explained that the trip home wouldn't cost him anything. The airline would fly him home free.

Carlos frowned. He did not understand. "Free? How could that be?"

Juan, speaking in slow careful Spanish as though he were addressing a very small child, explained how the airline had promised to send him home free the night he arrived. So since he hadn't taken them up on their offer then, he would do so at the end of the week.

"Listen, you stupid kid," Carlos said. "Sure they were going to send you home free when your uncle didn't show up. I

⊗ 290 ⊗

mean they can't let a little kid like you just be hanging around the airport at night all alone. But your uncle *did* show up. So the offer's over. Now you're *his* worry. Not theirs. How could they ever make any money if they kept dealing out free tickets to anyone wanting to make a trip back home?"

He spoke now in English. Juan kept nodding. Then he said, "*No entiendo*. I not onnerstan'."

So, with some effort, Carlos repeated it all in Spanish. Juan nodded again. This time he understood all too well, and knew with certainty that Carlos was correct. In fact, this very thought had been lurking in the back of his mind. But he hadn't allowed it to come forward before. Because he didn't want to know the truth. The truth that he *could* not go home.

"Listen, kid," Carlos said suddenly, in Spanish, "since you helped me with the boxes, how'd you like a free box seat for the game tomorrow afternoon?"

"What kind of game?" Juan asked.

"Stickball."

"What's stickball?"

"Stickball's what it says it is," Carlos said. "You hit a ball with a stick. Want me to show you?"

Juan nodded.

"C'mon," Carlos said. "I got my equipment upstairs." He shoved open the front door and Juan followed him into the hallway. The place smelled strongly of cats and rancid cooking oil and the garbage which sat outside each doorway in overflowing pails or paper bags.

⊗ 291 ⊗

No entiendo (nō en tyen´ dō) I do not understand.

Juan felt like holding his breath and holding his nose. Who would want to live in such a place when they could be back in the fresh mountain air of Barranquitas where the only smell one noticed was that of flowers?

When they reached the third floor Carlos took a ring of keys from his pocket and started unlocking one of the doors. "We got three different locks," he explained to Juan, "because we have been robbed five times."

Juan was impressed. Carlos must live in a pretty big place with some valuable things in it for anyone to bother robbing his apartment five times. After all, even though the hallways smelled, that didn't mean the apartments weren't beautiful inside.

But inside there was nothing much either. Just one room with a flowered curtain drawn across the middle. The whole place was not much bigger than the bedroom he shared at home with his two sisters. There was a wooden table and four wooden chairs all painted bright green. There was a picture of the Virgin Mary tacked to the wall. And in the corner a small stove and large sink, stacked with dishes. Sunlight fell in through the open window and lay in a long oblong pattern across the worn green linoleum on the floor. There was a flower box on the windowsill with some geraniums in it.

Not a bad place, Juan thought. At least it looked friendly. He'd a lot rather live here than in Uncle Esteban's fine basement apartment where all the windows had bars like a jail.

Carlos meanwhile had gone behind the curtain. He came back with a small rubber ball and a broom. "Of course," he said, "the bat we play with is a mop handle without the mop. But our captain keeps that in his house. I'm the manager of

the team," he added, with an edge of pride in his voice. "That means I set up the games and arrange everything. The big game we got on tomorrow is against the Young Princes. Come on. I'll show you how we play."

Juan followed Carlos into the hallway again, waited while his new friend locked the door with three different keys, and went down the stairs after him, taking two at a time as Carlos did.

In the street Carlos waited until a few cars had gone by. Then, when there was a lull in the traffic, he stepped out, threw the ball into the air, swung the broom handle hard. And missed.

Shamefaced, he picked up the ball. "Well, I myself am not so hot at this game," he said in English. "I'm better at organizing than playing. But the idea is, if you hit the ball past the

292

293

first sewer that's pretty good. If you hit it past the second sewer, that's sensational. And if you hit it past the third sewer, that's impossible. The third sewer's right down at the end of the street. You can hardly even see it from here."

Juan nodded. He had barely understood a word that Carlos said. But he was embarrassed to ask his friend to repeat it all over again in Spanish. So he asked instead, "I try?"

"Sure," Carlos said and threw him the broom which Juan caught in one hand. Then Carlos threw the ball which Juan caught in the other hand. And stepped out into the street.

"Hey! *Watch it!*" Carlos screamed in English.

Juan stepped back just as a yellow taxi sped by his toes. He'd been so intent about showing Carlos that he could hit this ball with the broom that he forgot about everything else—including getting run over. His heart now started thudding with fear at his narrow escape.

"Listen!" Carlos said sternly. "They got such things as cars in this city and don't you ever forget that!"

Juan nodded. He looked carefully up and down the street.

"It's okay now," Carlos said. "Nothing coming."

But still Juan felt afraid.

"Hurry up! *Avanza!*" Carlos said. "Take your chance while you got it."

So Juan, his heart still pounding, stepped out into the street, threw the rubber ball into the air, and hit it with the broom handle. Hard.

He watched the ball proudly as it sped through the air.

Carlos screamed again. And again Juan rushed back to the safety of the sidewalk. But this time there were no cars coming. This time Carlos screamed for another reason. "You hit

⊛ 294 ⊛

three sewers!" he kept screaming. "Man, don't you understand, you hit *three sewers!*"

"Yes," said Juan. "I onnerstan'." He did not know what "three sewers" meant. But he did understand that Carlos was impressed at how he had hit the ball.

"Listen," Carlos said. "You must be puttin' me on, man. Telling me you never played stickball before." He repeated the question in Spanish. The words were charged with suspicion. "You sure you never played stickball before?"

Juan shook his head. "No," he said. "I have never played stickball before." He saw no reason to explain that he had been playing stick-stone ever since he was seven years old. Hitting a stone with a stick across the Piñonas River in the Contest game he had invented.

"Listen, kid," Carlos said suddenly. "How'd you like to play on our team tomorrow afternoon?" Then, slowly, carefully he tried the words in Spanish. "*¿Vas a jugar con nosotros mañana?*"

Juan grinned. "Sure, man," he said in English. "Hokay!"

⊛ 295 ⊛

Avanza! (ä vän´ sä) Get going!

¿Vas a jugar con nosotros mañana? (väs a hoo gär´ kōn nō sō´ trōs män yä´ nä) Are you going to play with us tomorrow?

Discussing Strategy Use
Since the students have read this selection on their own, have volunteers share with the group any problems encountered while reading and any strategies used to solve those problems.

*

EXPLORING THROUGH DISCUSSION

Reflecting on the Selection
Whole-Group Discussion

The whole group discusses the selection and any personal thoughts or questions that it raises. During this time, students also **return to the clues, problems, and wonderings** they noted on the chalkboard during browsing.

TEACHING TIP In discussion of any selection, limit content questions from the teacher.

Assessment

To assess the students' understanding of the text, engage in a discussion to determine whether the students have grasped the following ideas:

- how the familiar sights and sounds of the West Side neighborhood helped Juan feel less homesick
- why Juan gives up on the idea of going back to Puerto Rico at the end of the week
- whether Juan and Carlos will see each other again

TIP FOR ENGLISH LANGUAGE LEARNERS

Provide an opportunity for English Language Learners to model for others. Encourage them to sum up the main ideas in the selection. Invite them to reread passages that support the main ideas. Praise their efforts in speaking and reading, especially their pronunciation of English and Spanish words in the text.

Response Journal

Students may wish to record their personal responses to the selection.

Exploring Concepts Within the Selection
Small-Group Discussion

Small groups discuss the relationship of the selection to family heritage. Circulate among the groups and observe the discussions. Refer the students to the Concept Board and the Question Board to keep them focused on their original ideas about family heritage and to see if those ideas have changed as a result of reading this selection.

Sharing Ideas About Explorable Concepts

Have the groups **report** and **discuss** their **ideas** with the rest of the class. It is crucial that the students' ideas determine this discussion.
- Students may discuss the idea that heritage is reflected in the customs, food, music, and language of one's homeland.

TIP FOR ENGLISH LANGUAGE LEARNERS

Draw on the knowledge of English Language Learners. Have them talk about anything they know about other cultures.

As this idea and others are stated, have the students **add them to** the **Question Board** or **Concept Board**.

Have the students look at the fine-art pieces on pages 312–313 of the student anthology and discuss the photograph by Lewis Hine. They may wish to express their thoughts and feelings about this work and any connections they think it has to the selection they have just read.
- The family shown in the photograph has just arrived in the United States. Students may make the connection that the people in this family, like Juan, are probably feeling homesick and confused.
- Some students may know that, after arriving in a city like New York, many immigrants made homes in neighborhoods where people spoke the language of their homeland. Perhaps the people in this photograph made a home for themselves in an Italian neighborhood.

Fine Art

Exploring Concepts Across Selections

Students may make connections with other selections in the unit.
- Students may observe that eating particular kinds of food is part of a family's heritage. In the selection *In Two Worlds,* the children of the Rivers family learn to hunt and prepare certain kinds of animals for

food. In "The Night We Started Dancing," Luisito describes the special food his family prepared for Christmas Eve. Juan is especially pleased to see familiar foods in the West Side grocery store.

Recording Ideas

As students complete the above discussions, ask them to **sum up what they have learned from their conversations and to tell how they might use this information** in further explorations. Any special information or insights may be recorded on the **Concept Board.** Any further questions that they would like to think about, pursue, or investigate may be recorded on the **Question Board.** They may want to discuss the progress that has been made on their questions.

➤ After discussion, the students should individually record their ideas on page 43 of their Explorer's Notebook.

Evaluating Discussions

Self-Assessment Questionnaire

➤ Distribute copies of Assessment Master 2, Self-Assessment Questionnaire, which can be found with the assessment materials provided in the Teacher Toolbox. Tell the students to answer the questionnaires after they have completed this lesson. Collect the completed questionnaires so that you can compare the students' current self-assessments with later self-assessments when they again answer the same questionnaires. You might also examine responses to see if the students' assessments of themselves are compatible with your assessments of them in your Teacher's Observation Log.

Explorer's Notebook, page 43

"The West Side" by Peggy Mann

_____

"Chinatown" by Laurence Yep

_____

"Women" by Alice Walker

_____

Assessment Master 2

Self-Assessment Questionnaire

1. How would you rate this selection?
   ○ easy   ○ medium   ○ hard

2. If you checked **medium** or **hard**, answer these questions.
   • Which part of the selection did you find especially difficult?
   • What strategy did you use to try and understand it?
   _____

   • Were some of the words hard?
   • What did you do to figure out their meaning?
   _____

3. What do you feel you need to work on to make yourself a better reader?
   _____

4. Give an example of something you said in the group. Tell why you said it.
   _____

5. Give an example of something that people in the group helped you understand about the selection.
   _____

Self-Assessment Questionnaire · · · Assessment Master 2

2 READING WITH A WRITER'S EYE

MINILESSON

Remind the students that in each selection they have read so far you have discussed something the writer did especially well. For example, in "The Night We Started Dancing," Ann Cameron used characterization effectively.

Tell the students that since they have read this selection on their own, you would like them to identify something the author has done especially well. Is there something in the writing that stands out? Remind the students to think back to any part of the story that they reacted to strongly or particularly enjoyed as they read. This might be a clue to especially good writing.

Allow time for the students to skim the story to refresh their memories. If they seem to be having difficulty expressing how they felt about the writing in this selection, model a response by talking about your own reactions to Mann's **use of language** or to her **characters** or **setting**.

WRITING

Linking Reading to Writing

Encourage the students to use in their own writing any of Mann's writing techniques that they especially liked.

* Writing Process

Although no specific writing assignment is recommended here, in any writing that they're working on, students may concentrate on an appropriate phase in the writing process. Encourage those students who have begun writing realistic fiction pieces to work at revising them. Remind them to use the Writing Strategy Posters whenever necessary.

VOCABULARY

Encourage the students to discuss words or phrases from the selection that they want to use in their speaking and writing or in their exploration for this unit. Concept-related words or phrases that you might discuss include *mainland* and *embarrassed.*

Remind students to add words and phrases to their personal dictionaries in their Writer's Notebook. Then provide an opportunity for students to fill out Vocabulary Exploration forms, Reproducible Master 14, for words they wish to learn or those that are important to the unit concept. For additional opportunities to build vocabulary, see **Teacher Tool Card 75.**

TIP FOR ENGLISH LANGUAGE LEARNERS

Some words in the selection may be unfamiliar to native English-speaking students. If applicable, encourage English Language Learners who speak Spanish to work with native English speakers to help them with pronunciation and word meanings, using pictures and context clues.

3 GUIDED AND INDEPENDENT EXPLORATION

EXPLORING CONCEPTS BEYOND THE TEXT

Guided
Exploration

Students will select activities in which they explore family heritage. Refer them to the **Exploration Activities poster** and give them time to choose an activity and to discuss what they wish to explore and how they wish to go about it. If the students need further help, here is a suggestion:

Ask one or more students to locate Puerto Rico on a large wall map or globe. You might remind students that residents of Puerto Rico are U.S. citizens. Have volunteers identify both New York and Puerto Rico so that students can see the distance between the two places. Encourage students who were born in other countries, or whose ancestors were, to locate those countries on the map or globe.

❯ Ask students to think about people in their own families who left their homelands to begin new lives in the United States. Encourage them to interview these people, using Home/School Connection 21. If a student has no family member who fits that category, he or she might interview a family friend. Have students share and compare the information they gather from these interviews.

✱ *Exploring Through Reflective Activities*

TIP FOR ENGLISH LANGUAGE LEARNERS

Encourage native English-speaking students and English Language Learners who share an interest in learning more about a certain culture to work together in cooperative/collaborative groups.

Home/School Connection 21

"The West Side"

A message from _____

Your child has read a story about a boy who learns he does not have to lose his family heritage even though he leaves his homeland.

Help your child set up an interview with a relative or friend who emigrated from another country. The questions that follow might be used for the interview. Please encourage your child to share this information with the rest of the class.

Name: _____

What country were you born in? _____

How old were you when you left? _____

Where did you live when you first arrived here? _____

_____

If you needed to learn English, how did you learn it? _____

_____

_____

Was it easy or difficult to make new friends? Tell more about that. _____

_____

_____

If you could give advice to somebody just arriving from another country, what would it be? _____

_____

_____

_____

_____

_____

_____

Copyright © 1995 Open Court Publishing Company

Unit 3/Family Heritage   H/SC 21

Exploring a Variety of Cultures

You have read about families who live in very different places and who have very different family heritages. Think about some of the different homes people live in, the different foods they eat, and the different ways they earn

Selection	Setting	Homes

50 EN   Family Heritage/Unit 3

money. Then fill in some of the spaces on the lines below. Continue to add information to these pages as you read other selections in the unit.

Foods	Ways People Earn Money	Other Differences

Unit 3/Family Heritage   EN 51

Explorer's Notebook, page 50

Explorer's Notebook, page 51

❯ To increase student's awareness of the variety of cultures represented in unit selections, encourage them to begin filling in the chart on Explorer's Notebook, pages 50–51.

Professional Checkpoint: Guided and Independent Exploration

The discussions and explorations are designed to expand and deepen students' understanding of the concepts related to family heritage. Encourage students to share with each other how their ideas have changed. They should readily accept and discuss each other's point of view.

Notes:

✳ INDEPENDENT WORKSHOP
Building a Community of Scholars

Student-Directed Reading, Writing, and Discussion

Remind the students to check the Concept Board and the Question Board for additional questions or ideas to aid them in their exploration. At this time, students may choose to complete any unfinished pages in their Explorer's Notebook or to discuss those pages with their classmates.

WORKSHOP TIP

You may wish to have a tape recorder available for students conducting interviews. Show the students how to take notes as they listen to their taped interviews. Have them write down important information and any direct quotations they wish to share with their classmates.

Additional Opportunities for Independent Reading, Writing, and Cross-curricular Activities

✱ Reading Roundtable

Some students may want to read the book from which the selection was taken, *How Juan Got Home.*

Encourage the students to look at the Tradebook Connection Cards for reading ideas. *In the Year of the Boar and Jackie Robinson,* by Bette Bao Lord, features a child who is newly arrived in New York and who is unfamiliar with the language and customs of her new home. Shirley Temple Wong, the heroine of this book, also gains friends when she begins playing baseball. Students may enjoy reading this book and comparing Shirley's situation with Juan's. If students choose to read this book, suggest that they complete the activities on the accompanying Tradebook Connection Card in the Student Toolbox. For additional ideas for Reading Roundtable, see **Learning Framework Card 6.**

✱ Writing Seminar

Remind students to use peer conferencing and teacher conferencing as they revise their realistic fiction pieces.

Cross-curricular Activity Cards

The following Cross-curricular Activity Cards in the Student Toolbox are appropriate for this selection:
- 11 Social Studies—Imports and Exports
- 12 Social Studies—Community Resources

Community Resources
Use after "The West Side"

12
Social Studies

Imports and Exports
Use after "The West Side"

11
Social Studies

In this selection, the shopkeeper talked about the price of *batatas.* He said that he had to *import* them. That means these vegetables were grown elsewhere and shipped out, or *exported,* from that country to the United States. When we *import* products, we buy those products from other countries. When we export products, we make or grow those products in our own country and then sell and ship them to other countries.

Choose a country. In an encyclopedia or another resource, look for information about the foods and other products that are imported and exported by that country. Make lists of its imports and exports to share with your classmates. *A country's economy is an important part of its culture.*

Additional Opportunities for Solving Learning Problems

Tutorial

Use this time to work with those students who need help in any area. Remember to use peer tutoring with those for whom it would be appropriate. Encourage the students to ask for help whenever they feel the need. The following teaching aids are available in the Teacher Toolbox for your convenience:
- Writer's Craft: Characterization, Teacher Tool Card 13
- Writer's Craft: Setting, Teacher Tool Card 14
- Grammar, Mechanics, and Usage: Using Possessive Pronouns, Teacher Tool Card 60

Chinatown

1 READING THE SELECTION
INFORMATION FOR THE TEACHER

About the
Selection

Casey Young is Chinese, but she has never lived among Chinese people nor even met her Chinese grandmother. So, when she comes to San
Francisco's Chinatown to live with her grandmother, she has a lot to
learn—about being Chinese, about her mother's early life, and especially
about herself.

Using vivid images and figurative language, the author describes how
Casey and her grandmother walk the streets of Chinatown one evening.
Casey sees the streets transformed into a magical place and feels for the
first time that she has found the place where she belongs.

Link to the
Unit Concepts

"Chinatown," pages 296–309, is an excerpt from *Child of the Owl* by
Laurence Yep. In this selection, Yep describes how Casey comes to appreciate the richness of her Chinese heritage and to feel that she is a part of
the Chinese community in Chinatown.

About the
Author

Laurence Yep is a prolific writer of fiction for young people. While
growing up, Yep often felt that he was an outsider in an "all-American"
culture. When he embarked on a writing career, he felt safer writing science fiction than he did writing about his own heritage. In time, as he
became more comfortable with his heritage, he began to write novels
with Chinese characters. *The Serpent's Children* and *Mountain Light* are
set in nineteenth-century China; the latter includes a description of conditions on a ship carrying immigrants to San Francisco. *Dragonwings*
gives a detailed picture of Chinese immigrants in San Francisco in the
early twentieth century. *The Star Fisher* tells the story of Yep's mother,
who grew up in West Virginia during the 1920s.

Child of the Owl won the *Boston Globe-Horn Book* Fiction Award and
the Jane Addams Book Award. Yep's other awards include the

LESSON OVERVIEW

"Chinatown" by Laurence Yep, pages 296–309

READING THE SELECTION

Materials

Student anthology, pp. 296–309
Explorer's Notebook, p. 43
Assessment Master 1

READING WITH A WRITER'S EYE

Minilesson

Writer's Craft: Sensory Details

Materials

Reading/Writing Connection, p. 25
Reproducible Masters 14, 20

FYI

Teacher Tool Card
• Spelling and Vocabulary: Building
  Vocabulary, 75

Options for Instruction

Writer's Craft: Characterization
Writer's Craft: Dialogue
Writer's Craft: Figurative Language
(Use Teacher Tool Cards listed below.)

GUIDED AND INDEPENDENT EXPLORATION

Materials

Explorer's Notebook, pp. 50–51
Home/School Connection 22

Independent Workshop

Optional Materials from Student Toolbox

Tradebook Connection Cards

Cross-curricular Activity Card
• 4 Drama—Writing Dialogue

Student Tool Cards
• Writer's Craft/Reading: Giving
  Descriptions, 39
• Writer's Craft/Reading:
  Characterization, 13
• Writer's Craft/Reading: Using
  Dialogue in a Story, 19
• Writer's Craft/Reading: Figurative
  Language, 20

FYI

Learning Framework Card
• Writing Seminar, 8

Teacher Tool Cards
• Writer's Craft/Reading: Elaboration
  Through Providing Descriptions, 39
• Writer's Craft/Reading:
  Characterization, 13
• Writer's Craft/Reading: Using
  Dialogue in a Story, 19
• Writer's Craft/Reading: Figurative
  Language, 20

N O T E S

Asterisks (*) throughout the lesson indicate learning frameworks. Learning Framework Cards and Teacher Tool Cards can be found in the Teacher Toolbox.

Christopher Award for *The Star Fisher; Parenting*'s Reading Magic Award for *The Rainbow People,* a book of Chinese folk tales; and the Friends of Children and Literature Award, the Carter G. Woodson Book Award, and the International Reading Association Children's Book Award for *Dragonwings.*

INFORMATION FOR THE STUDENT

Explain that "Chinatown" is an excerpt from the book *Child of the Owl* and that the owl in the title of the book refers to a traditional Chinese tale told in the chapter that precedes this selection.

One afternoon, Casey's grandmother sees that Casey is lonely and unhappy. She shows Casey a beautiful jade carving of an owl that she wears around her neck and tells her that it was given to the women of their family by an ancestor who was an owl spirit. This owl spirit was forced to take on human form for a time and lived as the wife of a human man. Although she bore him several children, she missed the freedom she had known as an owl. After many years, she left her human family and resumed her owl form. Casey's grandmother says that because the women of their family are descended from this owl spirit, they often feel lonely in the ordinary, human, world.

Casey feels better after hearing this story. She says, "It was like there had always been this person inside of me that I had never been able to name or describe—a small feathery me lost inside this body—and now I not only knew her name but I could tell part of her story."

A biographical sketch of Laurence Yep appears on page 309 of the student anthology. It may be read before or after the students read the selection.

COGNITIVE AND RESPONSIVE READING

*

Activating Prior Knowledge

The selection is set in San Francisco in 1964, in an area referred to as Chinatown. In many large cities there are neighborhoods where people who speak a language other than English or who have similar ethnic backgrounds live together. Ask students to tell what they know about such neighborhoods.

Setting Reading Goals and Expectations

Have the students **browse** the **first page** of the selection, using the clues/problems/wondering procedure. Students will return to these observations after reading.

Recommendations for Reading the Selection

Because the setting is unfamiliar and the character's feelings are complex, students might like to read the selection aloud. During oral reading, use and encourage think-alouds. During silent reading, allow discussion as needed. Discuss problems, strategies, and reactions after reading.

This would also be a good selection for **responding** to text by **visualizing** and **making connections** while reading aloud. Model this response, and then invite the students to respond similarly.

About the Reading Strategies

Think-Aloud Prompts for Use in Oral Reading

This selection includes figures of speech and sensory descriptions that will probably require interpretation. **Visualizing** will help students to **interpret** the many descriptions in the selection.

The think-aloud prompts are placed where students may encounter difficulties with the text. These are merely suggestions. Remind the students to refer to the **reading strategy posters** and to use any strategy they need to make sense of what they are reading. Encourage the students to collaborate with classmates when confronted with difficulties while reading.

THINK
ALOUD
PROMPTS
•
These prompts may be used as guides to promote cognitive and responsive reading.

1 The first paragraph refers to the story that Paw-Paw has just finished telling Casey. She began the story by saying that all the women of their family felt lonely at times because of their owl ancestor.

CHINATOWN
from CHILD OF THE OWL by Laurence Yep
illustrated by Yoriko Ito

In the time since her mother, Jeanie, died, Casey Young has traveled around California with her father, Barney. But when he becomes sick and has to be hospitalized, Casey goes to live with her grandmother, Paw-Paw, in San Francisco's Chinatown. Here she begins to learn more about her Chinese heritage and about her mother.

1 I lay in bed thinking for a long time after Paw-Paw had finished her story. I'd never asked her about Jeanie before this, I suppose, because Barney had taught me not to talk about her. Finally I rolled over on my side to face her. "When did Jeanie feel lonely?"

Paw-Paw picked up a deck of cards and began to play a game of solitaire. She could play even while she talked. A three on the four of one column. A jack on the queen of another column. Flip. Flip. Flip. Like her fingers had eyes and brains so Paw-Paw didn't even have to look down. Her hands could do everything. "Maybe I should let your daddy tell you."

I turned so I lay on my stomach, hugging a pillow under my chin. "Barney won't talk much about her. Was she lonely when she was my age?"

Paw-Paw must have sensed the longing in my voice. "Oh, no. Your mommy always had lots of friends. She was very pretty. And very sweet. She was always a big help to me." Paw-Paw finished her game and began to sweep the cards into the middle of the table so she could gather them into a deck. "And your daddy was thought to be a very good-looking boy so they were always a natural couple. From grammar school on."

"Grammar school?"

296

297

"They both went to Commodore Stockton just a little way from here. And then they went through junior high and high school together." Paw-Paw began to shuffle her cards to get them ready for the next time she wanted to play.

"Were they very popular?"

"Oh, yes. Very popular. You'd always see them together at all the dances in Chinatown. Your momma liked dancing."

Paw-Paw went to the bureau and opened a middle drawer, rummaging around till she took out an old, worn brown bag and drew a small pile of photos out of it. She set them down on the table and sorted through them. "That's your momma. She was going to a dance that night." Paw-Paw tapped one photo of a pretty girl of about sixteen in bobby sox and a long skirt like all the American girls used to wear—or at least that's what Barney and some of the older people used to tell me when we had watched late-night movies in different hotel lobbies. "I used to sew all your momma's clothes but only with the best material." She glanced at me briefly and then went through some of the other old photos of Jeanie, who had a different outfit in each one. And while I didn't much care about the clothes, somehow talking with Paw-Paw about Jeanie made me feel less lonely.

"But she couldn't have always gone out with Barney. What did she do with you for fun? I mean, besides playing cards."

🌀 298 🌀

"We went to see Chinese movies." Paw-Paw put her cards down in a neat stack by the little cup that held her tooth-picks. They were cinnamon-flavored and each was wrapped in a little paper envelope. "Would you like to see a movie like your mommy and I used to see?"

I wasn't doing much of anything so I figured why not. "I've got money for myself."

"Why spend your money? I can sew some extra shirts this week."

"Are you sure it's okay?" I asked.

"Of course, it's okay," she snapped and I could see there would be no arguing with her.

Paw-Paw bundled up as usual, putting on a blouse over her pajama top and then a sweater and a heavy silk jacket over the sweater so that by the time she had on her heavy cloth coat, she looked twice as round. Over her head she put her favorite vermilion chiffon scarf with the roses embroidered on it with gold thread.

Paw-Paw seemed very comfortable within the small world of Chinatown; I wondered if Jeanie had been too. It didn't cover more than half a square mile or so then, and within those boundaries, as I was to find out, it is a very small, tightly knit world where everyone knows your business and you know theirs. To the west lay the souvenir shops and on the east, delicatessens and grocery stores and meat markets, some of which had fish tanks in the bottom half of their windows in which a hundred fish would be squeezed, all staring out at you with cold, black eyes, or even turtles, or sometimes cages of snakes, all to be sold and eaten.

🌀 299 🌀

To the north was Stockton Street, where my school was. Mostly it was sewing-machine shops up that way: plain store-fronts sometimes with wallpaper covering the windows or old, sun-bleached curtains. From within would come the steady whir and whine of the machines of the ladies sewing dresses, shirts, even jeans and expensive wedding outfits for American stores. A lot of ladies with no English could only do that. Just above Stockton Street was the public grammar school, Commodore Stockton, or "Commodore" to the kids. Across from it lay the <u>YWCA</u> and Cameron House, a kind of club for Chinese kids. Above that, where Paw-Paw never went, were the cable-car lines and the apartment houses for Americans, including the fancy hotels and limousines of Nob Hill.

But at that moment I was thinking mainly about the movies we were going to see. I had my doubts because all I had seen up to then were Charlie Chan movies or silly house-boys on TV shows or funny laundrymen in westerns. But even

🌀 *300* 🌀

so, one of those kinds of movies was better than nothing because I knew Paw-Paw never left Chinatown to see any of the Hollywood movies just a few blocks away.

We went to the Chinese Globe that had a bright neon sign outside in front and looked like a regular theater except for the fact that there was a guy selling newspapers by the ticket booth. He had about a dozen different Chinese newspapers laid in neat piles on a board that he laid over some boxes. But I saw a dozen portable newsstands like that set up all over Chinatown—in doorways or in corners or in front of busy stores. He nodded familiarly to Paw-Paw as she bought our tickets at the booth.

When I finally got to see the movies, they were completely different than I thought. I could see why Jeanie had liked them. For one thing, the Chinese were actually people who could be brave or sad. They had subtitles in English, too, which was good. It was something to see Chinese do more than be the sidekick to some white guy in a fight, or see the Chinese actually win. I mean, I almost felt like crying when I saw it: a kind of bubbling feeling deep down inside that had me almost cheering and crying while this Chinese mother led her three sons in beating up the bad guys. And it was even better when I saw the Chinese girls fighting.

The second feature, you see, was *Princess of the Streets*, which is about this girl who grows up in the back streets of Hong Kong. She gets friendly with this other girl who does juggling and fighting displays in a medicine show. And together she and her friend wipe out the big crime boss. I don't think I ever saw anyone jump as high in the air to kick someone.

🌀 *301* 🌀

 In 1964, when the story is set, there were few movie or television roles for Chinese characters other than minor roles as servants or laundry workers. Charlie Chan was an exception. He was a detective in a series of movies made in the 1930s. The Charlie Chan movies featured Chinese characters who talked in broken English.

It must have rained while we were inside the theater because when we came out later, the streets were slick and black, like they were made of shining crystal. I saw a Chinatown I'd never seen before. It was the Chinatown Jeanie must have seen. Suddenly all the gaudy neon signs were no longer a bunch of words but were like snakes of colored lights crawling up the faces of the buildings and their reflections smashed themselves on the streets, looking like broken stars sliding back and forth and trying to put themselves back together. Funny, but it seemed, right then, like I'd just come home.

A radio store had begun playing music over an outside loudspeaker. Some of the stuff, especially the opera, sounded terrible to me—a high whiny kind of noise—but this sounded different. Some people might have thought there was too much of a clutter of sound with the cymbals crashing and the drums beating and everybody playing like mad, but there was something inside of me that liked it—like it <u>synchronized</u> right with the pulsing of my blood through my body. And the sound wound its way through the chatter of the night-time crowds.

Humming with the tune, Paw-Paw took my arm for support as we made our way along the slippery pavements of Grant Avenue. We passed by the delicatessens, where Paw-Paw pointed to the dark-brown, roasted ducks dangling from hooks in the windows. "That's what I like," she said. "Jeanie too."

"I've never had duck in my life," I said.

She patted my arm, the one she was holding on to. "Maybe I'll sew some extra shirts and dresses someday and we'll buy half of one so you can try it."

302

We went about two blocks before the rain started to fall again. It was falling pretty hard so we stopped under the awning of this one souvenir shop. Paw-Paw acted like the window display had been put there just to entertain us. "Look at that whirly thing." She pointed at one of those little solar windmills that rotate whenever they're near a source of light like the light bulb <u>illuminating</u> the window.

There was something wrong about the window. At first I couldn't figure it out but as Paw-Paw went on mentioning things in the window, I realized she hadn't talked about one Chinese thing yet. I started to study the window then. There didn't seem to be anything as beautiful or as old as the owl charm Paw-Paw wore about her neck. There was just a lot of silly stuff like two-headed back-scratchers. Paw-Paw didn't point at any of those or at some of the things that were downright nasty—like pellet guns and various types of knives, from simple pocket- and hunting knives to switch-blades and gravity blades that snap out with a flick of a wrist. The only thing vaguely Oriental that I saw at first in the window were the Japanese kimonos and geisha dolls they sold.

"It doesn't seem right somehow," I said. "I mean, if it's a Chinatown souvenir shop, shouldn't it be selling Chinese stuff?"

"The Americans won't let us bring in things from China." She shrugged. "And the Taiwan government's too busy to bother with souvenirs. You have to sell the Americans something."

"But we're selling things as if they're Chinese when it's really . . . well, I don't know . . . this stuff just seems like junk compared to your owl charm. There's no story behind most

303

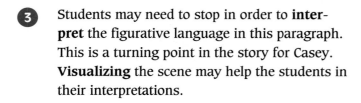

3 Students may need to stop in order to **interpret** the figurative language in this paragraph. This is a turning point in the story for Casey. **Visualizing** the scene may help the students in their interpretations.

4 There were few souvenirs from China in the store windows because political relations between communist China and the United States were strained in 1964 and few imports from China were available in the United States.

of this stuff. There's no meaning to this stuff. This junk is probably not even much fun."

"They do have a few real Chinese things. See?" She moved a little to the side and bent down, pointing to one dark corner of the window. "See down there in the back?"

I leaned forward slightly and looked where her finger was pointing and saw a bunch of dusty statues crowded together like they were making a last stand. "They've got some of the stuff you've got on your bureau. Look, there's that pretty lady with the flower."

Paw-Paw studied me. I hadn't laughed about the owl story and I had even liked the Chinese movies so I guess she decided to go ahead. "That lady is the Listener. She could have gone to heaven, but when she was just about to enter the gate, she could hear all the poor souls back on earth groaning and she turned her back on heaven, saying she could not enter until everyone else had gone before her, so she spends all her time trying to help the rest of us to heaven."

Though it was a cold, rainy night outside, I felt warm inside now that Paw-Paw was finally explaining things to me. "Hey, there's the guy with the big head."

"He's the spirit of long life," Paw-Paw corrected me. "His head swelled up because he's so full of life. He helps keep the record of your life and sometimes with special people he juggles his books and they live longer, so maybe someone dies when they're ninety-one instead of nineteen. He's got a magic peach in his hand, grown in heaven for the gods. A person eats that peach and that person lives forever."

And she told me the eight statues—not as small as hers—were the Eight Immortals who had once been simple men and women but had gained the secret of immortality. One of them had meditated so long and let his dream-soul wander so far away that his body died in the meantime and his dream-soul had to take the bony body of a crippled beggar when it got back.

She told me about a few more of the statues and when she stopped, I asked her a new question I'd been thinking about. "What would it be like if we were in China, Paw-Paw?"

Paw-Paw shut her eyes but kept her face turned toward the window as if she were trying to picture it herself. "It'd be very noisy and you'd have much less time to yourself than here. You have to go through the rain to the village lavatory. Or maybe you have to empty out a . . . a . . . what is the word? . . . a chamber pot."

"Ugh."

"No heat except the stuff in the stove so you have to go and look for every leaf and every bit of grass and all your neighbors would be doing the same thing."

"Would you have a whole bunch of families together in the same big house? Like Uncle Phil and Uncle Chester would live with you?" Uncle Chester was a year younger than Jeanie and lived down in L.A.

Paw-Paw shook her head. "Only if we were rich, but we'd probably be poor farmers if we had stayed back in China. Each of them would have their own little house and you and I would be crowded in somehow into one of those two."

I drew my finger down the glass slowly. Rain dribbled down from the awning overhead. "But still, would you like that better than the way you live now? I mean if we were in China, you'd really be in charge, like the mother was in the first movie, bossing all her grown-up sons around."

Paw-Paw sighed. "I don't know. It's too easy to worry about the way things might have been. I'd rather live with the way things are now. That's what the Owl Spirit did after all."

"Well, why don't you live with one of your children now?"

306

"I could live with your Uncle Phil anytime I want, but they always get this rotten chicken meat from the freezer, when chickens should be fresh. But no, the feathers make too much mess and they don't like it when I take out the blood and guts. And I say, 'What do you think's inside of you?' Or they give me steak in a huge chunk and they hand me a knife and that thing with the four sharp points."

"A fork?"

"Yes, and I say, 'When I come to the dinner table, I come to eat, not to cook. Meat should be cut up and cooked properly in the kitchen before dinner.'"

"They'd probably let you make your own meals," I said.

"Well, I guess I could make my peace with them on that, but there are other things." Her eyes glanced at the statues in the window. "They tell me those things are only for stupid, old people."

I realized that it all depended on how I looked around myself—if there were invisible walls around Chinatown for Paw-Paw, they were like the walls of a turtle, walls behind which you could remain warm and alive, and for someone like me, those walls didn't have to be any more of a trap than I let them. They could be like something to give me shape and form and when I couldn't grow anymore inside them, I could break out of those invisible walls.

Paw-Paw began to retie her scarf but her fingers had begun to stiffen in the cold and the wet. I reached my hands out. "Here, Paw-Paw, let me help you." So Paw-Paw leaned forward, waiting patiently until I had retied her scarf. She checked the knot under the chin of her reflection in the window, smoothing her hand over it.

307

5 The students may have wondered earlier why Paw-Paw left her homeland, China. This part answers some questions they may have had.

6 Students may conclude that this is another important turning point for Casey. She realizes that she can grow as a person in Chinatown and that she no longer feels trapped there.

She smiled, pleased. "You did that very well. Such strong young fingers."

She gripped my fingers tightly in her hand for a moment with what seemed like an immense strength. "Now help an old lady up the hills. It's wet and I'm afraid I'm going to fall."

7 I let her take my arm then and once again she was just a little old lady and we climbed slowly up the steeply slanting hillside, like two small owls clawing their way along a branch that twisted upward into the night sky.

MEET LAURENCE YEP, AUTHOR

Laurence Yep was born in San Francisco in 1948. Yep's father had come from China as a small boy, and his mother was born in West Virginia. It was his mother's mother, Marie Lee, who was the model for Paw-Paw in Child of the Owl. In his autobiography, The Lost Garden, Yep explains that, like Casey Young, he grew up speaking English and eating with a fork. He says of his grandmother: "She represented a 'Chineseness' in my life that was as unmovable and unwanted as a mountain in your living room. . . . So there I was with all of these strange, new pieces [of my background] that my grandmother had presented to me; pieces that had to be put into the puzzle that was myself but no clue where those pieces were to go.

"In part, to come up with some answers, I began to keep a file of family history. Whenever my mother, my aunts, or my grandmother told family stories, I would try to remember them so I could write them down later. It was only years later when I began to piece things together that I began to understand just how difficult a journey it had been for my grandmother from China, through Ohio and West Virginia and finally to her little home in Chinatown.

"More than anyone, I respected my grandmother. She had not only survived, but she had become her own person—which was something I wanted to do."

⚘ 309 ⚘

7 The students will probably notice that, in the last sentence, Casey is comparing herself and Paw-Paw with the characters in the story Paw-Paw told her. Encourage the students to **visualize** Casey's idea.

Discussing Strategy Use
Encourage students to discuss how they used the **visualizing** and **interpreting** strategies as they read the selection.

Reflecting on the Selection
Whole-Group Discussion

The whole group discusses the selection and any personal thoughts or questions that it raises. During this time, students also **return to the clues, problems, and wonderings** they noted on the board during browsing.

Assessment

To assess the students' understanding of the text, engage in a discussion to determine whether the students have grasped the following idea:
• why it was important to Casey to hear about her mother's childhood and about Chinese culture

Response Journal

Students may wish to record their personal responses to the selection.

Exploring Concepts Within the Selection
Small-Group Discussion

Small groups discuss the relationship of the selection to family heritage. Circulate among the groups and observe the discussions. Refer the students to the Concept Board and the Question Board to keep them focused on their original ideas about family heritage and to see if those ideas have changed as a result of reading this selection.

Sharing Ideas about Explorable Concepts

Have the groups **report** and **discuss** their **ideas** with the rest of the class. It is crucial that the students' ideas determine this discussion.
• Students may generalize that it is important for young people to be told about their parents' and grandparents' lives and about their cultural heritage.

As these ideas and others are stated, have the students **add them** to the **Question Board** or **Concept Board**.

Exploring Concepts Across Selections

Students may make connections with other selections in the student anthology.
• They may notice that both "The West Side" and "Chinatown" are set in ethnic neighborhoods.
• They may generalize that sometimes people who share a similar heritage like to live in the same neighborhood, surrounded by familiar things and by people who speak the language of their homeland.

Recording Ideas

As students complete the above discussions, ask them to **sum up what they have learned from their conversations and to tell how they might use this information** in further explorations. Any special information or insights may be recorded on the **Concept Board.** Any further questions that they would like to think about, pursue, or investigate may be recorded on the **Question Board.** They may want to discuss the progress that has been made on their questions. They may also want to cross out any questions that no longer warrant consideration.

▶ After discussion, the students should individually record their ideas on page 43 of their Explorer's Notebook.

TEACHING TIP Encourage students to identify with the selection by asking whether it reminds them of anything in their own lives—people, places, events, relationships, emotions, etc.

ASSESSMENT TIP This may be a good opportunity to observe students working in groups and to mark observations in the Teacher's Observation Log.

TIP FOR ENGLISH LANGUAGE LEARNERS
Provide a time for informal conversational practice. Conversational practice promotes using language as a social activity and as a means of personal discovery.

Evaluating Discussions

"The West Side" by Peggy Mann

_____
_____
_____
_____
_____
_____

"Chinatown" by Laurence Yep

_____
_____
_____
_____
_____
_____

"Women" by Alice Walker

_____
_____
_____
_____
_____
_____
_____

Unit 3/Family Heritage   EN 43

Explorer's Notebook, page 43

2 READING WITH A WRITER'S EYE

MINILESSON

Writer's Craft:
Sensory Details

Have the students discuss how **descriptive language helps a reader to picture a story's setting and action.** After discussion has shown that they understand the importance of sensory details, point out that throughout "Chinatown," **Laurence Yep uses descriptive language to help his readers relate to Casey's experiences** as she walks along the streets of Chinatown with Paw-Paw. For instance, on page 299, he describes Chinese meat markets: ". . . some of which had fish tanks in the bottom half of their windows in which a hundred fish would be squeezed, all staring out at you with cold, black eyes, or even turtles, or sometimes cages of snakes, all to be sold and eaten." It is almost impossible to read that passage without picturing the tanks and the hundreds of fish with their "cold, black eyes."

Selective Reading:
Focus on Sensory
Details

Have students go back to "Chinatown" and look for other examples of Laurence Yep's use of sensory details. Encourage volunteers to read aloud and comment on the examples they find.

Providing Descriptions

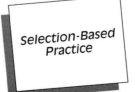

Selection-Based Practice

Here are other examples of the author's use of sensory details:

- page 300, the description of the sewing machine shops: "plain store-fronts sometimes with wallpaper covering the windows or old, sun-bleached curtains. From within would come the steady whir and whine of the machines of the ladies sewing."
- page 302, the description of Chinatown after a rain: "the streets were slick and black, like they were made of shining crystal. Suddenly all the gaudy neon signs were no longer a bunch of words but were like snakes of colored lights crawling up the faces of the buildings and their reflections smashed themselves on the streets, looking like broken stars sliding back and forth and trying to put themselves back together."
- page 302, the description of the music coming from a radio store: "Some people might have thought there was too much of a clutter of sound with the cymbals crashing and the drums beating and everybody playing like mad, but there was something inside of me that liked it—like it synchronized right with the pulsing of my blood through my body. And the sound wound its way through the chatter of the nighttime crowds."

Independent Practice: Sensory Details

❯ For additional practice in recognizing sensory details, have the students work in small groups to complete and discuss Reading/Writing Connection, page 25.

Reading/Writing Connection, page 25

"Chinatown"

Sensory Details

Tell which senses each of the following descriptions appeals to. Then find another descriptive passage in the story that appeals to one of the same senses. Give the page number and some of the descriptive details.

Suddenly all the gaudy neon signs were no longer a bunch of words but were like snakes of colored lights crawling up the faces of the buildings and their reflections smashed themselves on the streets, looking like broken stars sliding back and forth and trying to put themselves back together. (page 302)

Senses: _____

Page: _____ Descriptive details: _____

_____

Some people might have thought there was too much of a clutter of sound with the symbols crashing and the drums beating and everybody playing like mad, but there was something inside of me that liked it—like it synchronized right with the pulsing of my blood through my body. (page 302)

Senses: _____

Page: _____ Descriptive details: _____

_____

We climbed slowly up the steeply slanting hillside, like two small owls clawing their way along a branch that twisted upward into the night sky. (page 308)

Senses: _____

Page: _____ Descriptive details: _____

_____

Description

Unit 3/Family Heritage   R/WC 25

Name

Copyright © 1995 Open Court Publishing Company

WRITING

Linking Reading
to Writing

Remind the students that by providing good sensory details, a writer helps readers to picture the settings and action in his story. To provide opportunities for students to practice descriptive writing, encourage them to look through their writing folders to find passages that could be improved by adding sensory details.

✱ Writing Process

If students are revising the realistic fiction that they began two lessons ago, encourage them to look for passages that contain ideas that are hard to visualize. Suggest that such passages could be improved by adding more sensory details.

VOCABULARY

One interesting concept-related phrase from the story describes many newly arrived immigrants in America: *ladies with no English.* Other words from the story that children may find interesting and may wish to discuss include the following:

rummaging, gaudy, embroidered

Remind the students to add these or any other words or phrases from the story to the Personal Dictionary section of their Writer's Notebook. Some children may wish to share these additions with the class. Have Vocabulary Exploration forms, Reproducible Master 14, available for students who request them. For additional opportunities to build vocabulary, see **Teacher Tool Card 75.**

TIP FOR ENGLISH LANGUAGE LEARNERS

Provide opportunities for English Language Learners to practice listening, reading, and speaking. Encourage the students to discuss how the descriptions in their writing relate to the senses. Have partners exchange ideas about where to add or change sensory details.

VOCABULARY TIP Encourage the students to choose words *they* feel are important. Student choice leads to student ownership of words.

Professional Checkpoint: Reading with a Writer's Eye

Just as you and the students model reading strategies to help each other understand how good readers read, good writers can model effective writing strategies. Encourage the students to use techniques from the selections they read in their efforts to become better writers.

Notes:

3 GUIDED AND INDEPENDENT EXPLORATION

EXPLORING CONCEPTS BEYOND THE TEXT

Guided
Exploration

Students will select activities in which they explore family heritage. Refer them to the **Exploration Activities poster** and give them time to choose an activity and to discuss what they wish to explore and how they wish to go about it. If the students need further help, here is a suggestion:

➤ Have the students ask parents or other family members about folk tales or other stories from their cultural heritage. Students can record this information on Home/School Connection 22. Some students may want to write their own retelling of one of these stories and create illustrations to go with it. Others might want to look in the school or public library for folk tales from a particular culture.

Have the students return to Explorer's Notebook, pages 50–51, and record information about Paw-Paw's country of origin, China.

* Exploring
Through
Reflective
Activities

Home/School Connection 22

"Chinatown"

A message from _____

Your child has read a story about a girl who comes to live with her grandmother. She learns many things about her heritage, including a folk tale about an owl who lives as a human woman for many years.

Can you remember any folk tales you heard from older family members or friends when you were a child? Share these with your child and encourage her or him to take notes on the story or to rewrite it in his or her own way. Your child might illustrate the story by drawing a picture of a character or scene from the tale.

Characters in the story: _____
_____
_____

The country or area where the story originated: _____
_____

Some events in the story or descriptions of one or more characters:
_____
_____
_____
_____
_____
_____

If you have no information about folk tales or folk heroes from your family heritage, encourage your child to visit the library to find some stories. Collections of tales can be found listed in the library catalog under various countries or areas of origin.

Copyright © 1995 Open Court Publishing Company

Unit 3/Family Heritage   H/SC 22

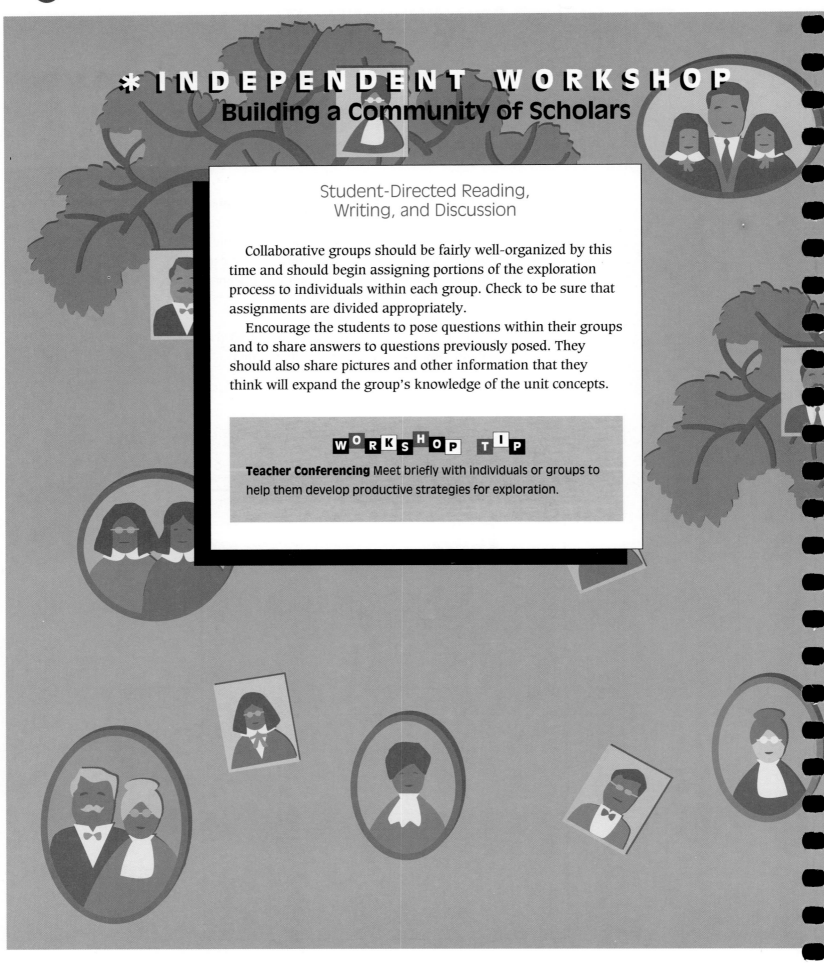

* INDEPENDENT WORKSHOP
Building a Community of Scholars

Student-Directed Reading, Writing, and Discussion

Collaborative groups should be fairly well-organized by this time and should begin assigning portions of the exploration process to individuals within each group. Check to be sure that assignments are divided appropriately.

Encourage the students to pose questions within their groups and to share answers to questions previously posed. They should also share pictures and other information that they think will expand the group's knowledge of the unit concepts.

WORKSHOP TIP

Teacher Conferencing Meet briefly with individuals or groups to help them develop productive strategies for exploration.

Additional Opportunities for Independent Reading, Writing, and Cross-curricular Activities

✱ Reading Roundtable

Encourage students to read and share other books by Laurence Yep, including his autobiography, *The Lost Garden.* This book includes background information about *Child of the Owl,* such as where he got his ideas for the characters and what motivated him to write the book.

✱ Writing Seminar

Remind students who are ready to proofread and publish their realistic fiction pieces to use the proofreading symbols on Reproducible Master 20 in their Writer's Notebook to help them as they proofread. For a review of Writing Seminar, see **Learning Framework Card 8.**

Cross-curricular Activity Cards

The following Cross-curricular Activity Card in the Student Toolbox is appropriate for this selection:

* 4 Drama—Writing Dialogue

Writing Dialogue
Use after "Chinatown"

4
Drama

With a classmate, dramatize a scene from "Chinatown" or from another selection in this unit. Decide who will play each character. Write out the dialogue so that each actor has a copy. Practice reading the parts, showing the characters' emotions. *Putting yourself in the place of a character helps you understand that character.*

Additional Opportunities for Solving Learning Problems

Tutorial

Steps Toward Independence By this point in the year students should be taking the initiative in identifying problem areas. Use this time to work with individuals or small groups of students who need help in some area. The following Teacher Tool Cards are available for your convenience:

* Writer's Craft/Reading: Elaboration Through Providing Descriptions, Teacher Tool Card 39
* Writer's Craft/Reading: Characterization, Teacher Tool Card 13
* Writer's Craft/Reading: Using Dialogue in a Story, Teacher Tool Card 19
* Writer's Craft/Reading: Figurative Language, Teacher Tool Card 20

Poetry
Women

1 READING THE POEM

INFORMATION FOR THE TEACHER

About the Poem

The poem "Women" by Alice Walker is a resounding tribute to the poet's mother and other women like her, African-American women who had little education themselves but who demanded education for their children.

Link to the Unit Concepts

"Women," on page 310, expresses Walker's admiration for her mother. Her mother's strength of character is an important part of the poet's family heritage.

About the Poet

Alice Walker has written novels, short stories, and essays as well as poetry. All of her books are intended for adults. Her books include *The Color Purple* and *In Search of Our Mothers' Gardens: Feminist Prose.* She has published three books of poetry: *Revolutionary Petunias and Other Poems; Once, Poems;* and *Good Night, Willie Lee, I'll See You in the Morning.*

Alice Walker often writes about women of older generations, especially poor southern African-American women of her mother's generation. In fact, her mother seems to have been one of the most important influences in her life. She writes of her mother:

> During the "working" day she labored beside—not behind—my father in the fields. Her day began before sunup, and did not end until late at night. There was never a moment for her to sit down, undisturbed, to unravel her own private thoughts: never a time free from interruption—by work or the noisy inquiries of her many children. And yet, it is to my mother—and all our mothers who were not famous—that I went in search of the secret of what has fed the

LESSON OVERVIEW

"Women" by Alice Walker, page 310–311

READING THE SELECTION

Materials

Student anthology, pp. 310–311
Explorer's Notebook, p. 43

READING WITH A WRITER'S EYE

Minilessons

Writer's Craft: Figurative Language in
Poetry

Materials

Reproducible Master 14

FYI

Teacher Tool Cards
- Writer's Craft/Reading: Genre—
  Poetry, 10
- Spelling and Vocabulary: Building
  Vocabulary, 75

GUIDED AND INDEPENDENT EXPLORATION

Independent Workshop

**Optional Materials from
Student Toolbox**

Tradebook Connection Cards

Student Tool Cards
- Writer's Craft/Reading: Figurative
  Language, 20
- Writer's Craft/Reading: Reading and
  Writing Poetry, 10

FYI

Learning Framework Card
- Reading Roundtable, 6

Teacher Tool Cards
- Writer's Craft/Reading: Figurative
  Language, 20
- Writer's Craft/Reading: Genre—
  Poetry, 10

Asterisks (*) throughout the lesson indicate learning frameworks. Learning Framework Cards and Teacher Tool Cards can be found in the Teacher Toolbox.

muzzled and often mutilated, but vibrant, creative spirit that the black woman has inherited, and that pops out in wild and unlikely places to this day.

About the
Illustrator

Tyrone Geter says about illustrating this poem:

Reading Alice Walker's poem "Women," I was very much reminded of my own childhood growing up in Alabama. I grew up in a single parent household of two sisters where dedication and strength of purpose were provided by my mother. Many of the women around my community were like my mother—they rarely had an elementary school education, yet they saw their children as graduates of universities and holders of the highest honors that these institutions had to offer.

They were strong women possessing superior mother wit and common sense. Many, like my mother, toiled as domestic workers. They worked long hours for small pay fueled by the desire that their children would be better off than they were.

I saw Alice Walker's poem "Women" as being a symbolic statement on the strength and perseverance of many black women who were very much like her mother. [For my illustration of this poem,] I depicted women of varying ages and social groups.

The struggle for civil rights in the United States has centered around the struggle for quality education. In the illustration, the climax of the triumph of our struggle is represented by the woman at the apex of the picture with her arms raised in victory. Children are reading on her right under the protective umbrella of her love. The patchwork represents the diversity of our people.

INFORMATION FOR THE STUDENT

Before reading the poem, the students should examine the illustration and read the information about the poet that follows the selection.
- You may want to share some of the information above about why Tyrone Geter chose to illustrate the poem as he did.
- Discuss with the students the gifts that Walker remembers her mother giving her when she was a teenager: a sewing machine, a suitcase, and a typewriter. Walker feels that these gifts expressed her mother's wishes for her: that she be independent and self-sufficient, that she feel free to travel far from home, and that she develop her talents as a writer.

Activating Prior Knowledge

Ask students to share what they know about opportunities for education for African-American children of Walker's generation in the South.

Setting Reading Goals and Expectations

Ask the students to look at this poem and tell in what ways it looks different from other poetry they have read. They will notice that many lines of this poem have only one word and that the lines do not rhyme.

Students will notice that the women Walker tells about in this poem are women of her "mama's generation." After having read of Walker's admiration for her mother, they will probably expect the poet to express admiration for these women.

Recommendations for Reading the Poem

Read the poem aloud and have the students follow the text as you read. Since this poem is difficult, you might practice reading it aloud a few times before you read it to the students.

- Emphasize the repetition of words, such as *knew, know,* and *knowing* in the last lines of the poem and of sounds such as /s/ in *stout of step, books, desks,* and *a place for us.*
- Pause at the end of each line of the poem. Pause longer at the end of each complete thought.
- There is no punctuation in the poem, but the first two lines form a "sentence"; lines 3 and 4 are phrases describing the women; lines 5–11, lines 12–21, and lines 22–26 form sentences, the last two of which begin with the word *how.*

Read the poem slowly two or three times. On the first reading, you may not want to interrupt the rhythm of the poem by stopping to clarify words and ideas. After they have heard the poem several times, let students take turns reading it aloud.

About the Reading Strategies

As with most poetry, "Women" will require the students to interpret as they listen or read. Be sure to allow them to stop and share questions and interpretations, and, as always, to ask for clarification when necessary.

TIP FOR ENGLISH LANGUAGE LEARNERS

Encourage English Language Learners to feel comfortable about speaking English. Encourage them to take turns tape recording individual readings of the poem with a partner. Then have them listen to and comment on each other's reading.

WOMEN
Alice Walker
illustrated by Tyrone Geter

They were women then
My mama's generation
Husky of voice—Stout of
Step
With fists as well as
Hands
How they battered down
Doors
And ironed
Starched white
Shirts
How they led
Armies
Headragged Generals
Across mined
Fields
Booby-trapped
Ditches
To discover books
Desks
A place for us
How they knew what we
Must know
Without knowing a page
Of it
Themselves.

310

MEET ALICE WALKER, POET

Alice Walker was born in Georgia in 1944, the eighth child of a sharecropper and a maid. She says about her mother: "She seemed a large, soft, loving-eyed woman who was rarely impatient in our home. Her quick, violent temper was on view only a few times a year, when she battled with the white landlord, who had the misfortune to suggest to her that her children did not need to go to school."

During her high school years, Walker's mother gave her three gifts that Walker believes showed her mother's wishes for her. The first was a sewing machine so that Walker could make her own clothes. "I even made my own prom dress, such as it was, something chartreuse net, I think. But the message about independence and self-sufficiency was clear." The second was a suitcase: "That suitcase gave me permission to travel and part of the joy in going very far from home was the message of that suitcase." The third was a typewriter. "Oh yes, she bought me a typewriter when I was in high school. How did my mama ever get that typewriter? She must have ordered it from Sears. A typewriter and a little typewriter table. She did all this on less than twenty dollars a week."

311

---

* **EXPLORING THROUGH DISCUSSION**

Reflecting on
the Poem

Have the students **discuss the poem** and any **personal reactions or questions** that it raised. Encourage them to think about how this poem has added to their understanding of family heritage.

- The students may comment that the poet believes the women of her mother's generation were wonderful examples of women, and that they were strong.

- The students may discuss the idea that although these women were usually gentle and worked hard, they could also be angry when they felt that their children were being denied advantages that white children had.

- Students may remember that Walker said that her mother became angry only when the white landlord suggested that her children did not need to go to school.

- The students may discuss the idea that although these women were not educated themselves they knew that the most important things their children could learn had to be learned from books.

- The students may remember that in "The Night We Started Dancing," Luisito's grandmother, like the women in the poem, insisted that her children get an education, although she herself had not learned to read until late in life.

Connections
Across Units

• Students might remember that Booker T. Washington, the author of "The Struggle for an Education," also believed that education was of paramount importance.

Response Journal

Poetry evokes very personal reactions. You might give students time to record their thoughts and feelings about this poem in their personal response journals.

Recording Ideas

➤ Have the students sum up their discussions and record their ideas and impressions about the poem and the concepts on the Concept Board and in their Explorer's Notebook, page 43.

Explorer's Notebook, page 43

"The West Side" by Peggy Mann

_____
_____
_____
_____
_____
_____
_____

"Chinatown" by Laurence Yep

_____
_____
_____
_____
_____
_____
_____

"Women" by Alice Walker

_____
_____
_____
_____
_____
_____
_____
_____

Unit 3/Family Heritage   EN 43

Copyright © 1995 Open Court Publishing Company

2 READING WITH A WRITER'S EYE

Writer's Craft:
Figurative
Language in
Poetry

Ask the students if there was anything about the poem that they especially enjoyed. Remind them that poets often use figures of speech to make difficult ideas easier to understand and to convey certain feelings about their subjects. A figure of speech is a comparison of two things that are not alike in most ways, but that are alike in a certain way, a way that the poet wants to emphasize.

In "Women," Walker compares women like her mother to generals. The generals led armies across fields that were mined or booby-trapped. The armies they were leading were their children, who were on a campaign to win a good education and a better position in the world. A figure of speech such as the one used in this poem is called a **metaphor.** Walker does not say that the women were *like* generals, she says that they *were* generals.

Figures of speech such as the one Walker uses help create the mood of a poem. Discuss how Walker's metaphor affects the mood of "Women." Encourage the students to share with the class the emotions elicited by this poem.

For more information about reading and writing **poetry,** see **Teacher Tool Card 10.**

WRITING

Linking Reading
to Writing

Invite volunteers to share with the group instances of how they or other writers have used figurative language in poetry or prose.

* Writing Process

If any students are working on poems, encourage them to try improving the poems by using figures of speech in the poems.

VOCABULARY

Words and phrases that students might discuss and record in the Personal Dictionary section of their Writer's Notebook include the following:

generation, battered, booby-trapped

Have Vocabulary Exploration forms, Reproducible Master 14, available for students who request them. Then provide an opportunity for volunteers to share words and phrases they've added and tell why they chose them. For additional opportunities to build vocabulary, see **Teacher Tool Card 75.**

3

GUIDED AND INDEPENDENT EXPLORATION

EXPLORING CONCEPTS BEYOND THE TEXT

Guided
Exploration

Students will select activities in which they explore learning. Refer them to the **Exploration Activities poster** and give them time to choose an activity and to discuss what they wish to explore and how they wish to go about it. If the children need further help, here are some suggestions:

Students might engage in a panel discussion on how parents' attitudes toward school and education affect their children and why this is an important part of family heritage.

* Exploring Through Reflective Activities

Professional Checkpoint: Guided and Independent Exploration

To promote intentional learning, keep the students aware of what they are learning and why, rather than letting them focus on the activities. It means to turn over—gradually, of course—the responsibility of learning to children themselves. It should not forever be the teacher who notices misconceptions and gaps in knowledge, who decides what is learned from an activity, who monitors learning and thinks of remedial actions. Eventually students must learn to do these things themselves if they are to go out into the world as life-long learners.

Notes:

✳ INDEPENDENT WORKSHOP
Building a Community of Scholars

Student-Directed Reading, Writing, and Discussion

The students should be working in their collaborative groups during the first part of Independent Workshop. Remind them that they may gain valuable insights by sharing ideas with their classmates.

WORKSHOP TIP

Remind the students to jot down questions and ideas as they read and do their independent exploring so that they will not forget to ask about things that pertain to their projects when collaborative groups meet.

Additional Opportunities for Independent Reading, Writing, and Cross-curricular Activities

✻ Reading Roundtable

Students may enjoy listening to or reading more poetry about family heritage. A good book to begin with is *Grandparents' Houses,* a collection edited by Corrine Streich. Encourage the students to practice reading some of the poems they find aloud. For additional ideas for Reading Roundtable, see **Learning Framework Card 6**.

✻ Writing Seminar

Encourage the students who have written or are writing poetry to share their poems with the class. Remind them to listen carefully to the comments and suggestions of their peers to determine if their poems are communicating the ideas and feelings they want them to.

Portfolio

Have the students spend some time considering which pieces of writing they might choose to put into their portfolios.

Additional Opportunities for Solving Learning Problems

Tutorial

You may want to use this time to work with students who need extra help. For your convenience, the following teaching aid is available in the Teacher Toolbox:

- Writer's Craft/Reading: Figurative Language, Teacher Tool Card 20
- Writer's Craft/Reading: Genre—Poetry, Teacher Tool Card 10

Fine Art

DISCUSSING FINE ART

Included here is some background information about the pieces of fine art shown on pages 312–313. Share with the students whatever you feel is appropriate. Some works may be familiar to them. Encourage them to express their reactions to each piece—for example, what the piece has to do with family heritage, whether it is related to this unit, and why. Encourage them to find out more about artists or artistic styles that interest them. For additional information on discussing fine art, refer to **Teacher Tool Card 123, Fine Art.**

Italian immigrants seeking lost luggage. 1904.
Lewis Hine. Silver gelatin print.

Lewis Hine (1874–1940) was born in Oshkosh, Wisconsin. From 1901 until 1908 he taught nature study and geography at the Ethical Culture School (ECS) in New York, a school that had pioneered the teaching of craft skills and industrial education. In 1905 Hine received an advanced degree in sociology from Columbia University. Also around that time, he began taking photographs of immigrants at Ellis Island. The superintendent of ECS encouraged Hine's photographic work because he wanted students to have the same regard for contemporary immigrants as they did for the Pilgrims who had come to New England.

In his pictures Hine does not attempt to hide the foreignness of the immigrants' clothing and appearance, but he reveals their pride and dignity. Looking at Hine's photographs, the viewer cannot doubt that these people will make a positive contribution to American society.

Later in his career, Hine became a photographer for the National Child Labor Committee, exposing the horrors of child-labor conditions in mines and factories throughout the country. Between 1916 and 1917, he traveled more than 50,000 miles.

Italian immigrants seeking lost luggage. 1904. Lewis Hine.
Silver gelatin print. Dorothy Norman Collection, Philadelphia Museum of Art

Detail of a Japanese scroll
depicting an Ainu family.
18th century. Woodblock print. Private collection.
Photo: Werner Forman Archive/Art Resource

Family Greeting. 1962. Eli Tikeayak,
Canadian Inuit, Rankin Inlet.
Light green-grey stone. Gift of Robert C.
Williamson, C.M., Art Gallery of Ontario,
Toronto. © Kissarvik Co-op Association Ltd.

313

Hine continued his social photography for the American Red Cross, for magazines, and for various agencies and businesses. However, by the late 1930s there was little demand for his work, and he sold few pictures. When he died in 1940, Hine, one of the country's greatest social photographers, was penniless and almost unknown.

The peak year for immigration to the United States was 1907, when more than one million people landed at Ellis Island in New York. One in four of these immigrants came from Italy; and of those from Italy, about eighty men came for every twenty women. Men worked, sometimes for years, to bring their families to the new land. In the Lewis Hine photograph shown here, a mother and her children search anxiously for their luggage. During the peak years of immigration, baggage might cover the entire first floor of the main building at Ellis Island. The husband and father of the family does not appear in this picture; perhaps he is one of those who arrived earlier in the United States and who now could finally afford to have his wife and children join him.

Between 1890 and 1914, fifteen million people came to the United States, most of them from Austria-Hungary, Russia, Italy, Greece, Romania, and Turkey. They came because of famine, persecution, and poverty at home and in hope of a better life in the United States. Every day as many as five to ten thousand people went through Ellis Island, processed by overworked doctors, clerks, translators, baggage handlers, ticket agents, and social workers.

Detail of a Japanese scroll depicting an Ainu family. 18th century. Woodblock print.

The Ainu are a native people who live primarily on the island of Hokkaido in northern Japan. Archeological evidence traces Ainu culture back three thousand or more years. The oldest existing document on the Ainu describes a Japanese expedition to Hokkaido between the years A.D. 658 and 660.

The traditional Ainu village was made up of from five to thirty-one homesteads. Each homestead included a dwelling, which was a rectangular wood-framed single room with a thatched roof. The center of family activity was a sunken hearth in the middle of the room. Fishnets, spears, bows, and arrows were stored in the southwest corner of the room, according to specific guidelines. Bowls, knives, weaving equipment, and treasured family possessions were kept in the northeast corner. The nuclear family—mother, father, and children—lived near the family of the father's father. Men hunted deer and bear and also fished. In their spare time, they carved wooden objects and decorations. Women collected firewood and roots of grasses for food, drew water, cultivated vegetable gardens, and wove cloth from the bark of elm and linden trees.

The Japanese introduced agriculture to the Ainu in the late nineteenth century, disrupting traditional hunting and fishing practices. Today many of the Ainu work in commercial fishing and farming, in the construction industry, or as day laborers.

Family Greeting. 1962.
Eli Tikeayak, Canadian Inuit, Rankin Inlet. Light green-grey stone.

The Eskimos live in and around the Arctic. They generally refer to themselves by words that mean "people": *Inuit* in Canada, *Inupiat* and *Yup'ik* in Alaska, and *Yuit* in Siberia and Saint Lawrence Island. For thousands of years, the Eskimo led a specialized way of life that helped them survive in the harsh Arctic environment. They hunted and fished, using every part of the animals and birds they caught for food, material for clothing and shelter, and tools.

Although Eskimos have had contact with whalers and explorers from outside their society for almost two hundred years, their way of life had changed little until the early twentieth century. The establishment of trading posts in the Canadian Arctic by the Hudson's Bay Company introduced the Canadian Inuit to the fur trade, manufactured goods, the credit system, and guns. Gradually, Eskimo society has gone from being a self-sufficient, nomadic society to being a settled society that is largely dependent on imported food, tools, and clothing. The dog team has been replaced by the snowmobile.

Until recently art other than that for purposes of ritual or ornamentation was not a central part of Eskimo life. Small models of animals were carved, to be used as toys by children and as gambling chips by adults. Charms and amulets were made from whale or bear teeth, to be worn attached to clothing. The arrival of Europeans introduced a demand for souvenirs. As long ago as the 1880s, carvings were being produced for trade with sailors.

Contemporary Eskimo sculpture first emerged in the late 1940s. By the 1960s, carving had become the major occupation of many adult Eskimo men. Its prestigious place in contemporary Eskimo culture is similar to the position formerly occupied by hunting and fishing. Thus carving is usually not practiced by women; printmaking is seen as more of a woman's art. Since hunting and fishing are not as important today as they once were, domestic and social scenes, as shown in *Family Greeting,* are becoming more common in sculpture. Previously, images of outdoor activities dominated the art.

Soapstone and serpentine deposits for the carvings are mined by the Eskimos themselves. The stone pieces are roughly cut with saws and axes, carved with chisels and knives, and polished with files and sandpaper. A man who attempts to carve the hardest stones is greatly admired. The carvings may weigh from one to two ounces to more than one hundred pounds.

The Eskimos have formed several cooperative organizations to market their art and oversee its quality. They view their sculptures and prints as expressions of their heritage—its history and its future. In Alaska and Canada, the Eskimos have gained political awareness and demanded land rights and concessions from the U.S. and Canadian governments, often successfully arguing their cases in court. Their centuries-old determination to survive in one of the harshest of the earth's environments has served them well in the modern world.

The Night Journey

1 READING THE SELECTION

INFORMATION FOR THE TEACHER

About the Selection

Thirteen-year-old Rache visits her great-grandmother Sashie every day and chats about school activities. Then one day Nana Sashie begins the story of her childhood in old Russia, a time when Jews were forced to serve in the tsar's army or were brutally murdered in pogroms. Soon Rache is caught up in this fascinating, suspenseful story—the story of how nine-year-old Sashie thought of a way for her family to escape. Sashie's story continues after school and then at night when the others are asleep. The "night journey" referred to in the title is this trip back in time that Rache and Nana Sashie take each night as well as the journey that nine-year-old Sashie takes in a wagon from Nikolayev.

Link to the Unit Concepts

"The Night Journey," pages 314–337, makes clear that the pain and hardships a family endures are as binding as its joyful celebrations. Also, Rache's excitement about the restored samovar, an object that plays a large part in Nana Sashie's story, emphasizes that not only are memories to be cherished, but so are objects such as the samovar—a symbol of her family's Russian heritage.

About the Author

Kathryn Lasky has written many books for children, from picture books to novels. She has also collaborated on several books with her photographer husband, Christopher G. Knight. These include *The Weaver's Gift,* a winner of the *Boston Globe-Horn Book* Award for non-fiction, and *Sugaring Time,* a Newbery Honor Book.

About the Illustrator

Trina Schart Hyman has illustrated over one hundred books, most of them for children. She has received many awards, including the 1985 Caldecott Medal for *St. George and the Dragon.* For a time, Hyman served as art director for *Cricket* magazine.

LESSON OVERVIEW

"The Night Journey" by Kathryn Lasky, pages 314–337

READING THE SELECTION

Materials
Student anthology, pp. 314–337
Explorer's Notebook, p. 44

READING WITH A WRITER'S EYE

Minilessons
Writer's Craft: Suspense
Writer's Craft: Dialogue

Materials
Reading/Writing Connection, pp. 26–27
Reproducible Master 14
Assessment Master 1

FYI
Teacher Tool Card
• Spelling and Vocabulary: Building
  Vocabulary, 75

Options for Instruction
Writer's Craft: Genre—Adventure
Writer's Craft: Characterization
Grammar, Mechanics, and Punctuation:
  Using and Punctuating Dialogue
(Using Teacher Tool Cards listed below.)

GUIDED AND INDEPENDENT EXPLORATION

Materials
Home/School Connection 23
Reproducible Master 38
Explorer's Notebook, p. 52

Independent Workshop

**Optional Materials from
Student Toolbox**
Tradebook Connection Cards

Cross-curricular Activity Cards
• 2 Music—Folk Dancing
• 4 Art—Making a Family Coat of Arms

Student Tool Cards
• Writer's Craft/Reading: Suspense and
  Surprise, 16
• Writer's Craft/Reading: Using
  Dialogue in a Story, 19
• Writer's Craft/Reading: Reading and
  Writing Adventure Tales, 7
• Writer's Craft/Reading:
  Characterization, 13
• Grammar, Mechanics, and Usage:
  Using and Punctuating Dialogue, 70

FYI
Learning Framework Card
• Reading Roundtable, 6

Teacher Tool Cards
• Writer's Craft/Reading: Suspense
  and Surprise, 16
• Writer's Craft/Reading: Using
  Dialogue in a Story, 19
• Writer's Craft/Reading: Genre—
  Adventure, 7
• Writer's Craft/Reading:
  Characterization, 13
• Grammar, Mechanics, and Usage:
  Using and Punctuating Dialogue, 70

NOTES

Asterisks (*) throughout the lesson indicate learning frameworks. Learning Framework Cards and Teacher Tool Cards can be found in the Teacher Toolbox.

INFORMATION FOR THE STUDENT

"The Night Journey" is an excerpt from a book by the same name. The book tells two stories: that of thirteen-year-old Rache, who lives in the present-day United States, and that of nine-year-old Sashie, who lives in Russia in 1900 with her parents, Joe and Ida; two babies, Louie and Cecil; her aunt Ghisa; and her grandfather, Zayde Sol. Sashie's family lives in Nikolayev, which is on the Black Sea, east of Odessa.

Sashie works out a plan for her family's escape. They will leave their village by hiding in a wagon. Once out of the village, they will dress as actors for the play traditionally performed at the festival of Purim, a play based on the Old Testament story of Esther. Gold coins needed for bribing the soldiers who guard the border will be baked into cookies that are traditionally eaten at this time.

Each family member is allowed to choose one thing to take on the journey, something small enough to be carried in his or her clothing. Ida however, decides to take something much larger—pieces of the family's samovar. The top of the samovar, she says, will serve as Queen Esther's crown; two tiers, unbolted, will be used as face shields during their ride under chicken coops at the beginning of their journey. The bottom of the samovar will serve as a bowl to hold the cookies.

The family is helped in their escape by Wolf Levinson, a frightening-looking man who arranges for their transportation to the border and who drives the chicken wagon on the first night of their journey.

*

COGNITIVE AND RESPONSIVE READING

Activating Prior
Knowledge

Have the students share what they know about situations in which people have fled their homelands in order to escape religious persecution.

Setting Reading
Goals and
Expectations

Have the students **browse** the **first page** of the selection, using the clues/problems/wondering procedure. Students will return to these observations after reading.

Recommen-
dations for
Reading the
Selection

Ask the students how they would like to read the selection. Because this is a long selection, students may prefer to read it silently, stopping after the first part to sum up before continuing. The second part of the selection begins on page 325 and is indicated by the large initial capital letter.

During oral reading, use and encourage think-alouds. During silent reading, allow discussion as needed. Discuss problems, strategies, and reactions after reading.

This would also be a good selection for **responding** to text by **visualizing** and **making connections** while reading aloud. Model this response, and then invite the students to respond.

About the Reading Strategies

Because the story is exciting and suspenseful, students will want to **make predictions** as they read the story. Students may also want to stop to **clarify unfamiliar words** and to **interpret** the behavior of characters at various points in the selection.

Think-Aloud Prompts for Use in Oral Reading

The think-aloud prompts are placed where students may encounter difficulties with the text. These are merely suggestions for strategy use. Remind the students to refer to the **reading strategy posters** and to use any strategy they need to make sense of what they are reading. Encourage the students to collaborate with classmates when confronted with difficulties while reading.

Note: As they read the selection, students will come across some Hebrew words that may be unfamiliar to them. Hebrew is an ancient language still used in Israel and in traditional prayers of Jewish people throughout the world. The Hebrew words in the selection can usually be clarified through context. Pronunciations of these words and phrases can be found with the reduced pages on which they appear. There are also several Russian place names in the selection. These names are pronounced as they are spelled and should be of little difficulty to the students.

THINK ALOUD
PROMPTS

These prompts may be used as guides to promote cognitive and responsive reading.

THE NIGHT JOURNEY

from the book by Kathryn Lasky
illustrated by Trina Schart Hyman

Rache lives with her parents, Ed and Leah; her grandmother, Rose; and her great-grandmother, Sashie. Rache's parents and grandmother warn her not to upset Nana Sashie by asking about tsarist Russia and the persecution Jewish people were subjected to there. However, Rache is fascinated by the story Nana Sashie has begun to tell about her family's dangerous escape from that country.

In an old trunk Rache finds a piece of the brass samovar, or tea urn, that figures largely in Nana Sashie's story. The samovar was the one thing that Sashie's mother, Ida, chose to take with her from Russia. The selection begins on the evening when Rache's father surprises the family with a rebuilt samovar. That night, Nana Sashie continues her story for Rache after the others have gone to bed.

314   315

"I have one last gift," said Ed.

"Oh, Ed, enough already!"

"This is actually a gift for the whole family."

"Oooooh!" Rache, Leah, and the nanas exclaimed in <u>unison</u>.

"Just one minute while I get it." Ed went to the pantry and returned with something large and fairly tall wrapped in cloth. "It was too big to wrap in paper so I just put this cloth around it." As he set it on the table he asked, "Who wants to unwrap it?"

Rache was puzzled. There were not the usual hesitations, the if-you-don't-like-it statements.

"Rache, why don't you unwrap it?"

"Well, okay," said Rache with slight <u>apprehension</u>. She leaned forwards and gave a light tug. The cloth fell off. There was a sharp gusty sound as each of the women sucked in her breath in shock. Then silence. A <u>samovar</u>—polished and bright—stood before them. Rache heard Nana Sashie whisper something in Yiddish. The top piece—the crown, Ida's crown—flickered <u>unquenchably</u> in the candlelight. The good soldier was back! Rache sat stunned as conversation bubbled up around her.

"It's a samovar!"

Even the babies liked a glass of tea from the samovar.

"Ed, however did you do it?"

From my bed I could see the samovar.

"Well, the part that Rache found started me off."

"Were you here that day?"

Like a polished good soldier.

1 The words floated back to Rache through the <u>din</u>.

◈ *316* ◈

"So I started hunting in antique shops and got some leads from the museum—you know, just to find the other brass parts."

Its brass catching the glow of the gas lamp in the street outside.

"I'll tell you who was really incredibly helpful and who did most of the rebuilding when we got the parts was . . ."

I used to pretend it was a good soldier . . .

"Bo Andersen of Andersen's Jewelry. You know, the son, the kid . . ."

"You mean the one who's about forty?"

"Yes. Well, he just loved working on this."

"Nana Sashie?" Leah suddenly looked worried. "Ed, I hope this doesn't . . . Nana Sashie, are you all right?"

1 Students may need to use the **context clues** to **clarify** that the sentences in italic type are Rache's thoughts as her family's conversation is going on around her. She is remembering pieces of Sashie's story.

A sentry in the darkness standing watch over us.

There were two small pockets of loud silence in the happy din—one was Nana Sashie, whose face seemed lost in a gentle <u>reverie</u>, and the other was Rache, who, now over her initial astonishment, felt a confusing mixture of emotions. When she had first discovered the samovar part, Rache had been disgusted by Leah's and Nana Rose's ignorance of Sashie's Russia. But now she felt a real apprehension, as if the gulf between the two worlds had closed too quickly and the one world that she had explored with Sashie would no longer be just theirs alone. Sashie! Funny, she had never thought of her as just Sashie before. She had always been Nana Sashie. It was odd. Odder still was her father. Did he know about the meetings with Nana Sashie? Had he seen her go into Nana's room that night?

"Rache! Come back to the world of the living. Thank you."

"Oh, sorry!"

"Nana Sashie asked you a question."

"Oh! What? What Nana?"

"Would you kindly fetch the toolbox. There are a few bolts that need tightening if we are going to use this for making tea—which we are!"

After tightening several bolts, Nana Sashie declared the samovar fit for a trial run and insisted that they bring it to her bedroom.

"I don't like the idea of her sleeping with that thing burning in her room," said Nana Rose to Ed and Leah.

"What do you mean? I slept with 'that thing' burning every night in my room for my first nine years!"

"Sparks could fly."

318

"No, it's very well designed," said Ed. "It's probably safer than our electric toaster."

"Well, I don't like the idea."

"Well, I do," Nana Sashie said bluntly.

"I thought it was supposed to be for the whole family?" Nana Rose persisted.

"It is. You can come up to my room for tea any time. It's easier for you to come upstairs than for me to come down."

That seemed to settle it; the samovar went to Nana Sashie's room. If people wanted a cup of tea, they had to go to her bedroom, which consequently became quite socially active.

But that first night the samovar would belong to Nana Sashie and Rache alone. At least, that was the thought in Rache's mind as she moved across the hall carpeting to Sashie's room. It was 2:30 in the morning and Rache had not even needed the alarm to wake her for this short hike toward the long journey through time, through Nana Sashie's time, to the world that might not be strictly their preserve for much longer. She stepped into the bedroom. The polished good soldier loomed before her in the night. The street lights were lawns away in the suburbs, and yet the samovar seemed <u>lambent</u> and luminous, as if catching the reflections from a distant mirror.

"I knew you'd come tonight."

Rache jumped in surprise. The voice sounded so young.

"Nana Sashie!"

"Who else?"

"You're awake?"

"Yes."

319

2 The space between paragraphs indicates a change of scene—from the family gathering at dinner to Nana Sashie's room later that night.

"How's your stomach?"

"What about my stomach?"

"The garlic didn't upset it?"

"Of course not! Stop with the stomach already! Come sit down here beside me." She patted the covers. "Quite remarkable, isn't it? With just one piece to start with, your father did an amazing job! And now he's back, the good soldier." Nana Sashie gave Rache's hand a squeeze.

Like iron filings pulled to a magnet, Rache's and Sashie's eyes were drawn to the glow of the samovar. The old eyes flickered with new color. Time melted. A century bent. There was a young voice.

"We're going with him?"

A strange waxy face with dreadful eyes had melted out of the mist of the cobbler's alley. Sashie felt a stinging cuff on her ear as soon as she asked the question.

"Be quiet!" Her father's voice was sharp. He leaned forward and greeted Wolf warmly.

As Sashie saw her father's hand actually touch the other man's flesh, she felt her stomach turn, and she recoiled in horror. She sought her mother's hand, but Ida was like a statue, rigid, her eyes unseeing sockets. Through the fog came the disembodied cluckings of chickens. Sounds, even the strangest ones, took on a peculiar intimacy in the thickness of a fog, and Sashie shivered as she heard these.

"Wolf Levinson," said Joe. "My family—Sashie; my wife, Ida; my sister, Ghisa; and my father, Sol."

Wolf nodded and touched his hand to his hat in his first social gesture in twenty-five years.

⚇ 320 ⚇

"We have no time to waste, Joe." Sashie felt her mother wince at hearing her husband's name spoken by this man. "So if you will follow me, the wagon's right here. I have arranged the coops so you can get in and lie flat. Then I'm afraid after you're settled I must put them back to cover you."

"Yes. Yes, Wolf, we understand," said Joe.

"Well then, this way and we can lay out the bedclothes to make it more comfortable." There was a bustling as bundles were taken off backs and rearranged in the wagon. Sashie was busy untying her own, but she suddenly was aware of a stony, inexorable stillness directly behind her. It was as if Ida were not even breathing. Joe put down his toolbox and moved quickly to her side. He spoke gently. "Come on now, Ida." He began to untie her bundle quickly. "It's going to be all right."

"The chickens are one thing, but the devil is something else!"

"Don't be silly, Ida." But Ida did not answer.

Crawling down a temporary center aisle Wolf had made, Sashie was helping Ghisa spread the bedclothes on the floor of the wagon. As long as she kept helping Ghisa she did not have to look at or really think about the strange face with the awful eyes. But now there was trouble. She could sense it. Ida was not moving and Joe was desperate. Sashie peeked around a coop. Her mother's bedrock stance shocked her. She felt the real possibility that the escape might never begin, that they were doomed to stand here until morning, when they would be discovered. And then what? She had absolutely no idea how her father could ever move her mother onto the wagon. It would take a miracle. Sashie suddenly thought of Moses standing by the Red Sea before it parted. Next to Ida, the Red

⚇ 321 ⚇

3 Here is another shift in the story—from the present to Sashie's past. Students may need to use a **clarification strategy** to clarify the relationships between the new characters introduced in this section.

Sea was a puddle to jump. Sashie had never seen anything as unmovable as Ida. Partially hidden by the coop, Sashie listened to the drama taking place between her parents.

"Ida, you must!" pleaded Joe.

"Who is this man?"

"Ida, he is our only chance."

"What hell has he been to?"

"Ida!" Joe swallowed hard and brought his face close to hers. "For the love of our children, get in that wagon!" What in the world was he going to do, Sashie wondered. Carry her?

"Ida, say this with me." And Joe began a soft chant: *"She'ma Y'Isroeal! Adonai Aloujanou! Adonai Echod!* Hear, O Israel! The Lord our God! The Lord is One!"

Sashie's eyes widened as she saw her mother lean on her father's arm and begin to move. As she took these first steps on the longest journey, Sashie could hear her mother whispering softly the words of the *Shema,* the Jewish statement of faith.

322

The blankets had been spread. Ida and Sashie stretched out in the most forward part of the wagon, each with a baby tucked in at her side. The space left between them was for Joe. At their toes were the tops of Ghisa's and Zayde Sol's heads, who were stretched out from the midsection of the wagon to the back end. Ida and Sashie settled in as best they could. With a small pillow under their heads, they had about twelve or fifteen inches clearance between their faces and the chicken coops. This seemed much more <u>ample</u> than Sashie had imagined. There was plenty of room to place a tier of the samovar over her face as a shield.

"This isn't bad, Mama," said Sashie, trying on the samovar face mask. "Here, try it." Sashie turned toward her mother to hand her the brass piece.

"No, I want to see," Ida said <u>emphatically</u>.

"So much for the samovar!" muttered Ghisa, whose voice floated up from Sashie's feet. There was no way that Sashie could see Ghisa's or Zayde Sol's face, and she found that she missed the smirk that must have punctuated her aunt's remark. She could just see her mother's face by turning her head to the side, and she could see Louie's chubby face, tucked in under her own arm and sleeping for now. Cecile's face was mostly buried under her mother's blouse, but Sashie listened hard and through the clucking gale of the chickens above could hear the deep, throaty sucking noises of the infant as she nursed, a sound she had heard a thousand times but which thrilled her in a new way. Her father had arranged himself between Ida and Sashie. His head was a little forward of theirs, so he did not block their view of each other, and in order to see Joe, Ida and Sashie needed only to crane their

323

She'ma Y'Isroeal! (shmä´ yis rō el´)

Adonai Aloujanou! (ä dō noi´ el ō hä´ nōō)

Adonai Echod! (ä dō noi´ e hôd´)

necks and look up a bit. He quickly put a hand on each of their shoulders.

"Well, is everything as comfortable as possible here? You know, you don't need to be on your backs; you can turn over on your stomachs. Everyone all right?" Joe asked. "Ida?"

"All right." She replied flatly.

"Sashie?"

"Fine, Papa."

"Ghisa?"

"Lovely!" Darn, Sashie thought. She wished she could see Ghisa's face.

"Papa?" Joe asked.

There was a slight pause, then, "I'm alive?"

"All ready?" Wolf's face loomed at the end of the aisle.

"All set," Joe answered. His voice seemed tinged with excitement that bordered more on joy than fear.

"All right, I'll put on the last coops."

There was a great clatter and clacking as Joe dropped the first coop into the center aisle where it rested on the edges of the flanking coops. A little chunk of white night disappeared, and Sashie felt her heart beat faster. More clatter and clucks, and another piece of the night vanished. One by one the coops were dropped, and piece by piece the world above Sashie and her family was eaten up. The clucking of chickens choked the air around her, and Sashie found herself gulping for breath. Terrified of inhaling one of the white feathers that tumbled crazily through the air, she tried to screen her mouth with her scarf, but then it was harder to breathe.

"Sashie!" Her father's voice came through strong and gentle. "Look at me, Sashela." She craned her neck towards her

324

father. "You breathe like me now. Do just what I do. First in through the nose, not too deep, then out through the mouth blowing softly. Slowly. Take your time, Sashela. There's plenty of air. And you think of nice things, like the smell of bread baking and kites flying and the first leaves of May and lighting Hanukkah candles."

"Harruh!" They heard Wolf grunt and slap the reins on the horse's back. The wagon groaned and lurched forwards, the wheels creaking, and they were on their way. Sashie thought she could count every cobblestone as the wagon rolled down the cobbler's alley. But she kept breathing just as her father had told her to and tried to think of nice things—things that now seemed rare and wondrous, like an open window on a starry summer night, a raindrop's path on glass, April branches with leaves curled tight as babies' fists.

They must be on Vaskeyevka Street. She would try and guess their route as they went. But she certainly could not see, and at this hour there were no sounds except the blizzard of cluckings that raged inches above them. She wondered if they would go by the park. And then after the park, what? She had never gone beyond the park. The Alexandra Gate of the park was the farthest perimeter of her life. Some chicken droppings splattered on her cheek, but just as disgust welled up inside Sashie a new noise split the cluckings—iron spikes hitting stone. The world above was laced with the rhythmic strikes.

"Whoa! Whoa!" She felt the wagon stop. Ghisa slid forwards a bit, her head pressing on Sashie's feet, and Sashie's head pressed against her father's arm. Louie's eyes flew open. Sashie opened her eyes as wide as she could and, staring

325

directly into the little boy's, commanded his silence with an unblinking and fierce gaze that was intended to freeze his tongue. Quickly she reached up her sleeve for a sugar stick and popped it into his mouth. It worked, this time. Outside she could hear Wolf conversing in Russian with some men. The street was being repaired and impassable for a four-wheel vehicle. They must turn around and take Zolodievka Street. There followed a great deal of jangling and jolting shot through with Wolf's grunts and barks at the horse. Sashie felt the wagon roll backwards a few feet, then forwards. There were more barks. From the noise Sashie thought that Wolf must be off the wagon and guiding the horse around by pushing and pulling on the harness. Louie cried out once, but the sound was drowned by the tumult of the horse whinnying in protest, chickens clucking, harness jangling, wheels creaking, not to mention the string of curses and barks emanating from Wolf.

"Old man!" said one of the street workers jovially. "Watch your tongue. You know there are not just roosters aboard your wagon. I see some hens!"

The swirl of feathers seemed to freeze in the air above Sashie. She felt Ghisa grab her foot and her father's hand bite into her shoulder.

"Just joking!" She heard the man protest innocently. "Can't you take a joke, old man?"

Sashie had not heard Wolf say anything to the street worker, but she had a sense that Wolf need not say much to fill another with dread. The wagon was finally turned around. The street worker stood just by Sashie's side of the wagon now. With only the boards between them, she could hear him

326

mutter nervously to the other, "Queer eyes!" Sashie could feel Wolf climbing into the driver's seat.

"Harruh!" he yelled. The wagon lurched forwards and clattered out of the street.

If they had to take Zolodievka Street instead of this one, it must be fairly near, and if it were fairly near, reasoned Sashie, the Alexandra Gate of the park was not that far away. Approaching the edge of her known world, Sashie felt a ripple of excitement run through her body. She remembered suddenly a book her father had shown her that had a picture of a map from long long ago, from before Columbus had discovered the new world. The map showed a world with the continents and oceans known in the early fifteenth century. At a certain distance from the land, sea serpents were drawn riding through the crests of waves, with the legend HERE BEGINNETH THE REGION OF THE DRAGONS. Except, thought Sashie, in Russia the dragons live everywhere, and she and her family were supposed to be escaping from them to the tsarless region of what angels? She was not sure. Although she herself had not dealt directly with the dragons, Sashie never once doubted their existence. One did not have to have tea with the tsar and tsarina to have his life sabotaged by them, or their ministers, or the notorious Black Hundreds, who were nothing but street thugs glorified by the tsar and given a license to kill Jews. She remembered her father's stories of the army and she had the feeling that that was not the half of it. And she would never forget the night the news came of her grandparents. She had been only three years old at the time, but she would never forget it—the hollow, stunned voice of

327

her mother repeating over and over, "Both of them?" No, Sashie believed in these dragons, and something deep, deep inside told her that the dragon's fire had scorched Wolf. His eyes were queer because he had looked straight down the fiery throat. She wondered what it was he had seen. She would probably never know, Sashie thought, and she could certainly never ask.

Louie had finished his sugar stick and was demanding more. Sashie felt the wagon turn another corner. They must be near the Alexandra Gate. Had Columbus been forced to begin the region of the dragons with a baby wailing for more and twisting his nose, as Louie was now twisting Sashie's? "Hush, hush!" commanded everyone, but Louie would not be quiet.

"Give him another one!" hissed Ghisa from Sashie's feet. Sashie groped up her sleeve for another sugar stick. "Here," she huffed, "what do I care if you grow up to have rotten teeth!"

4 Ida prayed a strange prayer—that her baby boy would grow old enough to have rotten teeth. And Joe, buoyed by Sashie's relentless optimism, smiled quietly to himself and patted his daughter on the shoulder.

Sashie had fifteen sugar sticks. At this rate, she calculated, they would not last the day. "We might need the b-o-t-t-l-e." Ida and Joe weren't overjoyed at the prospect of drugging babies, but such a possibility had had to be planned for on this trip and a bottle of milk with a light sleeping draught had been prepared. Just then Sashie heard a torrent of water from a slop bucket being thrown out a high window. The chickens on the left side of the wagon forward of her sent up a loud cackle. They must have caught some of it, and then under the layer of cackles was another noise—a steamy hiss of curses from Ghisa.

328

There seemed to be more street noises now—shutters being opened, dogs barking, more wheels creaking, fragments of early morning talk drifting out of doorways as shopkeepers readied for trade. But where were they? It sounded nothing like the noises one would hear around the Alexandra Gate. There were not any buildings near the gate from whose windows slop buckets would be emptied. They must be beyond the gate and near the outskirts of Nikolayev, Sashie thought. As if to answer her question, there was suddenly a new sound and a new motion as the wheels of the wagon rolled from cobblestones to wood. The bass tones of the wooden planks rumbled beneath the wheels and the rush of coursing spring waters muted the manic cluckings. Even Louie, who had managed to sit up, stopped sucking on his sugar stick.

"What dat?" the baby demanded softly.

"It's the river." Sashie whispered. "We're leaving Nikolayev now."

"Oh."

"Be a good boy, Louie!" Sashie patted his knee. Louie was now starting to crawl around, exploring under the chicken coops. It seemed to keep him quiet and drain off some of his energy, so nobody tried to stop him. There wasn't far he could go.

As the wagon moved from the bridge to the dirt road, the clucks and cackles rolled up once more in a suffocating swarm. Oh, to hear water again! thought Sashie. But the liquid resonance of the flowing river was soon a memory obliterated by the cackles that seemed to bristle right inside Sashie's brain. She would go mad if she listened to the chickens another minute! She would think of a song. But she

329

4 Students may need to **clarify** that Ida was praying for the survival of her baby, so that he would live to experience adulthood and decaying teeth.

could not think of one. She would try to hear the road under the wheels. But she could not hear it. The road did, however, feel different from the cobblestone streets. It was softer. The speed seemed slower—not just slower, but thicker, Sashie thought. How can motion feel thick? It was not a bad feeling. And the noise, it wasn't noise. She caught herself. How can I hear noise, Sashie thought, above the cackles? But she did. And it was different. It wasn't noise that was reflected from hard surfaces like cobblestones, wood, and granite. It came from a deep quiet center. They were soft and sucking sounds; the sound of things being absorbed, soaked up. It's mud sounds, thought Sashie, ecstatically. "I am listening to spring mud." It was like beautiful music to Sashie.

Just above the mud but not as high as the wagon top she heard another sound. It was the whispering of a south wind blowing through winter grass. Sashie had never in her life been outside the city. She had never known the sound of the vast quietness of the country, which absorbed noise to make new sound. She lay perfectly still, listening as the country sounds bloomed around her like huge flowers.

Through the minutes and in and out of hours they slept, whispered, ate a hunk of bread or piece of potato. The babies were doing tolerably well and the sleeping draught had not yet been needed. A huge baked potato kept Louie busy for twenty minutes. A medley of whispered nursery rhymes delivered by Sashie and her father averted a near tantrum.

Sashie had just finished drawing tiny faces on both her thumb and index finger for a puppet finger show to entertain Louie when she felt Wolf slow the horse.

"Whoa!" he said.

330

The horse and the wagon stopped. Just as Wolf had begun to speak to the horse, Sashie had heard distant rapid beats, like small explosions in the earth.

"Trouble!" Wolf's voice was tight with fear. "Everybody must be quiet! It's soldiers." He paused, and Sashie thought she could hear the breath catch in his throat. "My God, it's an imperial regiment!"

Then there was a timpani of cold metal as sabers and spurs jangled in the air. Sashie had managed to grab Louie and press him flat on the floor. Her father lay his leg over the little boy's kicking ones and Sashie clapped her hand over his mouth.

"Hail! In the name of their imperial majesties, the Tsar Nicholas and the Tsarina Alexandra!"

Wolf mumbled something conciliatory, but Sashie could not hear the exact words, for the only noise was that of metal clanging, leather squeaking, hooves striking the ground, animals panting, and occasional coughs. The chickens' clucking was eclipsed by the noises that accompanied the tsar's regiment of twenty on an exercise in the countryside. And beneath the chicken coops the human cargo lay in frozen terror.

"You carry chickens, I see . . ." The commander spoke. "And where are you bound for?"

"Oh, just to Borisov to deliver them for my boss to a client."

"How generous of your boss. I am sure he would not begrudge a few chickens for the tsar's regiment, and the client will never miss them."

"Lieutenant, if you please, two or three coops." Sashie heard a man jump from a horse.

331

"Aaaaagggg!" screamed Wolf. "Hold it!"

" 'Hold it!' You old Zhidi!" The last word hung in the air like a dagger dripping blood. "Zhidi," the abusive word for "Jew," had become quite popular with the latest wave of pogroms. Sashie trembled all over. She pressed her hand harder on Louie's mouth.

The commander spoke slowly. "You deny one of the tsar's most loyal and favored regiments a few chickens? To deny the tsar's officers is to deny the tsar, and to deny the tsar is to deny God!" the voice thundered.

"No! No! I do not deny anything to you, your . . . your excellency. It's just that the coops are in bad repair and if you carry them with you they are bound to come apart and the chickens escape. Better you take the chickens slaughtered."

"Fine. Lieutenant, skewer a few chickens then, if you will."

There was a bright flash and Sashie's breath suddenly locked in her throat. Her eyes widened in terror as she saw the

tip of a thin silver blade slice through the mesh and come within three inches of her face. Time stopped as her eyes focused on the glinting sliver of death that played above her. She could even see the scarlet sleeve of the officer's jacket. The three gold buttons blazed through a small flurry of white feathers, and the black decorative braid at the cuff was like four coiled snakes ready to strike. The silvery death dance went on raging above her face and throat. The moist still air from her half-open mouth fogged the blade tip.

"Here! I find you a fat one. Those are all skinny." The blade stilled. The silver death retreated through the slashed mesh to the world above, and Sashie fainted.

A few seconds later she came to and heard Wolf talking rapidly.

"Those are the scrawny ones. Good breeders, but no good eating. Now over here we have your scratchers."

"Scratchers?" asked the commander.

"Yeah, scratchers. They have to scratch for their food. Makes 'em tough. Stringy. They're big chickens, mind you. Weighty, but quite tough. No flavor. But here. Here in the middle we have our plumpsters—we call them plumpsters." Wolf prattled on faster than a runaway cart down Kliminsky Street on the science and technology of poultry. "With the plumpsters you get more meat per cubic centimeter than any other kind of chicken. Succulent! Juicy! You see, the plumpsters are not required to scratch for their food. And what food it is! Whole-grain bread soaked in gravy, pumpkin seeds, kasha. We Zhidi should only eat like that! The plumpsters' main job in life is eating, with an occasional stroll in a very small area. A chicken, one might say, truly fit for a tsar. Please

333

sire, your sword. I will fetch you the plumpest of the plumpsters. Yes, a rare bird indeed!"

Sashie felt the wagon shake as Wolf pulled himself up on the side. "Kosher is quick!" She heard Wolf mutter to himself in Yiddish. In less than three minutes he had slaughtered ten chickens. Blood dripped down the center aisle onto the bedclothes.

"Your chickens, your excellency. May you and your officers eat them in good health!"

"Your client will never miss them," came the reply.

As the spurs dug into flanks, whinnies mixed with leathery squeaks and metallic janglings filled the air. The command finally came—"Forward!"—and then the rapid explosive noises of eight hooves striking the earth as they moved off with their imperial load.

Zhidi, Sashie thought, when at last she could think again. Wolf called himself a Zhidi. How very strange that he could do this—abuse himself with this foul word even though it was done to ingratiate himself with the commander. For the first hours after the encounter with the regiment, Sashie lay in a state of total exhaustion. It was as if her nerves, her brain, and each muscle in her body had used every bit of energy available. Gradually, however, she began to realize that she was alive. It was a miracle. It was as if she were a newborn baby with an older mind that could appreciate the wonder of its own birth—of being born a whole, complete human being. She tingled all over with the sheer excitement of her own living body. She touched her throat and face. She traced the gullies and curves of her ears. She pressed hard through all the layers of clothing and felt a rib. She took a joyous inventory

🌀 334 🌀

of her body. Then after the miracle of survival was confirmed, she thought of Wolf and the word he had used in reference to himself. How absolutely confounding and unfathomable it was. She could not imagine ever calling herself by this horrible name, no matter what the danger was.

Sashie had stared unblinkingly as Death sliced the air just inches from her face and throat. She was sure Wolf had seen something worse, but what was it? The haunted man contained a death riddle. Sashie had been brought to the edge, but Wolf in some way had crossed over.

The fog had long ago burned off and slants of sunlight had pierced through the mesh and feather storm into the netherworld of the coops. But now the sun was at too low an angle to light the wagon, and Sashie felt a twilight chill. If she could only move more, she would feel warmer. Louie was warm as a puppy from crawling around under the coops, and though he was now sleeping, his short little body could curl up into a nice ball perfect for conserving energy. Sashie tucked him in closer to her own body to steal a little heat. Soon she drifted in and out of a troubled sleep that jolted and lurched and flashed with silver blades dripping blood. Then everything stopped and she woke up into a night-still world with her own hand fast at her throat.

"All right!" Wolf shouted. She felt him jump down from the driver's seat. "We're here."

"My God!"

"Thank God!"

"Am I dead or alive?"

"Or a chicken!"

"It's all right, Ida, we're here!"

🌀 335 🌀

"Oh, Joe!"

"Hang on, folks. I'll get the coops off in half a second." Sashie felt Wolf climb on the back end of the wagon. She heard the clatter of the first coop being removed.

"Ah!" exclaimed Ghisa with wonder as she saw the first piece of the world above. Another two coops were removed and Sashie heard Zayde Sol recite a *broche*, a prayer, upon seeing the evening again. Then another coop was removed and a square of night sky reappeared, black velvet chinked with stars. Piece by piece the sky came back and the wind, with the smell of winter grass and earth, blew across Sashie's face.

Each person had to be helped off the wagon by Wolf and, except for Louie, walked around a few feet by him until their legs and back regained their strength. Sashie needed Wolf's arm only for a couple of steps. Almost immediately she was off on her own trying out her new legs. First she tried walking a few meters, but the night was so warm, the air so gentle, and the field so vast that Sashie felt she must dance, leap, fly through this startling country. Under the starry dome of the Russian night Sashie whirled and jumped. Her head thrown back, she watched the stars spin and smelled the thawing earth and listened to the wind songs in the grass.

Ghisa too was soon running and skipping in jerky little circles around a moonlit tree stump. The babies squealed and Ida and Joe said soft prayers of thanksgiving and laughed gently with each other in the night. And Zayde Sol said more *broches*—*broches* for seeing stars again, *broches* for seeing the moon, *broches* for seeing a baby walk, and *broches* for seeing a granddaughter dance.

❺

🖉 *336* 🖉

❺ If students need help clarifying the word *broches,* you might model noticing that there is a **context clue** in the previous sentence: "Ida and Joe said soft prayers of thanksgiving," as well as at the beginning of the sentence in which the word appears: "And Zayde Sol said more broches." (The word *more* is a clue.)

broche (brô´ KHah)

Discussing Strategy Use

Have the students share how they used any of the reading strategies as they read "The Night Journey." If students used strategies they developed for themselves, encourage them to share these strategies with the rest of the class.

* EXPLORING THROUGH DISCUSSION

Reflecting on the Selection
Whole-Group Discussion

The whole group discusses the selection and personal thoughts or questions that it raises. During this time, students also **return to the clues, problems, and wonderings** they noted on the chalkboard during browsing.

Assessment

To assess the students' understanding of the text, engage in a discussion to determine whether the students have grasped the following ideas:
- why the samovar is significant to Rache
- how Sashie's family escaped from Nikolayev in a wagon full of chickens
- why it was important for Rache to hear the story of the escape and for her great-grandmother to tell it

Response Journal

Students may wish to record their personal responses to the selection.

Exploring Concepts Within the Selection
Small-Group Discussion

Small groups discuss the relationship of the selection to family heritage. Circulate among the groups and observe the discussions. Refer the students to the Concept Board and the Question Board to keep them focused on their original ideas about family heritage and to see if those ideas have changed as a result of reading this selection.

Sharing Ideas About Explorable Concepts

Have the groups **report** and **discuss** their **ideas** with the rest of the class. It is crucial that the students' ideas determine this discussion.
- Students may conclude that family heritage includes the bad things that have happened to families as well as the good things.
- Students may conclude that because of political and religious persecution, the only way for some families to preserve the culture that is important to them is to take it with them to another place.
- Students may discuss examples of families that cherish objects that represent their country of origin or their family heritage.
- Students may conclude that it is important for young people to be told about their parents' and grandparents' lives and about their cultural heritage.

As these ideas and others are stated, have the students add them to the **Question Board** or the **Concept Board**.

Exploring Concepts Across Selections

Students may make connections with other selections in the student anthology.
- Students may remember that in "The West Side," Juan had been sent to New York from Puerto Rico so that he might have a better life. Paw-Paw, the grandmother in "Chinatown," probably left her homeland for similar reasons. In the same way, Sashie's family hopes to find a better life somewhere outside Russia.
- Students may discuss that just as the Chinese statues and the owl charm have a special meaning for Paw-Paw and Casey, the samovar has a special meaning for Rache and Nana Sashie, and that just as it

TEACHING TIP Reinforce student commentary only when absolutely necessary (for example, when a student who has been especially reticent offers a comment and no reinforcement is coming from other students). Teacher reinforcement suggests that the teacher holds the definitive opinion or that the answers will come from the teacher rather than from the group as a whole.

TIP FOR ENGLISH LANGUAGE LEARNERS

Use information from English Language Learners' cultures as the background for discussing the concepts. If there are students from Russia in your class, invite them to talk about and to expand on anything from the story that is familiar to them.

is important for Casey to learn about being Chinese from Paw-Paw, it is important for Rache to learn from her great-grandmother what it meant to be a Jew in tsarist Russia.

- Students may remember that just as the owl charm and the samovar have stories that go with them, the candy box that Grandmother Sibble III shares with Lina in the selection "Storks" has a story that goes with it.

Connections Across Units

Recording Ideas

As students complete the above discussions, ask them to **sum up what they have learned from their conversations and to tell how they might use this information** in further explorations. Any special information or insights may be recorded on the **Concept Board.** Any further questions that they would like to think about, pursue, or investigate may be recorded on the **Question Board.** They may want to discuss the progress that has been made on their questions. They may also want to cross out any questions that no longer warrant consideration.

➤ After discussion, the students should individually record their ideas on page 44 of their Explorer's Notebook.

Explorer's Notebook, page 44

Recording Concept Information continued

"The Night Journey" by Kathryn Lasky

_____

"The Land I Lost" by Huynh Quang Nhuong

_____

"Parmele" by Eloise Greenfield and Lessie Jones Little

_____

44 EN   Family Heritage/Unit 3

Good readers develop their own strategies for dealing with difficult text. Encourage the students to share and discuss the strategies
they have developed on their own as well as those suggested on the
strategy posters.

Notes:

2 READING WITH A WRITER'S EYE
MINILESSONS

Writer's Craft:
Suspense

Ask the students to discuss what they know about the use of suspense in stories. Guide discussion to the understanding that **suspense is
the feeling of anxious uncertainty about what will happen next** and
that writers like to use that uncertainty to hold their readers' interest.

Point out that Kathryn Lasky's story is filled with suspense from the
moment that Nana Sashie begins the story of her family's flight from
Nikolayev. Will they be detected or won't they? That is the constant,
underlying uncertainty that Lasky builds on. As many good writers do,
she raises and lowers the level of suspense to keep her readers turning
the pages. As soon as the story characters escape from one dangerous
situation, they are involved in another dangerous situation.

On page 321, even before they climb into their hiding places in Wolf
Levinson's poultry wagon, Sashie is frightened when her mother suddenly balks at the idea. "[Sashie] felt the real possibility that the escape
might never begin, that they were doomed to stand here until morning,
when they would be discovered."

Then, on page 323, after everyone is finally on the wagon, everything
calms down again for a while. "This seemed much more ample than
Sashie had imagined. There was plenty of room to place a tier of the
samovar over her face as a shield." Things are quiet for a while as the
wagon makes its way along the town's streets.

On page 326, the wagon comes upon some men who are repairing the
road. Again, the reader wonders whether the family will be caught, and
this time it seems as though they have been discovered when one of the
men calls out, "You know there are not just roosters aboard your wagon.
I see some hens." Lasky immediately relieves the suspense. " 'Just joking!' She heard the man protest innocently. "Can't you take a joke, old
man?' "

Selective Reading:
Focus on Suspense

Now have the students go back to "The Night Journey" to find other
examples of how Lasky creates suspense. Encourage volunteers to read
aloud and explain any examples they find.

*Selection-Based
Practice*

Other examples include these situations:
- page 328: when the baby noisily demands more candy as the wagon continues along the town's streets
- page 331: when the tsar's soldiers stop the wagon
- page 331: when the commander demands some chickens instead of searching the wagon
- page 332: when the lieutenant sticks his saber into the chicken coops, narrowly missing Sashie's face

Independent Practice: Suspense

➤ For additional practice in recognizing suspense in stories, have the students work together to discuss and complete Reading/Writing Connection, page 26.

Writer's Craft: Dialogue

Ask the students to suggest some reasons why writers use dialogue in stories. They should understand that **writers use dialogue to move their stories along, to make the stories more realistic, or to help readers learn something about the characters who are talking.** Point out that good writers know that dialogue must serve one of these purposes. Dialogue used for no good reason can slow a story down and make it uninteresting.

ASSESSMENT TIP This may be a good opportunity to observe students working in groups and to mark observations in the Teacher's Observation Log.

Reading/Writing Connection, page 26

Suspense

"The Night Journey"

In "The Night Journey," Kathryn Lasky uses rising and falling suspense to hold readers' interest. Look again at "The Night Journey" or at other stories for more examples of suspense. Write the title of the selection, the page the suspenseful passage is on, and the reason the passage is suspenseful.

Title: _____ Page: _____
Why the passage is suspenseful: _____
_____
_____

Title: _____ Page: _____
Why the passage is suspenseful: _____
_____
_____

Title: _____ Page: _____
Why the passage is suspenseful: _____
_____
_____

Title: _____ Page: _____
Why the passage is suspenseful: _____
_____
_____

Look back at this page for ideas when you want to add suspense to your stories.

Mood
26 R/WC   Family Heritage/Unit 3

In "The Night Journey," Kathryn Lasky makes good use of dialogue to show how the characters feel toward each other. For example, beginning at the bottom of page 319, she relates the conversation between Rache and Nana Sashie. This simple conversation tells a lot about the relationship between Rache and Nana Sashie. They care about each other and are comfortable in each other's company.

Selective Reading: Focus on Dialogue

Have the children find other examples in "The Night Journey" of how **dialogue helps readers to understand the characters' feelings or helps to move the story along.** Encourage volunteers to read aloud and explain the examples they find.

Other examples of dialogue that provides insights about characters include the following:

- page 322: the conversation between Ida and Joe when Joe is trying to convince his wife to get into the poultry wagon
- pages 324 and 325: when Joe explains to Sashie how she should cope with the suffocating smell and the dust from the chickens
- pages 331 to 335: the conversation between the frightened Wolf Levinson and the arrogant officer of the tsar's soldiers.

Examples of dialogue that helps to move the action of the story along include the following:

- page 321: "We have no time to waste Joe. . . . So if you will follow me, the wagon's right here."
- page 335: "'All right!' Wolf shouted. . . . 'We're here!'"

Independent Practice: Dialogue

❯ For additional practice in recognizing how dialogue helps to reveal characters' emotions, have the students work in small groups to complete and discuss Reading/Writing Connection, page 27.

Selection-Based Practice

WRITING

Linking Reading to Writing

Remind students that dialogue can be used to make a story seem more real, to reveal something about the characters who are speaking, or to move along the action in a story. Remind them also that using suspense will help to hold their readers' interest. To provide opportunities for them to use these writing elements, encourage them to look through their writing folders for pieces of their own writing that could be improved by adding dialogue or by creating a suspenseful situation.

✷ Writing Process

If students are still revising the **realistic fiction** pieces that they began earlier, ask them to look for places where dialogue would be a useful way to move the plot along or to reveal something about the characters. Some students might also want to revise the plots of their stories to provide suspense.

Encourage any students who have decided to revise existing pieces to focus on ideas and content during this phase of the writing process. They can focus on correcting mechanical, grammatical, and spelling errors during proofreading.

"The Night Journey"

Dialogue

Kathryn Lasky uses dialogue to provide information about her characters, to make the story seem more realistic, and to move the action along. Look again at "The Night Journey" or at other stories you have read for examples of dialogue being used for these purposes. Write the title of the story, the page where the dialogue appears, and the purpose of the dialogue.

Title: _____ Page: _____

Purpose of the dialogue: _____
_____
_____

Title: _____ Page: _____

Purpose of the dialogue: _____
_____
_____

Title: _____ Page: _____

Purpose of the dialogue: _____
_____
_____

Title: _____ Page: _____

Purpose of the dialogue: _____
_____
_____

Look back at this page for ideas when you want to add dialogue to your stories.

Dialogue
Unit 3/Family Heritage   R/WC 27

Reading/Writing Connection, page 27

VOCABULARY

Words related to family heritage that students may find interesting and want to discuss include the following:
samovar, kosher, tantrum, ingratiate, poultry, skewer

Have Vocabulary Exploration forms, Reproducible Master 14, available for students who request them. Remind the students to add these or any other words and phrases from the story to the Personal Dictionary section of their Writer's Notebook. Some students may wish to share these additions with the class. For additional opportunities to build vocabulary, see **Teacher Tool Card 75.**

VOCABULARY TIP Model for students how to use context clues during reading to determine a word's meaning.

3 GUIDED AND INDEPENDENT EXPLORATION

EXPLORING CONCEPTS BEYOND THE TEXT

Guided Exploration

Students will select activities in which they explore family heritage. Refer them to the **Exploration Activities poster** and give them time to choose an activity and to discuss what they wish to explore and how they wish to go about it. If the students need further help, here is a suggestion:

Remind them that one important way to discover more about their own family heritage is to ask questions of older family members about it. If those relatives live in other cities, students can write letters to them.

▶ Ask students to take home and complete Home/School Connection 23 in order to learn more about whom they might write to and where these persons live.

▶ Have students work together to write letters to relatives in other towns. Then have them use Reproducible Master 38 to review the parts of a friendly letter—date, greeting, message, signature—and to check their letters.

Exploring Through Reflective Activities

Home/School Connection 23

"The Night Journey"

A message from _____

A character in "The Night Journey" hears about her family's history from a great-grandmother. Perhaps your child has an older relative or family friend who can give him or her some information about your family's history. Encourage your child to write a letter asking that relative for information on family history.

The guidelines for writing a friendly letter were distributed in class. Ask your child to share them with you. Help her or him to think of some questions to ask in the body of the letter. With your child, review the first draft of the letter and discuss its content. Review the final draft of the letter and check to see that the envelope is addressed and stamped correctly. When your child receives an answer to the letter, read it together and then decide whether parts of it can be shared with the class.

Name and address of somebody I can write to for information about my family's history: _____
_____
_____

Some questions I would like to ask in my letter: _____
_____
_____
_____

This is the date I wrote the letter: _____

This is the date I received a reply: _____

Did I remember to thank the person for helping me learn about my family's history?
_____

Unit 3/Family Heritage   H/SC 23

Reproducible Master 38

Personal Letter Checklist

_____ Did you write today's date in the top right-hand corner?

_____ Did you write a greeting in the first line of the letter?

_____ Did you say everything you wanted to say in the letter?

_____ Did you end with "Love" at the bottom right of the letter?

_____ Did you sign the letter?

_____ On the envelope, did you include the person's full name?

_____ Did you include the complete street address?

_____ Do you need to add an apartment number?

_____ Did you include the town or city name and ZIP code?

_____ Did you include a return address in the top left corner?

_____ Did you put a stamp on the envelope?

Name _____

RM 38   Writer's Notebook: Checking My Work

Organizing Information

This is what I learned about my family heritage from the answer I received to my letter.

Information about where my ancestors were born:

_____
_____
_____
_____
_____
_____
_____

Information about individual ancestors:

_____
_____
_____
_____
_____
_____
_____

Other information:

_____
_____
_____
_____
_____
_____
_____
_____

52 EN   Family Heritage/Unit 3

Explorer's Notebook, page 52

When students receive answers to their letters have them report what they learn to the class. With the sender's permission, copy and display parts of the letters.

❯ Have the students use Explorer's Notebook, page 52, to organize the information they collect from the letters they receive.

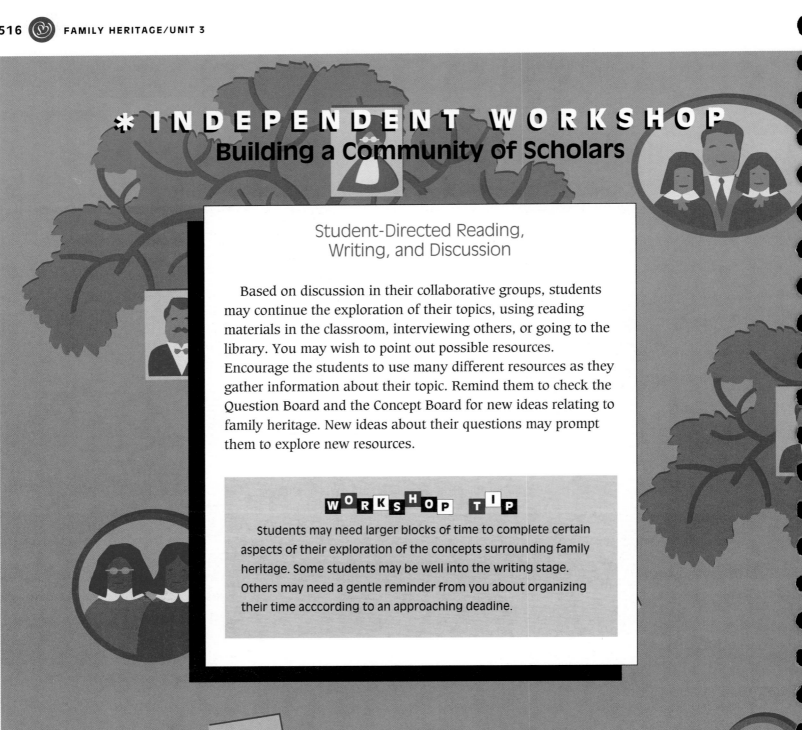

✱ INDEPENDENT WORKSHOP
Building a Community of Scholars

Student-Directed Reading, Writing, and Discussion

Based on discussion in their collaborative groups, students may continue the exploration of their topics, using reading materials in the classroom, interviewing others, or going to the library. You may wish to point out possible resources. Encourage the students to use many different resources as they gather information about their topic. Remind them to check the Question Board and the Concept Board for new ideas relating to family heritage. New ideas about their questions may prompt them to explore new resources.

WORKSHOP TIP

Students may need larger blocks of time to complete certain aspects of their exploration of the concepts surrounding family heritage. Some students may be well into the writing stage. Others may need a gentle reminder from you about organizing their time acccording to an approaching deadine.

Additional Opportunities for Independent Reading, Writing, and Cross-curricular Activities

✱ Reading Roundtable

Some students may be interested in reading the entire book from which the selection was taken—*The Night Journey.* For additional ideas for Reading Roundtable, see **Learning Framework Card 6.**

✱ Writing Seminar

Remind the students to use the writing process for any writing they are working on. If your class is using the optional Writer's Handbook, students should be encouraged to use it to help them as they write.

Cross-curricular Activity Cards

The following Cross-curricular Activity Cards in the Student Toolbox are especially appropriate for this selection:

- 2 Music—Folk Dancing
- 4 Art—Making a Family Coat of Arms

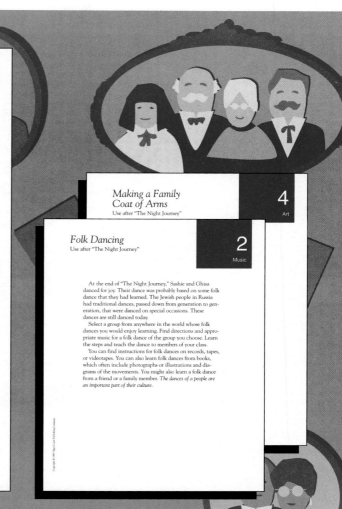

Additional Opportunities for Solving Learning Problems

Tutorial

Work with individuals or small groups who need help in any area. The following Teacher Tool Cards are available for your convenience:

- Writer's Craft/Reading: Suspense and Surprise, Teacher Tool Card 16
- Writer's Craft/Reading: Using Dialogue in a Story, Teacher Tool Card 19
- Writer's Craft/Reading: Genre–Adventure, Teacher Tool Card 7
- Writer's Craft/Reading: Characterization, Teacher Tool Card 13
- Grammar, Mechanics, and Punctuation: Using and Punctuating Dialogue, Teacher Tool Card 70

Assessment

The Land I Lost: Adventures of a Boy in Vietnam

1 READING THE SELECTION

INFORMATION FOR THE TEACHER

About the Selection

Huynh Quang Nhuong (Hwŏŏn Kwän Nyōōn) planned to live his life in Vietnam. He planned to be a teacher like his father, and a farmer and hunter like all the other men in his village. However, war and paralysis from a gunshot wound forced him to leave his beloved homeland. The warm and humorous stories that he writes about his childhood are, as he says, his memories of a land that was lost to him forever.

"The Land I Lost," pages 338–347, consists of two chapters from *The Land I Lost: Adventures of a Boy in Vietnam* by Huynh Quang Nhuong. The first part is the introduction and describes the way of life of Huynh's family before it was disrupted by war. The second part, "Opera and Karate," is from a chapter about Huynh's grandmother. This book is also a Tradebook Connection selection for Grade 5.

Link to the Unit Concepts

The heritage of this Vietnamese family is unique in many ways. One aspect of the family's heritage is the emphasis on working hard. Each family member, including children from the age of six, works hard to produce food. The cultural aspect of the family's heritage is reflected in the grandmother's interests and activities, which include theater and mythology. The loyalty and affection that family members feel for one another are apparent throughout the selection.

About the Author

Huynh Quang Nhuong graduated from the University of Saigon (now renamed the University of Ho Chi Minh City) with a degree in chemistry. He was drafted into the South Vietnamese army and was left permanently paralyzed by a gunshot wound. Huynh came to the United States for medical treatment and decided to remain here. Here he earned bachelor's and master's degrees in French and in comparative literature.

LESSON OVERVIEW

"The Land I Lost" by Huynh Quang Nhuong, pages 338–347

READING THE SELECTION

Materials

Student anthology, pp. 338–347
Explorer's Notebook, p. 44
Assessment Masters 1–2, 5

READING WITH A WRITER'S EYE

Minilesson

Assessment

Materials

Reproducible Master 14

FYI

Teacher Tool Card
• Spelling and Vocabulary: Building Vocabulary, 75

GUIDED AND INDEPENDENT EXPLORATION

Independent Workshop

Optional Materials from Student Toolbox

Tradebook Connection Cards
• *The Land I Lost* by Huynh Quang Nhuong

NOTES

....

Asterisks (*) throughout the lesson indicate learning frameworks. Learning Framework Cards and Teacher Tool Cards can be found in the Teacher Toolbox.

INFORMATION FOR THE STUDENT

Share the information given above about the author. Explain that in Vietnam one's surname, or family name, comes before one's given names; thus the author would be addressed as Mr. Huynh.

In 1954 Vietnam was divided into North Vietnam and South Vietnam as part of a peace settlement between the French, who formerly controlled the country as a colony, and communist forces. After this division, a communist government ruled North Vietnam, and former supporters of the French headed the government of South Vietnam. In 1957 the Vietnam War began when South Vietnamese communists, supported by North Vietnam, began to rebel against the government. The United States sent military forces to aid South Vietnam, while China and the Soviet Union sent troops to aid the North. In 1973 a cease-fire agreement was signed, and American troops left the country. In 1975 the capital of South Vietnam fell to the communists, and the country was unified under one government. Since that time many people have left the country as refugees.

Background Information

COGNITIVE AND RESPONSIVE READING

Activating Prior Knowledge

Ask the students to discuss what they know about Vietnam or the Vietnam War.

Setting Reading Goals and Expectations

Even though this selection has been designated as an Assessment selection, the **class will proceed as usual with the setting of reading goals and expectations.** To do this, they will **browse the selection,** using the clues/problems/wondering procedure. Students will return to these observations after reading.

Recommendations for Reading the Selection

Explain to the students that they will read this selection to assess what they have learned about family heritage. Place the students in small groups. Tell them that they will decide in their small groups how to read the selection. For example, the groups may choose from among the following options:
- to read silently but stay in groups, stopping to ask each other questions when they need help understanding. If any students are of Vietnamese origin or are familiar with Vietnamese customs, ask them to comment on or help to clarify any puzzling points in the text during the discussion of the selection
- to alternate reading aloud and summarizing a section at a time
- to read silently on their own

Encourage the students to use the strategies that they think will best help them understand and appreciate the selection. They should feel free to refer to the reading strategy posters as needed. Encourage them to collaborate with others in their groups by asking questions when they encounter difficulties and by offering suggestions to others who need help.

TIP FOR ENGLISH LANGUAGE LEARNERS

Give English Language Learners a chance to build a broad base of knowledge and cultural understanding. To help ensure their success, draw on their backgrounds. Have them talk about what they already know about Vietnam.

❯ Distribute copies of Assessment Master 5, Concept Connections for Unit 3, Family Heritage, which you will find in the booklet *Masters for Continuous Assessment* in the Teacher Toolbox. Tell the students that after reading the selection in their small groups, they will write responses on the master independently. They will then regroup and share their findings, changing any ideas they wish.

Assessment Master 5

Concept Connections

1. Explain what this selection is about. Write a short summary.

_____

_____

_____

_____

_____

2. Tell what this selection has to do with family heritage.

_____

_____

_____

_____

_____

3. Tell how this selection is like other selections you have read in this unit.

_____

_____

_____

_____

_____

4. You have read many selections about family heritage. How did *this* selection change your ideas about family heritage?

_____

_____

_____

_____

_____

Date

Name

Unit 3/Family Heritage   Assessment Master 5

THINK ALOUD PROMPTS

To foster independence, think-aloud prompts are not provided for Assessment lessons.

THE LAND I LOST:
ADVENTURES OF
A BOY IN VIETNAM
from the book by Huynh Quang Nhuong
illustrated by Allen Eitzen

I was born on the central highlands of Vietnam in a small <u>hamlet</u> on a riverbank that had a deep jungle on one side and a chain of high mountains on the other. Across the river, rice fields stretched to the slopes of another chain of mountains.

There were fifty houses in our hamlet, scattered along the river or propped against the mountainsides. The houses were made of bamboo and covered with coconut leaves, and each was surrounded by a deep trench to protect it from wild animals or thieves. The only way to enter a house was to walk across a "monkey bridge"—a single bamboo stick that spanned the <u>trench</u>. At night we pulled the bridges into our houses and were safe.

There were no shops or marketplaces in our hamlet. If we needed supplies—medicine, cloth, soaps, or candles—we had to cross over the mountains and travel to a town nearby. We used the river mainly for traveling to distant hamlets, but it also provided us with plenty of fish.

During the six-month rainy season, nearly all of us helped plant and <u>cultivate</u> fields of rice, sweet potatoes, Indian mustard, eggplant, tomatoes, hot peppers, and corn. But during the dry season, we became hunters and turned to the jungle.

Wild animals played a very large part in our lives. There were four animals we feared the most: the tiger, the lone wild hog, the crocodile, and the horse snake. Tigers were always trying to steal cattle.

Sometimes, however, when a tiger became old and slow it became a maneater. But a lone wild hog was even more dangerous than a tiger. It attacked every creature in sight, even when it had no need for food. Or it did crazy things, such as charging into the hamlet in broad daylight, ready to kill or to be killed.

The river had different dangers: crocodiles. But of all the animals, the most hated and feared was the huge horse snake. It was sneaky and attacked people and cattle just for the joy of killing. It would either crush its victim to death or poison it with a bite.

Like all farmers' children in the hamlet, I started working at the age of six. My seven sisters helped by working in the kitchen, weeding the garden, gathering eggs, or taking water to the cattle. I looked after the family herd of water buffaloes. Someone always had to be with the herd because no matter how carefully a water buffalo was trained, it always was ready to nibble young rice plants when no one was looking. Sometimes, too, I fished for the family while I guarded the herd, for there were plenty of fish in the flooded rice fields during the rainy season.

I was twelve years old when I made my first trip to the jungle with my father. I learned how to track game, how to recognize useful roots, how to distinguish edible mushrooms from poisonous ones. I learned that if birds, raccoons, squirrels, or monkeys had eaten the fruits of certain trees, then those fruits were not poisonous. Often they were not delicious, but they could calm a man's hunger and thirst.

My father, like most of the villagers, was a farmer and a hunter, depending upon the season. But he also had a college

340

education, so in the evenings he helped to teach other children in our hamlet, for it was too small to afford a professional schoolteacher.

My mother managed the house, but during the harvest season she could be found in the fields, helping my father get the crops home; and as the wife of a hunter she knew how to dress and nurse a wound and took good care of her husband and his hunting dogs.

I went to the lowlands to study for a while because I wanted to follow my father as a teacher when I grew up. I always planned to return to my hamlet to live the rest of my life there. But war disrupted my dreams. The land I love was lost to me forever.

These stories are my memories. . . .

OPERA AND KARATE

When she was eighty years old grandmother was still quite strong. She could use her own teeth to eat corn on the cob or to chew on sugar plants to extract juice from them. Every two days she walked for more than an hour to reach the marketplace, carrying a heavy load of food with her, and then spent another hour walking back home. And even though she was quite old, traces of her beauty still lingered on: Her hands, her feet, her face revealed that she had been an attractive young woman. Nor did time do much damage to the youthful spirit of my grandmother.

One of her great passions was theater, and this passion never diminished with age. No matter how busy she was, she never missed a show when there was a group of actors in

341

town. If no actors visited our hamlet for several months, she would organize her own show in which she was the manager, the producer, and the young leading lady, all at the same time.

My grandmother's own plays were always melodramas inspired by books she had read and by what she had seen on the stage. She always chose her favorite grandson to play the role of the hero, who would, without fail, marry the heroine at the end and live happily ever after. And when my sisters would tell her that she was getting too old to play the role of the young heroine anymore, my grandmother merely replied: "Anybody can play this role if she's young at heart."

When I was a little boy my grandmother often took me to see the opera. She knew Chinese mythology by heart, and the opera was often a dramatization of this mythology. On one special occasion, during the Lunar New Year celebrations—

342

my favorite holiday, because children could do anything they wanted and by tradition no one could scold them— I accompanied my grandmother to the opera. When we reached the theater I wanted to go in immediately. But my grandmother wanted to linger at the entrance and talk to her friends. She chatted for more than an hour. Finally we entered the theater, and at that moment the "Faithful One" was onstage, singing sadly. The "Faithful One" is a common character in Chinese opera. He could be a good minister, or a valiant general, or someone who loved and served his king faithfully. But in the end he is unjustly persecuted by the king, whose opinion of him has been changed by the lies of the "Flatterer," another standard character.

When my grandmother saw the "Faithful One" onstage she looked upset and gave a great sigh. I was too interested in what was happening to ask her the reason, and we spent the next five hours watching the rest of the opera. Sometimes I cried because my grandmother cried at the pitiful situation of the "Faithful One." Sometimes I became as angry as my grandmother did at the wickedness of the "Flatterer."

When we went home that night my grandmother was quite sad. She told my mother that she would have bad luck in the

343

following year because when we entered the theater, the "Faithful One" was onstage. I was puzzled. I told my grandmother that she was confused. It would be a good year for us because we saw the good guy first. But my mother said, "No, son. The 'Faithful One' always is in trouble and it takes him many years to <u>vindicate</u> himself. Our next year is going to be like one of his bad years."

So, according to my mother's and grandmother's logic, we would have been much better off in the new year if we had been lucky enough to see the villain first!

My grandmother had married a man whom she loved with all her heart, but who was totally different from her. My grandfather was very shy, never laughed loudly, and always spoke very softly. And physically he was not as strong as my grandmother. But he excused his lack of physical strength by saying that he was a "scholar."

About three months after their marriage, my grandparents were in a restaurant and a rascal began to insult my grandfather because he looked weak and had a pretty wife. At first he just made insulting remarks, such as, "Hey! Wet chicken! This is no place for a weakling!"

My grandfather wanted to leave the restaurant even though he and my grandmother had not yet finished their meal. But my grandmother pulled his shirt sleeve and signaled him to remain seated. She continued to eat and looked as if nothing had happened.

Tired of yelling insults without any result, the rascal got up from his table, moved over to my grandparents' table, and

❧ 344 ☙

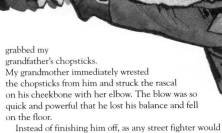

grabbed my grandfather's chopsticks. My grandmother immediately wrested the chopsticks from him and struck the rascal on his cheekbone with her elbow. The blow was so quick and powerful that he lost his balance and fell on the floor.

Instead of finishing him off, as any street fighter would do, my grandmother let the rascal recover from the blow. But as soon as he got up again, he kicked over the table between him and my grandmother, making food and drink fly all over the place. Before he could do anything else, my grandmother kicked him on the chin. The kick was so swift that my grandfather didn't even see it. He only heard a heavy thud, and then saw the rascal tumble backward and collapse on the ground.

All the onlookers were surprised and delighted, especially the owner of the restaurant. Apparently the rascal, one of the best karate fighters of our area, came to this restaurant every

❧ 345 ☙

day and left without paying for his food or drink, but the owner was too afraid to <u>confront</u> him.

While the rascal's friends tried to revive him, everyone else surrounded my grandmother and asked her who had taught her karate. She said, "Who else? My husband!"

After the fight at the restaurant people assumed that my grandfather knew karate very well but refused to use it for fear of killing someone. In reality, my grandmother had received special training in karate from my great-great uncle from the time she was eight years old.

Anyway, after that incident, my grandfather never had to worry again. Anytime he had some business downtown, people treated him very well. And whenever anyone happened to bump into him on the street, they bowed to my grandfather in a very respectful way.

One morning my grandmother wanted me to go outside with her. We climbed a little hill that looked over the whole area, and when we got to the top she looked at the rice field below, the mountain on the horizon, and especially at the river. As a young girl she had often brought her herd of water buffaloes to the river to drink while she swam with the other children of the village. Then we visited the graveyard where her husband and some of her children were buried. She touched her husband's tombstone and said, "Dear, I will join you soon." And then we walked back to the garden and she gazed at the fruit trees her husband had planted, a new one for each time she had given birth to a child. Finally, before we left the garden my sister joined us, and the two of them fed a few ducks swimming in the pond.

❧ 346 ☙

That evening my grandmother did not eat much of her dinner. After dinner she combed her hair and put on her best dress. We thought that she was going to go out again, but instead she went to her bed room and told us that she didn't want to be disturbed.

The family dog seemed to sense something was <u>amiss,</u> for he kept looking anxiously at everybody and whined from time to time. At midnight my mother went to my grandmother's room and found that she had died, with her eyes shut, as if she were sleeping normally.

It took me a long time to get used to the reality that my grandmother had passed away. Wherever I was, in the house, in the garden, out on the fields, her face always appeared so clearly to me. And even now, many years later, I still have the feeling that my last conversation with her has happened only a few days before.

❧ 347 ☙

Reflecting on the Selection

As the students read the selection, circulate among the groups to observe their understanding of the concepts as well as their collaboration in solving difficulties in understanding the selection.

As you note their collaborative group discussions, mark your Teacher's Observation Log for the individuals in one or two groups. Take a moment to reflect on how each student is changing from unit to unit in her or his ability to use strategies to solve problems.

Have the groups break while the students **respond independently** to Concept Connections, Assessment Master 5.

ASSESSMENT TIP This is an ideal time to mark observations in your Teacher's Observation Log.

Exploring Concepts Within the Selection

Allow the students to regroup to compare and discuss their responses to Concept Connections. During these discussions you will have more opportunities to observe students and to mark your Teacher's Observation Log.

Collect the Concept Connections pages and continue with the lesson as usual.

ASSESSMENT TIP This is another ideal time to mark observations in the log.

Response Journal

Some students may have experienced the death of a grandparent or great-grandparent. They may wish to record personal responses to the selection.

Sharing Ideas About Explorable Concepts

Have the groups **report** and **discuss** their **ideas** with the rest of the class. It is crucial that the students' ideas determine this discussion.

- Students may reflect on the author's feelings about Vietnam. He looks back to the country where he spent his childhood with affection because of the happy times he remembers there, and with sadness because he fears he will never be able to go back.
- Students may comment on the fact that, although the author's grandmother died when he was still a child, she seems very real to him when he is an adult.
- Students may comment on the idea that family stories about parents and grandparents are important for passing down family heritage.

As these ideas and others are stated, have the students **add them to** the **Question Board** or the **Concept Board**.

Exploring Concepts Across Selections

Ask the students whether this selection reminds them of any others they have already read in this unit. If so, in what ways? They might **make connections** with other selections in the unit.

- Students might notice that, like Luisito in "The Night We Started Dancing" and Rache in "The Night Journey," the author lived in a multigenerational family.
- Students might remark that, like Casey in "Chinatown," the author learned about his cultural heritage from his grandmother.

Recording Ideas

➤ As students complete the above discussions, ask them to **sum up what they have learned from their conversations and to tell how they might use this information** in further explorations. Any special information or insights may be recorded on the **Concept Board**. Any further questions that they would like to think about, pursue, or investigate may be recorded on the **Question Board**. They may want to discuss the progress that has been made on their questions. They may also want to cross out any questions that no longer warrant consideration. Have the students record their findings in their Explorer's Notebook, page 44.

Self-Assessment Questionnaire

➤ After these aspects of the lesson have been completed, you may wish to distribute copies of Self-Assessment Questionnaire, Assessment Master 2. Allow plenty of time for the students to complete this important assessment piece.

Evaluating Discussions

Explorer's Notebook, page 44

Recording Concept Information continued

"The Night Journey" by Kathryn Lasky

"The Land I Lost" by Huynh Quang Nhuong

"Parmele" by Eloise Greenfield and Lessie Jones Little

44 EN

Family Heritage/Unit 3

Self-Assessment Questionnaire

1. How would you rate this selection?
   ○ easy   ○ medium   ○ hard

2. If you checked **medium** or **hard**, answer these questions.
   • Which part of the selection did you find especially difficult?
   • What strategy did you use to try and understand it?
   _____
   _____

   • Were some of the words hard?
   • What did you do to figure out their meaning?
   _____
   _____

3. What do you feel you need to work on to make yourself a better reader?
   _____
   _____
   _____

4. Give an example of something you said in the group.
   Tell why you said it.
   _____
   _____
   _____

5. Give an example of something that people in the group helped you
   understand about the selection.
   _____
   _____
   _____

Self-Assessment Questionnaire   Assessment Master 2

INDIVIDUAL | GROUP | Date | Name

Copyright © 1995 Open Court Publishing Company

Assessment Master 2

2 READING WITH A WRITER'S EYE

MINILESSON

Assessment

Remind the students that in each selection they have read so far they have discussed something the author did especially well. For example, in "Chinatown" they discussed sensory images.

Tell the students that they will have the opportunity to decide what the author did especially well in "The Land I Lost." To focus their thinking, you might ask them to think about what they noticed in or liked about this selection. Encourage them to reread favorite sections. Did the author use a special way of writing that made the selection interesting or different?

If the students are having difficulty expressing what they noticed about the writing in this selection, model a response for them by pointing out things that you felt were noteworthy. For example, you might comment on the humor in the story or on the details Huynh includes to describe his grandmother.

WRITING

Linking Reading to Writing

Encourage the students to use in their own writing anything they particularly enjoyed about Huynh's writing. Invite them to go to their writing folders and see what piece of writing they might revise by adding details or by doing anything else that they noticed was done well in this selection.

✱ Writing Process

Although no specific writing assignment is recommended here, students may concentrate on an appropriate phase in the writing process with any writing on which they are currently working. Some students should be ready to proofread and publish the realistic fiction pieces they began earlier in the unit.

TEACHING TIP Reading is the ultimate source of good models for writing.

VOCABULARY

Words from the selection that are related to the unit concepts and for which the students may want to fill out Vocabulary Exploration forms, Reproducible Master 14, include *cultivate* and *hamlet.*

Remind the students to add these or any other words and phrases from the selection to the Personal Dictionary section of their Writer's Notebook. For additional opportunities to build vocabulary, see **Teacher Tool Card 75**.

Professional Checkpoint: Reading with a Writer's Eye

An environment in which writing is central provides a multifaceted context for the development of higher-order thinking. Students learn to plan, which allows them to work out ideas in their heads; to set goals, which promotes interest and the ability to monitor progress; to edit, which enables the creation of text that conforms to conventional standards and heightens its acceptability; and to revise content, which engages them in the reworking and rethinking activities that elevate writing from a craft to a tool for discovery.

Notes:

3 GUIDED AND INDEPENDENT EXPLORATION

EXPLORING CONCEPTS BEYOND THE TEXT

Guided
Exploration

Students will select activities in which they explore family heritage. Refer them to the **Exploration Activities poster** and give them time to choose an activity and to discuss what they wish to explore and how they wish to go about it. If the students need further help, here is a suggestion:

Remind the students that in the selection the author describes attending an opera based on Chinese mythology with his grandmother and that his grandmother sometimes wrote her own plays. Ask the students to think about unit selections or other books they have read about family heritage. Discuss any suggestions. Have them suggest specific episodes of these stories that might be dramatized. Remind them to consider everything they would need for a play—dialogue, sets, costumes, and props.

For example, if students decide to dramatize the scene in the restaurant on pages 344–346 of this selection, they would need loose pants and blouses as costumes for the grandmother and grandfather as a young couple and for the restaurant owner, the "rascal" and his friends, and a few onlookers. They would need a low table, chopsticks, and rice bowls. And, since the author provides only a few lines of dialogue for the scene, they would need to write lines for the rascal, the grandmother, the restaurant owner, and perhaps for others. For this scene, the actors would need to work at choreographing the fight scene between the rascal and the grandmother.

* Exploring Through Reflective Activities

Professional Checkpoint: Guided and Independent Exploration

Learning to work collaboratively in groups is essential for success. You should encourage students to take responsibility within the group. Give students time to work out group problems before offering advice.

Notes:

✳ INDEPENDENT WORKSHOP
Building a Community of Scholars

Student-Directed Reading, Writing, and Discussion

Provide time for students to meet with their collaborative groups during the first part of Independent Workshop to complete their exploration of family heritage. Those groups that want to share their explorations should be preparing their information for presentation.

Additional Opportunities for Independent Reading, Writing, and Cross-curricular Activities

* Reading Roundtable

Remind the students that *The Land I Lost* is one of the books in the Tradebook Connection. Activities relating to this book can be found on the accompanying Tradebook Connection Card in the Student Toolbox.

* Writing Seminar

Remind the students to use the writing process for any writing they are working on. If they are writing dialogue for a play, they should practice reading it aloud.

Portfolio

Have the students spend some time considering which pieces of writing they might choose to put into their portfolios.

Additional Opportunities for Solving Learning Problems

Tutorial

Work with individuals or small groups who need help in any area. This is also a good time for peer tutoring. Have the students refer to the appropriate Student Tool Cards to guide their work. Encourage them to discuss with you any questions they may have.

Parmele

1 READING THE SELECTION

INFORMATION FOR THE TEACHER

About the
Selection

"Parmele," pages 348–353, is an excerpt from *Childtimes,* a family memoir by Eloise Greenfield and her mother and grandmother. In this selection, Greenfield recalls her family's annual visits with her grandparents in Parmele, North Carolina. She remembers automobile trips along country roads and special times with her grandparents. Greenfield's vivid descriptions let readers feel that they themselves are along on this trip to Parmele.

Link to the
Unit Concepts

The experiences of this close-knit family mirror the heritage of many families from the early and mid-twentieth century. These were the "good old days" before television, video games, and other distractions reduced the time families spent together.

The children in this family live in the city. However, their parents grew up in the rural South and their grandparents still live there. The children learn about this aspect of their family heritage by visiting their grandparents.

About the
Author

When Eloise Greenfield realized there was a shortage of books for and about black children, she devoted herself to filling that void. Her works include short stories, novels, poetry, and biographies. *Paul Robeson* won the Jane Addams Children's Book Award; *Rosa Parks,* the Carter G. Woodson Award. She received the Coretta Scott King Award for *African Dream.* Her poetry collection, *Honey, I Love,* was an ALA Notable Book. (A poem from that collection, "Harriet Tubman," is found in Unit 4 of Grade 5 *Collections for Young Scholars.*) Greenfield lives in Washington, D.C., where she encourages aspiring authors—both children and adults—in her writing workshops.

LESSON OVERVIEW

"Parmele" by Eloise Greenfield, pages 348–353

READING THE SELECTION

Materials
Student anthology, pp. 348–353
Explorer's Notebook, p. 44
U.S. map

READING WITH A WRITER'S EYE

Minilesson
Writer's Craft: Elaboration

Materials
Reading/Writing Connection, p. 28
Reproducible Master 14

FYI
Teacher Tool Card
• Spelling and Vocabulary: Building Vocabulary, 75

Options for Instruction
Writer's Craft: Elaboration Through
 Providing Reasons or Causes
Writer's Craft: Elaboration Through
 Providing Descriptions
Grammar, Mechanics, and Usage:
 Capitalization
(Use Teacher Tool Cards listed below.)

GUIDED AND INDEPENDENT EXPLORATION

Materials
Explorer's Notebook, p. 53
Assessment Master 1

Independent Workshop

Optional Materials from Student Toolbox

Tradebook Connection Cards

Cross-curricular Activity Card
• 13 Social Studies—Comparing Modes of Transportation

Student Tool Cards
• Writer's Craft/Reading: Giving Examples, 38
• Writer's Craft/Reading: Telling Important Facts, 40
• Writer's Craft/Reading: Giving Reasons or Causes, 37
• Writer's Craft/Reading: Giving Descriptions, 39
• Grammar, Mechanics, and Usage: Capitalization, 57

FYI
Teacher Tool Cards
• Writer's Craft/Reading: Elaboration Through Providing Examples, 38
• Writer's Craft/Reading: Elaboration Through Providing Specific Facts, 40
• Writer's Craft/Reading: Elaboration Through Giving Reasons or Causes, 37
• Writer's Craft/Reading: Elaboration Through Providing Descriptions, 39
• Grammar, Mechanics, and Usage: Capitalization, 57

Asterisks (*) throughout the lesson indicate learning frameworks. Learning Framework Cards and Teacher Tool Cards can be found in the Teacher Toolbox.

Lessie Jones Little, Greenfield's mother, collaborated on one other book with her daughter. This book, *I Can Do It by Myself,* was named a Notable Children's Trade Book in the Field of Social Studies.

Greenfield and Little were inspired to write *Childtimes* by the stories of Little's mother, Pattie Ridley Jones. Jones began writing about her life when she was in her eighties. The authors used her written stories, along with stories she had told them through the years and stories other family members told about her, to write her part of the book.

Jones, who was born in 1884, tells about her grandparents, who were slaves in North Carolina, and about her parents. She also tells about Parmele, where many people worked for a lumber company, and about her home, her visits with her grandparents, and other memories from her childhood. Little, who was born in 1906, and Greenfield, whose parents moved from Parmele to Washington, D.C., shortly after her birth in 1929, also tell about their childhoods. Each writer recalls what she understood about important people, ideas, and events of the time, especially such things as racial segregation and African-American culture, when she was a child.

INFORMATION FOR THE STUDENT

Information about Eloise Greenfield and about the book from which the selection was taken can be found in the paragraphs about the author that follow the selection. Students may read these paragraphs before or after reading the selection.

COGNITIVE AND RESPONSIVE READING

Activating Prior Knowledge

Ask students who have been to North Carolina or to Washington, D.C., to tell what they know about these places. Then ask volunteers to find North Carolina and Parmele on a map. Parmele is in the northeast corner of the state, slightly west of Norfolk. Students should also find Washington, D.C., and Norfolk, Virginia. Some students may want to trace a route the family may have taken. If students have visited any of these places, have them tell what they know about them.

Setting Reading Goals and Expectations

Have the students **browse the selection,** using the clues/problems/ wondering procedure. Students will return to these observations after reading.

Recommendations for Reading the Selection

Ask the students how they would like to read the selection. "Parmele" has an easygoing style that is especially suited for oral reading.

During oral reading, use and encourage think-alouds. During silent reading, allow discussion as needed. Discuss problems, strategies, and reactions after reading.

This would also be a good selection for **responding** to text **by making connections** and **visualizing** while reading aloud. Model these responses, and then invite the students to respond.

About the Reading Strategies

Because the selection describes events that occurred in the 1940s, students may need to **clarify** unfamiliar words and passages in the text. **Visualizing** will help students to interpret the many descriptions in the selection.

Think-Aloud Prompts for Use in Oral Reading

Think-aloud prompts are placed at points in the text where students may encounter difficulties. Remind the students to refer to the **reading strategy posters** and to use any strategy they feel they need to help make sense of what they are reading. Encourage the students to collaborate with classmates when confronted with difficulties while reading.

THINK ALOUD PROMPTS

These prompts may be used as guides to promote cognitive and responsive reading.

① Students may find it helpful to look at the family photograph on page 351, so that they can identify the children in the family.

② The first set of grandparents mentioned here are on Eloise Greenfield's mother's side of the family, and the grandparents they are going to visit in Parmele are on her father's side.

③ These men were prisoners serving out their sentences by working on state highways. Because the guards were concerned about prisoners trying to escape, they carried guns.

PARMELE

from Childtimes: A Three-Generation Memoir by Eloise Greenfield and Lessie Jones Little

Every summer we took a trip down home. Down home was Parmele.

To get ready for our trip, Daddy would spend days working on our old car, putting it in shape to go on the road, and Mama would wash and iron all of our clothes. Then everything would be packed in the tan leather suitcase and the black cardboard suitcase, and we'd be ready to go.

① Mama and Daddy would sit in the front with Vedie in Mama's lap, and Wilbur, Gerald, and I sat in the back with our legs on top of the suitcases. This was before cars had trunks. Or radios. Or air conditioners or heaters. And there were no superhighways. The speed limit was forty-five miles an hour, and we went thirty-five to keep from straining the car.

It was an eight-hour trip to Norfolk, Virginia, where we always went first. Grandma Pattie Ridley Jones and Grandpa had moved there by that time, and we'd spend about a week **②** with them, then go on to Parmele for another week.

On the road, I played peek-a-boo with Vedie between her naps. Or my brothers and I would count all the cars on the road. We'd say, "There go one! That's twenty-two. There go another one!" And we'd read out loud the rhymes on the red

⬭ 348 ⬭

signs advertising Burma shaving cream, and wave at people sitting on their porches, and argue with each other until one of us got real mad and real loud and Mama told us we were giving her the jimjams and to be quiet.

One thing that we saw on the road frightened me. Chain gangs. We saw them often, the lines of black men in their black-and-white-striped jail suits, chained by their ankles and watched over, as they repaired the roads, by white men with guns.

③ I wasn't afraid of the men, and I didn't think about maybe getting shot. But for a reason I didn't understand, I was afraid of the whole thing. Those bent-over striped backs, the sharp points of the picks the men swung, the sound of the picks hitting the concrete, the sight of men with long guns, pacing. It scared me.

After a few miles, that scared feeling would fade away, and I'd start to have fun again, or I might take a nap, and it always seemed as if days had passed before we finally crossed the line into Parmele.

By the time of my visits there, only a few trains were still passing through. My Parmele wasn't a train town or a <u>mill</u> town. It was a quiet town. Chinaberry trees and pump water and tree swings and figs and fat, pulpy grapes on the vine. People saying, "hey" instead of "hi," the way they did in Washington, *hey-ey*, sending their voices up, then down, softly, singing it through their noses. Parmele was me running from the chickens when I was little, riding around the yard in a goat-pulled cart, sitting on the porch and letting people going by in their cars wave at me, reading in the rocking chair, taking long walks to the gas station for soda pop with

⬭ 349 ⬭

the children of Mama's and Daddy's childtime friends. Parmele was uncles and aunts and cousins. And Granny. And Pa.

They were Daddy's parents, Mack and Williamann Little. Black people in Parmele called them Mr. Mack and Miss Williamann. White people called them Uncle Mack and Ain' Williamann.

Granny was thin and whitehaired. She kept snuff tucked inside her bottom lip and wore aprons over her long dresses. I remember her most bending over the collards in her garden or feeding the chickens. She used to sew leftover material from my dresses into her patchwork quilts. She used to make apple jelly and green tomato pickles. Anything her grandchildren wanted, she wanted them to have.

And so did Pa.

"Leave the children alone," he used to tell mamas and daddies. "They ain't doing nothing."

4 Pa was a sharecropper. He worked in the fields, farming the land for the white man who owned it, and got paid in a share of the crops he raised. Along with that, he had almost always had some kind of little business going, even when Daddy was a boy—a meat market, an icehouse, a cleaner's, a grocery store.

Long before I was born, Pa had been a member of the Marcus Garvey group that used to meet in Parmele on Sunday afternoons. It was one of thousands of branches of the United Negro Improvement Association headed by Marcus Garvey. They met to talk about the beauty and strength of blackness, and to plan the return of black people to Africa.

I didn't think my grandfather was afraid of anything except the frogs that came out of the mud-filled ditches at night and flopped across the yard, and he knew plenty of names to call

350

Eloise Greenfield stands at the far right of this photograph taken at Parmele in 1941. With her are her grandfather, her mother, her grandmother, Wilbur, Vedie, and Gerald.

them. The thumb on his right hand looked like a little bald-headed man. The top joint had been cut off in a farm accident, and he had put it in a jar of preserving liquid that stayed on the front-room mantel. I never got tired of looking at it.

Children hung around Pa, nieces and nephews and neighbors, listening to his stories, giggling at his jokes. Some nights there would be just us—Wilbur, Gerald, and me, with our grandfather—sitting on the porch where the only light was that of the stars and the nearest house was a long way down the road. He'd tell scary stories, and get really tickled when we got scared. He swore his ghost stories were true.

"One night," he'd say, "me and my brother John was coming 'cross that field over yonder." He'd make his arm tremble

351

4 Sharecropping was a common way of earning a living for people who could not afford to buy their own farms. Sharecroppers usually began and remained very poor. Students may remember that Alice Walker's father was also a sharecropper.

and point toward the woods across the highway. "And we <u>commence</u> to hearing this strange sound. Ummmmm-*umph!* Ummmmm-*umph!* And we looked up and saw this . . . this *haint!*"

He'd twist his face and narrow his eyes in horror as he stared out into the darkness, and I could just feel all those haints <u>hovering</u> behind us, daring us to turn around and run for the door.

Sometimes Pa would stop right in the middle of a story.

"Then what happened, Pa?" one of us would ask.

"Oh, I left after that," he'd say, and he'd laugh. Then we'd laugh, small nervous laughs, wanting to believe that it had all been just a joke.

Every year when it was time for us to leave, a sudden change would come over Pa. One minute he'd be challenging Daddy to a foot race that never took place, and the next minute he was weak and sick, trying to get us to stay. He didn't think he would live to see us the following summer, he'd say. At breakfast he'd begin the blessing with, "Lord, I sure do thank You for allowing me to see my family one last time before You call me home," and he'd pray a long, sad prayer that brought tears to our eyes.

But finally, when nothing worked, Pa would give up and help Daddy load the car with suitcases and with sacks of fresh corn and peanuts. There'd be hugs and kisses and more tears, and then we'd drive away, leaving him and Granny standing on the side of the road, waving, waving, waving, getting smaller and smaller, until they blended into one and disappeared.

Pa never liked to leave home. Granny came to visit us a few times over the years, but Pa always made an excuse. He

352

couldn't get away right then, he had too much work to do, or something. One year, though, he had to come. He'd had a <u>stroke</u>, and Mama and Daddy brought him to Washington to take care of him. The stroke had damaged his body and his mind, so that he didn't understand much of what was going on around him, but he knew he wasn't where he wanted to be. Mama would take him for a walk and he'd ask people on the street, "Which way is Parmele?"

My grandfather never got back to Parmele. He lived in Washington for eighteen months, and then, in 1951, at the age of seventy-eight, he died.

MEET ELOISE GREENFIELD, AUTHOR
This selection from Childtimes *was written by Eloise Greenfield. Her grandmother, Patty Ridley Jones, and mother, Lessie Jones Little, wrote other parts of the book. Each of the three women tells about the times in which she grew up and the things she remembers from her childhood.*

In the preface to this book, the authors talk about family heritage: "This book is about family. Kinsfolk touching across the centuries, walking with one hand clasping the hands of those who have gone before, the other hand reaching back for those who will come after. . . .

"We came, one behind the other, to our childtimes— grandmother, mother, daughter—just three marchers in a procession that stretches long and wide. Stretches across the ocean to the continent of Africa, back to great-grandmothers and great-grandfathers and great-greats and great-great-greats, and on and on, all the way back to the beginning of human life on earth. Stretches outward to sisters and brothers and aunts and uncles and nephews and nieces and cousins. A long, wide, family procession with thousands of marchers. We are just three."

353

Discussing Strategy Use
Encourage the students to discuss how they used the strategies as they read the selection.

*

EXPLORING THROUGH DISCUSSION

Reflecting on the Selection
Whole-Group Discussion

The whole group discusses the selection and any personal thoughts or questions that it raises. During this time, students also **return to the clues, problems, and wonderings** they noted on the board during browsing.

Assessment

To assess the students' understanding of the text, engage in a discussion to determine whether the students have grasped the following ideas:

- why the author's family made a trip "down home" every year
- some of the many differences between Parmele and Washington, D.C., that the author noticed when she was a child
- how the author felt about her grandparents in Parmele

Response Journal

Students may wish to record their personal responses to the selection.

Exploring Concepts Within the Selection
Small-Group Discussion

Small groups discuss the relationship of the selection to family heritage. Circulate among the groups and observe the discussions. Refer the students to the Concept Board and the Question Board to keep them focused on their original ideas about family heritage and to see if those ideas have changed as a result of reading this selection.

Sharing Ideas About Explorable Concepts

Have the groups **report** and **discuss** their **ideas** with the rest of the class. It is crucial that the students' ideas determine this discussion.

- Students may conclude that the happy times that families spend together are important and build special memories.
- In talking about grandparents, students may generalize that children can learn about their heritage by spending time with older family members.

As these ideas and others are stated, have the students **add them to** the **Question Board** or the **Concept Board.**

Exploring Concepts Across Selections

Students might make connections with other selections in the unit.

- Students may notice that several of the selections feature grandparents in important roles. In each of these selections, there is a mutual respect between older and younger generations.
- Students may notice that, just as in "Chinatown" and "In Two Worlds," old ways and new ways are contrasted in "Parmele." For instance, the author points out that, when she was a child, cars traveled more slowly and had no air conditioning or radios.

Recording Ideas

As students complete the above discussions, ask them to **sum up what they have learned from their conversations and how they might use this information** in further explorations. Any special information or insights may be recorded on the **Concept Board**. Any further questions that they would like to think about, pursue, or investigate may

Recording Concept Information continued

"The Night Journey" by Kathryn Lasky

_____
_____
_____
_____
_____
_____
_____

"The Land I Lost" by Huynh Quang Nhuong

_____
_____
_____
_____
_____
_____
_____

"Parmele" by Eloise Greenfield and Lessie Jones Little

_____
_____
_____
_____
_____
_____
_____
_____

44 EN   Family Heritage/Unit 3

Explorer's Notebook, page 44

be recorded on the **Question Board**. They may want to discuss the progress that has been made on their questions. They may also want to cross out any questions that no longer warrant consideration.

❯ Ask students to record their findings in their Explorer's Notebook on page 44.

2

READING WITH A WRITER'S EYE

MINILESSON

Writer's Craft:
Elaboration

Ask the students to tell what they know about elaborating on main ideas in paragraphs by using examples or details. Remind them that **the most important idea in a paragraph is often stated at the beginning. The rest of the paragraph provides examples or details** that elaborate on this important idea.

In this selection, students will see paragraphs in which the important idea is not stated at all but must be inferred from the examples and details in the paragraph.

Have a volunteer read the last paragraph beginning on page 348. Ask students to tell what all of these sentences are about. The important idea

Name

"Parmele"

Elaboration

Choose four paragraphs from "Parmele." Write the page number on which each paragraph appears. Write the important idea in each paragraph. Then list the examples or the details that are used to elaborate on each important idea.

Page: _____ Important idea: _____
_____

Examples or details: _____
_____
_____
_____

Page: _____ Important idea: _____
_____

Examples or details: _____
_____
_____
_____

Page: _____ Important idea: _____
_____

Examples or details: _____
_____
_____
_____

Page: _____ Important idea: _____
_____

Examples or details: _____
_____
_____
_____

Elaboration
28 R/WC   Family Heritage/Unit 3

Reading/Writing Connection, page 28

of this paragraph is not stated, but all the examples tell about how the children passed the time on the long car trip.

Then have another student read the next two paragraphs. Ask students to state the important idea in the paragraphs. (Greenfield was frightened by the chain gangs she saw on the road.) Here the important idea is stated and the rest of the sentences in these paragraphs give details about what the chain gang looked like, so that the reader can better understand why Greenfield was frightened.

Selective Reading: Focus on Elaboration

Have the students look through the selection for other paragraphs in which a general idea is illustrated by specific examples or details. Remind them that **the general idea may be stated or unstated.** Paragraphs they might mention include the following:
- page 349, paragraph 4: specific things the author remembers about Parmele
- page 350, paragraph 2: specific details about Granny
- page 353, paragraph 1: examples of how Pa acted when the family went home

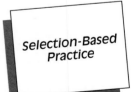

Selection-Based Practice

Independent Practice: Elaboration

❱ Have students complete Reading/Writing Connection page 28 individually or in small groups. If they work individually, have them share their work in small groups when they complete the page.

WRITING

Linking Reading to Writing

Have the students look through their writing folders to find paragraphs that can be improved by elaboration with examples or with details.

* Writing Process

Some students may want to write about their own visits with grandparents. Some may want to write anecdotes about family members such as those Greenfield wrote about her grandfather. If students wish to begin a new piece of writing, suggest that they begin the prewriting phase of the writing process by noting their ideas in the Writing Ideas section of their **Writer's Notebook** so they can refer to them when they are ready to write their first drafts.

VOCABULARY

Concept-related words from the selection that the students may want to discuss or remember and use include the following:

icehouse, patchwork quilts, jimjams, collards, haint

Have Vocabulary Exploration forms, Reproducible Master 14, available for students who request them. Remind the students to add these or any other words and phrases from the selection to the Personal Dictionary section of their Writer's Notebook. Some students may wish to share these additions with the class. For additional opportunities to build vocabulary, see **Teacher Tool Card 75.**

3 GUIDED AND INDEPENDENT EXPLORATION

EXPLORING CONCEPTS BEYOND THE TEXT

Guided Exploration

Students will select activities in which they explore family heritage. Refer them to the **Exploration Activities poster** and give them time to choose an activity and to discuss what they wish to explore and how they wish to go about it. If the students need further help, here is a suggestion:

On the chalkboard, draw the portion of Eloise Greenfield's family tree shown below. Help the students to see where her parents and her grandparents fit into the chart. Explain that the abbreviation *m.* stands for "married" and a vertical line below the *m.* shows the children from this marriage.

* Exploring Through Reflective Activities

Pattie Frances Ridley m. William Jones   Mack Little m. Williamann

(five other children)   Lessie Blanche Jones m. Weston Wilbur Little

Weston Wilber   Gerald   Vedie   Vera   Eloise Little m. Robert Greenfield

▶ On Explorer's Notebook, page 53, have the students practice filling in family trees for some of the characters they read about in this unit. Rache's family, for example, includes family members for six generations: first, Sashie's grandfather; next, Sashie's parents and aunt; next, Sashie and her siblings; next, Rache's Nana Rose; next, Rache's parents; and finally Rache herself. Remind them to reread the selection about the family whose family tree they decide to illustrate to be sure that they include all of the family members mentioned.

Some students may want to make family trees for their own families. Remind them to check with their parents or other family members to get the names of relatives they may not know.

Presenting Exploration Results

If any of the collaborative groups have information to present to the rest of the class, allow sufficient time for them to do so. Encourage the students to take their time and make their presentations as interesting to the audience as possible. Provide any audiovisual equipment the students need for their presentations.

After each presentation, encourage classmates to respond to the presentation. What did they most enjoy about the presentation? Which ideas were the most interesting? What new facts did they learn? Can they link information from the presentation with something they have learned during the course of the unit?

ASSESSMENT TIP This may be a good opportunity to observe students working in groups and to mark observations in the Teacher's Observation Log.

Explorer's Notebook, page 53

Drawing a Family Tree

Use the space below to draw a family tree for one of the families you read about in the unit. Remember to show the oldest generation at the top of the page and the youngest generation at the bottom of the page. You may not be able to fill in all of the spaces on the family tree for some families.

Copyright © 1995 Open Court Publishing Company

Unit 3/Family Heritage   EN 53

*INDEPENDENT WORKSHOP
Building a Community of Scholars

Student-Directed Reading, Writing, and Discussion

Collaborative groups should be bringing their exploration of family heritage to closure. Suggest that they think about whether they have any special ideas to share with the rest of the class. They should discuss how they want to present their ideas.

If any of the students have become very involved in a research project and are not yet ready to present their findings, allow as much time as they need. As students progress into the next unit provide time for these students to present their findings.

Unit Wrap-up

UNIT DISCUSSION

Initiate a general class discussion of the unit, centering on family heritage. The Concept Board and project displays can be used as stimuli for students to recall what knowledge they have gained from participating in this unit. In addition, the students might open their Explorer's Notebooks to page 41 to remind themselves of what they knew about family heritage as they began the unit and what they expected to learn from completing the unit. The discussion may be extended to include

- an evaluation of the unit selections
- an evaluation of the unit activities
- an evaluation of the overall unit (How well did the unit cover the explorable concepts? Was family heritage a good subject to examine? Why or why not?)
- a consideration of aspects of family heritage worth further exploration, beginning with any questions left on the Question Board.

Small-Group Discussion

As an alternative, you might have the students work in small groups to discuss the unit. Encourage group participants to refer to the Concept Board, browse the anthology selections, and review their Explorer's Notebook pages for Unit 3 to refresh their memories on important ideas raised in the unit. Then have the groups share with classmates important points and conclusions from their discussions.

ASSESSMENT

Informal Assessment

➤ Give the students the opportunity to make individual evaluations of their learning experiences during this unit by completing Explorer's

Knowledge About Family Heritage

This is what I know about family heritage before reading the unit.

_____
_____
_____
_____
_____
_____
_____
_____
_____
_____
_____

These are some things about family heritage that I would like to talk about and understand better.

_____
_____
_____
_____
_____
_____
_____
_____
_____
_____

Reminder: I should read this page again when I get to the end of the unit to see whether my ideas about family heritage have changed.

_____
Unit 3/Family Heritage   EN 41

Explorer's Notebook, page 41

Notebook pages 54–55. You may want to conference individually with each student to discuss each evaluation.

End-of-Unit Assessment

At this point, you might wish to carry out end-of-unit assessments for Unit 3: Family Heritage. You will find the following end-of-unit assessment booklets in the Teacher's Toolbox:

Comprehension Assessment
- Understanding the Selection
- Making Connections Across Selections
- Checking Skills
- Multiple-Choice Option

Essay and Writing Assessment

You may pick and choose among the various assessment components to find the right mix for assessing areas you want to stress. See *Formative Assessment: A Teacher's Guide* for specific suggestions on how to use these assessment materials.

Unit Wrap-up

How did you feel about this unit?
- ☐ I enjoyed it very much.
- ☐ I liked some of it.
- ☐ I liked it.
- ☐ I didn't like it.

How would you rate the difficulty of the unit?
- ☐ easy ☐ medium ☐ hard

How would you rate your performance during this unit?
- ☐ I learned a lot about family heritage.
- ☐ I learned some new things about family heritage.
- ☐ I didn't learn much about family heritage.

Why did you choose this rating?

What was the most interesting thing you learned about family heritage?

Is there anything else about family heritage that you would like to learn? What?

54 EN   Family Heritage/Unit 3

Explorer's Notebook, page 54

What did you learn about family heritage that you didn't know before?

What did you learn about yourself as a learner?

As a learner, what do you need to work on?

What resources (books, films, magazines, interviews, tool cards, other) did you use on your own during this unit? Which of these were the most helpful? Why?

Unit 3/Family Heritage   EN 55

Explorer's Notebook, page 55

UNIT CELEBRATION

Have students suggest ways to celebrate their completion and appreciation of the unit. The following are some suggestions:
- Invite family members in for a "tour" of the classroom. Different children could act as tour guides, explaining the various aspects of family heritage on display—such as the Concept Board postings and the project exhibits.
- Students who have articles of clothing or objects associated with their family heritage might wear them or bring them to school and share information about them.
- Plan an International Food Fair where students share food that is part of their family heritage and tell about family traditions, especially any traditions associated with this food. Students might want to wear special ethnic clothing on the day of this fair, and they might want to invite parents or grandparents. Arrange for someone to take pictures of this celebration.

Appendixes

Appendix 1   Scope and Sequence

STRATEGIES AND SKILLS	LEVEL					
	1	2	3	4	5	6
Print Awareness						
Capitalization	■					
Constancy of words	■					
End punctuation	■					
Follow left-to-right, top-to-bottom	■					
Letter recognition and formation	■					
Paragraph indention	■					
Relationship between illustrations and print	■					
Relationship between spoken and printed language	■					
Word boundaries in text	■					
READING STRATEGIES						
Setting Reading Goals and Expectations						
Activate prior knowledge.	■	■	■	■	■	■
Browse the text.	■	■	■	■	■	■
Consider why you are reading.	■	■	■	■	■	■
Decide what you expect from the text.	■	■	■	■	■	■
Responding to Text						
Make connections between what you are reading and what you already know.	■	■	■	■	■	■
Visualize, or picture, what is happening in the text.	■	■	■	■	■	■
Wonder freely as you read.	■	■	■	■	■	■
Predict what will happen next.	■	■	■	■	■	■
Think about how the text makes you feel.	■	■	■	■	■	■
Checking Understanding						
Interpret as you read.	■	■	■	■	■	■
Sum up to check your understanding as you read.	■	■	■	■	■	■
Ask questions to check your understanding as you read.		■	■	■	■	■
Clarifying Unfamiliar Words and Passages						
Apply decoding skills if there are unknown words.	■	■	■	■	■	■
Determine what is unclear.		■	■	■	■	■
Apply context clues if there are words whose meanings you don't know.	■	■	■	■	■	■

STRATEGIES AND SKILLS	LEVEL					
	1	2	3	4	5	6
READING STRATEGIES						
Clarifying Unfamiliar Words and Passages *continued*						
Check the dictionary.		■	■	■	■	■
Reread the passage that didn't make sense to you.	■	■	■	■	■	■
WRITING STRATEGIES						
Planning and Setting Writing Goals						
Use reading to improve your writing.	■	■	■	■	■	■
Record interesting and important topics to write about.	■	■	■	■	■	■
Note information you will need in order to write.		■	■	■	■	■
Decide on the main goals of the writing.		■	■	■	■	■
Revise your plans.		■	■	■	■	■
Considering Readers						
Make your topic interesting.		■	■	■	■	■
Decide what effect you want to have on your readers.		■	■	■	■	■
Determine if readers will understand.		■	■	■	■	■
Predict your readers' reactions, and then compare their reactions to what you expected.		■	■	■	■	■
Summarize audience reactions.		■	■	■	■	■
Revising Content						
Reread very carefully.	■	■	■	■	■	■
Pinpoint parts of your writing that can be made clearer.		■	■	■	■	■
Identify information confusing to readers.		■	■	■	■	■
Reorganize ideas or information.		■	■	■	■	■
Use a story frame or plot line.		■	■	■	■	■
Consider your own reactions and ideas.		■	■	■	■	■
CONVENTIONS/SKILLS						
Writer's Craft/Reading						
Causal indicators	■	■	■	■	■	■
Characterization	■	■	■	■	■	■
Choosing vivid verbs		■	■	■	■	■
Dialogue	■	■	■	■	■	■
Elaboration through comparisons and contrasts		■	■	■	■	■
Elaboration through forming questions and conjectures		■	■	■	■	■
Elaboration through giving opinions		■	■	■	■	■
Elaboration through giving reasons or causes	■	■	■	■	■	■

STRATEGIES AND SKILLS

Writer's Craft/Reading *continued*

Skill	LEVEL 1	2	3	4	5	6
Elaboration through including lists and examples		■	■	■	■	■
Elaboration through providing background				■	■	■
Elaboration through providing descriptions	■	■	■	■	■	■
Elaboration through providing explanations or definitions		■	■	■	■	■
Elaboration by providing opposing viewpoints				■	■	■
Elaboration through providing problems and solutions		■		■	■	■
Elaboration through providing specific facts	■	■	■	■	■	■
Exaggeration		■		■	■	■
Figurative language		■	■	■	■	■
Formal versus informal writing				■	■	■
Foreshadowing				■		■
Genre—adventure				■	■	■
Genre—biography and autobiography		■	■	■	■	■
Genre—expository text	■	■	■	■	■	■
Genre—fable	■	■	■	■	■	■
Genre—fairy tale	■	■	■		■	
Genre—fantasy	■	■	■	■	■	■
Genre—folk tale	■	■	■	■	■	■
Genre—historical fiction		■	■	■	■	■
Genre—legend		■	■	■	■	■
Genre—myth, tall tale	■		■	■	■	■
Genre—play/drama	■	■	■	■	■	■
Genre—poetry	■	■	■	■	■	■
Genre—realistic fiction	■	■	■	■	■	■
Genre—science fiction			■		■	■
Humor			■	■	■	
Indicators of additional information			■	■	■	
Indicators of differing information			■	■	■	
Indicators of place and location	■	■	■	■	■	■
Indicators of time and order	■	■	■	■	■	■
Irony						■
Persuasive writing		■	■	■	■	■
Plot		■	■	■	■	■
Point of view		■	■	■	■	■
Process description		■	■	■	■	■
Setting	■	■	■	■	■	■
Staying on subject	■		■	■	■	■
Strong topic sentences		■	■	■	■	■

STRATEGIES AND SKILLS

Writer's Craft/Reading *continued*

Skill	1	2	3	4	5	6
Suspense and surprise		■	■	■	■	
Using headings and captions	■	■	■	■	■	■
Using quotations in writing				■	■	■
Variety in writing		■	■	■	■	■
Writing good beginnings		■	■	■	■	■
Writing paragraphs		■	■	■	■	■
Writing personal experiences		■	■	■	■	■

Grammar, Mechanics, and Usage

Skill	1	2	3	4	5	6
Capitalization	■	■	■	■	■	■
Clauses and phrases			■	■	■	■
Comparing with adjectives and adverbs	■	■	■	■	■	■
Complete and incomplete sentences	■	■	■	■	■	■
Compound sentences		■	■	■	■	■
Compound subject and predicate			■	■	■	■
End punctuation	■	■	■	■	■	■
Kinds of sentences	■	■	■		■	■
Parts of a sentence		■	■	■	■	■
Parts of speech	■	■	■	■	■	■
Pronoun/antecedent agreement	■	■	■	■	■	■
Punctuating titles of works (books, movies etc.)		■	■	■	■	■
Subject/verb agreement		■	■	■	■	■
Using adjectives and adverbs		■	■	■	■	■
Using colons and semicolons				■	■	■
Using commas in dates, addresses, and parts of a letter		■	■	■	■	■
Using commas in introductory phrases			■	■		■
Using commas in a series		■	■	■	■	■
Using dashes and ellipses			■	■	■	■
Using gerund phrases				■	■	■
Using negatives correctly			■	■	■	■
Using parentheses		■	■	■	■	■
Using possessive nouns	■	■	■	■	■	■
Using possessive pronouns		■	■	■	■	■
Using prepositions and prepositional phrases		■	■	■		■
Using and punctuating dialogue	■	■	■	■	■	■
Using reflexive pronouns				■	■	■
Verb tense		■	■	■	■	■

STRATEGIES AND SKILLS

	LEVEL					
	1	2	3	4	5	6
Phonics/Decoding						
Blending sounds into words	■	*	*			
Consonant clusters	■	*	*			
Consonant digraphs	■	*	*			
Consonant sounds and spellings	■	*	*			
High-frequency words	■	*	*			
Phonemic awareness	■	*	*			
Syllables	■	*	*			
Vowel diphthongs	■	*	*			
Vowels: long sounds and spellings	■	*	*			
Vowels: *r*-controlled	■	*	*			
Vowels: short sounds and spellings	■	*	*			
Spelling and Vocabulary						
Adding prefixes and suffixes		■	■	■	■	■
Building vocabulary		■	■	■	■	■
Compound words	■	■	■	■	■	■
Frequently misspelled words		■	■	■	■	■
Homophones	■	■	■	■	■	■
Inflectional endings	■	■	■	■	■	■
Long-vowel spelling patterns		■	■	■	■	■
Regular and irregular plurals		■	■	■	■	■
Short-vowel spelling patterns	■	■	■	■	■	■
Spelling generalizations		■	■	■	■	■
Synonyms and antonyms	■	■	■	■	■	■
Unstressed vowel sounds (schwa)	■	■	■	■	■	■
Using and punctuating contractions	■	■	■	■	■	■
Study and Research						
Alphabetical order	■	■	■			
Choosing sources		■	■	■	■	■
Comparing information across sources		■		■	■	■
Formulating questions and conjectures		■	■	■	■	■
Interviewing		■	■	■	■	■
Making a bibliography		■		■	■	■
Making and using a time line		■	■	■	■	■
Note taking		■	■	■	■	■
Observing and recording details		■	■			

* Optional review at this level

STRATEGIES AND SKILLS

Study and Research *continued*

Skill	1	2	3	4	5	6
Organizing information in a chart		■	■	■	■	■
Outlining				■	■	■
Parts of a book	■			■	■	■
Using a dictionary or glossary	■			■	■	■
Using a thesaurus				■	■	■
Using an encyclopedia		■	■	■	■	■
Using and understanding diagrams				■	■	■
Using maps, globes, and atlases		■	■	■	■	■
Using primary sources				■	■	■
Using the card catalog (including electronic cc)		■	■	■	■	■
Using the *Reader's Guide*			■	■	■	■

SETTING READING GOALS AND EXPECTATIONS

Reading Strategies	Ask Yourself
ACTIVATE prior knowledge.	What do I already know about this?
BROWSE the text.	What kind of text is this? What seems important? What looks interesting? What might cause problems?
CONSIDER why you are reading.	Am I reading this for fun? Am I reading this to learn something? What do I want to learn?
DECIDE WHAT you expect from the text.	What might this be about? What do I want to find out?

RESPONDING TO TEXT

Reading Strategies

MAKE CONNECTIONS between what you are reading and what you already know.

VISUALIZE what is happening in the text.

WONDER freely as you read.

PREDICT what will happen next.

THINK ABOUT how the text makes you feel.

Ask Yourself

What does this text remind me of?
Have I read or experienced anything like this before?
Does any of this surprise me? Why?

Can I picture in my mind what is described in the text?
How might a picture or diagram help me picture and understand the text?

I wonder why this is the way it is?
I wonder what else there is to know about this?

What part of the text helped me predict?
What did I already know that helped me predict?
Which illustrations helped me predict?

How do I feel about what I'm reading?

CHECKING UNDERSTANDING

Reading Strategies

INTERPRET as you read.

SUM UP to check your understanding as you read.

ASK QUESTIONS to check your understanding as you read.

Ask Yourself

What does the text mean to me and others?
Does it have more than one meaning? What?
Does the text change my mind about anything? How?

Does this make sense?
What is this section about?
What is the whole selection about?
How would I explain this in my own words?
Can I find out more if I look back?

What might a teacher ask here?
What might be on a test?
What question is answered by the most important idea here?

CLARIFYING UNFAMILIAR WORDS AND PASSAGES

Reading Strategies

APPLY DECODING SKILLS if there are unknown words.

DETERMINE what is unclear.

APPLY CONTEXT CLUES if there are words whose meanings you don't know.

CHECK the dictionary.

REREAD the passage that didn't make sense to you.

Ask Yourself

Have I seen this word before?
What words that I already know are like this word?
Can I sound this out?
How can I break this long word into parts?
What prefixes or suffixes do I recognize?
What small words within the long word will help me read it?

Do I understand the meanings of all the words?
Which parts are unclear? How can I make sense of them?
What, if anything, did the author leave out?

What context clues can I find in the rest of the sentence or in sentences around the word?

Does the passage make sense now?

Discussion Starters

I didn't know that...

Does anyone know...

I figured out that...

I liked the part where...

I'm still confused about...

This made me think...

I agree with _____ because...

I disagree with _____ because...

The reason I think...

Phases in the Writing Process

Prewriting

Drafting

Revising

Proofreading

Publishing

PLANNING AND SETTING WRITING GOALS

Writing Strategies

Use reading to improve your writing.

Record interesting and important topics to write about.

Note information you will need in order to write.

Decide on the main goals of the writing.

Revise your plans.

Ask Yourself

What did this author do that I really liked?
How can I do this in my writing?

What is important or interesting to me and others?
Did something happen to me that I'd like to share?

What are the important ideas that I want others to know about this?
What do I already know?
What will I need to know?

What is my purpose for writing this?
What are the important points that I want to get across?

Have my writing ideas changed after thinking about my topic? How?
How does new information change what I will write?

CONSIDERING READERS

Writing Strategies	Ask Yourself
MAKE your topic interesting.	Will others be interested in this? What can I do or add to make this topic more interesting to others?
DECIDE what effect you want to have on your readers.	Who am I writing for? How do I want to make readers feel? What do I want readers to learn?
DETERMINE if readers will understand.	Will readers understand this? Is there enough information? If not, what can I add? Is it clear and well written?
PREDICT your readers' reactions, and then compare their reactions to what you expected.	If readers don't know anything about this topic, will they enjoy reading this? If they are reading this for the first time, what might they say about the topic? What will my audience say about the topic? Was I right?
SUMMARIZE audience reactions.	Did many readers have the same comments? What were they? What is good about my composition? What do I need to change?

REVISING CONTENT

Writing Strategies	Ask Yourself
REREAD very carefully.	Have I left out words or put in unnecessary words? Does my writing make sense?
PINPOINT parts of your composition that can be made clearer.	Is this passage descriptive enough for readers to visualize? Should I say more through examples or explanations?
IDENTIFY information confusing to readers.	Were my readers confused? Could this information be wrong? How can I check and correct it?
REORGANIZE IDEAS OR INFORMATION.	What's my purpose for writing this? Am I achieving that purpose? Do I need to include more facts? Do I need to take out any unnecessary information?
USE A STORY FRAME OR PLOT LINE.	Who are the main characters? What is the problem? What are the story events? Are there conflicts or blocks? Does my story build to a high point? Does the story come to a satisfactory conclusion? Would dialogue help to develop my story?
CONSIDER YOUR OWN REACTIONS AND IDEAS.	How do I feel about my writing? Am I pleased with my writing? Did I include all the information I had planned? What would I like to change?

THE RESEARCH CYCLE

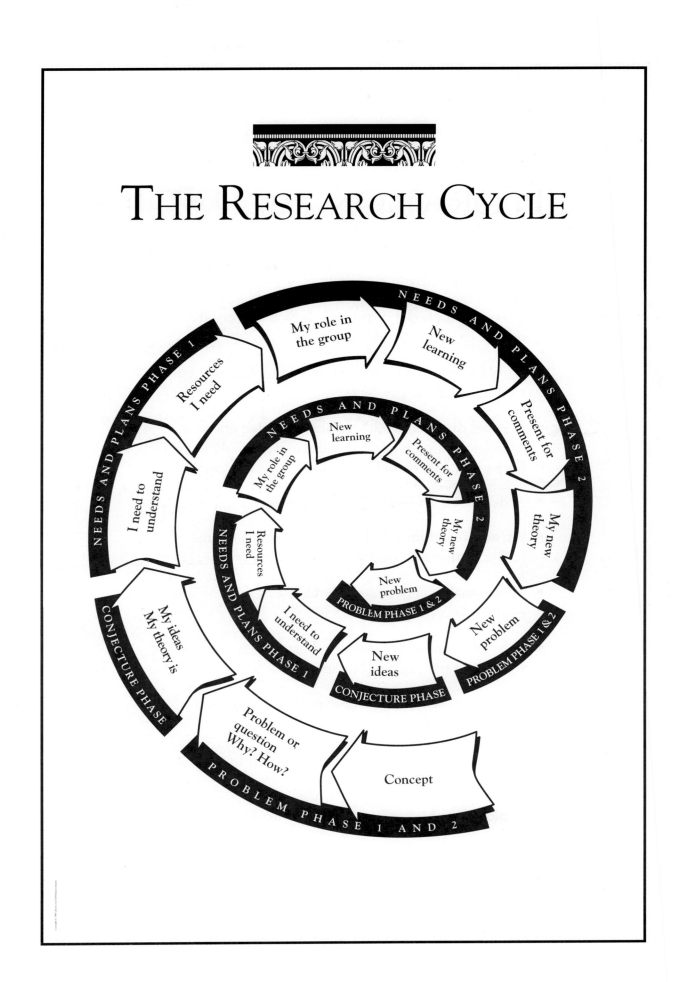

EXPLORATION ACTIVITIES

- A **literature search** to pursue a question or a problem. Discussion or writing may follow.

- An **original playlet** or **puppet show** based on situations related to the explorable concepts.

- A **role-playing game** to work out a problem related to the explorable concepts.

- A **panel discussion** with audience participation on a question or problem. (This discussion would have a leader and may be videotaped.)

- A **debate** on an issue related to the explorable concepts.

- An **advice column** dealing with problems related to the explorable concepts.

- A **personal experience story** related to the explorable concepts.

- The **questioning of visiting experts** about some aspect relating to the explorable concepts.

- An **interview** with someone on a subject related to the explorable concepts.

- A **survey** on an issue or question related to the explorable concepts.

- A **picture** or photo essay about the explorable concepts.

Appendix 3 Audiovisual Sources

BARR FILMS
12801 Schabarum Avenue
Irwindale, CA 91706
(800) 234-7878

BRITANNICA FILMS
310 South Michigan Avenue
Chicago, IL 60604
(312) 347-7000

CORONET/MTI
108 Wilmont Road
Deerfield, IL 60015
(800) 334-7830

CYNTHIA A. CHERBAK PRODUCTIONS
c/o The Media Guild
11722 Sorrento Valley Road
Suite E
San Diego, CA 92121
(619) 755-9191

LITTLE FORT MEDIA
c/o United Learning, Inc
6633 West Howard Street
P.O. Box 48718
Niles, IL 60648
(800) 424-0362

LUCERNE MEDIA
37 Ground Pine Road
Morris Plaines, NJ 07950
(800) 341-2293

PHOENIX/BFA
468 Park Avenue South
New York, NY 10016
(800) 684-5910

PUBLIC MEDIA VIDEO
5547 North Ravenswood Avenue
Chicago, IL 60640
(800) 323-4222

PYRAMID FILM AND VIDEO
Box 1038
2801 Colorado Avenue
Santa Monica, CA 90406
(800) 421-2304

TV ONTARIO
1140 Kildare Farm Road
Suite 308
Cary, NC 27511
(919) 380-0747

Appendix 4 Learning Framework Cards

1. **Cognitive and Responsive Reading**

    1A. Setting Reading Goals and Expectations

    1B. Responding to Text

    1C. Checking Understanding

    1D. Clarifying Unfamiliar Words and Passages

2. **Exploring Through Discussion**

3. **Exploring Through Reflective Activities**

4. **Exploring Through Research**

    4A. Problem Phase 1 and 2

    4B. Conjecture Phase

    4C. Needs and Plans Phase 1 and 2

5. **Independent Workshop**

6. **Reading Roundtable**

7. **Writing Process**

    7A. Prewriting

    7B. Drafting

    7C. Revising

    7D. Proofreading

    7E. Publishing

8. **Writing Seminar**

Appendix 5   Teacher/Student Tool Cards

TEACHER TOOL CARDS

STUDENT TOOL CARDS

Writer's Craft/Reading

	TEACHER TOOL CARDS		STUDENT TOOL CARDS
1	Genre—Folk Tale and Fable	1	Reading and Writing Folk Tales and Fables
2	Genre—Myth, Legend, and Tall Tale	2	Reading and Writing Myths, Legends, and Tall Tales
3	Genre—Realistic Fiction	3	Reading and Writing Realistic Fiction
4	Genre—Historical Fiction	4	Reading and Writing Historical Fiction
5	Genre—Fantasy	5	Reading and Writing Fantasy
6	Genre—Science Fiction	6	Reading and Writing Science Fiction
7	Genre—Adventure	7	Reading and Writing Adventure Tales
8	Genre—Biography and Autobiography	8	Reading and Writing Biography and Autobiography
9	Genre—Expository Text	9	Reading and Writing Expository Text
10	Genre—Poetry	10	Reading and Writing Poetry
11	Genre—Play/Drama	11	Reading and Writing Plays/Drama
12	Point of View	12	Point of View
13	Characterization	13	Characterization
14	Setting	14	Setting
15	Plot	15	Plot
16	Suspense and Surprise	16	Suspense and Surprise
17	Exaggeration	17	Exaggeration
18	Formal versus Informal Writing	18	Differences Between Formal and Informal Writing
19	Using Dialogue in a Story	19	Using Dialogue in a Story
20	Figurative Language	20	Figurative Language
21	Choosing Vivid Verbs	21	Choosing Vivid Verbs
22	Writing Paragraphs	22	Writing Paragraphs
23	Strong Topic Sentences	23	Strong Topic Sentences
24	Writing Good Beginnings	24	Writing Good Beginnings
25	Staying on Subject	25	Staying on Subject
26	Variety in Writing	26	Variety in Writing
27	Indicators of Time and Order	27	Signal Words Showing Time and Order
28	Indicators of Place and Location	28	Signal Words Showing Place and Location
29	Indicators of Additional Information or Emphasis	29	Signal Words Showing That There's More or Important Information
30	Indicators of Differing Information	30	Signal Words Showing That Something Is Changing

TEACHER TOOL CARDS

Writer's Craft/Reading *continued*

STUDENT TOOL CARDS

	TEACHER TOOL CARDS		STUDENT TOOL CARDS
31	Causal Indicators	31	Showing Cause and Effect
32	Using Quotations in Writing	32	Using Quotations in Writing
33	Persuasive Writing	33	Writing to Persuade
34	Process Description	34	Describing a Process
35	Using Headings and Captions	35	Using Headings and Captions
36	Elaboration Through Providing Comparison and Contrast	36	Comparing and Contrasting
37	Elaboration Through Giving Reasons or Causes	37	Giving Reasons or Causes
38	Elaboration Through Providing Examples	38	Giving Examples
39	Elaboration Through Providing Descriptions	39	Giving Descriptions
40	Elaboration Through Providing Specific Facts	40	Telling Important Facts
41	Elaboration Through Providing Background	41	Giving Background
42	Elaboration Through Providing Definitions in Text	42	Giving Definitions
43	Elaboration Through Providing Concept Information	43	Giving Concept Information
44	Elaboration Through Providing Problem and Solution	44	Giving Problem and Solution
45	Elaboration Through Forming Questions and Conjectures	45	Writing Questions and Conjectures

Grammar, Mechanics, and Usage

46	Complete and Incomplete Sentences	46	Complete and Incomplete Sentences
47	Compound Subject and Predicate	47	Compound Subject and Predicate
48	Compound Sentences	48	Compound Sentences
49	Phrases	49	Phrases
50	Clauses	50	Clauses
51	End Punctuation	51	End Punctuation
52	Using Commas in a Series	52	Using Commas in a Series
53	Using Commas in Dates, Addresses, Direct Address, and Parts of a Letter	53	Using Commas in Dates, Addresses, Direct Address, and Parts of a Letter
54	Using Parentheses, Dashes, and Ellipses	54	Using Parentheses, Dashes, and Ellipses
55	Using Colons and Semicolons	55	Using Colons and Semicolons
56	Punctuating Titles of Works	56	Punctuating Titles of Books, Stories, and Movies
57	Capitalization	57	Capitalization
58	Parts of Speech	58	Parts of Speech
59	Using Possessive Nouns	59	Using Possessive Nouns
60	Using Possessive Pronouns	60	Using Possessive Pronouns
61	Pronoun/Antecedent Agreement	61	Using the Right Pronoun for the Right Noun

TEACHER TOOL CARDS

Grammar, Mechanics, and Usage *continued*

STUDENT TOOL CARDS

Spelling and Vocabulary

	TEACHER TOOL CARDS		STUDENT TOOL CARDS

Study and Research

Classroom Supports / Classroom Participation

Appendix 6   Cross-curricular Activity Cards

ART
1 Picture Books
2 Making Sets for a Puppet Show
3 Drawing the Stars
4 Making a Family Coat of Arms
5 Talking Headlines
6 Designing an "Underground" House
7 Travel Brochure
8 Enlistment Posters
9 Artists of the American West
10 Pictographs and Petroglyphs
11 Travel Brochure for Dreamland
12 Souvenir Scrapbook
13 Dream Sketches
14 Stained Glass Windows

DRAMA
1 Dramatizing "The Library Card"
2 Sam Mott at School
3 Writing and Acting Out a Conversation
4 Writing Dialogue
5 Performing a Debate
6 Staging "The Telegram"
7 Remembering Slavery
8 Classmate Interviews
9 Famous Speeches
10 Language Pantomime
11 News from the West
12 Shipboard Conversations

MATH
1 Counting the Stars
2 Astronomy Word Problems
3 Planning for an Emergency
4 Calculating Cattle-Drive Distances
5 Reading a Train Schedule
6 Taking a Pioneer Poll
7 Weather
8 Surveying Travel
9 Sea Leagues
10 Spanish Money

MUSIC
1 Songs of Latin America
2 Folk Dancing
3 Write a Song
4 Pioneer Songs
5 Mood Music
6 Make a Lyre

SCIENCE
1 A Pile of Coal
2 Ecology
3 Lunar Log
4 Creating the Constellations
5 Create an Observatory
6 Measuring Time on a Dial
7 Making a Telescope
8 The Solar System
9 Understanding How Black Holes Form
10 Making Traditional Foods
11 Constellation Names
12 Photography
13 Medical Advancements
14 Women in Medicine
15 The Telegraph
16 Pioneer Medicine
17 Pioneer Technology
18 Horses
19 Animal Journeys
20 Animals Helping Animals
21 Technology of Exploration
22 Make a Sandglass
23 Make a Compass
24 Signs of Spring

SOCIAL STUDIES
1 Braille
2 The Manual Alphabet
3 Uganda
4 Conducting a Survey
5 France
6 Washington's Journey
7 The Netherlands
8 Planets and Days of the Week
9 Steps to Statehood
10 Cultures of Middle America
11 Imports and Exports
12 Community Resources
13 Means of Transportation
14 In the Land of Dixie
15 A Lincoln Log
16 Making Maps
17 Political Parties
18 Write a Poem About Harriet Tubman
19 Studying the Underground Railroad
20 Civil War Uniforms
21 Draw a Map of the Wilderness
22 State Nicknames
23 Military Tactics and Terminology
24 Vicksburg: Before and After
25 After the Battle
26 The End of Wars
27 Lincoln Scrapbook
28 Uses of the Buffalo
29 Native-American Pen Pals
30 Retelling Native-American Legends
31 The Bowl Game
32 Lone Star State Time Line
33 Meet a Pioneer
34 Cowboys Around the World
35 From Schooners to Railroads
36 Plains Indian Sign Language
37 The Transcontinental Railroad
38 Explorer Maps
39 Homes Diorama
40 Trails of the West
41 The Spanish Southwest
42 The American West Today: In the News
43 Tracing Younde's Travels
44 Native-American Games of Skill
45 Greek Gods and Goddesses
46 Words from Greek and Roman Mythology
47 Going to Warsaw
48 Map Your Dreams

Appendix 7   Tradebook Connection Cards

Buffalo Woman. Paul Goble. Bradbury Press, 1984. A young hunter aims an arrow at a buffalo only to find a young woman, whom he marries. When she goes back to her people, he follows and becomes a buffalo.

Bunnicula. Deborah and James Howe. Atheneum, 1979. Chester the cat tries to get rid of a new bunny whom he suspects of being a vampire. Meanwhile, Harold the dog tries to save the bunny.

Caddie Woodlawn. Carol Ryrie Brink. Macmillan, 1973. Caddie, a young girl allowed to "run wild" with her brothers, makes a daring visit to an Indian village amid rumors of an Indian attack.

Cat Walk. Mary Stolz. Harper & Row, 1983. An odd young barn cat wants to be a pet and have a name.

Dear Mr. Henshaw. Beverly Cleary. Morrow, 1983. A young boy begins corresponding with his favorite author.

The Double Life of Pocahontas. Jean Fritz. Putnam, 1983. Pocahontas moved between the Indian and white worlds, eventually marrying John Rolfe and moving to England.

I am the running girl. Arnold Adoff. Harper & Row, 1979. Free verse poetry tells of the preparations for and the exhilaration of running.

In the Year of the Boar and Jackie Robinson. Bette Bao Lord. Harper & Row, 1984. When a young Chinese girl, new to the Unites States, is called "Jackie Robinson," she learns everything she can about him and finally meets him.

The Land I Lost. Huynh Quang Nhuong. HarperCollins, 1982. A Vietnamese boy tells of his life in the central highlands from the time Tank, the water buffalo, is bought until it is accidentally killed by gunfire.

The Midnight Fox. Betsy Byars. Viking, 1968. Tom hates staying at his aunt and uncle's farm until he spies a fox. He becomes fascinated with the fox and eventually saves it from his uncle.

Pigs Might Fly. Dick King-Smith. Viking, 1982. A pig with deformed feet is saved from the Pigman, learns to swim, and saves his family and friends during a flood.

Song of the Trees. Mildred D. Taylor. Dial, 1975. When Mr. Andersen tries to force Cassie's grandmother to sell the family's trees, Cassie's father steps in.

Acknowledgments

Grateful acknowledgment is given to the following publishers and copyright owners for permission granted to reprint selections from their publications. All possible care has been taken to trace ownership and secure permission for each selection included.

Maxwell Aley Associates: "Galileo" from *Pioneer Astronomers* by Navin Sullivan, copyright © 1964 by Navin Sullivan.

Bantam Books, a division of Bantam Doubleday Dell Publishing Group, Inc.: "The Night We Started Dancing" by Ann Cameron, from *Free to Be . . . A Family,* by Marlo Thomas and Friends, copyright © 1987 by Free to Be Foundation, Inc.

Gwendolyn Brooks: "To Young Readers" by Gwendolyn Brooks, copyright © 1991 by Gwendolyn Brooks, published in *Very Young Poets* by Third World Press, 1991.

Curtis Brown, Ltd.: An excerpt entitled "Mukasa at School" from *Mukasa* by John Nagenda, copyright © 1973 by John Nagenda. An excerpt entitled "The West Side" from *How Juan Got Home* by Peggy Mann, copyright © 1972 by Peggy Mann.

Children's Better Health Institute, Benjamin Franklin Literary & Medical Society, Inc., Indianapolis, IN: "Sam at the Library" by Carol Combs Hole, from *Jack and Jill,* copyright © 1967 by Curtis Publishing Co.

Clarion Books, an imprint of Houghton Mifflin Co.: An excerpt from *Voyager to the Planets* by Necia H. Apfel, copyright © 1991 by Necia H. Apfel.

Education Development Center, Inc., Newton, MA, and William Bentzen, for the heirs of Knud Rasmussen: "History of the Tunrit" from *Songs and Stories of the Netsilik Eskimos,* translated by Edward Field from text collected by Knud Rasmussen, illustrated by Kiakshuk and Pudlo, copyright © 1967, 1968 by Education Development Center, Inc.

Farrar, Straus and Giroux, Inc.: An excerpt from *The Heavenly Zoo: Legends and Tales of the Stars,* retold by Alison Lurie, illustrated by Monika Beisner, text copyright © 1979 by Alison Lurie, illustrations copyright © 1979 by Monika Beisner.

Harcourt Brace & Company: An excerpt entitled "The Library Card" from *Rufus M.* by Eleanor Estes, illustrated by Louis Slobodkin, copyright 1943, copyright © renewed 1970 by Eleanor Estes. "Seventh Grade" from *Baseball in April and Other Stories* by Gary Soto, copyright © 1990 by Gary Soto. "Women" from *Revolutionary Petunias and Other Poems* by Alice Walker, copyright © 1970 by Alice Walker.

HarperCollins Publishers: An excerpt entitled "Storks" from *The Wheel on the School* by Meindert DeJong, illustrated by Maurice Sendak, text copyright 1954 by Meindert DeJong, illustrations copyright 1954 by Maurice Sendak. An excerpt from *The Land I Lost: Adventures of a Boy in Vietnam* by Huynh Quang Nhuong, text copyright © 1982 by Huynh Quang Nhuong. An excerpt entitled "Chinatown" from *Child of the Owl* by Laurence Yep, copyright © 1977 by Laurence Yep. "Parmele" from *Childtimes: A Three-Generation Memoir* by Eloise Greenfield and Lessie Jones Little, copyright © 1979 by Eloise Greenfield and Lessie Jones Little.

Houghton Mifflin Co.: An excerpt entitled "Into the Light of Day" from *Child of the Silent Night* by Edith Fisher Hunter, copyright © 1963 by Edith Fisher Hunter. An excerpt entitled "Sun and Star Calendars" from *Sky Watchers of Ages Past* by Malcolm E. Weiss, copyright © 1982 by Malcolm E. Weiss. An excerpt entitled "Telescopes" from *The Way Things Work* by David Macaulay, compilation copyright © 1988 by Dorling Kindersley Ltd., London, text copyright © 1988 by David Macaulay and Neil Ardley, illustrations copyright

© 1988 by David Macaulay. An excerpt from *In Two Worlds: A Yup'ik Eskimo Family* by Aylette Jenness and Alice Rivers, photographs by Aylette Jenness, text copyright © 1989 by Aylette Jenness and Alice Rivers, photographs copyright © 1989 by Aylette Jenness.

Lothrop, Lee & Shepard Books, a division of William Morrow & Co., Inc.: An excerpt from *Do Bananas Chew Gum?* by Jamie Gilson, text copyright © 1980 by Jamie Gilson.

Elsa Marston: "Circles, Squares and Daggers: How Native Americans Watched the Skies" by Elsa Marston, from the September 1990 issue of *Odyssey* magazine, copyright © 1990 by Elsa Marston.

Vonda N. McIntyre: An excerpt entitled "A Meeting in Space" from *Barbary* by Vonda N. McIntyre, copyright © 1986 by Vonda N. McIntyre.

Morrow Junior Books, a division of William Morrow & Co., Inc.: *Stars* by Seymour Simon, text copyright © 1986 by Seymour Simon.

Penguin Books Canada Limited: An excerpt entitled "A Real Job" from *Little by Little* by Jean Little, copyright © 1987 by Jean Little.

Marian Reiner, for the author, and Holiday House Inc., for the illustrator: "Sun" and "Secrets" from *Space Songs* by Myra Cohn Livingston, illustrated by Leonard Everett Fisher, text copyright © 1988 by Myra Cohn Livingston, illustrations copyright © 1988 by Leonard Everett Fisher, published by Holiday House.

Viking Penguin, a division of Penguin Books USA Inc.: An excerpt from *The Night Journey* by Kathryn Lasky, illustrated by Trina Schart Hyman, text copyright © 1981 by Kathryn Lasky, illustrations copyright © 1981 by Trina Schart Hyman.

Walker and Co., 720 Fifth Avenue, New York, NY 10019: An excerpt from *How Did We Find Out the Earth Is Round?* by Isaac Asimov, copyright © 1972 by Isaac Asimov.

Photography
 83 Guelph Daily Mercury
113 B. & C. Alexander/Black Star
139 AP/Wide World
309 K. Yep
311 Jean Weisinger

Diagrams
147, 148, 149 Accurate Art, Inc.

Illustrations
12F–14F Van Howell
19F–29F Barbara Kelley

Index